Lecture Notes in Computer Science 8808

Commenced Publication in 1973
Founding and Former Series Editors:
Gerhard Goos, Juris Hartmanis, and Jan van Leeuwen

More information about this series at http://www.springer.com/series/7407

Cristian S. Calude · Rūsiņš Freivalds
Iwama Kazuo (Eds.)

Computing with New Resources

Essays Dedicated to Jozef Gruska
on the Occasion of His 80th Birthday

Editors

Cristian S. Calude
Department of Computer Science
The University of Auckland
Auckland
New Zealand

Iwama Kazuo
School of Informatics
Kyoto University
Kyoto
Japan

Rūsiņš Freivalds
University of Latvia
Riga
Latvia

ISSN 0302-9743
Lecture Notes in Computer Science
ISBN 978-3-319-13349-2
DOI 10.1007/978-3-319-13350-8

ISSN 1611-3349   (electronic)

ISBN 978-3-319-13350-8   (eBook)

Library of Congress Control Number: 2014957956

LNCS Sublibrary: SL1 – Theoretical Computer Science and General Issues

Springer Cham Heidelberg New York Dordrecht London

Printed on acid-free paper

Springer International Publishing AG Switzerland is part of Springer Science+Business Media
(www.springer.com)

Preface

Jozef Gruska is a well-known computer scientist for his many and broad results, but also because he was "everywhere"—he had 33 long-term visiting positions in Europe, North America, Asia, and Africa.

Professor Gruska introduced the descriptional complexity (of grammars, automata, and languages) and is one of pioneers of parallel (systolic) automata. His other main research interests include parallel systems and automata and quantum information processing, transmission, and cryptography. They are all represented by various contributions to this volume. He is co-founder of four regular series of conferences in informatics and two in quantum information processing and the founding chair (1989–1996) of the IFIP Specialist Group on Foundation of Computer Science.

Professor Jozef Gruska

When in 1996 Professor Jozef Gruska was presented with the IEEE Computer Pioneer Award, the official citation was: *For the development of computer science in the former Czechoslovakia with fundamental contributions to the theory of computing and extraordinary organisational activities.*

Indeed, Jozef Gruska is the father of theoretical computer science research in Czechoslovakia and among the first Slovak programmers in the early 1960s. Gruska was one of the first lecturers on analog/digital computers at Comenius University in Bratislava and the first lecturer on foundations of computing. In addition, he was active in establishing the first computer science curricula at the Comenius University. He also helped the development of computer science education at Masaryk University in Brno and computing education in Slovak high schools.

In 1966 Gruska started the research seminar *Automata, Languages, and Algorithms,* largely credited for the development of a strong group of theoretical computer scientists in Bratislava. For a country on the east side of the iron curtain, Czechoslovakia vitally needed scientific contacts with foreign colleagues. Jozef Gruska was one of the main organizers of the first conference on theoretical computer science in Eastern Europe, *MFCS (Mathematical Foundations of Computer Science) 1972*, in Jablonna near Warsaw (Poland). The following year, in 1973, the continuation of this conference was organized in Štrbské Pleso, High Tatras (Czechoslovakia), with Jozef Gruska as conference chair. More than 150 participants, including 80 foreigners, was most unusual for a conference in former socialist countries. The main talks were presented by J. Bečvář

(Prague), A. Blikle (Warsaw), K. Čulík (Prague), B. Dömölki (Budapest), F. Gécseg (Szeged), S. Ginsburg (Los Angeles), J. Gruska (Bratislava), P. Hájek (Prague), J. Hartmanis (Ithaca, New York), P.J. Hayes (Colchester, Essex), G. Hotz (Saarbrücken), N. Nagornyj (Moscow), M. Nivat (Paris), M. Novotný (Brno), Z. Pawlak (Warsaw), C.A. Petri (Birlinghoven/Bonn), H. Rasiowa (Warsaw), A. Salomaa (Aarhus), C.P. Schnorr (Frankfurt am Main), and P.H. Starke (Berlin). Really an international conference! After this event the proceedings of *MFCS* were published in the *Lecture Notes in Computer Science* (LNCS) of Springer-Verlag.

Rather soon, *MFCS* became the main East-European conference on theoretical computer science competing with its West-European sister I*CALP (International Colloquium on Automata, Languages and Programming)*. *ICALP* was first organized in 1972 in Paris, France; the second *ICALP* was held in 1974, and since 1976 *ICALP* has been an annual event, also publishing its proceedings in LNCS.

Another successful enterprise by Jozef Gruska and his colleagues was *SOFSEM (SOFtware SEMinar)*. The first *SOFSEM* was organized in 1974. Nowadays it is an international conference, similar to *MFCS*. It was started in 1974 as a national event in Czech or Slovak languages. During those early days of computer science and technology *SOFSEM* supplemented the university education and academic research. Traditionally, the audience consisted of university professors, academic researchers, university teaching staff, advanced students, and professionals in the field. It was an event for two weeks during the Winter period. First local, and later on also international, experts were invited. Each of them presented a series of lectures related to recent topics on computer science.

The basic format of each *SOFSEM* consisted of several series of invited talks, each of 3–5 hours. They were complemented by selected contributions of participants presented during two half-days in two parallel sessions. The lectures always started early in the morning and lasted long in the evenings to facilitate long lunch-breaks. The seminar venue was always chosen as far as possible from big towns. An ideal location was such that you went several hours by train, continued by an infrequent bus, and finally walked several kilometers. This ensured (to some extent) that *SOFSEM* was an oasis of intellectual freedom not much disturbed by government officials.

MFCS and *SOFSEM* have always been an opportunity for East-European and Soviet scientists to contact their Western colleagues. Even now—when the iron curtain no more exists and it is possible to travel elsewhere—there always is a large group of Latvian students at *SOFSEM*.

Jozef Gruska deeply feels the importance of research to be modern. This relates not only to his own research but also to what his students do. In the 1960s his interests concentrated on language theory. This resulted not only in regular papers but also in surveys both in Slovak and English (published in *Information and Control* and *Proceedings of IFIP Congresses*). Later this interest included complexity of computation, finally leading to the monograph *Foundations of Computing* (still available from Amazon).

Systolic trellis automata are simple models for VLSI. They are models of hexagonally connected and triangular shaped systolic arrays. Gruska's research on systolic automata made him really famous. Now it is impossible to write a paper related to systolic automata and not to refer to Gruska. This was the topic where Jozef Gruska got many famous co-authors, including K. Culik II, A. Salomaa, J. Wiedermann, E. Fachini,

A. Maggiolo Schettini, D. Singiorgi, M. Napoli, D. Parente, I. Guessarian, A. Monti, and many others.

Quantum computing is not merely one of the research interests of Jozef Gruska. He understood its importance from the very beginning. The first monograph written in this area of computer science is Gruska's *Quantum Computing*, published in 1999 by McGraw-Hill.

It cannot also be forgotten that he made a great contribution to the ERATO IMAI Quantum Computation and Information project, Tokyo, Japan, started in 2000. This is the first project on quantum computation in Japan, chaired by Hiroshi Imai, University of Tokyo, and awarded by the Japan Science and Technology Agency (JST). Its total budget was more than 15 million US dollars and ended up with a great success, for instance, in theory and experiments of quantum cryptography. Jozef Gruska was deeply involved in this project from the beginning, as a secret "Big Boss", and gave it a lot of important advice. The big success of the project could never be imagined without his help.

He also established contacts with Chinese and Korean colleagues and co-founded in 2001 a series of conferences, named *EQIS (ERATO Quantum Information Science)* first and *AQIS (Asia Quantum Information Science Conference)* later. Since 2003 Jozef Gruska has been the Chairman of the Steering Committee of *AQIS*, which was held since 2001 annually in Japan, China, Korea, and India.

In 1989, the IFIP General Assembly (GA) appointed Jozef Gruska as the founding chair of the temporary IFIP Special Group SG'14 on Foundations of Computing. He created this group with 43 top TCS people and chaired it for two terms until 1996, when he convinced IFIP GA to transfer SG'14 to the permanent IFIP Technical Committee TC1. It was for the first time since the establishment of IFIP in 1962 that TCS had an appropriate representation within IFIP. The first chair of TC1 was then G. Ausiello.

Professor Gruska has spent many years visiting universities and research institutes around the globe. Here is a list of some of them:

1. 1963, 6 months, Moscow, Kyiv, Novosibirsk, USSR, PhD student
2. 1968–1970, 2 academic years, University of Minnesota, USA, visiting professor
3. 1980, 6 months, University of Jena, East Germany, visiting professor
4. 1984, 1987, 1989–1993, 8 semesters, University of Hamburg, West Germany, visiting professor
5. 1994, 1996, 2000, 6 months, University of Karlsruhe, West Germany, visiting professor
6. 1988, 1989, 1992, 4 months, University of Salerno, Italy, visiting professor
7. 1990, 1993, 1997, 5 months, University Paris 6, France, visiting professor
8. 1994, 4 months, École Normale Supérieure, Lyon, France, visiting professor
9. 1997–1999, 12 months, University of Nice, France, visiting professor
10. 2001, 2002, 2003, 2004, 2005, 10 months, ERATO Quantum Project, Tokyo, Japan.

We have already mentioned the Computer Pioneer Award (IEEE, 1996). Professor Gruska was awarded many other distinctions including Bolzano Medal of the Czech Academy of Sciences (2003), elected member of the Academia Europaea (2006), Doctor Honoris Causa, University of Latvia (2013), the IFIP Silver Core Award (1995), Slovak Literally Fond Awards (1998, 2000). In the period 2008–2011, he was a member of the Council of Academia Europaea.

His Laboratory of Quantum Information Processing and Cryptography at the Masaryk University, Brno, Czech Republic has many foreign and local students as well as a continuous stream of visitors. Jozef Gruska is active as ever—see http://www.fi.muni.cz/usr/gruska—always ready to give a talk or to start a new collaboration.

Many happy returns, Professor Gruska!

September 2014

Cristian S. Calude, Auckland
Rūsiņš Freivalds, Riga
Kazuo Iwama, Kyoto

Jozef Gruska's Publications

Academic Publications

1. Tables for determining the critical stresses of thin-walled bars and the use of a computer for calculation, in Slovak, co-authors: A. Mrázik,I. Plander, Stavebnický Časopis, V9 (1961) 461–484
2. Program for calculating forced vibrations in torsional vibrating systems by an automatic computer, co-author: I. Plander, Bulletinul Insitutului Politechnic, DIN IASI, V10 (1964) 269–278
3. Calculation of thin-walled bars, in Slovak, co-author A. Mrázik, Publishing House of the Slovak Academy of Sciences (1965). 120.
4. On structural ambiguity of formal languages, Czech. Math. J., V15 (1965) 283–294
5. Induction in formal languages - some properties of reducing transformations and of isolable sets, Czech. Math. J., V15 (1965) 406–415
6. Structural unambiguity of ALGOL MOD, Comment. Math. Univer. Caroline, V6 (1965) 281–328
7. Isolable and weakly isolable sets, Czech. Math. J., V16 (1966) 76–90
8. Two operations with formal languages and their influence upon structural unambiguity, Matematicko-fyzikálny Časopis, V16 (1966) 58–65
9. On sets generated by context-free grammars, Kybernetika, V2 (1966) 483–493
10. On a classification of context-free languages, Kybernetika, V3 (1967) 22–29
11. Solution of a system of linear algebraic equations with band matrices, Aplikace matematiky, V12 (1967) 493–498
12. Some classification of context-free languages, Information and Control, V14 (1969) 152–173
13. Complexity and unambiguity of context-free grammars and languages, Information and Control, V18 (1971) 502–519
14. Unambiguity of context-free grammars and languages, Information Processing 68, North-Holland (1971) 135–139
15. A characterization of context-free languages, Journal of Computer and System Sciences, V5 (1971) 353-363 (Reprinted in Russian, in "Kiberneticzeski sbornik", V9, Moscow (1972) 114–126)
16. A few remarks on the index of context-free grammars and languages, Information and Control, V19 (1971) 216–223
17. On the size of context-free grammars, Kybernetika, V8 (1972) 213–218
18. Generation and approximation of finite and infinite languages, Proceedings of MFCS'72, Warsaw (1972) 1–7
19. On star-height hierarchies of context-free languages, Kybernetika, V9 (1973) 231–236
20. Descriptional complexity of context-free languages, Proceedings of MFCS'73, High Tatras (1973) 71–85

21. Generalized context-free grammars, Acta Cybernetica, V2 (1973) 35–39
22. Algebraic characterization and complexity of context-free languages, Proceedings of Mini-conference on Algebraic Theory of Automata, Szeged (1973) 10–14
23. Grammatical levels and subgrammars of context-free grammars, Arch. Math. 1, Scripta Foc. Sci. Nat. UJEP Brunensis, IX (1974) 207–217
24. Complexity of algorithms – I. Analysis of algorithms, in Slovak, Informačné systémy, V3 (1974) 207–217
25. Complexity of algorithms – II. Optimal algorithms, in Slovak, Informačné systémy, V3 (1974) 335–348
26. Code optimization techniques, in Slovak, co-author J. Duplinský, Proceedings of Winter School SOFSEM'74, VVS Bratislava (1974) 127–171
27. Proceedings of Winter School SOFSEM'74 (editor), VVS Bratislava (1974) 272 p.
28. Analysis and effectivity of algorithms, in Slovak, Proceedings of Winter School SOFSEM'75, VVS Bratislava (1975) 33–94
29. Proceedings of Winter School SOFSEM'75 (editor), VVS Bratislava (1975) 344 p.
30. Divide-and conquer and other techniques to design effective algorithms, in Slovak, Proceedings of Symposium ALGORITMY'75, SVTS Bratislava (1975) 315–328
31. Complexity of concrete algorithms – I. Basic principles, in Slovak, Lecture Notes, VVS Bratislava (1975) 146 p.
32. A note on ϵ-rules in context-free grammars, Kybernetika, V11 (1975) 26-31
33. Structural unambiguity and context-free grammars, Information Processing Machines, V18 (1975) 17–54
34. Proving correctness of programs, in Slovak, co-author I. Prívara, Proceedings of Winter School SOFSEM'76, VVS Bratislava (1976) 331–376
35. Proceedings of Winter School SOFSEM'76 (editor), VVS Bratislava (1976) 399 p.
36. Complexity of concrete algorithms – II. Sorting, in Slovak, Lecture Notes, VVS Bratislava (1976) 121 p.
37. Descriptional complexity (of languages) – a short survey, Proceedings of MFCS'76, LNCS 45 (1976) 65–80
38. Mathematical Foundations of Computer Science, Proceedings of MFCS'77 (editor), LNCS 53, Springer-Verlag (1977) 605 p.
39. Proceedings of Winter School SOFSEM'77 (editor), VVS Bratislava, VVS Bratislava (1997) 381 p.
40. Data types and data structures, in Slovak, co-authors: J. Wiedermann, A. Černý, Proceedings SOFSEM'78, VVS Bratislava, (1978) 45–110
41. Proceedings of Winter School SOFSEM'78 (editor), VVS Bratislava (1978) 480 p.
42. Descriptional systems and descriptional complexity, in Slovak, In "Descriptional complexity of algorithms, automata and languages" I, VVS Bratislava (1978) 11–29
43. Algorithms, in Slovak, co-author: M. Franek, SPN Bratislava (1979) 250 p.
44. Descriptional and computational complexity, in Slovak, in "Descriptional complexity of algorithms. automata and languages" II, VVS Bratislava (1979) 11–26

45. Proceedings of Winter School SOFSEM'79 (editor), VVS Bratislava (1979) 420 p.
46. Computational complexity of algorithms, in Slovak, Lecture Notes, Technical University, Bratislava, 1980, 60 p.
47. Algorithms, in Slovak, Publisher SPN, Bratislava (1980, 1982), first and second edition, 192 p.
48. Programming and exercises in programming, in Czech, SPN Praha (1980) 224 p.
49. Proceedings of Winter School SOFSEM'80 (editor). VVS Bratislava (1980) 424 p.
50. Data type specifications. In "Data types, programs and algorithmic problems", in Slovak, VVS Bratislava, 1981, 8–39
51. Proceedings of Winter School SOFSEM'81 (editor). VVS Bratislava (1981) 451 p.
52. Proceedings of MFCS'81 (co-editor M. Chytil), LNCS 118, Springer Verlag (1981) 589 p.
53. On non-regular context-free languages and pumping, co-authors: K. Culik II, A. Salomaa, EATCS Bulletin, N16 (1982) 22–24
54. Specification and design of programs, in Slovak, Proceedings of SOFSEM'82, VVS Bratislava (1982) 333–337
55. Proceedings of Winter School SOFSEM'82 (editor), VVS Bratislava (1982) 420 p.
56. Systolic computations and automata, in Slovak, In "Theory and methodology of programming and data base systems", VVS Bratislava (1982) 82–106
57. Quo vadites data structures and algorithms, Bulletin of EATCS, N21 (1983) 183–189
58. Systolic systems, in Slovak, co-authors: P. Ružička, J. Wiedermann, I. Vrťo, in "Distributed and Parallel Systems", VVS Bratislava (1983) 11–185
59. Computational complexity of algorithms, lecture notes, in Slovak, Technical University of Bratislava (1982) 112 p.
60. Proceedings of Winter School SOFSEM'83 (editor), VVS Bratislava (1983) 491 p.
61. Systolic systems, in Slovak, co-authors: P. Ružička, J. Wiedermann, in Proceedings of SOFSEM'83, VVS Bratislava (1983) 267–308.
62. Computer revolution, in Slovak, co-authors: I. M. Havel, J. Wiedermann, J. Zelený, in "Proceedings of SOFSEM'83", VVS Bratislava (1983) 7–64
63. Special purpose systolic systems, in Slovak, Proceedings of Computer Control of Discrete Processes, High Tatras (1983) 10–18
64. Systolic automata for VLSI on balanced trees, co-authors: K. Culik II, A. Salomaa, Acta Informatica, V18 (1983) 10–18
65. On a family of languages resulting from systolic tree automata, co-authors: K. Culik II, A. Salomaa, Theoretical Computer Science, V23 (1983) 231–242
66. Systolic trellis automata, joint authors: K. Culik II, A. Salomaa, International Journal on Computer Mathematics (1984) V15, 195–212, V16, 3–22.
67. Systolic automata – power, characterization, non-homogeneity. Proceedings of MFCS'84, LNCS 176 (1984) 32–49
68. Design of parallel computational networks, in Slovak, in "Parallel and distributed systems", VVS Bratislava (1985) 35–76

69. Modular trellises, co-author: A. Černý, in "Book of L", Springer-Verlag (1986) 45–62

70. Cybernetics and Informatics, in Slovak, Proceedings of Symposium on Cybernetics Aspects of Computer Development (1986) 3–6

71. Modular trellis automata, co-author: A. Černý, Fundamenta Informaticae, V9 (1986) 253–282

72. Systolic trellis automata: stability, decidability and complexity, co-authors: K. Culik, A. Salomaa, Information and Control, V71, N3 (1986) 218–230

73. Pragmatic aspects of complexity theory (position statement): Proceedings of IFIP'86 Congress (1986) North-Holland, 1–10

74. Proceedings of MFCS'86 (co-editors: B. Rovan, J. Wiedermann). LNCS 233, Springer Verlag (1986) 640 p.

75. Information revolutions, in Slovak, co-author: J. Wiedermann, Vesmír, V65, N7 (1986) 373–378

76. Great personalities of computer history, in Slovak, Vesmír, V65, N8 (1986) 446–450

77. Systolic architectures, systems and computations, Proceedings of ICALP'88, LNCS 317, Springer-Verlag (1988) 254–270

78. On informatics and informatization, in Slovak, Proceedings of SOFSEM'88, VVS Bratislava (1988) I–XV

79. Arise of informatics as of a basic science and problems of its present development, in Slovak, Information Systems (1989) 221–231

80. Synthesis, structure, and power of systolic computations, Theoretical Computer Science, V71 (1990) 47–77

81. Simulation of systolic tree automata on trellis automata, co-authors: E. Fachini, A. Maggiolo Schettini, D. Singiorgi, International Journal on Foundations of Computer Science, V1, N2 (1990) 87–110

82. Matrices multiplication, in Slovak, co-author J. Vyskoč, Matematické Obzory, V38 (1992) 31–46

83. Methodological, social and ethical problems in programming and artificial intelligence, in "Intelligent systems – state of the art and future directions", Eds. W. Ras and M. Zemanková, Ellis Horwoodd (1990) 488–503

84. Informatics as the scientific environmnet for artificial intelligence, in "The future in research in artificial intelligence" (Eds. R. Meersman, Ir. P. A. Flach), Elsevier (1991) 11–23

85. Maturing of Informatics, co-author H. Jürgensen, in "Images of programming", Eds. D. Bjorner, V. Kotov, Elsevier Science Publisher (1991) I-55–I-69

86. Power of Interconnections and of Nondeterminism in Regular T-tree Systolic Automata, co-authors: E. Fachini, M. Napoli and D. Parente, Mathematical System Theory, V28 (1995) 245–266

87. Why we should not any longer only repair, polish and iron current computer science education, Proceedings of IFIP WG3.2 Working Conference "Informatics at university level: Teaching advanced subjects in the future", ETH Zurich, 1991, Education & Computing 8 (1993) 303–330

88. Normal forms and nondeterminism in Y-tree systolic automata, co-authors: E. Fachini, M. Napoli, D. Parente, in "Proceedings of the second International Colloquium on Words, Languages and Combinatorics", Kyoto (1992), Eds. M. Ito and H. Jürgensen, World Scientific (1994) 143–154

89. Informatics and its education – new horizons, aims, and principles, Proceedings of SOFSEM'93, INFOSTAT Bratislava (1993) 85–96

90. Fix-point semantics of synchronized systems and correctness of their basic transformations, co-author: I.Guessarian, Proceedings of the IFIP Congress'94, INFORMATION PROCESSING'94 (1994) 231–238

91. Optimization of systolic tree automata, co-authors: M. Napoli, D. Parente, Proceedings of IFIP Congress'94, INFORMATION PROCESSING'94 (1994) 247–252

92. Descriptional complexity, Commenius University, Bratislava, Thesis to defended for the highest degree in science (DrSc) (1995) 160 p.

93. Systolic tree and tree-like automata, Publications Mathematicae Debrecen, V514, 3-4 (1997) 807–855

94. State complexity of SBTA languages, co-authors: E. Fachini, M. Napoli, D. Parente, Proceedings of LATIN'95, LNCS 911, Springer-Verlag (1995) 346–357

95. Succinctness of descriptions of SBTA–languages, co-authors: A. Monti, M. Napoli, D. Parente, Theoretical Computer Science, V179, N 1-2 (1997) 251–271

96. Foundations of computing, International Thomson Computer Press, US (1997) 735 p.

97. Adjusting informatics education to information era, co-author R. Vollmar, in Foundations of Computer Science: Potential – Theory – Cognition, Eds. Ch. Freksa, M. Jantzen and R. Valk, LNCS 1337 (1997) 49–67

98. Informatics in curricula for non-informatics students: Engineering and Science. Joint author: R. Vollmar, in Proceedings of IFIP TC3/WG3.2 Workshop "Informatics as a discipline and in other disciplines: What is in common?", Eds. F. Mulder, T. van Weert, Entschede, 17-20.8 (1997) London, Chapman and Hall, 203–211

99. Fix-point semantics of systolic systems transformation, co-author I. Guessarian, Journal of Automata, Languages and Combinatorics, V2 (1997) 93–133

100. Quantum computing, McGraw-Hill (1999) 440 p.

101. Quantum computing – WEB supplement, 1999,
http://www.mcgraw-hill.co.uk/gruska.

102. Informatics in 21st century, Proceedings of the conference "Security of Information Systems in Financial Sphere', Bratislava (1999) Appendix, 1–6

103. Quantum challenges in descriptional complexity, Pre-proceedings of the International Workshop on Descriptional Complexity of Automata, Grammars and Related Structures, Universität Magdeburg, Dept. of Computer Science (1999) 23–38.

104. Quantum challenges, Proceedings of SOFSEM'99, Springer-Verlag, LNCS, 1523 (1999) 2–29

105. Quantumization of Informatics, Proceedings of Riga Workshop on Quantum Computation and learning, Mälardalen University and Riga University, Eds: R. Bonner and R. Freivalds (1999) 9–32

106. Descriptional complexity issues in quantum computing, Journal of Automata, Languages and Combinatorics, V5, N3 (2000) 191–218

107. New challenges for theoretical computer science, Proceedings of IFIP TCS2000, Springer-Verlag, LNCS 1872 (2000) 599–601

108. Quantumization of theoretical informatics, Proceedings of IFIP TCS2000, Springer-Verlag, LNCS 1872 (2000) 604–608

109. Quantumization of Informatics II, Proceedings of Sundbyholm Slott Workshop on Learning and Quantum Computing, University Mälardalen (2000) 1–12

110. Quantum implications of quantum automata, Proceedings of NATO Workshop on decoherence in quantum computing, Ed. A. Gonis, Mykonos, (2000) 329–339

111. Quantum models and modes of computation and communication. co-author R. Vollmar, Proceedings of RIMS Workshop, Kyoto, March 22-23 (2000) 76–85

112. Quantum finite automata, co-author R. Vollmar, Proceedings of the Kyoto International Conference on Words, Languages and Combinatorics III, Kyoto, March 15-19, 2000, World Scientific (2003) 192–211

113. Quantum puzzles, mysteries and paradoxes, co-author F. Peper, Proceedings of Vienna THEORIETAG 2000 and the "New computing paradigms: molecular and quantum computing", September 25 (2000) 105–126

114. Quantum computing challenges, In *"Mathematics unlimited: 2001 and beyond"*, Eds. B. Engquist and W. Schmid , Springer-Verlag (2001) 529–564

115. Puzzles, mysteries and power of quantum entanglement, co-author H. Imai, Proceedings of MCU'01, Chisinau, LNCS 2055, Springer-Verlag (2001) 25–69

116. Proceedings of the ERATO conference EQIS'01, ERATO, JST, Tokyo, co-editors, H. Imai and K. Matsumoto (2002) 65 p.

117. Security and cryptography in 21th century, Proceedings of 2nd International Conference on Security of Information Systems, Prague, May 30-31 (2001) 105–113

118. Power of quantum entanglement, co-authors H. Imai and K. Matsumoto, in Proceedings "Foundations of information technology in the era of network and mobile computing", IFIP'02 World Computer Congress, Kluwer Academic Publisher (2002) 3–22

119. Quantum information processing, Proceedings of the annual database conference DATACON, Masaryk University, Brno (2002) 77–112

120. Proceedings of the ERATO conference EQIS'02, ERATO, JST, Tokyo, co-editors, H. Imai and K. Matsumoto (2002) 168 p.

121. Succinctness in quantum information processing, Proceedings of DCFS Conference, MTA SZTAKI, Budapest, July (2003) 15–25

122. Quantum entanglement as a new quantum information processing resource, New Generation Computing, V21, N4 (2003) 279–296

123. Proceedings of ERATO conference EQIS'03, ERATO, JST, Tokyo, co-eds: H. Imai and M. Hayashi (2003) 168 p..

124. Special issue on quantum computing, EQIS'03, in the International Journal of Quantum Information, co-eds. H. Imai and M. Hayashi, V2, N1 (2004) 194 p.

125. Quantum complexity theory goals and challenges, Special issue of The International Journal on Quantum Information Processing, devoted to Camerino conference, V3, N1 (2005) 31–40

126. Universal sets of quantum information processing primitives and optimal use of such primitives, General Theory of information transfer and combinatorics, Proceedings of the Bielefeld Workshop in information transmission and combinatorics, edited by R. Ahlswede, LNCS 4123, Springer Verlag (2006) 356–377; also in Electronic Notes in Discrete mathematics, V21 (2005) 285–289

127. Universality in quantum computing, Pre-proceedings of MCU'04, Russian Academy of Sciences (2004) 33–37

128. Optimal time & communication solution of firing squad synchronization problems on square arrays, toruses and rings, co-authors Dominik Parente and Salvatore La Torre, Proceedings of DLT'04, LNCS 3340 (2004) 200–211

129. Main challenges and driving forces of IT in the era of globalization, Proceedings of Shanghai Forum, part Information Technology, May 16-17, Fudan University Press, Shanghai, May 16-17, (2005) 60–72

130. Quantum complexity theory tools, goals and challenges, In Quantum information and communication, Proceedings of QICC'05, Allied Publishers, Eds: S. P. Pal and S. Kumar, ISBN 81-8424-064-3 (2006) 1750-197

131. Universality and optimality of quantum information processing primitives, In Quantum information and communication, Proceedings of QICC'05, Allied Publishers, Eds: S. P. Pal and S. Kumar, ISBN 81-8424-064-3 (2006) 1–18

132. Security in quantum cryptography and quantum networks, in *Aspects of Network and Information Security*, Proceedings of the NATO Advance Study Institute on Network Security and Intrusion Detection, Yerevan, IOS Press, Eds. E. Kranakis, E. Haroutunian, E. Shahhazian, ISBN 978 1-58603 856 (2006) 19–46

133. Quantum finite automata: an invitation, (Eds. Z. Esik, C. Martin-Vide, V. Mitrana): Recent advances in Formal Languages and Applications, Studies in Computational Intelligence 25, Eds: Z. Esik, C. Martin-Vide, V. Mitrana, Springer Verlag (2006) 81–117

134. Different Time Solutions for the Firing Squad Synchronization Problem on Basic Grid Networks, RAIRO Theoretical Informatics and Applications, co-authors: S. La Torre, M. Napoli and M. Parente, V 40 (2006) 177–206

135. A broader view on limitations of information processing and communication by nature, Natural computing, Springer Verlag, V6 (2007) 75–112

136. From informatics to quantum informatics, Proceedings of the Fourth IFIP International Confeence on Theoretical Computer Science- TCS 2006 at the World Computer Congress, Springer Verlag (2006) 17–46

137. The emergence and challenges of quantum informatics, in Information technology (Special issue devoted to memory of Thomas Beth, Ed. Roland Vollmar), V48, issue 6 (2006) 336–343

138. Quantum informatics paradigms and tools for QIPC, Quantum computing, Proceedings of BackAction, a conference in Kanpur, March 2006, Ed. D. Goswami, AIP conference proceedings N864 (2007) 1–10

139. The firing squad synchronization problem on squares, toruses and rings (co-authors: S. La Torre, M. Parente), International Journal on Foundations of computer Science, V18, N3 (2007) 637–654

140. Quantum informatics and its relation to informatics, physics and mathematics (A dialog with Cris Calude), Bulletin of EATCS (2007) June issues N92, 20–30, October issue, N93, 33–49

141. Algebraic methods in quantum informatics, in "Algebraic Informatics", Springer, LNCS 4728 (2007) 87–111

142. Quantum computation, in "Willey Encyclopedia of Computer Science and Engineering" (2009) 2297–2310

143. Recent developments and challenges of quantum cryptography, Zborník Mikulašskej kryptobesiedky, Trusted network Solutions, co-author J. Bouda, ISBN 978-80-903083-9 (2008) 25–27

144. From classical cryptography to quantum physics through quantum cryptography, Journal of the India Institute of Science, V 89, N3 (2009) 271–282

145. Impacts of informatics on QIPC, Quantum signal and information, Nanjing University of Post and Telecommunication (2011) 40-48

146. A perception of Informatics, web page of Academia Europaea, http://www.AE-Info.org/ae/user/Gruska.Jozef, 49 p.

147. Impulses and roads to a new perception of informatics, in "Rainbow of Computer Science", Eds: C. Calude, A. Salomaa and G. Rozenberg, Springer Verlag (2011) 183–199

148. Multi-letter Quantum Finite Automata: Decidability of the Equivalence and Minimization of States; co-authors: D. Qiu, L. Li, X. Zou, P. Mateus, Acta Informatica, V48, N 5-6 (2011) 271–290

149. One-way finite automata with quantum and classical states, Co-authors: S. Zheng, D. Qiu, L. Li, LNCS 7300, Festschrift Series to Honor Juergen Dassow, Eds. H. Bordihn, M. Kutrib, B. Truthe (2011) 273–290

150. Quantum entanglement and new perception of informatics, AIP Conference Proceedings (Eds. D. Home, G. Kar and A. Majumdar), V1384 (2011) 59–65

151. De-quantisation, AIP Conference Proceedings V1444 (Eds. N. Mebarki et al.) (2012) 106–116

152. Quantum finite automata (Co-authors, D. Qiu, L. Li and P. Mateus), in CRC Handbook on Finite State based Models and Applications, Ed. J. Wang, CRC Press (2012) 113–144

153. State succinctness of two-way finite automata with quantum and classical states. co-authors: S. Zheng, D. Qiu, L. Li, P. Mateus. Theoretical Computer Science, V499 (2013) 98–112

154. Power of the interactive proof systems with verifiers modelled by semi-quantum two-way quantum automata. co-authors: S. Zheng; D. Qiu, submitted ti Quantum Information Processing Journal, April 2013

155. On the state complexity of semi-quantum finite automata, co-authors: S. Zheng, D. Qiu, RAIRO Theoretical Informatics and Applications, DOI 10.1051/ita/2014003, (2014) 21 p.

156. New vision and future of informatics, Pre-proceedings of the International Conference on Intelligent Information systems; Institute of Mathematics and Computer Science, Moldavian Academy of Science, Chisinau (2013) 11–14

157. Roads to new grand challenges of informatics, in Fourteenth Conference on Membrane Computing, Eds: A. Alhazov, S. Cojocaru, M. Gheorghe, Y. Rogozhin, G. Rozenberg, A. Salomaa, LNCS 8340 (2014) 10–18

158. New vision and goals of informatics and megachallenges of mankind, Computer science Journal of Moldova, V21, N3 (2013) 309–319

159. On the state-complexity of semi-quantum finite automata; co-authors S. Zheng and D. Qiu, Proceedings of LATA 2014, LNCS 8370 (2014) 601–612

Miscellania Publications

1. MFCS'77, Cocktail speech, Bulletin of EATCS, N3 (1978) 23–23
2. 10 years of MFCS, Bulletin of EATCS, N15 (1981) 21–30
3. Report on the 2nd International Workshop on Graph Grammars and their Application to Computer Science, Bulletin of EATCS, N19 (1983) 51-57.
4. ICALP'84, Bulletin of EATCS, N24 (1984) 152–156.
5. More consistently towards originality of thinking, Nové slovo, N36 (1987) 22–22
6. More consistently in PhD education – I. Could cosmetic changes help?, in Slovak, Nedeľná pravda, daily newspaper, N44 (1987) 10-10
7. More consistently in PhD education – II. Why so much of formalism, in Slovak, Nedeľná pravda, daily newspaper, N45 (1987) 10-10
8. More consistently in PhD education – III. Is it so difficult to make changes?, in Slovak, Nedeľná pravda, daily newspaper, N46 (1987) 12–10
9. 10th IFIP Congress, Bulletin of EATCS, N31 (1987), 131–134
10. Some observations on theory and practice in computer science, Bulletin EATCS, N32 (1987) 54–63
11. Better tools for specialists, in Slovak, Vesmír, V67, N5 (1988) 294–294
12. Goals and needs of basic research in informatics, in Slovak, Vesmír, V67, N7 (1988) 414–414
13. ICALP'88, Bulletin of EATCS, N36 (1988) 12–16.
14. International coordination of science, in Slovak, Vesmír, V67, N12 (1988) 685–686
15. Paradoxes of computation technology, in Slovak, Nové slovo, June 9 (1988), 6–6
16. From cybernetics and electronics to informatics, Tribuna, weakly newspaper, N24 (1988) 6–6
17. Science also needs truth, Nové slovo, January 21 (1990) 5–5
18. IFIP'89 Congress, Bulletin of EATCS, N40, 1990, 326–329.
19. Only the best have a chance, in Slovak, Národná obroda, daily newspaper, September 13 (1990) 11–11
20. IFIP Specialist Group, SIGACT NEWS, V21, N2 (1991) 113–116.
21. Quo vadis artificial intelligence, in Slovak, Vesmír, V70, N11 (1991) 645–646
22. Cybernetics versus Informatics, in Slovak, Informačné systémy, V19, N2 (1991) 228–232.
23. Information world. Do you think that people can think?, in Slovak, interview, Slobodný piatok (Daily newspaper), 26. 11 (1993) 10–10
24. New goals of science, in Slovak, Slobodný piatok, daily newspaper, V5, N26 (1994) 9–9
25. Thanks to enemies for success, in Slovak, interview, Práca (Daily newspaper), March 3 (1994) 5–5
26. IFIP creates a new specialist group. Computer Research News, V6, N3 (1995) 12–12
27. Information will be decisive, in Slovak, interview, Literárny týždenník, N13 (1995) 10–11

28. Theoretical computer science conference helps interaction of South America with International community, IFIP Newsletter, V12, N3 (1995) 1,6,7 1995
29. IFIP Specialist Group 14: Foundations of Computer Science, IFIP Newsletter, V13, N1 (1996) 5–6, 8
30. Specialist Group 14: Foundations of Computer Science, in *36 years of IFIP*,edited by H. Zemanek, Published by IFIP, Laxenburg (1997) 277–286
31. How is the world we live in?, in Slovak, Hospodarské noviny, daily newspaper, interview, 12.2 (1998) 7–7
32. Federated conference, in Slovak, Univerzitní noviny, Masaryk University, Brno, V5, N9 (1998) 8–11
33. Revolution is as a tornado, in Slovak, interview, Život, weekly journal, N27 (1998) 12–13
34. First monograph on quantum computing, In Slovak, PC-Revue, interview, N11 1999) 22–24
35. Interview with Prof. Jozef Gruska (V. Linhartova), in Slovak Univerzitní noviny, Masaryk university, Brno, V7, N2 (2000) 67-70; N 3 (2000) 65-67; N4 (2000) 47–50
36. Is quantum information era coming?, in Slovak, Universitní noviny, Brno, N6 (2001) 1–6
37. We try to explore laws and limitations of the information world, in Slovak,muni.cz, Masaryk University, Brno, N5 (2005) 5–5
38. Why should we try to reach stars? in Slovak, interview, TV OKO, weakly journal, N50 (2006) 4–8
39. More self assurance does not hurt, in Slovak, Hospodarské noviny (Daily newspaper), 23.2 (2010) 4-4
40. Another physics of universe, Research.eu, N55 (2008) 33–34
41. History of TC1 – Foundations of Computer Science, in *50 years of IFIP*, Eds: K. Brunnstein and H. Zemanek, 2011, 72-76, IFIP publisher (2011) 72–76
42. Best schools have stronger requirements, in Slovak, interview, Učiteľské noviny, V8, N1 (2014) 17, 20–21

TV Movies

1. *My seven wonders of the world*, in Slovak, director M. Čorba, Slovak TV (1989) 36 min.
2. *Bethlehem mystery – Slovak nativities from collection of J. Gruska*, in Slovak, director L. Halama, Slovak TV (2007) 25 min.
3. *Bethlehem mystery – Czech and Moravian nativities from collection of J. Gruska*, in Slovak, director L. Halama, Slovak TV (2007) 25 min.
4. *Bethlehem mystery – European and Asian nativities from collection of J. Gruska*, in Slovak, director L. Halama, Slovak TV (2007) 25 min.
5. *Bethlehem mystery – American and African nativities from collection of J. Gruska*, in Slovak, director L. Halama, Slovak TV (2007) 25 min.
6. *GEN.sk – Jozef Gruska*, in Slovak, director M Chodovský, Slovak TV (2010) 14 min.

Contents

Computing with Controlled Resources

Computing with Unconventional Resources

History and Philosophy of Computing

Computing with Automata:
Classical, Cellular and Systolic

Counting with Probabilistic and Ultrametric Finite Automata

Kaspars Balodis$^{(\boxtimes)}$

Faculty of Computing, University of Latvia,
Raiņa bulvāris 19, Riga LV-1586, Latvia
kbalodis@gmail.com

Abstract. We investigate the state complexity of probabilistic and ultrametric finite automata for the problem of counting, i.e. recognizing the one-word unary language $C_n = \{1^n\}$. We also review the known results for other types of automata.

For one-way probabilistic automata, we construct a minimal 3-state automaton for counting to n with isolated cutpoint (but with decreasing isolation radius as n increases). We construct a two-way probabilistic automaton that counts to n with a constant number of states. We also show a minimal 2-state ultrametric automaton for counting.

1 Introduction

One of the main problems in the field of computational complexity theory is to determine the advantages that probabilistic algorithms have, compared with deterministic algorithms. The simplest model to explore this is the finite automaton.

In 1981, Freivalds in his invited talk in the International Symposium on Mathematical Foundations of Computer Science (MFCS) (it is worth mentioning that he was invited by Jozef Gruska) showed that for every $\varepsilon > 0$ a nonregular language $L = \{0^n 1^n \mid n \geq 1\}$ can be recognized by a two-way probabilistic automaton with probability $1 - \varepsilon$ [9].

In this paper, we investigate the descriptional complexity advantages for probabilistic and ultrametric automata compared with deterministic, nondeterministic and alternating automata. In [1], Ambainis showed that probabilistic automata can be significantly smaller than deterministic automata by constructing a one-way probabilistic automaton with n states such that any equivalent deterministic automaton requires $\Omega\left(2^{n\frac{\log \log n}{\log n}}\right)$ states.

We limit our focus to unary languages containing exactly one word. We say that an automaton counts to n if it recognizes the language $C_n = \{1^n\}$. We show that probabilistic and ultrametric automata for the counting problem can be very succinct, requiring only a constant number of states in many models.

This work has been supported by the European Social Fund within the project "Support for Doctoral Studies at University of Latvia."

© Springer International Publishing Switzerland 2014
C.S. Calude et al. (Eds.): Gruska Festschrift, LNCS 8808, pp. 3–16, 2014.
DOI: 10.1007/978-3-319-13350-8_1

2   Finite Automata

We assume the familiarity of the reader with finite automata and give only the standard definitions of the automata. For a description of how the automata work, see, for example, [10,11].

Definition 1. *A one-way deterministic finite automaton (1DFA) is a tuple $\mathcal{A} = (Q, S, \delta, q_0, F)$ where*

> *Q is the finite set of states,*
> *S is the input alphabet,*
> *$\delta : Q \times S \to Q$ is the transition function,*
> *$q_0 \in Q$ is the starting state, and*
> *$F \subseteq Q$ is the set of accepting states.*

Definition 2. *A one-way nondeterministic finite automaton (1NFA) is a tuple $\mathcal{A} = (Q, S, \delta, q_0, F)$ where*

> *Q is the finite set of states,*
> *S is the input alphabet,*
> *$\delta : Q \times S \to 2^Q$ is the transition function,*
> *$q_0 \in Q$ is the starting state, and*
> *$F \subseteq Q$ is the set of accepting states.*

Here we summarize the known results about counting with non-probabilistic (deterministic, nondeterministic and alternating) automata. To keep the article self-contained, the simple proofs or the proof ideas are also provided.

Theorem 1. *For each n there exists a 1DFA with $n+1$ states that recognizes C_n.*

Proof. Consider the automaton $\mathcal{A}_n = (\{0, 1, \ldots, n\}, \{1\}, \delta_n, 0, \{n\})$ (see Fig. 1) where $\delta_n(i, 1) = i + 1$ for all $0 \leq i < n$ and undefined for $i = n$. It is easy to see that it indeed accepts the language C_n. □

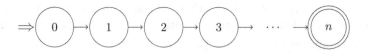

Fig. 1. 1DFA with $n+1$ states recognizing C_n. Double arrow shows the starting state. The double-circled state is final.

It is known that $n+1$ is also the necessary number of states even for 1NFA.

Theorem 2 ([14]). *$n+1$ states are necessary for recognizing C_n with a 1NFA.*

Proof. Assume that there are fewer than $n+1$ states for a 1NFA $\mathcal{A}$ recognizing C_n. An accepting run on $w = 1^n$ must visit at least one state more than once; therefore, it contains a cycle. It therefore follows that more than one word is accepted by $\mathcal{A}$. □

However, alternating automata can count to n with fewer states.

Definition 3. *A one-way alternating automaton (1AFA) is a tuple $M = (\Sigma, \Pi, S, \delta, q_0, F)$ where*

> *Σ and Π are the finite sets of existential and universal states, respectively, with $\Sigma \cap \Pi = \emptyset$ and $Q = \Sigma \cup \Pi$,*
> *S is the input alphabet,*
> *$\delta : Q \times S \to 2^Q$ is the transition function,*
> *$q_0 \in Q$ is the starting state, and*
> *$F \subseteq Q$ is the set of accepting states.*

In [15], Leiss proved that any deterministic n-state automaton has an equivalent alternating automaton with $\lceil \log n \rceil$ states. Therefore, as noted in [14], Theorem 1 immediately implies the following theorem:

Theorem 3. *For each n, there exists a 1AFA with $\lceil \log n \rceil$ states that recognizes C_n.*

A 1AFA is called *one-switch* if it cannot move from an existential state to a universal state. Thus, a one-switch 1AFA alternates between the branching modes at most once.

In [5], Birget proved the following theorem:

Theorem 4 ([5]). *For each n there exists a one-switch 1AFA that recognizes C_n with $O(\log^2 n / \log \log n)$ states.*

Proof. Consider the automaton in Fig. 2. The concept behind this automaton is to count the remainder modulo of each of the first k primes $p_1, p_2, \ldots, p_k$ such that $p_1 \cdot p_2 \cdot \ldots \cdot p_k \geq n$. The first part of the automaton (states a_j^i) accepts the word 1^m iff $\forall 1 \leq i \leq k \ \ m \equiv n \pmod{p_i}$. By the Chinese Remainder Theorem, the unique number less than $p_1 \cdot p_2 \cdot \ldots \cdot p_k$ that satisfies this property is n itself.

The second part of the automaton (states b_j^i) does the opposite – it rejects the subwords whose length is m such that $\forall 1 \leq i \leq k \ \ m \equiv n \pmod{p_i}$. This part is being run on every proper suffix of the input word.

Therefore, the automaton accepts exactly those words $w = 1^m$ for which $\forall 1 \leq i \leq k \ \ m \equiv n \pmod{p_i}$ and no proper suffix of w has this property. Therefore, the only word that is accepted is 1^n.

It is known that the sum of the first k primes is $\sum_{i=1}^{k} p_i = \frac{1}{2} k^2 \ln k + o(k^2 \ln k)$ and the product of the first k primes is $\prod_{i=1}^{k} p_i = e^{(1+o(1))k \ln k}$ (see for example [2]). From this basis, one can derive that the described automaton has $O(\log^2 n / \log \log n)$ states. □

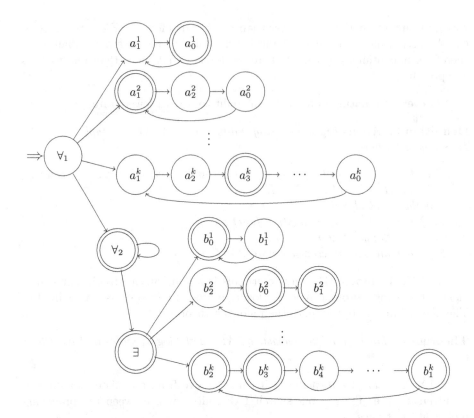

Fig. 2. 1AFA recognizing C_n. The final states in the first set of cycles are exactly those a^i_j for which $n \equiv j \pmod{p_i}$. State b^i_j is final iff a^i_j is not. States $\forall_1$ and $\forall_2$ are universal; all others states are existential.

3   Probabilistic Automata

Probabilistic finite automata (PFAs) were introduced by Rabin in [17].

Definition 4. *A one-way probabilistic finite automaton (1PFA) is a tuple* $\mathcal{A} = (Q, S, \delta, q_0, F)$ *where*

   Q is the finite set of states,
   S is the input alphabet,
   $\delta : Q \times S \times Q \to [0, 1]$ is the probabilistic transition matrix,
   $q_0 : Q \to [0, 1]$ is the starting vector, and
   $F \subseteq Q$ is the set of accepting states.

Definition 5. *A two-way probabilistic finite automaton (2PFA) is a tuple* $\mathcal{A} = (Q, S, \delta, q_0, F)$ *where*

   Q is the finite set of states,

S is the input alphabet,

$\delta : Q \times S \cup \{\vdash, \dashv\} \times Q \times \{L, N, R\} \rightarrow [0, 1]$ is the probabilistic transition matrix and $\vdash$ and $\dashv$ are the left and right endmarkers, respectively, and L, N, R denote the head movement,

$q_0 : Q \rightarrow [0, 1]$ is the starting vector, and

$F \subseteq Q$ is the set of accepting states.

Let $\mathcal{A}(x)$ denote the probability that a PFA $\mathcal{A}$ accepts the word x.

We say that a PFA $\mathcal{A}$ recognizes language L with cutpoint $\lambda \in [0, 1]$ if $\forall x \in L \ \mathcal{A}(x) > \lambda$ and $\forall x \notin L \ \mathcal{A}(x) < \lambda$. We say that a PFA $\mathcal{A}$ recognizes language L with an isolated cutpoint $\lambda \in [0, 1]$ if there exists $\delta > 0$ (called isolation radius) such that $\forall x \in L \ \mathcal{A}(x) > \lambda + \delta$ and $\forall x \notin L \ \mathcal{A}(x) < \lambda - \delta$.

We show that 3 states are necessary and sufficient to count to n with a 1PFA with an isolated cutpoint.

Theorem 5. *For each n, there exists a 1PFA that recognizes C_n with 3 states with an isolated cutpoint.*

Proof. Consider the following automaton $\mathcal{A}_n = (\{1, 2, 3\}, \{1\}, M_n, (1, 0, 0), \{2\})$ with the transition matrix

$$M_n = \begin{pmatrix} 1 - \varepsilon_1 & \varepsilon_1 & 0 \\ 0 & 1 - \varepsilon_2 & \varepsilon_2 \\ 0 & 0 & 1 \end{pmatrix}$$

where ε_1 and ε_2 depend on n (see Fig. 3).

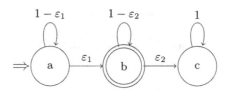

Fig. 3. 1PFA with 3 states recognizing C_n. The double arrow shows the starting state (with probability 1). The double-circled state is final.

We will show that it is possible to choose $\varepsilon_1, \varepsilon_2$ such that the acceptance probability is the highest on the word 1^n. Let $\varepsilon_1 = \varepsilon_2$. Then the probability of accepting 1^m is given by

$$(1 - \varepsilon_1)^{m-1} \varepsilon_1 m$$

The derivative of this quantity is

$$(1 - \varepsilon_1)^{m-1} \varepsilon_1 (1 + m \ln (1 - \varepsilon_1))$$

Solving it to be equal to 0 when $m = n$ gives $\varepsilon_1 = 1 - e^{-1/n}$.

Therefore, by setting $\varepsilon_1 = \varepsilon_2 = 1 - e^{-1/n}$, we get an automaton that has the maximal probability of acceptance on the word 1^n, and the acceptance probability decreases as the length of the word increases or decreases.

Note that although as n increases the difference between the probabilities of the automaton $\mathcal{A}_n$ to accept 1^n and 1^{n+1} (or 1^n and 1^{n-1}) decreases, for every n there exist λ and $\delta > 0$ such that the word 1^n is accepted with probability greater than $\lambda + \delta$, and the probability to accept any other word is less than $\lambda - \delta$, i.e. the cutpoint is isolated. $\square$

An example plot of the acceptance probability of words 1^x with $\varepsilon_1 = \varepsilon_2 = 1 - e^{-\frac{1}{200}}$ is shown in Fig. 4.

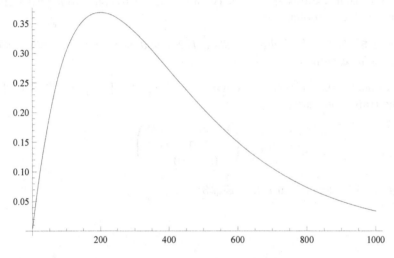

Fig. 4. The probability of accepting 1^x with $\varepsilon_1 = \varepsilon_2 = 1 - e^{-\frac{1}{200}}$

Theorem 6. *If $n > 1$ then any 1PFA that recognizes C_n has at least 3 states.*

Proof. Assume there exists a 1PFA with 2 states recognizing C_n for $n > 1$. Exactly one of the states must be final; otherwise, either all or none of the words would be accepted. Without loss of generality, assume that the first state is the non-final state and the second state is the final state. Let

$$M_1 = \begin{pmatrix} 1-p & p \\ m & 1-m \end{pmatrix}$$

be the transition matrix of the automaton.

$$M_1^2 = \begin{pmatrix} 1 - p(2-m-p) & p(2-m-p) \\ m(2-m-p) & 1 - m(2-m-p) \end{pmatrix}$$

If the automaton is in a probability distribution $\begin{pmatrix} a \\ 1-a \end{pmatrix}$ then after reading two symbols (twice applying M_1), the probability distribution becomes

$$\begin{pmatrix} m(2-m-p) + a(m+p-1)^2 \\ 1 - m(2-m-p) - a(m+p-1)^2 \end{pmatrix}$$

Notice that for every $a \in [0,1]$ the probability of being in a final state changes monotonically after every two symbols read; therefore, the automaton cannot recognize C_n for $n > 1$. □

Notice that although each individual automaton $\mathcal{A}_n$ from Theorem 5 has an isolated cutpoint, the isolation radius decreases as n increases. In [7], Freivalds showed how to construct a series of 1PFAs for recognizing C_n with a constant isolation radius.

Theorem 7 ([7]). *For each n, there exists a 1PFA with $O(\log^2 n / \log \log n)$ states that recognizes C_n with probability $\frac{3}{5}$.*

Proof. The automaton is similar to the 1AFA from the proof of Thm. 4. However, now the rejection of long words is performed by a probabilistic clock rather than an alternating behavior. The automaton is defined as follows:

$$\mathcal{A}_n = (\{b, a_0^1, \dots, a_{p_k-1}^k\}, 1, \delta, (0, \frac{1}{k}, 0, \dots, 0, \frac{1}{k}, 0, \dots, 0, \dots, \frac{1}{k}, 0, \dots, 0),$$
$$\{a_{n \bmod p_1}^1, \dots, a_{n \bmod p_k}^k\})$$

with p_i states $a_0^i, \dots, a_{p_i-1}^i$ for each of the first k primes $p_1, \dots, p_k$ (the value of k is to be determined later). The states $a_0^i, \dots, a_{p_i-1}^i$ form a cycle, which counts the remainder modulo p_i. State a_j^i is final iff $n \equiv j \pmod{p_i}$. The starting probability distribution of the automaton is $\frac{1}{k}$ in each of the states $a_0^1, a_0^2, \dots, a_0^k$ (see Fig. 5).

From every state there is a transition with probability $1 - \varepsilon$ to the state b.

By the Chinese Remainder Theorem, if $p_1 < p_2 < \dots < p_k$ are the first k primes and $p_1 \cdot p_2 \cdot \dots \cdot p_l \geq n$, then $\forall n' < p_1 \cdot p_2 \cdot \dots \cdot p_l$ if $n' \neq n$ at most $l - 1$ of the following congruences are satisfied:

$$n' \equiv n \pmod{p_1}$$
$$n' \equiv n \pmod{p_2}$$
$$\dots$$
$$n' \equiv n \pmod{p_k}$$

Let l be the minimal number such that $p_1 \cdot p_2 \cdot \dots \cdot p_l \geq 2n$.
Choose $k = 3l$.

Therefore, any word with length $n' < 2n \leq p_1 \cdot p_2 \cdot \dots \cdot p_l$ will be accepted with probability at most $\frac{l-1}{k} < \frac{l}{3l} = \frac{1}{3}$. Words with length n will be accepted with probability $1 - E(n)$ where $E(n)$ is the probability to be in state b after reading a word of length n. By the sum of geometric series, $E(n) = \varepsilon + (1-\varepsilon) \cdot \varepsilon + (1-\varepsilon)^2 \cdot \varepsilon + \cdots + (1-\varepsilon)^{n-1} \cdot \varepsilon = \sum_{i=0}^{n-1} \varepsilon \cdot (1-\varepsilon)^i = \varepsilon \frac{1-(1-\varepsilon)^n}{1-(1-\varepsilon)} = 1 - (1-\varepsilon)^n$. Words of length $n' \geq 2n$ will be accepted with probability at most $1 - E(2n)$.

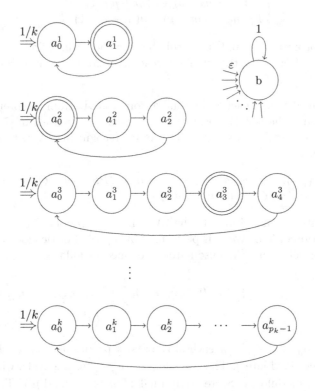

Fig. 5. 1PFA recognizing C_n. The accepting states in each cycle are exactly those that correspond to $n \bmod p_i$ For purposes of clarity, the transitions from each state to state b with probability ε are not drawn. All of the unlabeled transitions have probability $1-\varepsilon$.

By choosing $\varepsilon = 1 - \sqrt[n]{\frac{3}{5}}$ we get $1 - E(n) = \frac{3}{5}$ and $1 - E(2n) = \frac{9}{25} < \frac{2}{5}$. Therefore, 1^n is accepted with probability $\frac{3}{5}$, and every other word is accepted with probability $< \frac{2}{5}$.   □

As the next theorem shows, for the 2-way probabilistic finite automata, even a constant number of states suffices to recognize C_n with a fixed probability.

Theorem 8. *For each $\varepsilon > 0$ there exists a constant c_ε such that for each n there exists a 2PFA that recognizes C_n with c_ε states with probability $1 - \varepsilon$.*

Proof. In [9], Freivalds showed for every $\varepsilon > 0$ how to construct a 2PFA that recognizes the language EQUAL $= \{0^n 1^n \mid n \geq 1\}$ with probability $1 - \varepsilon$.

In [3], Balodis proved that if languages $\mathcal{L}, \mathcal{L}' \in S^*$ are such that there exists $u \in S^*$ such that $\forall x \in S^*(x \in \mathcal{L}' \Leftrightarrow ux \in \mathcal{L})$ then a 2PFA $\mathcal{A}$ recognizing $\mathcal{L}$ can be modified into a 2PFA $\mathcal{A}'$ recognizing $\mathcal{L}'$ with the same number of states. The idea is to change the transition matrix of $\mathcal{A}$ on the endmarker $\vdash$ in such a way that it considers symbol $\vdash$ as a string $\vdash u$.

One can see that for C_n and EQUAL, there exists u (namely $u = 0^n$) such that $\forall x \in \{1\}^* (x \in C_n \Leftrightarrow ux \in$ EQUAL$)$. We can therefore use this result to construct an equally-sized automaton and then restrict it to a smaller alphabet $\{1\}$ to obtain an automaton recognizing C_n.   □

4 Ultrametric Automata

Ultrametric finite automata and ultrametric Turing machines were first introduced by Freivalds in [8]. This has been followed by several papers in which various aspects of these machines are studied in depth. In [4], Balodis et al. have studied the descriptional complexity of ultrametric automata. They showed that ultrametric automata can achieve an exponential advantage in terms of the number of states required when compared with equivalent deterministic automata. In [13], the reversal complexity of ultrametric Turing machines has been studied.

Ultrametric automata are similar to probabilistic automata, the difference being that in probabilistic automata real numbers between 0 and 1 called probabilities are used to describe the branching of the automaton, while in ultrametric automata, p-adic numbers called amplitudes are used instead.

In [18], Turakainen generalized the probabilistic automaton model to allow the use of generalized probabilities – arbitrary real numbers – and showed that with such generalized automata, only the same class of languages – stochastic languages – can be recognized. Following this generalization, there are also no restrictions for ultrametric automata on the p-adic numbers that are allowed to be used as the amplitudes.

4.1 p-adic Numbers

In describing the notion of p-adic numbers, we follow the introductory text by David A. Madore [16].

Introduction to p-adic Numbers. A p-adic digit is a natural number in the range of 0 to $p-1$ (inclusive) where by p we denote an arbitrary prime number. A p-adic integer is a sequence $(a_i)_{i \in \mathbb{N}}$ in which each a_i is a p-adic digit. This is the same as $\cdots a_i \cdots a_2 a_1 a_0$. It corresponds to a natural number given by

$$\sum_{i=0}^{+\infty} a_i p^i,$$

where p is our chosen prime number. This sequence is infinite to the left side. Furthermore, a natural number represented in p-adic numbers will have only a finite number of non-zero digits. For any given $n \in \mathbb{N}$, the non-zero component of its representation in p-adic numbers will exactly match the representation of n in base p. Take the number 42 as an example, which is written as 132 in base 5. Its 5-adic representation is $\cdots 0 \cdots 0132$.

The situation is different for negative and rational p-adic numbers. Let us consider the number $\frac{1}{2}$ and its 5-adic representation as an example. 5-adic $\frac{1}{2}$ is a number that, when added to itself, gives 1. From this, we can devise that the 5-adic representation of $\frac{1}{2}$ is

$$
\begin{array}{r}
\cdots 2\,2\,2\,2\,2\,3 \\
+ \cdots 2\,2\,2\,2\,2\,3 \\
\hline
\cdots 0\,0\,0\,0\,0\,1
\end{array}
$$

Similarly, we devise subtraction and negative numbers. For example, in 5-adics

$$
\begin{array}{r}
\cdots 0\,0\,0\,1\,3\,2 \\
- \cdots 0\,0\,0\,2\,3\,4 \\
\hline
\cdots 4\,4\,4\,3\,4\,3
\end{array}
$$

Interestingly, almost all rational numbers can be expressed as p-adic integers. The exceptions for a given p are the numbers of the form $\frac{a}{b}$, where a is not divisible by p but b is divisible by p.

Numbers that cannot be expressed as p-adic natural numbers can, however, be expressed as p-adic rational numbers. Let us consider the number $\frac{1}{5}$ as an example. It cannot be expressed in 5-adic natural numbers, but it can be expressed as a 5-adic rational number

$$
\cdots 0 \cdots 000, 1.
$$

We can note that, as with p-adic natural numbers, p-adic rational numbers are expressed as a sequence that is infinite to the left side and finite to the right.

All of the usual arithmetic operations can be carried out on p-adic numbers as well, namely addition, subtraction, multiplication and division. Addition, subtraction and multiplication can be carried out in p-adic integers, but the results of division can be general p-adic numbers.

It is obvious that for every $q \in \mathbb{Q}$ there exists a prime number p such that q can be expressed as a p-adic number. The same does not hold for real numbers. For every p, there exists an irrational number such that it cannot be expressed as a p-adic number. However, this does not imply that for some p, p-adic numbers are a subset of real numbers. For every p, there is a continuum of p-adic numbers that cannot be expressed as a real number [8].

The field of p-adic numbers is denoted as $\mathbb{Q}_p$.

p-adic Absolute Values. A function $d : X \times X \to R_{\geq 0}$ where X is a non-empty set is called a metric iff it satisfies the following conditions:

1. $d(x,y) = 0$ iff $x = y$,
2. $d(x,y) = d(y,x)$,
3. $d(x,y) \leq d(x,z) + d(z,y)$ for all $z \in X$.

If the third property can be replaced by its stronger variant – the strong triangle inequality $d(x,y) \leq max\{d(x,z), d(z,y)\}$ – the norm is called ultrametric. Otherwise, it is called Archimedean. [8]

If the set X is equipped with the addition and multiplication operations (and forms a vector space), then a notion of norm can be introduced. The metric function is used to find the distances among the elements of a set. The distance of a given element to zero $d(x,0)$ is called the norm or absolute value of the element and is denoted by $\|x\|$.

The norm of an element satisfies the following properties:

1. $\|x\| = 0$ if and only if $x = 0$,
2. $\|x * y\| = \|x\| * \|y\|$,
3. $\|x + y\| \leq \|x\| + \|y\|$ (the triangle inequality).

For every non-zero rational number α there exists a unique prime factorization $\alpha = \pm 2^{\alpha_2} 3^{\alpha_3} 5^{\alpha_5} 7^{\alpha_7} \cdots$ where $\alpha_i \in \mathbb{N}$.

Definition 6. *The p-adic absolute value (also called the p-**norm**) of a rational number α is*

$$\|\alpha\|_p = \begin{cases} p^{-\alpha_p}, & \text{if } \alpha \neq 0 \\ 0, & \text{if } \alpha = 0. \end{cases}$$

p-adic numbers in more detail are discussed in [16]. The use of p-adics in other sciences can be seen in [6,12].

4.2 Automata

Ultrametric automata are defined as in [4].

Definition 7. *A finite one-way p-ultrametric automaton ($1U_pFA$) is a sextuple $(Q, S, s_0, \delta, F, \Lambda)$ where*

Q is the finite set of states,
S is the input alphabet,
$s_0 : Q \to \mathbb{Q}_p$ is the initial amplitude distribution,
$\delta : (S \cup \{\$\}) \times Q \times Q \to \mathbb{Q}_p$ is the transition function,
$F \subseteq Q$ is the set of final states, and
$\Lambda = (\lambda, \diamond)$ is the acceptance condition where $\lambda \in \mathbb{R}$ is the acceptance threshold and $\diamond \in \{\leq, \geq\}$.

The automaton works as follows. At every timestep, each of its states has an associated p-adic number called its amplitude. The automaton starts with the initial amplitude distribution s_0. Then it proceeds by processing the symbols of the input word $w = w_1 \ldots w_n$ one at a time. The amplitude distribution after processing the i-th symbol is denoted as s_i, with $s_i(y) = \sum_{x \in Q} s_{i-1}(x) \cdot \delta(w_i, x, y)$

for every $y \in Q$. After the n-th symbol, the end marker $ is processed in the same way, obtaining the final amplitude distribution s_{n+1}. If the sum of the p-norms of final amplitudes over final states is at least (or at most) the threshold, i.e., if $\sum_{x \in F} \|s_{n+1}(x)\|_p \diamond \lambda$, then the word w is said to be accepted; otherwise, it is rejected.

Here we show an optimal ultrametric automaton for counting.

Theorem 9. *For each n and each prime p there exists a $1U_pFA$ that recognizes C_n with 2 states.*

Proof. Consider the automaton $\mathcal{A}_n = (\{a, b\}, \{1\}, (p^n, p^{-n}), \delta, \{a, b\}, (\leq, 2))$ (see Fig. 6) where

$$\delta_1 = \begin{pmatrix} p & 0 \\ 0 & p^{-1} \end{pmatrix} \qquad \delta_\$ = \begin{pmatrix} 1 & 0 \\ 0 & 1 \end{pmatrix}$$

On a word 1^m, the sum of norms of the final states is $\|p^{n-m}\| + \|p^{-n+m}\| = p^{-n+m} + p^{n-m}$, which is equal to 2 if $m = n$ and greater otherwise. $\square$

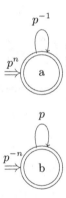

Fig. 6. $1U_pFA$ with 2 states recognizing C_n. Double arrows show the starting state amplitude distribution. Edges show the transitions on symbol 1 (the automaton has the identical transition on the endmarker).

Theorem 10. *If $n > 0$ then any $1U_pFA$ that recognizes C_n has at least 2 states.*

Proof. Assume there exists a $1U_pFA$ with 1 state a that recognizes C_n. Let $\alpha = \delta(1, a, a)$ be the coefficient that is multiplied to the amplitude of state a for every symbol of the input word. The final amplitude after processing word 1^m (and the endmarker) in the state a is $s_0(a) \cdot \alpha^m \cdot \delta(\$, a, a)$.

Assume α is a p-adic integer. If its rightmost p-adic digit is 0, then multiplying any p-adic number (except 0) by α decreases the norm. If α is not a p-adic integer (it has some non-zero digits to the right of the p-adic comma), then multiplication with α increases the norm. If α is a p-adic integer whose rightmost p-adic digit is not 0, then multiplication with α does not change the norm.

Therefore, as the length of the word increases, the norm increases or decreases monotonically or does not change, which eliminates the possibility to recognize C_n for $n > 0$. □

References

1. Ambainis, A.: The complexity of probabilistic versus deterministic. In: Nagamochi, H., Suri, S., Igarashi, Y., Miyano, S., Asano, T. (eds.) ISAAC 1996. LNCS, vol. 1178, pp. 233–238. Springer, Heidelberg (1996). http://dx.doi.org/10.1007/BFb0009499
2. Bach, E., Shallit, J.: Algorithmic Number Theory. MIT Press, Cambridge, MA, USA (1996)
3. Balodis, K.: One Alternation Can Be More Powerful Than Randomization in Small and Fast Two-Way Finite Automata. In: Gsieniec, L., Wolter, F. (eds.) FCT 2013. LNCS, vol. 8070, pp. 40–47. Springer, Heidelberg (2013). http://dx.doi.org/10.1007/978-3-642-40164-0_7
4. Balodis, K., Beriņa, A., Cīpola, K., Dimitrijevs, M., Iraids, J., Jēriņš, K., Kacs, V., Kalējs, J., Krišlauks, R., Lukstiņš, K., Raumanis, R., Scegulnaja, I., Somova, N., Vanaga, A., Freivalds, R.: On the state complexity of ultrametric finite automata. In: SOFSEM 2013: Theory and Practice of Computer Science, vol. 2, pp. 1–9 (2013)
5. Birget, J.C.: Two-way automata and length-preserving homomorphisms. Mathematical Systems Theory **29**(3), 191–226 (1996). http://dx.doi.org/10.1007/BF01201276
6. Dragovich, B., Dragovich, A.: A p-adic model of dna sequence and genetic code. p-Adic Numbers, Ultrametric Analysis, and Applications **1**(1), 34–41 (2009)
7. Freivalds, R.: On the growth of the number of states in result of the determinization of probabilistic finite automata. Avtomatika i Vicislitelnaja Tehnika **3**, 39–42 (1982). (in Russian)
8. Freivalds, R.: Ultrametric automata and turing machines. In: Voronkov, A. (ed.) Turing-100, EPiC Series, vol. 10, pp. 98–112. EasyChair (2012)
9. Freivalds, R.: Probabilistic two-way machines. In: Gruska, J., Chytil, M.P. (eds.) MFCS 1981. LNCS, vol. 118, pp. 33–45. Springer, Heidelberg (1981)
10. Gruska, J.: Foundations of Computing. International Thomson Computer Press, Boston, MA, USA (1997)
11. Hopcroft, J.E., Ullman, J.D.: Introduction to Automata Theory. Addison-Wesley, Languages and Computation (1979)
12. Kozyrev, S.V.: Ultrametric analysis and interbasin kinetics. In: 2nd International Conference on p-adic Mathematical Physics, vol. 826, pp. 121–128. AIP Publishing (2006)
13. Krišlauks, R., Rukšāne, I., Balodis, K., Kucevalovs, I., Freivalds, R., Nāgele, I.: Ultrametric turing machines with limited reversal complexity. In: SOFSEM 2013: Theory and Practice of Computer Science, vol. 2, pp. 87–94 (2013)
14. Kupferman, O., Ta-Shma, A., Vardi, M.Y.: Counting with automata (2001)

15. Leiss, E.: Succinct representation of regular languages by boolean automata. Theoretical Computer Science **13**(3), 323–330 (1981). http://www.sciencedirect.com/science/article/pii/S0304397581800059
16. Madore, D.A.: A first introduction to p-adic numbers (2000). http://www.madore.org/~david/math/padics.pdf
17. Rabin, M.O.: Probabilistic automata. Information and Control **6**(3), 230–245 (1963). http://www.sciencedirect.com/science/article/pii/S0019995863902900
18. Turakainen, P.: Generalized automata and stochastic languages. Proceedings of The American Mathematical Society **21**, 303–309 (1969)

Systolic Automata and P Systems

Roberto Barbuti[1], Andrea Maggiolo-Schettini[1], Paolo Milazzo[1],
Giovanni Pardini[1](✉), and Simone Tini[2]

[1] Dipartimento di Informatica, Università di Pisa,
Largo B. Pontecorvo 3, 56127 Pisa, Italy
{barbuti,maggiolo,milazzo,pardinig}@di.unipi.it
[2] Dipartimento di Scienza e Alta Tecnologia, Università dell'Insubria,
Via Valleggio 11, 22100 Como, Italy
simone.tini@uninsubria.it

Abstract. Systolic automata are models of highly-concurrent language
acceptors based on identical processors with one-way flow of information,
amenable to efficient hardware implementation as multiprocessor chips.

In this paper we investigate the relationship between Binary Systolic
Tree Automata (BSTA), in which the underlying communication structure
is an infinite complete binary tree with parallel bottom-up computation,
and P systems, a biologically-inspired formalism based on rewrite rules acting upon multisets of symbols with a maximally-parallel semantics.

In particular, we propose a variant of BSTA as multiset languages
acceptors, termed Multiset BSTA. By exploiting the similarity in the
parallel computation as performed in both BSTA and P systems, we
show how a Multiset BSTA can be simulated by a cooperative P system
while preserving the computational efficiency of systolic automata.

1 Introduction

Systolic automata are highly parallel language acceptors inspired by the functioning of VLSI architectures [14,17]. A systolic automaton is an infinite tree
associated with an input function g and a processing function f. Without loss
of generality, the tree of a systolic automaton is often assumed to be binary,
thus obtaining the class of Binary Systolic Tree Automata (BSTAs). The input
function g maps each symbol of the considered input alphabet into a working
symbol from an operating alphabet. The processing function f, instead, maps
two working symbols into one. The way in which a BSTA processes a candidate
string to determine whether it belongs or not to the accepted language is by
feeding its tree at a suitable level with such a string, and then by applying the
processing function at each level (from bottom to top) in order to produce, in
the root of the tree, a single operating symbol. If such a symbol belongs to the
accepting alphabet (subset of the operating alphabet) then the candidate string
is accepted, otherwise it is not accepted. Note that a string w of length m has
to be accepted at smallest level n of the tree such that $m \leq 2^n$. Moreover, if
$m < 2^n$, then $2^n - m$ instances of the special symbol ♯ are appended to the
string.

© Springer International Publishing Switzerland 2014
C.S. Calude et al. (Eds.): Gruska Festschrift, LNCS 8808, pp. 17–31, 2014.
DOI: 10.1007/978-3-319-13350-8_2

It has been proved that BSTAs can accept all regular languages [17]. Moreover, by exploiting the tree structure they can accept higher level languages such as $a^{2^n} b^{2^n}$. The class of languages accepted by a BSTA is a subset of the class E0L [24] called *Systolic E0L* [13]. Many variants of systolic automata have been proposed (see, e.g., [15,16,19]), and many studies have been performed on them (see, e.g., [18,20,21])

The processing of a candidate string by a BSTA is performed in a highly parallel way. Symbols to be associated with nodes at level i of the tree can be obtained by the symbols associated with nodes at level $i + 1$ by applying f, the processing function, 2^i times in parallel to each pair of children nodes of nodes at level i. This is repeated for each level of the tree until the root is reached. Hence, an execution of a BSTA can be seen as a sequence of highly parallel steps in which *all* of the currently available symbols are processed and "transformed" into symbols to be used in the next step. The form of parallelism at the basis of the functioning of BSTAs is hence very similar to the notion of *maximal parallelism* considered in the context of P Systems [23]. P Systems are a form of hierarchical multiset rewriting systems. Maximal parallelism in P systems states that, at each step of their execution, rewriting rules must be applied in parallel to a sub-multiset of the available symbols (possibly to *all* of them) so that no rule can be applied to the remaining symbols.

The aim of this paper is hence to investigate the relationship between BSTAs and P systems based on the similarity of the forms of parallelism they consider. Since P systems are used to process multisets, the first thing we do is to define a variant of BSTAs, called MBSTAs, that can be used to accept *multiset languages* rather than languages of strings. As usual when passing from string languages to multiset languages ([12]), we show that MBSTAs can accept every context-free multiset language. Then, we face the problem of translating a MBSTA into an equivalent P system (used as language acceptor [9]). To this aim we define another (equivalent) variant of MBSTAs, called Regular MBSTAs, in which some regularity conditions are assumed. Finally, we define a translation of RMBSTAs into P systems and prove that P systems obtained after translation are as efficient as the original RMBSTAs.

2   Background

Let $\mathbb{N}$ be the set of natural numbers and $\mathbb{N}^+$ denote $\mathbb{N} \setminus \{0\}$. Elements of sets are enumerated between $\{$ and $\}$, while elements of multisets are enumerated between $\{\!|$ and $|\!\}$. Given a finite alphabet Λ, we denote by Λ^* the set of all finite strings over Λ, namely $\epsilon \in \Lambda^*$, for ϵ the empty string, and $aw \in \Lambda^*$, for $a \in \Lambda$ and $w \in \Lambda^*$. Given two sets of strings Z_1, Z_2, their concatenation is denoted $Z_1.Z_2 = \{w_1 w_2 \mid w_1 \in Z_1, w_2 \in Z_2\}$. The number of occurrences of a symbol a in a string w is denoted $|w|_a$; moreover, given a set $Z \subseteq \Lambda$, $|w|_Z = \sum_{a \in Z} |w|_a$. The length of w is denoted $|w|$. The ith element of w is denoted w_i. We denote with Λ^+ the set $\Lambda^* \setminus \{\epsilon\}$. As usual, a language over Λ is a subset $L \subseteq \Lambda^*$. We denote $\mathcal{M}(\Lambda)$ the set of all the multisets with elements in Λ. The union of multisets is denoted by $\oplus$, \ denotes both the difference between sets and the difference between multisets, and $\emptyset$ denotes both the empty set and the empty multiset. Moreover, we denote with $\mathcal{P}(I)$ the powerset of I, that is the set of all subsets of the set I. Given a function $f : A \to A$, we define f^n as $f^0(x) = x$ and $f^n(x) = f(f^{n-1}(x))$.

Definition 1 (Parikh mapping). *Let* $\Lambda = \{a_1, a_2, \ldots, a_n\}$ *be an ordered alphabet. The* Parikh mapping *over strings* $\phi : \Lambda^* \to \mathbb{N}^n$ *is defined as follows:*

$$\phi(w) = (|w|_{a_1}, |w|_{a_2}, \ldots, |w|_{a_n}).$$

The Parikh mapping of a language $L \subseteq \Lambda^*$ *is defined as* $\phi(L) = \{\phi(w) \mid w \in L\}$.

In the rest of the paper, we always assume alphabets to be ordered. Therefore there is a one-to-one correspondence between Parikh vectors in $\mathbb{N}^{|\Lambda|}$ and multisets over Λ. For this reason, with a slight abuse of notation, we assume to denote by $\phi(w)$, for any string $w \in \Lambda^*$, both the Parikh vector and the multiset over Λ described by w.

We recall from [22] the definition of Binary Systolic Tree Automata [14,17].

Definition 2 (Binary Systolic Tree Automaton). *A* Binary Systolic Tree Automaton (BSTA)[1] *is a construct* $K = (\Lambda, Q, F, f, g)$, *where* Λ *is the finite input alphabet,* $Q \cup \{\natural\}$ *is the finite operating alphabet (with* $\natural$ *being a special symbol outside of* Λ, Q*),* $F \subseteq Q \cup \{\natural\}$ *is the accepting alphabet,* $f : (Q \cup \{\natural\}) \times (Q \cup \{\natural\}) \to Q \cup \{\natural\}$ *is the processing function and* $g : \Lambda \cup \{\natural\} \to Q \cup \{\natural\}$ *is the input function. Moreover, the processing function is such that* $f(x, y) = \natural$ *iff* $x = y = \natural$*; while the input function is such that* $g(x) = \natural$ *iff* $x = \natural$.

A BSTA is interpreted as an infinite complete binary tree, in which the processing function f is associated with each node. A BSTA can accept strings on the alphabet Λ in the following way. Given a string $w \in \Lambda^*$ having length m, we take the smallest level n of the tree with at least m nodes. If $m < 2^n$, let $\ell = 2^n - m$. The string $w\natural^\ell$ is transformed by means of the input function, by applying g to each one of its symbols, preserving the ordering. The string in $(Q \cup \{\natural\})^*$ obtained is then fed to the level n of the tree. Precisely, the symbols in the transformed string are given as input, in order, to the nodes of the cut at level n, starting from the leftmost node.

At the first step, once each node of the cut has an input in $Q \cup \{\natural\}$, all processing functions of the level $n - 1$ get, in parallel, the two inputs from their children nodes and produce their results, a symbol in $Q \cup \{\natural\}$ for each node. This process is iterated for n steps, resulting in a symbol $q \in Q \cup \{\natural\}$ being produced in the root of the tree. If $q \in F$ then the string is accepted, otherwise it is rejected by the BSTA.

The definition of BSTAs reported here, from [22], includes constraints on the behaviour of the processing and input function when dealing with the special symbol $\natural$ which were not assumed in the original definition ([14]). Note that

---

[1] Also known in the literature by the acronyms SBTA and BT-VLSI.

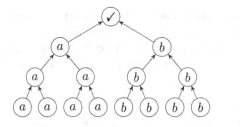

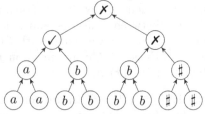

Fig. 1. BSTA accepting computation   **Fig. 2.** BSTA rejecting computation

such constraints on functions f and g imply that the value of function $f(\sharp, x)$, for $x \in Q$, is irrelevant, since it is never used by a BSTA. In fact, at each level of the tree, any and all $\sharp$ symbols may only occur at the end of the string.

Definition 3 (Language accepted by a BSTA). *Consider a BSTA, $K = (\Lambda, Q, F, f, g)$. We define $\overline{f} : (Q \cup \{\sharp\})^* \to (Q \cup \{\sharp\})^*$ and $\overline{g} : (\Lambda \cup \{\sharp\})^* \to (Q \cup \{\sharp\})^*$ as follows:*

$$\overline{f}(w_1 w_2 \ldots w_m) = f(w_1, w_2) f(w_3, w_4) \ldots f(w_{m-1}, w_m) \qquad \text{if } m \text{ is even;}$$
$$\overline{g}(w_1 w_2 \ldots w_m) = g(w_1) g(w_2) \ldots g(w_m).$$

Given a string $w \in \Lambda^*$, let $n \in \mathbb{N}$ be such that $|w| \leq 2^n$. Then w is accepted by K at level n iff $\overline{f}^n(\overline{g}(w \sharp^\ell)) \in F$, where $\ell = 2^n - |w|$. The string w is accepted by K iff it is accepted at the smallest level n with $|w| \leq 2^n$. Finally, the language accepted by K is the set of strings $L(K) = \{w \in \Lambda^* \mid w \text{ is accepted by } K\}$.

Example 1. Let us consider the BSTA $K = (\Lambda, Q, F, f, g)$ where $\Lambda = \{a, b\}$, $Q = \{a, b, \checkmark, \times\}$, $F = \{\checkmark\}$, g is the identity function, and f is defined as follows:

$$f(a, a) = a \quad f(b, b) = b \quad f(a, b) = \checkmark \quad f(\sharp, \sharp) = \sharp$$

and $f(x, y) = \times$ for any other pair of symbols not defined above. Two possible computations of K are shown in Figure 1 and 2. The language accepted by the BSTA is $L(K) = \{a^{2^n} b^{2^n} \mid n \in \mathbb{N}\}$.

A useful property for the definition of BSTAs is to be able to give the string as input to any level of the tree with enough nodes, by relaxing the constraint that requires it to be fed to the smallest possible level. We recall the definition of *stable* BSTA, for which the result of either acceptance or rejection of a string w is independent of the actual level n ($|w| \leq 2^n$) to which the string is fed. Moreover, each BSTA can be transformed into an equivalent *stable* BSTA, as shown by the theorem which follows.

Definition 4 (Stable BSTA). *A BSTA $K = (\Lambda, Q, F, f, g)$ is stable iff for each string $w \in \Lambda^*$ and for all $n_1, n_2 \in \mathbb{N}$ with $|w| \leq 2^{n_1} \leq 2^{n_2}$, it holds that*

w is accepted by K at level $n_1 \iff w$ is accepted by K at level n_2.

Theorem 1 ([14,22]). *For every BSTA K there exists a stable BSTA K' such that $L(K) = L(K')$.*

3   Multiset Binary Systolic Tree Automata

A *Multiset Binary Systolic Tree Automaton* (MBSTA) has the same structure of a BSTA, but it accepts multisets. Because multisets have no order among the elements, the elements of the multiset can be given as input to the nodes of the cut in any order. For a multiset to be accepted by a MBSTA there needs to be some order of the symbols yielding a final symbol in the root of the tree.

Definition 5 (Multiset language accepted by a MBSTA). *Consider a MBSTA, $M = (\Lambda, Q, F, f, g)$. Given a multiset $\mu \in \mathcal{M}(\Lambda)$, let $n \in \mathbb{N}$ be such that $|\mu| \leq 2^n$. Then μ is accepted by M at level n iff there exists a string $w \in \Lambda^*$ such that $\phi(w) = \mu$ and $\overline{f}^n(\overline{g}(w \sharp^\ell)) \in F$, where $\ell = 2^n - |\mu|$. The multiset μ is accepted by M iff it is accepted at the smallest level n such that $|\mu| \leq 2^n$. Finally, the* multiset language accepted by M *is set of multisets $L(M) = \{\mu \in \mathcal{M}(\Lambda) \mid \mu$ is accepted by $M\}$.*

The multiset language accepted by a MBSTA is obtained from the language accepted by the BSTA having the same structure through the Parikh mapping.

Proposition 1. *Assume a BSTA $K = (\Lambda, Q, F, f, g)$ and the MBSTA $M = (\Lambda, Q, F, f, g)$ having the same structure. Then*

1. *If a string $w \in \Lambda^*$ is accepted by K at level n then the multiset $\phi(w) \in \mathcal{M}(\Lambda)$ is accepted by M at level n;*
2. *If a multiset $\mu \in \mathcal{M}(\Lambda)$ is accepted by M at level n then there is a string $w \in \Lambda^*$ such that $\phi(w) = \mu$ and w is accepted by K at level n.*

Proof. Directly by Definition 5.

Corollary 1. *Assume a BSTA $K = (\Lambda, Q, F, f, g)$ and the MBSTA $M = (\Lambda, Q, F, f, g)$ having the same structure. Then $L(M) = \{\phi(w) \mid w \in L(K)\}$.*

The notion of stability is trivially extended to MBSTAs. Moreover, analogously to BSTAs, a MBSTA can always be transformed into an equivalent stable MBSTA.

Definition 6 (Stable MBSTA). *A MBSTA $M = (\Lambda, Q, F, f, g)$ is stable iff for each multiset $\mu \in \mathcal{M}(\Lambda)$ and $n_1, n_2 \in \mathbb{N}$ with $|\mu| \leq 2^{n_1} \leq 2^{n_2}$, it holds that*

$$\mu \text{ is accepted by } M \text{ at level } n_1 \iff \mu \text{ is accepted by } M \text{ at level } n_2.$$

Proposition 2. *Let $K = (\Lambda, Q, F, f, g)$ be a stable BSTA. Then the MBSTA $M = (\Lambda, Q, F, f, g)$ having the same structure is stable.*

Proof. Assume any multiset $\mu \in \mathcal{M}(\Lambda)$ and any pair of naturals $n_1, n_2 \in \mathbb{N}$ such that $|\mu| \leq 2^{n_1} \leq 2^{n_2}$. We prove that if μ is accepted by M at level n_1 then μ is accepted by M at level n_2, the converse case is analogous. If μ is accepted by M at level n_1, then by Proposition 1 (case 2) there exists some $w \in \Lambda^*$ such that $\phi(w) = \mu$ and w is accepted by K at level n_1. Since K is stable we infer that w is accepted by K at level n_2, thus implying, through Proposition 1 (case 1), that μ is accepted by M at level n_2.

Theorem 2. *For every MBSTA M there exists a stable MBSTA M' such that $L(M) = L(M')$.*

Proof. Given the MBSTA $M = (\Lambda, Q, F, f, g)$, we consider the BSTA $K = (\Lambda, Q, F, f, g)$ having the same structure of M. From Theorem 1 there exists a stable BSTA $K' = (\Lambda, Q', F', f', g')$ with $L(K) = L(K')$. Consider the MBSTA $M' = (\Lambda, Q', F', f', g')$ having the same structure of K'. From Proposition 2 we have that M' is stable. It remains to be shown that $L(M') = L(M)$. We prove that for any $\mu \in \mathcal{M}(\Lambda)$, $\mu \in L(M)$ implies $\mu \in L(M')$, the converse is analogous. If $\mu \in L(M)$, then by Corollary 1 we infer $w \in L(K)$ for some $w \in \Lambda^*$ with $\phi(w) = \mu$. From $L(K) = L(K')$ we infer $w \in L(K')$. Since K' and M' have the same structure, by Corollary 1 it follows $\mu \in L(M')$.

3.1   MBSTAs and MFAs

In this section we briefly study the expressive power of MBSTAs, by showing that they can accept all the languages recognized by Multiset Finite Automata. A *Multiset Finite automaton (MFA)* [12] is a finite automaton in which the input is given by a multiset of symbols of the alphabet. It starts in its initial state with the whole multiset of symbols, and changes its current state based on the state itself and on a symbol which is chosen from the multiset. The chosen symbol is removed from the multiset. The MFA stops when either no move is possible or the multiset is empty. We also recall the important fact that MFAs have the same expressive power as Multiset Context-Free Grammars ([12]), therefore they accept the class of *context-free multiset languages*.

Definition 7 (Multiset Finite Automaton). *A* Multiset Finite Automaton *is a construct $A = (\Lambda, Z, W, z_0, t)$, where Λ is the* input alphabet, *Z is the finite set of* states, *W is the set of* accepting states *($W \subseteq Z$), $z_0 \in Z$ is the* initial state, *and t is the* transition function *($t : Z \times \Lambda \to \mathcal{P}(Z)$).*

Definition 8 (Multiset language accepted by a MFA). *Given the* Multiset Finite Automaton *$A = (\Lambda, Z, W, z_0, t)$, a* configuration *of A is a pair (z, μ), where z is a state, $z \in Z$, and μ is a multiset of symbols, $\mu \in \mathcal{M}(\Lambda)$. Let $\vdash$ denote the following relation on configurations, whose reflexive and transitive closure is denoted $\vdash^*$:*

$$(z, \mu) \vdash (z', \mu') \iff z' \in t(z, a),\ a \in \Lambda,\ \mu' = \mu \backslash \{\!|a|\!\}.$$

A multiset $\mu \in \mathcal{M}(\Lambda)$ is accepted by A iff $(z_0, \mu) \vdash^* (z, \emptyset)$ for some $z \in W$. The multiset language accepted by A is $L(A) = \{\mu \in \mathcal{M}(\Lambda) \mid \mu$ is accepted by $A\}$.

Theorem 3. *Given an alphabet Λ, every context-free multiset language L is accepted by a MBSTA.*

Proof. The proof follows that in [17]. Consider the MFA $A = (\Lambda, Z, W, z_0, t)$ with $L(A) = L$, and build a MBSTA $K = (\Lambda, Q, F, f, g)$ with $L(K) = L$ as follows.

The processing alphabet Q of K is defined as $Q = \mathcal{P}(Z \times Z)$, where each symbol in Q corresponds therefore to a set of pairs (z_1, z_2) of states of A.

The input function $g : \Lambda \cup \{\sharp\} \to Q \cup \{\sharp\}$ is defined as follows:

$$g(a) = \{(z_i, z_j) \mid z_i, z_j \in Z,\ z_j \in t(z_i, a)\} \qquad a \in \Lambda;$$
$$g(\sharp) = \sharp;$$

while the processing function $f : Q \cup \{\sharp\} \times Q \cup \{\sharp\} \to Q \cup \{\sharp\}$ is defined as

$$f(I, J) = \{(z_i, z_j) \mid (z_i, z_k) \in I,\ (z_k, z_j) \in J\};$$
$$f(I, \sharp) = I;$$
$$f(\sharp, \sharp) = \sharp.$$

Finally, let $F_0 = \{I \in Q \mid \exists z \in W.\ (z_0, z) \in I\}$; then the accepting alphabet is

$$F = \begin{cases} F_0 \cup \{\sharp\} & \text{if } z_0 \in W; \\ F_0 & \text{if } z_0 \notin W. \end{cases}$$

Let us consider any node of the binary tree computed according to f and g from a string $w\sharp^\ell$ being fed at some level n, with $w \in \Lambda^*$ and $\ell = 2^n - |w|$. Assume $I \neq \sharp$ and let $\sigma(I)$ be the substring of w corresponding to the ordered sequence of leaves being descendants of I. It is easy to see that I contains precisely the pairs of states (z_1, z_2) such that there exists a path in A labelled by the symbols in $\sigma(I)$; i.e., given $\sigma(I) = a_1 a_2 \ldots a_k$, then $(z_i, z_k) \in I$ iff there exist states $z_1, z_2, \ldots, z_{k+1}$ such that for all $i < k$ we have $z_{i+1} \in t(z, a_i)$.

Assume now an arbitray multiset $\mu \in L(A)$. Then there exist a string $w = a_1 \ldots a_k \in \Lambda^*$ with $\phi(w) = \mu$ and configurations $(z_0, \mu_0) \vdash (z_1, \mu_1) \vdash \cdots \vdash (z_k, \mu_{k+1})$ such that for all i we have $\mu_{i+1} = \mu_i \setminus \{a_i\}$, and $z_k \in W$ is an accepting state. For n such that $k \leq 2^n$ consider the node $\widetilde{I} = \overline{f}^n(\overline{g}(w\sharp^{2^n - k}))$. We have $(z_0, z_k) \in \widetilde{I}$ and, since $x_k \in W$, we have $\widetilde{I} \in F$. Therefore $\mu \in L(K)$.

Assume $\mu \in L(K)$. Then there exist a n such that $k \leq 2^n$ and a string $w = a_1 \ldots a_k \in \Lambda^*$ with $\phi(w) = \mu$, a node $\widetilde{I} = \overline{f}^n(\overline{g}(w\sharp^{2^n - k})) \in F$ and configurations $(z_0, \mu_0) \vdash (z_1, \mu_1) \vdash \cdots \vdash (z_k, \mu_{k+1})$ such that for all i we have $\mu_{i+1} = \mu_i \setminus \{a_i\}$. From $\widetilde{I} \in F$ we infer $z_k \in W$. Therefore $\mu \in L(A)$. We conclude $L(K) = L(A)$.

3.2   Regular MBSTAs

We introduce variants of BSTAs and MBSTAs, called Regular BSTAs (RBSTAs) and Regular MBSTAs (RMBSTAs) respectively, in which some regularity conditions are assumed. Regular MBSTA will be used as an intermediate formalism to ease the construction of a P system which accepts the same multiset language as a given MBSTA.

Definition 9 (Regular (M)BSTA).   A Regular BSTA (resp. Regular MBSTA) is a BSTA $C = (\Lambda, Q, F, f, g)$ (resp. MBSTA $M = (\Lambda, Q, F, f, g)$) such that Q can be partitioned into the sets $Q_o = \{q_1, \ldots, q_h\}$ of plain symbols, and $Q_o^\sharp = \{q_{h+1}^\sharp, \ldots, q_n^\sharp\}$ of tagged symbols, and the following regularity conditions for the functions f and g are satisfied:

- $g(x) \in Q_o$, for all $x \in \Lambda$;
- $f(q_1, q_2) \in Q_o$, for all $q_1, q_2 \in Q_o$;
- $f(q_1, \sharp) \in Q_o^\sharp$, for all $q_1 \in Q_o \cup Q_o^\sharp$;
- $f(q_1, q_2) \in Q_o^\sharp$, for all $q_1 \in Q_o$, $q_2 \in Q_o^\sharp$.

Theorem 4. *Let $K = (\Lambda, Q, F, f, g)$ (resp. $M = (\Lambda, Q, F, f, g)$) be a stable BSTA (resp. stable MBSTA). Then we can effectively construct a stable RBSTA $K' = (\Lambda, Q', F', f', g)$ (resp. stable RMBSTA $M' = (\Lambda, Q', F', f', g)$) such that*

- $L(K) = L(K')$ *(resp. $L(M) = L(M')$);*
- Q' *can be partitioned into the sets $Q_o = Q$ and $Q_o^\sharp = \{x^\sharp \mid x \in Q\}$.*

Proof. Let $F' = F \cup \{x^\sharp \mid x \in F\}$, and let f' be defined as follows:

- for $x, y, z \in Q_o$, if $f(x, y) = z$ then $f'(x, y) = z$ and $f'(x, y^\sharp) = z^\sharp$;
- for $x, z \in Q_o$, if $f(x, \sharp) = z$ then $f'(x, \sharp) = z^\sharp$ and $f'(x^\sharp, \sharp) = z^\sharp$;
- $f'(\sharp, \sharp) = \sharp$.

We prove that the thesis holds for BSTAs and MBSTAs by showing that for all strings $w \in \Lambda^*$ and n such that $|w| \leq 2^n$, w can be accepted by K (resp. M) at level n iff w can be accepted by K' (resp. M') at level n.

Let $\ell = 2^n - |w|$, and let $u_i = (\overline{f})^i (\overline{g}(w \sharp^\ell))$, $u_i' = (\overline{f'})^i (\overline{g}(w \sharp^\ell))$, for $i \in \{0, \ldots, n\}$. Note that $|u_i| = |u_i'| = 2^{n-i}$. Moreover, let us define the function $\theta : (Q_o \cup Q_o^\sharp \cup \{\sharp\})^+ \to (Q_o \cup \{\sharp\})^+$ as follows:

$$\theta(x) = \theta(x^\sharp) = x \qquad\qquad x \in Q_o$$
$$\theta(\sharp) = \sharp$$
$$\theta(x_1 \ldots x_k) = \theta(x_1) \ldots \theta(x_k)$$

It suffices to show that for all $i \in \{0, \ldots, n\}$, $u_i = \theta(u_i')$, which can be proved by induction. As regards the base case, $u_0 = \theta(u_0')$, since $u_0' = u_0 \in (Q_o \cup \{\sharp\})^+$.

In the inductive case, assume $u_i = \theta(u_i')$; we need to prove that $u_{i+1} = \theta(u_{i+1}')$. By the definitions of g and f', for all i, each string u_i' is of the form $q_1 \ldots q_k \sharp \ldots \sharp$ with $q_i \in Q_o$ for all $i < k$ and $q_k \in Q_o \cup Q_o^\sharp$. As a consequence, only either one of the following two cases may occur (in the following, we assume $\overline{f}(\epsilon) = \epsilon$):

- *Case $u_i' = \alpha v$, with $\alpha \in Q_o^*$, $v \in \{\sharp\}^*$.* It holds that $u_i = \theta(u_i') = u_i'$.
  If $|\alpha|$ is even, then $u_{i+1}' = \overline{f'}(u_i') = \overline{f}(u_i) = u_{i+1}$, and hence $\theta(u_{i+1}') = \theta(u_{i+1}) = u_{i+1}$.
  If $|\alpha|$ is odd, let $u_i' = \alpha' x \sharp v'$, with $\alpha' \in Q_o^*$, $x \in Q_o$, $v' \in \{\sharp\}^*$. Then $u_{i+1}' = \overline{f'}(\alpha' x \sharp v') = \overline{f}(\alpha') f'(x, \sharp) \overline{f}(v') = \overline{f}(\alpha') (f(x, \sharp))^\sharp \overline{f}(v')$, and hence $\theta(u_{i+1}') = \overline{f}(\alpha') f(x, \sharp) \overline{f}(v') = \overline{f}(u_i) = u_{i+1}$.
- *Case $u_i' = \alpha x^\sharp v$, with $\alpha \in Q_o^*$, $x \in Q_o$, $v \in \{\sharp\}^*$.* It holds that $u_i = \theta(u_i') = \alpha x v$.

If $|\alpha|$ is odd, let $u'_i = \alpha' yx^\sharp v$, with $\alpha' \in Q^*_o$, $y \in Q_o$. Then $u'_{i+1} = \overline{f'}(\alpha' yx^\sharp v) = \overline{f}(\alpha')f'(y,x^\sharp)\overline{f}(v) = \overline{f}(\alpha')(f(y,x))^\sharp\overline{f}(v))$; hence $\theta(u'_{i+1}) = \overline{f}(\alpha')f(y,x)\overline{f}(v) = \overline{f}(u_i) = u_{i+1}$.

If $|\alpha|$ is even, let $u'_i = \alpha x^\sharp \natural v'$, with $v' \in \{\natural\}^*$. Then $u'_{i+1} = \overline{f'}(\alpha x^\sharp \natural v') = \overline{f}(\alpha)f'(x^\sharp, \natural)\overline{f}(v') = \overline{f}(\alpha)(f(x,\natural))^\sharp\overline{f}(v))$ (recall that $f(x,\natural) \neq \natural$ by definition). Hence $\theta(u'_{i+1}) = \overline{f}(\alpha)f(x,\natural)\overline{f}(v') = \overline{f}(u_i) = u_{i+1}$.

4 P Systems

P systems [23] are a bio-inspired computational formalism, where the behaviour is driven by evolution rules applied to multisets of objects. A P system is composed of a hierarchy of membranes, each containing a multiset of objects and a set of evolution rules. Evolution rules describe how the objects of the system evolve, for example they can be used to describe chemical reactions, i.e. rules in which some objects interact and, as a result, they are transformed into some other objects. Given a membrane m, its evolution rules in the set R_m can be applied only to the objects contained in the same membrane, and not in any other membrane. Many versions of P systems have been defined [2,4,7]. Formal semantics of different versions of P systems are presented in [1,3,5,8,10,11].

An evolution rule is of the form $u \rightarrow v$, where u and v are multisets whose elements are called *reactants* and *products*, respectively. When a rule is applied, the reactants are removed from the membrane and the products are added to the target membrane, which could be a different membrane than the one in which the rule is applied. Membranes are univocally labelled with natural numbers. Given a membrane m, the products of a rule associated with m are described by a multiset of (possibly) labelled objects having the following forms: a, meaning that the object a is added to the same membrane m; a_{out}, meaning that the object a is to be sent out of the membrane; a_{in_x}, meaning that the object a is to be sent into the child membrane labelled by x.

An evolution rule is said to be *cooperative* if it contains more than one reactant, otherwise the rule is called *non-cooperative*. This naming is also extended to P system models, that is, a *non-cooperative* P system is such that all its rules are non-cooperative, otherwise it is a *cooperative* P system.

A formal definition of P systems follows.

Definition 10. *A P system is a tuple* $\Pi = (V, \mu, w_1, \ldots, w_n, R_1, \ldots, R_n)$ *where:*

- *V is a finite* alphabet *whose elements are called* objects;
- *$\mu \subset \mathbb{N} \times \mathbb{N}$ describes the tree-structure of membranes, where $(i,j) \in \mu$ denotes that the membrane labelled by j is contained in the membrane labelled by i;*
- *w_i, with $1 \leq i \leq n$, are strings from V^* representing multisets over V associated with membranes $1, 2, \ldots, n$ of μ;*
- *R_i, with $1 \leq i \leq n$, are finite sets of evolution rules associated with membranes $1, 2, \ldots, n$ of μ.*

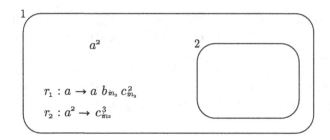

Fig. 3. An example of P system model

A characteristic of P systems is the way in which rules are applied in each step, namely with *maximal parallelism*. In each step, evolution rules are applied in a maximal non-deterministic way in all membranes, that is, in each membrane, a multiset of rules is selected non-deterministically to consume the membrane objects, in such a way that no other rule can be applied to the objects which are not involved in any rule application.

A *configuration* of a P system is given by an association of its membranes with multisets of objects. The multisets of objects $w_1, \ldots, w_n$ in the definition of a P system Π represent the initial configuration of Π. A *computation* is a sequence of transitions between configurations of a given P system Π starting from the initial configuration. Each transition of a computation describes a maximally parallel step. A computation is *successful* if and only if it reaches a configuration in which no rule is applicable. The result of a successful computation can be defined in different ways. Unsuccessful computations are those computations which never halt, thus yielding no result.

Example 2. Figure 3 depicts a P system with two membranes, labelled 1 and 2. The rules r_1 and r_2 are associated with membrane 1, while membrane 2 has no rules associated with it. An application of rule $r_1 = a \rightarrow a\, b_{in_2}\, c^2_{in_2}$ causes a copy of object b and two copies of object c to be sent into the inner membrane 2. The object a is still present after the application, since it appears in the right-hand part of the rule. Rule $r_2 = a^2 \rightarrow c^3_{in_2}$, instead, can be applied to a pair of objects a, and results in sending three copies of the object c into membrane 2. The initial state, as depicted, contains two copies of object a in membrane 1, and no objects in membrane 2.

At the first step, either rule r_1 or r_2 is applied. In fact, both the rules are enabled, since their reactants are present in the membrane. Actually, if r_1 is applied to an object a, then the maximality requires it to be applied also to the other copy of a. This application sends the objects $b^2 c^4$ into membrane 2. The objects contained in membrane 1 remain aa after the application, therefore the double application of rule r_1 can be repeated in the subsequent step. Whenever rule r_2 is applied, it causes the two copies of a in membrane 1 to disappear, thus terminating the computation. In such a case, the objects ccc are sent into membrane 2. Therefore, any computation of this P system is composed of a sequences of steps in which only r_1 is applied (twice per step), followed by a last step in which rule r_2 is applied once. Therefore, whenever the P system terminates, membrane 2 contains a multiset of objects $b^k c^{2k+3}$, for some $k \geq 0$.

A P system can be used either as an acceptor or as a generator of a multiset language over an alphabet Λ [9]. In the first case, a multiset over Λ is inserted in the outmost membrane of the P system and the result of its computations says whether such a multiset belongs to the multiset language accepted by the P system or not. In the second case the P system has a fixed initial configuration and can give as results (possibly in a non-deterministic way) all the possible multisets belonging to a given multiset language.

In order to investigate the relationship between (R)MBSTAs and P systems let us recall from [9] the definition of P system used as language acceptor. From [6] it follows that any P system Π can be translated into an equivalent P system Π' having a (flat) membrane structure that consists only of one membrane. Hence, we consider in this paper only *flat acceptor P Systems*.

Definition 11. *A flat acceptor P system over an alphabet Λ is a P system $\Pi = (\Lambda \cup \mathcal{C} \cup \{\mathbf{T}\}, \emptyset, \mu_1, R_1)$, where:*

- *$\mathcal{C}$ is a set of control objects such that $\Lambda \cap \mathcal{C} = \emptyset$;*
- *$\mathbf{T}$ is a special object not contained in $\Lambda \cup \mathcal{C}$;*
- *μ_1 is a multiset of objects in $\mathcal{C}$.*

A multiset μ of objects over Λ is accepted by Π iff, by adding μ to μ_1, then a final configuration can be reached with $\mathbf{T}$ occurring in the membrane.

The multiset language accepted by a flat acceptor P system Π is denoted $Ps(\Pi)$ (as Parikh set).

4.1   Simulating RMBSTAs with P Systems

Let $R = (\Lambda, Q, F, f, g)$ be a RMBSTA. Recall that Q can be partitioned into the sets $Q_o = \{q_1, \ldots, q_h\}$ of plain symbols, and $Q_o^\sharp = \{q_{h+1}^\sharp, \ldots, q_n^\sharp\}$ of tagged symbols. Moreover, assume, without loss of generality, that $\Lambda \cap Q = \emptyset$.

Let us consider two fresh symbols: $\diamond, \mathbf{F} \notin \Lambda \cup Q$. Symbol $\diamond$ is a special *trap* symbol that will be used to denote invalid computations, while $\mathbf{F}$ (dual to $\mathbf{T}$) will be used to denote computations that do not accept the input multiset. We construct an acceptor P system $\Pi_R = (\Lambda \cup \mathcal{C} \cup \{\mathbf{T}\}, \emptyset, \mu_1, R_1)$ where $\mathcal{C} = Q \cup \{\mathbf{F}, \sharp, \diamond\}$, $\mu_1 = \{\!|\sharp|\!\}$, and R_1 is composed of the rules shown in Figure 4.

Theorem 5. *Let $R = (\Lambda, Q, F, f, g)$ be a RMBSTA, and let $\Pi_R = (\Lambda \cup \mathcal{C} \cup \{\mathbf{T}\}, \emptyset, \mu_1, R_1)$ be the corresponding acceptor P system. Then, for any multiset $\mu \in \mathcal{M}(\Lambda)$ the following implications hold:*

1. *μ is accepted by R at level n $\implies$ μ can accepted by Π_R in no more than $n + 2$ steps;*

$$
\begin{array}{ll}
x \rightarrow y & \text{if } y = g(x),\ x \in \Lambda \\[4pt]
xy \rightarrow z & \text{if } z = f(x,y);\ x \in Q_o,\ y,z \in Q_o \cup Q_o^\sharp \\[4pt]
x\sharp \rightarrow z\sharp & \text{if } z = f(x,\sharp);\ x,z \in Q_o \cup Q_o^\sharp \\[4pt]
x\sharp \rightarrow \mathbf{T} & \text{if } x \in F \cap (Q_o \cup Q_o^\sharp) \\[4pt]
x\sharp \rightarrow \mathbf{F} & \text{if } x \in (Q_o \cup Q_o^\sharp) \setminus F \\[4pt]
\sharp \rightarrow \mathbf{T} & \text{if } \sharp \in F \\[4pt]
\sharp \rightarrow \mathbf{F} & \text{if } \sharp \notin F \\[4pt]
\sharp \rightarrow \sharp & \\[4pt]
x \rightarrow \Diamond & \text{if } x \in Q_o \cup Q_o^\sharp \\[4pt]
x\mathbf{T} \rightarrow \Diamond & \text{if } x \in Q_o \cup Q_o^\sharp \\[4pt]
x\mathbf{F} \rightarrow \Diamond & \text{if } x \in Q_o \cup Q_o^\sharp \\[4pt]
\Diamond \rightarrow \Diamond &
\end{array}
$$

Fig. 4. Evolution rules of a P system which simulates a RMBSTA

2. μ is accepted by Π_R in 1 step $\implies$ μ is accepted by R at level 0;

3. μ is accepted by Π_R in $n + 2$ steps, with $n \geq 0$ $\implies$ μ is accepted by R at level n.

As a consequence of these implications we have $L(R) = Ps(\Pi_R)$.

Proof. Item 1. Let us consider an accepting computation of the RMBSTA R, starting from a string $w \in \Lambda^*$ such that $\phi(w) = \mu$. Let $\ell = 2^n - |w|$, and $w_h = \overline{f}^{(n-h)}(\overline{g}(w\sharp^\ell))$, for $h \in \{0, \ldots, n\}$. It holds $w_0 \in F$.

If $|w| = 0$, then $\forall h \in \{0, \ldots, n\}.\ w_h \in \{\sharp\}^+$. Since μ is accepted, $w_0 = \sharp \in F$. The initial configuration of Π_R contains only $\sharp$, from which the transition $\sharp \longrightarrow \mathbf{T}$ can be performed, reaching a final accepting configuration.

Assume $|w| > 0$. For all $h \in \{0, \ldots, n\}$, $w_h = w_h'\sharp \ldots \sharp$, with $|w_h| = 2^h$, $w_h' = q_1 \ldots q_k$, $\forall j < k.\, q_j \in Q_o$, and $q_k \in Q_o \cup Q_o^\sharp$. Each application of the processing function f may only involve pairs of symbols (x,y) from one of these sets: $Q_o \times Q_o$; $Q_o \times Q_o^\sharp$; $Q_o \times \{\sharp\}$; $\{\sharp\} \times \{\sharp\}$. Note that, for the above cases (except for $f(\sharp,\sharp)$), Π_R contains evolution rules which simulate the behaviour of f. In fact, for the first two cases, Π_R contains an evolution rule $xy \rightarrow z$, with $z = f(x,y)$, while in the third case a rule $x\sharp \rightarrow z\sharp$, with $z = f(x,\sharp)$, is present. Since each symbol in w_h is used exactly in one application of f, according to the definition of the evolution rules of the P system Π_R, the resulting string w_{h+1} is such that the transition $\phi(w_h'\sharp) \longrightarrow \phi(w_{h+1}'\sharp)$ can be performed by Π_R. Therefore, the P system can perform, from the initial state $\phi(w\sharp)$, the sequence of $n + 2$ transitions $\phi(w\sharp) \longrightarrow \phi(w_n'\sharp) \longrightarrow \cdots \longrightarrow \phi(w_0'\sharp) \longrightarrow \phi(\mathbf{T})$, where the first transition corresponds to the application of function g, and the last transition is made possible because $w_0' = w_0 \in F$.

Item 2. In this case, only rule $\sharp \to \mathbf{T}$ may have been applied to the initial state $\mu \cup \{\!|\sharp|\!\}$, for the input multiset $\mu = \emptyset \in \mathcal{M}(\Lambda)$, which implies $\sharp \in F$; hence μ can be accepted by R at level 0. Otherwise, if $|\mu| > 0$, then the P system may not have reached a final accepting configuration in one step. In fact, the only way to yield $\mathbf{T}$ is to apply rule $\sharp \to \mathbf{T}$ while, at the same time, rules $x \to y$ with $y = g(x)$ are applied to each symbol in μ, thus yielding a non-final configuration.

Item 3. Let us consider an accepting computation $\gamma_0 \to \gamma_1 \to \cdots \to \gamma_{n+2}$, $n \geq 0$. It holds $\gamma_{n+2} = \{\!|\mathbf{T}|\!\}$, since no symbol in $Q \cup \{\mathbf{F}, \sharp, \Diamond\}$ may be present (note that no more than one of either $\mathbf{T}$ or $\mathbf{F}$ may be present in a configuration). In turn, either $\gamma_{n+1} = \{\!|\sharp|\!\}$ or $\gamma_{n+1} = \{\!|x\sharp|\!\}$. The former case implies that $\forall i \in \{0, \ldots, n\}$. $\gamma_i = \{\!|\sharp|\!\}$, since the only rule which may have been applied is $\sharp \to \sharp$. Hence $\mu = \emptyset$, which can be accepted by R at any level $n \geq 0$.

Let us consider the case $\gamma_{n+1} = \{\!|x\sharp|\!\}$, with $x \in F \cap Q$. Let $\widetilde{Q} = Q_o^* \cup (Q_o^* . Q_o^\sharp)$, namely $\widetilde{Q}$ contains all strings composed of symbols from Q_o, possibly ending with a symbol from $Q_o^\sharp$. We prove that $\forall i \in \{0, \ldots, n\}$, if $\gamma_{n+1-i} = \phi(\alpha\sharp)$ with $\alpha \in \widetilde{Q}$, $|\alpha| \leq 2^i$, and $\overline{f}^i(\alpha\sharp^\ell) \in F \cap Q$ where $\ell = 2^i - |\alpha|$, then $\gamma_{n-i} = \phi(\beta\sharp)$ with $\beta \in \widetilde{Q}$, $|\beta| \leq 2^{i+1}$, and $\overline{f}^i(\alpha\sharp^\ell) = \overline{f}^{i+1}(\beta\sharp^{\ell'})$, where $\ell' = 2^{i+1} - |\beta|$.

Assume $\gamma_{n-i} = \phi(\alpha\sharp)$. Due to the maximally-parallel semantics of P systems, $\gamma_{n-i-1} = \phi(\beta\sharp)$. In fact, $\phi(\alpha\sharp)$ may only have been obtained by either (i) $|\alpha|$ applications of rule $xy \to z$ yielding each symbol in α, and one application of $\sharp \to \sharp$; or (ii) $|\alpha| - 1$ applications of rule $xy \to z$ yielding each *but one* symbol in α, and one application of $x\sharp \to z\sharp$. Moreover, note that $|\beta|_{Q_o^\sharp} \leq |\alpha|_{Q_o^\sharp} \leq 1$. Therefore, in both cases, $\alpha\sharp^\ell = \overline{f}(\beta\sharp^{\ell'})$, and hence $\overline{f}^i(\alpha\sharp^\ell) = \overline{f}^{i+1}(\beta\sharp^{\ell'})$.

Note that, at the beginning, $\gamma_0 = \mu \cup \{\!|\sharp|\!\}$, hence $\gamma_1 = \{\!|g(x) \mid x \in \mu|\!\} \cup \{\!|\sharp|\!\}$. It follows that, since $\gamma_{n+1} = \{\!|x\sharp|\!\}$ with $x \in F \cap Q$, then $\overline{f}^n(w\sharp^\ell) \in F \cap Q$, for some string $w \in \widetilde{Q}$ such that $\phi(w\sharp) = \gamma_1$. Therefore $w = \overline{g}(w')$, for some w' such that $\phi(w') = \mu$, from which we conclude $\overline{f}^n(\overline{g}(w')\sharp^\ell) = \overline{f}^n(\overline{g}(w'\sharp^\ell)) \in F \cap Q$.

Finally, note that Item 1 implies $L(R) \subseteq Ps(\Pi_R)$, while *Items 2* and *3* imply $Ps(\Pi_R) \subseteq L(R)$ (note that the initial configuration of Π_R does not contain $\mathbf{T}$, hence it needs at least one step to reach a final accepting configuration).

5 Conclusions

In this paper we have related systolic automata and P systems. We have extended systolic automata to accept multisets of symbols, by introducing Multiset Binary Systolic Tree Automata (MBSTAs). In particular, we have shown how an equivalent variant of MBSTAs (called Regular MBSTAs) can be easily translated into cooperative P systems.

References

1. Andrei, O., Ciobanu, G., Lucanu, D.: A rewriting logic framework for operational semantics of membrane systems. Theoretical Computer Science **373**(3), 163–181 (2007)

2. Barbuti, R., Caravagna, G., Maggiolo-Schettini, A., Milazzo, P.: P systems with endosomes. International Journal of Computers, Communications and Control 4(3), 214–223 (2009)
3. Barbuti, R., Maggiolo-Schettini, A., Milazzo, P., Pardini, G.: Simulation of spatial P system models. Theoretical Computer Science 529, 11–45 (2014)
4. Barbuti, R., Maggiolo-Schettini, A., Milazzo, P., Pardini, G., Tesei, L.: Spatial P systems. Natural Computing 10(1), 3–16 (2011)
5. Barbuti, R., Maggiolo-Schettini, A., Milazzo, P., Tini, S.: Compositional semantics and behavioral equivalences for P systems. Theoretical Computer Science 395(1), 77–100 (2008)
6. Barbuti, R., Maggiolo-Schettini, A., Milazzo, P., Tini, S.: A P systems flat form preserving step-by-step behaviour. Fundamenta Informaticae 87(1), 1–34 (2008)
7. Barbuti, R., Maggiolo-Schettini, A., Milazzo, P., Tini, S.: P systems with transport and diffusion membrane channels. Fundamenta Informaticae 93(1–3), 17–31 (2009)
8. Barbuti, R., Maggiolo-Schettini, A., Milazzo, P., Tini, S.: Compositional semantics of spiking neural P systems. Journal of Logic and Algebraic Programming 79(6), 304–316 (2010)
9. Barbuti, R., Maggiolo-Schettini, A., Milazzo, P., Tini, S.: Membrane systems working in generating and accepting modes: Expressiveness and encodings. In: Gheorghe, M., Hinze, T., Păun, G., Rozenberg, G., Salomaa, A. (eds.) CMC 2010. LNCS, vol. 6501, pp. 103–118. Springer, Heidelberg (2010)
10. Barbuti, R., Maggiolo-Schettini, A., Milazzo, P., Tini, S.: An overview on operational semantics in membrane computing. International Journal of Foundations of Computer Science 22(1), 119–131 (2011)
11. Busi, N.: Using well-structured transition systems to decide divergence for catalytic P systems. Theoretical Computer Science 372(2–3), 125–135 (2007)
12. Csuhaj-Varjú, E., Martín-Vide, C., Mitrana, V.: Multiset Automata. In: Calude, C.S., Păun, G., Rozenberg, G., Salomaa, A. (eds.) Multiset Processing. LNCS, vol. 2235, pp. 69–83. Springer, Heidelberg (2001)
13. Culik II, K., Gruska, J., Salomaa, A.: On a family of L languages resulting from systolic tree automata. Theoretical Computer Science 23(3), 231–242 (1983)
14. Culik II, K., Gruska, J., Salomaa, A.: Systolic automata for VLSI on balanced trees. Acta Informatica 18(4), 335–344 (1983)
15. Culik II, K., Gruska, J., Salomaa, A.: Systolic trellis automata I. International Journal of Computer Mathematics 15(1–4), 195–212 (1984)
16. Culik II, K., Gruska, J., Salomaa, A.: Systolic trellis automata II. International Journal of Computer Mathematics 16(1), 3–22 (1984)
17. Culik II, K., Salomaa, A., Wood, D.: Systolic tree acceptors. RAIRO-Theoretical Informatics and Applications-Informatique Théorique et Applications 18(1), 53–69 (1984)
18. Fachini, E., Gruska, J., Maggiolo-Schettini, A., Sangiorgi, D.: Simulation of systolic tree automata on trellis automata. International Journal of Foundations of Computer Science 1(2), 87–110 (1990)
19. Fachini, E., Maggiolo-Schettini, A., Resta, G., Sangiorgi, D.: Nonacceptability criteria and closure properties for the class of languages accepted by binary systolic tree automata. Theoretical Computer Science 83(2), 249–260 (1991)
20. Fachini, E., Maggiolo-Schettini, A., Sangiorgi, D.: Comparisons among classes of Y-tree systolic automata. In: Rovan, B. (ed.) Mathematical Foundations of Computer Science 1990. LNCS, vol. 452, pp. 254–260. Springer, Berlin Heidelberg (1990)

21. Fachini, E., Maggiolo-Schettini, A., Sangiorgi, D.: Classes of systolic Y-tree automata and a comparison with systolic trellis automata. Acta Informatica **29**(6/7), 623–643 (1992)
22. Gruska, J., Monti, A., Napoli, M., Parente, D.: Succinctness of descriptions of SBTA-languages. Theoretical Computer Science **179**(1–2), 251–271 (1997)
23. Păun, G.: Membrane Computing: An Introduction. Springer, Heidelberg (2002)
24. Rozenberg, G., Salomaa, A.: The mathematical theory of L systems. Academic Press (1980)

Soliton Automata with Multiple Waves

Henning Bordihn[1], Helmut Jürgensen[2]([⊠]), and Heiko Ritter[1]

[1] Institut für Informatik, Universität Potsdam,
August-Bebel-Str. 89, 14482 Potsdam, Germany
[2] Department of Computer Science, Western University,
N6A 5B7, London, Ontario, Canada
hjj@csd.uwo.ca

Abstract. Soliton automata were defined by Dassow and Jürgensen about 1986 to model the changes of the bond structure in certain types of molecules as a result of a soliton wave travelling through the molecules. We extend the model to include the presence of more than just a single soliton. Certain situations are specific to the multi-soliton case and lead to changes to some of the basic definitions and result in a new class of soliton automata. In this paper we lay the foundations for a theory of multi-soliton automata, explain the modelling decisions, and discuss issues which are new when multiple solitons are considered.

1 Solitons

We consider the switching behaviour of bonds in a molecule when a disturbance, called a soliton in the sequel, is injected. The bonds are likely to change, leading to a different molecule. Taking these molecules as states, one gets a system which behaves like an automaton. It has been shown in particular, that such automata can simulate logical gates and memories; thus they could be composed to form a universal computer. However, "when considering unorthodox means of computation one needs to discard any preconceived ideas, but first investigate what the new means have to offer and, after that, how to use the new features to achieve the intended goals." This was stated by one of the present authors (HJ) in the 1980s in several talks. A similar opinion is found in [37] where Mario Ruben states "to do Boolean logic with molecules is to do violence against them". Hence, in this paper we investigate the potential of such automata without concern as to how they may be used in conventional Boolean circuits. Combining many of such molecules into a larger one forms something akin to a cellular automaton. One gets a powerful computer at the size of a few hundred Å. We consider only the components of such a powerful cellular computer and their capabilities.

Solitons can be considered as waves or particles travelling through some "substance" unhindered, without energy loss, and without interference. They travel slowly – at the speed of sound, but fast enough when only small distances need to be covered. They can, however, modify the "field" through which they travel. We suggest that the reader view solitons as waves because this helps in the understanding of the formal model. We use the terms of *molecule* and

© Springer International Publishing Switzerland 2014
C.S. Calude et al. (Eds.): Gruska Festschrift, LNCS 8808, pp. 32–48, 2014.
DOI: 10.1007/978-3-319-13350-8_3

soliton in a rather metaphorical sense, abstracting radically from the physical and chemical realities. We speculate about what could be achieved by the soliton effect in molecules. What can actually be achieved is for researchers in physics, chemistry and engineering to explore. Utopia may not be that far away. For the history of solitons we refer to [36, pp. 18–19]. In this paper we only consider solitons in molecules. For the physics of solitons in such situations we refer to [22] and [36].

We look at a single situation, that of a soliton travelling through a molecule. This idea was suggested by Carter in [8–16,30]. The kind of molecules under consideration is specified below. A soliton is sent through that molecule; the binding structure of the molecule changes. Hence, if one interprets the prior and the posterior binding structures as states of a system, the molecule together with the solitons behaves as an automaton or a switching device. In the early literature these are called *soliton valves*. A formal definition of *soliton automata* based on this physical or chemical phenomenon is given in [18].

Terminological confusion may arise: There is another definition of *soliton automata,* which is completely unrelated to the one used here. It was initiated by a paper on "Soliton-Like Behavior in Automata" by Park [38]. In that sense the term *soliton automaton* is found in many papers on cellular automata, but has no relation to the physics of solitons.

We return to the basic idea. Not all molecules would work. Polyacetylene chains and several other types of molecules are known to have a fairly controlled reaction to solitons. Accordingly, research on soliton-based switching or automata focussed on bond changes in polyacetylene chains or polymers. In essence, one considers molecules, the basic structure of which is a sequence of carbon atoms with bonds of alternating weights connecting them and with other atoms or molecules – of not always logical, but often physical relevance – connected to the carbon atoms. In this paper we only consider the soliton-induced state changes in polymers – more precisely, abstractions of them. In other words, we ignore physical and chemical details. In representing molecules, we show nothing but the carbon atoms and possibly some hydrogen atoms as illustrated in Fig. 1. Abstracting further, we consider graphs with special properties and transformations of such graphs into others with the same topology and the same properties. Such graphs are called soliton graphs in the sequel. In a soliton graph the nodes have degrees 1, 2 or 3. Nodes of degree 1 are said to be exterior; they form the entry and exit points for solitons. Nodes of degrees 2 or 3 are interior. The edges are undirected, there are no loops, and the edges have weights 1 or 2, these representing single and double bonds, respectively. From entry to exit a soliton travels along edges of alternating weights. Therefore, the two edges at a node of degree 2 must have different weights, and of the three edges at a node of degree 3, two have weight 1 and one has weight 2. Formal definitions of these concepts are given in Section 3 below.

Informally, a soliton transforms a soliton graph into another soliton graph. Consequently, a soliton automaton consists of a soliton graph acting as the generator for the automaton, solitons specified by their entry and exit locations as

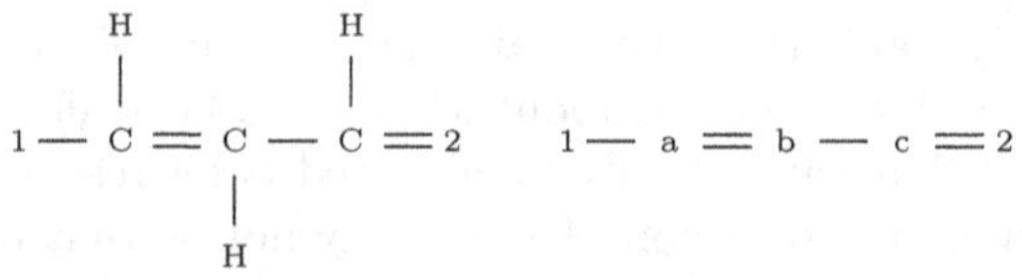

Fig. 1. A very simple polyacytelene molecule before and after abstraction. Interior nodes are specified by letters when required. Exterior nodes replacing some unknown attached molecules are represented by numbers.

the input alphabet, the potential state changes as the transition function, and all reachable soliton graphs as the state space. Regardless of physical and chemical realities, this leads to an interesting model of computation. Experiments have shown that, despite well-known quantum effects, this model could be realistic.

The theory of solitons in polymers suggests to study not only the effect of single solitons as proposed originally by Carter, but also to investigate the effect of multiple soliton waves. Multiple soliton waves introduce parallelism of a kind not usually encountered in computer science because soliton waves could pass each other unchanged.

2   Notation and Basic Notions

We introduce some notation and review basic notions. The sets of positive integers and of non-negative integers are denoted by $\mathbb{N}$ and $\mathbb{N}_0$, respectively. An alphabet is a finite non-empty set the elements of which are called symbols. Let Σ be an alphabet. The set of all (finite) words over Σ, including the empty word λ, is denoted by Σ^*; let $\Sigma^+ = \Sigma^* \setminus \{\lambda\}$.

A semi-automaton is a construct $\mathcal{A} = (Q, \Sigma, \tau)$ where Q is a non-empty set, Σ is an alphabet and $\tau : Q \times \Sigma \to 2^Q$ is a mapping. The elements of Q are called states; Σ is the input alphabet of $\mathcal{A}$; τ is the transition function of $\mathcal{A}$. We assume that Q is finite and that, for all $q \in Q$ and all $a \in \Sigma$, $\tau(q, a) \neq \emptyset$. Moreover, we drop the prefix "semi-" as we do not consider any other kind of automata.

Let $\mathcal{A} = (Q, \Sigma, \tau)$ be an automaton. The function τ is extended as follows: for $R \subseteq Q$ and $w \in \Sigma^*$, let

$$\tau(R, w) = \begin{cases} R, & \text{if } w = \lambda, \\ \tau\left(\bigcup_{q \in R} \tau(q, a), v\right), & \text{if } w = av \text{ with } a \in \Sigma \text{ and } v \in \Sigma^*. \end{cases}$$

For $w \in \Sigma^*$, let τ_w be the mapping defined by $\tau_w(R) = \tau(R, w)$ for all $R \subseteq Q$. Instead of $\tau_w(R)$ we write $R\tau_w$. With this convention, the mapping τ of Σ^* into the monoid $\mathfrak{T}_Q$ of all mappings of 2^Q into 2^Q, which maps $w \in \Sigma^*$ onto τ_w, is a homomorphism, that is, for $w = uv$ with $u, v \in \Sigma^*$ one has $\tau_w = \tau_{uv} = \tau_u \tau_v$. Let R be a non-empty subset of Q. Define $[R] = \bigcup_{w \in \Sigma^*} R\tau_w$. The construct $([R], \Sigma, \tau)$ is the subautomaton of $\mathcal{A}$ generated by R.

The automaton $\mathcal{A}$ is said to be deterministic if $|\tau_a(q)| = 1$ for all $a \in \Sigma$ and all $q \in Q$. In that case τ_a is considered as a mapping of Q into Q, that is as a transformation of Q. The set of transformations of Q induced by τ is a monoid with the multiplication defined as above, the *transition monoid* $T(\mathcal{A})$ of $\mathcal{A}$. The transformation τ_λ is the identity element of $T(\mathcal{A})$. Inputs u and v of $\mathcal{A}$ are said to be equivalent if and only if $\tau_u = \tau_v$. As the transition monoid $T(\mathcal{A})$ is a submonoid of the monoid of all mappings of Q into Q, the *full transformation monoid* $\mathfrak{T}_Q$ of Q, the order (cardinality) of $T(\mathcal{A})$ is at most $|Q|^{|Q|}$. The symmetric group $\mathfrak{S}_Q$ on Q is a maximal subgroup of $\mathfrak{T}_Q$. For $n = |Q|$, we identify the symmetric group on n elements in its natural representation $\mathfrak{S}_n$ with $\mathfrak{S}_Q$ via an arbitrary, but fixed numbering of the states in Q.

3 Soliton Graphs and Soliton Paths

In this section and the next one we list and elaborate on, a few definitions taken from [18]. The model of soliton automata considered there assumes that only a single soliton is present at any given moment. We summarize known facts regarding the computational power of soliton automata with this restriction. The presence of multiple solitons is considered further below. Many of the results summarized, but not used in the sequel, would require extensive formal definitions. Rather than copying these, we refer the reader to the original publications and supply only informal explanations.

Definition 1 ([18]). *A* soliton graph *is a weighted graph* $G = (N, E, w)$ *such that:*

1. *N is the finite, non-empty set of nodes.*
2. *$E \subseteq N \times N$ is the set of undirected edges, such that $(n, n') \in E$ implies that $(n', n) \in E$. For $n \in N$, $d(n)$ is the degree of n.*
3. *For no $n \in N$, $(n, n) \in E$.*
4. *$w : E \to \{1, 2\}$ is a mapping with $w(n, n') = w(n', n)$.*
5. *w extended to $w : N \to \{1, 2, 3, 4\}$ requires that*

$$w(n) = \sum_{(n,n') \in E} w(n, n') = d(n) + 1.$$

6. *Every connected component of G contains at least one node of degree 1.*

Nodes of degree 1 are exterior; *all other nodes are* interior.

In the sequel we assume, without special mention, that $|N| \geq 3$ to exclude trivial exceptions. Next we define which paths a soliton can take. This definition only works when no more than one soliton is present. Below we change this definition in a consistent fashion when we consider multiple solitons.

Definition 2. *Let $G = (N, E, w)$ be a soliton graph and let $n_0 \in N$ be an exterior node. A* partial soliton path P_k *of length $k \in \mathbb{N}_0$ from n_0 is a path $n_0, n_1, \ldots, n_k$ constructed from a sequence of partial soliton paths P_i with $i = 0, 1, \ldots, k$ as follows:*

1. *For* $i = 0$, *let* $G_0 = (N, E, w_0) = G$, *and let* P_0 *be the path consisting only of the node* n_0.

2. *Suppose* $0 < i \le k$, *that* $n_0, n_1, \ldots, n_{i-1}$ *is a partial soliton path* P_{i-1} *constructed so far and that* $G_0, G_1, \ldots, G_{i-1}$ *is the sequence of weighted graphs considered in the construction. Choose a node* $n_i \in N$ *such that* $(n_{i-1}, n_i) \in E$; *when* $i > 1$, n_i *must differ from* n_{i-2} *and satisfy* $w_{i-1}(n_{i-1}, n_i) \ne w_{i-2}(n_{i-2}, n_{i-1})$. *If no such node exists, the construction ends without success. Let* P_i *be the path* $n_0, n_1, \ldots, n_{i-1}, n_i$. *Define*

$$w_i(n, n') = w_i(n', n) = \begin{cases} 3 - w_{i-1}(n, n'), & \text{if } n = n_{i-1} \text{ and } n' = n_i \\ & \text{or vice versa,} \\ w_{i-1}(n, n'), & \text{otherwise.} \end{cases}$$

Let $G_i = (N, E, w_i)$. *Increase* i *by 1 and repeat this construction step if* $i \le k$.

Every path $n_0, n_1, \ldots, n_k$ *with* n_0 *exterior and* $n_1, \ldots, n_{k-1}$ *interior, constructed in this way, is called a* partial soliton path. *If* $k > 0$ *and* n_k *is exterior the path is a* (total) soliton path.

Definition 2 differs from, but is equivalent to, the corresponding definition of soliton paths in [18]. We use expressions like "a soliton moves from n_i to n_{i+1}" or "a soliton traverses a path" or "a soliton is at node n_i" in a metaphorical sense to indicate the sequence of changes in the sequence $G_0, G_1, \ldots, G_k$ of graphs. A soliton starting its path at the exterior node n_0 will first move to the unique node n_1 connected to n_0 and change the weight of the edge between these nodes. From then on it can move to a neighbouring node, not reversing direction, if the previous weight of the edge just traversed differs from the current weight of the next edge. In every move the weight of the edge being traversed is changed. A soliton can traverse the same edge several times, but never by just returning.

4 Single-Soliton Automata

Let $G = (N, E, w)$ be a soliton graph, and let X be its set of exterior nodes. For $n, n' \in X$, let $S(G, n, n')$ be the set of weighted graphs obtained by traversing a soliton path from n to n'. If no such soliton path exists, let $S(G, n, n') = \{G\}$. Let $S(G, n) = \bigcup_{n' \in X} S(G, n, n')$. Every graph in $S(G, n)$ is a soliton graph. Let $\Gamma = \Gamma(N, E)$ be the set of all soliton graphs with N and E as sets of nodes and edges, respectively. For $n, n' \in X$, define the mappings

$$\tau_{n,n'} : \Gamma \to 2^{\Gamma} : G \mapsto S(G, n, n')$$

and

$$\delta_n : \Gamma \to 2^{\Gamma} : G \mapsto S(G, n).$$

Let $\tau : (n, n') \mapsto \tau_{n,n'}$ and $\delta : n \mapsto \delta_n$ map $X \times X$ and X, respectively, to these mappings. The constructs $(\Gamma, X \times X, \tau)$ and (Γ, X, δ) are automata.

Definition 3 ([18]). *Let $G = (N, E, w)$ be a soliton graph. Let X be its set of exterior nodes. Let Γ and τ be as above. The subautomaton $\mathcal{A}(G)$ of $(\Gamma, X \times X, \tau)$ generated by G is the soliton automaton of G. Let $S(G)$ denote the set of states of $\mathcal{A}(G)$.*

A similar definition can be formulated with respect to δ. This latter variant, which involves much nondeterminism, has not been studied in the literature so far and is not considered in the present work either.

In soliton automata, two kinds of determinism can be observed: (1) Determinism in the usual automaton theoretic sense: $|S(G', n, n')| = 1$ for all $G' \in S(G)$ and all $(n, n') \in X \times X$. (2) *Strong determinism:* For all $G' \in S(G)$ and $(n, n') \in X \times X$, there is at most one soliton path from n to n'. As a physical building block, a soliton automaton should be deterministic, at least. Strong determinism is preferable as the behaviour of the soliton automaton with respect to timing is nondeterministic otherwise. Hence research focussed on deterministic soliton automata in either sense, on the graph structure implying determinism and on the computational power of deterministic soliton automata. The latter is considered in terms of the size and structure of the transition monoids of these automata. By saying that G is deterministic or strongly deterministic, we mean that $\mathcal{A}(G)$ is deterministic or strongly deterministic, respectively.

A soliton graph G may consist of several connected components. Each component defines a soliton automaton with its own input alphabet. Thus, if G has the connected components $G_1, G_2, \ldots, G_k$, then $T(\mathcal{A}(G)) = T(\mathcal{A}(G_1)) \times T(\mathcal{A}(G_2)) \times \cdots \times T(\mathcal{A}(G_k))$. Beyond the merely graph theoretical notion of connectedness, one also needs to consider another related concept which is based on the existence or non-existence of soliton paths. A path from n to n' in the graph theoretical sense is said to be *impervious* if none of its edges occurs in a partial soliton path in any $G' \in S(G)$ [18].

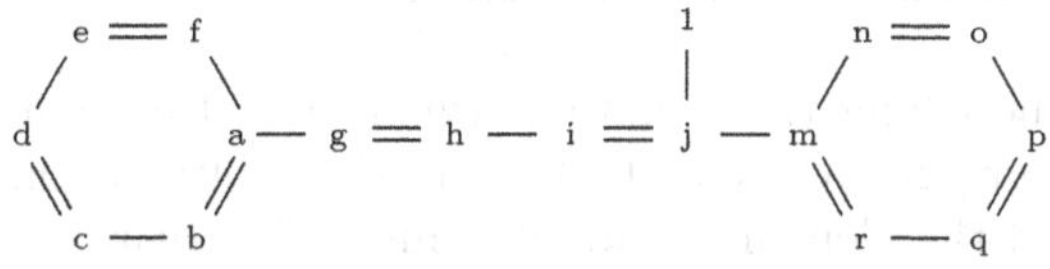

Fig. 2. A soliton graph with an impervious path from node j to the right

In Fig. 2 we show an example of a soliton graph with an impervious path. In the single-soliton model, impervious paths can be removed without any change to the transition monoid (see [20] for the precise statement). Removal of impervious paths may increase the number of connected components. The transition monoid of the resulting *reduced soliton graph* is trivially isomorphic with that of the original soliton automaton. Hence, one needs to consider only *indecomposable soliton graphs*, that is, soliton graphs which, after the removal of impervious paths, are connected. This holds only when single solitons are considered.

To measure the computational power of soliton automata we use their transition monoids as a yardstick. Their structure depends on the cycle structure of the underlying graphs. Multiple cycles usually cause non-determinism. Otherwise, mostly symmetric groups or alternating groups in their natural representations are encountered. For certain types of graphs with cycles of odd lengths, one finds groups of monomial matrices over the field with three elements [18–21]. The main open questions concern the transition monoids of soliton automata based on trees [31]. An attempt to connect the structure of soliton graphs to the corresponding soliton automata in terms of category theory was proposed in [1].

One can think of soliton graphs as being equivalent if and only if their soliton automata are isomorphic; for the single-soliton model this leads to the following simple observation, universally used, but obviously not true when multiple solitons are present.

Observation 1. *Let $G = (N, E, w)$ be a soliton graph. Let $n_0, n_1, \ldots, n_k$ be a partial soliton path such that $d(n_i) = 2$ for $i = 0, 1, \ldots, k - 1$ and $k > 3$. Let G' be the soliton graph obtained from G as follows: (1) Remove n_1 and n_2 from N. (2) Redirect edges going into and out of n_1 to go into and out of n_3. (3) Remove all edges involving n_2. The resulting graph G' is a soliton graph which is equivalent to G.*

A completely graph theoretic approach to the theory of soliton automata is taken by Bartha, Krész and others [2–7,32–35]. The approach is based on matching theory. It will be important to investigate to which extent matching theory can help in the multi-soliton model as well. A kind of switching theory for soliton automata is proposed by Groves in [29]. Unfortunately, little of this important work, except [23,24], is published in versions which would be easily accessible [25–28].

5   Multiple Soliton Waves Make a Difference

We now turn to modelling the situation, when more than one soliton travels through a soliton graph. We refer to this as the multi-soliton model. In the single-soliton model the elementary input symbols are pairs of external nodes. As mentioned, an alternative, not explored in detail, would be to consider just the external nodes as input symbols. For the multi-soliton model we define the input symbols as bursts of external nodes or pairs of external nodes as follows. The main difficulty in describing the behaviour of multiple solitons in a meaningful and – as one hopes – realistic way lies in the definition of soliton paths and the interaction of solitons when they happen to meet. We assume that waves cannot reverse nor unite, but that they can cross each other. This basic idea leads to the definition below of a legal configuration trail as the counterpart of a soliton path. Whether this is adequate at the molecular level is a matter for physicists to determine. Given that definition, one can then adjust the remaining definitions for soliton automata. However, several assertions about soliton graphs and soliton automata change due to the potential interaction of solitons.

Definition 4 (Bursts of Inputs). *Let S be a finite non-empty set not containing the symbols $\|$ and $\perp$. Moreover, let $S \cap \mathbb{N}_0 = \emptyset$.*

A burst over S is a word of the form

$$s_1\|_{k_1} s_2\|_{k_2} \cdots s_{m-1}\|_{k_{m-1}} s_m \perp$$

with the following properties:

1. *$m \in \mathbb{N}$;*
2. *$s_1, s_2, \ldots, s_m \in S$;*
3. *$k_1, k_2, \ldots, k_{m-1} \in \mathbb{N}_0$;*

The length *of such a burst is m.*

For $m \in \mathbb{N}$, let $B_m(S)$ be the set of all bursts of length m over S. Let $B_{\leq m}(S) = \bigcup_{i=1}^{m} B_i(S)$ and $B(S) = \bigcup_{i=1}^{\infty} B_i(S)$.

A burst over S is the basic input symbol to the automata under consideration. It is to be interpreted as follows. If the burst is initiated at time t, the symbol s_1 is input at time t; s_2 is input at time $t + k_1$; and, in general, s_j is input at time $t + \sum_{i=1}^{j-1} k_i$. Here the empty sum is defined to be 0. The symbol $\perp$ indicates that the input process pauses until the system has stabilized.

Let G be a soliton graph with set X of exterior nodes. A burst as input has two interpretations: (1) The set S could be the set X with the implied meaning that $x \in X$ indicates the node where the soliton is injected. (2) The set S could be the set $X \times X$ with the implied meaning that $(x, x') \in X \times X$ indicates the nodes where the soliton is injected and received, respectively. As in the single-soliton model, we only consider the latter case.

We consider a few simple examples which show that changes to Definition 2 are required for the multi-soliton model and that the multi-soliton model allows for state transitions which do not exist in the single-soliton model. We indicate the position of the solitons in the graphs by symbols: • for the first one and ∘ for the second one.

Example 1. The *3-tree* graph (*soliton valve* [8], *soliton junction* [29]):

For single solitons the automaton is strongly deterministic and has three states. The transition monoid is the symmetric group $\mathfrak{S}_3$.

Now consider selected bursts of length 2.

(1) The input $(1,2)\|_1(3,1)\perp$ is equivalent to $(2,3)\perp$.

(2) The input $(1,2)\|_0(3,2)\perp$ leads to the situation shown below. As both solitons need to leave on the same edge at the same time, it is not clear what happens to the weight of that edge. The input $(1,2)\|_0(3,1)\perp$ leads to the same situation. By the original definition of soliton paths of [18], one of the two solitons can leave, while the other one cannot. By Definition 2, both can leave, equivalent to $(2,3)\perp$. This implies that these two definitions are not equivalent in the multi-soliton case.

Also the input $(1,2)\|_1(1,2)\bot$ reveals that the two definitions are not equivalent. In both cases, Definition 2 leads to an intuitively more convincing result compared to the original definition of [18].

For the single-soliton model it is sufficient to consider the paths a soliton might travel through. In the multi-soliton model one needs to consider multiple paths. This idea is captured in the following definitions. For the sequel, we assume that $G = (N, E, w)$ is a soliton graph and that the nodes appearing in bursts are exterior nodes of G.

Definition 5 (Position Map). *For $m \in \mathbb{N}$, let $\mathfrak{m} = \{1, 2, \ldots, m\}$. Let $G = (N, E, w)$ be a soliton graph such that $N \cap \mathbb{N}_0 = \emptyset$. A* position map *for m is a mapping of $\mathfrak{m}$ into $N \cup \mathbb{N}_0$.*

If π is a position map for m, then $\pi(i)$ indicates at which node the ith soliton is or how many steps are still required until it will enter the graph. $\pi(i) = 0$ means that the ith soliton has left the graph.

Definition 6 (Intial Position Map for a Burst). *Let*

$$b = (n_1, n_1')\|_{k_1}(n_2, n_2')\|_{k_2} \cdots (n_m, n_m')\bot$$

be a burst of length m. The initial position map *π_b for b is defined as follows: Let r be minimal such that $k_1 = k_2 = \cdots k_r = 0$ and $k_{r+1} > 0$ or $r = m - 1$. Then*

$$\pi_b(i) = \begin{cases} n_i, & if\ 1 \leq i \leq r + 1, \\ k_{r+1}, & if\ i = r + 2, \\ \pi_b(i-1) + k_{i-1}, & if\ i > r + 2. \end{cases}$$

Definition 7 (Final Position Map). *A position map π for m is said to be* final *if $\pi(i) = 0$ for all $i \in \mathfrak{m}$.*

Now we consider the small steps occurring when a burst is the input to a soliton graph. The original graph undergoes a sequence of changes until it reaches a (stable) soliton graph again. The duration of the sequence as well as the actual changes can be non-deterministic. We refer to the (stable) soliton graphs as states and to the other graphs as intermediate states.

In general, for a soliton graph $G = (N, E, w)$ one considers the underlying graph $\hat{G} = (N, E)$ without weights. We need to consider arbitrary weighted graphs based on $\hat{G}$ (or G) where the weight does not need to satisfy the condition of soliton graphs. We still restrict the weights of edges to be either one or two. However, the weight of a node of degree 2 could be 2, 3, or 4 and the weight of a node of degree 3 could be between 3 and 6. Such weighted graphs serve to define the state transitions of a soliton automaton.

Definition 8 (Potential Successor Map). *Let G be a soliton graph. Let $m \in \mathbb{N}$, and let π and π' be position maps for m. Let*

$$b = (n_1, n_1') \|_{k_1} (n_2, n_2') \|_{k_2} \cdots (n_m, n_m') \perp$$

be a burst of length m. The map π' is a potential successor of π (with respect to $\sim b$), if and only if, for $i = 1, 2, \ldots, m$,

$$\pi'(i) = \begin{cases} \pi(i) - 1, & \text{if } \pi(i) \in \mathbb{N}_0 \text{ and } \pi(i) > 1, \\ n_i, & \text{if } \pi(i) \in \mathbb{N}_0 \text{ and } \pi(i) = 1, \\ n, & \text{if } \pi(i) \in N, \ n \in N \text{ and } \big(\pi(i), n\big) \in E, \\ 0, & \text{if } \pi(i) \in N \text{ is external or if } \pi(i) = 0. \end{cases}$$

Definition 9 (Configuration Trail). *Let $G = (N, E, w)$ be a soliton graph. Let $m \in \mathbb{N}$, and let π and π' be position maps for m. Let*

$$b = (n_1, n_1') \|_{k_1} (n_2, n_2') \|_{k_2} \cdots (n_m, n_m') \perp$$

be a burst of length m.

1. *A* configuration *(for b) is a pair (G', π) such that $G' = (N, E, w')$ is a weighted graph with weights in $\{1, 2\}$ and π is a position map for m.*
2. *A* configuration trail *for G and b is a finite sequence*

$$(G_0, \pi_0), (G_1, \pi_1), \ldots$$

   of configurations with the following properties.
   (a) $G_0 = G$, and π_0 is the initial position map for b.
   (b) Let $j \geq 1$. The sequence

$$(G_0, \pi_0), (G_1, \pi_1), \ldots, (G_j, \pi_j)$$

   is a configuration trail, if and only if

$$(G_0, \pi_0), (G_1, \pi_1), \ldots, (G_{j-1}, \pi_{j-1})$$

   is a configuration trail such that π_{j-1} is not final, and $G_j(N, E, w_j)$ and π_j and the sequence satisfy the following conditions for all i:
   i. π_j is a potential successor of π_{j-1}.
   ii. If $\pi_{j-1}(i) \in N$ is external and $j = 1$, then $\pi_j(i) \in N$.
   iii. If $j > 1$ and $\pi_{j-2}(i) = 1$, then $\pi_j(i) \in N$.
   iv. If $j > 1$, $\pi_{j-1}(i) \in N$ is external and equal to n_i', and if $\pi_{j-2}(i) \in N$, then $\pi_j(i) = 0$.
   v. If $\pi_{j-1}(i) \in N$ is internal and $\pi_{j-2}(i) \in N$, then

$$w_{j-2}\big(\pi_{j-2}(i), \pi_{j-1}(i)\big) \neq w_{j-1}\big(\pi_{j-1}(i), \pi_j(i)\big).$$

   vi. If $\pi_j(i) \neq 0$, then $\pi_j(i) \neq \pi_{j-1}(i)$ and, if $j > 1$, $\pi_j(i) \neq \pi_{j-2}(i)$.

vii. G_j is obtained from G_{j-1} by changing the weights of some edges as follows: If $\big(\pi_{j-1}(i), \pi_j(i)\big) \in E$, then

$$w_j\big(\pi_{j-1}(i), \pi_j(i)\big) = w_j\big(\pi_j(i), \pi_{j-1}(i)\big) = 3 - w_{j-1}\big(\pi_{j-1}(i), \pi_j(i)\big).$$

All other weights remain unchanged.

3. A configuration trail is legal, if it satisfies the following conditions for all $j \geq 1$:
    (a) If $\pi_{j-1}(i)$ and $\pi_{j-1}(i')$ are nodes and $\pi_{j-1}(i) = \pi_{j-1}(i')$ for some distinct i and i', then $\pi_j(i) \neq \pi_j(i')$.
    (b) If $\pi_{j-1}(i)$ and $\pi_{j-1}(i')$ are nodes with $\big(\pi_{j-1}(i), \pi_{j-1}(i')\big) \in E$, then $\pi_j(i) \neq \pi_{j-1}(i')$ or $\pi_j(i') \neq \pi_{j-1}(i)$.

4. A configuration trail

$$(G_0, \pi_0), (G_1, \pi_1), \ldots, (G_j, \pi_j)$$

is partial if π_j is not final. Otherwise it is total.

In the definition, as stated, part (2b) may be undefined without the legality conditions. We chose this slightly inconsistent presentation to make things easier to read. The definition restates those parts of Definition 2 which are independent of the number of solitons while keeping track of all soliton positions. The legality conditions state that no two solitons can traverse the same edge at the same time regardless of their mutual directions. As a consequence, no two solitons can enter the same external node at the same time; this holds true both for exterior nodes used as entry points and those used as exit points. They can be at an internal node simultaneously, but must leave it on different edges. Moreover, they cannot simply swap places.

Proposition 1. Let $G = (N, E, w)$ be a soliton graph and let

$$b = (n_1, n_1')\|_{k_1} (n_2, n_2')\|_{k_2} \cdots (n_m, n_m')\bot$$

be a burst. Let $(G_0, \pi_0), (G_1, \pi_1), \ldots, (G_j, \pi_j)$ be any legal configuration trail for G and b. Then, for $h = 0, 1, \ldots, j - 1$ and all interior nodes $n \in N$, $|\{i \mid i \in \mathfrak{m}, \pi_h(i) = n\}| < d(n)$.

Proof. Consider (G_h, π_h) with $0 \leq h < j$ and an interior node n. Because of the legality condition, no more than $d(n)$ solitons can arrive at the node n simultaneously. Hence, we have to show that $d(n)$ solitons cannot arrive at n simultaneously when there is another legal step in the trail. One distinguishes several cases according to the degree of n and to how many solitons are at n prior to the step. We omit the details here. They will be provided in a separate publication. $\qquad\square$

Using the assumptions of Proposition 1, the statement does not hold in general for $h = j$ when the legal configuration trail under consideration is not total. In that case $|\{i \mid i \in \mathfrak{m}, \pi_h(i) = n\}| = d(n)$ is possible. However not all solitons can leave node n because of the legality conditions. Hence, the legal partial configuration trail cannot be continued into a legal total configuration trail.

Definition 10 (Result of a Burst). *Let G be a soliton graph and let b be a burst. The result of burst b on G is the set $\mathsf{Result}(G, b)$ of weighted graphs G' such that there is a legal total configuration trail for b transforming G into G'.*

The set $\mathsf{Result}(G, b)$ should be considered as analogous, in the multi-soliton model, to the set $S(G, n, n')$ in the single-soliton model. We show below that every element of $\mathsf{Result}(G, b)$ is again a soliton graph.

We extend the operator Result to sets of graphs and bursts and then define its closure under iteration: As before, let Γ be the set of soliton graphs with the same underlying graph as G and let $\mathcal{G} \subseteq \Gamma$. Let X be the set of exterior nodes of these graphs. Let $B \subseteq B(X \times X)$ be a set of bursts. Define

$$\mathsf{Result}(\mathcal{G}, B) = \bigcup_{G \in \mathcal{G}} \bigcup_{b \in B} \mathsf{Result}(G, b).$$

For $i \in \mathbb{N}_0$ let

$$\mathsf{Result}^i(\mathcal{G}, B) = \begin{cases} \mathcal{G}, & \text{if } i = 0, \text{ and} \\ \mathsf{Result}\big(\mathsf{Result}^{i-1}(\mathcal{G}, B), B\big), & \text{if } i > 0. \end{cases}$$

Finally, let

$$\mathsf{Result}^*(\mathcal{G}, B) = \bigcup_{i \geq 0} \mathsf{Result}^i(\mathcal{G}, B).$$

For a given graph G, the set of soliton graphs with G as underlying graph is finite. Therefore, the set $\mathcal{G}$ is finite. Hence also $\mathsf{Result}^*(\mathcal{G}, B)$ is finite and there is a finite subset B' of B such that $\mathsf{Result}^*(\mathcal{G}, B)$ is equal to $\mathsf{Result}^*(\mathcal{G}, B')$ and $\mathsf{Result}^*(\mathcal{G}, B')$ can be computed in finitely many steps.

Proposition 1 establishes that no interior node n can have more than $d(n) - 1$ solitons occupying it. The following more precise statement clarifies the connection between the degree of an interior node, its weight, and the number of solitons at the node.

Proposition 2 (Interior Nodes without Solitons). *Let $G = (N, E, w)$ be a soliton graph and let $b = (n_1, n_1')\|_{k_1}(n_2, n_2')\|_{k_2} \cdots (n_m, n_m')\bot$ be a burst. Let $(G_0, \pi_0), (G_1, \pi_1), \ldots, (G_j, \pi_j)$ be any legal configuration trail for G and b with $j > 1$. Then, for $h = 0, 1, \ldots, j$ and all interior nodes $n \in N$, $w_h(n) = d(n) + 1$ whenever $\pi_h^{-1}(n) = \emptyset$.*

Proof. As the trail is legal, at most $d(n) - 1$ solitons can be at n at any step $h < j$. For $h = 0$ the statement holds true. Consider the smallest h such that solitons arrive at n for the first time. Let h' be smallest such that $h < h' \leq j$

such that no solitons are present at node n at step h'. If no such h and h' exists, the statement is trivially true.

Hence, suppose h and h' exist. One shows that the statement holds true at step h' using an extensive case distinction. By induction, this implies the claim. The details of the proof will be provided in another publication.   □

Proposition 3 (Preservation of Soliton Graphs under Bursts). *Let G be a soliton graph and let b a burst. Every $G' \in \mathsf{Result}(G, b)$ is a soliton graph.*

Proof. Every $G' \in \mathsf{Result}(G, b)$ is obtained by a legal total configuration trail. As the trail is total, there is no soliton on any node in the end. Hence, by Proposition 2, G' is a soliton graph.   □

Proposition 4 (Model Consistency). *Let G be a soliton graph. Let n and n' be exterior nodes of G and let $b = (n, n')\bot$. Then $S(G, n, n') = \mathsf{Result}(G, b)$. Moreover, there is a one-to-one correspondence between soliton paths from n to n' and legal total configuration trails for b.*

Proof. This is a direct consequence of the equivalence of Definition 2 with Definition 9 for the special case of bursts of length 1.   □

Definition 11 (Multi-Soliton Automaton). *Let G be a soliton graph with set X of external nodes. Let $B \subseteq B(X \times X)$ be a set of bursts. Let*

$$\mathsf{States}(G, B) = \mathsf{Result}^*(G, B).$$

The B-soliton automaton of G is the finite automaton $\mathcal{A}_B(G)$ with inputs $b \in B$, state set $\mathsf{States}(G, B)$ and non-deterministic transition function

$$\tau(G', b) = \begin{cases} \mathsf{Result}(G', b), & \text{if } \mathsf{Result}(G', b) \neq \emptyset, \\ \{G'\}, & \text{otherwise,} \end{cases}$$

for $G' \in \mathsf{States}(G, B)$ and $b \in B$.

Note that $\mathsf{States}(G, B)$ is finite and that B can always be assumed to be finite.

Proposition 5. *Let G be a soliton graph with set X of external nodes. Let $B \subseteq B(X \times X)$ be a set of bursts. Let $m \in \mathbb{N}$.*

1. *$\mathcal{A}_B(G)$ is connected (as automaton). Every state can be reached from G.*
2. *For $B = B_{\leq m}$, $\mathcal{A}_B(G)$ is strongly connected (as automaton).*
3. *$\mathcal{A}_{B_{\leq m}}(G)$ is a subautomaton of $\mathcal{A}_{B_{\leq m+1}}(G)$.*
4. *There is a soliton graph G such that $\mathcal{A}_{B_1}(G)$ is a proper subautomaton of $\mathcal{A}_{B_{\leq 2}}(G)$.*
5. *There is a $k \in \mathbb{N}$, depending on G, such that*

$$\mathsf{States}(G, B_{\leq k}) = \mathsf{States}(G, B_{\leq k+j})$$

for all $j \in \mathbb{N}$.

6. *There is a $k \in \mathbb{N}$, depending on G, such that $\mathcal{A}_{B_{\leq k}}(G) = \mathcal{A}_{B_{\leq k+j}}(G)$ for all $j \in \mathbb{N}$.*

7. *Observation 1 does not hold in general for bursts of length greater than 1.*

Proof. The first statement is a direct consequence of the definition of the set $\mathsf{States}(G, B)$. The second statement follows from the fact that $\mathcal{A}_{B_1}(G)$ is strongly connected. The third statement is a consequence of the inclusion $B_{\leq m} \subseteq B_{\leq m+1}$. For the fourth statement we provide an example: Let G be the soliton graph of Fig. 2. The path going to the right at node j is impervious for single solitons. However, it is used by the burst $(1, 1)\|_1(1, 1)\bot$, and this changes the weights on both cycles. The automaton $\mathcal{A}_{B_1}(G)$ has two states while $\mathcal{A}_{B_{\leq 2}}(G)$ has four states. The transition monoid of the former is $\mathfrak{S}_2$, that of the latter is $\mathfrak{S}_2 \times \mathfrak{S}_2$. The fifth statement is a consequence of the fact that the set of soliton graphs with the same underlying graph is bounded. The sixth statement follows from the fifth by finiteness. For the seventh statement one considers different values of k in the burst $(1, 1)\|_k(1, 1)\bot$ for the soliton graph considered above. $\square$

In the single-soliton model all inputs cause involutorial transformations; hence the soliton automaton is strongly connected and, moreover, the transition monoid is a group. We believe that this might be true also for the multi-soliton model, but expect that some kind of reversal on bursts may be needed. In the fifth statement of Proposition 5 we only assert that the state set will stabilize when a certain length of bursts has been reached. The sixth statement says that at some stage, the automata are the same. We don't know, whether this happens at the same stages.

The example used for the fourth statement enables an impervious path leading to a part of the graph which would be unaccessible otherwise. The example suggests that we should expect a direct product of transition monoids arising from the single-soliton model. We do not think that this is the whole picture.

6   From Here, Where?

Modelling the effect of more than a single soliton turned out to be significantly more complicated than expected. We believe that our model captures most of the essential facts; whether it does, in essence, should be answered by physics. One can, however, also treat our model, while originally motivated by physical or chemical processes, as a network model with complicated traffic, for instance that of a railway system, in which many trains move around nearly independently, only controlled by local signals.

Many natural questions remain unanswered and are left for a successor to this paper: One needs to clarify the distinction between determinism and strong determinism. What is the time or length bound for bursts, such that adding bursts exceeding these bounds will not change the transition monoid of the automaton? Are the transformations induced by bursts involutorial? Can resets be caused by bursts? Can matching theory help?

To some of these and further natural questions we have partial answers. It has become evident, however, that there are fundamental differences between the single-soliton and the multi-soliton models.

A complete version of the present paper including full proofs, detailed explanations and examples, and further results and discussions is about to be submitted to a journal.

Acknowledgments. This research was partially supported by the Natural Sciences and Engineering Research Council of Canada.

References

1. Bartha, M., Jürgensen, H.: Characterizing finite undirected multigraphs as indexed algebras. Technical Report Report 252, Department of Computer Science, The University of Western Ontario (1989)
2. Bartha, M., Krész, M.: Elementary decomposition of soliton automata. Acta Cybernet. **14**, 631–652 (2000)
3. Bartha, M., Krész, M.: Structuring the elementary components of graphs having perfect internal matching. Theoret. Comput. Sci. **299**, 179–210 (2003)
4. Bartha, M., Krész, M.: Deterministic soliton graphs. Informatica **30**, 281–288 (2006)
5. Bartha, M., Krész, M.: Splitters and barriers in open graphs having a perfect internal matching. Acta Cybernet. **18**, 697–718 (2008)
6. Bartha, M., Krész, M.: Deciding the deterministic property for soliton graphs. Ars Math. Contemp. **2**, 121–136 (2009)
7. Bartha, M., Krész, M.: Soliton circuits and network-based automata: Review and perspectives. In: Martín-Vide, C. (ed.) Scientific Applications of Language Methods Mathematics, Computing, Language, and Life: Frontiers in Mathematical Linguistics and Language Theory, vol. 2, pp. 585–631. Imperial College Press, London (2011)
8. Carter, F.L.: Conformational switching at the molecular level. In: Carter, F.L. (ed.) Molecular Electronic Devices, pp. 51–71. Marcel Dekker, New York (1982)
9. Carter, F.L.: The concepts of molecular electronics. In: Aizawa, M. (ed.) Bioelectronics. Research and Development Report, vol. 50, pp. 123–158. CMC Press, Denver (1984)
10. Carter, F.L.: The molecular device computer: Point of departure for large scale cellular automata. In: Farmer, D., Toffoli, T., Wolfram, S. (eds.) Cellular Automtata, Proceedings of an Interdisciplinary Workshop, pp. 175–194. North-Holland, Amsterdam (1983,1984); Published in Physica 10D(1&2)
11. Carter, F.L., Schultz, A., Duckworth, D.: Soliton switching and its implications for molecular electronics. In: Carter [17], pp. 149–182
12. Carter, F.L.: Problems and prospects of future electroactive polymers and "molecular" electronic devices. In: Lockhart, L.B. (ed.) The NRL Program on Electroactive Polymers, First Annual Report. NRL Memorandum Report, vol. 3960, pp. 121–175. Naval Research Laboratory, Washington (1979)
13. Carter, F.L.: Further considerations on "molecular" electronic devices. In: Fox, R.B. (ed.): The NRL Program on Electroactive Polymers, Second Annual Report. NRL Memorandum Report, vol. 4335, pp. 35–52. Naval Research Laboratory, Washington (1980)

14. Carter, F.L.: Searching for S-P analogues of (SN)$_x$. In: Fox, R.B. (ed.) The NRL Program on Electroactive Polymers, Second Annual Report. NRL Memorandum Report, vol. 4335, pp. 3–10. Naval Research Laboratory, Washington (1980)

15. Carter, F.L.: The chemistry in future molecular computers. In: Heller, S.R., Potenzone, Jr., S.R. (eds.) Proceedings of the 6th International Conference on Computers in Chemical Research and Education (ICCCRE) Computer Applications in Chemistry. Held in Washington, DC, July 11–16, 1982. Analytical Chemistry Symposia Series, vol. 15, pp. 225–262. Elsevier, Amsterdam (1983)

16. Carter, F.L.: Molecular level fabrication techniques and molecular electronic devices. J. Vac. Sci. Technol. B **1**(4), 959–968 (1983)

17. Carter, F.L. (ed.): Molecular Electronic Devices II. Marcel Dekker, New York (1987)

18. Dassow, J., Jürgensen, H.: Soliton automata. J. Comput. System Sci. **40**, 158–181 (1990)

19. Dassow, J., Jürgensen, H.: Deterministic soliton automata with a single exterior node. Theoret. Comput. Sci. **84**, 281–292 (1991)

20. Dassow, J., Jürgensen, H.: Deterministic soliton automata with at most one cycle. J. Comput. System Sci. **46**, 155–197 (1993)

21. Dassow, J., Jürgensen, H.: The transition monoids of soliton trees. In: Păun, G. (ed.) Mathematical Linguistics and Related Topics. Papers in Honour of Solomon Marcus on His 70th Birthday, pp. 76–87, Editura Academiei Române, Bucureşti (1995)

22. Davydov, A.S.: Solitons in Molecular Systems. D. Reidel Publ. Co., (1985)

23. Groves, M.P.: Dynamic circuit diagrams for some soliton switching devices. In: Carter [17], pp. 183–204

24. Groves, M.P.: Towards verification of soliton circuits. In: Carter, F.L., Siatkowski, R.E., Wohltjen, H. (eds.) Molecular Electronic Devices, pp. 287–302. North-Holland, Amsterdam (1988)

25. Groves, M.P.: Soliton circuit design using molecular gate arrays. In: Kotagiri, R., Patel, M. (eds.) Proceedings of the Twentieth Australasian Computer Science Conference, ACSC 1997, Sydney, Australia, pp. 245–252 (February 5–7, 1997), Published in Australian Computer Science Communications 19(1)

26. Groves, M.P., Carvalho, C.F., Marlin, C.D., Prager, R.H.: Using soliton circuits to build molecular memories. Australian Computer Science Communications 15(1), 37–45 (1993); This journal issue contains the "Proceedings of the Sixteenth Australian Computer Science Conference, ACSC-16, February 3–5, 1993, Brisbane, Queensland", edited by G. Gupta, G. Mohay and R. Topor

27. Groves, M.P., Carvalho, C.F., Prager, R.H.: Switching the polyacetylene soliton. Materials Science and Engineering **C3**, 181–185 (1995)

28. Groves, M.P., Marlin, C.D.: Using soliton circuits to build molecular computers. Australian Computer Science Communications **17**, 188–193 (1995)

29. Groves, M.P.: A Soliton Circuit Design System. PhD Thesis, University of Adelaide (1987)

30. Hashmall, J.A., Baker, L.C.W., Carter, F.L., Brant, P., Weber, D.C.: Semi-empirical calculations on electroactive polymeres. In: Fox, R.B. (ed.) The NRL Program on Electroactive Polymers, Second Annual Report. NRL Memorandum Report, vol. 4335, pp. 11–23. Naval Research Laboratory, Washington (1980)

31. Jürgensen, H., Kraak, P.: Soliton automata based on trees. Internat. J. Foundations Comput. Sci. **18**, 1257–1270 (2007)

32. Krész, M.: Soliton Automata: A Computational Model on the Principle of Graph Matchings. PhD thesis, University of Szeged, Hungary (2004)

33. Krész, M.: Simulation of Soliton Circuits. In: Farré, J., Litovsky, I., Schmitz, S. (eds.) CIAA 2005. LNCS, vol. 3845, pp. 347–348. Springer, Heidelberg (2006)
34. Krész, M.: Graph decomposition and descriptional complexity of soliton automata. J. of Automata, Languages and Combinatorics **12**, 237–263 (2007)
35. Krész, M.: Soliton automata with constant external edges. Theoret. Comput. Sci. **206**, 1126–1141 (2008)
36. Lu, Y.: Solitons & Polarons in Conducting Polymers. World Scientific, Singapore (1988)
37. Does molecular electronics compute? Nature Nanotechnology 8(6) (2013), 377. Editorial
38. Park, J.K., Steiglitz, K., Thurston, W.P.: Soliton-like behavior in automata. Physica **19D**, 423–432 (1986)

On Power Series over a Graded Monoid

Zoltán Ésik[1] and Werner Kuich[2(✉)]

[1] University of Szeged, Szeged, Hungary
[2] Technische Universität Wien, Vienna, Austria
werner.kuich@tuwien.ac.at

Abstract. We consider power series over a graded monoid M of finite type. We show first that, under certain conditions, the equivalence problem of power series over M with coefficients in the semiring $\mathbb{N}$ of nonnegative integers can be reduced to the equivalence problem of power series over $\{x\}^*$ with coefficients in $\mathbb{N}$. This result is then applied to rational and recognizable power series over M with coefficients in $\mathbb{N}$, and to rational power series over Σ^* with coefficients in the semiring $\mathbb{Q}_+$ of nonnegative rational numbers, where Σ is an alphabet.

1 Power Series over a Graded Monoid and a Decidability Result

In [4], Sakarovitch considers power series over a graded monoid. Let $\langle M, \cdot, 1 \rangle$ be a monoid and let $|\ | : M \to \mathbb{N}$ be a mapping, called *length*, such that

(i) $|m| > 0$ for all $m \in M$, $m \neq 1$;
(ii) $|m \cdot n| = |m| + |n|$ for all $m, n \in M$.

Then $\langle M, \cdot, 1 \rangle$ is called *graded monoid*. The definition implies that $|1| = 0$. If a graded monoid M is finitely generated, we call M a graded monoid of *finite type*. In Section 2 of [4], Sakarovitch proves the following results:

Proposition 1 (Sakarovitch [4]). *In a graded monoid of finite type, the number of elements whose length is less than an arbitrary given integer $n > 0$ is finite.*

A monoid is called *finitely decomposable* if, for all $m \in M$, the set of pairs (m_1, m_2) such that $m_1 m_2 = m$ is finite.

Corollary 1 (Sakarovitch [4]). *In a graded monoid of finite type, every element is finitely decomposable.*

Let S be a semiring and M be a graded monoid of finite type. Then any mapping from M into S is a *(formal) power series* (*over M with coefficients in S*). The set of all these power series is denoted by $S\langle\langle M \rangle\rangle$. If r is a power series

Partially supported by grant no. K 108448 from the National Foundation of Hungary for Scientific Research.
Partially supported by Austrian Science Fund (FWF): grant no. I1661-N25.

C.S. Calude et al. (Eds.): Gruska Festschrift, LNCS 8808, pp. 49–55, 2014.
DOI: 10.1007/978-3-319-13350-8_4

then the image of an element $m \in M$ under r is denoted by (r, m) which is called *coefficient* of m and the power series is written as

$$r = \sum_{m \in M} (r, m)m \,.$$

Power series where almost all coefficients are 0 are called *polynomials*. The set of all polynomials is denoted by $S\langle M \rangle$.

For all $r_1, r_2 \in S\langle\langle M \rangle\rangle$, we consider the following operations:

(i) the (pointwise) addition of r_1 and r_2, denoted by $r_1 + r_2$ and defined by

$$(r_1 + r_2, m) = (r_1, m) + (r_2, m) \text{ for all } m \in M;$$

(ii) the (Cauchy) product of r_1 and r_2, denoted by $r_1 \cdot r_2$ and defined by

$$(r_1 \cdot r_2, m) = \sum_{m_1 m_2 = m} (r_1, m_1)(r_2, m_2) \text{ for all } m \in M;$$

(iii) the (pointwise) Hadamard product of r_1 and r_2, denoted by $r_1 \odot r_2$ and defined by
$$(r_1 \odot r_2, m) = (r_1, m)(r_2, m) \text{ for all } m \in M;$$

Moreover, we consider the scalar multiplications of $s \in S$ and $r \in S\langle\langle M \rangle\rangle$ denoted by $s \cdot r$ and $r \cdot s$ and defined by

$$(s \cdot r, m) = s \cdot (r, m) \text{ and } (r \cdot s, m) = (r, m) \cdot s \text{ for all } m \in M, \text{ respectively.}$$

The power series 0 and 1 are defined by

$(0, m) = 0$ for all $m \in M$ and
$(1, 1) = 1, \quad (1, m') = 0$ for all $m' \in M$, $m' \neq m$, respectively.

Proposition 2 (Sakarovitch [4]). *Let M be a graded monoid of finite type and S a semiring. Then $\langle S\langle\langle M \rangle\rangle, +, \cdot, 0, 1\rangle$ and $\langle S\langle M \rangle, +, \cdot, 0, 1\rangle$ are semirings.*

In the sequel, $\langle M, \cdot, 1\rangle$ will always denote a graded monoid of finite type and S will denote a semiring.

A power series $r \in S\langle\langle M \rangle\rangle$ is called *cycle-free* if there exists an $n \geq 1$ such that $(r, 1)^n = 0$; it is called *proper* if $(r, 1) = 0$. Let $r \in S\langle\langle M \rangle\rangle$. Then the *proper part* of r is the power series $\sum_{m \in M, \, m \neq 1}(r, m)m$ and the *constant term* of r is the power series $(r, 1)1$, also written $(r, 1)$. If $r \in S\langle\langle M \rangle\rangle$ is cycle-free then $\{n \mid (r^n, m) \neq 0\}$ is locally finite, i.e., is a finite set for all $m \in M$. Hence, the infinite sum

$$r^* = \sum_{n \geq 0} r^n$$

is defined; it is called the *star of r*.

Proposition 3 (Sakarovitch [4]). *Let $r \in S\langle\langle M \rangle\rangle$ be a cycle-free power series with constant term r_0 and proper part r_1. Then*

$$r^* = (r_0^* r_1)^* r_0^* = r_0^* (r_1 r_0^*)^*.$$

Defining $\varphi : \mathbb{N}\langle\langle M \rangle\rangle \to \mathbb{N}\langle\langle \{x\}^* \rangle\rangle$, x a symbol, by

$$\varphi(r) = \sum_{m \in M} (r, m) x^{|m|},$$

it is easily shown that φ is a semiring morphism. The mapping φ is also compatible with the star operation applied to a cycle-free power series r, i.e.,

$$\varphi(r^*) = \varphi(r)^* \text{ if } r \in \mathbb{N}\langle\langle M \rangle\rangle \text{ is cycle-free.}$$

A power series $r \in S\langle\langle M \rangle\rangle$ is termed *rational* (over S and M) if r can be obtained from polynomials of $S\langle M \rangle$ by finitely many applications of the *rational operations* $+, \cdot, ^*$, where * is applied only to *proper* power series. The family of rational power series (over S and M) is denoted by $S^{\mathrm{rat}}\langle\langle M \rangle\rangle$. By Proposition 3, we get an equivalent definition of rational power series if we replace *proper* by *cycle-free*. The formula telling how a given rational power series r is obtained from these polynomials by rational operations is referred to as a *rational expression for r*.

Theorem 1. *Let M be a graded monoid of finite type and assume that $|\ | : M \to \mathbb{N}$ is recursive. Then φ, as a mapping $\mathbb{N}^{\mathrm{rat}}\langle\langle M \rangle\rangle \to \mathbb{N}^{\mathrm{rat}}\langle\langle \{x\}^* \rangle\rangle$, is recursive.*

Proof. We prove the theorem by induction on the structure of a rational power series $r \in \mathbb{N}^{\mathrm{rat}}\langle\langle M \rangle\rangle$. We show that from a rational expression for $r \in \mathbb{N}^{\mathrm{rat}}\langle\langle M \rangle\rangle$ we can compute a rational expression for $\varphi(r)$ since φ is a semiring morphism preserving *.

(i) For $r = n$, $n \in \mathbb{N}$, $\varphi(r) = n\varepsilon$. For $r = a$, $a \in M$, $\varphi(a) = x^{|a|}$. Since φ is a semiring morphism, $\varphi(p) \in \mathbb{N}\langle \{x\}^* \rangle$ for $p \in \mathbb{N}\langle M \rangle$.

(ii) Since φ is a semiring morphism, we obtain $\varphi(r_1 + r_2) = \varphi(r_1) + \varphi(r_2)$ and $\varphi(r_1 \cdot r_2) = \varphi(r_1) \cdot \varphi(r_2)$.

(iii) Since φ is a semiring morphism, we obtain, for a proper power series in $\mathbb{N}\langle\langle M \rangle\rangle$,

$$\varphi(r^*) = \sum_{n \geq 0} \varphi(r^n) = \sum_{n \geq 0} \varphi(r)^n = \varphi(r)^*.$$

$\square$

We call a power series $r \in S\langle\langle M \rangle\rangle$ *unambiguous* if, for all $m \in M$, $(r, m) \in \{0, 1\}$.

In the proof of our next theorem we use the following equality:

$$(\varphi(r), x^k) = \sum_{|m|=k} (r, m), \quad r \in \mathbb{N}\langle\langle M \rangle\rangle, \ k \geq 0.$$

This next theorem is a generalization of Theorems 16.21 and 16.22 of Kuich, Salomaa [3].

Theorem 2. *Let M be a graded monoid of finite type and assume that $|\ |$: $M \to \mathbb{N}$ is recursive. Then*

(i) *for $r_1, r_2 \in \mathbb{N}^{\mathrm{rat}}\langle\langle M \rangle\rangle$ with $(r_1, m) \geq (r_2, m)$ for all $m \in M$ the problem whether or not $r_1 = r_2$ is decidable;*

(ii) *if $\mathfrak{R} \subseteq \mathbb{N}^{\mathrm{rat}}\langle\langle M \rangle\rangle$ such that, for $s_1 \in \mathbb{N}^{\mathrm{rat}}\langle\langle M \rangle\rangle$ and $s_2 \in \mathfrak{R}$, $s_1 \odot s_2$ is in $\mathbb{N}^{\mathrm{rat}}\langle\langle M \rangle\rangle$, then for two unambiguous power series $r_1 \in \mathbb{N}^{\mathrm{rat}}\langle\langle M \rangle\rangle$ and $r_2 \in \mathfrak{R}$ the problem whether or not $r_1 = r_2$ is decidable.*

Proof. By Theorem 1 the mapping $\varphi : \mathbb{N}^{\mathrm{rat}}\langle\langle M \rangle\rangle \to \mathbb{N}^{\mathrm{rat}}\langle\langle \{x\}^* \rangle\rangle$ is recursive. By Corollary 8.18 of Kuich, Salomaa [3] the equivalence problem for power series in $\mathbb{N}^{\mathrm{rat}}\langle\langle \{x\}^* \rangle\rangle$ is decidable. Hence, for two given rational power series r_1 and r_2 in $\mathbb{N}^{\mathrm{rat}}\langle\langle \{x\}^* \rangle\rangle$ we can decide, whether or not $\varphi(r_1) = \varphi(r_2)$.

(i) If $\varphi(r_1) = \varphi(r_2)$ then, for all $k \geq 0$, $\sum_{|m|=k}(r_1, m) = \sum_{|m|=k}(r_2, m)$. Hence, $(r_1, m) \geq (r_2, m)$ for all $m \in M$ implies $(r_1, m) = (r_2, m)$. If $\varphi(r_1) \neq \varphi(r_2)$ then, for some $k \geq 0$, $\sum_{|m|=k}(r_1, m) \neq \sum_{|m|=k}(r_2, m)$. Hence, for some $m' \in M$ of length k we obtain $(r_1, m') \neq (r_2, m')$.

(ii) Since (r_1, m) and (r_2, m) are in $\{0, 1\}$ for all $m \in M$, we obtain $(r_1 \odot r_2, m) \leq (r_1, m)$ and $(r_1 \odot r_2, m) \leq (r_2, m)$ for all $m \in M$. By (i) it is decidable whether or not $r_1 \odot r_2 = r_1$ and $r_1 \odot r_2 = r_2$. Clearly, $r_1 = r_2$ iff $r_1 \odot r_2 = r_1$ and $r_1 \odot r_2 = r_2$. Hence, $r_1 = r_2$ is decidable. $\square$

2   Decidability Problems for Unambiguous Power Series

In the sequel, Σ, $1 \notin \Sigma$, denotes a finite generating set of M and S denotes a semiring. We write Σ^* for the set of all finite products of elements of Σ. Hence, we obtain $\Sigma^* = M$. By $S\langle \Sigma \cup \{1\}\rangle$ and $S\langle\{1\}\rangle$ we denote the set of polynomials of the form $p = (p, 1)1 + \sum_{x\in\Sigma}(p, x)x$ and $p = (p, 1)1$, respectively.

A *finite (weighted) automaton* (over Σ and S)

$$\mathfrak{A} = (Q, R, A, P)$$

is given by

(i) a finite nonempty set Q of *states*,
(ii) a *transition matrix* $A \in (S\langle \Sigma \cup \{1\}\rangle)^{Q \times Q}$,
(iii) an *initial state vector* $R \in (S\langle\{1\}\rangle)^{1 \times Q}$,
(iv) an *final state vector* $P \in (S\langle\{1\}\rangle)^{Q \times 1}$.

The finite automaton $\mathfrak{A}$ is *cycle-free* (resp. *proper*) if the isomorphic copy of A in $S^{Q \times Q}\langle \Sigma \cup \{1\}\rangle$ is cycle-free (resp. proper).

The behavior $||\mathfrak{A}||$ of a cycle-free finite automaton $\mathfrak{A}$ is defined by

$$||\mathfrak{A}|| = \sum_{q_1, q_2 \in Q} R_{q_1}(A^*)_{q_1, q_2} P_{q_2} = RA^*P.$$

(See Sakarovitch [4], Section 3 and Gruska [1], Chapter 3.)

By Proposition 3.14 of Sakarovitch [4], for each *cycle-free* finite automaton there exists a *proper* finite automaton with the same behavior.

By Theorem 3.10 of Sakarovitch [4], we obtain

$$S^{\mathrm{rat}}\langle\langle M\rangle\rangle = \{\|\mathfrak{A}\| \mid \mathfrak{A} \text{ is a proper finite automaton over } \Sigma \text{ and } S\}.$$

Let $\mu : M \to S^{Q \times Q}$, Q a finite index set, be a morphism, and let $\lambda \in S^{1 \times Q}$, $\nu \in S^{Q \times 1}$. Then (λ, μ, ν) is called *S-representation of M of dimension Q*. A power series $r \in S\langle\langle M\rangle\rangle$ is called *S-recognizable* if there exists a finite set Q and an S-representation of M of dimension Q (λ, μ, ν) such that

$$r = \sum_{m \in M} (\lambda\mu(m)\nu)m.$$

We say then that the S-representation (λ, μ, ν) *recognizes* r. The set of all S-recognizable formal power series is denoted by $S^{\mathrm{rec}}\langle\langle M\rangle\rangle$.

Theorem 3 (Sakarovitch [4], Theorem 4.38). *Suppose that S is a commutative semiring. Let $r \in S^{\mathrm{rec}}\langle\langle M\rangle\rangle$ and $u \in S^{\mathrm{rat}}\langle\langle M\rangle\rangle$. Then $r \odot u \in S^{\mathrm{rat}}\langle\langle M\rangle\rangle$. Moreover, if r is recognized by an S-representation and u is given by a rational expression then a rational expression for $r \odot u$ can be effectively constructed.*

Proof. The first sentence of our theorem is implied by Theorem 4.38 of Sakarovitch [4]. For the proof of the second sentence, we first show that the constructions of Theorems 4.13 and 4.35, and of Proposition 4.33 of Sakarovitch [4] are effective. We use the notation of Sakarovitch [4] as far as possible.

Theorem 4.13: If r and u in $S^{\mathrm{rec}}\langle\langle M\rangle\rangle$ are recognized by the S-representations (λ, μ, ν) and (η, κ, ξ), respectively, then $r \odot u$ is recognized by the S-representation $(\lambda \otimes \eta, \mu \otimes \kappa, \nu \otimes \xi)$, where $\otimes$ denotes the Kronecker product. Clearly, the construction is effective.

Theorem 4.35: Let M and N be graded monoids and $\theta : M \to N$ be a continuous monoid morphism, i.e., $m\theta$ is unequal to the unit of N for all $m \in M$.

(i) From a rational expression for $r \in S^{\mathrm{rat}}\langle\langle M\rangle\rangle$ a rational expression for $r\underline{\theta} \in S^{\mathrm{rat}}\langle\langle N\rangle\rangle$ can effectively be constructed.

(ii) If θ is surjective, then from a rational expression for $u \in S^{\mathrm{rat}}\langle\langle N\rangle\rangle$ a rational expression for some $r \in S^{\mathrm{rat}}\langle\langle M\rangle\rangle$ such that $r\underline{\theta} = u$ can effectively be constructed.

Proposition 4.33: Let $\theta : M \to N$ be a monoid morphism and $u \in S^{\mathrm{rec}}\langle\langle M\rangle\rangle$ be recognized by the S-representation (λ, μ, ν). Then $u\theta^{-1} \in S^{\mathrm{rec}}\langle\langle M\rangle\rangle$ is recognized by the S-representation $(\lambda, \theta\mu, \nu)$. Clearly, the construction of the latter S-representation is effective.

We now prove the second sentence of our theorem. Since M is finitely generated there exists a finite alphabet Σ' and a surjective continuous morphism $\theta : \Sigma'^* \to M$. Here Σ' has the same cardinality as the generating set Σ of M. Assuming $\Sigma = \{m_1, \ldots, m_k\}$ and $\Sigma' = \{x_1, \ldots, x_k\}$ we construct effectively $\theta(x_j) = m_j$, $1 \le j \le k$. By Theorem 4.35(ii) there exists a power series

$u' \in S^{\mathrm{rat}} \langle\!\langle (\Sigma')^* \rangle\!\rangle$ such that $u'\underline{\theta} = u$ and a rational expression for $u'\underline{\theta}$ can effectively be constructed by the given rational expression for u.

By Lemma 4.37 of Sakarovitch [4],

$$r \odot u = (r\underline{\theta^{-1}} \odot u')\underline{\theta}.$$

Proposition 4.33 ensures that $r\underline{\theta^{-1}} \in S^{\mathrm{rec}} \langle\!\langle \Sigma'^* \rangle\!\rangle = S^{\mathrm{rat}} \langle\!\langle \Sigma'^* \rangle\!\rangle$. It is wellknown that a rational expression for $r\underline{\theta^{-1}}$ can effectively be constructed from an S-representation that recognizes $r\underline{\theta^{-1}}$. Hence, a rational expression for $r\underline{\theta^{-1}}$ can effectively be constructed. Since $r\underline{\theta^{-1}} \odot u' \in S^{\mathrm{rec}} \langle\!\langle \Sigma'^* \rangle\!\rangle = S^{\mathrm{rat}} \langle\!\langle \Sigma'^* \rangle\!\rangle$ by Theorem 4.13 a rational expression for $r\underline{\theta^{-1}} \odot u'$ can effectively be constructed. Finally, by Theorem 4.35(i) the construction of a rational expression for $(r\underline{\theta^{-1}} \odot u')\underline{\theta} = r \odot u$ is effective. $\qquad\square$

A monoid M is called *rationally enumerable* if $\mathrm{char}(M) \in \mathbb{N}^{\mathrm{rat}} \langle\!\langle M \rangle\!\rangle$. Here char denotes the characterisic series.

Theorem 4 (Sakarovitch [4], Corollary 4.39)**.** *Suppose that S is a commutative semiring. If M is rationally enumerable then $S^{\mathrm{rec}} \langle\!\langle M \rangle\!\rangle \subseteq S^{\mathrm{rat}} \langle\!\langle M \rangle\!\rangle$. If an S-representation recognizing $r \in S^{\mathrm{rec}} \langle\!\langle M \rangle\!\rangle$ is given then a rational expression for r can effectively be constructed.*

Proof. We use the proof of Corollary 4.39 of Sakarovitch [4]. Since $r \in S^{\mathrm{rec}} \langle\!\langle M \rangle\!\rangle$ and, by hypothesis, $\mathrm{char}(M) \in S^{\mathrm{rat}} \langle\!\langle M \rangle\!\rangle$, we obtain $r \odot \mathrm{char}(M) = r \in S^{\mathrm{rat}} \langle\!\langle M \rangle\!\rangle$ and, by Theorem 3, a rational expression for r can be effectively constructed from a given S-representation recognizing r. $\qquad\square$

Corollary 2. *Let M be a graded monoid of finite type that is rationally enumerable and assume that $|\ | : M \to \mathbb{N}$ is recursive. Then φ, as a function $\mathbb{N}^{\mathrm{rec}} \langle\!\langle M \rangle\!\rangle \to \mathbb{N}^{\mathrm{rat}} \langle\!\langle \{x\}^* \rangle\!\rangle$, is recursive.*

Theorem 5. *Let M be a rationally enumerable graded monoid of finite type such that $|\ | : M \to \mathbb{N}$ is recursive. Then for two unambiguous power series $r \in \mathbb{N}^{\mathrm{rat}} \langle\!\langle M \rangle\!\rangle$ and $s \in \mathbb{N}^{\mathrm{rec}} \langle\!\langle M \rangle\!\rangle$ the problem whether or not $r = s$ is decidable.*

Proof. By Theorem 1 and Corollary 2, $\varphi : \mathbb{N}^{\mathrm{rat}} \langle\!\langle M \rangle\!\rangle \to \mathbb{N}^{\mathrm{rat}} \langle\!\langle \{x\}^* \rangle\!\rangle$ and $\varphi : \mathbb{N}^{\mathrm{rec}} \langle\!\langle M \rangle\!\rangle \to \mathbb{N}^{\mathrm{rat}} \langle\!\langle \{x\}^* \rangle\!\rangle$, respectively, are recursive. Now the application of Corollary 8.18 of Kuich, Salomaa [3] and of Theorems 3 and 2 (ii) proves our theorem. $\qquad\square$

Harju, Karhumäki [2] proved the famous result that the equivalence problem for deterministic finite multitape automata is decidable. The next corollary states a weak version of this result.

Corollary 3. *Let $\Sigma_1, \ldots, \Sigma_n$ be alphabets. Then for a deterministic finite automaton $\mathfrak{A}$ over $\Sigma = \{(a_1, \varepsilon, \ldots, \varepsilon) \mid a_1 \in \Sigma_1\} \cup \cdots \cup \{(\varepsilon, \varepsilon, \ldots, a_n) \mid a_n \in \Sigma_n\}$ and $\mathbb{N}$, and an unambiguous power series $r \in \mathbb{N}^{\mathrm{rec}} \langle\!\langle \Sigma_1^* \times \cdots \times \Sigma_n^* \rangle\!\rangle$ the problem, whether or not $\|\mathfrak{A}\| = r$ is decidable.*

An inspection of the proof of Theorem 2 shows that $\mathfrak{R} \subseteq \mathbb{N}^{\mathrm{rat}} \langle\!\langle M \rangle\!\rangle$ can be replaced by $\mathfrak{R} \subseteq S^{\mathrm{rat}} \langle\!\langle M \rangle\!\rangle$ if the semiring S is ordered and satisfies the following condition: For all $a_1, a_2, b_1, b_2 \in S$,

$$a_1 + a_2 = b_1 + b_2, \ a_1 \geq b_1, \ a_2 \geq b_2 \text{ imply } a_1 = b_1, \ a_2 = b_2.$$

A nontrivial complete ordered semiring does not satisfy this condition; the semirings $\mathbb{Q}_+$ and $\mathbb{R}_+$ do satisfy this condition.

Theorem 6. *Let Σ be an alphabet and $r \in \mathbb{Q}_+^{\mathrm{rat}} \langle\!\langle \Sigma^* \rangle\!\rangle$ such that $(r, w) \leq 1$ for all $w \in \Sigma^*$. Then it is decidable whether or not r is unambiguous.*

Proof. Since $(r, w) \leq 1$ for all $w \in \Sigma^*$ we have $r \odot r \leq r$. Since $\mathbb{Q}_+^{\mathrm{rat}} \langle\!\langle \Sigma^* \rangle\!\rangle$ is closed under Hadamard product, by Corollary 8.18 of Kuich, Salomaa [3] and by Theorem 2 (i) it is decidable whether or not $r \odot r = r$. The theorem is proved by the observation that $r \odot r = r$ iff $(r, w) \in \{0, 1\}$ for all $w \in \Sigma^*$. $\qquad\square$

References

1. Gruska, J.: Foundations of Computing. Thomson Learning (1997)
2. Harju, T., Karhumäki, J.: The equivalence problem of multitape finite automata. Theoretical Computer Science **78**, 347–355 (1991)
3. Kuich, W., Salomaa, A.: Semirings, Automata, Languages. EATCS Monographs on Theoretical Computer Science, Vol. 5. Springer (1986)
4. Sakarovitch, J.: Rational and recognisable power series. In: Droste, M., Kuich, W., Vogler, H. (eds.) Handbook of Weighted Automata, ch. 4. Springer (2009)

Advances on Random Sequence Generation by Uniform Cellular Automata

Enrico Formenti[1], Katsunobu Imai[2], Bruno Martin[1(✉)],
and Jean-Baptiste Yunès[3]

[1] I3S-CNRS, Univ. Nice Sophia Antipolis, Nice, France
{Enrico.Formenti,Bruno.Martin}@unice.fr
[2] Graduate School of Engineering, Hiroshima University, Hiroshima, Japan
imai@iec.hiroshima-u.ac.jp
[3] LIAFA, Univ. Paris Diderot, Paris, France
Jean-Baptiste.Yunes@univ-paris-diderot.fr

Abstract. The study of cellular automata rules suitable for cryptographic applications is under consideration. On one hand, cellular automata can be used to generate pseudo-random sequences as well as for the design of S-boxes in symmetric cryptography. On the other hand, Boolean functions with good properties like resiliency and non-linearity are usually obtained either by exhaustive search or by the use of genetic algorithms. We propose here to use some recent research in the classification of Boolean functions and to link it with the study of cellular automata rules. As a consequence of our technique, this also provides a mean to get Boolean functions with good cryptographic properties.

Keywords: Cellular automata · Random number generation · Boolean functions

1 Introduction

Cellular automata (CA) are models of finite state machines used in many applications. They form a discrete model of parallelism evolving within discrete time steps according to a local updating rule. CAs are employed for the generation of cryptographic binary pseudo-random sequences [18] and for solving the firing squad problem [10]. Pseudo-random sequences (PRS) have a long history of applications to computational (Monte Carlo sampling, numerical simulation) and communications problems (coding theory, stream ciphers). In the present work, we particularly focus on the search for good local CA rules by using mathematical tools from Boolean functions. For this, we consider a CA rule as a Boolean function in several variables (from three up to five) and we search for Boolean functions that fulfill good cryptographic properties such as non-linearity and resiliency. Next, we use those good Boolean functions as CA rules that can be iterated to provide 'extended' Boolean functions (in nine variables). This work (starting with Boolean functions in four variables) requires an exhaustive search among all possible Boolean functions. The methodology that we use can

© Springer International Publishing Switzerland 2014
C.S. Calude et al. (Eds.): Gruska Festschrift, LNCS 8808, pp. 56–70, 2014.
DOI: 10.1007/978-3-319-13350-8_5

provide Boolean functions satisfying non-linearity and resiliency properties with a large number of variables (up to nine here). Such Boolean functions are (yet) unreachable by a classical brute force search because of the combinatorial explosion.

Such Boolean functions (or CA rules) can be used in many applications. Either directly for pseudo-random sequences generation or as updating functions for providing lightweight random sources of good quality in sensor networks. Other target applications can be joined compression and data encryption (also called co*cryption [15]), or used in hardware devices like FPGA or GPU for quickly providing randomness.

The material is organized as follows. Section 2 introduces the definitions and notations from both cellular automata and Boolean functions theories. Section 3 recalls related results. More precisely, it provides evidence that there is no rule with three variables which provides cryptographic pseudo-random sequences. It also recalls a classification from [11] which lists all equivalence classes containing rules with four variables suitable for generating cryptographic pseudo-random sequences. Section 4 presents the main contribution of the paper and gives some of the five variable rules that can be used for generating cryptographic pseudo-random sequences. In Section 5, we present some statistical testing against the sequences generated by using five variable rules selected from Section 4. Finally, Section 6 concludes the paper and proposes future research directions.

2 Definition and Notation

This section recalls some basic notation and facts on pseudo-randomness, CAs and Boolean functions.

2.1 Pseudo-Randomness

In [20], three mechanisms responsible for random behavior in systems are described: (1) *Randomness from physics* like brownian motion; (2) *Randomness from the initial conditions* which is studied by chaos theory; and (3) *Randomness by design*, also called pseudo-randomness. Many algorithms generate PRS. The behavior of the system is fully determined by knowing the seed and the algorithm used. They are quicker methods than extracting "true" randomness from the environment, inaccessible to computers.

The applications of randomness have led to many different methods for generating random data. These methods may vary as to how unpredictable or statistically random they are, and how quickly they can generate random sequences. Before the age of computational PRS, generating large amount of random numbers required a lot of work and were distributed as random number tables.

In the sequel, we will consider *pseudo-random generators* (PRG). This corresponds to a deterministic algorithm which "stretches" a short truly random sequence (the *seed*) into a polynomially longer sequence that appears to be "random" (although it isn't). In other words, although the output of a PRG is not really random, it is (polynomially for probabilistic distinguishers) unfeasible to tell the difference. It turns out that pseudorandomness and computational complexity are linked in a fundamental way (see [8] for further details). More practically, this corresponds to the behavior of random number generators implemented in operating systems. In this case, the short truly random sequence corresponds to the pseudo-device `/dev/random` and the output of the PRG to the pseudo-device `/dev/urandom` for producing more random bits of weaker quality.

2.2 Cellular Automata

One-dimensional binary CAs consist of a line of cells taking their states among binary values. For practical implementations, the number of cells is finite. There are two cases: a CA has *periodic boundary conditions* if the cells are arranged in a ring and it has *null boundary conditions* when both extreme cells are continuously fixed to zero. All the cells are finite state machines with an updating function which gives the new state of the cell according to its current state and the current state of its nearest neighbors. For a presentation of CAs, see [9].

In [18], it was proposed to use CAs to produce PRS. Binary CAs with l cells ($l = 2N + 1$ for $N \in \mathbb{N}$) were considered. For a CA, the values of the cells at time $t \geq 0$ are updated synchronously by a Boolean function f with $n = r_1 + r_2 + 1$ variables by the rule $x_i(t + 1) = f(x_{i-r_1}(t), \dots, x_i(t), \dots, x_{i+r_2}(t))$. Elementary CAs are such that $r_1 = r_2 = 1$. For a fixed t, the sequence of the values $x_i(t)$ for $1 \leq i \leq 2N + 1$, is the *configuration* at time t. It is a mapping $c : [\![1, l]\!] \to \mathbb{F}_2$ which assigns a Boolean state to each cell. The initial configuration ($t = 0$) $x_1(0), \dots, x_l(0)$ is the *seed*, the sequence $(x_N(t))_t$ is the *output sequence* and, when $r_1 = r_2 = r$, the number r is the *radius* of the rule. The *Wolfram numbering* associates a rule number to any one of the 256 elementary CA; it takes the binary expansion of a rule number as the truth table of a 3-variable Boolean function.

2.3 Boolean Functions

A Boolean function is a mapping from $\mathbb{F}_2^n$ into $\mathbb{F}_2$. In the sequel, additions in $\mathbb{Z}$ (resp. $\mathbb{F}_2$) will be denoted by $+$ and Σ (resp. $\oplus$ and $\bigoplus$), products by $\times$ and $\prod$ (resp. $\cdot$ and $\prod$). When there is no ambiguity, $+$ will denote the addition of binary vectors. If x and y are binary vectors, their inner product is $x \cdot y = \sum_{i=1}^n x_i y_i$. A very handy representation of Boolean function is the *algebraic normal form*:

Definition 1 (ANF). *A Boolean function f with n variables is represented by a unique binary polynomial in n variables, called* algebraic normal form*: $f(x) = \bigoplus_{u \in \mathbb{F}_2^n} a_u (\prod_{i=1}^n x_i^{u_i})$ $a_u \in \mathbb{F}_2$, u_i is the i-th projection of u.*

Example 1. The ANF of rule (30) is $x_1 \oplus x_2 \oplus x_3 \oplus x_2 x_3$ or 1+2+3+23.

The *degree of the ANF* or *algebraic degree* of f corresponds to the number of variables in the longest term $x_1^{u_1} \dots x_n^{u_n}$ in the ANF of f. The *Hamming weight*

$w_H(f)$ of f is the number of $x \in \mathbb{F}_2^n$ such that $f(x)=1$. The *Hamming weight* $w_H(x)$ of $x \in \mathbb{F}_2^n$ counts the number of 1-valued coordinates in x. f is *balanced* if $w_H(f) = w_H(1 \oplus f) = 2^{n-1}$.

Definition 2. *f and g Boolean functions in n variables are* equivalent *iff*

$$f(x) = g\left((x \cdot A) \oplus a\right) \oplus \left(x \cdot B^T\right) \oplus b, \quad \forall x \in \mathbb{F}_2^n \tag{1}$$

where A is a non-singular binary $n \times n$ matrix, b a binary constant, a and $B \in \mathbb{F}_2^n$.

An important tool in the study of Boolean functions is the *Fourier-Hadamard transform*, a linear mapping which maps a Boolean function f to the real-valued function $\widehat{f}(u) = \sum_{x \in \mathbb{F}_2^n} f(x)(-1)^{u \cdot x}$, which describes the *spectrum* of the latter. When applied to the *sign function* $f_\chi(x) = (-1)^{f(x)}$, the Fourier-Hadamard transform is the *Walsh transform*: $\widehat{f_\chi}(u) = \sum_{x \in \mathbb{F}_2^n} (-1)^{f(x) \oplus u \cdot x}$. Since $f_\chi(u) = 1 - 2f(u)$, the Fourier-Hadamard transform is:

$$\widehat{f}(u) = \frac{1}{2} \sum_{x \in \mathbb{F}_2^n} (-1)^{u \cdot x} - \frac{1}{2}\widehat{f_\chi}(u) \quad , \tag{2}$$

Using Eq. (2), we obtain that $\widehat{f_\chi}(u) = 2^n \delta_0 - 2\widehat{f}(u)$, where δ_0 denotes the *Dirac symbol* defined by $\delta_0(u) = 1$ if u is the null vector and $\delta_0(u) = 0$ otherwise [4].

If f and g are two equivalent Boolean functions in n variables, it holds that:

$$\widehat{f_\chi}(u) = (-1)^{a \cdot A^{-1}(u^t + B^T) + b} \widehat{g_\chi}((u \oplus B)(A^{-1})^T) \quad . \tag{3}$$

This property is used by [3] for counting the number of functions satisfying some cryptographic properties.

The Walsh transform allows to study the *correlation-immunity* of a function.

Definition 3. *A Boolean function f in n variables is k-correlation-immune $(0 < k < n)$ if, given any n independent and identically distributed binary random variables $x_1, \cdots, x_n$ according to a uniform Bernoulli distribution, then the random variable $Z = f(x_1, \ldots, x_n)$ is independent from any random vector $(x_{i_1}, x_{i_2}, \ldots, x_{i_k})$, $1 \leq i_1 < \cdots < i_k < n$. When f is k-correlation immune and balanced, it is k-resilient.*

In [21], a spectral characterization of resilient functions was given:

Theorem 1. *A Boolean function f in n variables is k-resilient iff it is balanced and $\widehat{f}(u)=0$ for all $u \in \mathbb{F}_2^n$ s.t. $0 < w_H(u) \leq k$. Equivalently, f is k-resilient iff $\widehat{f_\chi}(u)=0$ for all $u \in \mathbb{F}_2^n$ s.t. $w_H(u) \leq k$.*

Theorem 1 concerns both transforms (refer to [4] for further details).

Theorem 2 (Siegenthaler Bound). *For a k-resilient $(0 \leq k < n-1)$ Boolean function in n variables, there is an upper bound for its algebraic degree d: $d \leq n - k - 1$ if $k < n - 1$ and $d = 1$ if $k = n - 1$.*

2.4   Some Properties of the Fourier-Hadamard Transform

Computing the Fourier-Hadamard transform We use the Fourier-Hadamard transform from [6] called the *Walsh or Sequency Ordered Transform* (WHT)$_w$. This transform is used to study the CA rules in order to find the best rules for generating PR sequences, like in [7,14]. To check the rules, we use the fast transform algorithm whose time complexity is $O(n \log n)$. The algorithm receives as an input an array $\mathbf{F}$ of size 2^n which contains the images by the t iterates of the local rule f of all the configurations of n cells naturally ordered: $f^t(0), \ldots, f^t(2^n - 1)$ and outputs the transform $\widehat{\mathbf{F}}$ in the reverse order: $\widehat{f^t}(2^n - 1), \ldots, \widehat{f^t}(0)$.

Application to CA rules We proceed step by step with increasing values of t, which counts the number of times the local rule in 5 variables, supposed to be 1-resilient, is iterated on an initial configuration. In this way, we consider the natural extension of $f : \mathbb{F}_2^5 \to \mathbb{F}_2$ to $f : \mathbb{F}_2^{n+4} \to \mathbb{F}_2^n$ where:

$$f(x_0, \ldots, x_{n+4}) = (y_1, \ldots, y_n) \text{ s.t. } y_j = f(x_{j-2}, x_{j-1}, x_j, x_{j+1}, x_{j+2}), j \in [\![1, n]\!]$$

Using the extended f, one can define the t-th iterate of f which is a function $f^t : \mathbb{F}_2^{4t+1} \to \mathbb{F}_2$. We compute next the maximum absolute value of the Fourier-Hadamard transform of the tth-iterate of f at all the points u of Hamming weight 1 and we select the rules with a minimum spectral value.

The computation is repeated with increasing values of t until we identify rules with flat spectral or relatively small values which are slowly growing.

Some properties on the iterates In order to find other CA rules which preserve resiliency upon iterates, one can remark that the Fourier-Hadamard transform is preserved under some transformations like the *reflection* (which just takes the mirror-image of the initial configuration). Unfortunately, the other classical transformations on CAs (conjugation and conjugation-reflection) do not preserve the resiliency upon iterates in general.

Let Φ denote the *reverse operator* $\Phi : \mathbb{F}_2^m \to \mathbb{F}_2^m$, $\Phi((v_1, \ldots, v_m)) = (v_m, \ldots, v_1)$.

Definition 4. *Let* $f : \mathbb{F}_2^{2m+1} \to \mathbb{F}_2$ *be the local function of a CA. Then,* $f_R(x_{-m}, \ldots, x_0, \ldots, x_m) = \Phi \circ f(x_m, \ldots, x_0, \ldots, x_{-m})$ *is the* reflection *of* f.

Another basic transformation is given by $\Psi(x) = 1 \oplus x$ for $x \in \mathbb{F}_2$. It corresponds to the negation of the variable and is used for designing the conjugation and the conjugation-reflection introduced in [19, p. 492]. With some abuse of notation, Ψ is extended to sequences of Boolean variables: for $u = (u_1, u_2, \ldots, u_n)$ with $u_i \in \mathbb{F}_2$, $\Psi(u) = (\Psi(u_1), \Psi(u_2), \ldots, \Psi(u_n))$. Moreover, $\Psi^{-1} = \Psi$.

Definition 5. *Let* $f : \mathbb{F}_2^{2m+1} \to \mathbb{F}_2$ *be the local function of a CA. Then* $f_N(x_{-m}, \ldots, x_0, \ldots, x_m) = \Psi \circ f(\Psi(x_m, \ldots, x_0, x_{-m}))$ *is the* negation *of* f.

One can see that for any $t \in \mathbb{N}$, $f^t \circ H = H \circ f_R^t$ for $H = \Psi$ or $H = \Phi$.

Lemma 1. *Let* $\Xi : \mathbb{F}_2^{2m+1} \to \mathbb{F}_2^{2m+1}$ *be 1:1 and* $f : \mathbb{F}_2^{2m+1} \to \mathbb{F}_2$ *a CA. Then,* $w_H(f) = w_H(f \circ \Xi)$.

Proposition 1 shows that resiliency is preserved by the reflection when the local rule is iterated.

Proposition 1. *Let* $f : \mathbb{F}_2^{2m+1} \to \mathbb{F}_2$ *be the local function of a CA. For any* $t \in \mathbb{N}$, *let* $0 < k \le 2mt + 1$. *Then,* f_R^t *is k-resilient iff* f^t *is k-resilient.*

Proof. The transformation Φ is bijective. Hence, by Lemma 1, we have $w_H(f_R) = w_H(f \circ \Phi) = w_H(f)$. Since f is balanced, $w_H(f_R) = w_H(\Psi \circ f)$. Now, applying Lemma 1 to $\Psi \circ f$ and using last equation, it holds $w_H(\Psi \circ f) = w_H(\Psi \circ f \circ \Phi) = w_H(\Psi \circ f_R)$. Let $a = B = (0, 0, \ldots, 0)$, $b = 0$ and A the reverse identity matrix. Remark that A is non-singular, then, by using Eq. 3, one obtains $\widehat{(f_R^t)}_\chi(u) = \widehat{f_\chi^t}(u \cdot (A^{-1})^T) = \widehat{f_\chi^t}(u \cdot A) = \widehat{f_\chi^t}(A \cdot u)$ which entails

$$\widehat{f_R^t}(u) = \widehat{f^t}(A \cdot u) \ . \tag{4}$$

Now, assume that f^t is k-resilient. Remark that $w_H(A \cdot u) = w_H(u)$ for any u, therefore, by Theorem 1, if $\widehat{f^t}(u) = 0$ for $0 < w_H(u) \le k$, then, by Eq. 4, $\widehat{f_R^t}(u) = 0$ too. For the converse, just remark that A^2 is the identity transformation and then, by Eq. 4, one finds $\widehat{f_R^t}(\Phi(u)) = \widehat{f^t}(u)$. Therefore if $\widehat{f_R^t}(\Phi(u)) = 0$, we have $\widehat{f^t}(u) = 0$. Since Φ is a bijection we have the thesis.

Lemma 2. *Let* $f : \mathbb{F}_2^{2m+1} \to \mathbb{F}_2$ *be the local function of a CA. For any* $t \in \mathbb{N}$, f_N^t *is balanced iff* f^t *is balanced.*

Proof. Assume f^t balanced for some $t \in \mathbb{N}$. By definition of f_N^t, $w_H(f_N^t) = w_H(\Psi \circ f^t \circ \Psi)$. Remark that $\Psi \circ f^t$ is a CA; then by Lemma 1, $w_H(\Psi \circ f^t \circ \Psi) = w_H(\Psi \circ f^t)$. Since f^t is balanced, $w_H(\Psi \circ f^t) = w_H(f^t)$. Finally, observing that Ψ^2 is the identity and by Lemma 1 again, it holds $w_H(f^t) = w_H(\Psi^2 \circ f^t) = w_H(\Psi^2 \circ f^t \circ \Psi) = w_H(\Psi \circ f_N^t)$. For the converse, assume that f_N^t is balanced for some $t \in \mathbb{N}$. Then, $w_H(f_N^t) = w_H(\Psi \circ f_N^t) = w_H(\Psi^2 \circ f^t \circ \Psi) = w_H(f^t \circ \Psi)$. By Lemma 1, $w_H(f^t \circ \Psi) = w_H(f^t)$ and therefore $w_H(f^t) = w_H(f_N^t)$. Again, by Lemma 1, $w_H(\Psi \circ f^t) = w_H(\Psi \circ f^t \circ \Psi) = w_H(f_N^t)$. Hence $w_H(f^t) = w_H(\Psi \circ f^t)$.

Proposition 2. *Let* $f : \mathbb{F}_2^{2m+1} \to \mathbb{F}_2$ *be the local function of a CA. For any* $t \in \mathbb{N}$, *let* $0 < k \le 2mt + 1$. *Then,* f^t *is k-resilient iff* f_N^t *is k-resilient.*

Proof. Fix $k \in \mathbb{N}$ as in the hypothesis. By Lemma 2, it suffices to prove that $\widehat{f_N}(u) = h(u) \cdot \widehat{f}(u)$ for any $u \in \mathbb{F}_2^{2m+1}$ such that $0 < w_H(u) \le k$ and $h : \mathbb{F}_2^{2m+1} \to \mathbb{R}^+$. Let $A = \text{Id}$, $a = (1, 1, \ldots, 1)$, $b = 1$ and $B = (0, 0, \ldots, 0)$. Then, by using Eq. 3, one obtains $\widehat{(f_N^t)}_\chi(u) = (-1)^{1+a \cdot u} \widehat{f_\chi^t}(u)$ for any $u \in \mathbb{F}_2^{2mt+1}$ with $0 < w_H(u) \le 2mt + 1$. This entails $\widehat{f_N^t}(u) = (-1)^{1+a \cdot u} \widehat{f^t}(u)$.

Consider the equivalence relation $\mathcal{R}$ on CA rules such that $f\mathcal{R}g$ iff $g = f_R$ or $g = f_N$ or $g = f_{RN}$. According to [5], there are $2^{2^m}(6 + 2^{2^m})$ distinct $\mathcal{R}$-classes. Propositions 1 and 2 say that all elements in a class have the same resiliency and hence only one element per class should be tested for studying this property. However the gain obtained by this quotient of the set of local rules is minor. Section 5 proposes (among other things) to consider affine transformations instead. Indeed, even if f and its Boolean equivalent, say f_A have the same resiliency, this does not hold, in general, for their iterates. This is essentially due to the fact that the above proofs are based on the existence of a bijection ϕ and a transformation τ on the local rules such that for any local rule f, it holds that $\forall t \in \mathbb{N}$, $[\tau(f)]^t \circ \phi = \phi \circ f^t$. This property is not true, in general for transformations different from negation or reflection.

3   Related Results

3.1   3-variable Boolean Update Function

An exhaustive search of 3-variable Boolean update function was done in [16]:

Theorem 3. *There is no non-linear correlation-immune elementary CA.*

The same result can be obtained by applying the Siegenthaler bound with $n = 3$ variables and testing for $k = 1$-resiliency. It tells that the algebraic degree is $d \leq n - k - 1 = 1$. Thus, only linear functions can be resilient.

Despite this, CA may be used for generating PRS by increasing the number of variables in the Boolean function which is used as a local CA rule. In the sequel, we recall which functions in four variables are suitable and we present a way to gather five variable functions for cryptographic purposes.

3.2   4-variable Boolean Update Function

In [11] the $2^{16} = 65536$ elementary CA rules with 4 variables were classified according to their resiliency and non-linearity. An exhaustive search by the Walsh transform of all Boolean functions with 4 variables was realized, to find a list of 1-resilient functions, with high non-linearity. There are exactly 200 non linear balanced functions which are 1-resilient.

A Boolean function in 4 variables is defined by an integer between 0 and 65536, extending Wolfram's notation for CA rules with 3 variables. For classifying the functions, we use their ANF. For instance the ANF of rule (280) ($=100011000$ in binary) corresponds to the polynomial $f(x_1, x_2, x_3, x_4) = x_1 x_2 \oplus x_3 \oplus x_4 = 12 + 3 + 4$.

For the classification of these functions, let σ denote a 4×4 permutation matrix. Recall that two Boolean functions f and g are affine equivalent if there exists a permutation σ such that $f(x) = g(\sigma(x))$ or $g(\sigma(x)) + 1$.

The following table gives the set of all 1-resilient function, with a representative of each class f, its corresponding ANF and the cardinal of each class:

f	|ANF|	ANF	card.
34680	280	12+3+4	12
6120	360	4+12+13+23	8
7140	300	2+4+12+13	48
11730	282	1+3+4+12	24
34740	1308	2+3+4+12+24	48
39318	4374	1+2+3+4+34	12
7128	5432	3+4+12+13+24+34	24
11220	380	2+3+12+13+24	24

The non-linearity of these functions is computed for an evaluation of the resistance against the attack of [1]. The 200 1-resilient Boolean functions with 4 variables have a non-linearity equal to 4.

4 Exploring Radius 2, 1-Resilient Elementary CA Rules

Unlike 3 and 4 variable Boolean update function, we will not explore the whole class of radius 2 elementary uniform CA rules. Instead, we use the classification of Boolean functions in 6 variables or less with respect to some cryptographic properties from [3] where an efficient algebraic approach to the classification of the affine equivalence classes of the cosets of the first order Reed-Muller error correcting code is proposed. Indeed, the study of the properties of Boolean functions is related to the study of Reed-Muller codes. The code-words of the r-th order Reed-Muller code of length 2^n, denoted by $RM(r,n)$ correspond to the truth tables of Boolean functions with degree less or equal to r. [2] classified all the 2^{26} cosets of $RM(1,5)$ into 48 equivalence classes under the action of the group $AGL(2,5)$. The method is used to classify with respect to the 48 classes into which the general affine group $AGL(2,5)$ partitions the cosets of $RM(1,5)$. The cryptographic properties considered by [3] are correlation immunity (CI), resiliency (R) and propagation characteristics as well as their combination.

Table 1. Number of functions satisfying $CI(1)$ and $R(1)$

Representative	$\mathcal{N}_{CI(1)}$	$\mathcal{N}_{R(1)}$
12	4840	4120
123	16640	11520
123+14	216 000	133 984
123+14+25	69120	24960
123+145+23	1 029 120	537600
123+145+23+24+35	233 472	96 960

Table 1 is a selection of the representatives of Boolean functions taken out from [3] which lists the representative and counts the number of equivalent Boolean functions in the equivalence class which satisfy 1-resiliency (denoted by $R(1)$ in the table) and correlation immunity of first order (denoted by $CI(1)$

in the table). In Table 1, for a property P, $\mathcal{N}_P$ counts the number of Boolean functions which fulfills P.

From the original table, we only select representatives of Boolean functions of algebraic degrees 2 and 3 since, because of the Siegenthaler bound, there cannot be 1-resilient Boolean function of degree one. The classification done by [3] also removes Boolean functions of degree 4 if 1-resiliency is considered. Thus, there are only 6 equivalence classes containing 1-resilient Boolean functions which are listed in Table 1; 12 is the single equivalence class of degree two Boolean functions and the remaining 5 are all of degree three.

4.1   Finding the Rules

From the classification by [3], representatives of Boolean functions fulfilling the property of 1-resiliency were found. We restricted the search of Boolean functions in the same algebraic coset instead of the equivalence class in order to limit the combinatorial explosion. Our goal was to find 1-resilient elements in the cosets. For this, we first explored the elements of the cosets listed in Table 1 by considering all the linear combinations of all possible linear/affine functions and by computing the Fourier-Hadamard transform on all those elements in the coset. More precisely, the first step is to generate all coset elements. If we denote by $R(x_1, x_2, x_3, x_4, x_5)$ the coset leader (which is the representative), we consider all elements of the form:

$$R(x_1, x_2, x_3, x_4, x_5) \oplus (ax_1) \oplus (bx_2) \oplus (cx_3) \oplus (dx_4) \oplus (ex_5) \oplus h$$

for a, b, c, d, e, h Boolean, spanning all the 2^6 elements of the coset. Then, for each element, we compute the Fourier-Hadamard transform, we next only select the balanced Boolean functions and finally the Boolean functions which are 1-correlation immune among the balanced Boolean functions. That is, among the balanced Boolean functions, all functions with zero spectral values at points whose binary decomposition has a Hamming weight of 1. This first step was done with Mathematica 9.0 and gave us Table 2.

Reading Table 2, we notice that two cosets seem not to contain 1-resilient functions, although listed in the table by [3]. The reason for this is that we did not make the complete exploration of the equivalence class. Recall that the table by [3] classifies the 48 equivalence classes of $RM(1,5)$ under the action of the general affine group $AGL(2,5)$. At first, to check if our approach is valid, we only generated the coset elements and not the Boolean functions which could be obtained by the action of $AGL(2,5)$ and which can be generated using Eq. (1). The size of the set of functions to explore is thus smaller. We run the fast transform algorithm on a set containing 6.2^6 elements which has to be compared with the whole set with 2^{32} elements. If we had taken into account the action of $AGL(2,5)$, we should have explored 6 classes among the 48 equivalence classes (a ratio of $1/8$) on the whole set.

Table 2. 1-resilient Boolean functions in the cosets. Hexadecimal numbers refer to the truth table.

Representative	1-resilient functions
12	3c3c3cc3 3c3cc33c 3cc33c3c 3cc3c3c3 5a5a5aa5 5a5aa55a 5aa55a5a 5aa5a5a5 66666699 66669966 66996666 66999999 69696996 69699669 69966969 69969696 96696969 96699696 96966996 96969669 99666666 99669999 99996699 99999966 a55a5a5a a55aa5a5 a5a55aa5 a5a5a55a c33c3c3c c33cc3c3 c3c33cc3 c3c3c33c
123	66696996 66699669 66966969 66969696 66996699 69666699 69696966 69996666 69999999 96666666 96669999 96996699 96999966 99696969 99699696 99966996 99969669
123+14	66695aa5 6669a55a 66965a5a 6696a5a5 696655aa 6966aa55 969955aa 9699aa55 99695a5a 9969a5a5 99965aa5 9996a55a
123+14+25	∅
123+145+23	1eb4663c 1eb499c3 e14b663c e14b99c3
123+145+23+24+35	∅

4.2 Testing the Iterates

We use the results from section 4.1 to select rules susceptible of preserving 1-resiliency, with the same procedure we used in section 2.4. More precisely, from the set of elementary, radius 2 rules (with a generic element denoted by f), we consider the natural extension of $f : \mathbb{F}_2^5 \rightarrow \mathbb{F}_2$ to $f : \mathbb{F}_2^{n+4} \rightarrow \mathbb{F}_2^n$ (with $n > 0$) where: $f(x_1, \ldots, x_{n+4}) = (y_1, \ldots, y_n)$ such that $y_j = f(x_j, x_{j+1}, x_{j+2}, x_{j+3}, x_{j+4}), j \in [\![1, n]\!]$. Using the extended f, one can define the t-th iterate of f which is a function $f^t : \mathbb{F}_2^{4t+1} \rightarrow \mathbb{F}_2$. We next test the second iterate for selecting rules preserving the 1-resiliency. In other words, we compute the maximum absolute value of the Fourier-Hadamard transform of the tth-iterate of f at all the points u of Hamming weight 1 and we select the balanced rules with a flat spectral value at those points (by Theorem 1).

For every f of Tab. 2, we built f^2 and tested its 1-resiliency property. This property is easily observable on the Fourier-Hadamard spectrum $\widehat{f^2}$: f^2 is m-resilient if $\forall u \in \mathbb{F}_2^9 / w_H(u) \leq m$, then $\widehat{f^2}(u) = 0$. The spectrum has been computed by the algorithm defined in subsection 2.4 and implemented in C. The results are in Tab. 3 and shows that few functions (exactly 4 of them) of coset 12 are not 1-resilient, that every function of coset 123 and coset 123+14 preserves 1-resiliency, and no function of coset 123+145+23 are 1-resilient after 2 iterations.

5   PRNG Testing

The quality of pseudo-randomness generated by the above mentioned Boolean functions has been evaluated by using the Diehard test suite, a widely used tool. It has been developed by Marsaglia from the Florida State University and consists of 17 different tests which have become something which could be considered as a "benchmarking tool" for PR number generators (see [12]). It is meant to evaluate if a stream of numbers is a good PRS. We will not explain how Diehard really works and we refer the reader to [13] for further details. Basically, Diehard uses Kolmogorov-Smirnov normality test to quantify the distance between the distribution of a given data set and the uniform distribution; and as the documentation says:

Table 3. 1-resilient Boolean functions after 2 iterations

	0x3C3C3CC3	yes	0x3C3CC33C	no	0x3CC33C3C	no
	0x3CC3C3C3	yes	0x5A5A5AA5	yes	0x5A5AA55A	yes
	0x5AA55A5A	yes	0x5AA5A5A5	yes	0x66666699	yes
	0x66669966	yes	0x66996666	yes	0x66999999	yes
	0x69696996	yes	0x69699669	yes	0x69966969	yes
Coset 12	0x69969696	yes	0x96696969	yes	0x96699696	yes
	0x96966996	yes	0x96969669	yes	0x99666666	yes
	0x99669999	yes	0x99996699	yes	0x99999966	yes
	0xA55A5A5A	yes	0xA55AA5A5	yes	0xA5A55AA5	yes
	0xA5A5A55A	yes	0xC33C3C3C	yes	0xC33CC3C3	no
	0xC3C33CC3	no	0xC3C3C33C	yes		
	0x66696996	yes	0x66699669	yes	0x66966969	yes
	0x66969696	yes	0x69666699	yes	0x69669966	yes
Coset 123	0x69996666	yes	0x69999999	yes	0x96666666	yes
	0x96669999	yes	0x96996699	yes	0x96999966	yes
	0x99696969	yes	0x99699696	yes	0x99966996	yes
	0x99969669	yes				
	0x66695AA5	yes	0x6669A55A	yes	0x66965A5A	yes
Coset 123+14	0x6696A5A5	yes	0x696655AA	yes	0x6966AA55	yes
	0x969955AA	yes	0x9699AA55	yes	0x99695A5A	yes
	0x9969A5A5	yes	0x99965AA5	yes	0x9996A55A	yes
	0x1EB4663C	no	0x1EB499C3	no	0x2D7855F0	no
	0x2D78AA0F	no	0x44EE3C66	no	0x44EEC399	no
Coset 123+145+23	0x4B1ECC69	no	0x77220FAA	no	0x7722F055	no
	0x88DD0FAA	no	0x88DDF055	no	0xB4E13396	no
	0xBB113C66	no	0xBB11C399	no	0xD28755F0	no
	0xD287AA0F	no	0xE14B663C	no	0xE14B99C3	no

Each Diehard test is able to provide probability values (p-value) which should be uniformly distributed on $[0, 1)$ if the sequence is made of truly independent bits. Those p-values are obtained by $p = F(X)$ where F is the assumed distribution of the sample random variable X–often normal. But that assumed F is just an asymptotic approximation, for which the fit will be worse in the tail of the distribution. Thus, we should not be surprised with occasional p-values close to 0 or 1. When a stream really fails, one gets p-values of 0 or 1 to six or more places. Otherwise, for each test, its p-value should lie in the interval $(0.025, 0.975)$.

So in order to test our data, we designed a C program in which we included the Diehard functions that were slightly modified to fit well with our needs. That is to directly use the results of the CA as a PRG. The 17 different and independent statistical tests require about 16 Mbyte of PR values in binary format.

Our goal was to generate different number sequences from the CA and test them against Diehard. Two different tests were made.

5.1   Randomness Preservation

In this section we describe the experimentation we made to test if a CA "preserves" the randomness through its dynamics. For this experiment, we consider a CA, whose transition function is $f : \mathbb{F}_2^5 \to \mathbb{F}_2$. Given such a CA, we set up an initial sequence of bits $(b_i)_{i \geq 0}$ that we extract from the /dev/random pseudo-device of a MacOSX system[1]. Then we compute the sequence of bits $(b'_i)_{i \geq 0}$ such that $\forall i \leq 0$, $b'_i = f(b_{5i}, b_{5i+1}, b_{5i+2}, b_{5i+3}, b_{5i+4})$. To ensure some statistical soundness, for a single CA we build 30^2 of such sequences from the same entropic source (each sequence being 16 Mbyte long as required by Diehard).

The measure, illustrated in Fig. 1, shows all the distributions of the indicators produced by each single sequence passing all the Diehard tests. And it can be observed that the p-values are well distributed for every data pack. Indeed, there are no accumulation points near zero or one.

This means that the input to the tests is made of independent bits. Thus, we can deduce that these functions are good at preserving the randomness. Or, in other terms, if we feed a CA with a truly random sequence (obtained by the entropy collector of the BSD kernel) as an input configuration and let the CA run, the output configuration is still PR, according to the Diehard test suite.

5.2   Random Number Generation

Much more classically, these tests were built to evaluate the possible generation of a good PR sequence by CAs. While it is well known that radius 1 elementary CAs are not suitable for generating PR sequences, it is not impossible to build good PR sequence from simple CAs. As we already tested if the radius-2 functions are good to preserve the randomness, it would be interesting to consider them as PRNG. So, we tried something very similar to [17].

We set up two rings of cells. Although Wolfram used a ring of 127 cells and Preneel (1993) suggested a ring of 1024 cells to ensure a better quality (both used a slightly different mechanisms for random bit extraction), we use perimeters 64 and 65 as done in [17]. The initial configuration of these rings is of Hamming weight 1. We let the CA iterate about 2 million times. Then, from each configuration obtained, we extract two 32-bits words: the "even" (resp. "odd"), word is built with the state of the first 32 "even" (resp. "odd") cells. The sequences of these "even" (resp. "odd") words constitute two different sequences of 16 Mbyte.

Then, we use Diehard to produce p-values for each test. We were able to find some CAs (like the one with rule 0x69999999 given as an example in Fig. 2). This suggests that it may be possible to obtain a good PRNG from such a CA.

---

[1] The entropy collector of the BSD kernel family is considered as a pretty good source of random numbers and MacOSX is built on top of a BSD kernel.

[2] The repetition of 30 independent experiments comes from statistics. Indeed sample sizes of at least 30 are for many tests considered as "large" and allows a better statistical treatment.

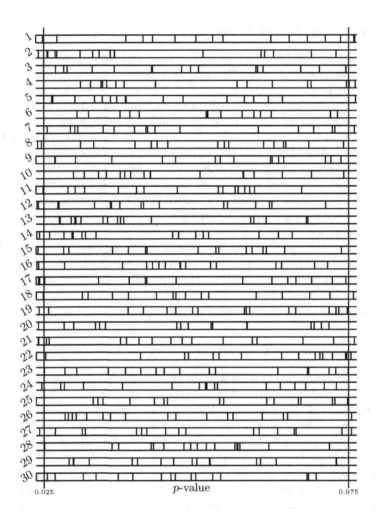

Fig. 1. 0x3C3C3CC3: distribution of the p-values for each data pack. p-values between the two lines (at 0.025 and 0.975) mean that the corresponding statistical test was successful.

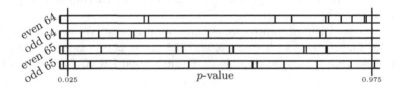

Fig. 2. Distribution of the p-values for the ring CA with rule 0x69999999. p-values between the two lines (at 0.025 and 0.975) mean that the corresponding statistical test was successful.

6 Conclusion

The main interest of this work concerns the hardware implementation. The target hardware model of CAs is the Field Programmable Gate Arrays (known as FPGAs). FPGAs are now a popular implementation style for digital logic systems and subsystems. These devices consist of an array of uncommitted logic gates whose function and interconnection is determined by downloading information to the device. When the programming configuration is held in static RAM, the logic function implemented by those FPGAs can be dynamically reconfigured in fractions of a second by rewriting the configuration memory contents. Thus, the use of FPGAs can speed up the computation done by the cellular automata. Putting all together allows high-rate pseudo-random generation of good quality that can be used as a basic component for lightweight cryptography requiring pseudo-random sources.

These results can be extended in many directions. If the number of variables of a Boolean function must be increased, our approach for extending good updating rules can be helpful. Increasing the number of variables in a Boolean function is a classical problem in symmetric cryptography.

Acknowledgments. The authors are grateful to C. Carlet who pointed out Reference [4] for explaining the difference between Fourier-Hadamard and Walsh transforms and to J. Mairesse for its help with statistical testing.

References

1. Apohan, A.M., Koc, C.K.: Inversion of cellular automata iterations. Computer and Digital Techniques **144**, 279–284 (1997)
2. Berlekamp, E., Welch, L.: Weight distribution of the cosets of the $(32, 6)$ Reed-Muller code. IEEE Trans. Inf. Theory **18**, 203–207 (1972)
3. Braeken, A., Borissov, Y., Nikova, S., Preneel, B.: Classification of Boolean functions of 6 variables or less with respect to some cryptographic properties. In: Caires, L., Italiano, G.F., Monteiro, L., Palamidessi, C., Yung, M. (eds.) ICALP 2005. LNCS, vol. 3580, pp. 324–334. Springer, Heidelberg (2005)
4. Carlet, C.: Boolean functions for cryptography and error-correcting codes. Technical report, University of Paris 8 (2011)
5. Cattaneo, G., Formenti, E., Margara, L., Mauri, G.: Transformations of the one-dimensional cellular automata rule space. Parallel Computing **23**(11), 1593–1611 (1997)
6. Elliott, D.E., Rao, K.R.: Fast transforms, algorithms, analysis, applications. Academic press (1982)
7. Formenti, E., Imai, K., Martin, B., Yunès, J.-B.: On 1-resilient, radius 2 elementary CA rules. In: Fatès, N., Goles, E., Maass, A., Rapaport, I. (eds.) Automata 2011, pp. 41–54 (2011)
8. Goldreich, O.: Pseudorandomness. Notices of the AMS **46**(10), 1209–1216 (1999)
9. Gruska. J.: Foundations of Computing. International Thomson Publishing (1997)
10. Gruska, J., La Torre, S., Parente, M.: The firing squad synchronization problem on squares, toruses and rings. Int. J. Found. Comput. Sci. **18**(3), 637–654 (2007)

11. Lacharme, P., Martin, B., Solé, P.: Pseudo-random sequences, boolean functions and cellular automata. In: Proceedings of Boolean Functions and Cryptographic Applications (2008)
12. Marsaglia, G.: A current view of random number generators. In: Computer Sciences and Statistics, pp. 3–10 (1985)
13. Marsaglia, G.: Diehard (1995). http://www.stat.fsu.edu/pub/diehard/
14. Martin, B.: A Walsh exploration of Wolfram CA rules. In: International Workshop on Cellular Automata, pp. 25–30. Hiroshima University, Japan (2006)
15. Martin, B.: Mixing compression and CA encryption. In: Bonnecaze, A., Leneutre, J., State, R. (eds.) SAR-SSI 2007, pp. 255–266. Université Jean Moulin, Lyon (2007)
16. Martin, B.: A Walsh exploration of elementary CA rules. Journal of Cellular Automata 3(2), 145–156 (2008)
17. Shackleford, B., Tanaka, M., Carter, R.J., Snider, G.: FPGA implementation of neighborhood-of-four cellular automata random number generators. In: Proceedings of the 2002 ACM/SIGDA Tenth International Symposium on Field-Programmable Gate Arrays, FPGA 2002, pp. 106–112. ACM (2002)
18. Wolfram, S.: Cryptography with cellular automata. In: Williams, H.C. (ed.) CRYPTO 1985. LNCS, vol. 218, pp. 429–432. Springer, Heidelberg (1986)
19. Wolfram, S.: Theory and applications of cellular automata. World Scientific, Singapore (1986)
20. Wolfram, S.: A new kind of science. Wolfram Media Inc., Champaign (2002)
21. Xiao, G.-Z., Massey, J.L.: A spectral characterization of correlation-immune combining functions. IEEE Trans. on Information Theory 34(3), 569 (1988)

On the Determinization Blowup for Finite Automata Recognizing Equal-Length Languages

Juhani Karhumäki and Alexander Okhotin[(✉)]

Department of Mathematics and Statistics,
University of Turku, FI-20014 Turku, Finland
{karhumak,alexander.okhotin}@utu.fi

Abstract. Motivated by the application to image compression (K. Čulík II, J. Kari, "Image compression using weighted finite automata", *Computers & Graphics*, 1993), the paper considers finite automata representing formal languages with all strings of the same length, and investigates relative succinctness of representation by deterministic and nondeterministic finite automata (DFA, NFA). It is shown that an n-state NFA recognizing a language of strings of length ℓ over a k-symbol alphabet can be transformed to a DFA with at most $\ell \cdot k^{\sqrt{\frac{2}{\log_2 k} n + 3\ell + 3}} = 2^{O(\sqrt{n})}$ states. At the same time, for every k-symbol alphabet with $k \geqslant 2$, and for every $n \geqslant 1$, there exists an n-state NFA recognizing an equal-length language, which requires a DFA with at least $k^{\sqrt{\frac{n}{k-1}} - 2} = 2^{\Omega(\sqrt{n})}$ states.

1 Introduction

There is an interesting application of finite automata to representing two-dimensional images, under which an image is defined by an automaton that computes the value of each pixel, where the pixel's coordinates are represented by a string. Then, automata can be used to generate, to compress or to tranform such images.

Apparently, these ideas were first proposed in a paper by Berstel and Morcrette [3]. The systematic research on representing images was initiated by Čulík and Dube [6], who related it to the theory of fractals [2]. The model was further studied by Čulík and Kari [8], who developed a practical automaton-based image compression algorithm [9]. For a survey of image processing using finite automata, the reader is referred to an upcoming handbook chapter by Karhumäki and Kari [15].

Consider a square picture with resolution $2^\ell \times 2^\ell$. The coordinates of each pixel in the image are defined by a string of length ℓ over a four-symbol alphabet $\Sigma = \{a, b, c, d\}$. In order to locate the pixel pointed to by a string, the image is progressively subdivided into smaller squares, using each symbol to choose one of the four quadrants, as illustrated in Figure 1(left). Thus, every string over Σ of length ℓ defines one of the pixels in an image. For instance, Figure 1(right) shows a pixel defined by the string bcd. Using this system of coordinates, a

Supported by the Academy of Finland under grant 257857.

C.S. Calude et al. (Eds.): Gruska Festschrift, LNCS 8808, pp. 71–82, 2014.
DOI: 10.1007/978-3-319-13350-8_6

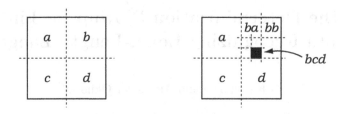

Fig. 1. (left) Subdivision of a square image into four quadrants; (right) Accessing a pixel of a 8×8 image by a string of length 3

black-and-white image of size $2^\ell \times 2^\ell$ can be defined by listing the coordinates of all black pixels; this will be a formal language over Σ, in which all strings are of length ℓ.

In the literature, this basic method is extended to define greyscale pictures using *weighted automata*, in which every transition has a probability of making it, and the automaton accordingly defines the probability of each input string; this probability can be interpreted as a shade of grey. Furthermore, using infinite strings to access any point in the unit square, one can use finite automata to define fractal images with an infinite resolution, that is, any sets of points. This is one of the cases of representing continuous objects by automata; some related work on representing real function by automata was done by Čulík and Karhumäki [7], by Derencourt et al. [10], and by Karhumäki and Sallinen [17]. These extensions are, however, beyond of the scope of this paper.

This paper investigates the size of finite automata used for representing black-and-white images of fixed resolution, such as those considered by Karhumäki et al. [16]. As these automata act as a compressed representation, their size measures the effectiveness of image compression. The problem studied here is comparing the size of two compressed formats for images: deterministic finite automata (DFA) and their nondeterministic counterparts (NFA).

The study of succinctness of finite automata has a long history. Since Rabin and Scott [24] defined the main types of automata and presented transformations between them, numerous authors contributed to determining precise succinctness tradeoffs between different automaton models. For instance, Rabin and Scott [24] showed how to transform an n-state NFA to a 2^n-state DFA recognizing the same language, whereas Lupanov [20] presented n-state NFAs, for which a DFA requires all 2^n states. Similar results for other types of automata were presented by Moore [22], by Leung [19] and by Kapoutsis [14]; Chrobak [5], Geffert et al. [11], Okhotin [23] and Kunc and Okhotin [18] studied tradeoffs between automata over a unary alphabet. Succinctness issues in formal grammars were first investigated by Gruska [12].

The automata used to represent images in this paper are special in two respects. Most importantly, the languages they recognize consist of strings of equal length; in the following, they shall be referred to as *equal-length languages*. Another restriction is that these languages are defined over a fixed 4-symbol alphabet. Though the general result on the exponential state complexity of the NFA to DFA transformation [20] uses a small alphabet as well, it relies on infinite languages, and hence does not apply to the equal-length case.

The most relevant prior work is the research on determinizing NFAs recognizing *finite languages*. For such an NFA with n states, defined over a 2-symbol alphabet, Mandl [21] showed that there is an equivalent DFA with only $2^{\frac{n}{2}+1}$ states. Salomaa and Yu [25] extended this result to finite languages over an alphabet with k symbols, for which an n-state NFA can be transformed to a DFA with $\frac{1}{k-1}k^{\lceil\frac{n}{\log_2 k+1}\rceil+1}$ states.

This paper establishes similar results under a stronger assumption that the language recognized by an NFA is not only finite, but equal-length. Such automata were studied, in particular, by Amilhastre et al. [1]. The general form of equal-length automata is explained in Section 2. Then, in Section 3, it is shown that every n-state NFA recognizing a language of strings of length ℓ over a k-symbol alphabet can be transformed to a DFA with as few as $\ell \cdot k^{\sqrt{\frac{2}{\log_2 k}n+3\ell+3}} = 2^{O(\sqrt{n})}$ states. This is substantially less than for arbitrary finite languages [25]. A fairly close lower bound of $k^{\sqrt{\frac{n}{k-1}}-2} = 2^{\Omega(\sqrt{n})}$ states is presented in Section 4.

2   Finite Automata and Image Representation

Consider a $2^\ell \times 2^\ell$ image, with $\ell \geqslant 0$. As explained in the introduction, each pixel in such an image is identified by a string of length ℓ over a four-symbol alphabet $\Sigma = \{a, b, c, d\}$. Every subsequent symbol in this string selects one of four quadrants in a further subdivision of the image, as illustrated in Figure 1 above. Then, any black-and-white image is described by a formal language over Σ, with all strings of length ℓ, which is accordingly called a *equal-length language*.

This papers considers the representation of equal-length languages by *finite automata* of two kinds: *deterministic* and *nondeterministic*.

Definition 1. *A deterministic finite automaton (DFA) is a quintuple $A = (\Sigma, Q, q_0, \delta, F)$, in which*

- *Σ is an input alphabet,*
- *Q is a finite set of states,*
- *$\delta \colon Q \times \Sigma \to Q$ is a total transition function,*
- *$q_0 \in Q$ is the initial state, and*
- *$F \subseteq Q$ is the set of accepting states.*

For every input string $w = a_1 \ldots a_\ell$, with $\ell \geqslant 0$ and $a_i \in \Sigma$, the computation of the automaton is a uniquely determined sequence of states $p_0, p_1, \ldots, p_\ell$, where $p_0 = q_0$ and $p_i = \delta(p_{i-1}, a_i)$ for each $i \in \{1, \ldots, \ell\}$. The string is accepted if $p_\ell \in F$.

The language recognized by the automaton, denoted by $L(A)$, is the set of all strings it accepts.

A state of a DFA is called *dead*, if no string can be accepted beginning from that state. A DFA recognizing a finite language must have at least one dead state, in which all excessively long strings are rejected. All dead states in any DFA can always be merged into one, and in the following, every DFA is assumed to have a unique dead state.

Let $A = (\Sigma, Q, q_0, \delta, F)$ be a DFA that recognizes an equal-length language, that is, $L(A) \subseteq \Sigma^\ell$ for some $\ell \geqslant 0$. Then, as long as A is not in its dead state q_{dead}, it must remember the length of the string in the current state (otherwise it would accept some strings of a wrong length). The set of its (non-dead) states is accordingly separated into $\ell + 1$ disjoint subsets as

$$Q \setminus \{q_{dead}\} = Q_0 \cup Q_1 \cup \ldots \cup Q_\ell,$$

where every state q in each layer Q_i is reachable from the initial state only by strings of length i. In particular, $Q_0 = \{q_0\}$, $F = Q_\ell$, and all transitions from any states in a layer Q_i may lead only to the states in the subsequent layer Q_{i+1}, or to the dead state.

Definition 2. *A nondeterministic finite automaton (NFA) is a quintuple $A = (\Sigma, Q, Q_0, \delta, F)$, with a set of initial states $Q_0 \subseteq Q$ and with a nondeterministic transition function $\delta \colon Q \times \Sigma \to 2^Q$ listing all possible next states.*

Let $w = a_1 \ldots a_\ell$, where $\ell \geqslant 0$ and $a_i \in \Sigma$, be an input string. An NFA may have multiple computations on w. A computation is any sequence $p_0, p_1, \ldots, p_\ell$, where $p_0 \in Q_0$ and $p_i \in \delta(p_{i-1}, a_i)$ for each $i \in \{1, \ldots, \ell\}$. Such a computation is accepting if $p_\ell \in F$. A string is considered accepted if at least one of these computations is accepting. The set of all such strings is the langyage recognized by the automaton, denoted by $L(A)$.

Unlike a deterministic automaton, an NFA need not have a dead state: instead of entering a dead state, it may use a transition to an empty set of states. Accordingly, all dead states can be removed from an NFA. Assume that every NFA has no dead states, that is, can accept some string from each of its states.

If an NFA $A = (\Sigma, Q, Q_0, \delta, F)$ recognizes an equal-length language $L(A) \subseteq \Sigma^\ell$, with $\ell \geqslant 0$, then it should also remember the length of the string in its state. Its set of states is split into $\ell + 1$ layers as

$$Q = Q_0 \cup Q_1 \cup \ldots \cup Q_\ell,$$

and again, all transitions from each layer Q_i may go only to the states in the next layer Q_{i+1}.

3   Determinizing Equal-Length Automata

Any NFA $A = (\Sigma, Q, Q_0, \delta, F)$ can be converted to a DFA $B = (\Sigma, Q', S_0, \delta', F')$ recognizing the same language by a well-known transformation, known as *the subset construction*. The states of the DFA are subsets of Q, that is, $Q' = 2^Q$.

The initial state of B is the set $S_0 = Q_0$. Its transition function is defined by $\delta'(S, a) = \bigcup_{q \in S} \delta(q, a)$. Finally, a subset is accepting if it contains any states accepting in the NFA: $F' = \{ S \subseteq Q \mid S \cap F \neq \varnothing \}$. Thus, if n is the number of states in the original NFA, the resulting DFA has at most 2^n states.

This section analyzes the subset construction for equal-length languages, and shows that in this special case, the number of reachable states in the DFA is much smaller than 2^n.

Let an NFA $A = (\Sigma, Q, Q_0, \delta, F)$ recognize an equal-length language $L(B) \subseteq \Sigma^\ell$, with $\ell \geqslant 0$. Let $Q = Q_0 \cup \ldots \cup Q_\ell$ be the partition of states into $\ell + 1$ layers, so that $\delta(q, a) \subseteq Q_{i+1}$ for all $q \in Q_i$ and $a \in \Sigma$. When the subset construction is applied to such a layered NFA, its layer structure is preserved in the resulting DFA: the latter has $\ell + 1$ layers, and the states in each i-th layer are subsets of Q_i. Another upper bound on the size of each layer of the DFA can be inferred from its transition structure: if there are $k = |\Sigma|$ symbols in the alphabet, then the number of states in every $(i+1)$-th layer of the DFA cannot be greater than k times the number of states in its i-th layer. These two conditions are formally stated in the following lemma.

Lemma 1. *Let $\ell \geqslant 0$ and let A be an NFA over an alphabet Σ, with $L(A) \subseteq \Sigma^\ell$. For each $i \in \{0, \ldots, \ell\}$, let m_i be the number of states in every i-th layer of A. Consider the DFA B obtained from A by the subset construction, and let M_i be the number of reachable states in every i-th layer of B. Then:*

$$M_i \leqslant 2^{m_i}, \qquad\qquad \text{for all } i \in \{0, \ldots, \ell\}, \qquad (1a)$$
$$M_{i+1} \leqslant k \cdot M_i, \qquad\qquad \text{for all } i \in \{1, \ldots, \ell\}. \qquad (1b)$$

The next lemma exploits these two conditions to obtain an upper bound on the size of the DFA.

Lemma 2. *Let Σ be a k-symbol alphabet, let $L \subseteq \Sigma^\ell$ be an equal-length language recognized by an n-state NFA A. For a layer i, and let m be the number of states in all layers from 0 to i. Then the DFA obtained from this NFA by the subset construction has at most $k^{\sqrt{\frac{2}{\log_2 k} m + 3i + 3}}$ states in the layer $i + 1$.*

Proof. In the notation of Lemma 1, $m = m_0 + \ldots + m_i$, $M = M_{i+1}$, and it is claimed that

$$M_{i+1} \leqslant k^{\sqrt{\frac{2}{\log_2 k}(m_0 + \ldots + m_i) + 3i + 3}}.$$

The first step of the proof is to estimate the expression under the square root in terms of M. By the first claim of Lemma 1, each m_j is greater than or equal to $\log_2 M_j$, and hence,

$$\frac{2}{\log_2 k}(m_0 + \ldots + m_i) + 3i + 3 \geqslant \frac{2}{\log_2 k}(\log_2 M_0 + \ldots + \log_2 M_i) + 3i + 3 =$$

$$= 2\log_k(M_0 \cdot \ldots \cdot M_i) + 3i + 3.$$

What is the least possible value of the product $M_0 \cdot \ldots \cdot M_i$? By the second claim of Lemma 1, each factor can be estimated in terms of $M = M_{i+1}$ as follows: first, $M_i \geqslant \frac{M}{k}$; then, $M_{i-1} \geqslant \frac{M_i}{k} \geqslant \frac{M}{k^2}$, etc. Furthermore, each M_j must be at least 1. Thus, the lower bound on $M_0 \cdot \ldots \cdot M_i$ is obtained by dividing each consecutive factor by k until 1 is reached:

$$M_i \cdot \ldots \cdot M_0 \geqslant \frac{M}{k} \cdot \frac{M}{k^2} \cdot \ldots \cdot \frac{M}{k^{\lfloor \log_k M \rfloor}} \cdot 1 \cdot \ldots \cdot 1$$

Using this inequality, the estimation of the expression under the square root continues as follows.

$$2\log_k(M_0 \cdot \ldots \cdot M_i) + 3i + 3 \geqslant 2\log_k \left(\frac{M}{k} \cdot \frac{M}{k^2} \cdot \ldots \cdot \frac{M}{k^{\lfloor \log_k M \rfloor}} \right) + 3i + 3 =$$

$$= 2\log_k(M^{\lfloor \log_k M \rfloor}) - 2\log_k(k^{1+2+\ldots+\lfloor \log_k M \rfloor}) + 3i + 3 =$$

$$= 2\lfloor \log_k M \rfloor \log_k M - 2\frac{\lfloor \log_k M \rfloor(\lfloor \log_k M \rfloor + 1)}{2} + 3i + 3 \geqslant$$

$$\geqslant 2\log_k M(\log_k M - 1) - \log_k M(\log_k M + 1) + 3i + 3 =$$

$$= (\log_k M)^2 - 3\log_k M + 3i + 3$$

In order to estimate the last expression, consider that $M_j \leqslant k^j$ for all j: indeed, this is true for $j = 0$, as the DFA has one state in layer 0, and the rest is proved inductively using the second claim of Lemma 1. Thus, $M \leqslant k^{i+1}$, and therefore $\log_k M \leqslant i + 1$. Using this estimation,

$$(\log_k M)^2 - 3\log_k M + 3i + 3 \geqslant (\log_k M)^2.$$

Now,

$$k\sqrt{\frac{2}{\log_2 k}(m_0+\ldots+m_i)+3i+3} \geqslant k\sqrt{(\log_k M_{i+1})^2} = M_{i+1},$$

as claimed.   □

In particular, Lemma 2 implies that the number of states in the last ℓ-th layer of the DFA—and hence, in each layer—is at most $k\sqrt{\frac{2}{\log_2 k}n+3\ell+3}$, where n is the total number of states in the original NFA. This estimation leads to the following theorem.

Theorem 1. *Let Σ be an alphabet, denote $k = |\Sigma|$. Let $L \subseteq \Sigma^\ell$, with $\ell \geqslant 1$, be an equal-length language recognized by an n-state NFA. Then the DFA obtained from this NFA by the subset construction has at most $\ell \cdot k\sqrt{\frac{2}{\log_2 k}n+3\ell+3} = 2^{O(\sqrt{n})}$ reachable states.*

Proof. In layer 0, the DFA has only one state. In each of the subsequent layers, it has at most $k\sqrt{\frac{2}{\log_2 k}m+3\ell+3}$ states by Lemma 2. This yields an upper bound of $1 + \ell k\sqrt{\frac{2}{\log_2 k}m+3\ell+3}$ states. In order to get rid of one extra state in this rough estimation, consider that there are at most k states in layer 1, whereas $k\sqrt{\frac{2}{\log_2 k}m+3\ell+3} \geqslant k\sqrt{6} > k+1$. With this correction, the desired upper bound is obtained.

Since $\ell < n$, this bound can be estimated as $2^{O(\sqrt{n})}$, where the constant in the exponent depends on the size of the alphabet. □

Theorem 1 shows that any given n-state NFA recognizing an equal-length language is simulated by a DFA with $2^{O(\sqrt{n})}$ states. It is natural to ask whether there could exist any improved construction that would yield a DFA with significantly fewer states. A negative answer, that $2^{\Theta(\sqrt{n})}$ states are necessary in the worst case, shall be given in the next section. In other words, there cannot exist a better transformation that would always produce $2^{o(\sqrt{n})}$ states.

4   A Lower Bound on the Determinization Blow-Up

In order to show that determinizing equal-length languages over any alphabet $\Sigma_k = \{a_1, \ldots, a_k\}$ incurs a $2^{\Omega(\sqrt{n})}$-state blow-up, it is sufficient to present a family of *witness languages*, which are recognized by small NFA, but any DFA recognizing them must have many states.

The proposed example is a language of all strings of length $2d$, with $d \geqslant 2$, which contain a pair of identical symbols at a distance of exactly d; furthermore, this repeated symbol shall not be a_k. An NFA recognizing this language can guess the position of the first symbol and then compare it to the other one, whereas a DFA will have to remember the first d symbols in its state. This leads to the blow-up established in the following lemma.

Lemma 3. *For each $k \geqslant 2$ and $d \geqslant 2$, the language*

$$L_{k,d} = \{\, s_1 \ldots s_{2d} \mid \exists i \in \{1, \ldots, d\} : \ s_i = s_{i+d} \in \{a_1, \ldots, a_{k-1}\} \,\},$$

defined over the alphabet $\Sigma_k = \{a_1, \ldots, a_{k-1}, a_k\}$, is recognized by an NFA with $(k-1)d^2 + 2d$ states, whereas every DFA recognizing this language must have at least k^d states in the d-th layer.

Proof. An NFA recognizing the language $L_{k,d}$ is illustrated in Figure 2 for a 4-symbol alphabet and for $d = 4$. For arbitrary values of k and d, such an NFA is equipped with an initial block of d states (see the 4 states at the left border of the figure), in which it reads up to $d-1$ first symbols while nondeterministically guessing the position $i \in \{1, \ldots, d\}$, in which it should begin comparing the symbol s_i to s_{i+d}. Then it remembers one of the $k-1$ possible values of s_i in its internal state, ignores $d-1$ following symbols, and then makes sure than the subsequent symbol is the same as the remembered symbol; this is implemented as $k-1$ sequential segments of d states each, for each of the d choices of i. Finally, the automaton ignores $d-i$ final symbols in the last block of d states (as in the 4 states at the right border of Figure 2). The total number of states is therefore $d + (k-1)d^2 + d$, as claimed.

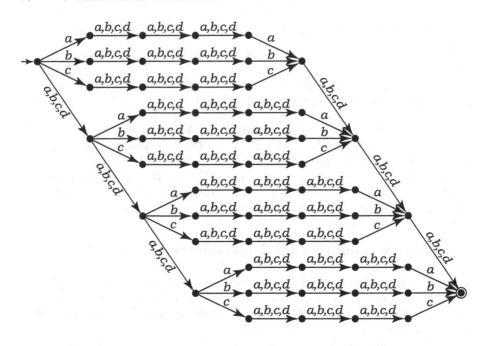

Fig. 2. A 56-state NFA recognizing the language $L_{k,d}$, with $k = 4$ and $d = 4$

Consider all strings of length d over Σ; there are k^d such strings. It is claimed that every DFA recognizing $L_{k,d}$ must reach different states after reading these strings.

For every two distinct strings $u = s_1 \ldots s_d$ and $u' = s'_1 \ldots s'_d$, let i be any position in which they differ, that is, $s_i \neq s'_i$. At least one of s_i, s'_i is not a_k; assume, without loss of generality, that $s_i \neq a_k$. Consider the string $v = t_1 \ldots t_d$, in which the symbol in the i-th position is $t_i = s_i$, whereas the rest of the symbols are $t_j = a_k$, for all $j \neq i$. Now the string uv belongs to the language $L_{k,d}$, because it has the same symbol s_i in the positions i and $i+d$. On the other hand, the string $u'v$ is not in $L_{k,d}$, because it may have matching symbols only in the positions i and $i+d$ (as all other positions have the prohibited symbol a_k in the second half of the string), and these symbols, s'_i and $t_i = s_i$, are known to be different. Then, in order to accept uv and to reject $u'v$, a DFA must reach different states after reading u and u'. Therefore, it should have k^d different states in the d-th layer.   □

Returning to the representation of images by languages over a 4-symbol alphabet, Lemma 2 with $k = 4$ defines a family of formal languages representing some $4^d \times 4^d$ images. These images can be compressed to NFA with $3d^2 + 2d$ states, whereas any DFA defining such an image needs at least 4^d states.

A 256×256 image defined by the language in Lemma 3, with $k = 4$ and $d = 4$, is presented in Figure 3. It is recognized by a 56-state NFA in Figure 2,

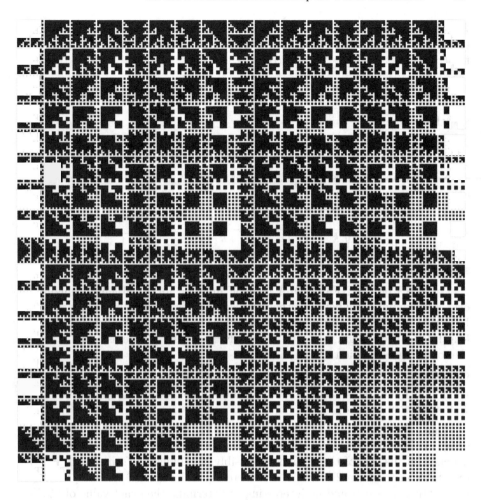

Fig. 3. The 256×256 image defined by the language in Lemma 3, with $k = 4$, $d = 4$

but every DFA for this language must have at least $4^4 = 256$ states. The latter lower bound can be observed in the image in Figure 3, where all 256 of its 16×16 pixel blocks are pairwise distinct, and hence require pairwise distinct states in the 4th layer of the DFA.

It remains to express the number of states in a DFA as a function of the number of states in the original NFA, leading to the following counterpart to Theorem 1.

Theorem 2. *Let Σ be any alphabet containing at least two symbols, denote $k = |\Sigma|$. Then, for every $n \geqslant 2$, there exists an equal-length language L over Σ that is recognized by an n-state NFA, whereas every DFA recognizing this language has at least $k^{\sqrt{\frac{n}{k-1}}-2} = 2^{\Omega(\sqrt{n})}$ states.*

Proof. The desired language L is provided by Lemma 3. Given k and n, consider the largest integer d, for which $(k-1)d^2 + 2d \leqslant n$. It is determined by solving the equation $(k-1)d^2 + 2d = n$: consider that

$$(k-1)d^2 + 2d = (k-1)\left(d^2 + \frac{2d}{k-1}\right) = (k-1)\left(\left(d + \frac{1}{k-1}\right)^2 - \frac{1}{(k-1)^2}\right),$$

and then define

$$d = \left\lfloor \sqrt{\frac{n}{k-1} + \frac{1}{(k-1)^2}} - \frac{1}{k-1} \right\rfloor.$$

Now, Lemma 3 gives a language recognized by an n-state NFA, for which every DFA requires at least

$$k^d = k^{\left\lfloor \sqrt{\frac{n}{k-1} + \frac{1}{(k-1)^2}} - \frac{1}{k-1} \right\rfloor} \geqslant k^{\sqrt{\frac{n}{k-1}} - 2}$$

states, as desired.   □

Let $f_k(n)$ be the NFA-to-DFA tradeoff function for equal-length languages over a k-symbol alphabet. In other words, $f_k(n)$ is the number of states in a DFA that is sufficient and in the worst case necessary to represent every equal-length language recognized by an n-state NFA. Then, Theorems 1 and 2 imply the following estimation of this function.

Corollary 1. *For every alphabet Σ containing at least two symbols, and for every $n \geqslant 1$, the NFA-to-DFA tradeoff function for equal-length languages over Σ is estimated as $f_k(n) = 2^{\Theta(\sqrt{n})}$.*

Thus, the complexity of determinizing NFA recognizing equal-length languages is known up to a constant factor in the exponent. This constant factor depends on the size of the alphabet. Possibly, the function $f_k(n)$ could be representable in the form $2^{(1+o(1))C_k\sqrt{n}}$, where C_k is the desired constant factor; if this is true, then it would be interesting to determine the exact value of C_k.

5   Further Work

State complexity of operations on finite automata is a common topic of research. For instance, for finite languages, it was studied by Câmpeanu et al. [4] and by Han and Salomaa [13].

With images represented by formal languages, operations on images become operations on languages, and it is useful to investigate the effect of these operations on the size of automata. One such result is known already: Karhumäki, Plandowski and Rytter [16] determined the state complexity of cropping an image, that is, taking an n-state DFA representing a $2^\ell \times 2^\ell$ image, and producing a DFA for any $2^k \times 2^k$ subimage of this image. This operation requires $\Theta(n^{2.5})$ states, and the bound is tight in the worst case [16].

It might be interesting to consider other questions of this kind. For instance, what is the complexity of inverting an image represented by an n-state NFA, or, in other words, of complementing an equal-length NFA?

References

1. Amilhastre, J., Janssen, P., Vilarem, M.-C.: FA Minimisation Heuristics for a Class of Finite Languages. In: Boldt, O., Jürgensen, H. (eds.) WIA 1999. LNCS, vol. 2214, p. 1. Springer, Heidelberg (2001)
2. Barnsley, M.F.: Fractals Everywhere, Academic Press Professional (1988)
3. Berstel, J., Morcrette, M.: Compact representation of patterns by finite automata. In: Gagalowicz, A. (Ed.) Pixim 1989: L'Image Numérique à Paris, pp. 387–402 (1989)
4. Seuring, M., Gössel, M.: A Structural Method for Output Compaction of Sequential Automata Implemented as Circuits. In: Boldt, O., Jürgensen, H. (eds.) WIA 1999. LNCS, vol. 2214, p. 158. Springer, Heidelberg (2001)
5. Chrobak, M.: Finite automata and unary languages, Theoretical Computer Science, 47, 149–158 (1986); Errata: 302, 497–498 (2003)
6. Čulík II, K., Dube, S.: Rational and affine expressions for image description. Discrete Applied Mathematics **41**(2), 85–120 (1993)
7. Čulík II, K., Karhumäki, J.: Finite automata computing real functions. SIAM Journal on Computing **23**(4), 789–814 (1994)
8. Čulík II, K., Kari, J.: Image compression using weighted finite automata. Computers & Graphics **17**(3), 305–313 (1993)
9. Čulík II, K., Kari, J.: Image-data compression using edge-optimizing algorithm for WFA inference. Information Processing & Management **30**(6), 829–838 (1994)
10. Derencourt, D., Karhumäki, J., Latteux, M., Terlutte, A.: On continuous functions computed by finite automata. RAIRO Informatique Théorique et Applications **28**, 387–404 (1994)
11. Geffert, V., Mereghetti, C., Pighizzini, G.: Converting two-way nondeterministic unary automata into simpler automata. Theoretical Computer Science **295**(1–3), 189–203 (2003)
12. Gruska, J.: Descriptional complexity of context-free languages. In: Mathematical Foundations of Computer Science (MFCS 1973 Strbské Pleso, High Tatras, Czechoslovakia, 3–8 September), 71–83 (1973)
13. Han, Y.-S., Salomaa, K.: State complexity of union and intersection of finite languages. International Journal of Foundations of Computer Science **19**(3), 581–595 (2008)
14. Kapoutsis, C.A.: Removing Bidirectionality from Nondeterministic Finite Automata. In: Jedrzejowicz, J., Szepietowski, A. (eds.) MFCS 2005. LNCS, vol. 3618, pp. 544–555. Springer, Heidelberg (2005)
15. Karhumäki, J., Kari, J.: Finite automata, image manipulation and automatic real functions. In: Pin, J.-É. (Ed.) Handbook of Automata, European Mathematical Society, to appear
16. Karhumäki, J., Plandowski, W., Rytter, W.: The complexity of compressing subsegments of images described by finite automata. Discrete Applied Mathematics **125**(2–3), 235–254 (2003)
17. Karhumäki, J., Sallinen, T.: Weighted Finite Automata: Computing with Different Topologies. In: Calude, C.S., Kari, J., Petre, I., Rozenberg, G. (eds.) UC 2011. LNCS, vol. 6714, pp. 14–33. Springer, Heidelberg (2011)
18. Černo, Peter, Mráz, František: Δ-Clearing Restarting Automata and CFL. In: Mauri, Giancarlo, Leporati, Alberto (eds.) DLT 2011. LNCS, vol. 6795, pp. 153–164. Springer, Heidelberg (2011)

19. Leung, H.: Descriptional complexity of NFA of different ambiguity. International Journal of Foundations of Computer Science **16**(5), 975–984 (2005)
20. Lupanov, O.B.: A comparison of two types of finite automata (in Russian). Problemy Kibernetiki **9**, 321–326 (1963)
21. Mandl, R.: Precise bounds associated with the subset construction on various classes of nondeterministic finite automata. In: 7th Princeton Conference on Information and System Sciences, 263–267 (1973)
22. Moore, F.R.: On the bounds for state-set size in the proofs of equivalence between deterministic, nondeterministic, and two-way finite automata. IEEE Transactions on Computers **20**, 1211–1214 (1971)
23. Okhotin, A.: Unambiguous finite automata over a unary alphabet. Information and Computation **212**, 15–36 (2012)
24. Rabin, M.O., Scott, D.: Finite automata and their decision problems. IBM Journal of Research and Development **3**, 114–125 (1959)
25. Salomaa, K., Yu, S.: NFA to DFA transformation for finite languages over arbitrary alphabets. Journal of Automata, Languages and Combinatorics **2**(3), 177–186 (1997)

Aspects of Reversibility for Classical Automata

Martin Kutrib[✉]

Institut für Informatik, Universität Giessen,
Arndtstr. 2, 35392 Giessen, Germany
kutrib@informatik.uni-giessen.de

Abstract. Some aspects of logical reversibility for computing devices with a finite number of discrete internal states are addressed. These devices have a read-only input tape, may be equipped with further resources, and evolve in discrete time. The reversibility of a computation means in essence that every configuration has a unique successor configuration and a unique predecessor configuration. The notion of reversibility is discussed. In which way is the predecessor configuration computed? May we use a universal device? Do we have to use a device of the same type? Or else a device with the same computational power? Do we have to consider all possible configurations as potential predecessors? Or only configurations that are reachable from some initial configurations? We present some selected aspects as gradual reversibility and time-symmetry as well as results on the computational capacity and decidability mainly of finite automata and pushdown automata, and draw attention to the overall picture and some of the main ideas involved.

1 Introduction

Computers are information processing devices which are physical realizations of abstract computational models. So, it is interesting to know whether an abstract model is able to obey physical laws. Since reversibility is a fundamental principle in physics, it is interesting to study the models from this point of view. Moreover, the observation that loss of information results in heat dissipation [26] strongly suggests to study reversible computations without loss of information.

First studies of this kind have been done for the massively parallel model of cellular automata since the sixties of the last century. Nowadays it is known from [29] that every, possibly irreversible, one-dimensional cellular automaton can always be simulated by a reversible one-dimensional cellular automaton in a constructive way. Later, in [4] reversible sequential machines, more precisely, Turing machines have been introduced. Again, a fundamental result is that every Turing machine can be made reversible. These two types of devices received a lot of attention in connection with reversibility. They are beyond the scope of this discussion. Valuable surveys with further references to literature are, for example, [15] for cellular automata and [30], where one may find a summary of results on reversible Turing machines, reversible cellular automata, and other reversible models such as logic gates, logic circuits, or logic elements with memory (see also [3,17,18,21] for further investigations). Logical reversibility has

© Springer International Publishing Switzerland 2014
C.S. Calude et al. (Eds.): Gruska Festschrift, LNCS 8808, pp. 83–98, 2014.
DOI: 10.1007/978-3-319-13350-8_7

been studied also for other computational devices such as space-bounded Turing machines [27], two-way multi-head finite automata [2,31], one-way multi-head finite automata [20], and queue automata [22].

Here we focus on some aspects of reversibility in sequential devices, where we mainly restrict the discussion exemplarily to finite automata and pushdown automata. In Section 2 the notion of reversibility and its possible definitions are discussed. In Section 3 the simplest device in question is considered. Gradual reversibility, computational capacity, and decidability of finite automata are the topics presented. The next level in the basic hierarchy of automata are deterministic pushdown automata. Their reversible variants are dealt with in Section 4. Finally, a further aspect of reversibility, the so-called time-symmetry, is discussed in Section 5. Basically, this means that one can go back in time by applying the same transition function as for forward steps after a specific transformation of the phase-space. So, time-symmetric machines themselves cannot distinguish whether they run forward or backward in time.

The reader is assumed to be familiar with the basic notions of automata theory as contained, for example, in [11,14]. In the present paper we will use the following notational conventions. An *alphabet* Σ is a non-empty finite set, its elements are called *letters* or *symbols*. We write Σ^* for the *set of all words* over the finite alphabet Σ. The *empty word* is denoted by λ, and $\Sigma^+ = \Sigma^* \setminus \{\lambda\}$. The *reversal* of a word w is denoted by w^R and for the *length* of w we write $|w|$. We use $\subseteq$ for *inclusions* and $\subset$ for *strict inclusions*. The *family of languages* accepted by devices of type X is denoted by $\quad(X)$. In the following, two devices are said to be *equivalent* if they accept the same language.

2 Reversibility of Automata – What Is It?

In general, here we consider computing machines with a finite number of discrete internal states. The machines have a read-only input tape, may be equipped with further resources, and evolve in discrete time, where each computation step is driven by a *deterministic transition function*. Given a *configuration* representing the complete "global state" of a device, the transition function is used to compute the successor configuration. The transition function depends on the current internal state and on the status of further resources the machine is equipped with. It gives the successor state and maybe changes the status of the resources.

Since we are particularly interested in reversible computations of such devices, we discuss the notion of reversibility first. Basically, reversibility is meant with respect to the possibility of stepping the computation back and forth. To this end, the devices have to be also backward deterministic. That is, any configuration must have at most one predecessor. This simple observation raises several questions.

For example, in which way is the predecessor configuration computed? May we use a universal device? Do we have to use a device of the same type? Or else a device with the same computational power? While the idea to step the computation back and forth anticipates not to use a universal machine in general,

Fig. 1. A DFA accepting the language a^*b^+ (left), and its reverse DFA with lookahead two (right). The labels on the edges indicate the *complete* content of the input window (but only 1 symbol is "consumed").

the answer to the latter questions is not that clear. Consider the deterministic finite automaton of Figure 1 that accepts the language a^*b^+. If the predecessor configuration has to be computed by a device of the same type, the DFA is irreversible since there are two different transitions entering the same state s_1 with the same input symbol b (see Figure 2). On the other hand, if the predecessor configuration may be computed by a device with the same computational power, the DFA is reversible. In this case we may provide a lookahead of size two, that is, the input window of the backward DFA has size two while nevertheless only one symbol is processed per time step. The lookahead helps to overcome the crucial situation of the computation at the borderline between the a's and b's (Figure 3). However, a lookahead does not increase the computational capacity of DFA. Such devices still characterize the regular languages only.

Another question that comes up in connection with the computability of predecessor configurations concerns the set of configurations that count. Do we have to consider all possible configurations as potential predecessors? Or only configurations that are reachable from some initial configurations, that is, configurations that actually occur in computations? Consider for example the DFA

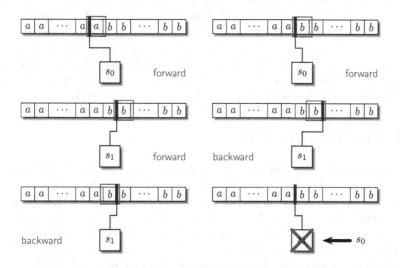

Fig. 2. An irreversible computation of the DFA accepting the language a^*b^+

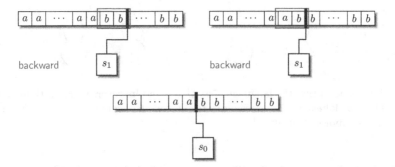

Fig. 3. Backward computation of the DFA with lookahead 2

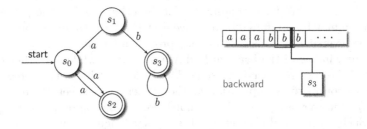

Fig. 4. A DFA (left) and an unreachable configuration (right)

in Figure 4. The configuration on the right-hand side is unreachable from any initial configuration. Is the DFA reversible? It is for all reachable configurations, but it is irreversible if all possible configurations count. Reversibility on reachable configurations is a wider notion than reversibility on all configurations. A gentle argument towards the former notion is given by the big bang theory. If one believes in it everything we are living in evolved from an initial situation.

So, in the sequel we carefully have to distinguish which notion of reversibility is meant. Unless stated otherwise, we require that the backward steps of a computation are performed by another device of the same type.

3   Finite-State Machines

Here we turn to the simplest type of device in question. Reversible deterministic finite automata (REV-DFA) have been introduced and studied in the context of algorithmic learning theory in [1] (see also [16]). Given a DFA M, the inverse $M^{\leftarrow}$ of M is defined by interchanging initial and final states and reversing each transition arrow. In [1], the finite automaton M is defined to be reversible if and only if both M and $M^{\leftarrow}$ are deterministic. Incomplete transition functions are allowed. In particular, this definition implies that for reversible DFA only one final state is allowed. Since there are regular languages that are not accepted by any DFA with a sole accepting state, by definition, there are non-reversible regular languages in this setting.

The reversible DFA of [1] are called *bideterministic* in [33]. The definition of reversibility has been extended in the latter reference. Now multiple accepting as well as multiple initial states are allowed. So, reversible DFA in the sense of [33] may have limited nondeterminism plugged in from the outside world at the outset of the computation. On the other hand, there are no non-reversible languages per definition any more.

Here we stick with standard definitions. That is, a REV-DFA has a unique initial state and may have multiple accepting states. Essentially, in [33] it has been shown that the regular language a^*b^+ of Figure 1 cannot be accepted by any REV-DFA.

Theorem 1 ([1, 33]). *There are regular languages which are not reversible, so there are deterministic finite automata that cannot be simulated by any reversible finite automaton.*

An observation in [1] is that the inherent irreversibility of some regular language may depend on the size of the input window of the devices. If this size is increased *for backward computations*, more languages become reversible. For example, the inherent irreversible language a^*b^+ of Figure 1 is reversibly accepted with lookahead size 2. This result led to the definition of so-called k-reversible languages. In [7] this notion has been generalized to DFA in the definition of [33], and in [24] to pushdown automata (and DFA in standard definition).

We denote DFA with lookahead size $k \geq 1$ by (k)-DFA. So, a classical deterministic finite automaton is a (1)-DFA. A forward DFA is said to be *reversible of degree k* (REV(k)-DFA) if the predecessor configuration is unique for all computations that lead to the current configuration along the last k symbols read in a forward computation. Note, the lookahead for the forward DFA is still 1 (see [24] for formal definitions). So, the lookahead of the backward DFA is used to determine the unique predecessor configuration from all computations that lead to the current configuration along the symbols seen in the input window.

This definition includes also non-reachable configurations. Consider once more the language a^*b^+ from above that is accepted by some REV(2)-DFA. The configuration $(baab, s_1, bb)$ is unreachable in any computation starting from an initial configuration, where $baab$ is the input read so far, s_1 is the current state, and bb is the unread input. The configuration $(aaab, s_1, bb)$ is reachable. Both have two predecessor configurations, namely $(baa, s_0, bbb), (baa, s_1, bbb)$ and $(aaa, s_0, bbb), (aaa, s_1, bbb)$. However, in both cases the predecessor configuration is unique, when the computation comes along the last two input symbols. For the first case we have $(ba, s_0, abbb) \vdash (baa, s_0, bbb) \vdash (baab, s_1, bb)$ and $(ba, s_1, abbb) \not\vdash^* (baab, s_1, bb)$.

The next example yields an infinite and strict hierarchy of regular languages dependent on the *degree of reversibility*.

Example 1. Let $k \geq 1$ be an integer. Then the language $\{\, a^m b^n \mid m \geq 0, n \geq k \,\}$ is accepted by some REV($k + 1$)-DFA as indicated in Figure 5. However, the language *cannot* be accepted by any REV(k)-DFA.   □

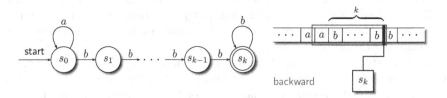

Fig. 5. A REV($k + 1$)-DFA accepting the language $a^* b^k b^*$. This DFA is not a REV(k)-DFA, and there is no other REV(k)-DFA accepting this language.

Theorem 2 ([1,24]). *For any integer $k \geq 1$, there are regular languages accepted by REV($k + 1$)-DFA that cannot be accepted by any REV(k)-DFA.*

So far, it turned out that lookaheads on the input gradually increase the capability to perform reverse computations. Now we are interested in the question whether all regular languages are captured by REV-DFA. Or else, whether there are regular languages that cannot be accepted by any REV-DFA of any degree. For the important subclass of *finite* languages, the answer to the latter question is *no*.

Proposition 1 ([24]). *Any finite language is accepted by some REV(1)-DFA.*

For a second important subclass, the *unary* languages, reversibility is always obtained as well, but the degree for REV-DFA cannot be bounded by any number.

Proposition 2 ([24]). *For any unary regular language L, there is an integer $k \geq 1$ so that L is accepted by some REV(k)-DFA.*

Finally, we consider the general cases where there are languages for which even an arbitrarily large degree cannot help.

Theorem 3 ([24]). *There are regular languages which cannot be accepted by any REV(k)-DFA for any degree $k \geq 1$.*

The idea of the proof is to use a language L over an alphabet Σ that is accepted with lookahead size 2 but cannot be accepted with lookahead size 1, and a regular substitution $s(a) = a\#^*$, for $a \in \Sigma$ and a new symbol #. Language $s(L)$ consists of all words from L with an arbitrary number of # between each two symbols from Σ. Clearly, $s(L)$ is still accepted by some DFA. On the other hand, for any $k \geq 1$, language $s(L)$ contains all words from $s(L) \cap (\Sigma \#^k)^*$. So, when accepting such words there is always at most one symbol of Σ in the lookahead. Therefore, if $s(L)$ would be reversible for input lookahead size k, a direct construction would show that it is reversible for input lookahead size 1 as well, a contradiction.

Summarizing the results so far, there is an infinite proper hierarchy of k-reversible languages. The union (REV(*)-DFA) = $\bigcup_{k \geq 1}$ (REV(k)-DFA) of all levels of the hierarchy is properly included in the family of regular languages. In order to justify the power of REV(k)-DFA we compare the union with other well-known subregular language families (see, for example, [5,12] for further results and references on subregular language families). It turned out that (REV(*)-DFA) includes finite as well as unary regular languages properly. Moreover, in [1] it is shown that (REV(*)-DFA) includes the definite languages [32] and the reverse definite languages [10] properly. On the other hand, (REV(*)-DFA) is incomparable with the subregular language families of generalized definite [10] and locally testable languages [28].

Coming to another aspect, we recall that it is well know that the minimal DFA accepting a given regular language is unique. So there is the natural question asking for the relations between minimality and reversibility. It turned out that in this connection the different notions of reversibility do matter. In [33], the following proposition is cited.

Proposition 3. *A language L is accepted by a bideterministic finite automaton if and only if the minimal finite automaton of L is reversible and has a unique final state.*

This answers the question about the notion of reversibility in [1]. However, for the other notions of reversibility considered, the *minimal reversible* finite automaton for some language can be exponentially larger than the minimal automaton.

Example 2. Let L be the finite language $\{aa, ab, ba\}$. The minimal DFA accepting the $2n$-fold concatenation of L is depicted in Figure 6. It has $6n + 1$ states. Since L^{2n} is finite, it is reversible. □

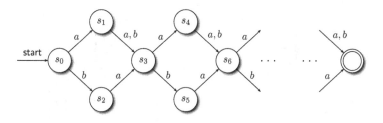

Fig. 6. A minimal DFA accepting the language L^{2n}, for $n \geq 1$

Theorem 4 ([13]). *Let $n \geq 1$. The minimal REV-DFA accepting L^{2n} has $\Omega(r^n)$ states, for some $r > 1$.*

Another aspect concerns the problem to decide whether a given language or automaton is reversible. In case of finite automata, deciding this problem for devices is almost trivial. An inspection of the transition function and the set of accepting states suffices. This observation transfers to languages in the notion of [1] by Proposition 3. In general, the problem is more involved.

Theorem 5 ([33]). *There is a polynomial time algorithm for testing whether the language accepted by a minimal finite automaton can be accepted by a reversible finite automaton.*

4 Pushdown Automata

The next level in the basic hierarchy of automata are deterministic pushdown automata (DPDA). Their reversible variants have been introduced and studied in [19], where only reachable configurations are relevant for reversibility and the predecessor configurations have to be computed by a device of the same type. Recall that the transition function δ of DPDA maps the current state, the current input symbol or λ, and the symbol at the top of the stack to the successor state and a new (possibly empty) string at the top of the stack. We denote the relation from one configuration to the next by $\vdash$.

A DPDA M with transition function δ is said to be reversible (REV-DPDA), if there exists a reverse transition function $\delta^{\leftarrow}$ inducing a relation $\vdash^{\leftarrow}$ from one configuration to the next, so that $c_{i+1} \vdash^{\leftarrow} c_i$, $0 \leq i \leq n-1$, for any sequence $c_0 \vdash c_1 \vdash \cdots \vdash c_n$ of configurations passed through by M beginning with an initial configuration c_0 (cf. Figure 7). See [19,23] for detailed definitions.

Example 3 ([19]). The linear context-free languages $\{\, wcw^R \mid w \in \{a,b\}^* \,\}$ as well as $\{\, a^n cb^n \mid n \geq 0 \,\}$ are accepted by REV-DPDA. A sketch of the basic idea is shown in Figure 8. □

A simple observation reveals that the transitions of a REV-DPDA either pop a symbol, change the symbol at the top of the pushdown store, or push a single

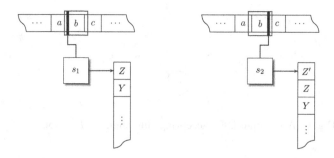

Fig. 7. Successive configurations of a reversible deterministic pushdown automaton, where $\delta(s_1, b, Z) = (s_2, Z'Z)$ (left to right) and $\delta^{\leftarrow}(s_2, b, Z') = (s_1, \lambda)$ (right to left)

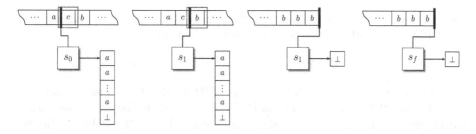

Fig. 8. Scheme of a forward computation of a REV-DPDA accepting $\{\, a^n cb^n \mid n \geq 0 \,\}$. The crucial point for backward computations is to determine the time step at which state s_0 has to be reentered. This is given by the c in the input.

symbol. The reason is that the reverse transition has only access to the topmost symbol. The next result clarifies the role played by λ-steps.

Theorem 6 ([19]). *For every REV-DPDA an equivalent realtime REV-DPDA can effectively be constructed, that is, a REV-DPDA without λ-steps.*

It is well known that general deterministic pushdown automata which are not allowed to perform λ-steps are weaker than DPDA that may move on λ input [11]. So, Theorem 6 provides a class of irreversible deterministic context-free languages. Every deterministic context-free language that is not realtime is not accepted by any REV-DPDA. For example, the language

$$\{\, a^m eb^n ca^m \mid m, n \geq 0 \,\} \cup \{\, a^m eb^n da^n \mid m, n \geq 0 \,\}$$

does not belong to the family   (REV-DPDA) (see, for example, [8,11]). This result immediately raises the question of whether *all realtime* deterministic context-free languages are reversible. The next theorem answers this question negatively. In particular, it shows that the c in the center of the input of Example 3 is essential.

Theorem 7 ([19]). *The realtime deterministic linear context-free language $\{\, a^n b^n \mid n \geq 0 \,\}$ is not accepted by any REV-DPDA.*

So, we conclude that the family   (REV-DPDA) is strictly included in the family of languages accepted by realtime deterministic pushdown automata. Not only in connection with reversibility it is interesting to consider realtime deterministic context-free languages whose reversals are also realtime deterministic context-free languages. It turned out that this family is incomparable with the family   (REV-DPDA). Furthermore, it is known that the families of linear context-free languages and   (REV-DPDA) are incomparable [19].

In [33], it has been shown that there are regular languages which are not accepted by any reversible finite automaton. However, the regular languages are strictly included in   (REV-DPDA) [19]. Summarizing the results so far, we have obtained the following strict hierarchy, where REG denotes the regular and $_{rt}$(DPDA) the realtime deterministic context-free languages:

$$\text{REG} \subset \quad (\text{REV-DPDA}) \subset \quad _{rt}(\text{DPDA}) \subset \quad (\text{DPDA}).$$

Let us now turn to decidability aspects of REV-DPDA. Problems which are decidable for DPDA are decidable for REV-DPDA as well. Therefore, emptiness, universality, equivalence, and regularity are decidable for REV-DPDA. On the other hand, inclusion is known to be undecidable for DPDA. By reduction of the Post's correspondence problem it has been shown that inclusion is undecidable for REV-DPDA, too [19].

The following theorem contrasts the situation for finite automata, where the problem is decidable in polynomial time (Theorem 5).

Theorem 8 ([19]). *It is undecidable whether the language accepted by a nondeterministic pushdown automaton can be accepted by a REV-DPDA.*

The same problem for deterministic pushdown automata is open. However, if we consider devices instead of accepted languages, we have the decidability of reversibility. The size of a pushdown automaton is the length of its representation.

Theorem 9 ([19]). *Let M be a deterministic pushdown automaton of size n. Then it is decidable in time $O(n^4)$ whether M is a REV-DPDA. Moreover, the decision problem is P-complete.*

Given a nondeterministic pushdown automaton, by inspecting the transition function one can decide whether or not it is a DPDA. If the answer is yes, then it can be decided whether it is a REV-DPDA by the previous theorem. If it is not a DPDA, then it cannot be a REV-DPDA. Therefore, the previous result transfers to nondeterministic devices.

Corollary 1. *Let M be a nondeterministic pushdown automaton of size n. Then it is decidable in time $O(n^4)$ whether M is a REV-DPDA. Moreover, the decision problem is P-complete.*

Next, the degree of reversibility is considered for pushdown automata. Compared with DFA the additional resource pushdown storage allows a more involved definition of lookaheads and, thus, degrees of reversibility. On the one hand, there is the possible lookahead on the input as for (k)-DFA. On the other hand, we consider a lookahead on the stack, that is, the machine can see the topmost l stack symbols.

Without going into the details of the definition, we say that a *deterministic pushdown automaton with lookaheads k and l ((k, l)-DPDA)* is a pushdown automaton having an input lookahead of size k and a lookahead of size l on the stack. A classical deterministic pushdown automaton is a DPDA with lookaheads $k = 1$ and $l = 1$.

In this connection we consider all configurations, not only reachable ones. As for DFA, a DPDA is said to be *reversible of degree* (k, l) (REV(k, l)-DPDA) if and only if there exists a reverse (k, l)-DPDA with transition function δ^- inducing a relation $\vdash^-$ from one configuration to the next, so that any configuration has a unique predecessor for all computations that lead to the configuration along the symbols seen in the input window and are consistent with the symbols at the top of the stack. Details of the definition can be found in [24].

Example 4. For any integer $k \geq 1$, the deterministic linear context-free language $\{\, a^n b a^m b a^n \mid n \geq 1, m \geq k \,\}$ is accepted by some REV$(k + 1, 1)$-DPDA.   □

The languages of Example 4 are used as witnesses for an infinite and tight hierarchy of languages acceptable by reversible pushdown automata of a degree that depends on the size of the input window only. Large stack windows do not help.

Theorem 10 ([24]). *For any integer $k \geq 1$, there are deterministic linear context-free languages accepted by REV$(k + 1, 1)$-DPDA that cannot be accepted by any REV(k, l)-DPDA, for an arbitrary $l \geq 1$.*

On the other hand, it turned out that the lookahead on the stack is interesting from a descriptional complexity point of view only. The question whether there are hierarchies with respect to the size of the stack lookahead has been answered negatively. In fact, any reversible pushdown automaton of degree $(k, l + 1)$ can be simulated by a reversible pushdown automaton of degree $(k, 1)$. So, in general, a lookahead on the stack does not help to obtain reversibility. We present the results obtained from two different simulation principles based on where the information of the topmost stack symbols is maintained. This could be in additional registers of the states or in the stack symbols. Both methods are constructive. From a practical point of view, states are somehow more active resources while stack symbols are more passive. So, it depends on the application which principle is more suitable.

Theorem 11 ([24]). *Let $k, l \geq 1$ be integers and M be a REV(k, l)-DPDA with m states and n stack symbols. Then an equivalent REV$(k, 1)$-DPDA with n stack symbols and at most $m \cdot \frac{n^{l+1}}{n-1}$ states can effectively be constructed.*

The second construction groups up to l stack symbols into one. However, the construction has to overcome the problem, that, when the original automaton pops a symbol, the simulating one has to access the symbol below the topmost.

Theorem 12 ([24]). *Let $k, l \geq 1$ be integers and M be a REV(k, l)-DPDA with m states and n stack symbols. Then an equivalent REV$(k, 1)$-DPDA with m states and at most $\frac{n^{l+1}}{n-1} \cdot (n^l + 1)$ stack symbols can effectively be constructed.*

So, as for DFA it turned out that lookaheads on the input gradually increase the capability to perform reversible computations. On the other hand, lookaheads on the stack do not. Now we take a look beyond the degrees. Are all realtime deterministic context-free languages captured by REV-DPDA? From above it is known that any finite language is accepted by some REV(1)-DFA and, thus, by a REV(1, 1)-DPDA. However, the necessity to provide arbitrary degrees to DFA to accept unary regular languages is not applicable for pushdown automata.

Proposition 4 ([24]). *Any unary (deterministic) context-free language is accepted by some REV(1, 1)-DPDA.*

Finally, by a similar idea of translation as for regular languages the next result is obtained.

Theorem 13 ([24]). *There are realtime deterministic context-free languages which cannot be accepted by any REV(k, l)-DPDA for any degree (k, l), $k, l \geq 1$.*

5   Time Symmetry

A further aspect of reversibility in real systems is discussed, for example, in [25]. In particular, physical reality reveals that often one can go back in time by applying the same transition function after a specific transformation of the phase-space. In [6] it is motivated that, for example, in Newtonian mechanics, relativity, or quantum mechanics one can go back in time by applying the same dynamics, provided that the sense of time direction is changed by a specific transformation of the phase-space. For Newtonian mechanics, the transformation leaves masses and positions unchanged but reverses the sign of the momenta. This aspect is called *time symmetry*. So, time-symmetric machines themselves cannot distinguish whether they run forward or backward in time. In this connection, computational models with discrete internal states, more precisely cellular automata, have been studied for the first time in [6].

Aspects of time-symmetry for reversible DFA and reversible DPDA have been considered in [23]. The "direction of time" is adjusted by a weak transformation of the phase-space, that is, an involution.

Let A, B, C be arbitrary sets, and $f : B \to C$, $g : A \to B$ two mappings. For their *composition* we write $f \circ g : A \to C$. A mapping $\tau : A \to A$ is said to be an *involution* if $\tau \circ \tau = \text{id}$, where id denotes the identity mapping. In general, we say that an automaton M is *time symmetric* if there exists an involution τ on the phase-space so that $\tau \circ \delta \circ \tau = \delta^{\leftarrow}$. So, given a configuration c, an application of the involution τ transforms it, then δ is used to compute a new configuration, which is again transformed by a second application of τ. The result is the predecessor configuration of c. Precise definitions naturally depend on the specific type of automaton considered.

First we turn to REV-DFA. A reversible DFA with state set S is *time symmetric* if and only if there is an involution $\tau : S \to S$ so that $\delta_x^{-1} = \tau \circ \delta_x \circ \tau$ holds for all input symbols x, where δ_x is the next-state function for input symbol x. Looking at two successive steps, we obtain $\delta_x^{-1} \circ \delta_y^{-1} = \tau \circ \delta_x \circ \tau \circ \tau \circ \delta_y \circ \tau = \tau \circ \delta_x \circ \delta_y \circ \tau$. Obviously, this generalizes to arbitrary numbers of steps. In some sense τ reverses the direction in time permanently (that is, until τ is applied again).

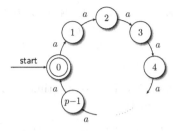

Fig. 9. Example of a unary reversible DFA accepting the language $\{\, a^{j \cdot p} \mid j \geq 0 \,\}$

Example 5. Consider the p-state DFA M depicted in Figure 9. It turns out that M *is* time symmetric. As witness involution one can take $\tau(i) = p - i - 1$ (see Figure 10 for $p = 8$). We have $\tau(\delta_a(\tau(i))) = \tau(\delta_a(p - i - 1)) = \tau(p - i) = i - 1 = \delta_a^{-1}(i) = \delta^{\leftarrow}(i, a)$, for all i (all arithmetic being done mod p). $\qquad\square$

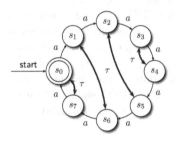

Fig. 10. Time symmetry of a reversible DFA accepting the language $\{\, a^{j \cdot 8} \mid j \geq 0 \,\}$

The natural question whether all reversible DFA are already time symmetric has been answered in the negative.

Theorem 14 ([23]). *There are reversible DFA which are not time symmetric.*

Figure 11 shows a witness for Theorem 14. Nevertheless, the relation between reversible and time-symmetric DFA is different from the relation between arbitrary and reversible DFA.

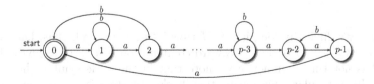

Fig. 11. Example of a reversible DFA that is not time symmetric

Theorem 15 ([23]). *Let $p \geq 1$ and M be a p-state reversible DFA. Then there exists an equivalent 2p-state time-symmetric DFA. This upper bound is tight, that is, for $p \geq 6$ there is a p-state reversible DFA so that every equivalent time-symmetric DFA has at least 2p states.*

While there are reversible DFA that are not time symmetric in general, every *unary* REV-DFA *is* time-symmetric.

Theorem 16 ([23]). *Each reversible unary DFA is time symmetric.*

The second type of devices we are going to discuss from the viewpoint of time symmetry are reversible pushdown automata. The handling of the additional resource makes the definition of time symmetry more involved. While the usual presentation of DPDA uses the transition function δ, in the present context it is advantageous to consider its induced *extended transition function* $\hat{\delta} : S \times (\Sigma \cup \{\lambda\}) \times \Gamma^* \rightarrow S \times \Gamma^*$, where Γ denotes the set of stack symbols, as follows. For any $p, q \in S$, $x \in \Sigma \cup \{\lambda\}$, $Z \in \Gamma$, and $\beta, \gamma \in \Gamma^*$ set $\hat{\delta}(q, x, Z\gamma) = (p, \beta\gamma)$ if and only if $\delta(q, x, Z) = (p, \beta)$.

While in Section 4 reversibility is considered for reachable configurations, here – to remain in context – we require reversibility for all configurations.

A reversible DPDA is *time symmetric* if and only if there is an involution $\tau : S \times \Gamma^* \rightarrow S \times \Gamma^*$ so that, $\hat{\delta}_x^{-1} = \tau \circ \hat{\delta}_x \circ \tau$ holds for all input symbols x.

For example, the linear context-free language $\{\, wcv \mid w \in \{a, b\}^*, w^R = vu \,\}$ is accepted by a time-symmetric DPDA showing that time-symmetric DPDA can accept non-regular languages. However, the next result contrasts the situation for DFA.

Theorem 17 ([23]). *There are reversible unary DPDA which are not time symmetric.*

The unary language $\{\, a^i \mid i \geq n \,\}$ is a witness for Theorem 17 (see Figure 12 for an example). Since it is regular, it is accepted by a REV-DPDA M. To this

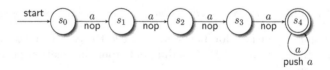

Fig. 12. A non-time-symmetric but reversible REV-DPDA that accepts $a^4 a^*$

end, on any sufficiently long input M runs into a cycle and, thus, has to push the history to get out of it in backward computations. In order to give evidence that M is not time symmetric we note that in the cycle symbols have to be pushed. In particular, this means that backward steps have to pop symbols. However, there are no states in the cycle that pop a symbol. So, there is no state to which a push state could be mapped by an involution witnessing the time symmetry.

As for DFA any reversible DPDA can be simulated by a time-symmetric DPDA with at most twice as many states.

Theorem 18 ([23]). *Let $p \geq 1$ and M be a p-state reversible DPDA. Then there exists an equivalent $2p$-state time-symmetric DPDA.*

Though it is well known that every unary context-free language is regular [9], the families of reversible and time-symmetric unary languages are different.

Theorem 19 ([23]). *(1) The family of languages accepted by time-symmetric (unary) DFA is properly included in the family of languages accepted by time-symmetric (unary) DPDA.*

(2) The family of languages accepted by reversible (unary) DFA is properly included in the family of languages accepted by reversible (unary) DPDA.

Finally, without going into further details, we just mention that the technique to put a reversible device and its inverse "side by side" also works for other types of reversible automata. However, whether the increase in size caused by doubling the number of states is always necessary is an interesting and almost untouched question.

References

1. Angluin, D.: Inference of reversible languages. J. ACM **29**, 741–765 (1982)
2. Axelsen, H.B.: Reversible Multi-head Finite Automata Characterize Reversible Logarithmic Space. In: Dediu, A.-H., Martín-Vide, C. (eds.) LATA 2012. LNCS, vol. 7183, pp. 95–105. Springer, Heidelberg (2012)
3. Axelsen, H.B., Glück, R.: A simple and efficient universal reversible turing machine. In: Dediu, A.-H., Inenaga, S., Martin-Vide, C. (eds.) LATA 2011. LNCS, vol. 6638, pp. 117–128. Springer, Heidelberg (2011)
4. Bennett, C.H.: Logical reversibility of computation. IBM J. Res. Dev. **17**, 525–532 (1973)
5. Bordihn, H., Holzer, M., Kutrib, M.: Determinization of finite automata accepting subregular languages. Theoret. Comput. Sci. **410**, 3209–3222 (2009)
6. Gajardo, A., Kari, J., Moreira, A.: On time-symmetry in cellular automata. J. Comput. System Sci. **78**, 1115–1126 (2012)
7. García, P., Vázquez de Parga, M., Cano, A., López, D.: On locally reversible languages. Theoret. Comput. Sci. **410**, 4961–4974 (2009)
8. Ginsburg, S., Greibach, S.A.: Deterministic context-free languages. Inform. Control **9**, 620–648 (1966)
9. Ginsburg, S., Rice, H.G.: Two families of languages related to ALGOL. J. ACM **9**, 350–371 (1962)
10. Ginzburg, A.: About some properties of definite, reverse-definite and related automata. IEEE Trans. Elect. Comput. **EC–15**, 806–810 (1966)
11. Harrison, M.A.: Introduction to Formal Language Theory. Addison-Wesley, Reading (1978)

12. Havel, I.M.: The theory of regular events II. Kybernetica **6**, 520–544 (1969)
13. Héam, P.C.: A lower bound for reversible automata. RAIRO Inform. Théor. **34**, 331–341 (2000)
14. Hopcroft, J.E., Ullman, J.D.: Introduction to Automata Theory, Languages, and Computation. AddisonWesley, Reading (1979)
15. Kari, J.: Reversible cellular automata. In: De Felice, C., Restivo, A. (eds.) DLT 2005. LNCS, vol. 3572, pp. 57–68. Springer, Heidelberg (2005)
16. Kobayashi, S., Yokomori, T.: Learning approximately regular languages with reversible languages. Theoret. Comput. Sci. **174**, 251–257 (1997)
17. Kutrib, M., Malcher, A.: Fast reversible language recognition using cellular automata. Inform. Comput. **206**, 1142–1151 (2008)
18. Kutrib, M., Malcher, A.: Real-time reversible iterative arrays. Theoret. Comput. Sci. **411**, 812–822 (2010)
19. Kutrib, M., Malcher, A.: Reversible pushdown automata. J. Comput. System Sci. **78**, 1814–1827 (2012)
20. Kutrib, M., Malcher, A.: One-Way reversible multi-head finite automata. In: Glück, R., Yokoyama, T. (eds.) RC 2012. LNCS, vol. 7581, pp. 14–28. Springer, Heidelberg (2013)
21. Kutrib, M., Malcher, A.: Real-time reversible one-way cellular automata. In: Cellular Automata and Discrete Complex Systems (AUTOMATA 2014) (to appear, 2014)
22. Kutrib, M., Malcher, A., Wendlandt, M.: Reversible Queue Automata. In: Non-Classical Models of Automata and Applications (NCMA 2014), vol. 304, pp. 163–178. Autralian Computer Society (2014)
23. Kutrib, M., Worsch, T.: Time-symmetric machines. In: Dueck, G.W., Miller, D.M. (eds.) RC 2013. LNCS, vol. 7948, pp. 168–181. Springer, Heidelberg (2013)
24. Kutrib, M., Worsch, T.: Degrees of Reversibility for DFA and DPDA. In: Yamashita, S., Minato, S. (eds.) RC 2014. LNCS, vol. 8507, pp. 40–53. Springer, Heidelberg (2014)
25. Lamb, J.S., Roberts, J.A.: Time-reversal symmetry in dynamical systems: A survey. Phys. D **112**, 1–39 (1998)
26. Landauer, R.: Irreversibility and heat generation in the computing process. IBM J. Res. Dev. **5**, 183–191 (1961)
27. Lange, K.J., McKenzie, P., Tapp, A.: Reversible space equals deterministic space. J. Comput. System Sci. **60**, 354–367 (2000)
28. McNaughton, R., Papert, S.: Counter-Free Automata. No. 65 in Research Monographs. MIT Press (1971)
29. Morita, K.: Reversible simulation of one-dimensional irreversible cellular automata. Theoret. Comput. Sci. **148**(1), 157–163 (1995)
30. Morita, K.: Reversible computing and cellular automata - a survey. Theoret. Comput. Sci. **395**, 101–131 (2008)
31. Morita, K.: Two-way reversible multi-head finite automata. Fund. Inform. **110**, 241–254 (2011)
32. Perles, M., Rabin, M.O., Shamir, E.: The theory of definite automata. IEEE Trans. Elect. Comput. **EC–12**, 233–243 (1963)
33. Pin, J.E.: On reversible automata. In: Simon, I. (ed.) Latin 1992. LNCS, vol. 583, pp. 401–416. Springer, Heidelberg (1992)

A Weakly Universal Cellular Automaton in the Pentagrid with Five States

Maurice Margenstern[(✉)]

Université de Lorraine, LITA, EA 3097 Campus du Saulcy,
57045 Metz, Cédex 1, France
margenstern@gmail.com

Abstract. In this paper, we construct a cellular automaton on the pentagrid which is planar, weakly universal and which have five states only. This result much improves the best result which was with nine states.

Keywords: Cellular automata · Universality · Tilings · Hyperbolic geometry

1 Introduction

In this paper, we construct a weakly universal cellular automaton on the pentagrid, see Theorem 2 at the end of the paper. Two papers, [1,7] already constructed such a cellular automaton, the first one with 22 states, the second one with 9 states. In this paper, the cellular automaton we construct has five states only. It uses the same principle of simulating a register machine through a railway circuit, but the implementation takes advantage of new ingredients introduced by the author in his quest to lower down the number of states, see [5]. The reader is referred to [3–5] for an introduction to hyperbolic geometry turned to the implementation of cellular automata in this context. A short introduction can also be found in [2]. However, it is not required to be an expert in hyperbolic geometry in order to read this paper.

Section 2 reminds the definition we take for weak universality. Section 3 is devoted to the proof of Theorem 2. In that section, Subsection 3.1 reminds the basic model used in the paper, Subsection 3.2 explains its implementation in the pentagrid, the tiling $\{5,4\}$ of the hyperbolic plane, Subsection 3.2 explains the scenario of the simulation performed by the automaton proving Theorem 2.

2 Universality and Weak Universality

Universality is a well know notion in computer science. However, the single word 'universality' is understood in different ways, sometimes somehow divergent.

Let us go back to the definition.

© Springer International Publishing Switzerland 2014
C.S. Calude et al. (Eds.): Gruska Festschrift, LNCS 8808, pp. 99–113, 2014.
DOI: 10.1007/978-3-319-13350-8_8

Definition 1. *Let $\mathcal{K}$ be a class of processes. Say that $\mathcal{K}$ **possesses a universal element** U if, a finite alphabet A being fixed once and for all, there is an encoding c of $\mathcal{K}$ elements into the words on A and of the data for a $\mathcal{K}$-element into the words on A such that for all element χ of $\mathcal{K}$ and for all data d of χ, U applied to $(c(\chi), c(d))$ ends its computation if and only if χ ends its own one when it is applied to d and, in that case, if $U(c(\chi), c(d)) = c(\chi(d))$.*

We also say that U **simulates** χ or that χ is **simulated** by U. If $\mathcal{K}$ possesses a universal element, we also say that $\mathcal{K}$ possesses the property of being universal. Note that we get again the standard definition of a universal Turing machine.

In the above definition, there are four elements. Data χ and d, the encoding of c and the universal element U. From the definition itself, the notion of encoding is an essential feature. Indeed, among the elements of $\mathcal{K}$, it is not difficult to construct some of them whose encoding is bigger than that of U. Indeed, it may be assumed that the encoding is an increasing function in this sense that if χ and ξ are elements of $\mathcal{K}$ transforming words on A onto words on A, then $c(\xi_{\circ}\chi) > c(\chi), c(\xi)$. Consequently, encoding the elements of $\mathcal{K}$ into a fixed alphabet is an essential feature. It allows U to simulate objects which are bigger than itself. Of course, changing the encoding may result in a change on the computation of U which may then be either faster or slower. At last, when U stops its computation, the result is an encoding of the result of the element of $\mathcal{K}$ simulated by U.

Now, since a few decades, these three items: the data, the encoding and the result are not always considered in the same way. From the definition, d is finite, as a word on A; when the computation of χ on d stops, that of U on $c(\chi)$ and $c(d)$ also stops. Now, whether this latter condition is observed or not, it happens that when U is applied to $c(\chi)$ and $c(d)$, it does not yield $c(d)$ when χ completes its computation on d, but something else, call it $e(d)$, where e can be considered as another encoding of d, e being also fixed once and for all. Indeed, $U(c(\chi), c(d)) = c(\chi(d))$ can also be rewritten $c^{-1}(U(c(\chi), c(d))) = \chi(d)$, so that $\chi(d)$ is restored by **decoding** $U(c(\chi), c(d))$. Introducing e consists in accepting that the decoding function can be independent from the encoding one.

Now, the conditions of finiteness on d and on the computation of U when that of χ on the considered data stops are not always observed. When all conditions of Definition 1. are observed we say that U is **strongly universal**. In this definition of strong universality, it is not required that the decoding be the inverse function of the encoding. However, it is required that e and c belong to comparable classes of complexity. Specifically, it is required that there is a primitive recursive function u such that for any d, $c(d), e(d) \leq u(|d|)$, where $|d|$ is the size of $c(d)$, i.e. the number of symbols in $c(d)$.

When the conditions of strong universality are not observed, we say that U is **weakly universal**. In case d is in some sense infinite, it is required that $c(d)$, which is an infinite word be of the form u^*wv^*, where u, v and w are words on A. The repeated words u and v are called the periodic patterns and it is not required that $u = v$. Note that during the computation, we may consider that each step t of U works on something of the form $u^*w_tv^*$. It is this situation that we shall consider, with this difference that we work in a $2D$-space and so, accordingly, we require a condition of periodicity restricted to the outside of a big enough disc, this condition being able to involve two different periodic patterns.

3   The Scenario of Our Simulation

Most of the cellular automata in hyperbolic spaces I constructed, myself or with a co-author, apply the same model of computation. We implement a railway circuit devised by Ian Stewart, see [8] which we rework in order to simulate a register machine. This general scenario is described in detail in [4,5]. Here, we simply give the guidelines in order to introduce the changes which are specific to this implementation.

3.1   Basic Features

The railway circuits consists of tracks, crossings and switches, and a single locomotive runs over the circuit. The tracks are pieces of straight line or arcs of a circle. In the hyperbolic context, we shall replace these features by assuming that the tracks travel either on **verticals** or **horizontals** and we shall make it clear a bit later what we call by these words. The crossing is an intersection of two tracks, and the locomotive which arrives at an intersection by following a track goes on by the track which naturally continues the track through which it arrived. Again, later we shall make it clear what this natural continuation is. Below, Figure 1 illustrates the switches and Figure 2 illustrates the use of the switches in order to implement a memory element which exactly contains one bit of information.

The three kinds of switches are the **fixed switch**, the **flip-flop** and the **memory switch**. In order to understand how the switches work, notice that in all cases, three tracks abut the same point, the **centre** of the switch. On one side switch, there is one track, say a, and on the other side, there are two tracks, call them b and c. When the locomotive arrives through a, we say that it is an **active** crossing of the switch. When it arrives either through b or c, we say that it is a **passive** crossing.

In the fixed switch, in an active passage, the locomotive is sent either always to b or always to c, we say that the **selected track** is always b or it is always c. In the passive crossing, the switch does nothing, the locomotive leaves the switch through a. In the flip-flop, passive crossings are prohibited: the circuit must be managed in such a way that a passive crossing never occurs at any flip-flop. During an active passage, the selected track is changed just after the passage of the locomotive: if it was b, c before the crossing, it becomes c, b respectively after it. In the memory switch, both active and passive crossing are allowed. The selected tracks also may change and the change is dictated by the following rule: after the first crossing, only in case it is active, the selected track is always defined as the track taken by the locomotive during its last passive crossing of the switch. The selected track at a given switch defines its **position**.

Fig. 1. The switches of the railway circuit. From left to right: the fixed switch, the flip-flop and the memory switch.

The current configuration of the circuit is the position of all the switches of the circuit. Note that it may be coded in a finite word, even if the circuit is infinite, as at each time, only finitely many switches have been visited by the locomotive.

Figure 2 illustrates how a flip-flop and a memory switch can be coupled in order to make a one bit memory element.

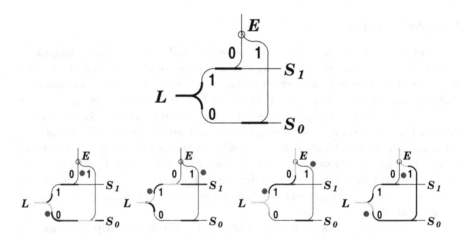

Fig. 2. The basic element of the circuit. Second row: Firs two drawings: reading the element. Last two drawings: writing the element.

3.2   In the Pentagrid

As mentionned in the introduction, the first weakly universal cellular automaton on the pentagrid was done by the author and a co-author, see [1]. The paper implements the solution sketchily mentioned in Subsection 3.1 with 22 states. In the next paper about a weakly universal cellular automaton on the pentagrid, see [7], the same model is implemented with 9 states. The difference with the former paper is that in the second paper, the cell which is at the centre of the switch has the same colour as another cell of the track. The centre of the switch is signalized by the neighbouring of the centre.

Former Implementations. Figure 4 illustrates the implementation of the crossing and of the switches performed in [7], showing in particular, the feature at which we just pointed. Figure 3 shows the implementation of the verticals, second row in the figure, and of the horizontal, first row. Both these figures show how to implement the basic element of Figure 2 in Subsection 3.1. Figure 5 show a global view of how the tree structure of the tiling can be used to implement a basic element in the pentagrid.

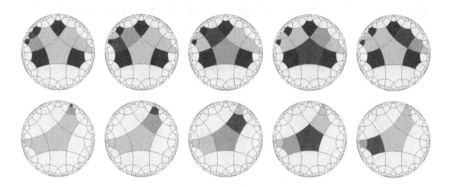

Fig. 3. Implementation of the tracks in the pentagrid. On the top, running a horizontal track from left to right. On the bottom, running a vertical track from top to bottom.

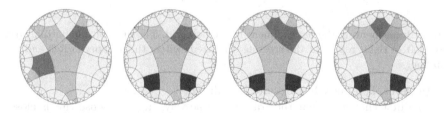

Fig. 4. Implementing the crossing and the switches in the pentagrid. From left to right; crossing, fixed switch, memory switch and flip-flop.

In this implementation, as well as in that of [1], the locomotive is implemented as two contiguous cell with different colours, which allows the implemented vehicle to find the direction of its motion along the tracks. The colours were chosen as green and red, green pointing at the front and red at the rear. The direction is then obvious. These are the elements which allowed us to prove the following result.

Theorem 1. (Margenstern, Song), *cf.*[7] − *There is a planar cellular automaton on the pentagrid with 9-states which is weakly universal and rotation invariant.*

By planar, we mean that the trajectory of the cells of the cellular automaton which at some point change their state is a planar structure which contains infinitely many cycles which cannot be reduced to a $1D$-structure. This is in particular the case of the units which constitute the registers of the register machine implemented by the railway circuit.

The New Scenario. In this paper, we take benefit of various improvements which I brought in the construction of weakly universal cellular automaton constructed in other contexts: in the heptagrid, another grid of the hyperbolic plane, in the hyperbolic 3D-space and in the tiling $\{13, 3\}$ of the hyperbolic plane, that latter automaton having two states only, see [5] for details.

Our implementation follows the same general simulation as the one described in Subsection 3.1. In particular, Figure 5 is still meaningful in this new setting.

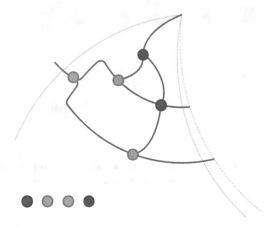

Fig. 5. Implementing the basic ellment in the petagrid. The discs on the bottom row, from left to right, represent the crossing, the fixed switch, the memory switch and the flip-flop.

However, here, new features are introduced.

The first change is that the tracks are one-way. In some sense this is closer to what we can see for railways in real life, in particular for highspeed ones. This change entails a big change in the switches and in the crossings. There is no change for the flip-flop which was already a one-way structure from the very beginning as passive crossings are ruled out for this kind of switches. For fixed switches it introduces a very small change: we keep the structure for a passive crossing and for the active one, as the selected track is the same, it is enough to continue the active way without branching at the centre of the switch, see Figure 6. In the same picture, we can see that the situation is different for the memory switch. This time, as there are two possible crossings of the switch and as the selected track may change, we have two one-way switches: an active one and a passive one. At first glance, the active switch looks like a flip-flop and the passive switch looks like a one-way fixed one. However, due to the working of the memory switch, we could say that the active memory switch is passive while the passive memory switch is active. Indeed, during an active crossing, the selected track is not changed contrary to what happens in the case of the flip-flop. Now, during a passive crossing, the switch looks at which track is crossed: the selected or the non-selected one. If it is the non-selected one, then the selection is changed and this change is also transferred to the active switch. Accordingly, there is a connection between the active and the passive one-way memory switches.

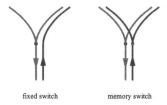

Fig. 6. The new switches for a one-way structured circuit: the fixed and the memory ones. Note that the flip-flop remains the same as in Figure 1.

Now, if we wish to significantly reduce the number of states, we also have to change the tracks themselves, as it appears that giving them the same colour as the background is better than assigning a special colour to identify the tracks. The consequence is that we have to place *milestones* in order to do so. This was performed in previous works, see [5]. But this is not enough: we also have to change the crossings. Contrary to what happens in the 3*D*-space where crossings can be replaced by bridges, which makes the situation significantly easier, crossings cannot be avoided in the plane.

In [5] we indicate a solution which allowed me to build a weakly universal cellular automaton in the hyperbolic plane with 2 states only. However, this was not performed in the pentagrid nor in the heptagrid, but in the tiling {13, 3}. This solution can be implemented here and this allowed me to reduce the number of states from 9 down to 5. There is a slight improvement in the present solution which might allow us to reduce the number of neighbours for a two-state weakly universal cellular automaton in the hyperbolic plane.

First, we look at a crossing of two one-way tracks. The main idea is that we organize the crossing in view of a **round-about**: an interference of road trafic in our railway circuit. We may notice that the locomotive arriving either from **A** or **B** in Figure 7 has to turn right at the second pattern it meets on its way. So that it is enough to devise a pattern which allows to count from 1 up to 2 in some way. In the two-states world of the weakly universal cellular automaton on {13, 3} described in [5], there were four patterns: a first one appears when the locomotive arrives at the round-about. At this point, a second locomotive is appended to the arriving one. At the second pattern, one locomotive is removed and so, as a single locomotive arrives through the round-about at the third pattern, then it knows that it has to turn right. Here, this scheme is slightly changed as follows. At the first pattern it meets the locomotive, which, arriving in a state S, is changed into T. At the second pattern, as a locomotive in the state T arrives, it is sent on the track which leaves the round-about. This is why three patterns are needed in Figure 7.

Figure 8 shows us how to assemble four one-way round-abouts in order to perform a true crossing for the intersection of two two-ways tracks.

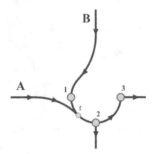

Fig. 7. The new crossing: the one-way tracks from **A** and **B** intersect. We have a three-quarters round-about. The small disc at **f** represents a fixed switch. Discs **1**, **2** and **3** represent the pattern which dispatches the motion of the locomotive on the appropriate way. Patterns **1** and **3** are needed as explained in the description of the scenario.

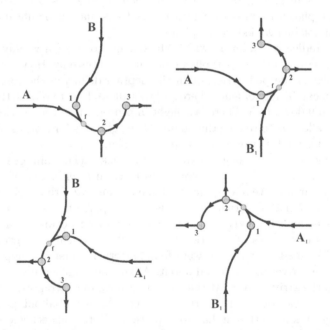

Fig. 8. The new crossing: four possible one-way track. Assembling them allows us to perform a two-way crossing. The notations are those of Figure 7. A_1, B_1 go opposite to **A**, **B**, respectively.

Now that we have seen the scenario to implement the circuit, we have to precisely look at how to implement it with five states only. We turn now to this question.

Implementing the New Scenario. As already announced, we need to use five states only. The first state is the quiescent state which we denote by W. Remember it is defined by the following rule: if a cell c and all its neighbours are in the state W, then at the next top of the clock, the cell c remains in the state W. We shall also call W the blank and we also shall say that a cell in W is white. The other states are B, G, R and Y. The cells in these states are said to be blue, green, red or yellow, respectively. The state B is mainly used for the milestones which delimit the tracks. The state G is the basic state of the locomotive. In crossings, the locomotive turns to R. The state Y is used for special markings in the passive memory switch. The states B, G and R are also used for marking in the crossings and in the other switches. The state G also appears in the milestones for the tracks.

Checking the new scenario requires to first study the implementation of the tracks. We have to define verticals and horizontals.

<u>Vertical and horizontal tracks</u>

The verticals are easy to define, they correspond to branches of the Fibonacci tree. In fact they are finite sequences of cells for which a side lies on a fixed line. The line can be changed inside the sequence as illustrated by Figure 9 for a green locomotive running on a top-down track.

Fig. 9. Top-down traversal of a vertical with a green locomotive

Fig. 10. The elements of the tracks. Leftmost picture: the standard element. Second and third pictures from left: the element which allows to perform sharp turns. Fourth and fifth pictures, illustration for a sharp turn.

The structure of an element of the track is simple. Assume that the locomotive leaves the cell through its side 1. Then, the milestones are always on sides 2 and 5. It enters either through sides 3 or 4. Both cases occur as illustrated in

Figure 9. Now, if we consider the standard numbering of the sides, then the place of the milestones depends on the direction of the motion. Assume that in the central cell, side 3 is the horizontal side. Then, for the cell 1(1), cell 1 of sector 1, the milestones are on the sides 3 and 5 in a bottom-up motion while they are on the sides 2 and 5 in the top-down one. The leftmost picture of Figure 10 illustrates the milestones as just defined.

The other pictures of Figure 10 illustrate two other patterns for the tracks. The second and third picture of the figure illustrates an element of the track which allows the locomotive, either green or red, to perform a sharp turn: this means that the locomotive enters through a side and exits through a contigous one. Such a turn is absolutely needed in the pentagrid in order to have cycles in the trajectory of the locomotive. If such a possibility would not be allowed, the locomotive would run to infinity without returning to any tile it had already visited.

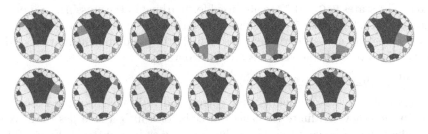

Fig. 11. A horizontal with a green locomotive, left-right run

The last two patterns of Figure 10 illustrate how to perform a sharp turn. A blue milestone is replaced by a green one. There are two possiblities and each of them is used for a direction of the motion. Rules are devised in such a way that the green milestone prevents a backward motion of the locomotive as can be checked on the pictures from the above descriptions.

It is the place to remark that as horizontal tracks run on three consecutive levels, a two-way portion of the tracks require at least seven consecutive levels as we need at least one level to separate the tracks run on each direction. A similar remark also holds for vertical lines. A two-way section must be separated by several nodes on the same level at the level where the distance between the supporting line is minimal: this distance must be positive, which guarantees that the lines are not secant. These constraints require much space for the implementation, but in the hyperbolic plane, we are never short of space.

Implementing the crossings

As indicated in Subsubsection 3.2, the tracks are organized according to what is depicted in Figures 7 and 8. From the latter figure, it is enough to focus on the implementation of Figure 7. From the implementation of the tracks, we only have to look at the implementatation of the patterns symbolically denoted as **1**, **2**, **3** and **f** in the figure. As **f** is a fixed switch whose implementation is indicated a bit further, we simply implement **1** as the other patterns are strict copies of this one. Figure 12 illustrates this implementation and the behaviour of the locomotive when it crosses the pattern. We can see that the difference strongly depends on the colour of the locomotive.

From Figure 7, the locomotive always arrives to the pattern from the same cell, namely 4(4). Then the locomotive goes to the centre, cell 0.

Fig. 12. The key pattern of the crossings. Notice the difference of behaviour depending on the colour of the locomotive.

When the locomotive is green, it goes to cell 1(1) arriving there as a red cell, and then it goes out onto the round-about towards the next pattern, still as a red locomotive. When the locomotive which arrives at cell 4(4) is red, it also goes to 0 but from there, it goes to 1(5) where it arrives as a green cell. Indeed, cell 1(5) remains white until it sees a red cell through its side 1. Note that side 1 is clearly indentified thanks to the pattern of the neighbours of cell 1(5). It is the pattern of an element of the tracks with a red milestone in place of the green one.

Implementation of a fixed switch

Figure 13 illustrates the passive crossing of a fixed switch for a green locomotive.

With one-way tracks, we need a single kind of passive fixed switch as there is no need of an active fixed switch, see Figure 6.

Fig. 13. The fixed switch: passive crossing by the green locomotive

Implementation of a flip-flop

With the flip-flop, we introduce the fifth state, Y. Figure 14 illustrates the configuration of a flip-flop and its active crossing by a locomotive.

Note that the change of the selected track occurs some time after the locomotive left the switch. The white cell at 2(2), it has three red neighbours, detects the passage of the locomotive just before the latter leaves the switch. Then, it passes the information to the cell 2(1) through 1(1). This makes 2(1) to flash, turning from Y to R and then turning back to Y. This flash makes both 1(1) and 1(5) to change their states in a way which triggers 2(2) and 2(5) to change their states. When the cell 2(2) is red, a symmetric process occurs.

Fig. 14. The flip-flop

Implementation of a memory switch

Now, we arrive to the most difficult situation. We have to implement two switches with a connection between them. As already noticed in Subsection 3.2, the active switch has a passive behaviour when crossed by the locomotive and the passive switch has an active behaviour when the locomotive takes the non-selected track. This action of the passive switch triggers the change of selection in the active switch: hence we have to organize the connection from the passive switch to the active one. The pattern of these switches, when the locomotive is not present, is illustrated by Figure 15.

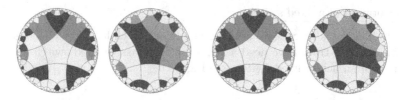

Fig. 15. The stable configuration of the active and passive memory switches. To left, the switches selected the right-hand side track. To right, they selected the left-hand side track.

Figure 16 illustrates the crossing of the active switch by the locomotive. Due to its way of working, the memory switch has two basic positions according to which is the selected track. We say that the left-, right-hand side switch selects the left-, right-hand side track respectively. We can check on the figure that the switch remains unchanged after the traversal of the locomotive.

We can see that the pattern of the active memory switch looks like that of the flip-flop. The difference is restricted to the cell 2(1) and its neighbours. In the flip-flop, the cell 2(1) is in Y and three consecutive neighbours are in B: cells 5, 6 and 7 of sector 1. In the active memory switch, the cell 2(1) is in B and the

Fig. 16. The active memory switch. The left-hand side switch.

cell $6(1)$ is white. Moreover, the cells $15(1)$ and $18(1)$ are in G. We shall see the role of these green cells in a while.

Before, we look at the crossing of the passive memory switch. We have four situations as the switch has two positions and as for each position, the locomotive may arrive either through the selected track or through the non-selected one.

Fig. 17. The passive memory switch. Here a left-hand side switch and a passive crossing through the non-selected track. Note that the selected track is changed in the right-hand side half of the figure.

As is clear on Figure 15, the pattern of the passive memory switch is very different from the active one. Although a part of it is taken from a fixed switch whose centre would be at the cell $2(3)$, the surrounding of this cell and the passive tracks is very specific.

Figure 17 illustrates the case when the locomotive crosses the non-selected track. We can see that this changes the selection according to the definition of the memory switch: the non-selected track becomes the new selected track.

Now, this information has to be transferred to the active memory switch. This is performed by the pattern of the passive memory switch. The crossing through the non-selected track is detected by the cell $1(5)$ which is in contact with the central cell. That latter one has a B-neighbour on the side of the selected track and a Y-one on the side of the non-selected track. When the locomotive becomes a neighbour of the central cell, it abuts the cell on the side of the Y-neighbour or of the B-one. This allows the central cell to know through which track the locomotive has run. Accordingly, if the run went through the non-selected one, the central cell flashes: it turns from B to R and then turns back to B. Now, this flash makes the cells $1(1)$ and $1(4)$ to take the opposite colour, from B to Y or from Y to B: this changes the signalization of the non-selected track. But the cell $1(5)$ also can see the flash of the central cell. This makes the cell $1(5)$ to also flash: it turns to G and then turns back to Y. Now, the cells $5(1)$ and $11(5)$ are milestones for the cell $4(5)$ which, accordingly, appears to be a possible element of a track. Consequently, the flash of $1(5)$ creates a second locomotive which can go along the track whose starting point is cell 4(5). It is enough to define a track going to the active memory switch to make the needed connection between the two parts of the memory switch.

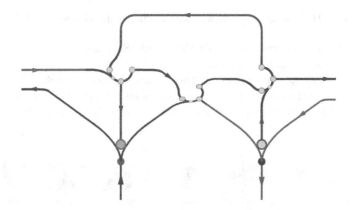

Fig. 18. The organisation of the memory switch

Figure 18 illustrates the global setting for implementing the memory switch with its tow parts, the passive and the active one and the connection between them. Now, the path whose starting point is the cell 4(5) in the passive switch, see Figure 15, goes to the active switch as indicated in Figure 18 and it arrives at the cell 6(1) of the active switch, see Figure 15.

Fig. 19. The change of selection in the active memory switch triggered by the arrival of the second locomotive at the cell 6(1). To left the case when the left-hand side track is selected, to right, when it is the case for the right-hand side track. The presence of the locomotive in 6(1) can be seen in the first picture of each series.

The cells 15(1) and 17(1) allow to make the second locomotive sent from the passive switch go to the cell 16(1) from where it is driven to the cell 6(1). Now, when the cell 2(1) can see the second locomotive, it flashes, turning to R and then back to B, which makes the cells 1(1) and 1(5) trigger the signal to the cells 2(2) and 2(5) which then take the opposite colour.

Figure 19 illustrates the situation when the second locomotive arriving at the cell 6(1) triggers the change of selection. As can be seen in the figure, the second locmotive vanishes just after it arrived at 6(1). This arrival makes the cell 2(1) flash and then the same mechanism as seen for the flip-flop apply: the situation for cells 2(2) and 2(5) is exactly the same.

And so, outside the locomotive which yields the simulation of the computation in this model, call it the **main locomotive**, from time to time a second locomotive appears for a while in order to transmit the appropriate signal to an active memory switch. It is important to notice that the motion of this second locomotive does not interfer with the motion of the main one. Indeed, although the track from a passive memory cell to its corresponding active one is very long, the distance between whole switches is much larger. In any case it can be made much larger: this can easily be seen on Figure 5. Also note that the second locomotive may sometimes be red. Indeed, as indicated by Figure 18, the second locomotive travels through two crossings.

With this study illustrated by the figures and the rules which can be found in [6], we completed the proof of the following result:

Theorem 2.   *There is a rotation invariant cellular automaton on the pentagrid with 5 states which is planar and weakly universal.*

References

1. Herrmann, F., Margenstern, M.: A universal cellular automaton in the hyperbolic plane. Theoretical Computer Science **296**, 327–364 (2003)
2. Margenstern, M.: Cellular Automata and Combinatoric Tilings in Hyperbolic Spaces, a survey. In: Calude, C., Dinneen, M.J., Vajnovszki, V. (eds.): DMTCS 2003. LNCS, vol. 2731, pp. 48–72. Springer, Heidelberg (2003)
3. Margenstern, M.: Cellular Automata in Hyperbolic Spaces. In: Adamatzky, A. (ed.) Theory, Collection: Advances in Unconventional Computing and Cellular Automata, vol. 1, p. 422. Old City Publishing, Philadelphia (2007)
4. Margenstern, M.: Cellular Automata in Hyperbolic Spaces. In: Adamatzky, A. (ed.) Implementation and computations. Collection: Advances in Unconventional Computing and Cellular Automata, vol. 2, p. 360. Old City Publishing, Philadelphia (2008)
5. Margenstern, M.: Small Universal Cellular Automata in Hyperbolic Spaces: A Collection of Jewels, Collection: Emergence, Complexity and Computation. In: Zelinka, I., Adamtzky, A., Chen, G. (eds.) p. 331. Springer (2013), doi:10.1007/978-3-642-36663-5
6. Margenstern, M.: A weakly universal cellular automaton in the pentagrid with five states, p. 23. arXiv:1403.2373
7. Margenstern, M., Song, Y.: A new universal cellular automaton on the pentagrid. Parallel Processing Letters **19**(2), 227–246 (2009). doi:10.1142/S0129626409000195
8. Stewart, I.: A Subway Named Turing, Mathematical Recreations in Scientific American, 90–92 (1994)

Minimum and non-Minimum Time Solutions to the Firing Squad Synchronization Problem

Margherita Napoli and Mimmo Parente[⊠]

Dipartimento di Informatica, Università di Salerno, Salerno, Italy
{napoli,parente}@unisa.it

Abstract. In this paper we present a survey on the minimum and non minimum time solutions to the Firing Squad Synchronization Problem. Particular emphasis is on the contribution given by Jozef Gruska, in honor of which this article is dedicated.

The problem consists in synchronizing a Cellular Automata (CA) whose cells work at discrete steps at unison. The first cell is initially in a particular state, called the *General*, and all the others are in a *Latent* state. The problem is solved when, all the cells enter for the first time and simultaneously a *Firing* state. In its original and basic formulation, the cells are arranged as a line, here we consider also other shapes like rings, rectangular grids and toruses. Also other variations of the problem are considered, such as the limited link capacitiesand different numbers and positions of the General state.

We consider both the minimum time needed to synchronize the CA and some algorithms synchronizing in particular times. Some open problems are also proposed.

Keywords: FSSP · Cellular Automata · Synchronous Computations · Channel Capacity

1 Introduction

Cellular Automata (CA) are perhaps the most intriguing and fascinating model of computation, and Quantum Cellular Automata, perhaps, the most important model of information processing by nature. It is therefore of great interest and large importance to study in depth many natural variants of the basic models of cellular automata and relations among them. CA have been investigated from many points of view and applied in fascinating ways in so many areas of science and technology. One of the first, and still fascinating, problems concerning cellular automata is the Firing Squad Synchronization Problem (FSSP). When and how one can make interaction of isolated and simply interconnected identical

---

Work partially supported by Italian FARB project grant cod. ORSA124598, 2012. The first author acknowledges also the Italian PRIN project grant 2010-2011 "Logical Methods of Information Management", cod. 2010FP79LR 001.

© Springer International Publishing Switzerland 2014
C.S. Calude et al. (Eds.): Gruska Festschrift, LNCS 8808, pp. 114–128, 2014.
DOI: 10.1007/978-3-319-13350-8_9

finite automata, to cooperate so effectively that they achieve almost impossible tasks, to completely synchronize their actions.[1]

The FSSP was originally proposed by John Myhill in 1957 and printed later in [Moo64]. Roughly speaking, its setting consists of a network of identical cells (finite automata) working synchronously at discrete time steps and connected linearly, see Fig. 1a. The cells are all in a quiescent state until the leftmost, stimulated by the external environment, enters a *General* state and issues a *Fire when ready* command and later all the cells (soldiers) enter simultaneously a *Fire* state.

In his seminal paper, Myhill said that at most four hours are needed to solve the FSSP, also by non computer science experts, as reported in [GK12]. However, though this may sound a little intimidating, we think that, as often happens in describing math problems, the simplicity of its formulation, and why not, also the elegance, can lead to this idea. What is certainly true is that the basic solution is quite simple to understand. The next natural step was to find the fastest solution and at the best of our knowledge, as reported by Umeo in [Ume96], Goto gave the first minimum time solution in a course note of Harvard University [Got62], and since then other minimum time solutions have been given, as we will see in in section 3.1.

In the original formulation of the problem, the cells are arranged as a line. We discuss time solutions also when cells are arranged in different shapes, such as ring-shaped or rectangular arrays, and spend few words on higher dimensional arrays. Besides the time, also the *size* of the finite automata is important, in fact processors with few states can function at higher clock rates and the solutions are faster in absolute time (see [GK12]). In section 3 we will discuss also on this aspect, and emphasize some open problems.

The importance of FSSP lies clearly also in the fact that synchronizing algorithms are useful when it is necessary to automatically start at the same moment various activities (e.g. different algorithms). This essentially motivated our studies reported in section 4, concerning the problem of synchronizing a network at given times.

Let us underline that this paper does not pretend to be a complete survey on the FSSP. Actually, in literature there is abundance of material and several beautiful survey papers have been written by Hiroshi Umeo.

The rest of the paper is organized as follows. In section 2 we give the basic definitions of the FSSP and of the different networks we consider. In section 3 we present the minimum time solutions. In the last section 4 we survey some algorithms that synchronize at particular times.

2   The Firing Squad Synchronization Problem

Cellular Automata. A cellular automaton (CA) consists of a regular *network* of *cells*, each in one of a finite number of *states* (Q denotes the set of such states).

---

[1] This paragraph is the incipit of the introduction written by Jozef in [GLP07], that we chose to quote in full here for the passion about the CA that it contains and still distils.

A *neighborhood* relation is defined, indicating the *neighbors* of each cell. All the cells have the same number N of neighbors, except a fixed number of *boundary cells* which have less neighbors. A boundary cell has less than N neighbors. A cell is intended to be linked to each of its neighbors through *communication channels*, and can send and receive, in each time step, binary sequences whose length is bounded by the capacity of the channels.

Time in the model is discrete. On each time step, every cell updates its state in accordance to a transition rule that takes as input the state of the cell itself and the sequences obtained from the cells in its neighborhood. The cells are then finite automata which operate synchronously, at discrete time unit. At each time t, a *configuration* specifies the state of each cell. A *computation step* modify the configuration, in accordance to the transition function and depending on both the current configuration and the sequences sent by the cells. An *initial configuration* is a configuration at time 1. Observe that in the classical definition of CA, the transition function takes as input the state of the cell itself and those of its neighbors at the previous step. Such classical definition is captured here when the capacity of the channels is $log|Q|$ and then each cell can send its whole state in a step.

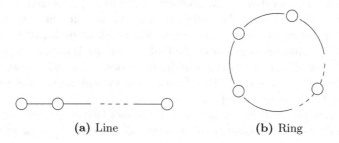

(a) Line   (b) Ring

Fig. 1. One dimensional networks

The FSSP Problem. We assume that among the states of the considered cellular automaton three are distinguished states: G, the *General* state, L, the *Latent* state, and F, the *Firing* state. The state L has the property that a cell in this state can send only 0 to its neighbors, and remains in the same state unless it receives a different from 0 sequence from one of its neighbors.

The initial configuration for the FSSP problem is such that a cell in a predetermined position in the network is in the state G, and is called GENERAL, and all the others cells, called LATENT, are in the state L (in some generalization of the problem, more then one GENERAL may occur in the initial configuration). The problem is to determine a description of a CA (state set and transition function), which does not depend on the number of cells, such that, starting from the initial configuration, at some future time, all the cells will simultaneously and, for the first time, enter the firing state F (*synchronization*).

We are interested in the time when the cells enter F, and we express it as a function of a parameter n of the size of the network. (e.g. for a LINE or a RING

n is its length, for a SQUARE it is the number of rows). A cellular automaton which provides a synchronization in time $t(n)$ is also called a *solution in time* $t(n)$ of the FSSP, or simply a *solution*.

Communication Networks. The original FSSP problem was defined over a linear sequence of cells. Later, a number of variations and generalizations of the problem have been introduced. We deal with FSSP defined over different *Communication Networks*: the network may have different shape, number of dimensions[2], and neighborhood relation, and the channels may vary for capacity and for direction of the information flow (either *two-way* or *one-way*).

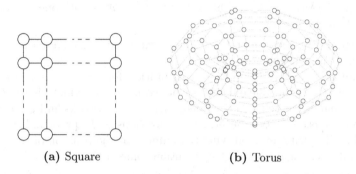

(a) Square   (b) Torus

Fig. 2. Two-dimensional networks

- One-dimensional networks:
  - LINE: a linear sequence of cells, with the first and the last cell being the boundary cells. Boundary cells have just one neighbor, the other cells have two neighbors. Channels are two-way, and connect every pair of adjacent cells. The capacity of the channels is $log|Q|$, that is, they have the ability to transmit a state of the CA, (see Figure 1a).
  - RING: a one-dimensional network with two-way communication channels with capacity $log|Q|$. The peculiarity is that there are no boundary cells, and all the adjacent cells are linked to each other, (see Figure 1b). Cells are numbered $1, \cdots, n$, as for a LINE, with the first cell arbitrarily chosen.
  - oneWay-RING: a RING in which the communication channels are *one-way*, that is, they are directed links from cell i to the cell $i + 1$, modulo n. Thus, at each step the i-th cell receives the information from the the cell $i - 1$, and sends the information to the cell $i + 1$.
  - 1-LINE and a 1-RING: similar to the LINE and to the RING, respectively, with communication channels having capacity 1. In this way, they have the ability to transmit just one bit in a time.
- Two-dimensional networks

---

[2] We use the term *dimension* here with the intended meaning to indicate the number of coordinates needed to locate a cell.

- SQUARE: a regular grid of $n \times n$ cells, numbered (i, j), for $1 \leq i, j \leq n$. Channels, with capacity $log|Q|$, are two-way, and connect every pair of adjacent cells, i.e. each cell (i, j), except for the boundary cells, is connected to cells $(i-1, j)$, $(i, j-1)$, $(i+1, j)$ and $(i, j+1)$ (a boundary cell may have two or three neighbors, depending on the values of i and j) (see Figure 2a).
- RECTANGLE: similar to the SQUARE, but with a grid of $m \times n$ cells.
- TORUS: Simplifying, it is obtained as a rotation of rings and can be seen as a two-dimensional regular grid of $n \times n$ cells, without boundary cells: as shown in Figure 2b, every cell has four neighbors.
- oneWay-TORUS: similar grid to the TORUS, with one-way channels from each cell (i, j) to the cells $(i, j+1)$ and $(i+1, j)$, modulo n.
- 1-SQUARE and 1-TORUS: SQUARE and TORUS with one-bit communication channels.

In a natural way, these definitions can be extended to communication networks with higher dimensions.

As already said, in the initial configuration for FSSP, a GENERAL is a cell in the state G. In the above described networks, the GENERAL is the first cell in the grid, that is the cell 1 in the one-dimensional networks and the cell $(1, 1)$ in the two-dimensional cases. Several generalizations of the problem have been considered in literature, by modifying the number or the position of the GENERALs in the initial configuration. Let us mention some of them.

- *Two-End FSSP*, also called *Two-End Synchronization*: the network is a LINE of n cells, and the synchronization starts from an initial configuration with a GENERAL at each end (i.e., at cells 1 and n).
- *Four-End FSSP*: the network is a SQUARE of $n \times n$ cells, and the synchronization starts from an initial configuration with GENERALs at the four corners (i.e., at cells $(1, 1)$, $(1, n)$, $(n, 1)$ and (n, n)).
- *Generalized FSSP* (GFSSP): the GENERAL is located on an arbitrary cell.
- *Multi-General FSSP* (MG-FSSP): in the initial configuration there is an arbitrary number of GENERALs, in arbitrary positions.
- *Asynchronous Multi-General FSSP* (A-MG-FSSP): a generalization of the MG-FSSP, in which the GENERALs start their work in an asynchronous way.

3   Minimum Time Solutions to the FSSP

In this section we present minimum time synchronization for several models of communication networks.

3.1   One-Dimensional Networks

Let us first consider one-dimensional models. We will discuss the optimum time for each variant of the problem and show that in almost all the considered cases, optimum time solutions exist.

Line. It is well known that any solution to FSSP over a LINE of n cells requires at least time $2n - 1$. Actually, the time required for the GENERAL to wake up all the LATENT cells is n, and other $n - 1$ steps need to get back the information that all the cells have been awakened.

First minimal solution to FSSP over a LINE, using a rather huge number of states (several thousands), was given in 1962 by Goto. Then, Waksman in [Wak66] showed a 16-state CA which is a well known algorithm, often considered to be the first minimum time solution to FSSP. In the same years, Balzer gave an 8-state solution, [Bal67]. Twenty years later Mazoyer constructed a 6-state minimum time solution which is the best known solution with respect to the number of states, [Maz87]. Optimum time solutions to the FSSP over a LINE have been analyzed and compared in [UHS05].

In the generalized version of FSSP problem (GFSSP) the GENERAL is located on any cell, that is an arbitrary cell may be in state G in the initial configuration. Moore and Langdon, in [ML68], showed a 17-state solution to GFSSP in time $n - 1 + max(p; n - p + 1)$, which is the minimum time required to synchronize the cells of a LINE where p is the number of cells between the GENERAL and the closest end of the LINE.

Other variations of the problem have been considered in literature, by modifying the number of the GENERALs in the initial configuration of the given CA. In the Multi-General FSSP problem (MG-FSSP), there are a number k of GENERAL cells, each being p_i cells far from the leftmost one, for $i \in [1, \cdots, k]$. In [SW04] a minimum time solution has been given in time $n + max(min_i(p_i); n - 1 - max_i(p_i))$. In the same paper, a more general case has also been considered in which the GENERALs start their work in an asynchronous way, each at a time t_i (A-MG-FSSP problem). In this case a lower bound has been provided but it has been proved that for each CA solving A-MG-FSSP, there are infinitely many instances for which the CA does not synchronize in the optimum time.

An interesting case is when two GENERALs occur in both the boundary cells, and the problem arising is known as Two-End synchronization of a LINE, [Cul89]. A Two-End synchronization of a LINE of n cells can be obtained in time n by considering the line as being split into two halves. Each of these half-lines can be seen as a LINE with one GENERAL, and is synchronized by a minimum time solution which starts from the boundary cells. In the case n is odd, the central cell belongs to both half-lines, and each half-line has $(n + 1)/2$ cells. Thus, all the cells fire simultaneously in time $2(n+1)/2 - 1 = n$. When n is even, the line is divided in two sub-lines of $n/2$ cells. Anyway, each of the two central cells can act as the last cell of its half-line only when it receives an input from the other half-line, thus the synchronization of each half-line needs a further unit of time, and then it works in time n also in this case.

Concerning cellular automata with the ability to transmit just one bit of information, Mazoyer, in [Maz96], showed that a minimum time solution exists even for a 1-LINE. Observe that in general 1-CA, i.e. CA using 1-bit channels, can simulate standard CA but this simulation causes a slow down of a factor $log|Q|$, where $|Q|$ is the number of states of the CA.

The Two-End synchronization outlined above does not work if one uses the solution to the case of 1-bit communication channel. The main reason is that the synchronization of 1-CA makes an important use of the information on the parity of the bits received by each cell. In [GLNP06, GLP07], the authors show that a unit time of delay is then necessary when the number of cells is even. This leads to a Two-End synchronization in time $2\lfloor n/2 \rfloor + 1$.

Ring and oneWay-Ring. A solution to the FSSP over a RING of n cells can simulate a Two-End synchronization of a LINE of $n + 1$ cells. Actually, the cell number 1 of the RING can act as both the boundary cells of the LINE. This idea is due to Culik, but he considered that an n cell RING could simulate a Two-End synchronization of an n cell LINE, thus obtaining an imprecise solution in time n, [Cul89].

We have already said that a Two-End synchronization of a LINE of $n + 1$ cells can be obtained in time $n + 1$, which is indeed the minimum time for an n cell RING. This is actually the time required for the GENERAL to wake all the cells up and receive the information back (see [GLP07] for a proof).

When the channels can communicate just one bit of information, the simulation of a Two-End synchronization of a LINE of $n + 1$ cells leads to a solution to 1-RING in time $2\lceil n/2 \rceil + 1$, [GLNP06, GLP07]. Hence, there is a gap between the lower and the upper bounds for the synchronization of a 1-RING with an odd number of cells.

The lower bound for the synchronization time, has been refined in [LNP96], in the case of oneWay-RINGs: it has been proved by contradiction that any solutions over a oneWay-RING requires at least time $2n$. Suppose that a solution in time less than $2n$ exists for FSSP over a oneWay-RING A with n cell, the same solution does not work correctly for a oneWay-RING B of $2n$ cell. One can see that the state entered by the n-th cell of A in any time $t < 2n$ may be the same as the state entered by the n-th cell of B at the same time. Hence, if the cells of A enter the FIRING state in a time $t < 2n$, then, when the algorithm runs on B, the n-th cell enters the FIRING state (the same state entered in A), while the last cell of B is still LATENT (it has not been awakened yet). Observe that in [Cul89], an imprecise solution in time $2n - 1$ was given.

It is easy to see that any synchronization of a LINE A of n processors in time $t(n)$ can be simulated on a oneWay-RING B in time $2t(n) - 1$. Actually, suppose that a cell i of A enters a state p in one step, in accordance to the transition function, and depending on the states q_L, q and q_R, of the cells $i - 1$, i and $i + 1$, respectively. By using two steps, the cell $i + 1$ of B can get both q_L and q from the cells $i - 1$ and i, and then can enter the state p. Thus, if A and B start from the same initial configuration at time 1 and A execute $t(n) - 1$ steps to reach a firing configuration, then, with the above simulation, all the cells of B fire after $2(t(n) - 1)$ steps, in time $2t(n) - 1$. The above idea can be exploited to get a solution to the FSSP for oneWay-RING in time $2n$. Consider a Two-End synchronization S of a LINE which takes time n. In the first step, a solution over the oneWay-RING lets also the second cell enters the state G. Now, the oneWay-RING can be seen as beginning from the second cell and ending to the first cell, thus having the same initial configuration as the LINE when S starts. With an algorithm implementing the above described simulation, the oneWay-RING is synchronized in time $2n$, see [LNP96].

The main results of the section are now summarized.

Theorem 1. *The following results hold:*

- *Every solution to FSSP over a* LINE *of n cells requires at least time $2n - 1$ and optimum time solutions to FSSP over a* LINE *and a* 1-LINE *exist;*
- *Every solution to FSSP over a* RING *of n cells requires at least time $n + 1$ and an optimum time solution exists;*
- *Every solution to FSSP over an oneWay-*RING *requires at least time $2n$, and an optimum time solution exists;*
- *Every solution to FSSP over* 1-RING *requires at least time $n + 1$ and there is a synchronization of a* 1-RING *in time $2\lceil n/2 \rceil + 1$.*

The table in Fig. 3 schematically summarizes the results of this subsection.

Model	Variation	Synchronization time	Reference	Minimum time?
LINE	–	$2n - 1$	[Wak66]	YES
LINE	Generalized	$n - 1 + max(p; n - p + 1)$	[ML68]	YES
LINE	k GENERALS	$n - 1 + max(min_i(p_i); n - max_i(p_i) + 1)$	[SW04]	YES
LINE	1-bit	$2n - 1$	[Maz96]	YES
LINE	Two-End	n	[Cul89]	YES
LINE	Two-End, 1-bit	$2\lfloor n/2 \rfloor + 1$	[GLNP06, GLP07]	for odd n
RING	–	$n + 1$	[Cul89]	YES
RING	1-bit	$2\lceil n/2 \rceil + 1$	[GLNP06, GLP07]	for even n
RING	$\geq$ 2-bit	$n + 1$	[GLNP06, GLP07]	YES
RING	oneWay	$2n$	[LNP96]	YES

Fig. 3. Solutions for one-dimensional Communication Networks

3.2 Two and Higher Dimensions

Square. Also in this case, a plethora of scenarios and algorithms have been given. The spark for the two-dimensional case with the general in a corner cell, was given by the results contained in the Ph.D. thesis of Wendel Terry Beyer, [Bey69] and of Ilka Shinahr, this latter then published in [Shi74]. For an $n \times n$ SQUARE, lower and upper bounds were given in time $2n - 1$. The solution in [Shi74] used 17 states, and still today there is an active research for this case. In [UK10] were used only 7 states adopting the so-called zebra mapping, and recently another algorithm has been presented in [UUN11], based on a new technique called one-sided recursive halving markings and using 37 states and 3271 rules, which is quite different from the well known classical algorithms of [Bey69, Shi74]. We omit here even the basic idea of classical algorithms, since it has been exposed several times in literature, see for example Wikipedia.

Rectangle. In the case of a RECTANGLE of $m \times n$ cells, $m \neq n$, in [Shi74] the author gave the lower bound for a solution in time $n + m + \max(m, n) - 2$ along with a matching time algorithm. For this case too there is an active research: in [UKT13] a new algorithm has been given which has some nice properties, like the easiness in the verification of its correctness and the fact that it can be extended to a solution for generalized FSSP, where the general is at an arbitrary position in the array (for this feature see also [UK12]). Another peculiarity is that it is isotropic with respect to the shape of a given rectangle array, that is there is no need to control the FSSP algorithm for longer-than-wide and wider-than-long input rectangles.

1-*Square.* In the case the communication channel is restricted to just 1-bit a trivial lower bound on the minimum firing time of a square $n \times n$ is clearly $2n - 1$. For this model, in [GLP04, GLP07], a tight upper bound of time $2n - 1$ has been shown, for the first time in this case.

As regards Four-End FSSP, where there are GENERALs positioned in the four corners of an $n \times n$ SQUARE, some synchronization algorithms have been given. When the channels have the capacity to transmit a state, it is in time n, while for the 1 bit case, it is in time $2\lfloor n/2 \rfloor + 1$, in a similar way as for Two-End synchronization of a LINE.

It should be noted that many of the optimum time solutions proposed for the two-dimensional case, are derived from well-known solutions for the one-dimensional case, for example those in [UK12, GLP07], embed the synchronization algorithms given by Mazoyer, the former resembles the one of [Maz87] using only 6-states, and the latter, given for 1-bit communication channels, combines that in [Maz96] and the classical of [Shi74].

Torus. As in the one-dimensional case for the RINGs, the minimum time to synchronize is at least the time necessary by the GENERAL to send and hence receive back a message to/from all the other cells. In [GLP07] it has been shown that in the case of a TORUS (sometime called also Square of Rings) this time is $n+ 1$. It is not trivial at all to establish that, in the case of one-way communication, this time rises to $3n - 1$, as shown in [LNP96], along with matching upper bound algorithms. This lower bound is shown by contradiction, in a similar way as for the lower bound of the synchronization time of a RING.

In the case of a 1-bit channel, by extensively using the result for Four-End FSSP, in [GLNP06, GLP07], an almost optimum upper bound is given in time $2\lceil n/2 \rceil + 1$. Let us underline that the restriction on the channel capacity is to be meant strictly and not as a shorthand for a big-O notation of some constant. In fact, it is worth noting that in the case of a channel with capacity strictly greater than 1-bit, in this same paper Gruska et al. showed an algorithm synchronizing in time $n + 1$, thus optimum in time. The idea exploited there was to use the second bit to recognize the type of messages, a thing that in the case of 1-bit channel was done exploiting the arrival time delay of the messages, thus not allowing to get the tightness of the bound.

Still for 1-bit communication channel, in [UMK03] some nice non optimum-time algorithms for synchronize any $n \times n$ SQUARE and $m \times n$ RECTANGLE in $2n$ and $m + n + max(m, n) + 1$ steps, have been given, respectively. The time complexities for these two algorithms are one step larger than the optimum ones.

Array of Dimension Greater than 2. In [UNK12] lower and upper bounds on optimum synchronization time for arrays of dimension $k > 2$ have been given. In particular it has been shown that, in case of one GENERAL in a corner of an array of size $n_1 \times n_2 \times \ldots \times n_k$, the minimum time is $\sum_{i=1}^{k} n_i + \max(n_1, n_2, \ldots, n_k) - k$ steps. In the same paper, this result has been generalized also for a GENERAL in any position.

We can now summarize the main results of this subsection.

Theorem 2. *The following results hold:*

- *Every synchronization of a* SQUARE *of* $n \times n$ *cells requires at least time* $2n - 1$, *and an optimum time solution exists over a* SQUARE *and a* 1-SQUARE;
- *Every synchronization of a* TORUS *of* $n \times n$ *cells requires at least time* $n + 1$, *and an optimum time solution exists;*
- *Every synchronization of a oneWay-*TORUS *of* $n \times n$ *cells requires at least time* $3n - 1$, *and an optimum time solution exists;*
- *Every synchronization of a* 1-TORUS *of* $n \times n$ *cells requires time at least time* $n + 1$ *and a solution exists in time* $2\lceil n/2 \rceil + 1$.

The table in Fig. 4 schematically summarizes the results cited in this subsection.

Model	Variation	Synchronization time	Reference	Minimum time?
RECTANGLE	–	$n + m + \max(m, n) - 2$	[Shi74]	YES
SQUARE	–	2n-1	[Bey69, Shi74]	YES
SQUARE	1-bit	$2n - 1$	[GLP04, GLP07]	YES
SQUARE	Four-End, 1-bit	$2\lfloor n/2 \rfloor + 1$	[GLNP06, GLP07]	for odd n
TORUS	–	$n + 1$	[GLNP06, GLP07]	YES
TORUS	1-bit	$2\lceil n/2 \rceil + 1$	[GLNP06, GLP07]	for even n
TORUS	2-bit	$n + 1$	[GLNP06, GLP07]	YES
TORUS	one-way	$3n - 1$	[LNP96]	YES

Fig. 4. Solutions for two-dimensional Communication Networks

A particular mention deserves the, somewhat orthogonal, work on the FSSP of Kojiro Kobayashi started, at the best of our knowledge, in 1977 with the paper [Kob77] till the beautiful recent one [GK12]. The trait of Kobayashi's studies is easily recognized as his research has been almost always focused on non regular shapes of the network cells and the FSSP has been related to a combinatorial problem for which only exponential algorithms are known. For example in [Kob01] the cells of the network are placed along a path of two-dimensional array space, and along with Goldstein, in [GK05, GK12], it has been shown that if a minimum-time solution exists, (for example for the path problem mentioned above), then there must exist polynomial time algorithms for solving the diameter problem in the standard RAM model of computation, this implying that P = NP.

The FSSP has been also studied in a setting where the processors do not share a global clock, though working in synchrony, and can be faulty [CDDS89]. In this paper upper and lower bounds are shown on the number of faulty processors that can be tolerate and still reach a solution. Recently this fault tolerant scenario has been resumed in [DHM12] and enriched by the first self-stabilizing firing squad algorithm, allowing thus recovery from arbitrary transient errors. This algorithm is optimum with regards to two aspects: if the algorithm is in a safe state, it reaches the consensus as fast as any other algorithm does once a cell receives a start signal, and the second is that starting from an arbitrary state, it converges to a safe state as fast as any other algorithm does.

Finally let us also mention a series of interesting papers related to the FSSP which have been very recently published by Arnold L. Rosenberg, see for example [Ros14, Ros13], that model robots with teams of cellular automata whose aim is to identify and search within squares of $n \times n$ mesh of tiles.

3.3   Open Problems

One of the best known open problem in this area regards the minimum number of states necessary to synchronize a LINE. Clearly, any CA solving FSSP has at least three states (G, L and F). Sanders, in [San94], showed that no 4-state CA can solve FSSP. Since the known solution with the least number of states is the one due to Mazoyer, with 6 states, it is unknown whether the minimum number of states is indeed 6 or there is a CA beating Mazoyer's solution.

All the solutions in Theorem 1 and in Theorem 2 are optimum in time, and thus the lower bounds are tight, except for a gap between the lower and the upper bounds for synchronization of both a 1-RING and a 1-TORUS with an odd number of cells. In these cases, the best known synchronization algorithms require time $n + 2$, whilst the known lower bound is $n + 1$. In [GLNP06, GLP07], solutions in time $n + 1$ have been shown for a RING and for a TORUS with 2-bit communication channels, thus showing the tightness of the given lower bound in the case of $O(1)$-bit channels. It is still an open problem to state whether such an optimum time solution exists for 1-RING, or the given lower bound can be made tighter.

Finally, another interesting matter regards the synchronization of CA over a RING and over a TORUS with both the restrictions: one-way and 1-bit communication channels. Clearly, no solution can consume less than $2n$ time, for a 1-bit oneWay-RING and less than $3n - 1$ time, for a 1-bit oneWay-TORUS. Anyway we do not know whether such solutions. The idea of the algorithms given for oneWay-RING and oneWay-TORUS does not work in the same time when 1-bit communication channels are used, since the number of steps necessary for a cell to send its state is greater than one in this case.

4   Synchronization Algorithms in Particular Time

In this section we will survey some of the main results known in literature to get *non minimum time* synchronization problems. More precisely, particular times in which, and also particular ways to, synchronize cellular automata ([LNP98, LNP00, GLNP06]).

The general pattern to get a synchronization in a particular given (not minimum) time, is the following simple idea: given a communication network A of parameter n, a signal[3] is generated from the General cell and comes back to it in time $(t(n) - min(n))$ where $min(n)$ is the minimum time for a CA to solve the FSSP over A, and $t(n) \geq n$. Then a minimum time solution starts, synchronizing thus A in time $t(n)$. For example, in the case A is an n-cell LINE or an $n \times n$ SQUARE, then $min(n) = 2n - 1$. However, despite its simplicity, sometimes the implementation of this idea is far from trivial, since it implies different compositions of different signals and synchronization algorithms. All the results have been obtained for the most general case, the 1-bit communication channel thus they hold *sic et simpliciter* for all types of channel capacities.

Theorem 3. *Synchronization algorithms in time n^2, 2^n, $n\lceil \log n \rceil$, and $n\lceil \sqrt{n} \rceil$ exist, for a 1-LINE, 1-SQUARE, 1-RING, and a 1-TORUS.*

Moreover other results have been given in the case of one-way communication.

Theorem 4. *Synchronization algorithms in time n^2, 2^n, and $n\lceil \log n \rceil$ exist, for a 1-oneWay-RINGand 1-oneWay-TORUS.*

To obtain other particular synchronization times, some signal and synchronization compositional operations have been introduced: *parallel, sequential* and *iterated*. Also sufficient conditions when these operations may be applied have been provided.

It is easy to implement the standard cross product of automata between two CA's A_1, A_2, using a greater channel capacity: the communication channels are kept distinct and therefore $A_1 \times A_2$ can run in parallel the synchronization algorithms. On top of this a CA that *selects* between two distinct synchronization algorithms, according to a given condition $P(n)$, has also been given. Examples of $P(n)$ are the parity of n or the fastest/slowest synchronization times. In particular this last feature can be realized as follows: given two CA's synchronizing in time $t_1(n)$ and $t_2(n)$, respectively, another CA is obtained as the cross product of the two and of a third one that *selects* according to the result of the test $t_1(n) \leq t_2(n)$.

Theorem 5. *Let A and B be solutions to FSSP with channel capacity a and b, respectively. It is possible to design a CA with channel capacity $a + b + c$, for some integer c, synchronizing in the minimum (maximum) times of A and B.*

Other particular times have been obtained, such as the sum and the product, holding for all the 1-bit models considered so far. In particular, the technique to obtain the product is interesting. It extends the cross product to let a solution in time $t_1(n)$ to be iterated $t_2(n)$ times, without using extra capacity of the channels.

---

[3] The concept of signal is often used in literature as a way to facilitate the description of a CA. Informally speaking, a signal can be seen in the space-time unrolling of the CA as a set of cells that, at a given time, receive/send words, different from all-zero words, from/to adjacent cells.

Theorem 6. *Given two solutions to the FSSP in time $t_1(n)$ and $t_2(n)$, and an integer $d \geq 0$, solutions in time $t_1(n) + t_2(n) + d$, and $t_1(n) \cdot t_2(n)$ exist.*

The next result provides solutions for a 1-SQUARE and for a 1-RECTANGLE, starting from that for a 1-LINE. Actually, in an $(n \times m)$-cell RECTANGLE, several LINEs of $n + m - 1$ cells can be individuated, starting from cell $(1, 1)$ and ending to cell (n, m) (for example, the cells in the first row and in the last column form one of such LINEs). Analogously, $(2n - 1)$-cell LINEs can be individuated in an $n \times n$ SQUARE. All such LINEs can be synchronized in parallel, using the same algorithm.

Theorem 7. *If there is a synchronization of a 1-LINE in time $t(n)$, then a synchronization on a 1-SQUARE in time $t(2n - 1)$ and a synchronization on a 1-RECTANGLE in time $t(n + m - 1)$ exist.*

From this last result and Theorem 3, the next theorems follow.

Theorem 8. *Synchronizations on a $n \times n$ 1-SQUARE in time $K^2, 2^K, K \cdot \lceil \log K \rceil$ and $K \cdot \lceil \sqrt{K} \rceil$, for $K = 2n - 1$, exist.*

Theorem 9. *Synchronizations on a $n \times m$ 1-RECTANGLE in time $J^2, 2^J, J \cdot \lceil \log J \rceil$ and $J \cdot \lceil \sqrt{J} \rceil$, for $J = n + m - 1$, exist.*

Finally let us also mention that synchronizing algorithms for all the models we have dealt with in this paper, exist in any time that can be expressed as a polynomial of n, formally stated in the following theorem.

Theorem 10. *Let $h \geq 2$ and $a_0, \ldots, a_h$ be integers with $a_h \geq 1$. A synchronization in time $a_h n^h + a_{h-1} n^{h-1} + \ldots + a_1 n + a_0$ exists on an n-cell 1-LINE, 1-RING, 1-oneWay-RING, and on an $(n \times n)$-cell 1-SQUARE, 1-TORUS, 1-oneWay-TORUS.*

References

[Bal67] Balzer, R.: An 8-state minimal time solution to the firing squad synchronization problem. Information and Control **10**(1), 22–42 (1967)

[Bey69] Beyer, W.T.: Recognition of topological invariants by iterative arrays. PhD thesis, Massahcusetts Institute of Technology (1969)

[CDDS89] Coan, B.A., Dolev, D., Dwork, C., Stockmeyer, L.J.: The distributed firing squad problem. SIAM J. Comput. **18**(5), 990–1012 (1989)

[Cul89] Karel Culik, I.I.: Variations of the firing squad problem and applications. Inf. Process. Lett. **30**(3), 153–157 (1989)

[DHM12] Dolev, D., Hoch, E.N., Moses, Y.: An optimal self-stabilizing firing squad. SIAM J. Comput. **41**(2), 415–435 (2012)

[GK05] Goldstein, D., Kobayashi, K.: On the complexity of network synchronization. SIAM J. Comput. **35**(3), 567–589 (2005)

[GK12] Goldstein, D., Kobayashi, K.: On minimal-time solutions of firing squad synchronization problems for networks. SIAM J. Comput. **41**(3), 618–669 (2012)

[GLNP06] Gruska, J., La Torre, S., Napoli, M., Parente, M.: Different time solutions for the firing squad synchronization problem on basic grid networks. RAIRO - Theoretical Informatics and Applications, ITA **40**(2), 177–206 (2006)

[GLP04] Gruska, J., La Torre, S., Parente, M.: Optimal time and communication solutions of firing squad synchronization problems on square arrays, toruses and rings. In: Calude, C.S., Calude, E., Dinneen, M.J. (eds.) DLT 2004. LNCS, vol. 3340, pp. 200–211. Springer, Heidelberg (2004)

[GLP07] Gruska, J., La Torre, S., Parente, M.: The firing squad synchronization problem on squares, toruses and rings. Int. J. Found. Comput. Sci. **18**(3), 637–654 (2007)

[Got62] Goto, E.: A minimum time solution of the firing squad problem. In: Course Notes for Applied Mathematics 298, Harvard University, pp. 52–59 (1962)

[Kob77] Kobayashi, K.: The firing squad synchronization problem for two-dimensional arrays. Information and Control **34**(3), 177–197 (1977)

[Kob01] Kobayashi, K.: On time optimal solutions of the firing squad synchronization problem for two-dimensional paths. Theor. Comput. Sci. **259**(1–2), 129–143 (2001)

[LNP96] La Torre, S., Napoli, M., Parente, M.: Synchronization of one-way connected processors. Complex Systems **10**(4), 239–256 (1996)

[LNP98] La Torre, S., Napoli, M., Parente, D.: Synchronization of a line of identical processors at a given time. Fundam. Inform. **34**(1–2), 103–128 (1998)

[LNP00] La Torre, S., Napoli, M., Parente, M.: A compositional approach to synchronize two dimensional networks of processors. Theoretical Informatics and applications, ITA **34**(6), 549–564 (2000)

[Maz87] Mazoyer, J.: A six-state minimal time solution to the firing squad synchronization problem. Theor. Comput. Sci. **50**, 183–238 (1987)

[Maz96] Mazoyer, J.: On optimal solutions to the firing squad synchronization problem. Theor. Comput. Sci. **168**(2), 367–404 (1996)

[ML68] Moore, F.R., Langdon, G.G.: A generalized firing squad problem. Information and Control **12**(3), 212–220 (1968)

[Moo64] Moore, E.F. (ed.): Sequential Machines: Selected Papers. Addison-Wesley Longman Ltd., Essex, UK, UK (1964)

[Ros13] Rosenberg, A.L.: Finite-state robots in a warehouse: Achieving linear parallel speedup while rearranging objects. In: Parallel Processing (ICPP), 2013 42nd International Conference on, pp. 379–388. IEEE (2013)

[Ros14] Rosenberg, A.L.: Region management by finite-state robots. The Computer Journal **57**(1), 59–72 (2014)

[San94] Sanders, P.: Massively parallel search for transition-tables of polyautomata. In: Parcella, pp. 99–108 (1994)

[Shi74] Shinahr, I.: Two- and three-dimensional firing-squad synchronization problems. Information and Control **24**(2), 163–180 (1974)

[SW04] Schmid, H., Worsch, T.: The firing squad synchronization problem with many generals for one-dimensional ca. In: Exploring New Frontiers of Theor. Inf., IFIP (TCS2004), pp. 111–124. Kluwer (2004)

[UHS05] Umeo, H., Hisaoka, M., Sogabe, T.: A survey on optimum-time firing squad synchronization algorithms for one-dimensional cellular automata. International Journal of Unconventional Computing **1**(4), 403–426 (2005)

[UK10] Umeo, H., Kubo, K.: A seven-state time-optimum square synchronizer. In: Bandini, S., Manzoni, S., Umeo, H., Vizzari, G. (eds.) ACRI 2010. LNCS, vol. 6350, pp. 219–230. Springer, Heidelberg (2010)

[UK12] Umeo, H., Kubo, K.: Recent developments in constructing square synchronizers. In: Sirakoulis, G.C., Bandini, S. (eds.) ACRI 2012. LNCS, vol. 7495, pp. 171–183. Springer, Heidelberg (2012)

[UKT13] Umeo, H., Kubo, K., Takahashi, Y.: An isotropic optimum-time fssp algorithm for two-dimensional cellular automata. In: Malyshkin, V. (ed.) PaCT 2013. LNCS, vol. 7979, pp. 381–393. Springer, Heidelberg (2013)

[Ume96] Umeo, H.: A note on firing squad synchronization algorithms. In: Worsch, T., Kutrib, M., (ed.), IFIP Cellular Automata Workshop 96, pp. 65 (1996)

[UMK03] Umeo, H., Michisaka, K., Kamikawa, N.: A synchronization problem on 1-bit communication cellular automata. In: Sloot, P.M.A., Abramson, D., Bogdanov, A.V., Gorbachev, Y.E., Dongarra, J., Zomaya, A.Y. (eds.) ICCS 2003, Part I. LNCS, vol. 2657, pp. 492–500. Springer, Heidelberg (2003)

[UNK12] Umeo, H., Nishide, K., Kubo, K.: A simple optimum-time fssp algorithm for multi-dimensional cellular automata. In: 18th international workshop on Cellular Automata and Discrete Complex Systems and 3rd international symposium Journées Automates Cellulaires, AUTOMATA & JAC, volume 90 of EPTCS, pp. 151–165 (2012)

[UUN11] Umeo, H., Uchino, H., Nomura, A.: How to synchronize square arrays in optimum-time - a new square synchronization algorithm. In: International Conference on High Performance Computing & Simulation, HPCS, pp. 801–807. IEEE (2011)

[Wak66] Waksman, A.: An optimum solution to the firing squad synchronization problem. Information and Control 9(1), 66–78 (1966)

Time-Optimum Smaller-State Synchronizers for Cellular Automata

Hiroshi Umeo[✉]

University of Osaka Electro-Communication, Neyagawa-shi, Hastu-cho,
18-8, Osaka 572-8530, Japan
umeo@cyt.osakac.ac.jp

Abstract. Synchronization of large-scale networks is an important and
fundamental computing primitive in parallel and distributed systems.
The synchronization in cellular automata, known as the firing squad
synchronization problem (FSSP), has been studied extensively for more
than fifty years, and a rich variety of synchronization algorithms has been
proposed not only for one-dimensional but also for two-dimensional, even
multi-dimensional cellular arrays. In the present paper, we construct an
overview of the study of the FSSP algorithms developed so far, focusing
on time-optimum smaller-state solutions to the FSSP.

1 Introduction

Synchronization of large-scale networks is an important and fundamental computing primitive in parallel and distributed systems. The synchronization in ultra
fine-grained parallel computational model of cellular automata has been known
as the firing squad synchronization problem (FSSP) since its development, in
which it was originally proposed by J. Myhill in the book edited by Moore [1964]
to synchronize all/some parts of self-reproducing cellular automata. We study
the FSSP solution that gives a finite-state protocol for synchronizing cellular
automata. The problem has been studied extensively for more than fifty years,
and a rich variety of synchronization algorithms has been proposed not only for
one-dimensional (1D) but also for two-dimensional (2D), even multi-dimensional
cellular arrays.

In the present paper, we construct an overview of the study of FSSP algorithms developed so far, focusing on smaller-state optimum-time solutions to the
FSSP. In Section 2 we give a description of the 1D FSSP and review some basic
results on 1D FSSP algorithms. Section 3 presents two smallest solutions, known
at present in the number of states of the automata realizing optimum-time protocols for 2D square and rectangle arrays. In Section 4 we introduce a simple
synchronizing schema based on recursive halving marking for multi-dimensional
arrays. It is shown that the schema is a natural extension of a family of the
classical well-known optimum-time FSSP algorithms developed by Waksmann
[1966], Balzer [1967], and Gerken [1987].

© Springer International Publishing Switzerland 2014
C.S. Calude et al. (Eds.): Gruska Festschrift, LNCS 8808, pp. 129–145, 2014.
DOI: 10.1007/978-3-319-13350-8_10

2   FSSP on One-Dimensional Arrays

2.1   Definition of the FSSP

The firing squad synchronization problem (FSSP) is formalized in terms of a model of cellular automata. Figure 1 shows a finite one-dimensional (1D) cellular array consisting of n cells, denoted by C_i, where $1 \leq i \leq n$. All cells (except the end cells) are identical finite state automata. The array operates in lock-step mode such that the next state of each cell (except the end cells) is determined by both its own present state and the present states of its right and left neighbors. All cells (*soldiers*), except the left end cell, are initially in the *quiescent* state at time $t = 0$. The quiescent state has a property whereby the next state of a quiescent cell having quiescent neighbors is the quiescent state. At time $t = 0$ the left end cell (*general*) is in the *fire-when-ready* state, which is an initiation signal to the array for the synchronization.

The firing squad synchronization problem is stated as follows. Given an array of n identical cellular automata, including a *general* on the left end which is activated at time $t = 0$, we want to give the description (state set and next-state function) of the automata so that, *at some future time*, all of the cells will *simultaneously* and, *for the first time*, enter a special *firing* state. The set of states must be independent of n. Without loss of generality, we assume $n \geq 2$. The tricky part of the problem is that the same kind of soldier having a fixed number of states must be synchronized, regardless of the length n of the array.

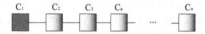

Fig. 1. One-dimensional (1D) cellular automaton

2.2   A Brief History of the Developments of Optimum-Time FSSP Algorithms

The problem known as the *firing squad synchronization problem* was devised in 1957 by J. Myhill, and first appeared in print in a paper by E. F. Moore [1964]. This problem has been widely circulated, and has attracted much attention. The firing squad synchronization problem first arose in connection with the need to simultaneously turn on all/some parts of a self-reproducing machine. The problem was first solved by J. McCarthy and M. Minsky who presented a $3n$-step algorithm. In 1962, the first optimum-time, i.e. $(2n - 2)$-step, synchronization algorithm was presented by Goto [1962], with each cell having several thousands of states. Waksman [1966] presented a 16-state optimum-time synchronization algorithm. Afterward, Balzer [1967] and Gerken [1987] developed an eight-state algorithm and a seven-state synchronization algorithm, respectively, thus decreasing the number of states required for the synchronization. In 1987, Mazoyer [1987] developed a six-state synchronization algorithm which, at present, is the algorithm having the fewest states. Figure 2 shows some snapshots for synchronizing a cellular array of size 17, implemented by Waksmann [1966], Balzer [1967], Gerken [1987], and Mazoyer [1987].

2.3   Complexity Measures and Properties in FSSP Algorithms

- **Time**

  Any solution to the original 1D FSSP with the general at one end can be easily shown to require $(2n - 2)$ steps for synchronizing n cells, since signals on the array can propagate no faster than one cell per step, and the time from the general's instruction until the final synchronization must be at least $2n - 2$.

  Theorem 1. [Goto [1962] (Lower Bound)] The minimum time in which the firing squad synchronization could occur is $2n - 2$ steps, where the general is located at one end.

  Theorem 2. [Goto [1962]] There exists a cellular automaton that can synchronize any 1D array of length n in optimum $2n - 2$ steps, where the general is located at one end.

- **Number of States**

  Number of states of the automata realizing solutions to the FSSP has been an important complexity measure in the study of the FSSP. The following three distinct states:

  Quiescent state,

  General state, and

  Firing state

  are required in order to define any cellular automaton that can solve the FSSP. Note that the boundary state for C_0 and C_{n+1} is not counted historically as an internal state. Balzer [1967] and Sanders [1994] showed that no four-state optimum-time solution exists. Umeo and Yanagihara [2009], Yunès [2008], and Umeo, Kamikawa, and Yunès [2009] gave some 5- and 4-state *partial* solutions that can solve the synchronization problem for infinitely many sizes n, but not all, respectively. The solution is referred to as *partial* solution, which is compared with usual *full* solutions that can solve the problem for all cells. Yunès [2008] and Umeo, Yunès, and Kamikawa [2009] developed 4-state partial solutions based on Wolfram's rules 60 and 150. They can synchronize any array/ring of length $n = 2^k$ for any positive integer k. Details can be found in Yunès [2008], Umeo, Kamikawa, and Yunès [2009], and Ng [2011]. Ng [2011] presented a list of 4-state asymmetric solutions to the ring FSSP.

  Theorem 3. [Balzer [1967], Sanders [1994]] There is no four-state *full* solution that can synchronize n cells.

  Theorem 4. [Yunès [2008], Umeo et al. [2009], Ng [2011]] There exist 4-state *partial* solutions to the FSSP.

Fig. 2. Some snapshots for optimum-time 1D FSSP algorithms (from top to bottom, left to right in each row), each realizing a 16-state solution (Waksmann [1966]), an 8-state solution (Balzer [1967]), a 6-state solution (Mazoyer [1987]), a 7-state solution (Gerken [1987]) and a 155-state solution (Gerken [1987])

- **Number of Transition Rules**
  Any k-state (excluding the boundary state) transition table for the synchronization has at most $(k-1)k^2$ entries in $(k-1)$ matrices of size $k \times k$. The number of transition rules reflects a complexity of synchronization algorithms.

- **Filled-In Ratio**
  To measure the density of entries in the transition table, we introduce a measure *filled-in ratio* of the state transition table. The filled-in ratio of the state transition table $\mathcal{A}$ is defined as follows: $f_{\mathcal{A}} = e/e_{total}$, where e is the number of exact entries of the next state defined in the table $\mathcal{A}$ and e_{total} is the number of possible entries defined such that $e_{total} = (k-1)k^2$, where k is the number of internal states of the table $\mathcal{A}$.

- **Symmetry vs. Asymmetry**
  Herman [1971, 1972] investigated a computational power of symmetrical cellular automata, motivated by a biological point of view. Szwerinski [1985] and Kobuchi [1987] studied a computational relation between symmetrical and asymmetrical CAs with von Neumann neighborhood. A transition table for a given CA is said to be *symmetric* if and only if the transition table $\delta : \mathcal{Q}^3 \to \mathcal{Q}$ such that $\delta(x, y, z) = \delta(z, y, x)$ holds, for any state x, y, z in $\mathcal{Q}$. A symmetrical cellular automaton has a property that the next state of a cell depends on its present state and the states of its two neighbors, but it is same if the states of the left and right neighbors are interchanged. Thus, the symmetrical CA has no ability to distinguish between its left and right neighbors. Those transition tables developed by Waksmann [1966], Balzer [1967], and Gerken [1987] are nearly symmetric, but the smallest one implemented by Mazoyer [1987] is asymmetric.

- **State-Change Complexity**
  Vollmar [1982] introduced a *state-change complexity* in order to measure the efficiency of cellular automata, motivated by energy consumption in certain physical memory systems. The state-change complexity is defined as the sum of *proper* state changes of the cellular space during the computations. Vollmar [1982] showed that $\Omega(n \log n)$ state-change is required by the cellular space for the synchronization of n cells in $(2n-2)$ steps. Gerken [1987] presented an optimum-time $\Theta(n \log n)$ state-change synchronization algorithm.

  Theorem 5. [Vollmar [1982] (Lower Bound)] $\Omega(n \log n)$ state-change is necessary for synchronizing n cells.

  Theorem 6. [Gerken [1987]] $\Theta(n \log n)$ state-change is sufficient for synchronizing n cells in $2n - 2$ steps.

Here, we present some tables based on quantitative and qualitative comparisons of those FSSP algorithms.

Table 1. A quantitative comparison of transition rule sets for optimum-time FSSP algorithms. The "*" symbol in parenthesis shows the correction and reduction of transition rules made in Umeo et al. [2005]. The "**" symbol indicates the number of states and rules obtained after the expansion of the original two-layer construction.

Algorithm	# of states	# of transition rules	State change complexity
Goto [1962]	many thousands	—	$\Theta(n \log n)$
Waksman [1966]	16	3216(202*)	$O(n^2)$
Balzer [1967]	8	182 (165 *)	$O(n^2)$
Gerken I [1987]	7	118 (105*)	$O(n^2)$
Mazoyer [1987]	6	120 (119*)	$O(n^2)$
Gerken II [1987]	32(155**)	347(2371**)	$\Theta(n \log n)$

Table 2. A qualitative comparison of optimum-time FSSP algorithms with respect to one/two-sided recursive properties and the number of signals being used for simultaneous space divisions

Algorithm	One-/ two-sided	Recursive/ non-recursive	# of signals
Goto [1962]	—	non-recursive	finite
Waksman [1966]	two-sided	recursive	infinite
Balzer [1967]	two-sided	recursive	infinite
Gerken I [1987]	two-sided	recursive	infinite
Mazoyer [1987]	one-sided	recursive	infinite
Gerken II [1987]	two-sided	recursive	finite

2.4   Generalized FSSP

The *generalized* FSSP (GFSSP, for short) is an extended FSSP version which allows the initial general to be located at any cell of the array. A key idea behind the GFSSP algorithm proposed by Moore and Langdon [1968] is to reconstruct the original FSSP algorithm as if an initial general had been at the left or right end with being the general state at time $t = -(k-1)$, where k is the number of cells between the general and the nearest end. Figure 3 illustrates a space-time diagram for the GFSSP and some snapshots for the 17-state realization in Moore and Langdon [1968].

The initial general emits a left- and right-going signal with 1/1 speed and keeps its position by marking a special symbol. The propagated signals generate a new general at each end. On reaching the end, they generate the necessary signals assuming that that end is the far end. The special marking symbol tells the first 1/1 signal generated by the left and right end generals that that side was the right nearest end. At that point the slope 1/1 signal is generated and it changes the slope of all the preceding signals to the next higher one, that is, $1/(2^\ell - 1)$ becomes $1/(2^{\ell+1} - 1)$. Note that the original optimum-time solution is working below the dotted line in the Fig. 3 (left). Most of the GFSSP algorithm proposed afterwards is based on the space-time diagram shown in Fig. 3. Therefore the optimum-time complexity for the GFSSP is $\min(k-1, n-k)$ steps smaller than the original FSSP with a general at one end. Thus, the time complexity is

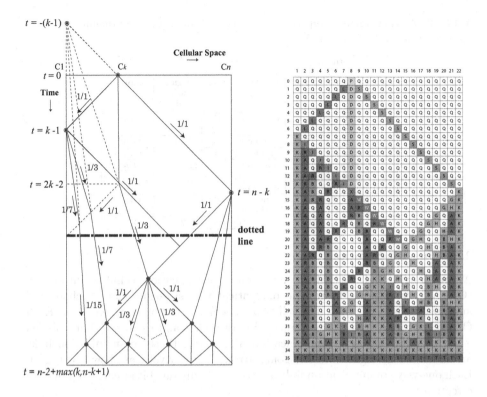

Fig. 3. Space-time diagram for the GFSSP algorithms on 1D array of length n with a general on C_k (left) and some snapshots for the 17-state realization on 22 cells with the general on C_8 (right)

$$2n - 2 - \min(k - 1, n - k) = n - 1 + \max(k - 1, n - k) = n - 2 + \max(k, n - k + 1).$$
See Umeo, Kamikawa, Nishioka, and Akiguchi [2010] for a detailed survey on the GFSSP algorithms.

As for the state-change complexity of the GFSSP algorithms, we have:

Theorem 7. [Umeo, Kamikawa, Nishioka, Akiguchi [2010]] Each GFSSP algorithm developed by Moore and Langdon [1968], Varshavsky, Marakhovsky and Peschansky [1970], Szwerinski [1982], Settle and Simon [2002], Umeo, Hisaoka, Michisaka, Nishioka and Maeda [2002], and Umeo, Maeda, and Hongyo [2006] has an $O(n^2)$ state-change complexity, respectively.

Here, we present a table based on a quantitative comparison of those GFSSP algorithms.

Table 3. A quantitative comparison of transition rule sets for optimum- and non-optimum-time GFSSP algorithms

Algorithm	Time complexity	# of states	# of revised (original) transition rules	State change complexity
Moore and Langdon [1968]	optimum	17	252 (—)	$O(n^2)$
Varshavsky et al. [1969]	optimum	10	273 (—)	$O(n^2)$
Szwerinski [1982]	optimum	10	324 (345)	$O(n^2)$
Settle and Simon [2002]	optimum	9	310 (326)	$O(n^2)$
UHMNM [2002]	optimum	9	203	$O(n^2)$
Umeo, Maeda, and Hongyo [2006]	non-optimum	6	115	$O(n^2)$
Umeo et. al [2010]	optimum	8	222	$O(n^2)$

2.5   One-Bit Solutions

A one-dimensional (1D) 1-bit inter-cell communication cellular automaton (CA_{1-bit}) consists of a finite array of identical finite state automata, each located at a positive integer point. The cell at point i is denoted by C_i where $i \geq 1$. Each C_i, except for C_1 and C_n, is connected with its left and right neighbor cells via a left or right one-way communication link, where those communication links are indicated by right- and left-going arrows, respectively, as shown in Fig. 4. Each one-way communication link can transmit only one bit at each step in each direction.

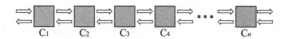

Fig. 4. A one-dimensional (1D) cellular automaton connected with 1-bit inter-cell communication links

A cellular automaton with 1-bit inter-cell communication (abbreviated as CA_{1-bit}) consists of a finite array of finite state automaton $A = (Q, \delta)$ such that

1. Q is a finite set of internal states.
2. δ is a function that defines the next state of any cell and its binary outputs to its left and right neighbor cells such that δ: $Q \times \{0, 1\} \times \{0, 1\} \rightarrow Q \times \{0, 1\} \times \{0, 1\}$ where $\delta(p, x, y) = (q, x', y')$, $p, q \in Q$, $x, x', y, y' \in \{0, 1\}$, has the following meaning: We assume that, at step t, the cell C_i is in state p and receives binary inputs x and y from its left and right communication links, respectively. Then, at the next step $t+1$, C_i takes a state q and outputs x' and y' to its left and right communication links, respectively. Note that binary inputs to C_i at step t are also outputs of C_{i-1} and C_{i+1} at step t. A quiescent state $q \in Q$ has a property such that $\delta(q, 0, 0) = (q, 0, 0)$.

Table 4. Transition table for a 35-state implementation of the optimum-time synchronization algorithm (Umeo and Yanagihara [2011])

1 Q	R=0	R=1		2 RGW	R=0	R=1		3 RPW	R=0	R=1		4 RA	R=0	R=1
L=0	(Q,0,0)	(Q,0,0)		L=0	(RGW,0,1)	(F,0,0)		L=0	(RPW,0,1)	(LGW,1,1)		L=0	(RQoS,0,0)	--
L=1	(RA,0,1)	(LGW,1,1)		L=1	(RGW,1,1)	(F,0,0)		L=1	--	--		L=1	(RP,0,0)	--

5 RQoS	R=0	R=1		6 RQeS	R=0	R=1		7 RQ1A	R=0	R=1		8 RQ0A	R=0	R=1
L=0	(RQ0A,0,1)	(LP,1,0)		L=0	(RQ1B,1,0)	--		L=0	(RQ0A,0,0)	(LG,1,0)		L=0	(RQ1A,0,0)	(RQ1A,1,0)
L=1	(RQeS,0,0)	(LP,1,0)		L=1	(RG1,0,1)	--		L=1	--	--		L=1	(RQ1A,0,0)	(RP1,1,1)

9 RQ1B	R=0	R=1		10 RQ0B	R=0	R=1		11 RQ1C	R=0	R=1		12 RQ0C	R=0	R=1
L=0	(RQ0B,0,0)	(LP,1,0)		L=0	(RQ1B,0,0)	(RQ1B,1,0)		L=0	(LQ1B,0,0)	(LQ1C,0,0)		L=0	(LQ1A,0,1)	--
L=1	--	--		L=1	(RQ1B,0,0)	(RG1,1,1)		L=1	(RQ0C,0,0)	(LP,1,0)		L=1	(RQ1C,0,0)	(RG1,0,1)

13 RG1	R=0	R=1		14 RG0	R=0	R=1		15 RP1	R=0	R=1		16 RP0	R=0	R=1
L=0	(RG0,0,0)	(LPW,1,0)		L=0	(RG1,0,1)	(RQ1B,0,0)		L=0	(RP0,0,0)	(LGW,1,1)		L=0	(RP1,0,1)	(RQ1A,1,0)
L=1	(RG0,0,0)	(LPW,1,0)		L=1	(RG1,0,1)	(RQ1C,0,0)		L=1	--	--		L=1	--	--

17 RG	R=0	R=1		18 RP	R=0	R=1		19 LGW	R=0	R=1		20 LPW	R=0	R=1
L=0	(LQ1C,0,0)	(LPW,1,0)		L=0	(LQ0C,0,0)	(LGW,1,1)		L=0	(LGW,1,0)	(LGW,1,1)		L=0	(LPW,1,0)	--
L=1	(LQ1C,0,0)	(LPW,1,0)		L=1	(RP,0,1)	(LGW,1,1)		L=1	(F,0,0)	(F,0,0)		L=1	(RGW,1,1)	--

21 LQ1A	R=0	R=1		22 LQ1B	R=0	R=1		23 LQ0A	R=0	R=1		24 LQ0B	R=0	R=1
L=0	(LQ0A,0,0)	(LQ1B,0,0)		L=0	(LQ0B,0,0)	(LQ1A,0,0)		L=0	(LQ1A,0,0)	(LQ1A,0,0)		L=0	(LQ1B,0,0)	(LQ1B,0,0)
L=1	(RG,0,1)	(LP1,1,0)		L=1	(RP,0,1)	(RP,0,0)		L=1	(LQ1A,0,1)	(LP1,1,1)		L=1	(LQ1B,0,1)	(LG1,1,1)

25 LQ1C	R=0	R=1		26 LQ0C	R=0	R=1		27 LG1	R=0	R=1		28 LG0	R=0	R=1
L=0	(RQ1B,0,0)	(LQ0C,0,0)		L=0	(RQ1A,1,0)	(LQ1C,0,0)		L=0	(LG0,0,0)	(LG0,0,0)		L=0	(LG1,1,0)	(LG1,1,0)
L=1	(RQ1C,0,0)	(RP,0,1)		L=1	--	(LG1,1,0)		L=1	(RPW,0,1)	(RPW,0,1)		L=1	(LQ1B,0,0)	(LQ1C,0,0)

29 LP1	R=0	R=1		30 LP0	R=0	R=1		31 LG	R=0	R=1		32 LP	R=0	R=1
L=0	(LP0,0,0)	(LP0,0,0)		L=0	(LP1,1,0)	(LP1,1,0)		L=0	(RQ1C,0,0)	(RQ1C,0,0)		L=0	(RQ0C,0,0)	(LP,1,0)
L=1	(RGW,1,1)	(RPW,0,0)		L=1	(LQ1A,0,1)	(LQ1B,0,0)		L=1	(RPW,0,1)	(RPW,0,1)		L=1	(RGW,1,1)	(RGW,1,1)

33 LP'	R=0	R=1		34 F	R=0	R=1		35 QW	R=0	R=1
L=0	--	(LQ1A,0,0)		L=0	--	--		L=0	(QW,0,0)	--
L=1	--	(RPW,0,0)		L=1	--	--		L=1	(LGW,1,0)	--

Thus, the CA_{1-bit} is a special subclass of *normal* (i.e., *conventional*) cellular automata. Let N be any normal cellular automaton with a set of states Q and a transition function $\delta : Q^3 \to Q$. The state of each cell on N depends on the cell's previous state and states on its nearest neighbor cells. This means that the total information exchanged per step between neighboring cells is O(1) bits. Each state in Q can be encoded with a binary sequence of length $\lceil \log_2 |Q| \rceil$ and then sending the binary sequences sequentially bit-by-bit in each direction via each one-way communication link. The sequences are then received bit-by-bit and decoded into their corresponding states in Q. Thus, the CA_{1-bit} can simulate one step of N in $\lceil \log_2 |Q| \rceil$ steps.

Umeo and Yanagihara [2011] constructed a smaller optimum-time implementation based on Gerken's synchronization algorithm [1987] on O(1)-bit-communication model. The constructed CA_{1-bit} has 35 internal states and 114 transition rules. Table 4 presents its transition rule set for the 35-state synchronization protocol and Figure 5 shows snapshots for synchronization processes on 17 cells,

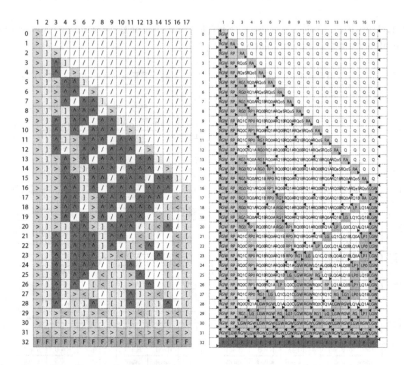

Fig. 5. Snapshots for synchronization processes on 17 cells, each for Gerken's algorithm [1987] on O(1)-bit-communication model (left) and the 35-state implementation (Umeo and Yanagihara [2011]) on CA_{1-bit} (right)

each for Gerken's algorithm [1987] on O(1)-bit-communication model (left) and the 35-state algorithm on CA_{1-bit} (right).

Theorem 8. [Umeo, Yanagihara [2011]] There exists a 35-state CA_{1-bit} that can synchronize n cells with the general on the left end in $2n - 2$ steps.

3 FSSP on Two-Dimensional Arrays

Figure 6 shows a finite 2D cellular array consisting of $m \times n$ cells. Each cell is an identical (except the border cells) finite-state automaton. The array operates in lock-step mode in such a way that the next state of each cell (except border cells) is determined by both its own present state and the present states of its north, south, east and west neighbors. The FSSP on the 2D array can be defined similarly. All cells (*soldiers*), except the north-west corner cell (*general*), are initially in the quiescent state at time $t = 0$ with the property that the next state of a quiescent cell with quiescent neighbors is the quiescent state again. At time $t = 0$, the north-west corner cell $C_{1,1}$ is in the *fire-when-ready* state, which is the initiation signal for the array. The FSSP is to determine a description (state set and next-state function) for cells that ensures all cells enter the *fire*

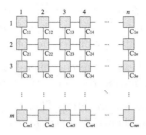

Fig. 6. A two-dimensional (2D) cellular automaton

state at exactly the same time and for the first time. The tricky part of the problem is that the same kind of soldier having a fixed number of states must be synchronized, regardless of the size $m \times n$ of the array. The set of states and next state function must be independent of m and n.

3.1 Rectangular Arrays

A large number of FSSP algorithms on 2D arrays has been proposed by Beyer [1969], Grasselli [1975], Shinahr [1974], Szwerinski [1982], Umeo, Hisaoka, and Akiguchi [2005], and Umeo, Nishide, and Kubo [2012]. It has been shown in Beyer [1969] and Shinahr [1974] independently that there exists no 2D cellular automaton that can synchronize any 2D array of size $m \times n$ in less than $m + n + \max(m, n) - 3$ steps. In addition they first proposed an optimum-time synchronization algorithm that can synchronize any 2D array of size $m \times n$ in optimum $m + n + \max(m, n) - 3$ steps. Shinahr [1974] gave a 28-state implementation. Umeo, Hisaoka and Akiguchi [2005] presented a new 12-state synchronization algorithm operating in optimum-step, realizing a smallest solution to the rectangle synchronization problem, known at present. As for the time optimality of the 2D FSSP algorithms, the following theorems have been shown.

Theorem 9. [Beyer [1969], Shinahr [1974]] There exists no cellular automaton that can synchronize any 2D array of size $m \times n$ in less than $m + n + \max(m, n) - 3$ steps, where the general is located at one corner of the array.

Theorem 10. [Beyer [1969], Shinahr [1974]] There exists an cellular automaton that can synchronize any 2D array of size $m \times n$ in exactly $m + n + \max(m, n) - 3$ steps, where the general is located at one corner of the array.

Umeo, Hisaoka and Akiguchi [2005] presented a 12-state synchronization algorithm operating in optimum-step, realizing the smallest, known at present, solution to the rectangle synchronization problem. The constructed 12-state cellular automaton has 1532 transition rules. The details can be found in Umeo, Hisaoka, and Akiguchi [2005].

Theorem 11. [Umeo et al. [2005]] There exists a 12-state cellular automaton that can synchronize any 2D array of size $m \times n$ at exactly $m + n + \max(m, n) - 3$ steps, where the general is located at one corner of the array.

Concerning its generalized cases where a general is initially positioned at any point on the 2D array, the following theorems are developed.

Theorem 12. [Umeo, Nishide, Kubo [2012]] There exists no 2D cellular automaton that can synchronize any 2D array of size $m \times n$ with an initial general on $C_{r,s}$ in less than $m + n + \max(m, n) - \min(r, m - r + 1) - \min(s, n - s + 1) - 1$ steps, where $1 \leq r \leq m, 1 \leq s \leq n$.

Theorem 13. [Szwerinski [1982], Umeo, Nishide, Kubo [2012]] There exists an optimum-time synchronization algorithm that can synchronize any $m \times n$ rectangular array with a general at $C_{r,s}$ in optimum $m + n + \max(m, n) - \min(r, m - r + 1) - \min(s, n - s + 1) - 1$ steps, where $1 \leq r \leq m, 1 \leq s \leq n$.

3.2   Square Arrays

Concerning the square synchronization which is a special class of rectangles, several square synchronization algorithms have been proposed by Beyer [1969], Shinahr [1974], and Umeo, Maeda, and Fujiwara [2002]. In recent years, Umeo and Kubo [2010] developed a seven-state square synchronizer, which is a smallest implementation, known at present, of the optimum-time square FSSP algorithm. One can easily see that it takes $2n - 2$ steps for any signal to travel from $C_{1,1}$ to $C_{n,n}$ due to the von Neumann neighborhood. For some typical square synchronization algorithms, see Umeo [2012].

Concerning the time optimality of the two-dimensional square synchronization algorithms, the following theorems have been established.

Theorem 14. [Beyer [1969], Shinahr [1974]] There exists no cellular automaton that can synchronize any 2D square array of size $n \times n$ in less than $2n - 2$ steps, where the general is located at one corner of the array.

Theorem 15. [Shinahr [1974]] There exists a 17-state cellular automaton that can synchronize any 2D square array of size $n \times n$ at exactly $2n - 2$ optimum steps.

Umeo and Kubo [2010] constructed a seven-state optimum-time square synchronizer based on a zebra-like mapping. It is known as the smallest implementation at present. The constructed seven-state cellular automaton has 787 transition rules. Details can be found in Umeo and Kubo [2010].

Theorem 16. [Umeo, Kubo [2010]] There exists a seven-state cellular automaton that can synchronize any 2D square array of size $n \times n$ in optimum $2n - 2$ steps.

In Table 5 we present a list of implementations of those FSSP algorithms for square cellular automata with O(1)-bit and 1-bit communications. The O(1)-bit communication model is a usual cellular automaton in which the amount of communication bits exchanged in one step between neighboring cells is assumed to be $O(1)$ bits. The 1-bit communication model is a subclass of the usual cellular automata, in which inter-cell communication is restricted to 1-bit communication discussed in Section 2.5.

Table 5. 2D FSSP algorithms for square arrays

Implementations	# of states	# of rules	Time complexity	Communication model
Beyer [1969]	—	—	$2n - 2$	$O(1)$-bit
Shinahr [1974]	17	—	$2n - 2$	$O(1)$-bit
Umeo, Maeda and Fujiwara [2002]	9	1718	$2n - 2$	$O(1)$-bit
Umeo and Kubo [2010]	7	787	$2n - 2$	$O(1)$-bit
Ishii et al. [2006]	15	1614	$2n - 2$	$O(1)$-bit
Umeo, Uchino and Nomura [2011]	37	3271	$2n - 2$	$O(1)$-bit
Gruska, Torre and Parente [2007]	—	—	$2n - 2$	1-bit
Umeo and Yanagihara [2011]	49	237	$2n - 2$	1-bit

4   FSSP for Multi-Dimensional Arrays

In this section, we review FSSP algorithms for multi-dimensional arrays, which has been presented in Umeo, Nishide, and Kubo [2012]. A kD FSSP algorithm is sketched as follows:

Optimum-Time kD FSSP Algorithm _____

Step 1. Start the recursive-halving marking on cells along each dimension, **find** a *center cell(s)* of the array, **generate** a general(s) on the center cell(s), and **pre-synchronize** the center point(s): zero-dimensional sub-array of the array.
Step 2. Pre-synchronize a 1D sub-array along the 1st dimension containing the synchronized center cell.
Step 3. to Step $k - 1$. for $j = 1$ to $k - 1$, by increasing the number of dimensions, **pre-synchronize** a jD sub-array containing the pre-synchronized $(j - 1)$D sub-array.
Step k. Synchronize the kD array. This yields the final synchronization of the given array.

4.1   3D FSSP/GFSSP Algorithms

We give several theorems for 3D FSSP with a general at one corner or an arbitrary position of the array.

Theorem 17. [Umeo, Nishide, Kubo [2012]] The minimum time in which the firing squad synchronization could occur is no earlier than $n_1 + n_2 + n_3 + \max(n_1, n_2, n_3) - 4$ for any 3D array of size $n_1 \times n_2 \times n_3$ with a general at $C_{1,1,1}$.

Theorem 18. [Umeo, Nishide, Kubo [2012]] There exists an optimum-time synchronization algorithm that can synchronize any 3D array of size $n_1 \times n_2 \times n_3$ with a general at $C_{1,1,1}$ in optimum $n_1 + n_2 + n_3 + \max(n_1, n_2, n_3) - 4$ steps.

Theorem 19. [Umeo, Nishide, Kubo [2012]] The minimum time in which the firing squad synchronization could occur is no earlier than $n_1 + n_2 + n_3 + \max(n_1, n_2, n_3) - \min(r_1, n_1 - r_1 + 1) - \min(r_2, n_2 - r_2 + 1) - \min(r_3, n_3 - r_3 + 1) - 1$ for any 3D array of size $n_1 \times n_2 \times n_3$ with a general at C_{r_1, r_2, r_3}.

Theorem 20. [Umeo, Nishide, Kubo [2012]] There exists an optimum-time synchronization algorithm that can synchronize any 3D array of size $n_1 \times n_2 \times n_3$ with a general at C_{r_1, r_2, r_3} in optimum $n_1 + n_2 + n_3 + \max(n_1, n_2, n_3) - \min(r_1, n_1 - r_1 + 1) - \min(r_2, n_2 - r_2 + 1) - \min(r_3, n_3 - r_3 + 1) - 1$ steps.

4.2   kD FSSP/GFSSP Algorithms

Theorems 17-20 can be expanded to k-dimensional arrays.

Theorem 21. [Umeo, Nishide, Kubo [2012]] There exists no cellular automaton that can synchronize any kD array of size $n_1 \times n_2 \times ... \times n_k$ with a general at $C_{1,1,...,1}$ in less than $\sum_{i=1}^{k} n_i + \max(n_1, n_2, ..., n_k) - k - 1$ steps

Theorem 22. [Umeo, Nishide, Kubo [2012]] There exists an optimum-time synchronization algorithm that can synchronize any kD array of size $n_1 \times n_2 \times ... \times n_k$ with a general at $C_{1,1,...,1}$ in optimum $\sum_{i=1}^{k} n_i + \max(n_1, n_2, ..., n_k) - k - 1$ steps.

Theorem 23. [Umeo, Nishide, Kubo [2012]] There exists no cellular automaton that can synchronize any kD array of size $n_1 \times n_2 \times ... \times n_k$ with a general at $C_{r_1, r_2, ..., r_k}$ in less than $\sum_{i=1}^{k} n_i + \max(n_1, n_2, ..., n_k) - \sum_{i=1}^{k} \min(r_i, n_i - r_i + 1) - 1$ steps.

Theorem 24. [Umeo, Nishide, Kubo [2012]] There exists an optimum-time synchronization algorithm that can synchronize any kD array of size $n_1 \times n_2 \times ... \times n_k$ with a general at $C_{r_1, r_2, ..., r_k}$ in optimum $\sum_{i=1}^{k} n_i + \max(n_1, n_2, ..., n_k) - \sum_{i=1}^{k} \min(r_i, n_i - r_i + 1) - 1$ steps.

5   Conclusions

In the present article, we have constructed a survey on recent developments in constructing FSSP algorithms for 1D, 2D, 3D and multi-dimensional arrays, focusing on time-optimum smaller-state solutions to the FSSP.

References

1. Balzer, R.: An 8-state minimal time solution to the firing squad synchronization problem. Information and Control 10, 22–42 (1967)
2. Beyer, W.T.: Recognition of topological invariants by iterative arrays. Ph.D. Thesis. MIT, pp. 144 (1969)
3. Gerken, H.: Über Synchronisations - Probleme bei Zellularautomaten. Diplomarbeit, Institut für Theoretische Informatik, Technische Universität Braunschweig, pp. 50 (1987)
4. Goto, E.: A minimal time solution of the firing squad problem. Dittoed course notes for Applied Mathematics 298, Harvard University, with an illustration in color, pp. 52–59 (1962)
5. Grasselli, A.: Synchronization of cellular arrays: The firing squad problem in two dimensions. Information and Control 28, 113–124 (1975)
6. Gruska, J., Torre, S.L., Parente, M.: The firing squad synchronization problem on squares, toruses and rings. Intern. J. of Foundations of Computer Science 18(3), 637–654 (2007)
7. Herman, G.T.: Models for cellular interactions in development without polarity of individual cells, I. General description and the problem of universal computing ability. International Journal of Systems Sciences 2(2), 271–289 (1971)
8. Herman, G.T.: Models for cellular interactions in development without polarity of individual cells, II. Problems of synchronization and regulation. International Journal of Systems Sciences 3(2), 149–175 (1972)
9. Kobuchi, Y.: A note on symmetrical cellular spaces. Information Processing Letters 25, 413–415 (1987)
10. Mazoyer, J.: A six-state minimal time solution to the firing squad synchronization problem. Theoretical Computer Science 50, 183–238 (1987)
11. Moore, E.F.: The firing squad synchronization problem. In: Moore, E.F. (ed.) Sequential Machines, Selected Papers, pp. 213–214. Addison-Wesley, Reading (1964)
12. Moore, F.R., Langdon, G.G.: A generalized firing squad problem. Information and Control 12, 212–220 (1968)
13. Ng, W.L.: 20119: Partial solutions for the firing squad synchronization problem on rings. UMI Dissertation Publishing, Ann Arbor, pp. 363 (2011)
14. Sanders, P.: Massively parallel search for transition-tables of polyautomata. In: Jesshope, C., Jossifov, V., Wilhelmi, W. (eds.) Proc. of the VI International Workshop on Parallel Processing by Cellular Automata and Arrays. Akademie, pp. 99–108 (1994)
15. Settle, A., Simon, J.: Smaller solutions for the firing squad. Theoretical Computer Science 276, 83–109 (2002)
16. Shinahr, I.: Two- and three-dimensional firing squad synchronization problems. Information and Control 24, 163–180 (1974)
17. Szwerinski, H.: Time-optimum solution of the firing-squad-synchronization-problem for n-dimensional rectangles with the general at an arbitrary position. Theoretical Computer Science 19, 305–320 (1982)
18. Szwerinski, H.: Symmetrical one-dimensional cellular spaces. Information and Control 67, 163–172 (1985)
19. Umeo, H.: Firing squad synchronization algorithms for two-dimensional cellular automata. International Journal of Cellular Automata 4, 1–20 (2008)

20. Umeo, H.: Firing squad synchronization problem in cellular automata. In: Meyers, R.A. (ed.) Encyclopedia of Complexity and System Science, vol. 4, pp. 3537–3574 (2009)

21. Umeo, H.: Problem solving on one-bit-communication cellular automata. In: Hoekstra, A.G., Kroc, J., Sloot, P.M.A.: Simulating Complex Systems by Cellular Automata, ch. 6. Springer, Heidelberg, pp. 117–144 (2010)

22. Umeo, H.: Recent Developments in Firing Squad Synchronization Algorithms: Smaller Solutions. In: Proc. of the 3rd International Conference on Networking and Computing, pp. 371–378 (2012)

23. Umeo, H.: Synchronizing square arrays in optimum-time. Int. J. General Systems 41(6), 617–631 (2012)

24. Umeo, H., Hisaoka, M., Akiguchi, S.: A twelve-state optimum-time synchronization algorithm for two-dimensional rectangular cellular arrays. In: Calude, C.S., Dinneen, M.J., Păun, G., Jesús Pérez-Jímenez, M., Rozenberg, G. (eds.) UC 2005. LNCS, vol. 3699, pp. 214–223. Springer, Heidelberg (2005)

25. Umeo, H., Hisaoka, M., Sogabe, T.: A survey on optimum-time firing squad synchronization algorithms for one-dimensional cellular automata. Intern. J. of Unconventional Computing 1, 403–426 (2005)

26. Umeo, H., Hisaoka, M., Michisaka, K., Nishioka, K., Maeda, M.: Some new generalized synchronization algorithms and their implementations for large scale cellular automata. In: Calude, C.S., Dinneen, M.J., Peper, F. (eds.) UMC 2002. LNCS, vol. 2509, pp. 276–286. Springer, Heidelberg (2002)

27. Umeo, H., Kamikawa, N., Yunès, J.B.: A family of smallest symmetrical four-state firing squad synchronization protocols for ring arrays. Parallel Processing Letters 19(2), 299–313 (2009)

28. Umeo, H., Kamikawa, N., Nishioka, K., Akiguchi, S.: Generalized Firing Squad Synchronization Protocols for One-Dimensional Cellular Automata - A Survey. Acta Physica Polonica B,Proceedings Supplement 3, 267–289 (2010)

29. Umeo, H., Kubo, K.: A seven-state time-optimum square synchronizer. In: Bandini, S., Manzoni, S., Umeo, H., Vizzari, G. (eds.) ACRI 2010. LNCS, vol. 6350, pp. 219–230. Springer, Heidelberg (2010)

30. Umeo, H., Maeda, M., Fujiwara, N.: An efficient mapping scheme for embedding any one-dimensional firing squad synchronization algorithm onto two-dimensional arrays. In: Bandini, S., Chopard, B., Tomassini, M. (eds.) ACRI 2002. LNCS, vol. 2493, pp. 69–81. Springer, Heidelberg (2002)

31. Umeo, H., Maeda, M., Hisaoka, M., Teraoka, M.: A state-efficient mapping scheme for designing two-dimensional firing squad synchronization algorithms. Fundamenta Informaticae 74(4), 603–623 (2006)

32. Umeo, H., Maeda, M., Hongyo, K.: A design of symmetrical six-state 3n-step firing squad synchronization algorithms and their implementations. In: El Yacoubi, S., Chopard, B., Bandini, S. (eds.) ACRI 2006. LNCS, vol. 4173, pp. 157–168. Springer, Heidelberg (2006)

33. Umeo, H., Nishide, K., Kubo, K.: A Simple Optimum-Time FSSP Algorithm for Multi-Dimensional Cellular Automata. DCM 2012, 151–165 (2012)

34. Umeo, H., Uchino, H., Nomura, A.: How to synchronize square arrays in optimum-time. In: Proc. of the 2011 International Conference on High Performance Computing and Simulation (HPCS 2011), pp. 801–807. IEEE (2011)

35. Umeo, H., Yamawaki, T., Nishide, K.: An optimu-time firing squad synchronization algorithm for two-dimensional rectangle arrays - Freezing-thawing technique based. International Journal of Cellular Automata 7, 31–46 (2012)

36. Umeo, H., Yanagihara, T.: A small five-state non-optimum-time solution to the firing squad synchronization problem - A geometrical approach. Fundamenta Informaticane **91**, 161–178 (2009)
37. Umeo, H., Yanagihara, T.: Smallest implementations of optimum-time firing squad synchronization algorithms for one-bit-communication cellular automata. In: Malyshkin, V. (ed.) PaCT 2011. LNCS, vol. 6873, pp. 210–223. Springer, Heidelberg (2011)
38. Varshavsky, V.I., Marakhovsky, V.B., Peschansky, V.A.: Synchronization of Interacting Automata. Mathematical Systems Theory **4**(3), 212–230 (1970)
39. Vollmar, R.: Some remarks about the "Efficiency" of polyautomata. International Journal of Theoretical Physics **21**(12), 1007–1015 (1982)
40. Waksman, A.: An optimum solution to the firing squad synchronization problem. Information and Control **9**(1966), 66–78 (1966)
41. Yunès, J.B.: A 4-states algebraic solution to linear cellular automata synchronization. Information Processing Letters **107**(2), 71–75 (2008)

Computing with Quantum Resources

Computing Boolean Functions
via Quantum Hashing

Farid Ablayev[✉] and Alexander Vasiliev

Kazan Federal University, Kazan, Russian Federation
fablayev@gmail.com

Abstract. In this paper we show a computational aspect of the quantum hashing technique. In particular we apply it for computing Boolean functions in the model of read-once quantum branching programs based on the properties of specific polynomial presentation of those functions.

1 Introduction

Hashing is widely used in computer science, it is especially useful in cryptographic protocols and data integrity check. In [1] we have introduced a nonbinary quantum hash function for cryptographic scenarios. For instance, the proposed quantum hashing is a suitable one-way function for quantum digital signature protocol from [10]. In this paper we consider another application of the quantum hashing and use it to construct efficient quantum algorithms in a restricted computational model.

Due to severe limits of existing physical implementations of quantum computer it is natural to consider the restricted models of quantum computations. The one we consider in this paper is based upon *quantum branching programs*. Two variants of quantum branching programs were introduced by Ablayev, Gainutdinova, Karpinski [3] (*leveled programs*), and by Nakanishi, Hamaguchi, Kashiwabara [12] (*non-leveled programs*). Later it was shown by Sauerhoff [14] that these two models are polynomially equivalent. The most commonly used restricted variant of quantum branching programs is the model of *Ordered Read-Once Quantum Branching Programs*. In computer science this model is also known as Ordered Binary Decision Diagrams (OBDDs). This restriction implies that each input variable may be read at most once, which is the least possible for any function essentially depending on its variables. Thus, the read-once restriction corresponds to minimizing of computational steps for quantum algorithms.

Essentially, the model of quantum OBDDS is a non-uniform equivalent of one-way quantum finite automata (QFA) and thus the technique given in this paper can be used in the QFA model as well.

In order to compute Boolean functions in the quantum OBDD model we exploit the specific polynomial presentation, which we have called *characteristic* [5]. The polynomial presentations of Boolean functions are widely used in theoretical computer science. For instance, an algebraic transformation of Boolean functions has been applied in [11] and [7] for verification of Boolean functions. In the quantum

© Springer International Publishing Switzerland 2014
C.S. Calude et al. (Eds.): Gruska Festschrift, LNCS 8808, pp. 149–160, 2014.
DOI: 10.1007/978-3-319-13350-8_11

setting polynomial representations were used for proving lower bounds on communication complexity in [8] as well as for investigating query complexity in [16]. Our approach combines the ideas similar to the definition of characteristic polynomial from [11], [7] and to the notion of *zero-error polynomial* (see, e.g. [16]).

In this paper we show how the proposed quantum hashing can be used to compute Boolean functions given by their polynomials in a very restricted computational model of quantum OBDDs. Due to the known general lower bound on the complexity of quantum OBDDs some of our algorithms turn out to be optimal.

2   Quantum Branching Programs

We use the notation $|i\rangle$ for the vector from Hilbert space $\mathcal{H}^d$, which has a 1 on the i-th position and 0 elsewhere. An orthonormal basis $|1\rangle, \ldots, |d\rangle$ is usually referred to as the *standard computational basis*. In this paper we consider all quantum transformations and measurements with respect to this basis.

Definition 1. *A Quantum Branching Program Q over the Hilbert space $\mathcal{H}^d$ is defined as*

$$Q = \langle T, |\psi_0\rangle, \text{Accept}\rangle \ , \tag{1}$$

where T is a sequence of l instructions: $T_j = \left(x_{i_j}, U_j(0), U_j(1)\right)$ is determined by the variable x_{i_j} tested on the step j, and $U_j(0)$, $U_j(1)$ are unitary transformations in $\mathcal{H}^d$.

Vectors $|\psi\rangle \in \mathcal{H}^d$ are called states (state vectors) of Q, $|\psi_0\rangle \in \mathcal{H}^d$ is the initial state of Q, and Accept $\subseteq \{1, 2, \ldots d\}$ is the set of indices of accepting basis states.

We define a computation of Q on an input $\sigma = \sigma_1 \ldots \sigma_n \in \{0,1\}^n$ as follows:

1. *A computation of Q starts from the initial state $|\psi_0\rangle$;*
2. *The j-th instruction of Q reads the input symbol σ_{i_j} (the value of x_{i_j}) and applies the transition matrix $U_j = U_j(\sigma_{i_j})$ to the current state $|\psi\rangle$ to obtain the state $|\psi'\rangle = U_j(\sigma_{i_j})|\psi\rangle$;*
3. *The final state is*

$$|\psi_\sigma\rangle = \left(\prod_{j=l}^{1} U_j(\sigma_{i_j})\right) |\psi_0\rangle \ . \tag{2}$$

4. *After the l-th (last) step of quantum transformation Q measures its configuration $|\psi_\sigma\rangle = (\alpha_1, \ldots, \alpha_d)^T$, and the input σ is accepted with probability*

$$Pr_{\text{accept}}(\sigma) = \sum_{i \in \text{Accept}} |\alpha_i|^2 \ . \tag{3}$$

Note, that using the set *Accept* we can construct M_{accept} – a projector on the accepting subspace $\mathcal{H}^d_{accept}$ (i.e. a diagonal zero-one projection matrix, which determines the final projective measurement). Thus, the accepting probability can be re-written as

$$Pr_{accept}(\sigma) = \langle \psi_\sigma M_{accept}^\dagger | M_{accept} \psi_\sigma \rangle = ||M_{accept}|\psi_\sigma\rangle||_2^2 \ . \tag{4}$$

Circuit Representation. Quantum algorithms are usually given by using quantum circuit formalism [9], [17], because this approach is quite straightforward for describing such algorithms.

We propose, that a QBP represents a classically-controlled quantum system. That is, a QBP can be viewed as a quantum circuit aided with an ability to read classical bits as control variables for unitary operations.

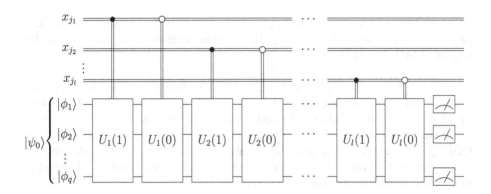

Fig. 1. Circuit presentation of a quantum branching program. Here $x_{i_1}, \ldots, x_{i_l}$ is the sequence of (not necessarily distinct) variables denoting classical control (input) bits. Using the common notation single wires carry quantum information and double wires denote classical information and control.

Example. As an example consider the Boolean function $MOD_m(x_1, \ldots, x_n)$ which tests whether the number of ones in it's input is a multiple of m. For this function the simple algorithm can be proposed (see Figure 2).

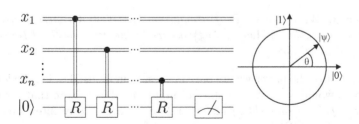

Fig. 2. Quantum branching program for MOD_m Boolean function. Here R denotes the rotation by an angle $\theta = \pi/m$ about the $\hat{y}$ axis of the Bloch sphere.

The algorithm starts with a qubit in basis state $|0\rangle$. At j-th step the value of x_j is tested. Upon input symbol 0 identity transformation I is applied. But if the value of x_j is 1, then the state of the qubit is transformed by the operator R, rotating it by the angle proportional to π/m.

The final state is measured in the standard computational basis. The input $\sigma = \sigma_1 \ldots \sigma_n$ is accepted if the result is the basis state $|0\rangle$, otherwise the input σ is rejected. For arbitrary input σ the acceptance probability equals to

$$Pr_{accept}(\sigma) = \cos^2\left(\frac{\pi \sum_i \sigma_i}{m}\right) . \tag{5}$$

Thus, if $MOD_m(\sigma) = 1$ then $Pr_{accept}(\sigma) = 1$. If $MOD_m(\sigma) = 0$ then the probability of erroneously obtaining the $|0\rangle$ can be close to 1, but this can be improved by using more qubits.

Complexity Measures. The width of a QBP Q, denoted by width(Q), is the dimension d of the corresponding state space $\mathcal{H}^d$, and the length of Q, denoted by length(Q), is the number l of instructions in the sequence T.

In this paper we're mostly interested in another important complexity for a QBP Q – a number of quantum bits, denoted by qubits(Q), physically needed to implement a corresponding quantum system with classical control. From definition it follows that $\log \text{width}(Q) \leq \text{qubits}(Q)$.

Acceptance Criteria. A QBP Q computes the Boolean function f with *bounded error* if there exists an $\epsilon \in (0, 1/2)$ (called *margin*) such that for all inputs the probability of error is bounded by $1/2 - \epsilon$.

In particular, we say that a QBP Q computes the Boolean function f with *one-sided error* if there exists an $\epsilon \in (0, 1)$ (called *error*) such that for all $\sigma \in f^{-1}(1)$ the probability of Q accepting σ is 1 and for all $\sigma \in f^{-1}(0)$ the probability of Q erroneously accepting σ is less than ϵ.

Read-Once Branching Programs. Read-once BPs is a well-known restricted variant of branching programs [15].

Definition 2. *We call a QBP Q a quantum OBDD (QOBDD) or read-once QBP if each variable $x \in \{x_1, \ldots, x_n\}$ occurs in the sequence T of transformations of Q at most once.*

For the rest of the paper we are only interested in QOBDDs, i.e. the length of all programs would be n (the number of input variables). Note that for OBDD model $size(Q) = n \cdot width(Q)$ and therefore we are mostly interested in the width of quantum OBDDs.

The "obliviousness" is inherent for a QBP and therefore this definition is consistent with the usual notion of an OBDD.

General Lower Bound. The following general lower bound on the width of QOB-DDs was proven in [4].

Theorem 1. *Let $f(x_1, \ldots, x_n)$ be a Boolean function computed by a quantum read-once branching program Q with bounded error for some margin ϵ. Then*

$$\text{width}(Q) \geq \frac{\log \text{width}(P)}{2 \log \left(1 + \frac{1}{\epsilon}\right)}, \tag{6}$$

where P is a deterministic OBDD of minimal width computing $f(x_1, \ldots, x_n)$.

That is, the width of a quantum OBDD cannot be asymptotically less than logarithm of the width of the minimal deterministic OBDD computing the same function. And since the deterministic width of many "natural" functions is exponential [15], we obtain the linear lower bound for these functions.

Let bits(P) be the number of bits (memory size) required to implement the minimal deterministic OBDD P for f and Q is an arbitrary quantum OBDD computing the same function.

Then Theorem 1 implies the following lower bound in terms of the number of bits and qubits as the complexity measure.

Corollary 1.

$$\text{qubits}(Q) = \Omega(\log \text{bits}(P)) \ . \tag{7}$$

3 Quantum Hashing

In this section we recall a quantum hashing function from [1].

Let $q = 2^n$ and $B = \{b_1, b_2, \ldots, b_d\} \subset \mathbb{Z}_q$. We define a quantum hash function $\psi_{q,B} : \{0,1\}^n \to (\mathcal{H}^2)^{\otimes(\log d + 1)}$ as follows. For an input $x \in \{0,1\}^n$ we let

$$|\psi_{q,B}(x)\rangle = \frac{1}{\sqrt{d}} \sum_{i=1}^{d} |i\rangle \left(\cos \frac{2\pi b_i x}{q} |0\rangle + \sin \frac{2\pi b_i x}{q} |1\rangle \right) \ . \tag{8}$$

It follows from this definition that the quantum hash $|\psi_{q,B}(x)\rangle$ of an n-bit string x consists of $\log d + 1$ qubits. We will show that d can be about $O(n)$ without loosing the quality of hashing.

The set $B = \{b_1, b_2, \ldots, b_d\}$ of hashing parameters not only defines the size of the hash but also gives the function $\psi_{q,B}$ an ability to withstand collisions, i.e. to distinguish different hashes with bounded error probability. We have called this property δ-*resistance*.

Formally, for $\delta \in (0,1)$ we call a function $\psi : \mathbb{X} \to (\mathcal{H}^2)^{\otimes s}$ δ-resistant if for any pair w, w' of different inputs

$$|\langle \psi(w) | \psi(w') \rangle| \leq \delta \ . \tag{9}$$

The value of δ for the hash function $\psi_{q,B}$ entirely depends on q (which is fixed here by the size of the input) and the set B, i.e. $\delta = \delta(q, B)$. In [1] we have shown a construction for the set of polylogarithmic size (in n) based on [13]. We have also proved the following result.

Theorem 2. *For arbitrary* $\delta \in (0,1)$ *there exists a set* $B = \{b_1, b_2, \ldots, b_d\}$ *of size* $d = \lceil (2/\delta^2) \ln(2q) \rceil$ *such that quantum hash function* $\psi_{q,B}$ *is a* δ-*resistant.*

In other words, for arbitrary $\delta \in (0,1)$ it is possible construct a δ-resistant quantum hash function $\psi_{q,B}$ that would produce an $\log d + 1 = O(\log \log q) = O(\log n)$-qubit hash out of n-bit input.

Implementation of the quantum hashing. In order to describe the implementation of the quantum hashing we introduce the following notations.

We define a *Compound Controlled Rotation* operator (CCR):

$$CCR_{q,B}(\theta) = CCR_{q,B,1}(\theta) \cdot CCR_{q,B,2}(\theta) \cdots CCR_{q,B,d}(\theta), \qquad (10)$$

where operator $CCR_{q,B,i}(\theta)$ rotates the target qubit by the angle θ if the control qubits were in the state $|i\rangle$ and is given in Figure 3.

$$CCR_{q,B,i}(\theta) =$$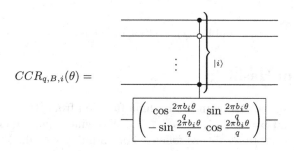

Fig. 3. A circuit for the operator $CCR_{q,B,i}(\theta)$, that rotates the target qubit by the angle θ if the control qubits were in the state $|i\rangle$. Here, the single-qubit rotation is made around the $\hat{y}$ axis of the Bloch sphere.

The compound operator $CCR_{q,B}(\theta)$ obviously has the following properties.

Property 1. CCR-property

$$CCR_{q,B}(0) = I,$$
$$CCR_{q,B}(\theta)|\psi_{q,B}(x)\rangle = |\psi_{q,B}(x+\theta)\rangle, \qquad (11)$$
$$CCR_{q,B}(\theta_1)CCR_{q,B}(\theta_2) = CCR_{q,B}(\theta_1 + \theta_2) .$$

Thus, the procedure of quantum hashing the input w by the function $\psi_{q,B}$ consists of the following steps:

0. Initialization of the $\log d + 1$ qubits in the state $|0 \ldots 0\rangle|0\rangle$.
1. Application of Hadamard transform to the first $\log d$ qubits:

$$\frac{1}{\sqrt{d}} \sum_{i=1}^{d} |i\rangle|0\rangle = |\psi_{q,B}(0)\rangle . \qquad (12)$$

2. Application of $CCR_{q,B}(w)$ creates the quantum hash of the input bit string $w = w_0 \ldots w_{n-1}$, which is also treated as a number $w = w_0 + w_1 2^1 + \ldots + w_{n-1} 2^{n-1}$:

$$CCR_{q,B}(w)|\psi_{q,B}(0)\rangle = |\psi_{q,B}(w)\rangle \ . \tag{13}$$

Note, that for the model of quantum branching programs this step consists of n substeps: for each input bit w_j there is an instruction $\langle w_j, I, CCR_{q,B}(2^j)\rangle$ of the quantum branching program, i.e. when $w_j = 1$ we apply $CCR_{q,B}(2^j)$, and do nothing otherwise. Obviously,

$$CCR_{q,B}(w) = CCR_{q,B}(w_0) \cdot CCR_{q,B}(w_1 2^1) \cdots CCR_{q,B}(w_{n-1} 2^{n-1}) \ . \tag{14}$$

Thus, an overall number of controlled rotations $CCR_{q,B,i}(\theta)$ is $nd = O(n^2)$.

From the description above it follows that the input bits are read only once, and the quantum branching program is actually a quantum OBDD. An illustrative presentation for this program is given in Figure 4.

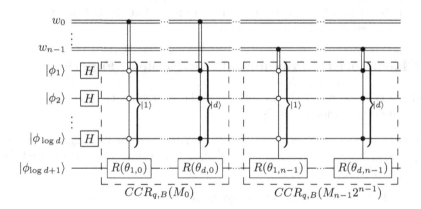

Fig. 4. A quantum OBDD in circuit presentation, that hashes an n-bit input $w = w_0 \ldots w_{n-1}$ into the state $|\psi_{q,B}(M)\rangle$ of $O(\log n)$ qubits. $R(\theta_{i,j})$ denotes a rotation by an angle $\frac{4\pi b_i 2^j}{q}$ around the $\hat{y}$ axis of the Bloch sphere.

Physical implementation. In [2,6] we have proposed an effective physical implementation of compound multiply controlled operators for the model of solid state quantum computer on multiatomic ensembles in the QED cavity. $CCR_{q,B,i}(\theta)$ is exactly such operator and thus can be accelerated in this architecture.

REVERSE-test. Whenever we need to check if a quantum state $|\psi(w)\rangle$ is a hash of a classical string v, one can use the procedure that we call a *REVERSE-test* [1].

Essentially the test applies the procedure that inverts the creation of a quantum hash, i.e. it "uncomputes" the hash to the initial state (usually the all-zero state).

Formally, let the procedure of quantum hashing the string w be given by unitary transformation $U(w)$, applied to initial state $|0\rangle$, i.e. $|\psi(w)\rangle = U(w)|0\rangle$. Then the REVERSE-test, given v and $|\psi(w)\rangle$, applies $U^{-1}(v)$ to the state $|\psi(w)\rangle$ and measures the resulting state. It outputs $v = w$ iff the measurement outcome is $|0\rangle$. So, if $v = w$, then $U^{-1}(v)|\psi(w)\rangle$ would always give $|0\rangle$, and REVERSE-test would give the correct answer. Otherwise, by δ-resistance property

$$\langle 0|U^{-1}(v)\psi(w)\rangle < \delta \ , \tag{15}$$

which bounds the probability of erroneously outputting $v = w$.

Overall, this test has one-sided error bounded by δ^2 if the quantum hash function is δ-resistant.

In case of quantum hash function $CCR_{q,B}$ the REVERSE-test consists of the following steps.
1. Application of $CCR_{q,B}(-v)$ to the state $|\psi(w)\rangle$.
2. Application of the Hadamard transform to all but the last qubit.
3. Measurement of the resulting state.

4   Characteristic Polynomials for Boolean Functions

In this section we recall the definition of the characteristic polynomial for a Boolean function proposed in [5].

Definition 3. *We call a polynomial $g(x_1, \ldots, x_n)$ over the ring $\mathbb{Z}_q$ a characteristic polynomial of a Boolean function $f(x_1, \ldots, x_n)$ and denote it g_f when for all $\sigma \in \{0,1\}^n$ $g_f(\sigma) = 0$ iff $f(\sigma) = 1$.*

Note, that such a polynomial always exists.

Lemma 1. *For any Boolean function f of n variables there exists a characteristic polynomial g_f over $\mathbb{Z}_{2^n}$.*

Proof. One way to construct such characteristic polynomial g_f is transforming a sum of products representation for $\neg f$.

Let $K_1 \vee \ldots \vee K_l$ be a sum of products for $\neg f$ and let $\tilde{K}_i$ be a product of terms from K_i (negations $\neg x_j$ are replaced by $1 - x_j$). Then $\tilde{K}_1 + \ldots + \tilde{K}_l$ is a characteristic polynomial over $\mathbb{Z}_{2^n}$ for f since it equals $0 \iff$ all of $\tilde{K}_i$ (and thus K_i) equal 0. This happens only when the negation of f equals 0.

Generally, there are many polynomials for the same function. For example, the function EQ_n, which tests the equality of two n-bit binary strings, has the following polynomial over $\mathbb{Z}_{2^n}$:

$$\sum_{i=1}^{n} (x_i(1 - y_i) + (1 - x_i)y_i) = \sum_{i=1}^{n} (x_i + y_i - 2x_iy_i) \ . \tag{16}$$

On the other hand, the same function can be represented by the polynomial

$$\sum_{i=1}^{n} x_i 2^{i-1} - \sum_{i=1}^{n} y_i 2^{i-1} \; . \tag{17}$$

5   Computing Boolean Functions with Quantum Hashing

Now we describe the class of Boolean functions that can be efficiently computed in the quantum OBDD model using the quantum hashing technique.

Let $f(x_1, \ldots, x_n)$ be a Boolean function and g be its characteristic polynomial. The following theorem holds.

Theorem 3. *Let $\delta \in (0, 1)$. If there exists is a linear polynomial g for a Boolean function f over $\mathbb{Z}_q$, then f can be computed with one-sided error δ^2 by a quantum OBDD on $O\left(\log \log q + \log 1/\epsilon\right)$ qubits.*

Proof. The key idea is to evaluate the characteristic polynomial and hash the result simultaneously while reading the input. Below we show that this can be easily done when the polynomial is linear. After the hash is prepared the value of the Boolean function f can be obtained by performing the REVERSE-test, checking whether 0 is hashed or not.

Since the polynomial g is linear, i.e. $g = c_1 x_1 + \ldots c_n x_n + c_0$, hashing its value can be done by a sequence of $CCR_{q,B}$ operators:

$$CCR_{q,B}(w) = CCR_{q,B}(c_0) \cdot CCR_{q,B}(c_1 x_1) \cdots CCR_{q,B}(c_n x_n) \; , \tag{18}$$

and this is easily done while reading the input only once.

Then the REVERSE-test applies $CCR_{q,B}(0)$, which is identity operator, and finishes with Hadamard transform and measurements. It outputs the correct answer with the one-sided error probability δ^2.

Thus, f can be computed with one-sided error δ^2 by a quantum OBDD on s qubits, where $s = O\left(\log \log q + \log 1/\epsilon\right)$.

5.1   Examples

The following functions have the aforementioned linear polynomials and thus are effectively computed with quantum hashing.

MOD_m The function MOD_m tests whether the number of 1's in the input is 0 modulo m. The linear polynomial over $\mathbb{Z}_m$ for this function is

$$\sum_{i=1}^{n} x_i.$$

The lower bound for the width of deterministic OBDDs computing this function is $\Omega(m)$ [15]. Thus, our method provides an exponential advantage of quantum OBDD over any deterministic one.

MOD'_m This function is the same as MOD_m, but the input is treated as binary number. Thus, the linear polynomial is

$$\sum_{i=1}^{n} x_i 2^{i-1}.$$

The lower and upper bounds are equal to those of MOD_m.

EQ_n The function EQ_n, which tests the equality of two n-bit binary strings, has the following polynomial over $\mathbb{Z}_{2^n}$

$$\sum_{i=1}^{n} x_i 2^{i-1} - \sum_{i=1}^{n} y_i 2^{i-1}.$$

This function is easy in the deterministic case for a clever choice of the variable ordering. But for the ordering, where all of x's are tested first, it is exponentially hard. In quantum setting, this function can be effectively computed regardless of the variable ordering.

$Palindrome_n(x_1, \ldots, x_n)$ This function tests the symmetry of the input, i.e. whether $x_1 x_2 \ldots x_{\lfloor n/2 \rfloor} = x_n x_{n-1} \ldots x_{\lceil n/2 \rceil + 1}$ or not. The polynomial over $\mathbb{Z}_{2^{\lfloor n/2 \rfloor}}$ is

$$\sum_{i=1}^{\lfloor n/2 \rfloor} x_i 2^{i-1} - \sum_{i=\lceil n/2 \rceil}^{n} x_i 2^{n-i}.$$

The situation with lower and upper bounds for this function is similar to that of EQ_n.

$PERM_n$ The *Permutation Matrix* test function ($PERM_n$) is defined on n^2 variables x_{ij} ($1 \le i, j \le n$). It tests whether the input matrix contains exactly one 1 in each row and each column. Here is a polynomial over $\mathbb{Z}_{(n+1)^{2n}}$

$$\sum_{i=1}^{n} \sum_{j=1}^{n} x_{ij} \left((n+1)^{i-1} + (n+1)^{n+j-1} \right) - \sum_{i=1}^{2n} (n+1)^{i-1}.$$

Note, that this function cannot be effectively computed by a deterministic OBDD – the lower bound is $\Omega(2^n n^{-5/2})$ regardless of the variable ordering [15]. The width of the best known probabilistic OBDD, computing this function with one-sided error, is $O(n^4 \log n)$ [15]. Our algorithm has the width $O(n \log n)$. Since the lower bound $\Omega(n - \log n)$ follows from Theorem 1, our algorithm is almost optimal.

The following functions have linear polynomials as well, but we are not aware of exponential lower bounds in the deterministic case.

$Period_n^s(x_0, \ldots, x_{n-1})$ This function equals 1 iff $x_i = x_{i+s \bmod n}$ for all $i \in \{0, \ldots, n-1\}$. The polynomial over $\mathbb{Z}_{2^n}$ is

$$\sum_{i=0}^{n-1} x_i \left(2^i - 2^{i-s \bmod n}\right).$$

$Semi - Simon_n^s(x_0, \ldots, x_{n-1})$ This function equals 1 iff $x_i = x_{i\oplus s}$ for all $i \in \{0, \ldots, n-1\}$. The polynomial over $\mathbb{Z}_{2^n}$ is

$$\sum_{i=0}^{n-1} x_i \left(2^i - 2^{i\oplus s}\right).$$

Acknowledgments. The work is performed according to the Russian Government Program of Competitive Growth of Kazan Federal University. Work was in part supported by the Russian Foundation for Basic Research (under the grants 12-07-97016, 14-07-00878).

References

1. Ablayev, F.M., Vasiliev, A.V.: Cryptographic quantum hashing. Laser Physics Letters 11(2), 025202 (2014). http://stacks.iop.org/1612-202X/11/i=2/a=025202
2. Ablayev, F., Andrianov, S., Moiseev, S., Vasiliev, A.: Encoded universality of quantum computations on the multi-atomic ensembles in the qed cavity. Tech. Rep. arXiv:1109.0291 [quant-ph]. Cornell University Library (September 2011). http://arxiv.org/abs/1109.0291
3. Ablayev, F., Gainutdinova, A., Karpinski, M.: On Computational Power of Quantum Branching Programs. In: Freivalds, R. (ed.) FCT 2001. LNCS, vol. 2138, pp. 59–70. Springer, Heidelberg (2001)
4. Ablayev, F., Gainutdinova, A., Karpinski, M., Moore, C., Pollett, C.: On the computational power of probabilistic and quantum branching programs of constant width. Information and Computation 203, 145–162 (2005). http://dx.doi.org/10.1016/j.ic.2005.04.003
5. Ablayev, F., Vasiliev, A.: Algorithms for quantum branching programs based on fingerprinting. Electronic Proceedings in Theoretical Computer Science 9, 1–11 (2009). http://arxiv.org/abs/0911.2317
6. Ablayev, F., Andrianov, S., Moiseev, S., Vasiliev, A.: Quantum computer with atomic logical qubits encoded on macroscopic three-level systems in common quantum electrodynamic cavity. Lobachevskii Journal of Mathematics 34(4), 291–303 (2013). http://dx.doi.org/10.1134/S1995080213040094
7. Agrawal, V., Lee, D., Wozniakowski, H.: Numerical computation of characteristic polynomials of boolean functions and its applications. Numerical Algorithms 17, 261–278 (1998). http://dx.doi.org/10.1023/A:1016632423579
8. Buhrman, H., Cleve, R., Watrous, J., de Wolf, R.: Quantum fingerprinting. Phys. Rev. Lett. 87(16), 167902 (2001). www.arXiv.org/quant-ph/0102001v1
9. Deutsch, D.: Quantum computational networks. Royal Society of London Proceedings Series A 425, 73–90 (1989). http://dx.doi.org/10.1098/rspa.1989.0099

10. Gottesman, D., Chuang, I.: Quantum digital signatures. Tech. Rep. arXiv:quant-ph/0105032. Cornell University Library (November 2001). http://arxiv.org/abs/quant-ph/0105032

11. Jain, J., Abraham, J.A., Bitner, J., Fussell, D.S.: Probabilistic verification of boolean functions. Formal Methods in System Design **1**, 61–115 (1992)

12. Nakanishi, M., Hamaguchi, K., Kashiwabara, T.: Ordered Quantum Branching Programs Are More Powerful than Ordered Probabilistic Branching Programs under a Bounded-Width Restriction. In: Du, D.-Z., Eades, P., Sharma, A.K., Lin, X., Estivill-Castro, V. (eds.) COCOON 2000. LNCS, vol. 1858, pp. 467–476. Springer, Heidelberg (2000)

13. Razborov, A.A., Szemeredi, E., Wigderson, A.: Constructing small sets that are uniform in arithmetic progressions. Combinatorics, Probability & Computing **2**, 513–518 (1993)

14. Sauerhoff, M., Sieling, D.: Quantum branching programs and space-bounded nonuniform quantum complexity. Theoretical Computer Science 334(1–3), 177–225 (2005). http://arxiv.org/abs/quant-ph/0403164

15. Wegener, I.: Branching Programs and Binary Decision Diagrams. SIAM Monographs on Discrete Mathematics and Applications. SIAM Press (2000)

16. de Wolf, R.: Quantum Computing and Communication Complexity. Ph.D. thesis, University of Amsterdam (2001)

17. Yao, A.C.C.: Quantum circuit complexity. In: Proceedings of Thirty-fourth IEEE Symposium on Foundations of Computer Science, pp. 352–361. IEEE Computer Society, Palo Alto (1993)

Complexity of Promise Problems on Classical and Quantum Automata

Maria Paola Bianchi, Carlo Mereghetti$^{(\boxtimes)}$, and Beatrice Palano

Dipartimento di Informatica, Università degli Studi di Milano via Comelico 39,
20135 Milano, Italy
{bianchi,mereghetti,palano}@di.unimi.it

Abstract. We consider the promise problem A^{N,r_1,r_2} on a *unary* alphabet $\{\sigma\}$ studied by Gruska et al. in [21]. This problem is formally defined as the pair $A^{N,r_1,r_2} = (A_{yes}^{N,r_1}, A_{no}^{N,r_2})$, with $0 \leq r_1 \neq r_2 < N$, $A_{yes}^{N,r_1} = \{\sigma^n \mid n \equiv r_1 \bmod N\}$ and $A_{no}^{N,r_2} = \{\sigma^n \mid n \equiv r_2 \bmod N\}$. There, it is shown that a measure-once one-way quantum automaton can solve exactly A^{N,r_1,r_2} with only 3 basis states, while any one-way deterministic finite automaton requires d states, d being the smallest integer such that $d \mid N$ and $d \nmid (r_2 - r_1) \bmod N$. Here, we introduce the promise problem $\text{DIOF}_{r_1,r_2}^{a,N}$ as an extension of A^{N,r_1,r_2} to *general* alphabets. Even for this problem, we show the same descriptional superiority of the quantum paradigm over one-way deterministic automata. Moreover, we prove that even by adding features to classical automata, namely nondeterminism, probabilism, two-way motion, we cannot obtain automata for A^{N,r_1,r_2} and $\text{DIOF}_{r_1,r_2}^{a,N}$ smaller than one-way deterministic.

Keywords: Classical and quantum automata · Promise problem · Descriptional complexity

1 Introduction

Several features have been added to the original model of *one–way deterministic* finite automaton (1DFA) [38]. Thus, we saw one-way nondeterminism (1NFA) [38], one-way probabilism (1PFA) [37], and the ability of scanning input strings back and forth, yielding the definition of *two-way* devices (e.g., 2DFA) [39]. However, simulation results show that the computational power of 1NFAs, 1PFAs with isolated cut point, and 2DFAs does not exceed that of 1DFA, i.e., the class of *regular languages*.

Beside these classical models, other types of finite automata based on the quantum paradigm [18] are introduced and investigated in the literature [2,4, 9,16,22,25,28,29,35]. The first and simplest variant of *one-way quantum finite automaton* (1QFA) is the measure-once model, where the probability of accepting words is evaluated by "observing" just once, at the end of input processing.

Partially supported by MIUR under the project "PRIN: Automi e Linguaggi Formali: Aspetti Matematici e Applicativi."

C.S. Calude et al. (Eds.): Gruska Festschrift, LNCS 8808, pp. 161–175, 2014.
DOI: 10.1007/978-3-319-13350-8_12

Surprisingly enough, measure-once 1QFAs working with isolated cut point are proved to single out a proper subclass of regular languages, namely group (or reversible) languages [5,14].

In addition to computational power, several works in the literature investigate the descriptional power of these models, i.e., their ability to provide succinct language representations. To this regard, a fundamental tool is to study how the number of states changes when turning one automaton into another. The first widely known result in this realm compares nondeterminism with determinism for one-way finite automata: each n-state 1NFA can be simulated by a 1DFA with 2^n states [38]. Moreover, this bound is tight [33]. Another tool to get deeper insights into the descriptional power of different models of finite automata is to test them on very specific tasks, such as recognizing *unary languages*, i.e., languages over single-letter alphabets [15,32]. Some results along this line of research for probabilistic and quantum automata can be found in [8,11,12,31]. Further results on the descriptional power of quantum automata are contained in [7,10,27,30].

The same questions on the computational and descriptional power of different models of finite automata have been extended from language recognition to more general tasks known as *promise problem* solving. A promise problem on an alphabet Σ is specified by two nonempty disjoint subsets of Σ^* called *yes*-instances and *no*-instances. Unlike language recognition, the union of the *yes*-instances and *no*-instances may be a proper subset of Σ^*. A device which solves the promise problem accepts *yes*-instances, rejects *no*-instances and is allowed arbitrary behavior on the remaining strings. Intuitively, this device is "promised" that the input is either a *yes*-instance or a *no*-instance, and is only required to distinguish between these two cases.

Recently, the study of promise problems has focused on quantum devices. The first result in this realm is given by Murakami et al. [34], who showed the existence of a promise problem solvable exactly by a quantum pushdown automaton, but not by any deterministic pushdown automaton. Concerning finite automata, Ambainis and Yakaryilmaz [3] showed the existence of a family of promise problems which can be solved exactly by a 2-state 1QFA, whereas the size of corresponding 1DFAs and exact 1PFAs grows without bound. Gruska et al. showed further results on the succinctness of 1QFAs for promise problems in [20,21,42–44].

In this paper, we consider the *unary* promise problem introduced in [21] as $A^{N,r_1,r_2} = (A_{yes}^{N,r_1}, A_{no}^{N,r_2})$, with $0 \le r_1 \ne r_2 < N$, $A_{yes}^{N,r_1} = \{\sigma^n \mid n \equiv r_1 \bmod N\}$ and $A_{no}^{N,r_2} = \{\sigma^n \mid n \equiv r_2 \bmod N\}$. Gruska et al. show that a measure-once 1QFA can solve exactly A^{N,r_1,r_2} with only 3 basis states, while a 1DFA requires d states, d being the smallest integer such that $d \mid N$ and $d \nmid (r_2 - r_1) \bmod N$. Here, we introduce the promise problem $\mathrm{DIOF}_{r_1,r_2}^{a,N}$ as an extension of A^{N,r_1,r_2} to *general* alphabets. Even for this problem, we show the same descriptional superiority of 1QFAs over 1DFAs. Moreover, we prove that adding features to classical automata, namely nondeterminism, probabilism, two-way motion, does not lead to finite automata smaller than 1DFAs for solving the promise problems A^{N,r_1,r_2} and $\mathrm{DIOF}_{r_1,r_2}^{a,N}$. To analyze these latter devices, we use the tool of normal forms for unary automata, namely: the Chrobak normal form for one-way nondeterministic finite automata [15], the cyclic normal form for one-way probabilistic finite automata [13], and a simplified form for two-way deterministic finite automata called sweeping [26,41]. Putting automata in such forms, enables us to point out their ultimate periodic behavior, from which we determine optimal lower limits for their descriptional power.

2   Preliminaries

2.1   Arithmetics and Linear Algebra

The set of natural (integer) numbers is denoted by $\mathbb{N}$ ($\mathbb{Z}$). The *greatest common divisor* of $a_1, \ldots, a_s \in \mathbb{Z}$ is denoted by $\gcd(a_1, \ldots, a_s)$. Their *least common multiple* is denoted by $\operatorname{lcm}(a_1, \ldots, a_s)$. For $a, b \in \mathbb{N}$, the notation $a \mid b$ ($a \nmid b$) stands for a divides (does not divide) b. For $N > 0$, the notation $a \equiv b \bmod N$ means that $a \bmod N = b \bmod N$. Clearly, $a \mid b$ if and only if $b \equiv 0 \bmod a$. By the Fundamental Theorem of Arithmetic, any integer $z > 1$ can be univocally expressed as a product $z = \prod_{i=1}^{s} z_i^{k_i}$, where $z_1 < \cdots < z_s$ are primes and $k_1, \ldots, k_s$ are positive integers. This product is the *prime factorization* of z. Given $a_1, \ldots, a_s, z \in \mathbb{Z}$, a linear Diophantine equation with variables $x_1, \ldots, x_s$ ranging over $\mathbb{Z}$ writes as $a_1 x_1 + \cdots + a_s x_s = z$. It is a very well known fact that this equation has solutions in $\mathbb{N}$ if and only if $\gcd(a_1, \ldots, a_s) \mid z$.

We quickly recall some notions of linear algebra, useful to describe the quantum world. For more details, we refer the reader to, e.g., [40]. The field of real (complex) numbers is denoted by $\mathbb{R}$ ($\mathbb{C}$). Given a complex number $z = a + ib$, we denote its *conjugate* by $z^* = a - ib$ and its *modulus* by $|z| = \sqrt{zz^*}$. We let $\mathbb{C}^{n \times m}$ and $\mathbb{C}^n$ (shorthand for $\mathbb{C}^{1 \times n}$) denote, respectively, the set of $n \times m$ matrices and n-dimensional row vectors with entries in $\mathbb{C}$. The identity matrix is denoted by I. We let $e_j = (0, \ldots, 0, 1, 0, \ldots, 0)$ be the characteristic vector having 1 in its jth component and 0 elsewhere.

Given a matrix $M \in \mathbb{C}^{n \times m}$, we let M_{ij} denote its (i, j)th entry. The *transpose* of M is the matrix $M^T \in \mathbb{C}^{m \times n}$ satisfying $M^T{}_{ij} = M_{ji}$, while we let M^* be the matrix satisfying $M_{ij}^* = (M_{ij})^*$. The *adjoint* of M is the matrix $M^\dagger = (M^T)^*$. For matrices $A, B \in \mathbb{C}^{n \times m}$, their *sum* is the $n \times m$ matrix $(A + B)_{ij} = A_{ij} + B_{ij}$. For matrices $C \in \mathbb{C}^{n \times m}$ and $D \in \mathbb{C}^{m \times r}$, their *product* is the $n \times r$ matrix $(CD)_{ij} = \sum_{k=1}^{m} C_{ik} D_{kj}$.

A *Hilbert space* of dimension n is the linear space $\mathbb{C}^n$ of n-dimensional complex row vectors equipped with sum and product by elements in $\mathbb{C}$, in which the *inner product* $\langle \varphi, \psi \rangle = \varphi \psi^\dagger$ is defined, for $\varphi, \psi \in \mathbb{C}^n$. The *norm* of a vector $\varphi \in \mathbb{C}^n$ is given by $\|\varphi\| = \sqrt{\langle \varphi, \varphi \rangle}$. If $\langle \varphi, \psi \rangle = 0$ (and $\|\varphi\| = 1 = \|\psi\|$), then φ and ψ are *orthogonal* (*orthonormal*). The set of orthonormal vectors $\{e_1, \ldots, e_n\}$ is called the *canonical basis* of $\mathbb{C}^n$. Two subspaces $X, Y \subseteq \mathbb{C}^n$ are orthogonal if any vector in X is orthogonal to any vector in Y. In this case, we denote by $X \dotplus Y$ the linear space generated by $X \cup Y$.

A matrix $M \in \mathbb{C}^{n \times n}$ is said to be:

- *Boolean:* whenever its entries are either 0 or 1.
- *Stochastic:* whenever its entries are reals from the interval $[0, 1]$ and each row sums to 1.
- *Unitary:* whenever $MM^\dagger = I = M^\dagger M$; equivalently, M is unitary if and only if it preserves the norm, i.e., $\|\varphi M\| = \|\varphi\|$ for any $\varphi \in \mathbb{C}^n$. It is easy to see that the product of unitary matrices is unitary as well.

A matrix $H \in \mathbb{C}^{n \times n}$ is said to be *Hermitian (or self-adjoint)* whenever $H = H^\dagger$. A matrix $P \in \mathbb{C}^{n \times n}$ is a *projector* if and only if P is Hermitian and idempotent, i.e., $P^2 = P$. The eigenvalues of a projector are either 0 or 1. More generally, given the Hermitian matrix H, let $c_1, \ldots, c_s$ be its eigenvalues and $E_1, \ldots, E_s$ the corresponding eigenspaces. It is well known that each eigenvalue c_k is real, that E_i is orthogonal to E_j for $i \neq j$, and that $E_1 \dotplus \cdots \dotplus E_s = \mathbb{C}^n$. Thus, every vector $\varphi \in \mathbb{C}^n$ can be uniquely decomposed as $\varphi = \varphi_1 + \cdots + \varphi_s$ for unique $\varphi_j \in E_j$. The linear transformation $\varphi \mapsto \varphi_j$ is the projector P_j onto the subspace E_j. Actually, the Hermitian matrix H is biunivocally determined by its eigenvalues and projectors as $H = \sum_{i=1}^s c_i P_i$, where $\sum_{i=1}^s P_i = I$.

2.2   Languages and Classical Finite Automata

We assume familiarity with basics in formal language theory (see, e.g., [23]). The set of all words (including the empty word ε) over a finite alphabet Σ is denoted by Σ^*. For a word $\omega \in \Sigma^*$, we let $|\omega|$ denote its length and ω_i its ith symbol. For $\sigma \in \Sigma$, we let $|\omega|_\sigma$ denote the number of occurrences of σ in ω. A language on Σ is any set $L \subseteq \Sigma^*$.

In what follows, we quickly outline the types of classical finite automata we shall be dealing with. For extensive presentations, the reader is referred to [23] for deterministic and nondeterministic automata, and to [36] for probabilistic automata.

A *one-way deterministic finite automaton* (1DFA) is defined by the 5-tuple $A = \langle S, \Sigma, \tau, s_1, F \rangle$, where $S = \{s_1, \ldots, s_{|S|}\}$ is the finite set of states, Σ the input alphabet, $s_1 \in S$ the initial state, $F \subseteq S$ the set of accepting states, and $\tau : S \times \Sigma \to S$ is the transition function. An input word is *accepted* by A if the induced computation starting from the initial state ends in some accepting state after consuming the whole input. A linear representation for the 1DFA A is the 3-tuple $\langle \alpha, \{M(\sigma)\}_{\sigma \in \Sigma}, \beta \rangle$, where $\alpha \in \{0, 1\}^{|S|}$ is the characteristic row vector of the initial state, $M(\sigma) \in \{0, 1\}^{|S| \times |S|}$ is the boolean stochastic matrix satisfying $M(\sigma)_{ij} = 1$ if and only if $\tau(s_i, \sigma) = s_j$, and $\beta \in \{0, 1\}^{|S| \times 1}$ is the characteristic column vector of the final states. The behavior of A on an input $\omega \in \Sigma^*$ is given by $p_A(\omega) = \alpha M(\omega) \beta$, where we let $M(\omega) = \prod_{i=1}^{|\omega|} M(\omega_i)$. The language accepted by A is the set $L = \{\omega \in \Sigma^* \mid p_A(\omega) = 1\}$.

A *one-way nondeterministic finite automaton* (1NFA) is defined similarly to a 1DFA, but the transition function now maps to possibly empty subsets of S, i.e., $\tau : S \times \Sigma \to 2^S$. This dynamic describes the possibility to have zero or more than one next state at each move. A word is accepted if there exists a computation starting from the initial state and ending in some accepting state after consuming the whole input. More formally, the linear representation for a 1NFA A is the 3-tuple $\langle \alpha, \{M(\sigma)\}_{\sigma \in \Sigma}, \beta \rangle$, where α, β are as before, while $M(\sigma) \in \{0,1\}^{|S| \times |S|}$ is the boolean (not necessarily stochastic) matrix satisfying $M(\sigma)_{ij} = 1$ if and only if $s_j \in \tau(s_i, \sigma)$. The accepted language is now defined as the set $L = \{\omega \in \Sigma^* \mid p_A(\omega) \geq 1\}$.

A *one-way probabilistic finite automaton* (1PFA) is defined similarly to above devices but now, for any given state and input symbol, the transition function returns a probability distribution over the possible next states. As a consequence, an accepting probability is associated with each input word. More formally, the linear representation for a 1PFA A is the 3-tuple $\langle \alpha, \{M(\sigma)\}_{\sigma \in \Sigma}, \beta \rangle$, where β is defined as above, $\alpha \in [0,1]^{|S|}$ is a stochastic row vector representing the initial probability distribution on S, and $M(\sigma) \in [0,1]^{|S| \times |S|}$ is the stochastic matrix where $M(\sigma)_{ij}$ is the *probability* that A moves from the ith to the jth state upon reading σ. Thus, the behavior $p_A(\omega)$ now returns the probability that A accepts the input word $\omega \in \Sigma^*$. The function $p_A : \Sigma^* \to [0,1]$ is also called the stochastic event induced by A. Given $\lambda \in [0,1]$, the language accepted by A with cut point λ is the set $L = \{\omega \in \Sigma^* \mid p_A(\omega) > \lambda\}$. Moreover, λ is said to be *isolated* if there exists a positive δ such that $|p_A(\omega) - \lambda| \geq \delta$, for any $\omega \in \Sigma^*$.

In a *two-way deterministic finite automaton* (2DFA), moves are dictated by a partial transition function[1] $\tau : S \times (\Sigma \cup \{\vdash, \dashv\}) \to S \times \{-1, +1\}$, where $\vdash, \dashv \notin \Sigma$ are two special symbols called left and right endmarker, respectively. In a move, the 2DFA reads an input symbol, changes its state, and moves the input head one cell to the right or to the left depending on whether τ returns $+1$ or -1, respectively. An input word $\omega \in \Sigma^*$ for A is stored on an input tape surrounded by the two endmarkers, so that the tape content is $\vdash \omega \dashv$. The machine accepts ω if the induced computation starting from the initial state with the head on the left endmarker reaches an accepting state with the head on either of the endmarkers. Although 2DFAs do not have a finite linear representation, we let $p_A(\omega) = 1$ ($p_A(\omega) = 0$) to denote that ω is accepted (not accepted) by A. Clearly, the accepted language is the set $L = \{\omega \in \Sigma^* \mid p_A(\omega) = 1\}$.

It is well known that 1DFAs, 1NFAs, isolated cut point 1PFAs and 2DFAs share the same computational power, i.e., they characterize the class of regular languages. Nevertheless, they have different descriptional power: representation of regular languages may be much more ?economical? — in terms of number of states — in one system than another. For instance, the following are the state costs of simulating n-state automata models by 1DFAs:

- 1NFAs: 2^n [33,38],
- 1PFAs with δ-isolated cut point: $(1 + 1/(2\delta))^{n-1}$ [1,36,37],
- 2DFAs: $n(n^n - (n-1)^n)$ [24,39].

These costs are optimal, except the one for isolated cut point 1PFAs which is "quasi optimal".

---

[1] In the deterministic case, we do not consider stationary moves since they can be easily removed without augmenting the number of states.

A language $L \subseteq \Sigma^*$ is called *unary* whenever $|\Sigma| = 1$. Unary regular languages are accepted by unary finite automata, i.e., automata having single-symbol input alphabets. It is folklore that any unary 1DFA consists of an initial path followed by a cycle (see Figure 1).

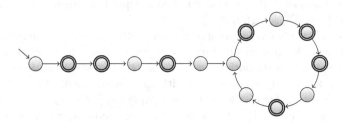

Fig. 1. A unary 1DFA. When depicting unary automata we will always omit the symbol label, since it would be redundant.

It is well known that unary automata show relevant differences from automata on general alphabets. For instance, it is proved in [15] that the optimal state cost of simulating n-state unary 1NFAs and 2DFAs by 1DFAs is "only" $e^{(1+o(1))\sqrt{n \cdot \ln n}}$. For unary 1PFAs, several recent simulation results may be found, e.g., in [11,13, 17,31]. All these simulations crucially rely on the fact that unary automata can be put in some "normal forms". In Section 4, we will recall such forms, and use them to get our results on promise problems.

2.3 Quantum Mechanics and Quantum Automata

Before outlining the model of quantum automaton we shall consider, we quickly present the main ingredients of the mathematical description of a quantum system possessing $Q = \{q_1, \ldots, q_m\}$ *basis states* and reacting to a set of impulses represented by the alphabet $\Sigma = \{\sigma_1, \ldots, \sigma_H\}$. (For more details, we refer the reader to, e.g., [18].) Every basis state $q_i \in Q$ can be represented by its characteristic vector $e_i \in \{0,1\}^m$. At any given time, the *quantum state* of the system is represented by a superposition $\pi = \sum_{k=1}^{m} \alpha_k e_k$, where the coefficients α_k are complex *amplitudes* and $\|\pi\| = 1$. With every symbol $\sigma_i \in \Sigma$, we associate a unitary transformation $U(\sigma_i) : \mathbb{C}^m \to \mathbb{C}^m$. An *observable* is described by an Hermitian matrix $\mathcal{O} = c_1 P_1 + \cdots + c_s P_s$. With the system being in the quantum state π, we can operate:

1. *Evolution $U(\sigma_i)$*: the new state $\xi = \pi U(\sigma_i)$ is reached; this dynamics is *reversible*, since $\pi = \xi U^\dagger(\sigma_i)$.
2. *Measurement of $\mathcal{O}$*: every outcome in $\{c_1, \ldots, c_s\}$ can be observed; c_j is obtained with probability $\|\pi P_j\|^2$ and, after measurement, the state collapses to the new state $\pi P_j / \|\pi P_j\|$. The state transformation induced by a measurement is typically *irreversible*.

Let us now see how quantum finite automata fit in this picture. *One-way quantum finite automata* (1QFAs) are computational devices particularly interesting because of their simplicity. Moreover, their analysis provides a good insight into the nature of quantum computation, since 1QFAs are a theoretical model for a quantum computer with finite memory. From the point of view of computational capabilities, 1QFAs present both advantages and disadvantages with respect to their classical (deterministic, nondeterministic or probabilistic) counterpart. Essentially, quantum superposition offers some computational advantages on probabilistic superposition seen for 1PFAs. On the other hand, quantum dynamics are reversible: because of limitation of memory, it is generally impossible to simulate classical automata by quantum automata. Limitations due to reversibility can be partially attenuated by systematically introducing measurements of suitable observables as computational steps.

Several models of quantum automata are proposed in the literature [2,6?]. Basically, they differ in measurement policy. In this paper, we only focus on the *measure-once model* [5,14,28], where the transformation on an input symbol is realized by a unitary operator and a *unique* measurement is performed at the end of computation. More formally, a measure-once 1QFA with m basis states and input alphabet Σ is a system $A = \langle Q, \Sigma, \{U(\sigma)\}_{\sigma \in \Sigma \cup \{\vdash, \dashv\}}, e_1, Q_a \rangle$, where:

- $Q = \{e_1, \ldots, e_m\}$ is the canonical basis of the Hilbert space $\mathbb{C}^m$; its elements are the basis states,
- Σ is a finite alphabet of input symbols, and $\vdash, \dashv \notin \Sigma$ are the left and right endmarkers,
- with any $\sigma \in \Sigma \cup \{\vdash, \dashv\}$, a unitary matrix $U(\sigma) \in \mathbb{C}^{m \times m}$ is associated,
- $e_1 = (1, 0, \ldots, 0) \in \mathbb{C}^m$ is the initial basis state,
- $Q_a \subseteq Q$ is the set of accepting basis states, identifying the projection matrix $P_a = \sum_{\{i \mid e_i \in Q_a\}} e_i^T e_i \in \mathbb{C}^{m \times m}$ which biunivocally determines the observable $\mathcal{O} = 1 \cdot P_a + 0 \cdot (I - P_a)$.

The behavior of A is the stochastic event $p_A : \Sigma^* \to [0, 1]$ defined, for any $x = x_1 x_2 \cdots x_n \in \Sigma^*$, by

$$p_A(x) = \|e_1 U(\vdash) U(x_1) U(x_2) \cdots U(x_n) U(\dashv) P_a\|^2.$$

The language accepted by A with (isolated) cut-point λ is defined as in Section 2.2 for 1PFAs.

From a computational power point of view, in [5,28] it is proved that measure-once 1QFAs are strictly less powerful than classical automata. In fact, with isolated cut point, they characterize the class of group (or reversible) languages, a proper subclass of regular languages. However, from a descriptional power point of view, they are shown to greatly outperform classical models. E.g., in [7,8,30], several families of regular languages are provided, on which measure-once 1QFAs are exponentially smaller than classical paradigms.

We remark that measure-once 1QFAs are originally introduced in [5,28] without the endmarkers, with an arbitrary initial unitary vector, and with an arbitrary accepting subspace. More precisely, the automaton is represented as $B =$

$\langle Q, \Sigma, \{U(\sigma)\}_{\sigma \in \Sigma}, \pi, P \rangle$, where Q, Σ and $U(\sigma)$ are defined as above, $\pi \in \mathbb{C}^m$ is a unitary vector and P is a projector. In this case, the event induced by B on x is $p_B(x) = \|\pi U(x_1)U(x_2) \cdots U(x_n)P\|^2$. Actually, the two models are equivalent:

- The automaton A is equivalent to $A' = \langle Q, \Sigma, \{U'(\sigma)\}_{\sigma \in \Sigma}, \pi', P_a \rangle$, where $U'(\sigma) = U(\dashv)^\dagger U(\sigma) U(\dashv)$ and $\pi' = e_1 U(\vdash) U(\dashv)$. In fact

$$p_{A'}(x) = \|e_1 U(\vdash)U(\dashv)U^\dagger(\dashv)U(x_1)U(\dashv) \cdots U^\dagger(\dashv)U(x_n)U(\dashv)P_a\|^2 = p_A(x).$$

- The automaton B is equivalent to $B' = \langle Q, \Sigma, \{U(\sigma)\}_{\sigma \in \Sigma \cup \{\vdash, \dashv\}}, e_1, Q_a \rangle$, where $U(\vdash)$ is a unitary matrix with π as the first row, so that $e_1 U(\vdash) = \pi$. To set Q_a, we notice that P is similar to the diagonal matrix P_a built on the eigenvalues of P, i.e., $P = V P_a V^\dagger$ with V being a unitary matrix [40]. Moreover, as recalled in Section 2.1, such eigenvalues are either 0 or 1. So, we let Q_a be the unique subset of Q such that $P_a = \sum_{\{i \mid e_i \in Q_a\}} e_i^T e_i$ holds. In addition, V being unitary, we let $U(\dashv) = V$, and notice that multiplying a vector by $V^\dagger$ does not change the vector norm. So, we can write

$$p_{B'}(x) = \|e_1 U(\vdash)U(x_1)U(x_2) \cdots U(x_n)U(\dashv)P_a\|^2$$
$$= \|\pi U(x_1)U(x_2) \cdots U(x_n)V P_a V^\dagger\|^2 = p_B(x).$$

Throughout the rest of the paper, we will simply write 1QFA, understanding the designation "measure-once".

3   Quantum Automata for Promise Problems

We recall that a *promise problem* over an alphabet Σ is a pair $A = (A_{yes}, A_{no})$, where $A_{yes}, A_{no} \subseteq \Sigma^*$ are nonempty disjoint sets. An automaton M solves A *with isolated cut point* λ if there exists a $\delta \in \left(0, \frac{1}{2}\right]$ such that

- for any $\omega \in A_{yes}$, $p_M(\omega) \geq \lambda + \delta$, and
- for any $\omega \in A_{no}$, $p_M(\omega) \leq \lambda - \delta$.

If $\lambda = \delta = \frac{1}{2}$, then A is solved by M *exactly*.

It is easy to see that the classical membership problem for a nonempty language $L \subseteq \Sigma^*$ may be regarded as the promise problem $(L, \Sigma^* \setminus L)$.

In [21], Gruska et al. propose the promise problem $A^{N,r_1,r_2} = (A_{yes}^{N,r_1}, A_{no}^{N,r_2})$ on the unary alphabet $\{\sigma\}$, with $0 \leq r_1 \neq r_2 < N$,

$$A_{yes}^{N,r_1} = \{\sigma^n \mid n \equiv r_1 \bmod N\} \quad \text{and} \quad A_{no}^{N,r_2} = \{\sigma^n \mid n \equiv r_2 \bmod N\}.$$

For the sake of readability, when referring to this problem throughout the rest of the paper, we let

$$l = (r_2 - r_1) \bmod N.$$

The following result is proved in [21]:

Theorem 1. *The promise problem A^{N,r_1,r_2} can be solved exactly by a 3 basis states 1QFA, while the minimal 1DFA has d states, where d is the smallest positive integer such that $d \mid N$ and $d \nmid l$.*

We recall that the minimal 1DFA for A^{N,r_1,r_2} addressed in Theorem 1 consists of a cycle of length d with a unique final state at distance r_1 from the initial state. We also notice that, by fixing $N = 2^{k+1}$, $r_1 = 0$ and $r_2 = 2^k$, we obtain the promise problem studied in [3], for which an unbounded size gap between quantum and deterministic finite automata solution is established. So, Theorem 1 extends this gap to other values of N (e.g., for prime N).

Let us now introduce a generalization of the promise problem A^{N,r_1,r_2} on the multi-letter alphabet $\Sigma = \{\sigma_1, \sigma_2, \ldots, \sigma_H\}$. For $0 \leq r_1 \neq r_2 < N$ and $a = (a_1, a_2, \ldots, a_H) \in \mathbb{N}^H$ satisfying $\gcd(a_1, a_2, \ldots, a_H, N) = 1$, we define the promise problem $\text{DIOF}^{a,N}_{r_1,r_2} = (\text{DIOF}^{a,N,r_1}_{yes}, \text{DIOF}^{a,N,r_2}_{no})$ as

$$\text{DIOF}^{a,N,r_1}_{yes} = \{\omega \in \Sigma^* \mid (a_1|\omega|_{\sigma_1} + a_2|\omega|_{\sigma_2} + \cdots + a_H|\omega|_{\sigma_H}) \equiv r_1 \bmod N\},$$

$$\text{DIOF}^{a,N,r_2}_{no} = \{\omega \in \Sigma^* \mid (a_1|\omega|_{\sigma_1} + a_2|\omega|_{\sigma_2} + \cdots + a_H|\omega|_{\sigma_H}) \equiv r_2 \bmod N\}.$$

As above, when referring to this problem, we let $l = (r_2 - r_1) \bmod N$. Notice that the condition $\gcd(a_1, a_2, \ldots, a_H, N) = 1$ ensures that $\text{DIOF}^{a,N,r_1}_{yes}$ and $\text{DIOF}^{a,N,r_2}_{no}$ are nonempty sets for any r_1, r_2. In addition, the condition $r_1 \neq r_2$ ensures disjointness. By suitably adapting the technique in [21], we exhibit succinct 1QFAs for the family $\text{DIOF}^{a,N}_{r_1,r_2}$:

Theorem 2. *The promise problem $\text{DIOF}^{a,N}_{r_1,r_2}$ can be solved exactly by a 3 basis states 1QFA.*

Proof. To get our 1QFA, we apply the same construction exhibited in Theorem 1 in [21]. The only difference is that, instead of having the unique matrix U_a performing a rotation of an angle θ, we here have matrices $U(\sigma_j)$ performing rotations of angles θa_j, for $1 \leq j \leq H$. As a consequence, the product $U(\omega) = \prod_{i=1}^{|\omega|} U(\omega_i)$ describing the computation of the 1QFA on any given input word ω now yields the matrix

$$U(\omega) = \begin{pmatrix} 1 & 0 & 0 \\ 0 & \cos\left(\theta \sum_{j=1}^{H} a_j|\omega|_{\sigma_j}\right) & \sin\left(\theta \sum_{j=1}^{H} a_j|\omega|_{\sigma_j}\right) \\ 0 & -\sin\left(\theta \sum_{j=1}^{H} a_j|\omega|_{\sigma_j}\right) & \cos\left(\theta \sum_{j=1}^{H} a_j|\omega|_{\sigma_j}\right) \end{pmatrix}.$$

The rest of the proof proceeds as in [21].   □

4   Classical Automata for Promise Problems

Let us now analyze the size required by classical automata for solving the promise problems A^{N,r_1,r_2} and $\text{DIOF}^{a,N}_{r_1,r_2}$. First we consider one-way models: both in the nondeterministic and probabilistic case, we obtain the same size lower bound as for 1DFAs (Theorem 1). Then, we extend this result to 2DFAs.

To study the solution of the promise problem A^{N,r_1,r_2} on 1NFAs, we recall the Chrobak normal form for unary automata [15]. This form extends the structure of unary 1DFAs displayed in Figure 1 and, roughly speaking, consists of an initial path at the end of which a nondeterministic move leads to more than one cycle (see Figure 2).

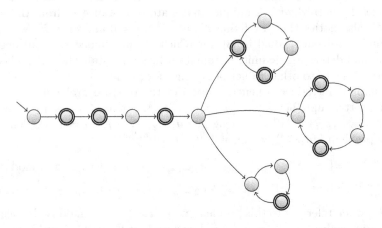

Fig. 2. A unary 1NFA in Chrobak normal form with 3 cycles

More formally, a unary 1NFA $A = \langle S, \{\sigma\}, \tau, s_0, F \rangle$ is in *Chrobak normal form* if S can be partitioned into $m + 1$ disjoint sets $S_0, C_1, \ldots, C_m$ such that:

- $S_0 = \{s_0, s_1, \ldots, s_t\}$,
- for $1 \le i \le m$, $C_i = \{p_{i,0}, p_{i,1}, \ldots, p_{i,y_i-1}\}$,
- for $1 \le i \le m$ and $0 \le j < y_i$, $\tau(p_{i,j}, \sigma) = \{p_{i,(j+1) \bmod y_i}\}$, i.e., C_i is a cycle of length y_i,
- for $0 \le i < t$, $\tau(s_i, \sigma) = \{s_{i+1}\}$, i.e., S_0 is a path of length t,
- $\tau(s_t, \sigma) = \{p_{1,0}, p_{2,0}, \ldots, p_{m,0}\}$, i.e., s_t is the only state where a nondeterministic move takes place, leading to a single state in each cycle.

In [15], it is proved the following:

Lemma 1. *Each unary n-state 1NFA can be simulated by a 1NFA in Chrobak normal form having $O(n^2)$ states in the initial path and at most n states in the cycles.*

The Chrobak normal form is crucial to obtain the following result:

Theorem 3. *The minimal 1NFA solving the promise problem A^{N,r_1,r_2} has d states, where d is the smallest positive integer such that $d \mid N$ and $d \nmid l$.*

Proof. The minimal 1DFA addressed in Theorem 1, is an example of d-state 1NFA for A^{N,r_1,r_2}. So, we only need to prove minimality.

Suppose there exists a 1NFA which solves A^{N,r_1,r_2} with $p < d$ states. By Lemma 1, we can convert this 1NFA into an equivalent 1NFA M in Chrobak normal form having t (which is $O(p^2)$) states in the initial path and at most p states in the cycles.

Let $\alpha \in \mathbb{N}$ satisfy $\alpha N > t$. Since $\sigma^{\alpha N + r_1} \in A_{yes}^{N,r_1}$, there exists an accepting state s reachable by M on input $\sigma^{\alpha N + r_1}$. Moreover, since $\alpha N + r_1$ exceeds the length of the initial path, s belongs to a cycle of length $\ell \le p$. This implies that the same state s is reachable by M on input $\sigma^{\alpha N + r_1 + \beta \ell}$, and therefore this word is accepted. Let $g = \gcd(\ell, N)$. If $g \mid l$, then there exist $\beta, \gamma \in \mathbb{N}$ such that the Diophantine equation $\beta \ell = \gamma N + l$ holds. However, for a suitable $\alpha' \in \mathbb{N}$, we get

$$\sigma^{\alpha N + r_1 + \beta \ell} = \sigma^{(\alpha + \gamma) N + r_1 + l} = \sigma^{(\alpha + \gamma) N + r_1 + (r_2 - r_1) \bmod N} = \sigma^{\alpha' N + r_2} \in A_{no}^{N,r_2},$$

and we have a contradiction. Therefore it must be $g \nmid l$. But since by definition

$$g \le \ell \le p < d$$

and $g \mid N$, we get a contradiction with the minimality of d. Hence, any 1NFA for A^{N,r_1,r_2} must have at least d states.   □

Theorem 3 shows that for the promise problem A^{N,r_1,r_2} nondeterminism does not help in saving states. We are going to show that even the use of probabilism does not lead to smaller automata.

To this aim, we recall the *cyclic normal form* [13] for unary 1PFAs. This form is similar to Chrobak normal form, the main difference being in accepting states and the move from s_t, i.e., the last state of the initial path. Each cycle must contain exactly one accepting state, however from s_t many different states, even belonging to the same cycle, can be reached by the only allowed probabilistic move (see Figure 3).

In [13], it is proved the following:

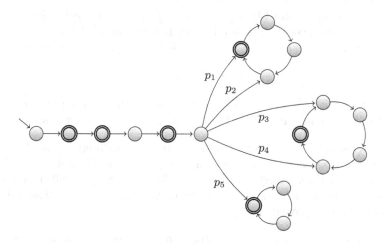

Fig. 3. A unary 1PFA in cyclic normal form with the constraint $\sum_i p_i = 1$

Lemma 2. *Each unary n-state 1PFA with isolated cut point can be converted into an equivalent 1PFA in cyclic normal form with isolated cut point (not necessarily keeping the same cut point and isolation) and with at most n states in the cycles.*

The cyclic normal form allows us to obtain the following result:

Theorem 4. *The minimal 1PFA solving with isolated cut point the promise problem A^{N,r_1,r_2} has d states, where d is the smallest positive integer such that $d \mid N$ and $d \nmid l$.*

Proof. The minimal 1DFA addressed in Theorem 1 can obviously be regarded as a d-state 1PFA solving exactly A^{N,r_1,r_2}.

To show minimality, suppose there exists a 1PFA which solves A^{N,r_1,r_2} with isolated cut point and $p < d$ states. By Lemma 2, we can convert this 1PFA into an isolated cut point 1PFA M in cyclic normal form having t states in the initial path and a set of cycles of lengths $\ell_1, \ell_2, \ldots \ell_z$, such that $\sum_{i=1}^{z} \ell_i \leq p$.

We choose $\alpha \in \mathbb{N}$ satisfying $\alpha N > t$. The word $\sigma^{\alpha N + r_1}$ brings M from the initial state to a state s in a cycle with a given probability. By letting $L = \text{lcm}(\ell_1, \ell_2, \ldots \ell_z)$, for any $\beta \in \mathbb{N}$ the word $\sigma^{\beta L}$ brings M from s back to s with certainty. Since this holds for any state s reachable by M on input $\sigma^{\alpha N + r_1}$, we have that $p_M(\sigma^{\alpha N + r_1}) = p_M(\sigma^{\alpha N + r_1 + \beta L})$.

Let $g = \gcd(L, N)$. If $g \mid l$, then there exist $\beta, \gamma \in \mathbb{N}$ such that the Diophantine equation $\beta L = \gamma N + l$ holds. So, for a suitable $\alpha' \in \mathbb{N}$, we have $\sigma^{\alpha N + r_1 + \beta L} = \sigma^{\alpha' N + r_2} \in A_{no}^{N,r_2}$, and we get

$$p_M(\sigma^{\alpha N + r_1}) = p_M(\sigma^{\alpha N + r_1 + \beta L}) = p_M(\sigma^{\alpha' N + r_2}).$$

However, $\sigma^{\alpha N + r_1} \in A_{yes}^{N,r_1}$ and we have a contradiction on M having an isolated cut point. Therefore, it must be $g \nmid l$. Let $g = \prod_{i=1}^{h} g_i^{b_i}$ be the prime factorization of g. Then, there exists $g_\kappa^{b_\kappa} \nmid l$. In addition, notice that $g_\kappa^{b_\kappa} \mid L$ and since $g_\kappa^{b_\kappa}$ is a prime power there exists $1 \leq j \leq z$ such that $g_\kappa^{b_\kappa} \mid \ell_j$. This implies that

$$g_\kappa^{b_\kappa} \leq \ell_j \leq p < d.$$

This, together with $g_\kappa^{b_\kappa} \mid N$ and $g_\kappa^{b_\kappa} \nmid l$, contradicts the minimality of d. Hence, any isolated cut point 1PFA for A^{N,r_1,r_2} must have at least d states. □

Even by using two-way motion, we do not manage to design automata smaller than 1DFAs, 1NFAs, and 1PFAs for solving the promise problem A^{N,r_1,r_2}. To this aim, we consider a simplified form for unary 2DFAs: a 2DFA is called *sweeping* if its input head changes its direction at the endmarkers only [41]. The following simulation result is proved in [26]:

Lemma 3. *For each unary n-state 2DFA, there exists an equivalent sweeping 2DFA with $n + 1$ states.*

This lemma allows us to show the following result:

Theorem 5. *The minimal sweeping* 2DFA *solving the promise problem* A^{N,r_1,r_2} *has* d *states, where* d *is the smallest positive integer such that* $d \mid N$ *and* $d \nmid l$. *Moreover, any* 2DFA *for* A^{N,r_1,r_2} *must have at least* $d - 1$ *states.*

Proof. Again, the minimal 1DFA addressed in Theorem 1 can obviously be regarded as a d-state sweeping 2DFA solving A^{N,r_1,r_2}. We now prove that this automaton is a minimal sweeping 2DFA for A^{N,r_1,r_2}.

Suppose there exists, a sweeping 2DFA M with $p < d$ states. Consider the computation of M accepting $\sigma^{N+r_1} \in A_{yes}^{N,r_1}$ in z traversals. Since $p < N$, in every traversal M must enter a cycle. Let C_i be the cycle entered along the ith traversal and ℓ_i the length of C_i. By letting $L = \mathrm{lcm}(\ell_1, \ldots, \ell_z)$, it is not hard to see that the computation of M on input $\sigma^{N+r_1+\beta L}$ leads to the same accepting state as for σ^{N+r_1}. Indeed, this computation has again z traversals and in the ith traversal the cycle C_i is repeated $\frac{\beta L}{\ell_i}$ more times. Now, consider $g = \gcd(L, N)$ and $\prod_{i=1}^{s} g_i^{b_i}$ its prime factorization. If $g \mid l$, then there exist $\beta, \gamma \in \mathbb{N}$ such that the Diophantine equation $\beta L = \gamma N + l$ holds. So, for a suitable $\alpha \in \mathbb{N}$, we have that

$$\sigma^{N+r_1+\beta L} = \sigma^{\alpha N + r_2} \in A_{no}^{N,r_2}$$

is accepted, leading to a contradiction. Therefore, $g \nmid l$ must hold. In this case, by proceeding analogously to the proof of Theorem 4, we get a contradiction with the minimality of d. Hence, any sweeping 2DFA for A^{N,r_1,r_2} must have at least d states.

Finally, since converting a 2DFA into sweeping costs at most one additional state (Lemma 3), we get that any 2DFA solving A^{N,r_1,r_2} must have at least $d-1$ states. $\qquad\square$

We conclude this section by addressing the size cost of solving the promise problem $\mathrm{DIOF}_{r_1,r_2}^{a,N}$ with classical automata.

Theorem 6. *To solve the promise problem* $\mathrm{DIOF}_{r_1,r_2}^{a,N}$, *the minimal* 1DFA, 1NFA, *isolated cut point* 1PFA, *and sweeping* 2DFA *have* d *states, where* d *is the smallest positive integer such that* $d \mid N$ *and* $d \nmid l$. *Moreover, any* 2DFA *for* $\mathrm{DIOF}_{r_1,r_2}^{a,N}$ *must have at least* $d - 1$ *states.*

Proof. For the upper bound, we can design 1DFAs, 1NFAs, 1PFAs, and 2DFAs solving $\mathrm{DIOF}_{r_1,r_2}^{a,N}$ with the same cyclic structure of the 1DFA for A^{N,r_1,r_2}. The only difference is that, while the automaton for A^{N,r_1,r_2} moves one state forward in the cycle upon reading σ, the automaton for $\mathrm{DIOF}_{r_1,r_2}^{a,N}$ moves a_i states forward on input σ_i, for $1 \le i \le H$.

For the lower bound, it suffices to notice that A^{N,r_1,r_2} is a particular case of $\mathrm{DIOF}_{r_1,r_2}^{a,N}$ with $|\Sigma| = 1$ and $a = 1$. $\qquad\square$

References

1. Ambainis, A.: The complexity of probabilistic versus deterministic finite automata. In: Asano, T., Igarashi, Y., Nagamochi, H., Miyano, S., Suri, S. (eds.) ISAAC 1996. LNCS, vol. 1178, pp. 233–238. Springer, Heidelberg (1996)

2. Ambainis, A., Beaudry, M., Golovkins, M., Kikusts, A., Mercer, M., Thérien, D.: Algebraic results on quantum automata. Theory of Comp. Sys. **39**, 165–188 (2006)
3. Ambainis, A., Yakaryilmaz, A.: Superiority of exact quantum automata for promise problems. Information Processing Letters **112**, 289–291 (2012)
4. Ambainis, A., Watrous, J.: Two-way finite automata with quantum and classical states. Theoretical Computer Science **287**, 299–311 (2002)
5. Bertoni, A., Carpentieri, M.: Regular languages accepted by quantum automata. Information and Computation **165**, 174–182 (2001)
6. Bertoni, A., Mereghetti, C., Palano, B.: Quantum computing: 1-way quantum automata. In: Ésik, Z., Fülöp, Z. (eds.) DLT 2003. LNCS, vol. 2710, pp. 1–20. Springer, Heidelberg (2003)
7. Bertoni, A., Mereghetti, C., Palano, B.: Small size quantum automata recognizing some regular languages. Theoretical Computer Science **340**, 394–407 (2005)
8. Bertoni, A., Mereghetti, C., Palano, B.: Some formal tools for analyzing quantum automata. Theoretical Computer Science **356**, 14–25 (2006)
9. Bertoni, A., Mereghetti, C., Palano, B.: Trace monoids with idempotent generators and measure-only quantum automata. Natural Computing **9**, 383–395 (2010)
10. Bianchi, M.P., Mereghetti, C., Palano, B.: Size Lower Bounds for Quantum Automata. In: Mauri, G., Dennunzio, A., Manzoni, L., Porreca, A.E. (eds.) UCNC 2013. LNCS, vol. 7956, pp. 19–30. Springer, Heidelberg (2013)
11. Bianchi, M.P., Mereghetti, C., Palano, B., Pighizzini, G.: On the size of unary probabilistic and nondeterministic automata. Fund. Informaticae **112**, 119–135 (2011)
12. Bianchi, M.P., Palano, B.: Behaviours of unary quantum automata. Fund. Informaticae **104**, 1–15 (2010)
13. Bianchi, M.P., Pighizzini, G.: Normal forms for unary probabilistic automata. Theoretical Informatics and Applications **46**, 495–510 (2012)
14. Brodsky, A., Pippenger, N.: Characterizations of 1-way quantum finite automata. SIAM J. Computing **5**, 1456–1478 (2002)
15. Chrobak, M.: Finite automata and unary languages. Theoretical Computer Science **47**, 149–158 (1986)
16. Golovkins, M., Kravtsev, M.: Probabilistic Reversible Automata and Quantum Automata. In: Ibarra, O.H., Zhang, L. (eds.) COCOON 2002. LNCS, vol. 2387, pp. 574–583. Springer, Heidelberg (2002)
17. Gramlich, G.: Probabilistic and Nondeterministic Unary Automata. In: Rovan, B., Vojtáš, P. (eds.) MFCS 2003. LNCS, vol. 2747, pp. 460–469. Springer, Heidelberg (2003)
18. Gruska, J.: Quantum Computing. McGraw-Hill, London, New York (1999)
19. Gruska, J.: Descriptional complexity issues in quantum computing. J. Automata, Languages and Combinatorics **5**, 191–218 (2000)
20. Gruska J., Qiu, D., Zheng, S.: Generalizations of the distributed Deutsch-Jozsa promise problem (2014), http://arxiv.org/abs/1402.7254arXiv:1402.7254
21. Gruska J., Qiu, D., Zheng, S.: Potential of quantum finite automata with exact acceptance (2014). http://arxiv.org/abs/1404.1689arXiv:1404.1689
22. Hirvensalo, M.: Quantum automata with open time evolution. Int. J. Natural Computing Research **1**, 70–85 (2010)
23. Hopcroft, J.E., Motwani, R., Ullman, J.D.: Introduction to Automata Theory, Languages, and Computation. Addison-Wesley, Reading (2001)
24. Kapoutsis, C.A.: Removing bidirectionality from nondeterministic finite automata. In: Jedrzejowicz, J., Szepietowski, A. (eds.) MFCS 2005. LNCS, vol. 3618, pp. 544–555. Springer, Heidelberg (2005)

25. Kondacs A., Watrous, J.: On the power of quantum finite state automata. In: Proc. 38th Symposium on Foundations of Computer Science (FOCS 1997), pp. 66–75 (1997)

26. Kunc, M., Okhotin, A.: Describing Periodicity in Two-Way Deterministic Finite Automata Using Transformation Semigroups. In: Mauri, G., Leporati, A. (eds.) DLT 2011. LNCS, vol. 6795, pp. 324–336. Springer, Heidelberg (2011)

27. Mercer, M.: Lower bounds for generalized quantum finite automata. In: Martín-Vide, C., Otto, F., Fernau, H. (eds.) LATA 2008. LNCS, vol. 5196, pp. 373–384. Springer, Heidelberg (2008)

28. Moore, C., Crutchfield, J.: Quantum automata and quantum grammars. Theoretical Computer Science 237, 275–306 (2000)

29. Mereghetti, C., Palano, B.: Quantum finite automata with control language. Theoretical Informatics and Applications 40, 315–332 (2006)

30. Mereghetti, C., Palano, B.: Quantum automata for some multiperiodic languages. Theoretical Computer Science 387, 177–186 (2007)

31. Mereghetti, C., Palano, B., Pighizzini, G.: Note on the succinctness of deterministic, nondeterministic, probabilistic and quantum finite automata. Theoretical Informatics and Applications 5, 477–490 (2001)

32. Mereghetti, C., Pighizzini, G.: Optimal simulations between unary automata. SIAM J. Comput. 30, 1976–1992 (2001)

33. Meyer, A., Fischer, M.: Economy of description by automata, grammars, and formal systems. In: Proc. 12th Annual IEEE Symposium on Switching and Automata Theory, pp. 188–91 (1971)

34. Murakami, Y., Nakanishi, M., Yamashita, S., Watanabe, K.: Quantum versus classical pushdown automata in exact computation. IPSJ Digital Courier 1, 426–435 (2005)

35. Nayak, A.: Optimal lower bounds for quantum automata and random access codes. In: Proc. 40th Symposium on Foundations of Computer Science (FOCS 1999), pp. 369–376 (1999)

36. Paz, A.: Introduction to Probabilistic Automata. Academic Press, New York, London (1971)

37. Rabin, M.O.: Probabilistic automata. Information and Control 6, 230–245 (1963)

38. Rabin, M., Scott, D.: Finite automata and their decision problems. IBM J. Res. Develop. 3, 114–125 (1959)

39. Shepherdson, J.C.: The reduction of two-way automata to one-way automata. IBM J. Res. Develop. 3, 198–200 (1959)

40. Shilov,G: Linear Algebra. Prentice Hall (1971) (Reprinted by Dover, 1977)

41. Sipser, M.: Lower bounds on the size of sweeping automata. J. Comput. System Sci. 21, 195–202 (1980)

42. Zheng, S., Gruska, J., Qiu, D.: On the State Complexity of Semi-quantum Finite Automata. In: Dediu, A.-H., Martín-Vide, C., Sierra-Rodríguez, J.-L., Truthe, B. (eds.) LATA 2014. LNCS, vol. 8370, pp. 601–612. Springer, Heidelberg (2014)

43. Zheng, S., Qiu, D., Gruska, J., Li, L., Mateus, P.: State succinctness of two-way finite automata with quantum and classical states. Theoretical Computer Science 499, 98–112 (2013)

44. Zheng, S., Qiu, D., Li, L., Gruska, J.: One-Way finite automata with quantum and classical states. In: Bordihn, H., Kutrib, M., Truthe, B. (eds.) Languages Alive. LNCS, vol. 7300, pp. 273–290. Springer, Heidelberg (2012)

Quantum Complexity of Boolean Matrix Multiplication and Related Problems

François Le Gall[✉]

Department of Computer Science Graduate, School of Information
Science and Technology, The University of Tokyo, Tokyo, Japan
legall@is.s.u-tokyo.ac.jp

Abstract. This paper surveys the state of the art of research on quantum algorithms for problems related to matrix multiplication, such as triangle finding, Boolean matrix multiplication and Boolean product verification. The exposition highlights how simple tools from quantum computing, and in particular the technique known as quantum search, can be used in a multitude of situations to design quantum algorithms that outperform the best known classical algorithms. Some open problems in this area are also described.

1 Introduction

Quantum computation is a computing paradigm based on the laws of quantum physics, which is now a recognized branch of computer science. Even restricting ourselves to applications of this paradigm to algorithm design (i.e., the design of algorithms for quantum computers, or *quantum algorithms*), it is now hardly possible to give a comprehensive description of all the main achievements of this field. Let us first instead discuss some motivations for studying quantum algorithms today, when quantum computers have still to be constructed.

A first motivation for studying quantum algorithms is to discover potential applications of quantum computers, and motivate the significant efforts that will be needed towards constructing a large-scale quantum computer. Perhaps the most famous example is Shor's quantum algorithm [25] that factorizes an integer in time polynomial in its number of digits, while the best known classical algorithm uses exponential time. Since several widely used cryptosystems are based on the assumption that factoring integers is hard, this represents one of the most noted possible applications of quantum computers.

A second motivation is to unravel properties of concrete computational problems by studying their complexity in the quantum setting. Research on quantum algorithms, or more generally insights from quantum computing, can shed a new light on the complexity of problems well studied in the classical setting, and can even lead to the construction of new classical algorithms. We refer to the recent survey by Drucker and de Wolf [8] for several examples of classical results inspired by quantum arguments.

The third motivation is more theoretical, but also perhaps the most fundamental, and consists in understanding the power and the limitations of quantum

© Springer International Publishing Switzerland 2014
C.S. Calude et al. (Eds.): Gruska Festschrift, LNCS 8808, pp. 176–191, 2014.
DOI: 10.1007/978-3-319-13350-8_13

computation. As Jozef Gruska wrote in 1999, until recently computing was considered as "machine processes", while in the 21th century computing will be seen as "Nature process" [12]. One of the goals of research on quantum algorithms is thus also to understand computation allowed by Nature, which at a microscopic level follows the laws of quantum mechanics. Much success has been achieved in this direction, by discovering quantum algorithmic techniques with no classical equivalent, studying the role of resources intrinsic to quantum mechanics (such as entanglement), or comparing the quantum and classical settings via the model of query complexity.

This paper considers essentially the second and third motivations, and focuses on analyzing computational problems related to matrix multiplication. The main two questions that we will ask ourselves are: For which problems related to matrix multiplication do quantum algorithms outperform the best classical (i.e., conventional) algorithms? and How do investigations on quantum algorithms give new insights into these problems ? Note that quantum physics is based on linear algebra and a multitude of algebraic techniques have been developed for studying quantum computation (a detailed description of some of these techniques can be found in Jozef Gruska's survey [14]). Our approach is converse, as we aim at analyzing how quantum techniques can be applied to better understand the complexity of algebraic problems.

The reasons why we choose to focus on matrix multiplication and related problems are that, while these problems are fundamental in theoretical computer science and easy to state, their complexities are not well understood and have been the subject of several recent developments. Moreover, interesting quantum algorithms for these problems can be constructed with simple tools from quantum computing (in particular, quantum search), which enables us to describe in this paper partial answers to the above two questions without having to introduce sophisticated quantum techniques. Indeed, this paper is intended to be comprehensible without prior knowledge of quantum computing.

The paper is organized as follows. In Section 2 we introduce the main computational problems considered in this work (triangle finding, Boolean matrix multiplication, Boolean product verification), the notion of query complexity, quantum computation and quantum search. In Section 3 we give a survey of the state of the art of algorithms for these three problems, while in Section 4 we describe a recent breakthrough by Vassilevska Williams and Williams [27] and its potential applications. Finally, in Section 5 we present several variants of Boolean matrix multiplication for which fast quantum algorithms have been constructed recently.

2 Preliminaries

In this section we formally define the three main computational problems studied in this paper (triangle finding, Boolean matrix multiplication and Boolean product verification) while introducing the notion of query complexity, in both the classical and quantum settings.

2.1   Classical Query and Time Complexities

Consider the following computational task. Let X be a finite set, and $f\colon X \to \{0,1\}$ be a Boolean function over X. Assume that the function f is given as a black box: a procedure $\mathcal{P}_f$ is available that, on input $x \in X$, outputs the value $f(x)$. The goal is to compute several properties of the function f in this model. We formally define below the triangle finding problem, the Boolean matrix multiplication problem and the Boolean product verification problem in this model.

Triangle finding. Let $G = (V, E)$ be an undirected and unweighted graph, where V represents the set of vertices and E represents the set of edges. Let $\mathcal{E}(V)$ denote the set of unordered pairs of vertices in V. In this case, the domain is $X = \mathcal{E}(V)$, and the function considered is $f_G\colon \mathcal{E}(V) \to \{0,1\}$ defined as follows (the dependence on G is made explicit by using a subscript): for any $\{u, v\} \in \mathcal{E}(V)$,

$$f_G(\{u, v\}) = \begin{cases} 1 & \text{if } \{u, v\} \in E, \\ 0 & \text{if } \{u, v\} \notin E. \end{cases}$$

The triangle finding problem asks to find three distinct vertices $u, v, w \in V$ such that $f_G(\{u, v\}) = f_G(\{u, w\}) = f_G(\{v, w\}) = 1$, or to report that no such triple of vertices exists.

Boolean matrix multiplication (BMM). Let A and B be two Boolean matrices (i.e., matrices in which the entries are either zero or one) of size $n \times n$. In this case we have $X = \{1, \dots, n\} \times \{1, \dots, n\} \times \{0, 1\}$ and the function considered is $f_{A,B}\colon X \to \{0,1\}$ defined as follows (again, the dependence on A and B is made explicit by using subscripts): for any $(i, j, d) \in X$,

$$f_{A,B}((i, j, d)) = \begin{cases} A[i, j] & \text{if } d = 0, \\ B[i, j] & \text{if } d = 1. \end{cases}$$

The Boolean matrix multiplication problem asks to compute the Boolean matrix product of A and B, denoted $A * B$ and defined as follows: $A * B$ is the $n \times n$ Boolean matrix such that the entry in the i-th row and the j-th column is

$$\bigvee_{k=1}^{n} A[i, k] \wedge B[k, j],$$

for each $(i, j) \in \{1, \dots, n\} \times \{1, \dots, n\}$, where $\vee$ denotes the logical OR, and $\wedge$ denotes the logical AND.

Boolean product verification (BPV). Let A, B and C be three Boolean matrices of size $n \times n$. In this case we have $X = \{1, \dots, n\} \times \{1, \dots, n\} \times \{0, 1, 2\}$ and the function considered is $f_{A,B,C}\colon X \to \{0,1\}$, defined as follows: for any $(i, j, d) \in X$,

$$f_{A,B,C}((i, j, d)) = \begin{cases} A[i, j] & \text{if } d = 0, \\ B[i, j] & \text{if } d = 1, \\ C[i, j] & \text{if } d = 2. \end{cases}$$

The Boolean product verification problem asks to decide whether $A * B = C$.

We will be interested in the query and time complexities of solving such problems. In the classical query complexity setting, we consider only the number of calls to the oracle $\mathcal{P}_f$. In the classical time complexity setting, we consider all the computational steps of the algorithm, assuming that each call to the oracle $\mathcal{P}_f$ can be done using one computation step (for the three concrete problems described above, this corresponds to a model where the entries of the adjacency matrix of a graph, or the entries of the input matrices, are stored in a random access memory). Boolean matrix multiplication illustrates well the difference between time and query complexity. Observe that, with $2n^2$ queries, one can obtain all the entries of A and B. Since $A * B$ can then be computed without any further query, the query complexity of Boolean matrix multiplication is thus $O(n^2)$. We will explain however in the next section that the best known upper bound on the time complexity of this problem is $O(n^{2.373})$.

2.2 Generic Search Problems

In this subsection we define a class of problems that we call *generic search problems about* f, in order to characterize situations where quantum computation (introduced in the next subsection) can outperform classical computation.

A generic search problem about f is defined by a finite set Y and a function $g : Y \to \{0, 1\}$ over Y. The goal is to find one element $y \in Y$ such that $g(y) = 1$, if such an element exists, or otherwise report that no solution exists. In the classical setting, we say that the function g can be computed at cost (c_q, c_t), where c_q and c_t are two non-negative integers, if the following conditions hold:

- for any given $y \in Y$, the value $g(y)$ can be computed using at most c_q calls to the oracle $\mathcal{P}_f$;
- for any given $y \in Y$, the value $g(y)$ can be computed using at most c_t computational steps, assuming that each call to the oracle $\mathcal{P}_f$ can be done using one computation step.

As a simple example of this concept, let us recast triangle finding as an instance of generic search. An instance of triangle finding over a graph G can be converted into an instance of generic search by taking Y as the set of unordered triples of vertices and $g : Y \to \{0, 1\}$ as the following function: for any $\{u, v, w\} \in Y$,

$$g(\{u, v, w\}) = \begin{cases} 1 & \text{if } f_G(\{u, v\}) = f_G(\{u, w\}) = f_G(\{v, w\}) = 1, \\ 0 & \text{otherwise.} \end{cases}$$

Note that $g(\{u, v, w\})$ can be computed using three evaluations of the function f_G, so the query cost is $c_q = 3$. The time cost depends on the precise computation model adopted, but can typically (e.g., when considering Boolean circuits) be upper bounded as $c_t = O(1)$.

Assume that the number of solutions (i.e., the size of $\{y \in Y \mid g(y) = 1\}$) of an instance of generic search is either zero or is greater than m, where m is a known positive integer. This generic search problem can be solved classically with high (e.g., greater than 2/3) probability by repeating the following process $O(|Y|/m)$ times: take one element y uniformly at random in Y, and then check if $g(y) = 1$ using the oracle $\mathcal{P}_f$. The query and time complexities of this classical randomized algorithm are

$$O\left(c_q \times \frac{|Y|}{m}\right) \quad \text{and} \quad O\left(c_t \times \frac{|Y|}{m}\right), \tag{1}$$

respectively, assuming that taking one element in Y uniformly at random can be done in negligible time. For instance, if we assume that the graph has either zero or at least m triangles, then the triangle finding problem over this graph can be solved in time $O(n^3/m)$. Note that the bounds of Eq. (1) are essentially tight. In particular, in the case $c_q = 1$, it is easy to show that there exist generic search problems for which $\Omega(|Y|/m)$ queries are needed.

2.3   Quantum Query and Time Complexities

In the quantum setting setting, the function f can be accessed *in a quantum way*. Technically, this means that there exists a quantum unitary operation $\mathcal{O}_f$ defined as follows that can be applied on a physical system at unit cost (the reader should feel free to skip this technical definition; the details are given here only for completeness, and will not be used later in the paper): for any element $x \in X$, any bit $b \in \{0, 1\}$, and any binary string $z \in \{0, 1\}^*$, the operation $\mathcal{O}_f$ maps the basis state $|x\rangle|b\rangle|z\rangle$ to the state $\mathcal{O}_f|x\rangle|b\rangle|z\rangle = |x\rangle|b\rangle|z \oplus f(x)\rangle$, where $\oplus$ denotes the bit parity (i.e., the logical XOR).

We say that a quantum algorithm computing some property of f uses k queries if the operation $\mathcal{O}_f$, given as an oracle, is called k times by the algorithm. The time complexity is defined by assigning a unit cost to each call to $\mathcal{O}_f$, and considering all the other computational steps of the quantum algorithm (i.e., considering the number of elementary quantum gates in a quantum circuit implementing the algorithm, see [13] for a complete treatment of quantum circuits and elementary gates). In the quantum setting, the cost (c_q, c_t) of a generic search problem about f is defined as in the classical setting, but considering calls to $\mathcal{O}_f$ instead of calls to $\mathcal{P}_f$.

One of the most striking examples showing the power of quantum computation is Grover algorithm [5,11], which corresponds to the following statement.

Theorem 1 (Quantum search). *Consider a generic search problem with cost (c_q, c_t) such that the number of solutions is either zero or is greater than m. There exists a quantum algorithm that solves, with high probability, this problem with query and time complexities*

$$O\left(c_q \times \sqrt{\frac{|Y|}{m}}\right) \quad \text{and} \quad \tilde{O}\left(c_t \times \sqrt{\frac{|Y|}{m}}\right),$$

respectively.[1]

---

[1] In this paper the notation $\tilde{O}(\cdot)$ suppresses the polylogarithmic factors.

By comparing these bounds with those of Eq. (1), we see that this gives a quadratic improvement with respect to classical computation. For instance, using the interpretation given in Section 2.2 of triangle finding as a generic search problem, Theorem 1 (applied with $m = 1$) immediately gives the following result.

Proposition 1. *There exists a quantum algorithm that solves, with high probability, the triangle finding problem with query complexity $O(n^{3/2})$ and time complexity $\tilde{O}(n^{3/2})$.*

Consider an instance of Boolean matrix multiplication, i.e., two $n \times n$ Boolean matrices given as function $f_{A,B}$. Suppose that, given a pair $(i,j) \in \{1,\dots,n\} \times \{1,\dots,n\}$, we want to compute the entry $(A*B)[i,j]$. This task can be converted into a generic search problem with $Y = \{1,\dots,n\}$, and function $g \colon Y \to \{0,1\}$ defined as

$$g(k) = \begin{cases} 1 & \text{if } f_{A,B}(i,k,0) = f_{A,B}(k,j,1) = 1, \\ 0 & \text{otherwise}, \end{cases}$$

for any $k \in \{1,\dots,n\}$. The costs for this search problem are $c_q = 2$ and $c_t = O(1)$. Since this problem has a solution if and only if $(A*B)[i,j] = 1$, Theorem 1 shows that the value of $(A*B)[i,j]$ can be computed with high probability in $O(\sqrt{n})$ queries and $\tilde{O}(\sqrt{n})$ time using a quantum computer.

Let us conclude by mentioning that, while (c_q, c_t) have been defined above as the costs of computing one value of g without error, the upper bounds of Theorem 1 hold even if (c_q, c_t) are defined as the costs of computing one value of g with constant (e.g., larger than $2/3$) success probability [15]. With this version of Theorem 1, we can analyze the complexity of Boolean product verification.

Proposition 2. *There exists a quantum algorithm that solves, with high probability, Boolean product verification with query complexity $O(n^{3/2})$ and time complexity $\tilde{O}(n^{3/2})$.*

Proof. Consider an instance of Boolean product verification. Note that $A*B \neq C$ if and only if there exists a pair $(i,j) \in \{1,\dots,n\} \times \{1,\dots,n\}$ such that $(A*B)[i,j] \neq C[i,j]$.

Consider the generic search problem about $f_{A,B,C}$ with $Y = \{1,\dots,n\} \times \{1,\dots,n\}$, and function $g \colon Y \to \{0,1\}$ defined as

$$g(i,j) = \begin{cases} 1 & \text{if } (A*B)[i,j] \neq C[i,j], \\ 0 & \text{otherwise}, \end{cases}$$

for any $(i,j) \in \{1,\dots,n\} \times \{1,\dots,n\}$. The costs for this search problem are $c_q = O(\sqrt{n})$ and $c_t = \tilde{O}(\sqrt{n})$, since we one entry of $A*B$ can be computed with this complexity. Theorem 1 (with $m = 1$) shows that this generic search problem can thus be solved with $O(n^{3/2})$ queries and $\tilde{O}(n^{3/2})$ time. □

3   Complexity of Triangle Finding, BPV and BMM

In this section we describe the complexity of triangle finding, Boolean product verification and Boolean matrix multiplication. We start by explaining standard reductions between these three problems in Section 3.1, and then in Section 3.2 give a survey of the best known lower and upper bounds on their complexities.

3.1   Standard Reductions Between the Three Problems

A concise, while slightly informal, statement of the relations described in this subsection is

$$\text{triangle} \leq \text{BPV} \leq \text{BMM}, \tag{2}$$

where the symbol $\leq$ represents a reduction from an instance of the problem on the left side to an instance of the problem on the right side.

Obviously, an algorithm for Boolean matrix multiplication can be used to solve an instance of Boolean product verification. Triangle finding reduces to Boolean matrix multiplication as well. The standard reduction works as follows, and was first explicitly mentioned by Itai and Rodeh [16]. Consider an undirected and unweighted graph G, and let A_G denote the adjacency matrix of the graph. Then G has a triangle if and only if there exists a pair $(i, j) \in \{1, \ldots, n\} \times \{1, \ldots, n\}$ such that $(A_G * A_G)[i, j] = A_G[i, j] = 1$. It is thus enough to compute the Boolean product of A_G by itself to decide if G has a triangle.

Triangle finding can be reduced to Boolean product verification as well. The idea is, given an undirected and unweighted graph G, to create an instance of Boolean product verification with the following three $2n \times 2n$ matrices

$$A = \begin{pmatrix} A_G & I \\ 0 & 0 \end{pmatrix}, \quad B = \begin{pmatrix} A_G & 0 \\ A_{\bar{G}} & 0 \end{pmatrix}, \quad C = \begin{pmatrix} A_{\bar{G}} & 0 \\ 0 & 0 \end{pmatrix},$$

as inputs, where I denotes the identity matrix of size $n \times n$, A_G denotes the adjacency matrix of G and $A_{\bar{G}}$ denotes the adjacency matrix of the complement of G (i.e., $A_{\bar{G}}(i, j) = 1$ if and only if $A_G(i, j) = 0$). Note that $A*B \neq C$ if and only if there exists a pair $(i, j) \in \{1, \ldots, n\} \times \{1, \ldots, n\}$ such that $(A_G * A_G)[i, j] = 1$ and $A_{\bar{G}}[i, j] = 0$, which means that G has a triangle.

3.2   Status of These Problems

Table 1 summarizes the best known upper and lower bounds on the query and time complexities, in both the classical and quantum settings, of triangle finding, Boolean product verification and Boolean matrix multiplication. We give below more details and explanations about these bounds.

The classical time complexity of Boolean matrix multiplication is one of the main open problems in theoretical computer science. The Boolean product of two $n \times n$ Boolean matrices A and B can be obviously computed in $O(n^3)$ time. The best known algorithm for this problem relies on matrix multiplication over a ring: in order to compute the Boolean matrix product, we interpret A and B as integer matrices (with entries zero or one), compute the usual product of A and B over the ring of integers, and then convert each non-zero entry of the product matrix into one. Since such a matrix product can be computed with time complexity $O(n^{\omega+\epsilon})$ for any $\epsilon > 0$, where ω is the exponent of matrix multiplication over a

Table 1. Best known upper and lower bounds on the classical and quantum complexities of triangle finding, Boolean product verification and Boolean matrix multiplication. The notation $O(n^{\omega+\epsilon})$ means that the upper bound is $O(n^{\omega+\epsilon})$ for any $\epsilon > 0$, where $\omega < 2.373$ denotes the exponent of square matrix multiplication.

	quantum time complexity	classical time complexity	quantum query complexity	classical query complexity
triangle	$\tilde{O}(n^{3/2})$	$O(n^{\omega+\epsilon})$	$O(n^{9/7})$ $\Omega(n)$	$\Theta(n^2)$
BPV	$\tilde{O}(n^{3/2})$	$O(n^{\omega+\epsilon})$	$O(n^{3/2})$ $\Omega(n^{19/18})$	$\Theta(n^2)$
BMM	$O(n^{\omega+\epsilon})$	$O(n^{\omega+\epsilon})$	$\Theta(n^2)$	$\Theta(n^2)$

ring (the best known upper bound on ω is $\omega < 2.373$, see [21, 26]), the product $A * B$ can be computed with the same complexity. The same upper bound holds for the complexity of triangle finding and Boolean product verification, from Relation (2). This is the best known upper bound for all these three problems, even if randomized algorithms are considered. Note that, interestingly, matrix product verification over a ring (instead of the Boolean semiring) can be solved, with high probability, in quadratic time [10].

It is easy to show that the classical query complexity of these three problems is $\Theta(n^2)$. The upper bound $O(n^2)$ follows trivially from the observation that with this amount of queries, we can queries all edges of the graph, or all the entries of the matrices, as mentioned in Section 2. The matching lower bounds follow from elementary arguments as well. For instance, the $\Omega(n^2)$-query lower bound for triangle finding follows from the observation that removing one edge from a graph can transform a graph containing a triangle into a triangle-free triangle. Any classical algorithm (even randomized) would need to query this edge in order to decide whether the graph contains a triangle or not, which cannot be done unless $\Omega(n^2)$ queries are made.

Let us now discuss the quantum time complexity of these problems. We have already shown (in Propositions 1 and 2) that the quantum time complexity of triangle finding and Boolean product verification is $\tilde{O}(n^{3/2})$. These simple upper bounds, obtained by a direct application of quantum search, are still the best known upper bounds. For computing the Boolean matrix product of two $n \times n$ Boolean matrices, no quantum algorithm outperforming the best known classical algorithm is known. Indeed, constructing a better quantum algorithm for Boolean matrix multiplication is one of the main open problems in this area (in Section 5 we will nevertheless mention some variants of the Boolean matrix multiplication problem for which quantum algorithms better than the best known classical algorithms have been constructed, in the time complexity setting).

Finally, consider the quantum query complexity of these three problems. The quantum query complexity of triangle finding has been the subject of much research recently. Magniez, Santha and Szegedy [24] showed how to design quantum algorithms faster than the straightforward algorithm of Proposition 1 and obtained query complexity $\tilde{O}(n^{13/10})$, using techniques based on quantum walks developed by Ambainis [1]. Belovs [4] recently introduced a method called learning graph and used it to improve the quantum query complexity of triangle finding to $O(n^{35/27}) = O(n^{1.296\cdots})$. Lee, Magniez and Santha [23] then showed, again using learning graphs, how to further improve this query complexity to $O(n^{9/7}) = O(n^{1.285\cdots})$, which is currently the best known upper bound. Jeffery, Kothari and Magniez [18] showed how this complexity can also be achieved, up to polylogarithmic factors, using quantum walks. Interestingly, the best known lower bound for triangle finding is still $\Omega(n)$. For Boolean product verification, it is unknown whether quantum algorithms better than straightforward quantum search (i.e., the algorithm of Proposition 2) exist. A $\Omega(n^{19/18})$-query lower bound has been obtained by Childs et al. [7], which suggests that this problem may be harder than triangle finding. For Boolean matrix multiplication, the classical lower bound $\Omega(n^2)$ holds also for quantum algorithms (this can formally proved, for instance, by using a reduction from a threshold problem, see [17]).

4   Boolean Matrix Multiplication and Triangle Finding

As mentioned in Section 3, there is an immediate reduction from triangle finding to Boolean matrix multiplication. In this section we describe a recent breakthrough by Vassilevska Williams and Williams [27]: a reduction from Boolean matrix multiplication to (several instances of) triangle finding. We also discuss its implications for the design of both classical and quantum algorithms for Boolean matrix multiplication.

4.1   Graph-Theoretical Interpretation of BMM

The reduction by Vassilevska Williams and Williams is based on an interpretation of the problem of computing the Boolean matrix product of two $n \times n$ Boolean matrices A and B as the problem of finding triangles in a tripartite graph of size $3n$ depending of both A and B. We describe this interpretation below.

Let n be any positive integer. Let I, J and K be three arbitrary disjoint sets of size n. Let us write $I = \{u_1, \ldots, u_n\}$, $J = \{v_1, \ldots, v_n\}$ and $K = \{w_1, \ldots, w_n\}$.

For any $n \times n$ Boolean matrices A and B, and any set $S \subseteq \{1, \ldots, n\} \times \{1, \ldots, n\}$, define the following three sets:

$$E_A = \Big\{ \{u_i, w_k\} \mid (i, k) \in \{1, \ldots, n\} \times \{1, \ldots, n\} \text{ and } A[i, k] = 1 \Big\},$$

$$E_B = \Big\{ \{v_j, w_k\} \mid (j, k) \in \{1, \ldots, n\} \times \{1, \ldots, n\} \text{ and } B[k, j] = 1 \Big\},$$

$$E_S = \Big\{ \{u_i, v_j\} \mid (i, j) \in S \Big\}.$$

We denote by $\mathcal{G}_{A,B,S}$ the undirected graph with vertex set $I \cup J \cup K$ and edge set $E_A \cup E_B \cup E_S$. Note that this graph is tripartite. For convenience, we will write

$$\mathcal{G}_{A,B} = \mathcal{G}_{A,B,\{1,\ldots,n\} \times \{1,\ldots,n\}}.$$

For any subsets $I' \subseteq I$, $J' \subseteq J$ and $K' \subseteq K$, we denote by $\mathcal{G}_{A,B,S}(I', J', K')$ the subgraph of $\mathcal{G}_{A,B,S}$ induced by the vertices in $I' \cup J' \cup K'$.

We now describe the reduction from Boolean matrix multiplication to triangle finding. The key insight is the following simple observation.

Lemma 1. *Let A and B be two $n \times n$ Boolean matrices, and write $C = A * B$. Then, for any $(i,j) \in \{1, \ldots, n\} \times \{1, \ldots, n\}$, $C[i,j] = 1$ if and only if there exists an index $k \in \{1, \ldots, n\}$ such that $\{u_i, v_j, w_k\}$ is a triangle of $\mathcal{G}_{A,B}$.*

Proof. By definition of the Boolean product, $C[i,j] = 1$ if and only if there exists an index $k \in \{1, \ldots, n\}$ such that $A[i,k] = B[k,j] = 1$. This latter condition means that both $\{u_i, w_k\}$ and $\{v_j, w_k\}$ are edges of $\mathcal{G}_{A,B}$, and thus $\{u_i, v_j, w_k\}$ is a triangle of $\mathcal{G}_{A,B}$.   □

Lemma 1 shows that, in order to compute the Boolean product $A * B$, it is enough to compute all pairs $(i,j) \in \{1, \ldots, n\} \times \{1, \ldots, n\}$ such that $\{u_i, v_j\}$ is an edge of a triangle of $\mathcal{G}_{A,B}$. A straightforward implementation of this strategy gives time complexity $O(n^2 \times T(3n))$, where $T(3n)$ denotes the time complexity of finding a triangle in a graph over $3n$ vertices. This is of course not efficient, but we show in the next subsection how to refine these ideas.

4.2   Efficient Reduction

We now describe the efficient reduction obtained in [27] from Boolean matrix multiplication to triangle finding.

The key ideas is to partition the set I into $m = \Theta(n^{2/3})$ subsets $I_1, \ldots, I_m$, each containing at most $n^{1/3}$ vertices. Similarly, partition the sets J and K into m subsets $J_1, \ldots, J_m$ and $K_1, \ldots, K_m$, respectively, each containing at most $n^{1/3}$ vertices. Consider the following strategy: starting with $S = \{1, \ldots, n\} \times \{1, \ldots, n\}$, we successively examine each triple $(a, b, c) \in \{1, \ldots, m\}^3$ and find all triangles in the graph in $\mathcal{G}_{A,B,S}(I_a, J_b, K_c)$ while immediately removing the corresponding pair from S as soon as a triangle is reported. The detailed algorithm is described in Fig. 1, and named Algorithm $\mathcal{A}$.

We now analyze Algorithm $\mathcal{A}$. First observe that, from Lemma 1, the matrix C output at Step 4 is the Boolean matrix product of A and B. Let us now analyze the time complexity of this algorithm. The complexity is dominated by the number of calls to the triangle finding procedure. Let e_{abc} denote the number of triangles reported when processing the triple $(a, b, c) \in \{1, \ldots, m\}^3$. Note that $\sum_{a,b,c=1}^m e_{abc} \leq n^2$, since the size of S is decreased by one each time a triangle is reported. The number of calls to the triangle finding procedure when processing the triple (a, b, c) is $e_{abc} + 1$, since one additional call is needed to decide that no more triangle exists. The total amount of calls to the triangle finding procedure is thus

$$\sum_{a,b,c=1}^m (e_{abc} + 1) \leq m^3 + n^2 = O(n^2),$$

Algorithm $\mathcal{A}$

Input: two $n \times n$ Boolean matrices A and B
Assumption: a triangle-finding procedure is available

1. Construct the graph $\mathcal{G}_{A,B}$;
2. $S \leftarrow \{1, \ldots, n\} \times \{1, \ldots, n\}$;
3. for a from 1 to m do
       for b from 1 to m do
           for c from 1 to m do

              repeat

                   find a triangle $\{u_i, v_j, w_k\}$ in $\mathcal{G}_{A,B,S}(I_a, J_b, K_c)$;
                   $S \leftarrow S \setminus \{(i,j)\}$;

              until no triangle is found
4. Output the $n \times n$ Boolean matrix C such that, for any $(i,j) \in \{1, \ldots, n\} \times \{1, \ldots, n\}$, $C[i,j] = 0$ if $(i,j) \in S$ and $C[i,j] = 1$ if $(i,j) \notin S$;

Fig. 1. Algorithm $\mathcal{A}$ reducing the computation of the Boolean product of two matrices A and B to several instances of triangle finding

and each call asks to find a triangle in a graph over at most $3 \times n^{1/3}$ vertices. We thus obtain the following result.

Theorem 2 ([27]). *Assume that we have a procedure that, for any $N \geq 1$, solves the triangle finding problem over a graph of N vertices in time $T(N)$. Then the Boolean product of two $n \times n$ Boolean matrices can be computed in time $O(n^2 \times T(3n^{1/3}))$.*

This result was a breakthrough since it showed, for the first time, how fast algorithms for triangle finding can be used to construct fast algorithms for Boolean matrix multiplication, as discussed in the next subsection.

Note that the above reduction implicitly assumed that the available procedure for triangle finding is classical and deterministic, which means in particular that the algorithm for Boolean matrix multiplication of Proposition 2 is also classical and deterministic. It is easy to see that the same result holds for other modes of computations. In particular, if the procedure for triangle finding is quantum, then the resulting Boolean matrix multiplication algorithm is quantum.

4.3 Implications: Towards Combinatorial Algorithms for BMM

In Section 3 we showed that the best known classical (and also the best known quantum) algorithm for computing the Boolean matrix product of two $n \times n$ Boolean matrices has time complexity $O(n^{2.373})$, which was obtained by using the best known (classical) algorithm for matrix multiplication over a ring. This algorithm, based on algebraic techniques, is nevertheless not practical, due to the huge multiplicative constant involved in its complexity.

In the classical setting, a fundamental open problem is to design fast algorithms for Boolean matrix multiplication that do not rely on algebraic techniques. Such algorithms are sometimes referred to as *combinatorial algorithms*.

Note that, by preprocessing the data using the so-called "method of four Russians" [2], it is easy to construct a $O(n^3/\log n)$-time algorithm. Recently, Bansal and Williams [3] (see also [27]) constructed an algorithm for Boolean matrix multiplication with time complexity $O\left(n^3/(\log n)^{2.25}\right)$ by combining this idea with algorithmic versions of the Szemerédi regularity lemma, via the graph-theoretic interpretation of Boolean matrix multiplication described in Section 4.1. The main open problem is still to construct a *truly subcubic* combinatorial algorithm for this problem, i.e., an algorithm with complexity $O(n^{3-\delta})$ for some constant $\delta > 0$. One of the most exciting potential applications of Theorem 2 is that we now know that any truly subcubic-time combinatorial algorithm for triangle finding immediately leads to a solution to this open problem (indeed, observe that the reduction used to prove Theorem 2 is combinatorial, in that it does not use algebraic techniques).

In the quantum setting, remember that in Section 2 we showed that computing one entry of the Boolean product of two $n \times n$ matrices can be done in $\tilde{O}(\sqrt{n})$ time. This means that all the n^2 entries of the output matrix can be computed in $\tilde{O}(n^{2.5})$ time. Moreover, this algorithm relies on quantum search only, and can then be considered as "combinatorial". A natural quantum version of the above open problem is whether there exists a quantum algorithm based on search (or other quantum techniques like quantum walks, but not relying on a reduction to matrix multiplication over a ring) with complexity $O(n^{2.5-\delta})$ for some constant $\delta > 0$. Theorem 2 gives us a natural approach to solve this problem: try to find a "combinatorial" quantum algorithm for triangle finding with time complexity $O(n^{3/2-\delta})$ for some constant $\delta > 0$. This is an open problem, even without any assumption on the nature of the quantum algorithm.

Open problem 1. *Is there a quantum algorithm that solves, with high probability, the triangle finding problem in time $O(n^{3/2-\delta})$, for some constant $\delta > 0$?*

We believe that this is one of the most fundamental open questions related to Boolean matrix multiplication in the quantum setting.

5   Fast Quantum Algorithms for Matrix Multiplication

In this section, we discuss variants of Boolean matrix multiplication for which quantum algorithms performing better than the best known classical algorithms have been constructed.

5.1   Rectangular Boolean Matrix Multiplication

A basic, but fundamental, example showing the power of quantum algorithms for problems related to matrices is *rectangular* Boolean matrix multiplication. By applying quantum search as described in Section 2, we immediately obtain the following result.

Theorem 3. *There exists a quantum algorithm that computes, with high probability, the Boolean product of an $n_1 \times n_2$ Boolean matrix by an $n_2 \times n_3$ Boolean matrix in time $\tilde{O}(n_1 n_3 \sqrt{n_2})$.*

For instance, if $n_1 = n_3 = n$ and $n_2 = n^3$, we obtain complexity $\tilde{O}(n^{3.5})$. This is better than the best known classical algorithm [19], which has complexity $O(n^{4.208})$. Actually, it is easy to show that any classical algorithm computing this rectangular matrix product requires $\Omega(n^4)$ time, since the size of each input matrix is n^4. For rectangular Boolean matrix multiplication quantum algorithms can thus outperform classical algorithms.

5.2   Sparse Boolean Matrix Multiplication

Consider again the task of multiplying two $n \times n$ Boolean matrices A and B, but assume that we know that the Boolean matrix product $C = A * B$ contains ℓ non-zero entries, where $1 \leq \ell \leq n^2$ is a parameter. Buhrman and Špalek [6] observed that C can then be computed in time $\tilde{O}(n^{3/2}\sqrt{\ell})$, which is better than the best known classical algorithm for the same task for moderately small values of ℓ (we refer to [6,20] for a precise comparison with the performance of classical algorithms). The idea is to search successively the non-zero entries of C. Remember that we can compute the value of a specific entry of C in time $\tilde{O}(\sqrt{n})$ using quantum search. Using Theorem 1, and using the fact that there are ℓ non-zero entries, we can thus find the first non-zero entry of C using a generic search over the search space $\{1, \ldots, n\} \times \{1, \ldots, n\}$, in time $\tilde{O}(c \times \sqrt{n^2/\ell})$, where $c = \tilde{O}(\sqrt{n})$. We can then do another generic search for finding the second entry of C, but this time excluding the entry just found from the search space. The time complexity will be $\tilde{O}(c \times \sqrt{n^2/(\ell-1)})$. We can continue this strategy to find all the ℓ non-zero entries of C, which gives overall time complexity

$$\tilde{O}\left(\sqrt{n} \times \left(\sqrt{\frac{n^2}{\ell}} + \sqrt{\frac{n^2}{\ell-1}} + \cdots + \sqrt{\frac{n^2}{2}} + \sqrt{\frac{n^2}{1}}\right)\right) = \tilde{O}(n^{3/2}\sqrt{\ell}),$$

where the equality follows from Cauchy-Swartz inequality and asymptotic bounds on harmonic series.

Jeffery, Kothari and Magniez [17] have recently shown how to do better in the query complexity setting, and constructed a quantum algorithm solving this problem with query complexity $\tilde{O}(n\sqrt{\ell})$. They also showed that this upper bound is tight, in the query complexity setting, up to possible polylogarithmic factors. Le Gall [20] showed that the time complexity of this problem is $\tilde{O}(n\sqrt{\ell} + \ell\sqrt{n})$. Let us give an outline of how these results can be obtained. Let us focus on finding the first entry. The two above results state that this can be done with complexity $\tilde{O}(n)$, i.e., better than the $\tilde{O}(n^{3/2})$ upper bound from the approach by Buhrman and Špalek. The idea is that, as mentioned in Section 4.1, finding the first non-zero entry reduces to finding a triangle in the graph $\mathcal{G}_{A,B}$. Since in $\mathcal{G}_{A,B}$ all the vertices between I and J are connected, this is equivalent to finding one index $k \in \{1, \ldots, n\}$ such that w_k is connected to both a vertex of I and a vertex of J. Checking if k satisfies this condition can be done in time $\tilde{O}(\sqrt{n} + \sqrt{n})$ by using two successive quantum searches. Thus finding an index k satisfying this condition can be done in time $\tilde{O}((\sqrt{n} + \sqrt{n}) \times \sqrt{n}) = \tilde{O}(n)$, by using Theorem 1 with $Y = \{1, \dots, n\}$ and $m = 1$. Once such a k is known, it is easy, using again quantum search, to find two indexes $i, j \in \{1, \dots, n\}$ such that $A[i, k] = B[k, j] = 1$, and thus $C[i, j] = 1$, in $\tilde{O}(\sqrt{n})$ time. This strategy does not work directly for finding the next non-zero entries of C since I and J will not be completely connected anymore (there will be m missing edges, if m non-zero entries of C have been found so far), but Refs. [17,20] show how to adapt this idea for this situation.

5.3 Matrix Multiplication Over Semirings

Boolean matrix multiplication is an example of matrix product over a *semiring*, namely, the Boolean semiring $(\{0, 1\}, \vee, \wedge)$. Given a set $R \subseteq \mathbb{Z} \cup \{-\infty, \infty\}$ and two binary operations $\oplus \colon R \times R \to R$ and $\odot \colon R \times R \to R$, the structure $(R, \oplus, \odot)$ is a semiring if it behaves like a ring except that there is no requirement on the existence of an inverse with respect to the operation $\oplus$. The definition of matrix multiplication can naturally be generalized to any semiring, as follows.

Definition 1. *Given two $n \times n$ matrices A and B over R, the matrix product over $(R, \oplus, \odot)$ is the $n \times n$ matrix C defined as $C[i, j] = \bigoplus_{k=1}^{n} (A[i, k] \odot B[k, j])$ for any $(i, j) \in \{1, \dots, n\} \times \{1, \dots, n\}$.*

Note that, whenever the operation $\oplus$ is such that a term as $\bigoplus_{k=1}^{n} x_k$ can be computed in $\tilde{O}(\sqrt{n})$ time using quantum techniques, the matrix product over the semiring $(R, \oplus, \odot)$ can be computed in time $\tilde{O}(n^{2.5})$ on a quantum computer. This is true for the Boolean semiring, but also for instance for the semiring $(\mathbb{Z} \cup \{\infty\}, \min, +)$ using a quantum algorithm based on quantum search for minimum finding [9]. The matrix product over this latter semiring is known as the *min-plus matrix product*, and is a key ingredient in a multitude graph algorithms, but, despite much effort (including a recent breakthrough by Williams [28]), no truly subcubic-time classical algorithm is known for this problem. This gives an example of multiplication of square matrices, widely used in practice, for which quantum computation outperforms the best known classical algorithms.

We conclude by mentioning that Le Gall and Nishimura [22] recently developed quantum algorithms improving over these $\tilde{O}(n^{2.5})$-time straightforward quantum algorithms over several semirings.

References

1. Ambainis, A.: Quantum walk algorithm for element distinctness. SIAM Journal on Computing **37**(1), 210–239 (2007)
2. Arlazarov, V.L., Dinic, E.A., Kronrod, M.A., Faradzev, I.A.: On economical construction of the transitive closure of a directed graph. Soviet Mathematics Doklady (English translation) **11**(5), 1209–1210 (1970)

3. Bansal, N., Williams, R.: Regularity lemmas and combinatorial algorithms. Theory of Computing **8**(1), 69–94 (2012)
4. Belovs, A.: Span programs for functions with constant-sized 1-certificates: extended abstract. In: Proceedings of STOC, pp. 77–84, 2012 (2012)
5. Boyer, M., Brassard, G., Høyer, P., Tapp, A.: Tight bounds on quantum searching. Fortschritte der Physik **46**(4–5), 493–505 (1998)
6. Buhrman, H., Špalek, R.: Quantum verification of matrix products. In: Proceedings of SODA, pp. 880–889 (2006)
7. Childs, A.M., Kimmel, S., Kothari, R.: The Quantum Query Complexity of Read-Many Formulas. In: Epstein, L., Ferragina, P. (eds.) ESA 2012. LNCS, vol. 7501, pp. 337–348. Springer, Heidelberg (2012)
8. Drucker, A., de Wolf, R.: Quantum Proofs for Classical Theorems. Number 2 in Graduate Surveys. Theory of Computing Library (2011)
9. Dürr, C., Høyer, P.: A quantum algorithm for finding the minimum. arXiv:quant-ph/9607014 (1996)
10. Freivalds, R.: Probabilistic machines can use less running time. In: IFIP Congress, pp. 839–842 (1977)
11. Grover, L.K.: A fast quantum mechanical algorithm for database search. In: Proceedings of STOC, pp. 212–219 (1996)
12. Gruska, J.: Quantum Challenges. In: Bartosek, M., Tel, G., Pavelka, J. (eds.) SOFSEM 1999. LNCS, vol. 1725, pp. 1–28. Springer, Heidelberg (1999)
13. Gruska, J.: Quantum Computing. Mcgraw Hill (2000)
14. Gruska, J.: Algebraic Methods in Quantum Informatics. In: Bozapalidis, S., Rahonis, G. (eds.) CAI 2007. LNCS, vol. 4728, pp. 87–111. Springer, Heidelberg (2007)
15. Høyer, P., Mosca, M., de Wolf, R.: Quantum search on bounded-error inputs. In: Baeten, J.C.M., Lenstra, J.K., Parrow, J., Woeginger, G.J: ICALP 2003. LNCS, vol. 2719, pp. 291–299. Springer, Heidelberg (2003)
16. Itai, A., Rodeh, M.: Finding a minimum circuit in a graph. SIAM Journal on Computing **7**(4), 413–423 (1978)
17. Jeffery, S., Kothari, R., Magniez, F.: Improving Quantum Query Complexity of Boolean Matrix Multiplication Using Graph Collision. In: Czumaj, A., Mehlhorn, K., Pitts, A., Wattenhofer, R. (eds.) ICALP 2012, Part I. LNCS, vol. 7391, pp. 522–532. Springer, Heidelberg (2012)
18. Jeffery, S., Kothari, R., Magniez, F.: Nested quantum walks with quantum data structures. In: Proceedings of SODA, pp. 1474–1485 (2013)
19. Le Gall, F.: Faster algorithms for rectangular matrix multiplication. In: Proceedings of FOCS, pp. 514–523 (2012)
20. Le Gall, F.: A Time-Efficient Output-Sensitive Quantum Algorithm for Boolean Matrix Multiplication. In: Chao, K.-M., Hsu, T., Lee, D.-T. (eds.) ISAAC 2012. LNCS, vol. 7676, pp. 639–648. Springer, Heidelberg (2012)
21. Le Gall, F.: Powers of tensors and fast matrix multiplication. In: Proceedings of ISSAC 2014, pp. 296–303 (2014)
22. Le Gall, F., Nishimura, H.: Quantum Algorithms for Matrix Products over Semirings. In: Ravi, R., Gørtz, I.L. (eds.) SWAT 2014. LNCS, vol. 8503, pp. 331–343. Springer, Heidelberg (2014)
23. Lee, T., Magniez, F., Santha, M.: Improved quantum query algorithms for triangle finding and associativity testing. In: Proceedings of SODA, pp. 1486–1502 (2013)
24. Magniez, F., Santha, M., Szegedy, M.: Quantum algorithms for the triangle problem. SIAM Journal on Computing **37**(2), 413–424 (2007)

25. Shor, P.W.: Polynomial-time algorithms for prime factorization and discrete logarithms on a quantum computer. SIAM Journal on Computing **26**(5), 1484–1509 (1997)
26. Vassilevska Williams, V.: Multiplying matrices faster than Coppersmith-Winograd. In: Proceedings of STOC, pp. 887–898 (2012)
27. Vassilevska Williams, V., Williams, R.: Subcubic equivalences between path, matrix and triangle problems. In: Proceedings of FOCS, pp. 645–654 (2010)
28. Williams, R.: Faster all-pairs shortest paths via circuit complexity. In: Proceedings of STOC 2014, pp. 664–673 (2014)

Quantum Distributed Computing Applied to Grover's Search Algorithm

Debabrata Goswami[(⊠)]

Indian Institute of Technology Kanpur, Kanpur 208016, India
dgoswami@iitk.ac.in

Abstract. Grover's Algorithm finds a unique element in an unsorted stock of N-elements in $\sqrt{N}$ queries through quantum search. A single-query solution can also be designed, but with an overhead of $N \log_2 N$ steps to prepare and post process the query, which is worse than the classical $N/2$ queries. We show here that by distributing the computing load on a set of quantum computers, we achieve better information theoretic bounds and relaxed space scaling. Howsoever small one quantum computing node is, by virtue of networking and sharing of data, we can virtually work with a sufficiently large qubit space.

Keywords: Distributed quantum computing · Grover's quantum search · Optical networking

1 Introduction

Today's digital computer is the cumulation of technological advancements that began with the mechanical clockwork ideas of Charles Babbage in the nineteenth century. However, it is surprising that logically, the high speed modern day computer is not fundamentally different from its gigantic 30 ton ancestors, the first of which were built in 1941 by the German engineer Konrad Zuse. Although computers nowadays have become more compact and considerably faster in their performance, their primary execution methodology has remained the same, which is to derive a computationally useful result via the manipulation and interpretation of encoded bits. The underlying mathematical principles are indistinguishable from those outlined in the visionary Church-Turing hypothesis, proposed in the year 1936, much ahead of the birth of the first computer. Bits, the fundamental units of information, are the smallest working units of a digital computer and are classically represented as either 0 or 1 in a digital computer. Classical bits are recognized by alluding to arbitrary thresholds of high (1) or low (0), and so each classical bit is physically realized through a macroscopic physical system, such as the magnetization of a hard disk or the charge on a capacitor. Information is thus realized as series of such bits, and these bits are manipulated via Boolean logic gates arranged in succession to produce an end result [1].

The idea of quantum mechanical computational devices started in the late 1970s when scientists, while trying to determine the fundamental limits of computation, realized that if technology continued to adhere to the Moore's Law,

© Springer International Publishing Switzerland 2014
C.S. Calude et al. (Eds.): Gruska Festschrift, LNCS 8808, pp. 192–199, 2014.
DOI: 10.1007/978-3-319-13350-8_14

the proposal of continuous diminishment in the circuits' sizes on silicon chips would eventually reach a point, where individual elements would not be larger than a few atoms. At such sizes, the physical laws governing the behavior and properties of such miniaturized circuits would inherently be not classical but quantum mechanical in nature. Consequently, the question of whether a fundamentally new kind of computer could be devised based on the principles of quantum physics surfaced.

Feynman was the first to make efforts to answer this question by producing an abstract model in the year 1982, which showed the process of computation using quantum systems [2]. He also explained the capacity of this machine to efficiently act as a simulator for quantum physics. In other words, a physicist can effectively carry out experiments related to quantum physics inside a quantum mechanical computer. Later, in 1985, Deutsch reaffirmed Feynman's assertion, showing that any physical process could, in principle, be modeled perfectly by a quantum computer, which eventually could result in the creation of a general purpose quantum computer [3]. The search for important applications for such a general purpose quantum computing machine began with this theoretical work of Deutsch.

An important breakthrough came in 1994, when Shor [4] devised a method for using quantum computers to crack factorization, an age-old problem in Number Theory. In this paper, Shor proposed the use of a group of mathematical operations, organized and designed specifically for a quantum computer, to factorize huge numbers extremely rapidly compared to conventional computers. With this, quantum computing went from being a mere scientific curiosity to a world-wide research interest.

A quantum computer exerts control over qubits by executing a series of quantum gates, each a unitary transformation acting on qubits. These quantum gates, when performed in succession, initially result into a complicated unitary transformation of a set of qubits at some point. The measurements of the qubits constitute the final computational result. However, on observation, qubits (similar to their classical counterpart, bits) show that they are of discrete nature and are individually represented by two states. Such inherent similarities in the calculation process of classical and quantum computers suggest that theoretically, a classical computer should be able to simulate a quantum computer. Thus, a classical computer should theoretically be able to do everything that a quantum computer does, naturally raising questions pertaining to the need for a quantum computer. Such questions were refuted by the fact that, though a classical computer is theoretically able to simulate a quantum computer, it is highly inept, and is practically incapable of performing most tasks that a quantum computer can perform at ease. John S. Bell, for the first time, explained that correlations among quantum bits differ qualitatively from the correlations among classical bits [5], making the simulation of a quantum computer on a classical one, a computationally hard problem that is practically irrelevant.

In fact, the amount of data processing required for a classical computer to simulate even a hundred qubit quantum computer is prohibitive. A classical computer trying to simulate a quantum computer would have to work with exponentially large matrices to perform calculations for each individual state, which is also represented as a matrix; thus requiring an exponentially longer time compared to the time taken by even a primitive quantum computer with only a hundred qubits that exist in a Hilbert space of $\sim 10^{30}$ dimensions. Thus, a system with only 100 qubits is impossible to simulate classically in any comprehensible time frame as it represents a quantum superposition of as many as 2^{100} states. Each of these states is classically equivalent to a single list of one hundred 1's and 0's. Any quantum operation on that system—a particular pulse of radio waves, for instance, whose action might be to execute a quantum gate operation on the 50th and 51st qubits—would simultaneously operate on all the 2^{100} states. Hence in a single step, in one tick of the computer's clock, a quantum operation, unlike the serial computers, computes not just on one machine state, but on 2^{100} machine states at a given time. Eventually, however, the system would collapse to a single quantum state corresponding to a single answer, a single list of one hundred 1's and 0's, dictated by the fundamental measurement axiom of quantum mechanics [6]. This is an amazing observation as it showcases the inherent disparity between quantum and classical computers in computational matters as; what is achieved via the quantum parallelism of superposition by a primitive quantum computer of 100 qubits would require a classical super computer perform the operation simultaneously on $\sim 10^{30}$ distinct processors; a practically impossible feat.

With the clever usage of the properties of superposition, interference, entanglement, non-clonability and non-determinism, exhibited by all quantum systems, a new form of "quantum parallelism" seems to be achievable, wherein an exponential number of computational paths can be explored simultaneously as opposed to sequentially in a single device. The challenge remains in framing computational questions in a way so that the most useful and probabilistic answer is extracted. With the help of right algorithm, it is possible to use this parallelism to solve certain problems in a fraction of the total time taken by a classical computer. Such algorithms are notoriously difficult to formulate, and till date, the most significant examples are Shor's algorithm [4] and Grover's algorithm [7]. Shor's algorithm allows for the extremely quick factorization of large numbers, in polynomial time [4] as compared to exponential time required by classical computers, which in principle, means that in solving some problems, only quantum computers not conventional digital computers, can provide viable solutions.

The other epochal quantum algorithm is the search algorithm [7,8,10], since most of the computable problems in quantum computing can be transformed into the problem of finding the correct answer amongst all the probable possibilities. Taking advantage of the quantum parallelism, Grover's algorithm searches an unsorted database of N entries in $\sqrt{N}$ attempts, while a conventional computer would take an average of $N/2$ attempts. The discovery of the quantum error correction is as significant as the algorithms taking advantage of the quantum parallelism. In fact, the prospects for quantum computing technology would have remained bleak but for the quantum error correction development. Another important aspect lies in the scaling issues related to quantum computing, which questions the limitations of the current technologies in quantum computing and hence derives continuous efforts towards newer, more reliable approaches. Even conforming to the current practical situation of restricting ourselves to the use of a small interacting molecular system, where only a small number of qubits are available for computation; we show that it is possible to achieve higher computational power provided that the computer systems, each consisting of only a few atoms or molecules acting as compute nodes are networked. Here we shall specifically explore the aspects of quantum distributed computing in light of the possible implementations of Grover's Algorithm.

2   Problem Statement

Grover's search algorithm shows that a quantum mechanical system needs at least $O(\sqrt{N})$ steps in order to identify a unique candidate satisfying a condition out of an unsorted dataset of N candidates [7,8]. This quadratic improvement is less optimal than the possible exponential improvement through quantum computing [6,9] as is seen, for example, in Shore's factorization algorithm [4], but is highly significant as the search problem is a universal necessity in quantum computing. Grover's subsequent work [10] concludes that one can overcome $O(\sqrt{N})$ bottleneck by making more elaborate queries, however, these increase the overhead in preparing and post-processing queries by $O(N \log_2 N)$ steps resulting in a decreased efficiency compared to classical situations.

   In this paper, we present a distributed quantum computing approach wherein we propose to solve the classical search problem by performing the computation on all the nodes in the network, thereby providing a better lower bound on the resource usage of Grover's Algorithm. We show that though we are still restricted by the quadratic bound at best, we get more relaxed resource usage. This study is motivated primarily by the fact that at present, achieving a large qubit space is difficult, which is one of the basic bottlenecks for the effective implementation success of many of the proposed algorithms. Given that decoherence [11] is a major concern in quantum computing, the success of quantum teleportation [12] could be utilized as an effective approach towards scaling quantum computing power by establishing a network of smaller qubit space quantum computers and distributing the computing load. The required coherent transfer of information in the network could also benefit from recent developments in coherent optical networking schemes [13]. This network of quantum computers would virtually produce the required qubit space for the effective implementation of various algorithms [14]. Another advantage of such networking lies in the high security offered by quantum information processing [15].

3   Theoretical Model

Let us first outline the search problem and pose it mathematically to suit our quantum distribution needs. Given a database of N elements $(X_1 X_2 X_3 ... X_n)$

with exactly one element satisfying a condition (say the required element is X_k). Now there exists a function which knows that the element required is X_k but it functions like a black box answering queries only as high/low. More explicitly if asked whether X_i satisfies the condition it sets output signal high only if $X_i = X_k$ otherwise low. We will refer to such as element satisfying this condition as the qualified element. The problem is to get the high signal in the minimum number of queries. Classically, the optimal way is to ask questions that eliminate half the elements under consideration with each question resulting in approximately $\log_2 N$ queries to reach the answer [7,8].

In Grover's single query approach [10], he considered a quantum system composed of multiple subsystems where each subsystem has an N dimensional state and each basis state of a subsystem corresponds to an element in the database. An appropriate single quantum query, pertaining to information regarding all N elements, resulted in the probability of the state corresponding to the qualified element(s) of each subsystem being amplified by a small amount. This small difference in amplitudes was estimated by making a measurement to determine that the element of the database in each subsystem corresponds to the element indicated by the most subsystems is the qualified element, provided the number of subsystems was sufficiently large. The sole purpose was to amplify the probability of qualified element by performing unitary operations on the subsystems.

Let us now discuss our design of distributed quantum computing wherein we consider a network of quantum computers which can communicate through quantum teleportation. The individual computing nodes in the network function like subsystems as described in Grover's approach earlier. Let us amplify the probability of qualified element by sequence of unitary operations. We move ahead by first applying selective inversion and then performing inversion about selection operation.

Let us define the black box which answers the query as high/low (0/1) is a function $f(z)$ such that $f(z) = 1$ for qualified element, *i.e.*, X_k, otherwise $f(z) = 0$ for all X_i, where $i \neq k$. The work of Boyer *et. al.* [16] shows that there exists a quantum circuit such that state $|x, b\rangle$ can be converted to $|x, f(x) \oplus b\rangle$, and if bit 'b' is placed in superposition of $\frac{1}{\sqrt{2}}(|0\rangle - |1\rangle)$, we keep intact the amplitudes of all elements but the qualified element. The amplitude of qualified element gets inverted. Next we apply inversion about average operator to amplify the probability of the qualified item. The inversion about average operation is by definition the unitary operation $D : D_{ij} = \frac{2}{N}$ if $i \neq j$; $D_{ii} = -1 + \frac{2}{N}$; where D can be shown to be physically implemented as a product of three local unitary matrices [8]. Assume that D is applied to a superposition with each element of the superposition having amplitude equal to $\frac{1}{\sqrt{N}}$, excepting one. Then, the single component that is different has an amplitude of $-\frac{1}{\sqrt{N}}$. After the unitary operation, the one that had the negative amplitude now becomes positive and its magnitude increases to approximately $\frac{3}{\sqrt{N}}$; while the rest stay unchanged. This would boost up the amplitude of the qualified element in each subsystem and we have sufficiently large number of identical subsystems (say total η such subsystems) to observe for which element the probability is higher. Each subsystem has N dimensional state space and each of N basis states actually corresponds to an element in the database. Consider each subsystem to have equal amplitude in all N states. Thus the state vector for the system (which is a tensor product of these η identical subsystems) would be $(|S_1 S_1 S_1...S_1\rangle + |S_2 S_2 S_2...S_2\rangle + ...N^{\eta}$ such terms) if $S_1, S_2, ...S_N$ denote N states.

Let us now query the database: whether the number of subsystems in the state corresponding to the marked item is odd or even. If it is odd, the phase is left untouched otherwise it is inverted. This is selective inversion as discussed earlier. If S_k is the state which stands for the qualified element, we can write the state vector as $(|S_1\rangle + |S_2\rangle + ... + (-|S_k\rangle) + ... + |S_N\rangle)^{\eta}$. We then perform the inversion about average operation independently on each of subsystems to boost the amplitude of the qualified element. As we discussed before, inversion about average operation allows us to amplify the probability of the state in negative phase by a factor of 3 in the positive direction. Mathematically, therefore, we can represent the vector state as $(|S_1\rangle + |S_2\rangle + ... + (3|S_k\rangle) + ... + |S_N\rangle)^{\eta}$. We cycle these steps for n times.

4   Results and Discussions

We will now try different values of n to see when it reaches an optimum.

For a generalized case: After n such cycles, the state vector can be written as $(|S_1\rangle + |S_2\rangle + ... + ((2n+1)|S_k\rangle) + ... + |S_N\rangle)^{\eta}$. The probability of obtaining the basis state corresponding to the qualified element in each of the η subsystems is approximately $\frac{(2n+1)^2}{N}$ and the probability of obtaining a different basis state is approximately $\frac{1}{N}$. Thus, it follows by the law of large numbers [17] that out of η subsystems, $\frac{(2n+1)^2 \eta}{N} \pm O(\frac{\sqrt{\eta}}{N})$ lie in state S_k. Assuming n to be large enough the equation is simplified to $\frac{4n^2 \eta}{N} \pm O(\frac{\sqrt{\eta}}{N})$ and if we let $\eta = KN$, then the equation can be rewritten as $4n^2 K \pm O(\sqrt{K})$. We can test the extreme values of 'n' for which the system will give an optimum value and hence provide both the upper and lower bounds.

For small size case, such as $n = \sqrt{\log_2 N}$: The state vector can be written as $(|S_1\rangle + |S_2\rangle + ... + (2\sqrt{\log_2 N} + 1)|S_k\rangle + ... + |S_N\rangle)^{\eta}$. The probability of obtaining the basis state corresponding to the marked state in each of the η subsystems is approximately $\frac{4\log_2 N}{N}$ and the probability of obtaining a different basis state is approximately $\frac{1}{N}$. Again it follows by the law of large numbers [17] that out of η subsystems, $4K\log_2 N \pm O(\sqrt{K})$ lie in state S_k, where $K = \frac{\eta}{N}$. In fact, it follows by the central limit theorem [18] that the probability of a particular variable deviating by more than $\pm\gamma\sqrt{K}$ from its expected value is less than $\exp[-O(\gamma^2)]$. Thus, if η is of the order of N then the equation becomes $4\log_2 N \pm O(1)$, which means that the overall effectiveness of the algorithm in this case has no improvement over the classical case.

It is important to note here that the value of n has to be less than $\frac{\sqrt{N}}{2}$ or else it will become a certain condition, with the probability reaching 1, thus all of the subsystems will be in the qualified state. Let us test this other limit now.

Testing the upper limit for $n = \frac{\sqrt{N}}{2}$: The state vector can be written as $(|S_1\rangle + |S_2\rangle + ... + (\sqrt{N} + 1)|S_k\rangle + ... + |S_N\rangle)^\eta$. The probability of obtaining the basis state corresponding to the qualified state in each of the η subsystems is approximately 1 and the probability of obtaining a different basis state is approximately $\frac{1}{N}$. By the law of large numbers [17], therefore, it follows that out of η subsystems, $\eta \pm O(\frac{\sqrt{\eta}}{N})$ lie in state S_k. Typically, $\eta \ll N$, so the uncertainty due to $O(\frac{\sqrt{\eta}}{N})$ can be neglected. There will be post processing steps of the order $O(\sqrt{\eta})$. Thus, the overall effectiveness of the algorithm increases to $O(\sqrt{N})$, since $\eta \ll N$.

We have, therefore, managed to show that the distributed quantum computing approach essentially preserves the benefits of Grover?s search algorithm for big data problems while for small problems the situation converges to the limit of the classical case. Since the scaling issue is prevalent for large computing sizes, distributing the computing load over smaller quantum nodes is an important feasibility criterion related to the scaling issues in quantum computing.

5   Conclusions

We distributed the computational load of Grover's search algorithm over a quantum network, which is facilitated through ideal teleportation communications. Grover's single-query method carries a lot of overhead pertaining to the preparation and post-processing of the query $[O(N \log_2 N)$ steps]. Hence, we relax the single-query constraint in order to achieve more optimal performance, which is significantly better than classical methodology $[O(\log_2 N)]$. Essentially this extension of Grover's approach, being assisted by quantum-networking ideas is crucial for scaling the problem. We have managed to show that if we replicate Grover's algorithmic approach of amplifying the probability of the eligible candidate in database 'n' times, we are bound by $O(\sqrt{N})$ for a much improved upper limit of n ($n = \frac{\sqrt{N}}{2}$) though the lower bound is an unchanged classical case of $O(N)$ for small n. However, since we would only be distributing the computing load for a large enough data-size, the advantages are evident. Furthermore, our approach addresses and substantially dilutes the practical concern regarding the limited qubit space associated with one quantum computer. Hence it should be seen as a promising computing framework. These results also provide substantial encouragement and impetus for scaling quantum computation by coupling quantum teleportation of multiple small quantum computer nodes.

Acknowledgments. Funds for this research were available from the ISRO STC Funding and Ministry of Human Resource Development (Govt. of India). DG thanks the efforts put in by Devesh Tewari during his BTP project. DG is grateful to S. Goswami and R. Goswami for help with manuscript language editing. DG is highly indebted to the constant support and encouragement from Prof. Gruska for pursing research and teaching in quantum information processing.

References

1. Gruska, J.: Foundations of Computing, ITCP Computer Science Series: (International Thomson Computer Press), 716 pages (1997)
2. Feynman, R.P.: Int. J. Theor. Physics **21**, 467 (1982)
3. Deutsch, D.: Proc. Roy. Soc. London **97**, 400 (1985)
4. Shor, P.W.: Proceedings of the Symposium on the Foundations of Computer Science: Los Alamos, California, pp. 124–134. IEEE Computer Society Press, New York (1994)
5. Bell, J.S.: The Speakable and Unspeakable in Quantum Mechanics. Cambridge University Press (1987)
6. Nielsen, M.A., Chuang, I.L.: Quantum Computing and Quantum Information. Cambridge University Press, Cambridge (2000)
7. Grover, L.K.: Proceedings of the Twenty-Eighth Annual Symposium on the Theory of Computing: Philadelphia, Pennsylvania, pp. 212–218. ACM Press, New York (1996)
8. Grover, L.K.: Quantum Mechanics Helps in Searching for a Needle in a Haystack. Phys. Rev. Letters, 325–328 (1997)
9. Bennett, C.H., Bernstein, E., Brassard, G., Vazirani, U.: SIAM J. Computing, 1510–1524 (1997)
10. Grover, L.K.: Quantum Computers Can Search Arbitrarily Large Databases by a Single Query. Phys. Rev. Letters, 4709 (1997)
11. Goswami, D.: Laser Phase Modulation Approaches towards Ensemble Quantum Computing. Phys. Rev. Letters, 177901 (2002)
12. Gottesman, D., Chuang, I.L.: Demonstrating the viability of universal quantum computation using teleportation and single-qubit operations. Nature, 390–393 (1999)
13. Sinha, M., Goswami, D.: System and method for improved coherent pulsed communication system having spectrally shaped pulses. US Patent (2004) US2004/0208613 A1 (October 21, 2004)
14. Schuch, N., Siewert, J.: Programmable Networks for Quantum Algorithms. Phys. Rev. Letters, 027902 (2003)
15. Miranowicz, A., Tamaki, K.: An Introduction to Quantum Teleportation. Math. Sciences, 28–34 (2002)
16. Boyer, M., Brassard, G., Hyer, P., Tapp, A.: Proceedings of 4th Workshop on Physics and Computation, Boston, MA, pp. 36–43 (1996)
17. Feller, W.: An Introduction to Probability Theory and Its Applications, vols. I and II. John Wiley, New York (1971),
18. Knuth, D.E.: Fundamentals of Algorithms: The Art of Computer Programming. Addison-Wesley, Reading(1973)

Maximally Entangled State
in Pseudo-Telepathy Games

Laura Mančinska[⊠]

Centre for Quantum Technologies, National University of Singapore,
Singapore, Singapore
laura@locc.la

Abstract. A pseudo-telepathy game is a non-local game which can
be won with probability one using quantum strategies but not using
classical ones. Our central question is whether there exist two-party
pseudo-telepathy games which cannot be won with probability one
using a maximally entangled state. Towards answering this question,
we develop conditions under which maximally entangled state suffices.
Our main result shows that for any game G, there exists a game $\tilde{G}$ such
that G admits a perfect strategy using a maximally entangled state if
and only if $\tilde{G}$ admits some perfect finite-dimensional quantum strategy.

Keywords: Nonlocal game · Entanglement · Projection game · Maximally entangled state · Pseudo-telepathy

1 Introduction

Entanglement is a central feature of quantum information processing (see [Gru99]
or [NC10] for a general introduction). In many cases it can be used to perform
nonlocal tasks that would otherwise be impossible or very inefficient. Therefore,
entanglement is a resource and one is interested in means of measuring the
entanglement content of a quantum state. Many such entanglement measures
have been introduced and studied (see [PV07] for a survey). The usual approach
is to define entanglement as the resource that cannot be increased using local
quantum operations and classical communication (LOCC). Here, we will only
be concerned with the two-party scenarios. In such a case, any desired shared
state can be obtained via LOCC from the so-called *maximally entangled state*

$$|\Psi_d\rangle := \frac{1}{\sqrt{d}} \sum_{i=1}^{d} |ii\rangle.$$

Therefore, according to any entanglement measure, the state $|\Psi_d\rangle$ possesses the
highest entanglement content among all states in $\mathbb{C}^d \otimes \mathbb{C}^d$. It would perhaps
be natural to expect that maximally entangled states are the most useful ones
for accomplishing nonlocal tasks. It turns out that this intuition fails and there
are known examples where less entangled states allow for better performance

© Springer International Publishing Switzerland 2014
C.S. Calude et al. (Eds.): Gruska Festschrift, LNCS 8808, pp. 200–207, 2014.
DOI: 10.1007/978-3-319-13350-8_15

[ADGL02, AGG05, ZG08]. Moreover, in some cases, maximally entangled states are shown to be suboptimal even if we do not restrict the dimension d of the maximally entangled states [JP11, VW11, LVB11, Reg12]. Most of these examples are given in terms of Bell inequality violations and when stated in terms of nonlocal games they yield games at which entangled players cannot succeed with probability one. Therefore, it could be possible that maximally entangled states are sufficient to achieve perfect performance, whenever this can be done using some entangled state.

In a one-round two-party nonlocal game $G = (S, T, A, B, V, \pi)$, two isolated parties, commonly known as Alice and Bob, play against the verifier. The verifier chooses a pair of questions $(s, t) \in S \times T$ according to some probability distribution π and sends s to Alice and t to Bob. The players need to respond with $a \in A$ and $b \in B$ respectively. They win if $V(a, b|s, t) = 1$, where $V : A \times B \times S \times T \rightarrow \{0, 1\}$ is a public verification function. The players' goal is to coordinate strategies so as to maximize their probability of winning; quantum players can use shared entanglement to improve their chances of winning. We say that a strategy is *perfect* if it allows the players to win with probability one. Games which admit perfect quantum but not classical strategies are known as *pseudo-telepathy* games [BBT05]. It is a challenging open question to understand if the optimal success probability of a game can always be achieved using a finite-dimensional strategy. Therefore, in this paper we focus on pseudo-telepathy games that admit a finite dimensional perfect strategy. In this terminology the central question of this paper is as follows:

Do there exist pseudo-telepathy games that cannot be won using maximally entangled state?

Answering the above question in the negative would imply that maximally entangled state is sufficient for zero-error communication over a noisy classical channel. This is due to the equivalence of zero-error communication protocols and a certain type of nonlocal games outlined in [CLMW10].

Previous results. It is known that maximally entangled state is sufficient for binary[1] and unique games[2] [CHTW04]. However, this is due to a trivial reason, since no entanglement is needed to win these games with probability one if it can be done in principle. Therefore, these two classes of games do not contain any pseudo-telepathy games and hence are not relevant to our question. Maximally entangled state is also sufficient for the games based on graph homomorphisms [RM12] and binary constraint system games [CM12]. These two classes are more relevant to our question, since they contain pseudo-telepathy games.

Our results. We partially answer the above question by exhibiting a class of games for which maximally entangled state is sufficient to reach perfect performance (see Theorem 1). The definition of this class is similar to that of projection

---

[1] In a binary game Alice and Bob need to answer bits, *i.e.*, $S = T = \{0, 1\}$.
[2] In a unique game for every pair of questions $(s, t) \in S \times T$ there exists a permutation σ_{st}, such that $V(a, b|s, t) = 1$ if and only if $a = \sigma(b)$.

games. This class subsumes both pseudo-telepathy graph homomorphism games and pseudo-telepathy binary constraint system games. Our proof technique is inspired by the one used in [CMN+07] in the context of quantum chromatic number. Finally, our main result is a characterization of pseudo-telepathy games for which maximally entangled states is sufficient (see Theorem 2).

2   Preliminaries

We use the mapping vec : $\mathrm{M}(d_A, d_B) \to \mathbb{C}^{d_A} \otimes \mathbb{C}^{d_B}$ defined via

$$\mathrm{vec} : |i\rangle\langle j| \mapsto |i\rangle|j\rangle$$

for all $i \in [d_A], j \in [d_B]$ and extended by linearity.

We now derive a formula that will often be used later. Applying the fact that $\mathrm{vec}(AXB^{\mathrm{T}}) = A \otimes B\,\mathrm{vec}(X)$ and $\mathrm{vec}(A)^\dagger\,\mathrm{vec}(B) = \mathrm{Tr}(A^\dagger B)$, and choosing matrix D such that $\mathrm{vec}\, D = |\psi\rangle$ we obtain

$$
\begin{aligned}
\mathrm{Tr}(A \otimes B|\psi\rangle\langle\psi|) &= \langle\psi|(A \otimes B)|\psi\rangle \\
&= \mathrm{vec}(D)^\dagger (A \otimes B)\,\mathrm{vec}(D) \qquad (1) \\
&= \mathrm{vec}(D)^\dagger\,\mathrm{vec}(ADB^{\mathrm{T}}) \\
&= \mathrm{Tr}(D^\dagger ADB^{\mathrm{T}})
\end{aligned}
$$

for all $A \in \mathrm{M}(d_A, d_A), B \in \mathrm{M}(d_B, d_B)$ and $|\psi\rangle \in \mathbb{C}^{d_A} \otimes \mathbb{C}^{d_B}$.

Consider a state $|\psi\rangle \in \mathbb{C}^{d_A} \otimes \mathbb{C}^{d_B}$ of full Schmidt rank. Then $d_A = d_B$ and $\mathrm{Tr}_A |\psi\rangle\langle\psi| = \mathrm{Tr}_B |\psi\rangle\langle\psi|$. Moreover, if we work in a Schmidt basis of $|\psi\rangle$, we have that

$$\mathrm{vec}\,\sqrt{\mathrm{Tr}_B(|\psi\rangle\langle\psi|)} = \mathrm{vec}\,\sqrt{\textstyle\sum_i \lambda_i^2|i\rangle\langle i|} = |\psi\rangle.$$

3   Results

In the context of nonlocal games the following lemma states that maximally entangled state can be used in place of any shared entangled state whose reduced state on either party commutes with the corresponding party's measurement operators.

Lemma 1. *Let* $\{E_i\}_{i\in[n]}, \{F_i\}_{i\in[m]} \subseteq \mathrm{Pos}(\mathbb{C}^d \otimes \mathbb{C}^d)$ *be measurements. Also let* $|\psi\rangle \in \mathbb{C}^d \otimes \mathbb{C}^d$ *be a state of full Schmidt rank and* $D := \sqrt{\mathrm{Tr}_B |\psi\rangle\langle\psi|} = \sqrt{\mathrm{Tr}_A |\psi\rangle\langle\psi|}$.

If $[D, E_i] = 0$ *for all* $i \in [n]$ *or* $[D, F_i] = 0$ *for all* $i \in [m]$ *then for all* $i \in [n], j \in [m]$ *we have*

$$\mathrm{Tr}(E_i \otimes F_j|\psi\rangle\langle\psi|) = 0 \Leftrightarrow \mathrm{Tr}(E_i \otimes F_j|\Psi\rangle\langle\Psi|) = 0,$$

where $|\Psi\rangle := \frac{1}{\sqrt{d}} \sum_i |\alpha_i\rangle|\beta_i\rangle$ *and* $|\alpha_i\rangle|\beta_i\rangle$ *is a Schmidt basis of* $|\psi\rangle$.

Proof. Let us work in a Schmidt basis of $|\psi\rangle$. Then $\text{vec}\,D = \text{vec}\,\sqrt{\text{Tr}_B\,|\psi\rangle\langle\psi|} = |\psi\rangle$. Since $\text{Tr}(E_i \otimes F_j |\psi\rangle\langle\psi|) = \text{Tr}(D^\dagger E_i D F_j^{\text{T}})$ by Equation (1) and $D^\dagger E_i D, F_j^{\text{T}} \succeq 0$, we obtain that

$$\text{Tr}(E_i \otimes F_j |\psi\rangle\langle\psi|) = 0 \Leftrightarrow D^\dagger E_i D F_j = 0.$$

We now assume that $[D, E_i] = 0$ for all $i \in [n]$ (the other case can be proven similarly). Since $D^\dagger E_i D F_j^{\text{T}} = D^\dagger D E_i F_j^{\text{T}}$ and D has full rank, we have

$$D^\dagger E_i D F_j^{\text{T}} = 0 \Leftrightarrow E_i F_j^{\text{T}} = 0.$$

Observe that $\text{vec}\,|\Psi\rangle = \text{Id}$ and hence $\text{Tr}(E_i \otimes F_j |\Psi\rangle\langle\Psi|) = \text{Tr}(\text{Id}^\dagger E_i \,\text{Id}\, F_j^{\text{T}}) = \text{Tr}(E_i F_j^{\text{T}})$. Thus we obtain

$$E_i F_j^{\text{T}} = 0 \Leftrightarrow \text{Tr}(E_i \otimes F_j |\Psi\rangle\langle\Psi|) = 0$$

which completes the proof.

In the context of local measurements, the following lemma states that only *projective* local measurements can give rise to perfectly correlated outcomes. Moreover, in such a case maximally entangled state $|\Psi\rangle$ can be used as the shared entangled state.

Lemma 2. *Let $\{E_i\}_{i\in[n]}, \{F_i\}_{i\in[n]} \subseteq \text{Pos}(\mathbb{C}^d \otimes \mathbb{C}^d)$ be two measurements and $|\psi\rangle \in \mathbb{C}^d \otimes \mathbb{C}^d$ be a state of full Schmidt rank and $D := \sqrt{\text{Tr}_B\,|\psi\rangle\langle\psi|}$. If for all distinct $i, j \in [n]$*

$$\text{Tr}(E_i \otimes F_j |\psi\rangle\langle\psi|) = 0 \tag{2}$$

then for all $i \in [n]$ we have that

- *operators E_i, F_i are projectors and*
- $[D, E_i] = [D, F_i] = 0$.

Proof. First, note that D can be assumed to be diagonal, if we work in the Schmidt basis of $|\psi\rangle$ and hence $D^\dagger = D^{\text{T}} = D$. Now we rewrite Equation (2) as

$$\text{Tr}(D^\dagger E_i D F_j^{\text{T}}) = 0, \tag{3}$$

for all distinct $i, j \in [n]$. It now follows that $\text{Tr}\left(D^\dagger E_i D(\text{Id} - F_i^{\text{T}})\right) = 0$ and hence

$$\text{supp}(D^\dagger E_i D) \subseteq \text{supp}\, F_i^{\text{T}},$$

where $\text{supp}(M)$ denotes the span of the columns of M. Similarly, the fact that $\text{Tr}\left((\text{Id} - E_i)D F_i^{\text{T}} D^\dagger\right) = 0$ gives

$$\text{supp}(D F_i^{\text{T}} D^\dagger) \subseteq \text{supp}(E_i).$$

Since conjugation by full rank matrix D does not change the rank, the two above inclusions imply that

$$\text{supp } F_i^{\text{T}} = \text{supp}(D^\dagger E_i D) \quad \text{and} \quad \text{supp}(E_i) = \text{supp}(DF_i^{\text{T}} D^\dagger).$$

Combining this with the orthogonality constraints (3), we get that

$$\text{supp } F_i^{\text{T}} \perp \text{supp } F_j^{\text{T}} \quad \text{and} \quad \text{supp } E_i \perp \text{supp } E_j$$

for all distinct $i, j \in [n]$. Hence, both $\{E_i\}_{i \in [n]}$ and $\{F_i\}_{i \in [n]}$ are projective measurements and moreover

$$E_i = \text{supp}(DF_i^{\text{T}} D^\dagger) \quad \text{and} \quad F_i^{\text{T}} = \text{supp}(D^\dagger E_i D),$$

where by slight abuse of notation we use $\text{supp}(M)$ to denote the *projector* onto the span of the columns of M.

We now show that $[D, E_i] = 0$ for all $i \in [n]$ (the proof for $[D, F_i] = 0$ is similar). From the orthogonality condition (3) and the fact that $D^\dagger E_i D, F_j^{\text{T}} \succeq 0$, we obtain that for all distinct $i, j \in [n]$

$$0 = D^\dagger E_i D F_j^{\text{T}} = D^\dagger E_i D \, \text{supp}(D^\dagger E_j D).$$

Hence, for all distinct $i, j \in [n]$ we also have $D^\dagger E_i D D^\dagger E_j D = 0$ and thus $E_i D^2 E_j = 0$, since D has full rank and $D^\dagger = D$. Now, $E_i D^2 E_j = 0$ implies that D^2 is block-diagonal with respect to the partition of the space corresponding to projectors E_i. Since in such a partition each E_i is block-diagonal with the blocks being $c\,\text{Id}$, where $c \in \{0, 1\}$, it follows that $[D^2, E_i] = 0$. Hence also $[D, E_i] = 0$ for all $i \in [n]$ as desired.

It follows from Lemma 2 that maximally entangled state is essentially the only state that gives rise to perfectly correlated outcomes. Since the operators E_i and F_i commute with D, their off-diagonal entries corresponding to different Schmidt coefficients of $|\psi\rangle$ must be zero. Thus E_i and F_i are block-diagonal, where the blocks are labeled by distinct Schmidt coefficients of $|\psi\rangle$. Hence, measurements $\{E_i\}$ and $\{F_i\}$ are direct sums of measurements each of which is performed on a maximally entangled state.

We now establish a result similar to Lemma 2 for two measurements with different number of outcomes.

Corollary 1. Let $\{E_i\}_{i \in [n]}, \{F_i\}_{i \in [m]} \subseteq \text{Pos}(\mathbb{C}^d \otimes \mathbb{C}^d)$ be two measurements and $|\psi\rangle \in \mathbb{C}^d \otimes \mathbb{C}^d$ be a state of full Schmidt rank and $D := \sqrt{\text{Tr}_B |\psi\rangle\langle\psi|}$. If there exists a function $f : [n] \to [m]$ such that for all $i \in [n]$ and $j \neq f(i)$

$$\text{Tr}(E_i \otimes F_j |\psi\rangle\langle\psi|) = 0 \tag{4}$$

then for all $i \in [m]$ we have that

- operators $F_j, E_j' := \sum_{i : f(i) = j} E_i$ are projectors and
- $[D, E_j'] = [D, F_j] = 0$.

Proof. This is exactly the statement of Lemma 2 for measurements $\{E'_j\}_{j\in[m]}$ and $\{F_j\}_{j\in[m]}$.

We now define a class of nonlocal games for which we will later show that maximally entangled state can be used to win with certainty, whenever it can be done using some finite-dimensional quantum strategy.

Definition 1. *We say that a nonlocal game $G = (S, T, A, B, V, \pi)$ is weakly projective for Bob, if for each of Bob's inputs $t \in T$ there exists an input $s \in S$ for Alice and a function $f_{st} : A \to B$ such that $V(s, t, a, b) = 1$ if and only if $b = f_{st}(a)$.*

The definition for a nonlocal game that is weakly projective for Alice is similar. The term "weak projection game" was chosen since G is called a projection game if for *all* pairs $(s, t) \in S \times T$ there exists a function f_{st} such that $V(s, t, a, b) = 1$ if and only if $f_{st}(a) = b$. Any projection game is weakly projective for both Alice and Bob; the converse, however, does not hold.

Theorem 1. *Suppose that a nonlocal game $G = (S, T, A, B, V, \pi)$ is weakly projective for Bob. If a shared entangled state $|\psi\rangle \in \mathbb{C}^d \otimes \mathbb{C}^d$ of full Schmidt rank and measurements $\mathcal{E}^{(s)} := \{E_i^s\}_{i \in A}$ and $\mathcal{F}^{(t)} := \{F_i^t\}_{i \in B}$ specify a perfect strategy for G then*

1. *operators F_j^t are projectors for all $t \in T, j \in B$;*
2. *a maximally entangled state $|\Psi\rangle$ can be used in place of $|\psi\rangle$.*

Proof. To prove the theorem, for each $t \in T$ we apply Corollary 1 to measurements $\mathcal{E}^{(s(t))}$ and $\mathcal{F}^{(t)}$, where $s(t)$ is Alice's input corresponding to t from Definition 1. This gives us item (1) and that $[F_j^t, D] = 0$ for all values of t, j. Now, by Lemma 1 we get item (2).

Definition 2. *Given game $G = (S, T, A, B, V, \pi)$, let $\tilde{G}_B := (S, T, \tilde{A}, B, \tilde{V}, \pi)$, where*

$$\tilde{S} := \{(s, 0), (t, 1) : s \in S, t \in T\},$$

$\tilde{A} := A \cup B$, and

$$\tilde{V}(a, b | (s, i), t) := \begin{cases} V(a, b | s, t) & \text{if } i = 0 \\ \delta_{ab} & \text{if } i = 1 \end{cases}$$

The game $\tilde{G}_A$ is defined similarly.

It is easy to see that $\tilde{G}_A$ ($\tilde{G}_B$) is a weak projection game for Alice (Bob) and therefore can be won using a maximally entangled state whenever some perfect quantum strategy exists. Also, any strategy used to win $\tilde{G}_A$ or $\tilde{G}_B$, can be used to win G. Hence, we obtain the following:

Theorem 2. *A nonlocal game G admits a perfect finite-dimensional quantum strategy if and only if $\tilde{G}_A$ or $\tilde{G}_B$ admits some perfect finite-dimensional quantum strategy.*

The above theorem can be used to show that a maximally entangled state is sufficient for both binary constraint system and homomorphism games.

In a binary constraint system game G, Alice is asked to assign values to the binary variables in a constraint c_s and Bob is asked to assign a value to a binary variable x_t. To win, their answers need to be consistent and Alice's assignment has to satisfy the constraint c_s. Any strategy used to win game G can also be used to win $\tilde{G}_B$. This is because upon receiving input $(t, 1)$ Alice can perform any measurement corresponding to a constraint c_s that contains variable x_t and respond with the value she would have assigned to the variable x_t.

In a homomorphism game G, Alice and Bob have the same input and output sets ($S = T$ and $A = B$) and their answers need to agree when they are given the same outputs. Therefore, any strategy used to win G can be used to win both $\tilde{G}_A$ and $\tilde{G}_B$ (essentially by ignoring the extra bit in the modified game).

4   Discussion

In this paper we have looked at the question of whether there exist pseudo-telepathy games that cannot be won with certainty using a maximally entangled state in some dimension d. As partial progress towards answering this question we have exhibited a class of pseudo-telepathy games for which maximally entangled state is always sufficient. Additionally, we have characterized pseudo-telepathy games which admit perfect strategies with a maximally entangled state. We hope that this characterization might help in producing an example of pseudo-telepathy which does not admit a maximally entangled perfect strategy (assuming such games exist).

An intersting open question is whether Lemma 2 admits an approximate version. More formally: suppose two measurements produce almost perfectly correlated outcomes, does it imply that the measurement operators almost commute with the reduced state D?

Acknowledgments. Laura Mančinska is supported by the Ministry of Education (MOE) and National Research Foundation Singapore, as well as MOE Tier 3 Grant "Random numbers from quantum processes" (MOE2012-T3-1-009).

References

ADGL02. Acín, A., Durt, T., Gisin, N., Latorre, J.I.: Quantum nonlocality in two three-level systems. Phys. Rev. A **65**(5), 523–525 (2002). arXiv:quant-ph/0111143

AGG05. Acín, A., Gill, R., Gisin, N.: Optimal Bell tests do not require maximally entangled states. Phys. Rev. Lett. **95**(21), 210–402 (2005). arXiv:quant-ph/0506225

BBT05. Brassard, G., Broadbent, A., Tapp, A.: Quantum pseudo-telepathy. Foundations of Physics **35**(11), 1877–1907 (2005). arXiv:quant-ph/0407221

CHTW04. Cleve, R., Hoyer, P., Toner, B., Watrous, J.: Consequences and limits of nonlocal strategies. In: Proceedings of the 19th IEEE Annual Conference on Computational Complexity, pp. 236–249 (2004). arXiv:quant-ph/0404076

CLMW10. Cubitt, T.S., Leung, D., Matthews, W., Winter, A.: Improving zero-error classical communication with entanglement. Phys. Rev. Lett. **104**, 230503–230506 (2010). arXiv:0911.5300

CM12. Cleve, R., Mittal, R.: Characterization of binary constraint system games (2012). arXiv:1209.2729

CMN+07. Cameron, P.J., Montanaro, A., Newman, M.W., Severini, S., Winter, A.: On the quantum chromatic number of a graph. Electr. J. Comb., 14(1) (2007). arXiv:quant-ph/0608016

Gru99. Gruska, J.: Quantum Computing. Osborne/McGraw-Hill (1999)

JP11. Junge, M., Palazuelos, C.: Large violation of Bell inequalities with low entanglement. Commun. Math. Phys. **306**(3), 695–746 (2011). arXiv:1007.3043

LVB11. Liang, Y.-C., Vértesi, T., Brunner, N.: Semi-device-independent bounds on entanglement. Phys. Rev. A, 83(2), 022108, (2011). arXiv:1012.1513

NC10. Michael, A.: Nielsen and Isaac L. Cambridge University Press, Chuang. Quantum computation and quantum information (2010)

PV07. Plenio, M.B., Virmani, S.: An introduction to entanglement measures. Quant. Inf. Comput. **7**, 1–51 (2007). arXiv:quant-ph/0504163

Reg12. Oded Regev. Bell violations through independent bases games. Quantum Inf. Comput. 12(1–2), 9–20, (2012). arXiv:1101.0576

RM12. Roberson, D.E., Mančinska, L.: Graph homomorphisms for quantum players (2012). arXiv:1212.1724

VW11. Vidick, T., Wehner, S.: More nonlocality with less entanglement. Phys. Rev. A, 83:052310 (May 2011). arXiv:1011.5206

ZG08. Zohren, S., Gill, R.D.: Maximal violation of the Collins-Gisin-Linden-Massar-Popescu inequality for infinite dimensional states. Phys. Rev. Lett. **100**(12), 120–406 (2008). arXiv:quant-ph/0612020

Quantum Finite Automata: A Modern Introduction

A.C. Cem Say[1] and Abuzer Yakaryılmaz[2]([✉])

[1] Department of Computer Engineering, Boğaziçi University,
34342 Bebek, İstanbul, Turkey
say@boun.edu.tr
[2] National Laboratory for Scientific Computing, Petrópolis, RJ 25651-075, Brazil
abuzer@lncc.br

Abstract. We present five examples where quantum finite automata (QFAs) outperform their classical counterparts. This may be useful as a relatively simple technique to introduce quantum computation concepts to computer scientists. We also describe a modern QFA model involving superoperators that is able to simulate all known QFA and classical finite automaton variants.

1 Introduction

Due to their relative simplicity, quantum finite automata (QFAs) form a sound pedagogical basis for introducing quantum computation concepts to computer scientists. Early QFA models were problematic, in the sense that they did not embody the full power provided by quantum physics, and led to confusing results where a "quantum" machine was not able to simulate its classical counterpart. In this paper, we present several simple QFA algorithms which demonstrate the superiority of quantum computation over classical computation. We then systematically construct the definition of a general QFA model, which is able to simulate all known QFA and classical finite automaton variants.

2 Preliminaries

Throughout the paper, Σ denotes the input alphabet, not including the left and right end-markers, ¢ and \$, respectively. We fix unary and binary alphabets as $\Sigma = \{a\}$ and $\Sigma = \{a,b\}$, respectively. A real-time finite automaton does not need to store the input. The given input is fed to the real-time machine from left to right, symbol by symbol. Moreover, a real-time machine can read ¢ before

Some parts of the material are based on the lectures given by the second author during his visits to Kazan Federal University, Ural Federal University, and Boğaziçi University in 2013.

Yakaryılmaz was partially supported by CAPES with grant 88881.030338/2013-01, ERC Advanced Grant MQC, and FP7 FET project QALGO.

© Springer International Publishing Switzerland 2014
C.S. Calude et al. (Eds.): Gruska Festschrift, LNCS 8808, pp. 208–222, 2014.
DOI: 10.1007/978-3-319-13350-8_16

the input and \$ after the input for pre- and post-processing, respectively. This ability does not increase the computational power of the standard automaton models, but a more detailed analysis is needed for the restricted models. In this paper, our real-time QFA algorithms and models do not use end-markers. Two-way models, on the other hand, have a read-only semi-infinite input tape, composed of infinitely many cells indexed by the natural numbers, on which the input $w \in \Sigma^*$ is placed as $\text{¢}w\$$ in the cells indexed 0 to $|w| + 1$. This tape is scanned by a head which can move one square to the left or right, never moving beyond the end-markers, in each step.

We assume that the reader is familiar with the basics of automata theory. An n-state real-time probabilistic finite automaton (rtPFA) M is a 5-tuple

$$M = (S, \Sigma, \{A_\sigma \mid \sigma \in \Sigma\}, s_1, S_a),$$

where $S = \{s_1, \ldots, s_n\}$ is the set of states, s_1 is the initial state, $S_a \subseteq S$ is the set of accepting states, and A_σ is a left stochastic transition matrix for $\sigma \in \Sigma$ such that $S_\sigma(i, j)$ is the probability of going from s_j to s_i upon reading σ. The computation starts in state s_1, and the given input is accepted if it finishes in an accepting state. The overall computation on input $w \in \Sigma^*$ can be traced by a stochastic column vector representing the probabilistic distribution of states in each step, whose initial value is $v_0 = (1 \ \ 0 \ \ \cdots \ \ 0)^T$. After reading the tth symbol $(1 \leq t \leq |w|)$, the new state vector can be calculated as

$$v_t = A_{w_t} v_{t-1}.$$

The overall acceptance probability of w by M is then

$$f_M(w) = \sum_{s_j \in S_a} v_{|w|}(j).$$

Note that the input is rejected with probability $1 - f_M(w)$. If the transition matrices are restricted to contain only zeros or ones as their entries, we obtain a real-time deterministic finite automaton (rtDFA).

3 Basics of Quantum Computation

An n-state quantum register is represented by an n-dimensional Hilbert space $\mathcal{H}_n$ for some positive integer n. We denote the standard bases for $\mathcal{H}_n$ as $\mathcal{B}_n = \{|q_1\rangle, \ldots, |q_n\rangle\}$, where $|q_j\rangle$ is an n-dimensional vector whose jth entry is 1, and all other entries are zeros for $1 \leq j \leq n$. Each q where $|q\rangle \in \mathcal{B}_n$ can be seen as a classical state, with the basis state $|q\rangle$ as its quantum counterpart. We denote the set $\{q_1, \ldots, q_n\}$ by Q.

A (pure) quantum state of the register is a column vector in $\mathcal{H}_n$, say,

$$|\psi\rangle = \begin{pmatrix} \alpha_1 \\ \vdots \\ \alpha_n \end{pmatrix} = \alpha_1 |q_1\rangle + \cdots + \alpha_n |q_n\rangle,$$

which is a linear combination of basis states such that the length of $|\psi\rangle$ is 1, i.e.

$$\sqrt{\langle\psi|\psi\rangle} = 1, \text{ or equivalently, } |\alpha_1|^2 + \cdots + |\alpha_n|^2 = 1,$$

where $\langle\cdot|\cdot\rangle$ is the inner product of any two given vectors, and, for any $j \in \{1,\ldots,n\}$, $\alpha_j \in \mathbb{C}$ is called the *amplitude* of $|q_j\rangle$, with $|\alpha_j|^2$ representing the probability of being in the jth state.

To observe the classical state of the system, *a measurement in the computational basis*, which determines whether the system is in $|q_1\rangle$, $|q_2\rangle$,..., or $|q_n\rangle$, is applied. This measurement therefore has n outcomes, respectively "1",...,"n". If the system is in the quantum state $|\psi\rangle$ exemplified above before the measurement, the outcome "j" can be obtained with probability $p_j = |\alpha_j|^2$.

If a system is closed, i.e. there is no interaction (including measurements) with the environment, quantum mechanics dictates that its evolution is governed by some unitary operators. Any operator defined on complex numbers is *unitary* if it is length-preserving, i.e. it maps any quantum state to another quantum state. Thus, we can say that $|\psi'\rangle = U|\psi\rangle$ is also a quantum state and so its length is 1 too. If $U \in \mathbb{C}^{n\times n}$ is unitary, then it also has the following equivalent properties: (i) all rows form an orthonormal set, (ii) all columns form an orthonormal set, and (iii) $U^\dagger U = UU^\dagger = I$, where $U^\dagger$ is the conjugate transpose of U.

One of the earliest quantum finite automaton definitions [8,20] was obtained by "quantumizing" the rtPFA model of Section 2 by positing that the transition matrix for each symbol should be unitary. According to that definition,

$$M = \{Q, \Sigma, \{U_\sigma \mid \sigma \in \Sigma\}, q_1, Q_a\}$$

denotes a real-time quantum finite automaton (rtQFA) with state set Q, as described above, and alphabet Σ. The machine starts out in the quantum state $|q_1\rangle$, which evolves by being multiplied with the unitary matrix U_σ whenever the symbol σ is consumed, until the end of the left-to-right scanning of the input. At that point, the state is measured, and the input is accepted if any member of the set of accept states $Q_a \subseteq Q$ is observed.

We will see later (Sections 4.5 and 5) that one needs somewhat more general operators to reach the full potential of QFAs. But this simple introduction is already sufficient to demonstrate several examples where quantum machines outperform their classical counterparts, as we are going to do in the next section.

4   Quantum Beats Classical: Five QFA-Based Examples

The algorithms to be presented in this section are based on a simple common component, which we now describe.

Consider a QFA whose entire memory can have only two states forming the set $Q = \{q_1, q_2\}$, i.e. just a *quantum bit (qubit)*. We restrict ourselves to real numbers as amplitudes. Any quantum state of such a single-qubit machine can then be represented as a point on the unit circle of $\mathbb{R}^2$, and any possible

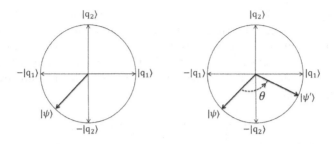

Fig. 1. The representation of rotation U_θ

unitary operator on it is either a reflection or a rotation. Let θ be the angle of a counterclockwise rotation denoted U_θ (see also Figure 1):

$$U_\theta = \begin{pmatrix} \cos\theta & -\sin\theta \\ \sin\theta & \cos\theta \end{pmatrix} \quad \text{or} \quad \begin{matrix} U_\theta|q_1\rangle \rightarrow \cos\theta|q_1\rangle + \sin\theta|q_2\rangle \\ U_\theta|q_1\rangle \rightarrow -\sin\theta|q_1\rangle + \cos\theta|q_2\rangle \end{matrix}.$$

Note that the (i,j)th entry of U_θ represents the amplitude of the transition from state q_j to state q_j, where $1 \le i, j \le 2$.

It is a well-known fact that if θ is a rational multiple of π, then U_θ is periodic, and its repeated application causes the quantum state to visit a finite number of points on the unit circle, returning to the same point after a finite number steps. On the other hand, if θ is an irrational multiple of π, then U_θ is aperiodic and dense on the unit circle, i.e. the quantum state would never visit the same position on the unit circle.

We proceed with several examples that use such rotations in interesting ways.

4.1 A QFA Can Recognize Far More Tally Languages with Cutpoint

Define a rtQFA R_θ with state set Q as described above, and $|q_1\rangle$ as the initial state. Our alphabet is unary, $\Sigma = \{a\}$, and R_θ simply applies U_θ to the qubit upon reading each a. At the end of the computation, the qubit is measured in the computational basis, and the input is accepted if $|q_1\rangle$ is observed.

It is clear that the empty string is accepted with probability 1. After reading the string a^k $(k > 0)$, the qubit will be in state

$$|\psi_k\rangle = \cos k\theta|q_1\rangle + \sin k\theta|q_2\rangle.$$

Therefore, the acceptance probability of a^k by R_θ is $\cos^2 k\theta$.

As can be noticed by the reader, a QFA defines a probability distribution over the strings on its input alphabet, $\{(w, f_M(w)) \mid w \in \Sigma^*\}$. So, for the empty string ε, $f_{R_{\alpha\pi}}(\varepsilon)$ is always 1 for any $\alpha \in \mathbb{R}$. If α is irrational, then there is no nonempty string a^k such that $f_{R_{\alpha\pi}}(a^k)$ is 0 or 1. On the other hand, if α is rational, then there is a minimum positive k such that $f_{R_{\alpha\pi}}(a^k)$ is 1 (and so $f_{R_{\alpha\pi}}(a^{jk})$ for any $j \in \mathbb{N}$). We leave it as an exercise to the reader to determine the values of α for which $f_{R_{\alpha\pi}}(a^k)$ would equal 0.

Since a QFA, say M, associates each string with a number in $[0, 1]$, we can split the set of all strings into three groups by picking a cutpoint λ in the interval $[0, 1]$: the strings whose acceptance probabilities are less than, greater than, or equal to the cutpoint. The strings accepted with probability greater than λ form *the language recognized* (or *"defined,"* in somewhat older terminology) *by M with cutpoint* λ [23]:

$$L(M, \lambda) = \{ w \in \Sigma^* \mid f_M(w) > \lambda \}.$$

So, any QFA (or PFA) defines a language with a cutpoint. A language recognized by a PFA with a cutpoint is called *stochastic*, and, it was shown that any language recognized by a QFA with a cutpoint is guaranteed to be stochastic, too [27].

In his seminal paper on probabilistic automata, Rabin showed that there are uncountably infinitely many stochastic languages [23]. He presented a 2-state PFA on a binary alphabet, and then showed that a different language is recognized by that PFA for each different cutpoint. This is not so for tally languages, since 2-state PFAs can define only regular languages, and any n-state PFA can define at most n nonregular languages with any cutpoint if the input alphabet is unary [21]. On the other hand, a 2-state QFA can define uncountably infinitely many tally languages [25], as we argue below:

Let $U_{\alpha\pi}$ be a rotation with an irrational α, e.g.

$$U_{\alpha\pi} = \begin{pmatrix} \frac{3}{5} & -\frac{4}{5} \\ \frac{4}{5} & \frac{3}{5} \end{pmatrix}.$$

Since $U_{\alpha\pi}$ is dense on the unit circle, there is always a k for any given two different cutpoints λ_1 and λ_2 such that the accepting probability of a^k lies between λ_1 and λ_2. Thus, $L(R_{\alpha\pi}, \lambda_1)$ and $L(R_{\alpha\pi}, \lambda_2)$ are different. Since there are uncountably many different possible cutpoints, the rtQFA $R_{\alpha\pi}$ defines uncountably many unary languages.

4.2   Nondeterministic QFAs Can Recognize Nonregular Languages

Quantum nondeterminism is defined as language recognition with cutpoint 0 [1]. In the classical case, realtime nondeterministic finite automata (equivalently, rtP-FAs with cutpoint 0) define only regular languages. On the other hand, rtQFAs with cutpoint 0 can recognize every language in a superset of regular languages known as the exclusive stochastic languages ($S^{\neq}$) [26], where a language is defined to be in $S^{\neq}$ if there exists a PFA such that all and only the non-members are accepted with probability $\frac{1}{2}$. Here, we present a very simple example.

Let M be a 2-state QFA defined on the binary alphabet $\Sigma = \{a, b\}$, with initial state q_1, and q_2 as the single accept state. After reading an a (resp., a b), M applies the rotation $U_{\sqrt{2}\pi}$ (resp., the rotation $U_{-\sqrt{2}\pi}$). We consider the language recognized by M with cutpoint 0.

It is clear that if M reads an equal number of a's and b's, the quantum state will be in its initial position $|q_1\rangle$, and so the accepting probability will be

0. That is, each string containing equal number of a's and b's is definitely not in the recognized language. For any other string, the quantum state ends up on a point of the unit circle that does not intersect the main axes, and so the acceptance probability will be nonzero, leading to the conclusion that each such string is in the language. Therefore, M recognizes the nonregular language

$$\text{NEQ} = \{w \mid |w|_a \neq |w|_b\},$$

where $|w|_\sigma$ denotes the number of occurrences of the symbol σ in string w, with cutpoint 0 [8].

4.3   Succinct Exact Solution of Promise Problems

From a practical point of view, a useful algorithm should classify the input strings with no error, or at least with high probability of correctness. We continue with an exact QFA algorithm.

A *promise problem* $P = (P_{yes}, P_{no})$ (defined on Σ) is a pair of two disjoint sets $P_{yes} \subseteq \Sigma^*$ and $P_{no} \subseteq \Sigma^*$. A promise problem P is said to be solved by a QFA M exactly if M accepts each $w \in P_{yes}$ with probability 1, and M accepts each $w \in P_{no}$ with probability 0. Note that there can be strings outside $P_{yes} \cup P_{no}$, and we do not care about the acceptance probabilities of these strings.

Real-time QFAs cannot be more succinct than real-time DFAs in the case of exact language recognition [17], but things change for certain promise problems [7]. For any $k > 0$, the promise problem EVENODD^k is defined as

$$\begin{aligned}\text{EVENODD}^k_{yes} &= \{a^{j2^k} \mid j \text{ is a nonnegative even integer}\} \\ \text{EVENODD}^k_{no} &= \{a^{j2^k} \mid j \text{ is a nonnegative odd integer}\}\end{aligned} .$$

If we pick $\theta = \frac{\pi}{2^{k+1}}$, then the rtQFA R_θ (from Section 4.1) can solve EVENODD^k exactly: It starts in state $|q_1\rangle$ and, after reading each block of a^{2^k}, it visits $|q_2\rangle, -|q_1\rangle, -|q_2\rangle, |q_1\rangle, \cdots$. So we can solve each EVENODD^k by a 2-state QFA. On the other hand, any rtDFA solving EVENODD^k requires at least 2^{k+1} states [7].[1] The interested reader may find it enjoyable to obtain the result for rtDFAs as an exercise. We also refer the reader to the recent works by Gruska and colleagues [14,15,28] for further results on the succinctness of exact QFAs.

4.4   Succinct Bounded-Error Language Recognition

Consider the language

$$\text{MOD}^p = \{a^{jp} \mid j \text{ is a nonnegative integer}\}$$

for some prime number p. Any rtPFA that recognizes MOD_p with bounded error has at least p states [4].

---

[1] In fact, any bounded-error PFA or any two-way NFA also requires at least 2^{k+1} states for this problem [11,24].

If we pick a $\theta = \frac{2\pi}{p}$, the familiar rtQFA R_θ can accept each member of MOD$_p$ exactly, and each non-member with some nonzero probability less than 1. The maximum possible erroneous acceptance probability for non-members is realized for input strings that bring the quantum state closest to $-|q_1\rangle$ at the end of its journey on the unit circle, as shown in Figure 2. The acceptance probabilities for non-members can therefore be bound by

$$\cos^2\left(\frac{\pi}{p}\right) = 1 - \sin^2\left(\frac{\pi}{p}\right),$$

and the rejection probability would be at least $\sin^2\left(\frac{\pi}{p}\right)$. As such, the error

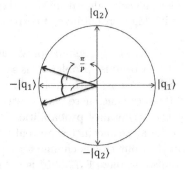

Fig. 2. These two vectors are the closest that the quantum state can get to $-|q_1\rangle$

committed by this family of algorithms nears 1 as p gets larger. But one can obtain a $O(\log p)$-state machine for any MOD$_p$ for any desired (nonzero) amount of tolerable error by combining several small machines with carefully selected rotation angles. That means that the succinctness gap between QFAs and PFAs can be exponential in the case of bounded-error language recognition [4,5]. In fact, this bound is tight for the simple rtQFA model, employing only unitary transformations, discussed in this section. We note that any language recognized by an n-state (general) QFA with bounded-error can be recognized by a $2^{O(n^2)}$-state DFA, but whether this bound is tight is still an open question [6].

4.5 Bounded-Error Recognition of Nonregular Languages in Polynomial Time

Our final example is about two-way automata, which can move their tape head back and forth over the input string, and for which runtime is therefore an issue. It is known that two-way PFAs cannot recognize any nonregular language with bounded error in polynomial (expected) time [10]. We will show how to construct a two-way QFA that recognizes the nonregular language

$$EQ = \{w \mid |w|_a = |w|_b\},$$

with bounded error in polynomial time [2].

Our two-way QFA is actually just a two-way deterministic finite automaton augmented with a qubit (see [2] for the general definition). The state set is partitioned to three subsets, namely, the accept, reject, and non-halting states. In each step of the execution, the classical portion of the machine determines either a unitary operator or a measurement in the computational basis to be applied to the quantum register.[2] After this quantum evolution, the machine makes a classical transition based on the scanned input symbol, current classical state, and latest measurement outcome, updating the classical state and head position accordingly. Execution ends when an accept or reject state is entered.

Note that we encountered a quantum machine which recognizes the complement of EQ with cutpoint 0 in Section 4.2. Modifying that machine by setting q_1 as a non-halting state and designating q_2 as a reject state, we obtain a QFA M that is guaranteed to reject any member of EQ with probability 0, and to reject non-members with some nonzero probability, in a single pass of the input from the left to the right.

One of the nice properties of the rotation with angle $\sqrt{2}\pi$ used by M is that, if you start on the x-axis ($|q_1\rangle$), the rotating vector always ends up in an orientation that is no closer than an amount proportional to the inverse of the number of rotation steps to the x-axis (see Figure 3). As indicated in the figure, the rejection probability of any non-member is the square of $\frac{1}{\sqrt{2}(|w|_a - |w|_b)}$, which can be at least $p_{rej} = \frac{1}{2|w|^2}$, where w is the input string.

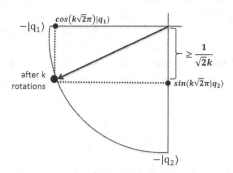

Fig. 3. The minimum distance to the x-axis after k rotations (see [2] for the proof)

Consider what happens if we augment M to run in a loop, moving its head back to the beginning of the tape and restarting if its left-to-right pass ends in the non-halting state: For input strings in EQ, this new machine would run forever. If the input is not in EQ, however, it would halt with rejection in polynomial expected time.

---

[2] Note that this machine does not fit the simplistic model of Section 3, since it allows more than just unitary transformations of the quantum register. See Section 5.

All that remains is to fix this machine so that it would eventually halt with acceptance, rather than run forever, with high probability for input strings in EQ, making sure that this fix does not spoil the property of non-members being rejected with high probability. This is achieved by inserting a call to a polynomial-time subroutine which accepts the input with probability $p_{acc} = \frac{p_{rej}}{2}$ at the end of each iteration of the loop.

So our algorithm for EQ is:

-Run M

-Accept with probability $\frac{1}{4|w|^2}$

-If not halted yet, restart.

Since M never rejects a member of EQ erroneously, it is clear that this algorithm accepts every member with probability 1. Any non-members would be rejected with probability at least

$$\sum_{j=0}^{\infty} (1 - p_{acc} - p_{rej})^j (p_{rej}) = \frac{1}{p_{acc} + p_{rej}} p_{rej} = \frac{2p_{acc}}{3p_{acc}} = \frac{2}{3},$$

meaning that the probability of erroneous acceptance is at most $\frac{1}{3}$, that is the error bound. By repeating this procedure t times, and accepting only when all t runs accept, the error bound can be reduced to $\frac{1}{3^t}$. The expected runtime is polynomially bounded, since we made sure that each iteration of the loop has a sufficiently great probability of halting.

And how do we implement the polynomial-time subroutine that accepts with just the probability described above? This task is in fact realizable by classical automata. A two-way PFA can easily implement a random walk: The head starts on the first symbol of the input. Then, in each step, a fair coin is flipped, and the head moves to the right (resp. left) if the result is heads (resp. tails), and, the walk is terminated if the head reaches an end-marker. The details of such a walk are given in Figure 4. A fair coin toss can be obtained by applying a rotation of angle $\frac{\pi}{4}$, i.e.

$$\begin{pmatrix} \frac{1}{\sqrt{2}} & -\frac{1}{\sqrt{2}} \\ \frac{1}{\sqrt{2}} & \frac{1}{\sqrt{2}} \end{pmatrix},$$

to a qubit in a computational basis state, and then measuring it.

It is another exercise for the reader to show how this subroutine can be designed to accept the input with probability $p_{acc} = \frac{1}{4|w|^2}$ by using random walks.

5   General QFAs

As mentioned earlier, the requirement that the program of a QFA should consist wholly of unitary transformations is an overly restrictive one, and several subclasses of regular languages that cannot be recognized by the rtQFA model of Section 3 have been identified [8]. In fact, this is true even for some proposed

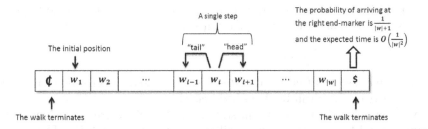

Fig. 4. The details of a random walk on the input w

generalizations of this QFA model, e.g., [3,12,18]. In Section 4.5, we saw a two-way QFA model that has classical as well as quantum states, and the classical states govern the computation flow and the determination of whether intermediate measurements or unitary transformations should be performed, depending on both input symbols and previous measurement results. A real-time version of such a model, realizing a unitary transformation, a projective measurement (see Figure 5), and classical evolution in each step, has been defined formally in [29], and can easily simulate any rtPFA, for instance. In this section, we focus on a restricted version of this model, and show that the full power of superoperators, generalizing unitary evolution and measurement transformations, is still retained.

Projective measurements are a generalization of measurements in the computational basis. Let Q be the set of states, and $|\psi\rangle$ be the current state. The state set may have been decomposed into some disjoint subsets, e.g. $Q = Q_1 \cup \cdots \cup Q_k$ for some $k \in \{1, \dots, n\}$. Based on this, we can decompose the whole space:

$$\mathcal{H}_n = \mathcal{H}_n^1 \oplus \cdots \oplus \mathcal{H}_n^k, \quad \mathcal{H}_n^j = span\{|q\rangle \mid q \in Q_j\} \quad (1 \le j \le n).$$

Similarly, we can decompose $|\psi\rangle$ as $|\widetilde{\psi_1}\rangle + \cdots + |\widetilde{\psi_k}\rangle$ where $|\widetilde{\psi_j}\rangle \in \mathcal{H}_j$ $(1 \le j \le n)$ and we use the $\sim$ notation for vectors whose lengths can be less than 1. A measurement operator based on this decomposition forces the system to collapse into one of these sub-systems when it is applied: There are k outcomes, say "1",…,"k", and the outcome "j" can be obtained with probability

$$p_j = \sum_{q_l \in Q_j} |\alpha_l|^2 = \langle \widetilde{\psi_j} | \widetilde{\psi_j} \rangle \quad (1 \le j \le k).$$

After getting the outcome "j" ($p_j > 0$), the system collapses into the jth subspace, and the new state is the normalization of $|\widetilde{\psi_j}\rangle$, which is $\frac{|\widetilde{\psi_j}\rangle}{\sqrt{p_j}}$.

Fig. 5. Projective measurements

Suppose that the quantum register of our rtQFA is composed of two systems called the main system (with the set of states $Q = \{q_1, \dots, q_n\}$) and the auxiliary system (with the set of states $\Omega = \{\omega_1, \ldots, \omega_l\}$, for some $l, n > 0$. So the state space is $\mathcal{H}_l \otimes \mathcal{H}_n$, and the set of quantum states is

$$\{(\omega_j, q_k) \mid 1 \leq j \leq l \text{ and } 1 \leq k \leq n\}.$$

Our machine also has l classical states $\{s_1, s_2, \ldots, s_l\}$, in correspondence with the members of Ω, as will be described below.

Now suppose that the quantum state is $|\omega_j\rangle \otimes |\psi\rangle$, where $|\omega_j\rangle$ is one of the computational basis states of the auxiliary system, and $|\psi\rangle \in \mathcal{H}_n$. That is, the quantum states of the auxiliary and main systems are $|\omega_j\rangle$ and $|\psi\rangle$, respectively. It will be guaranteed that the classical state in this case will be s_j, mirroring the auxiliary system state.

We will trace the execution of our machine for a single computational step. The unitary operator $U_{s_j, \sigma}$ to be applied to the quantum register is determined by the classical state s_j, and the scanned symbol σ. All such operators of this machine are products of two matrices

$$U_{s_j, \sigma} = U_\sigma U_{s_j},$$

where the functionality of U_{s_j} is to rotate the auxiliary state to ω_1 from ω_j, so that the operator U_σ finds the quantum state of the overall system to be

$$|\Psi\rangle = (|\psi\rangle(1), \ldots, |\psi\rangle(n), \underbrace{0, \ldots, 0}_{n \text{ times}}, \ldots, \underbrace{0, \ldots, 0}_{n \text{ times}})^\dagger$$

before it acts. Note that only the first n columns of U_σ determine the state attained after the evolution. Let us partition U_σ to $n \times n$ blocks. There are l^2 of these blocks, but only the "leftmost" l, designated E_1 through E_l below, are significant for our purposes:

$$U_\sigma = \begin{pmatrix} \begin{array}{|c|ccc|} \hline E_1 & * & \cdots & * \\ \hline E_2 & * & \cdots & * \\ \hline \vdots & \vdots & \ddots & \vdots \\ \hline E_l & * & \cdots & * \\ \hline \end{array} \end{pmatrix}.$$

The reader can also verify that the state obtained after applying U_σ to $|\Psi\rangle$ is

$$|\Psi'\rangle = \begin{pmatrix} |\widetilde{\psi_1}\rangle \\ |\widetilde{\psi_2}\rangle \\ \vdots \\ |\widetilde{\psi_l}\rangle \end{pmatrix},$$

where $|\widetilde{\psi_i}\rangle = E_i|\psi\rangle$ for $i \in \{1, \cdots, l\}$. Following this evolution, the auxiliary system is measured in the computational basis, which amounts to a projective measurement on the composite system. (This measurement is independent of the input symbol processed at the current step.) The probability of obtaining outcome "k" (where $1 \leq k \leq l$) is $p_k = \langle \widetilde{\psi_k} | \widetilde{\psi_k} \rangle$, and if "$k$" is observed ($p_k > 0$), the quantum state of the main system collapses to $|\psi_k\rangle = \frac{|\widetilde{\psi_k}\rangle}{\sqrt{p_k}}$. As the final action of every computational step for any input symbol, the classical state is set to s_k to mirror the observation result "k".

The reader might have noticed that all the information relevant to the computation is kept in the main system, and only the first l columns of the unitary operator actually affect the computation. It is therefore possible to trace the entire computation by just knowing $\mathcal{E} = \{E_1, \ldots, E_l\}$, and forgetting about the classical state and the auxiliary system. $\mathcal{E}$ is in fact what is called a *superoperator*, and each of the E_j are said to be its *operation elements*. Since they are composed of l orthonormal columns of a unitary operator, the operation elements satisfy the following equation that the reader can prove as an exercise:

$$\sum_{j=1}^{l} E_j^{\dagger} E_j = I.$$

We can now focus only on the main system as our machine, and think of the classical state and the auxiliary system as representing the environment that the machine interacts with. In that view, the computational step described above has caused the machine to be in a mixture of pure states, appropriately called a *mixed state*, which can be represented as

$$\{(p_j, |\psi_j\rangle) \mid 1 \leq j \leq l\}.$$

But there is a more convenient way to represent such a mixture as a single mathematical object, called a *density matrix*. Here is how to obtain the density matrix describing the mixture above:

$$\rho = \sum_{j=1}^{l} p_j |\psi_j\rangle\langle\psi_j|.$$

($\langle\psi_j|$ is defined to be the conjugate transpose of $|\psi_j\rangle$.) The reader can verify that, for each j, the jth diagonal entry of ρ represents the probability of the system being observed in the jth state. Therefore, the sum of all diagonal entries, the trace of the matrix ($Tr(\rho)$), is equal to 1.

A simple derivation reveals how this mixed state resulted from the pure state $|\psi\rangle$ through the application of our superoperator, as we represent ρ in terms of $|\psi\rangle$ and the operation elements:

$$\rho = \sum_{j=1}^{l} p_j |\psi_j\rangle\langle\psi_j| = \sum_{j=1}^{l} p_j \frac{|\widetilde{\psi_j}\rangle}{\sqrt{p_j}} \frac{\langle\widetilde{\psi_j}|}{\sqrt{p_j}} = \sum_{j=1}^{l} |\widetilde{\psi_j}\rangle\langle\widetilde{\psi_j}| = \sum_{j=1}^{l} E_j |\psi\rangle\langle\psi| E_j^{\dagger}.$$

In general, this is how you apply a superoperator to a state ρ to obtain the new state ρ':

$$\rho' = \mathcal{E}(\rho) = \sum_{j=1}^{l} E_j \rho E_j^{\dagger}.$$

A density matrix ρ has the following properties: (i) $Tr(\rho) = 1$, (ii) it is Hermitian, and (iii) it is semi-positive. Moreover, any density matrix corresponds to an actual mixed state.

We are ready to give the formal definition of a general QFA [16,27]. An n-state QFA $\mathcal{M}$ is a five-tuple

$$\{Q, \Sigma, \{\mathcal{E}_\sigma \mid \sigma \in \Sigma\}, q_1, Q_a\},$$

where (i) $Q = \{q_1, \ldots, q_n\}$ is the set of states, $q_1 \in Q$ is the initial state, and $Q_a \subseteq Q$ is the set of accepting states; (ii) Σ is the alphabet; and, (iii) $\mathcal{E}_\sigma$ is the superoperator defined for $\sigma \in \Sigma$ with l_σ operation elements: $\{E_{\sigma,1}, \ldots, E_{\sigma,l_\sigma}\}$.

Let $w \in \Sigma^*$ be the input. The computation starts in state $\rho_0 = |q_1\rangle\langle q_1|$. After reading each symbol, the defined superoperator is applied,

$$\rho_t = \mathcal{E}_{w_t}(\rho_{t-1}) = \sum_{j=1}^{l_\sigma} E_{w_t,j} \rho_{t-1} E_{w_t,j}^\dagger,$$

where $1 \leq t \leq |w|$. After reading the whole input, a measurement in the computational basis is made, and the input is accepted if one of the accepting states is observed. The overall accepting probability can be calculated as

$$f_M(w) = \sum_{q_j \in Q_a} \rho(j, j).$$

Simulation of Classical Machines. Let v be the state of an n-state probabilistic system, say P:

$$\begin{pmatrix} p_1 \\ p_2 \\ \vdots \\ p_n \end{pmatrix}, \quad \sum_{j=1}^{n} p_i = 1.$$

An n-state quantum system, say M, can represent v as

$$|v\rangle = \begin{pmatrix} \sqrt{p_1} \\ \sqrt{p_2} \\ \vdots \\ \sqrt{p_n} \end{pmatrix}.$$

Suppose that P is updated by a stochastic matrix A, i.e. $v' = Av$. Let us focus on the jth state, whose probability is p_j in v. Operator A maps p_j to

$$p_j \begin{pmatrix} A(1, j) \\ A(2, j) \\ \vdots \\ A(n, j) \end{pmatrix},$$

that represents the contribution of the jth state of v to v'. Now, we define a superoperator $\mathcal{E}$ with n operation elements $\{E_1, \ldots, E_n\}$ that simulates the effect of A as follows: The jth column of E_j is $(\sqrt{A_{1,j}}, \sqrt{A_{2,j}}, \ldots, \sqrt{A_{n,j}})^T$, and all other entries are zeros. (The reader can easily verify that $\mathcal{E}$ is a valid superoperator.) Then E_j maps $|v\rangle$ to

$$
\sqrt{p_j}
\begin{pmatrix}
\sqrt{A(1,j)} \\
\sqrt{A(2,j)} \\
\vdots \\
\sqrt{A(n,j)}
\end{pmatrix},
$$

that reflects the contribution of the jth column of A. By considering all operation elements, we can follow that the whole effect of A on v can be simulated by $\mathcal{E}$. Therefore, the evolution of P can be simulated by M by using a corresponding superoperator for each stochastic operator if a measurement in the computational basis is applied at the end of the computation of $\mathcal{M}$.

A straightforward conclusion is that any rtPFA can be simulated by a rtQFA having the same number of states. Moreover, since the tensor product of two superoperators is another superoperator, a rtQFA can simulate the computations of two rtQFAs in parallel. Therefore, rtQFAs are sufficiently general to simulate all known classical and quantum real-time finite state automata.[3]

For two recent surveys on QFAs, we refer the reader to [22] and [6].

Acknowledgments. We first met quantum finite automata in Prof. Gruska's book on quantum computing [13], for which we would like to extend him our thanks.

References

1. Adleman, L.M., DeMarrais, J., Huang, M.-D.A.: Quantum computability. SIAM Journal on Computing **26**(5), 1524–1540 (1997)
2. Ambainis, A., Watrous, J.: Two-way finite automata with quantum and classical states. Theoretical Computer Science **287**(1), 299–311 (2002)
3. Ambainis, A., Beaudry, M., Golovkins, M., Kikusts, A., Mercer, M., Thérien, D.: Algebraic results on quantum automata. Theory of Computing Systems **39**(1), 165–188 (2006)
4. Ambainis, A., Freivalds, R.: 1-way quantum finite automata: strengths, weaknesses and generalizations. In: FOCS 1998, pp. 332–341 (1998). http://arxiv.org/abs/quant-ph/9802062
5. Ambainis, A., Nahimovs, N.: Improved constructions of quantum automata. Theoretical Computer Science **410**(20), 1916–1922 (2009)
6. Ambainis, A., Yakaryılmaz, A.: Automata: from Mathematics to Applications, chapter Automata and quantum computing (in preparation)
7. Ambainis, A., Yakaryılmaz, A.: Superiority of exact quantum automata for promise problems. Information Processing Letters **112**(7), 289–291 (2012)
8. Bertoni, A., Carpentieri, M.: Analogies and differences between quantum and stochastic automata. Theoretical Computer Science **262**(1–2), 69–81 (2001)

---

[3] We refer the reader to [9,19,29] as some examples of classically enhanced rtQFAs .

9. Bertoni, A., Mereghetti, C., Palano, B.: Quantum computing: 1-way quantum automata. In: Èsik and Z. Fülöp (eds.): DLT 2003. LNCS, vol. 2710, pp. 1–20. Springer, Heidelberg (2003)
10. Dwork, C., Stockmeyer, L.: A time complexity gap for two-way probabilistic finite-state automata. SIAM Journal on Computing 19(6), 1011–1123 (1990)
11. Geffert, V., Yakaryılmaz, A.: Classical Automata on Promise Problems. In: Jürgensen, H., Karhumäki, J., Okhotin, A. (eds.) DCFS 2014. LNCS, vol. 8614, pp. 126–137. Springer, Heidelberg (2014)
12. Golovkins, M., Kravtsev, M., Kravcevs, V.: Quantum Finite Automata and Probabilistic Reversible Automata: R-trivial Idempotent Languages. In: Murlak, F., Sankowski, P. (eds.) MFCS 2011. LNCS, vol. 6907, pp. 351–363. Springer, Heidelberg (2011)
13. Gruska, J.: Quantum Computing. McGraw-Hill (1999)
14. Gruska, J., Qiu, D., Zheng, S.: Generalizations of the distributed Deutsch-Jozsa promise problem. Technical report (2014). arXiv:1402.7254
15. Gruska, J., Qiu, D., Zheng, S.: Potential of quantum finite automata with exact acceptance. Technical Report (2014). arXiv:1404.1689
16. Hirvensalo, M.: Quantum automata with open time evolution. International Journal of Natural Computing 1(1), 70–85 (2010)
17. Klauck, H.: On quantum and probabilistic communication: Las vegas and one-way protocols. In: STOC 2000, pp. 644–651 (2000)
18. Kondacs, A., Watrous, J.: On the power of quantum finite state automata. In: FOCS 1997, pp. 66–75 (1997)
19. Li, L., Qiu, D., Zou, X., Li, L., Lihua, W., Mateus, P.: Characterizations of one-way general quantum finite automata. Theoretical Computer Science 419, 73–91 (2012)
20. Moore, C., Crutchfield, J.P.: Quantum automata and quantum grammars. Theoretical Computer Science 237(1–2), 275–306 (2000)
21. Paz, A.: Introduction to Probabilistic Automata. Academic Press, New York (1971)
22. Qiu, D., Li, L., Mateus, P., Gruska, J.: Quantum finite automata. Discrete Mathematics and Its Applications. In: Handbook on Finite State based Models and Applications. Chapman and Hall/CRC (2012)
23. Rabin, M.O.: Probabilistic automata. Information and Control 6, 230–243 (1963)
24. Rashid, J., Yakaryılmaz, A.: Implications of Quantum Automata for Contextuality. In: Holzer, M., Kutrib, M. (eds.) CIAA 2014. LNCS, vol. 8587, pp. 318–331. Springer, Heidelberg (2014)
25. Shur, A.M., Yakaryılmaz, A.: Quantum, Stochastic, and Pseudo Stochastic Languages with Few States. In: Ibarra, O.H., Kari, L., Kopecki, S. (eds.) UCNC 2014. LNCS, vol. 8553, pp. 327–339. Springer, Heidelberg (2014)
26. Yakaryılmaz, A., Cem Say, A.C.: Languages recognized by nondeterministic quantum finite automata. Quantum Information and Computation 10(9&10), 747–770 (2010)
27. Yakaryılmaz, A., Cem Say, A.C.: Unbounded-error quantum computation with small space bounds. Information and Computation 279(6), 873–892 (2011)
28. Zheng, S., Gruska, J., Qiu, D.: On the State Complexity of Semi-quantum Finite Automata. In: Dediu, A.-H., Martín-Vide, C., Sierra-Rodríguez, J.-L., Truthe, B. (eds.) LATA 2014. LNCS, vol. 8370, pp. 601–612. Springer, Heidelberg (2014)
29. Zheng, S., Qiu, D., Li, L., Gruska, J.: One-Way Finite Automata with Quantum and Classical States. In: Bordihn, H., Kutrib, M., Truthe, B. (eds.) Languages Alive. LNCS, vol. 7300, pp. 273–290. Springer, Heidelberg (2012)

Physical Aspects of Oracles for Randomness and Hadamard's Conjecture

Karl Svozil[⊠]

Institute for Theoretical Physics, Vienna University of Technology, Wiedner
Hauptstraße 8-10/136, A-1040 Vienna, Austria
svozil@tuwien.ac.at
http://tph.tuwien.ac.at/~svozil

Abstract. We analyze the physical aspects and origins of currently proposed oracles for (absolute) randomness.

Keywords: Stochastic processes · Oracle computation · Indeterminism · Random number generator · Quantum measurement

1 Metamathematical and Metaphysical Origin of Oracles for Randomness

Jozef Gruska's extensive reviews of the *foundations of computing* [11], and *quantum computing* [12] documents his continued interest in the foundations of,
and the connections between, computation and physics. This encouraged me
to contribute to the physics of computation, in particular, by discussing non-
algorithmic oracles for randomness certified by physical principles.

The very existence of physical unknowables [17] and indeterminism is subject
to an ongoing debate that can be expected not to terminate at any time soon.
Thereby, like *Odysseus* trapped between *Scylla* and *Charybdis*, our perception
of how the universe is organized has been vacuously oscillating between, and
irritated by, claims of complete physical determinism on the one hand, as well
as indeterminism on the other hand.

Rather than arguing for one side or another, I would like to state upfront
that both positions are metaphysical; more precisely: from a physical perspective,
these claims are non-operational. And, formally, by reduction to the *halting problem* [11, Sec. 642], both of them are provably unprovable. Because, from a purely
phenomenological point of view, that is, in terms of the symbolic behaviour of
physical systems, any proof of determinism would imply solvability of the *rule
inference problem*, as well as total predictability even beyond the *Busy Beaver*
bound. Likewise, any claim of total indeterminism encounters the problem of
enumerating an infinity of "candidate theories of everything", let alone their
future behaviour, as mentioned earlier.

Nevertheless, one way of corroborating physical indeterminism, which could
then be used for the construction of evidence-based oracles for randomness, would

© Springer International Publishing Switzerland 2014
C.S. Calude et al. (Eds.): Gruska Festschrift, LNCS 8808, pp. 223–230, 2014.
DOI: 10.1007/978-3-319-13350-8_17

be to "screw open" physical boxes which allegedly produce random bits. We may not be able to do so, because, say, relative to certain physical assumptions and formal theorems such as complementarity and value indefiniteness, "nothing could be in" such boxes. But even then we may, at least, put forward some theoretical arguments which are based on what we are inclined to believe [3, 866]. In what follows we shall do exactly this: we mention such oracles for randomness; that is, some boxes containing allegedly indeterministic physical resources, and why we believe (or not believe) that they act as physical sources of random bits.

A necessary and sufficient condition for this is the existence of *gaps in the natural laws,* as discussed by Frank [8, Chapter III, Sec. 12]. Such gaps allow, or rather necessitate, "unlawful behaviour" which could be utilized for physical oracles of randomness.

2   Spontaneous Symmetry Breakdown and Deterministic Chaos

Already in 1873, Maxwell identified a certain kind of *instability* at *singular points* as rendering a gap in the natural laws [4, 211-212]: *"... when an infinitely small variation in the present state may bring about a finite difference in the state of the system in a finite time, the condition of the system is said to be unstable. It is manifest that the existence of unstable conditions renders impossible the prediction of future events, if our knowledge of the present state is only approximate, and not accurate. ... the system has a quantity of potential energy, which is capable of being transformed into motion, but which cannot begin to be so transformed till the system has reached a certain configuration, to attain which requires an expenditure of work, which in certain cases may be infinitesimally small, and in general bears no definite proportion to the energy developed in consequence thereof."*

Fig. 1 depicts a one dimensional gap configuration envisioned by Maxwell: a *"rock loosed by frost and balanced on a singular point of the mountain-side, the little spark which kindles the great forest, ..."* On top, the rock is in perfect balanced symmetry. A small perturbation or (pressure or thermal) fluctuation causes this symmetry to be broken, thereby pushing the rock either to the left or to the right hand side of the potential divide. This dichotomic alternative can be coded by 0 and by 1, respectively.

One may object to this scenario of *spontaneous symmetry breaking* by maintaining that, if indeed the symmetry is perfect, there is no movement, and the particle or rock stays on top of the tip (potential). Any slightest movement might either result from a microscopic asymmetry of the initial state of the particle, or from fluctuations of any form, either in the particle's position, or by the surrounding environment of the particle. For instance, any collision of gas molecules with the rock may push the latter over the edge by thermal fluctuations. Therefore, the randomness resides in the fluctuations, amplified by the instability. Whether or not any such fluctuation may be considered as creating a gap is a question related to debates in statistical physics mentioned later.

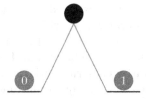

Fig. 1. (Color online) A gap created by a black particle sitting on top of a potential well. The two final states are indicated by grey circles. Their positions can be coded by 0 and 1, respectively.

A somewhat related scenario is that of *deterministic chaos,* because, as Poincaré pointed out [15, Chapter 4, Section 2, p.+56–57] *"it can be the case that small differences in the initial values produce great differences in the later phenomena; a small error in the former may result in a large error in the latter. The prediction becomes impossible and we have a "random phenomenon."*

3 Quantum Beam Splitter

A quantum mechanical gap can be realized by a beam splitter, such as a *half-silvered mirror*, with a 50:50 chance of transmission and reflection, as depicted in Fig. 2. A gap certified by quantum value indefiniteness necessarily has to operate with more than two exclusive outcomes [2]. Ref. [1] presents such a qutrit configuration.

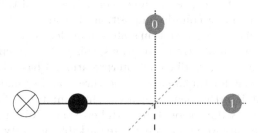

Fig. 2. (Color online) A gap created by a quantum coin toss. A single quantum (symbolized by a black circle from a source (left crossed circle) impinges on a semi-transparent mirror (dashed line), where it is reflected and transmitted with a 50:50 chance. The two final states are indicated by grey circles. The exit ports of the mirror can be coded by 0 and 1, respectively.

One may object to this scenario of *quantum indeterminism* by pointing out that it is merely based on a belief – actually, Born's *inclinations "to give up determinism in the world of atoms"* [3, p. 866] – with provable formal improvability. We shall come back to related issues later.

One may also object that a lossless beam splitter has a quantum mechanical representation as an invertible unitary operator **U**, and therefore is reversible.

Indeed, this can be readily demonstrated operationally by serially composing a lossless Mach-Zehnder interferometer with two beam splitters, thereby reconstructing the original quantum state (signal); that is, more formally, $\mathbf{U}^\dagger \mathbf{U} = \mathbf{I}$, where "$\dagger$" indicates the Hermitian adjoint, and $\mathbf{I}$ stands for the identity operator. How this kind of unitarity conforms with the view that a beam splitter can be considered an "active element" of quantum randomness remains unresolved, and is actually highly questionable [6,20]. Often vacuum fluctuations originating from the second, empty, input port are mentioned, but, pointedly stated [10, p. 249], these *"mysterious vacuum fluctuations ... may be regarded as sugar coating for the bitter pill of quantum theory."*

A lossless 50:50 beam splitter can be modelled by a normalized 2×2 Hadamard transformation $\mathbf{U} = \frac{1}{\sqrt{2}}\mathbf{H}_2$ with rows $(\frac{1}{\sqrt{2}}, \frac{1}{\sqrt{2}})$ and $(-\frac{1}{\sqrt{2}}, \frac{1}{\sqrt{2}})$, respectively.

More generally, suppose we would like to construct a $\underbrace{\frac{1}{n} : \frac{1}{n} : \ldots : \frac{1}{n}}_{n \text{ times}}$ beam splitter represented by a normalized Hadamard matrix $\frac{1}{\sqrt{n}}\mathbf{H}_n$; that is, an Hadamard matrix $\mathbf{H}_n$ divided by the square of (the dimension) n. An $n \times n$ Hadamard matrix $\mathbf{H}_n$ has entries in $\{-1,1\}$ such that any two distinct rows or columns of $\mathbf{H}_n$, interpreted as vectors in a Hilbert space, have scalar product zero; that is, they are orthogonal (or, equivalently, by requiring that its transpose $\mathbf{H}_n^T$ satisfies $\mathbf{H}_n\mathbf{H}_n^T = n\mathbf{I}_n$).

A *necessary* condition for such a construction is that $n = 1$, $n = 2$, or $n = 4k$ for any $k \in \mathbb{N}$. *Hadamard's conjecture* claims that this is also a *sufficient* condition for the existence of an n-dimensional Hadamard transformation; and thus, for a corresponding equi-decomposition of quantum states into coherent superpositions. (Of course, a quantum state can be decomposed into any fraction of unity by suitable unitary transformations; this just represents a permutation of the original state, or, in a different interpretation, a base change [16].)

A quantum oracle for Hadamard's conjecture would be one which would, for any $k \in \mathbb{N}$, output $4k$ orthogonal $\frac{1}{4k}$-equi-weighted mixtures of orthogonal states spanning the entire $4k$-dimensional (real) Hilbert space. A beam splitter realizing Hadamard's conjecture would possess the remarkable property that it converts a signal input in any one of the $4k$ input ports into a coherent equi-superposition of all output ports; with relative phase differences equal to 0 (corresponding to equal relative sign), and π (corresponding to relative sign "$-$").

At the same time, in terms of quantum states forming bases (or, by other namings, blocks, subalgebras or contexts), Hadamard's conjecture translates into the existence of a particular kind of pure states equivalent to the projectors corresponding to the row (column) vector of a normalized Hadamard matrix. The set of row vectors of $\frac{1}{\sqrt{4k}}\mathbf{H}_{4k}$ correspond to an orthogonal basis which is *(mutually) unbiased* with respect to the Cartesian standard basis in $\mathbb{R}^{4k}$.

Schwinger's construction [16] can be used for the rendition of mutually unbiased bases in arbitrary dimensions n; alas the base vectors may have complex coordinates. The construction starts with the Cartesian standard basis

$\{|e_1\rangle, |e_2\rangle, \ldots, |e_n\rangle\}$ and involves three steps: (i) a cyclic shift of the basis vectors $\{|f_1 = e_2\rangle, \ldots, |f_{n-1} = e_n\rangle, |f_n = e_1\rangle\}$, (ii) the construction of a unitary operator $\mathbf{U}$ by $\mathbf{U} = \sum_{i=1}^{n} |e_i\rangle\langle f_i|$; and finally (iii) the identification of the normalized eigenvectors of $\mathbf{U}$ with the elements of a basis which is unbiased with respect to the Cartesian standard basis. The associated normalized complex Hadamard matrix is just the row (column) matrix of the elements of this basis. For the sake of an example, we can readily write an algorithm [18] yielding a complex Hadamard matrix of dimension 8; that is,

$$\begin{pmatrix}
1 & 1 & 1 & 1 & 1 & 1 & 1 & 1 \\
-1 & 1 & -1 & 1 & -1 & 1 & -1 & 1 \\
i & -1 & -i & 1 & i & -1 & -i & 1 \\
-i & -1 & i & 1 & -i & -1 & i & 1 \\
(-1)^{1/4} & i & (-1)^{3/4} & -1 & -(-1)^{1/4} & -i & -(-1)^{3/4} & 1 \\
-(-1)^{3/4} & -i & -(-1)^{1/4} & -1 & (-1)^{3/4} & i & (-1)^{1/4} & 1 \\
(-1)^{3/4} & -i & (-1)^{1/4} & -1 & -(-1)^{3/4} & i & -(-1)^{1/4} & 1 \\
-(-1)^{1/4} & i & -(-1)^{3/4} & -1 & (-1)^{1/4} & -i & (-1)^{3/4} & 1
\end{pmatrix} .$$

Whether the Schwinger construction, for $n = 4k$, $k \in \mathbb{N}$, can be extended to produce only the real entries in $\{-1, 1\}$ instead of complex numbers of modulus unity remains unknown. One may conjecture that in this case the Dita decomposition [5] of unitary matrices into products of diagonal phase matrices (with modulus one entries) and orthogonal matrices – which in turn can be written as compositions of rotations in two-dimensional subspaces – yields the appropriate real Hadamard matrices by substituting 0 or π for all phases in the phase matrices (thereby rendering diagonal elements 1 and -1, respectively), as well as by identifying all rotation angles with $\pm\pi/4$ (thereby rendering factors whose absolute value is $1/\sqrt{2}$).

4   Quantum Vacuum Fluctuations

As stated by Milonni [13, p. xiii] and others, "... *there is no vacuum in the ordinary sense of tranquil nothingness. There is instead a fluctuating quantum vacuum.*" One of the observable vacuum effects is the *spontaneous emission of radiation* [19]: "... *the process of spontaneous emission of radiation is one in which "particles" are actually created. Before the event, it consists of an excited atom, whereas after the event, it consists of an atom in a state of lower energy, plus a photon.*" Recent experiments achieve single photon production by spontaneous emission, for instance by electroluminescence. Indeed, most of the visible light emitted by the sun or other sources of blackbody radiation, including incandescent bulbs, is due to spontaneous emission [13, p. 78] and thus is subject to *creatio ex nihilo*.

A gap based on vacuum fluctuations is schematically depicted in Fig. 3. It consists of an atom in an excited state, which transits into a state of lower energy, thereby producing a photon. The photon (non-)creation can be coded by the symbols 0 and 1, respectively.

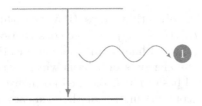

Fig. 3. (Color online) A gap created by the spontaneous creation of a photon

5 Analogies in Statistical Physics

In the following we shall briefly glance at two related physical issues – the purported (ir-)reversibility of quantum measurements, as well the character of the second law of thermodynamics [14].

5.1 Wigner's and Everett's Arguments Against Quantum Measurement

An extension of the observation context is what Wigner [20] and, in particular, Everett [6,7] had in mind when they argued against (irreversible and, in principal, for reversible) measurement, because quantum mechanics allows for two types of evolution: (i) the first type comprises irreversible measurements, whereas (ii) the second mode is characterized by the unitary, that is, reversible permutation, of quantum states in-between aforementioned measurements.

Alas, this is true only *for all practical purposes*, that is, relative to the physical means [14] available to resolve the huge number of degrees of freedom involving a "macroscopic" measurement apparatus. And yet, at least in principle, if the unitary quantum evolution is taken to be universally valid, then any distinction or cut between the observer and the measurement apparatus on the one side, and the quantized object on the other side, is not absolute or ontic, but epistemic, means-relative, subjective and conventional.

5.2 Analogies to the Second Law of Thermodynamics

There are good reasons to believe that also irreversibility in statistical physics is means relative [14] and thus epistemic: if we cannot resolve individual constituents of a group, and their degrees of freedom, then irreversibility is the epistemic expression of our incapacity to do so. In contradistinction, suppose the molecules are taken individually. In this case the second law might "dissolve into thin air" because of reversibility on the micro-description level. In Maxwell's own words [9, Document 15, p. 422] *"I carefully abstain from asking the molecules which enter where they last started from. I only count them and register their mean velocities, avoiding all personal enquiries which would only get me into trouble."*

6   *Caveats* and Afterthoughts

Stated pointedly, we have essentially been talking about the emergence of events *out of nothing* (e.g. *creatio ex nihilo*), and without any cause. Thereby, and for the sake of accepting classical and quantum oracles for randomness, we are denying the *principle of sufficient reason,* as well as negating Parmenides' *nothing comes from nothing,* which so powerfully guided the ancient Greek and modern western Enlightenments.

More technically, we note without further discussion that any "diluted" indeterminism, or gap mechanism, could be "concentrated" to Borel normality by assuming independence of bits in binary sequences.

As a last speculation, it might not be too unreasonable to contemplate that all gap scenarios, including spontaneous symmetry breakdown and quantum oracles, are ultimately based on vacuum fluctuations.

Acknowledgments. This research has been partly supported by FP7-PEOPLE-2010-IRSES-269151-RANPHYS.

References

1. Abbott, A.A., Calude, C.S., Conder, J., Svozil, K.: Strong Kochen-Specker theorem and incomputability of quantum randomness. Physical Review A 86, 062109, (December 2012). http://dx.doi.org/10.1103/PhysRevA.86.062109
2. Abbott, A.A., Calude, C.S., Svozil, K.: Value-indefinite observables are almost everywhere. Physical Review A 89, 032109, (March 2014). http://dx.doi.org/10.1103/PhysRevA.89.032109
3. Born, M.: Zur Quantenmechanik der Stoßvorgänge. Zeitschrift für Physik **37**, 863–867 (1926). http://dx.doi.org/10.1007/BF01397477
4. Campbell, L., Garnett, W.: The Life of James Clerk Maxwell: With a Selection From His Correspondence and Occasional Writings and a Sketch of His Contributions to Science. MacMillan, London (1882). http://www.sonnetsoftware.com/bio/maxbio.pdf
5. Dita, P.: Factorization of unitary matrices. Journal of Physics A: Mathematical and General **36**(11), 2781 (2003). http://dx.doi.org/10.1088/0305-4470/36/11/309
6. Everett III, H.: 'Relative State' formulation of quantum mechanics. Reviews of Modern Physics **29**, 454–462 (1957). http://dx.doi.org/10.1103/RevModPhys.29.454
7. Everett III, H.: The Everett Interpretation of Quantum Mechanics: Collected Works 1955–1980 With Commentary. Princeton University Press, Princeton, NJ (2012). http://press.princeton.edu/titles/9770.html
8. Frank, P., Cohen, R.S. (eds.): The Law of Causality and Its Limits (Vienna Circle Collection). Springer, Vienna (1997). http://link.springer.com/book/10.1007/978-94-011-5516-8
9. Garber, E., Brush, S.G., Everitt, C.W.F.: Maxwell on Heat and Statistical Mechanics: On "Avoiding All Personal Enquiries" of Molecules. Associated University Press, Cranbury, NJ (1995)
10. Garrison, J.C., Chiao, R.Y.: Quantum Optics. Oxford University Press, Oxford (2008)

11. Gruska, J.: Foundations of Computing. International Thompson Computer Press, London (1997)
12. Gruska, J.: Quantum Computing. McGraw-Hill, London (1999). http://www.fi.muni.cz/usr/gruska/qbook1.pdf
13. Milonni, P.W.: The Quantum Vacuum: An Introduction to Quantum Electrodynamics. Academic Press, San Diego (1994)
14. Myrvold, W.C.: Statistical mechanics and thermodynamics: A Maxwellian view. Studies in History and Philosophy of Science Part B: Studies in History and Philosophy of Modern Physics **42**(4), 237–243 (2011). http://dx.doi.org/10.1016/j.shpsb.2011.07.001
15. Poincaré, H.: Wissenschaft und Hypothese. Teubner, Leipzig (1914)
16. Schwinger, J.: Unitary operators bases 46, 570–579 (1960). http://dx.doi.org/10.1073/pnas.46.4.570
17. Svozil, K.: Physical unknowables. In: Baaz, M., Papadimitriou, C.H., Putnam, H.W., Scott, D.S. (eds.) Kurt Gödel and the Foundations of Mathematics, pp. 213–251. Cambridge University Press, Cambridge, UK (2011). http://arxiv.org/abs/physics/0701163
18. Svozil, K.: Mathematica code for the generation of mutually unbiased bases (2012, 2104). http://tph.tuwien.ac.at/svozil/publ/2012-schwinger.m
19. Weinberg, S.: The search for unity: Notes for a history of quantum field theory. Daedalus **106**(4), 17–35 (1977). http://www.jstor.org/stable/20024506
20. Wigner, E.P.: Remarks on the mind-body question. In: Good, I.J. (ed.) The Scientist Speculates, pp. 284–302. Heinemann and Basic Books, London and New York (1961). http://www.phys.uu.nl/igg/jos/foundQM/wigner.pdf

From Quantum Query Complexity to State Complexity

Shenggen Zheng[1] and Daowen Qiu[2(✉)]

[1] Faculty of Informatics, Masaryk University, 602 00 Brno, Czech Republic
zhengshenggen@gmail.com
[2] Department of Computer Science, Sun Yat-sen University,
Guangzhou 510006, China
issqdw@mail.sysu.edu.cn

Abstract. State complexity of quantum finite automata is one of the interesting topics in studying the power of quantum finite automata. It is therefore of importance to develop general methods how to show state succinctness results for quantum finite automata. One such method is presented and demonstrated in this paper. In particular, we show that state succinctness results can be derived out of query complexity results.

1 Introduction

An important way to get deeper insights into the power of various quantum resources and operations is to explore the power of various quantum variations of the basic models of classical automata. Of a special interest is to do that for various quantum variations of the classical automata, especially for those models that use very limited amounts of quantum resources: states, correlations, operations and measurements. This paper aims to contribute to such a line of research.

Number of (basis) states used is a natural complexity measure for (quantum) finite automata. The size of a (quantum) finite automaton is defined as the number of (basis) states of the (Hilbert) space on which the automaton will operate. In case of a hybrid, that is quantum/classical finite automata, it is natural to consider both complexity measures – the number of classical states and also the number of quantum (basis) states.

Quantum finite automata were introduced by Kondacs and Watrous [28] and also by Moore and Crutchfields [33], and since that time they were intensively explored [1,13,34,38]. State complexity and succinctness results are an important research area of the classical finite automata theory, see [37], with a variety of applications. Once quantum versions of classical finite automata were introduced and explored, it started to be of large interest to find out, also through

Work of the first author was supported by the Employment of Newly Graduated Doctors of Science for Scientific Excellence project/grant (CZ.1.07./2.3.00/30.0009) of Czech Republic. Work of second author was supported by the National Natural Science Foundation of China (Nos. 61272058, 61073054).

C.S. Calude et al. (Eds.): Gruska Festschrift, LNCS 8808, pp. 231–245, 2014.
DOI: 10.1007/978-3-319-13350-8_18

succinctness results, a relation between the power of classical and quantum finite automata models. This has turned out to be an area of surprising outcomes that again indicated that the relations between the classical and the corresponding quantum finite automata models are intriguing. In the past twenty years, state complexity of several variants of quantum finite automata were deeply and broadly studied [2–5,10,11,19,22–24,29–31,39,41–43].

State succinctness results were proved for some special languages and promise problems and for several automata models. The methods used to prove those results are various and often ad hoc. It is therefore natural to try to find out whether there are quite general methods to get state succinctness results for quantum finite automata. The answer is yes. We will show, in this paper, that state succinctness results can be derived in a nice way out of query complexity results. Here is the basic idea: State complexity is deeply related to communication complexity [27]. Buhrman et al. proved that various communication complexity results can be derived out of query complexity results [14]. If a communication protocol is simple enough, then we can use quantum finite automata to implement it. By using this line of thought, state succinctness results can be derived.

Quantum query complexity is the quantum generalization of the model of decision tree complexity. In this model, an algorithm to compute a Boolean function $f : \{0, 1\}^n \rightarrow \{0, 1\}$ is charged for "queries" to the input bits, while any intermediate computation is considered as free (see [15]).

Communication complexity was introduced by Yao [36] in 1979. In the setting of two parties, Alice is given $x \in \{0, 1\}^n$, Bob is given $y \in \{0, 1\}^n$ and their task is to communicate in order to determine the value of some Boolean function $f : \{0, 1\}^n \times \{0, 1\}^n \rightarrow \{0, 1\}$, while exchanging as small number of bits as possible. In this model, local computation is considered to be free, but communication is considered to be expensive and has to be minimized. Moreover, for computation, Alice and Bob can use all power available. There are usually three types of communication complexities considered according to the models of protocols used by Alice and Bob: deterministic, probabilistic and quantum.

Query complexity and communication complexity are related to each other. By using a simulation technique that transforms quantum query algorithms to quantum communication protocols, Buhrman et al. [14,16] obtained new quantum communication protocols and showed the first impressively (exponential) gap between quantum and classical communication complexity. In the reverse direction, Buhrman et al. showed that how to use lower bounds for quantum communication protocols to derive lower bounds for quantum query algorithms.

State complexity of finite automata and communication complexity are also related to each other. We can use communication complexity results to prove lower bounds on state complexity [25–27]. On the other hand, if the communication protocols are easy enough, then they can be simulated by finite automata and obtain new state complexity results (upper bounds) for finite automata.

Therefore, we can build connections from query complexity to state complexity. This could be a potential framework to get state succinctness results for quantum finite automata comparing to classical finite automata. We will demonstrate for several cases in this paper, that how to use quantum query complexity results to derive state succinctness results of finite automata.

We first consider the promise problem (partial function) studied in [32]. Namely, the problem

$$\mathrm{DJ}'(x) = \begin{cases} 1 \text{ if } W(x) \in \{0, 1, n-1, n\} \\ 0 \text{ if } W(x) = \frac{n}{2}, \end{cases} \tag{1}$$

where $W(x)$ is the Hamming weight of x. Montanaro et al. [32] gave a quantum query algorithm for DJ$'$ with 2 queries. However, their proof is quite complicated. Motivated by the method from [7], we give a simpler quantum query algorithm with 2 queries for DJ$'$.

Based on this simple query algorithm, we design a quantum communication protocol for the following promise problem

$$\mathrm{EQ}'(x, y) = \begin{cases} 1 & \text{if } H(x, y) \in \{0, 1, n-1, n\} \\ 0 & \text{if } H(x, y) = \frac{n}{2}, \end{cases} \tag{2}$$

where $H(x, y)$ is the Hamming distance between bit strings x and y. We further prove that the exact quantum communication complexity of EQ$'$ is $\mathbf{O}(\log n)$ while the deterministic communication complexity is $\mathbf{\Omega}(n)$.

Finally, we consider the promise problem $A(n) = (A_{yes}(n), A_{no}(n))$, where $A_{yes}(n) = \{x\#y\#\#x\#y \,|\, H(x, y) \in \{0, 1, n-1, n\}, \ x, y \in \{0, 1\}^n\}$ and $A_{no}(n) = \{x\#y\#\#x\#y \,|\, H(x, y) = \frac{n}{2}, \ x, y \in \{0, 1\}^n\}$. We will prove that the promise problem $A(n)$ can be solved exactly by a one-way finite automata with quantum and classical state (1QCFA) with $\mathbf{O}(n^2)$ quantum basis states and $\mathbf{O}(n^3)$ classical states, whereas the sizes of the corresponding one-way deterministic finite automata (1DFA) are $2^{\mathbf{\Omega}(n)}$.

The paper is structured as follows. In Section 2 basic concepts and notations are introduced and models involved are described in some details. A new quantum query algorithm is given for DJ$'$ in Section 3. Communication complexity of EQ$'$ is explored in Section 4. State complexity results for the promise problem $A(n)$ are showed in Section 5.

2   Preliminaries

In this section, we recall some basic definitions about query complexity, communication complexity and quantum finite automata. Concerning basic concepts and notations of quantum information processing and finite automata, we refer the reader to [20–22, 35].

2.1   Exact Query Complexity

Exact quantum query complexity for partial functions was dealt with in [12, 17, 23] and for total functions in [6–9, 32]. Concerning more basic concepts and notations concerning query complexity, we refer the reader to [15].

An exact classical (deterministic) query algorithm for computing a Boolean function $f : \{0,1\}^n \to \{0,1\}$ can be described by a decision tree. A decision tree T is a rooted binary tree where each internal vertex has exactly two children, each internal vertex is labeled with a variable x_i and each leaf is labeled with a value 0 or 1. T computes a Boolean function f as follows: The start is at the root. If this is a leaf then stop. Otherwise, query the variable x_i that labels the root. If $x_i = 0$, then recursively evaluate the left subtree, if $x_i = 1$ then recursively evaluate the right subtree. The output of the tree is the value of the leaf that is reached at the end of this process. The depth of T is the maximal length of a path from the root to a leaf (i.e. the worst-case number of queries used on any input). The *exact classical query complexity* (deterministic query complexity, decision tree complexity) is the minimal depth over all decision trees computing f.

Let $f : \{0,1\}^n \to \{0,1\}$ be a Boolean function and $x = x_1 x_2 \cdots x_n$ be an input bit string. An exact quantum query algorithm for f works in a Hilbert space with some fixed number of basis states. It starts in a fixed starting state, then performs on it a sequence of transformations $U_1, Q, U_2, Q, \ldots, U_t, Q, U_{t+1}$. Unitary transformations U_i do not depend on the input bits, while Q, called the query transformation, does, in the following way. Each of the basis states corresponds to either one or none of the input bits. If the basis state $|\psi\rangle$ corresponds to the i-th input bit, then $Q|\psi\rangle = (-1)^{x_i}|\psi\rangle$. If it does not correspond to any input bit, then Q leaves it unchanged: $Q|\psi\rangle = |\psi\rangle$. Finally, the algorithm performs a measurement in the standard basis. Depending on the result of the measurement, the algorithm outputs either 0 or 1 which must be equal to $f(x)$. The *exact quantum query complexity* is the minimum number of queries made by any quantum algorithm computing f.

2.2   Communication Complexity

We recall here only very basic concepts and notations of communication complexity, and we refer the reader to [27] for more details. We will deal with the situation that there are two communicating parties and with very simple tasks of computing two inputs Boolean functions for the case one input is known to one party and the other input to the other party. We will completely ignore computational resources needed by parties and focus solely on the amount of communication need to be exchanged between both parties in order to compute the value of a given Boolean function.

More technically, let X, Y be finite subsets of $\{0,1\}^n$. We will consider two-input functions $f : X \times Y \to \{0,1\}$ and two communicating parties. Alice is given $x \in X$ and Bob is given $y \in Y$. They want to compute $f(x,y)$. If f is defined only on a proper subset of $X \times Y$, f is said to be a partial function or a promise problem.

The computation of $f(x,y)$ will be done using a communication protocol. During the execution of the protocol, the two parties alternate roles in sending messages. Each of these messages is a bit-string. The protocol, whose steps are based on the communication so far, specifies also for each step whether the communication terminates (in which case it also specifies what is the output).

If the communication is not to terminate, the protocol specifies what kind of message the sender (Alice or Bob) should send next, as a function of its input and communication so far.

A deterministic communication protocol $\mathcal{P}$ computes a (partial) function f, if for every (promised) input pair $(x, y) \in X \times Y$ the protocol terminates with the value $f(x, y)$ as its output. In a probabilistic protocol, Alice and Bob may also flip coins during the protocol execution and proceed according to its output and the protocol can also have an erroneous output with a small probability. In a quantum protocol, Alice and Bob may use quantum resources to produce the output or (qu)bits for communication.

Let $\mathcal{P}(x, y)$ denote the output of the protocol $\mathcal{P}$. For an exact protocol, that always outputs the correct answer, $Pr(\mathcal{P}(x, y) = f(x, y)) = 1$.

The communication complexity of a protocol $\mathcal{P}$ is the worst case number of (qu)bits exchanged. The communication complexity of f is, with which respect to the communication mode used, the complexity of an optimal protocol for f.

We will use $D(f)$ to denote the *deterministic communication complexity* and $Q_E(f)$ to denote the *exact quantum communication complexity*.

2.3   One-way Finite Automata with Quantum and Classical States

In this subsection we recall the definition of 1QCFA.

Two-way finite automata with quantum and classical states were introduced by Ambainis and Watrous [1] and then explored in [39–44]. 1QCFA are one-way versions of 2QCFA, which were introduced by Zheng et al. [41]. Informally, a 1QCFA can be seen as a 1DFA which has access to a quantum memory of a constant size (dimension), upon which it performs quantum transformations and measurements. Given a finite set of quantum basis states Q, we denote by $\mathcal{H}(Q)$ the Hilbert space spanned by Q. Let $\mathcal{U}(\mathcal{H}(Q))$ and $\mathcal{O}(\mathcal{H}(Q))$ denote the sets of unitary operators and projective measurements over $\mathcal{H}(Q)$, respectively.

Definition 1. *A one-way finite automaton with quantum and classical states $\mathcal{A}$ is specified by a 10-tuple*

$$\mathcal{A} = (Q, S, \Sigma, \Theta, \Delta, \delta, |q_0\rangle, s_0, S_{acc}, S_{rej}) \tag{3}$$

where:

1. Q *is a finite set of orthonormal quantum basis states.*
2. S *is a finite set of classical states.*
3. Σ *is a finite alphabet of input symbols and let $\Sigma' = \Sigma \cup \{\cent, \$\}$, where $\cent$ will be used as the left end-marker and $\$ $ as the right end-marker.*
4. $|q_0\rangle \in Q$ *is the initial quantum state.*
5. s_0 *is the initial classical state.*
6. $S_{acc} \subset S$ *and $S_{rej} \subset S$, where $S_{acc} \cap S_{rej} = \emptyset$, are sets of the classical accepting and rejecting states, respectively.*

7. Θ *is a quantum transition function*

$$\Theta : S \setminus (S_{acc} \cup S_{rej}) \times \Sigma' \to \mathcal{U}(\mathcal{H}(Q)), \tag{4}$$

assigning to each pair (s, γ) a unitary transformation.

8. Δ *is a mapping*

$$\Delta : S \times \Sigma' \to \mathcal{O}(\mathcal{H}(Q)), \tag{5}$$

where each $\Delta(s, \gamma)$ corresponds to a projective measurement (a projective measurement will be taken each time a unitary transformation is applied; if we do not need a measurement, we denote that $\Delta(s, \gamma) = I$, and we assume the result of the measurement to be a fixed c).

9. δ *is a special transition function of classical states. Let the results set of the measurement be $\mathcal{C} = \{c_1, c_2, \ldots, c_s\}$, then*

$$\delta : S \times \Sigma' \times \mathcal{C} \to S, \tag{6}$$

where $\delta(s, \gamma)(c_i) = s'$ means that if a tape symbol $\gamma \in \Sigma'$ is being scanned and the projective measurement result is c_i, then the state s is changed to s'.

Given an input $w = \sigma_1 \cdots \sigma_l$, the word on the tape will be $w = \text{¢}w\$$ (for convenience, we denote $\sigma_0 = \text{¢}$ and $\sigma_{l+1} = \$$). Now, we define the behavior of 1QCFA $\mathcal{A}$ on the input word w. The computation starts in the classical state s_0 and the quantum state $|q_0\rangle$, then the transformations associated with symbols in the word $\sigma_0\sigma_1 \cdots, \sigma_{l+1}$ are applied in succession. The transformation associated with a state $s \in S$ and a symbol $\sigma \in \Sigma'$ consists of three steps:

1. Firstly, $\Theta(s, \sigma)$ is applied to the current quantum state $|\phi\rangle$, yielding the new state $|\phi'\rangle = \Theta(s, \sigma)|\phi\rangle$.
2. Secondly, the observable $\Delta(s, \sigma) = \mathcal{O}$ is measured on $|\phi'\rangle$. The set of possible results is $\mathcal{C} = \{c_1, \cdots, c_s\}$. According to quantum mechanics principles, such a measurement yields the classical outcome c_k with probability $p_k = ||P(c_k)|\phi'\rangle||^2$, and the quantum state of $\mathcal{A}$ collapses to $P(c_k)|\phi'\rangle/\sqrt{p_k}$.
3. Thirdly, the current classical state s will be changed to $\delta(s, \sigma)(c_k) = s'$.

An input word w is assumed to be accepted (rejected) if and only if the classical state after scanning σ_{l+1} is an accepting (rejecting) state. We assume that δ is well defined so that 1QCFA $\mathcal{A}$ always accepts or rejects at the end of the computation.

Language acceptance is a special case of so called promise problem solving. A *promise problem* is a pair $A = (A_{yes}, A_{no})$, where $A_{yes}, A_{no} \subset \Sigma^*$ are disjoint sets. Languages may be viewed as promise problems that obey the additional constraint $A_{yes} \cup A_{no} = \Sigma^*$.

A promise problem $A = (A_{yes}, A_{no})$ is solved exactly by a finite automaton $\mathcal{A}$ if

1. $\forall w \in A_{yes}, Pr[\mathcal{A} \text{ accepts } w] = 1$, and
2. $\forall w \in A_{no}, Pr[\mathcal{A} \text{ rejects } w] = 1$.

3   An Exact Quantum Query Algorithm for DJ$'(x)$

Montanaro et al. [32] gave a quantum algorithm for DJ$'$ with 2 queries. However, their proof is complicated. Motivated by the method from [7], we give a simpler algorithm with 2 queries for DJ$'$ as follow:

We use basis states $|0,0\rangle$, $|i,0\rangle$, $|i,j\rangle$ and $|k\rangle$ with $0 \leq i < j \leq n$ and $1 \leq k \leq n-2$. A basis state $|i,j\rangle$ corresponds to an input bit x_i for $1 \leq i \leq n$; a basis state $|k\rangle$ corresponds to an input bit y_k for $1 \leq k \leq n-2$ (y_k is some certain bit x_i) and the other basis states do not correspond to any input bit.

1. The algorithm $\mathcal{A}$ begins in the state $|0,0\rangle$ and then a unitary mapping U_1 is applied on it:

$$U_1|0,0\rangle = \sum_{i=1}^{n} \frac{1}{\sqrt{n}}|i,0\rangle. \tag{7}$$

2. $\mathcal{A}$ then performs the query:

$$\sum_{i=1}^{n} \frac{1}{\sqrt{n}}|i,0\rangle \rightarrow \sum_{i=1}^{n} \frac{1}{\sqrt{n}}(-1)^{x_i}|i,0\rangle. \tag{8}$$

3. $\mathcal{A}$ performs a unitary mapping U_2 to the current state such that

$$U_2|i,0\rangle = \sum_{j>i\geq 1} \frac{1}{\sqrt{n}}|i,j\rangle - \sum_{1\leq j<i} \frac{1}{\sqrt{n}}|j,i\rangle + \frac{1}{\sqrt{n}}|0,0\rangle \tag{9}$$

and the resulting quantum state will be

$$U_2 \sum_{i=1}^{n} \frac{1}{\sqrt{n}}(-1)^{x_i}|i,0\rangle = \frac{1}{n}\sum_{i=1}^{n}(-1)^{x_i}|0,0\rangle + \frac{1}{n}\sum_{1\leq i<j}((-1)^{x_i}-(-1)^{x_j})|i,j\rangle. \tag{10}$$

4. $\mathcal{A}$ measures the resulting state in the standard basis. If the outcome is $|0,0\rangle$, then $\sum_{i=1}^{n}(-1)^{x_i} \neq 0$ and DJ$'(x) = 1$. Otherwise, suppose that we get the state $|i,j\rangle$, then we have $x_i \neq x_j$. Let $y = x \setminus \{x_i, x_j\}$, we have $W(y) \in \{0, n-2, \frac{n-2}{2}\}$. If $W(y) = \frac{n-2}{2}$, then DJ$'(x) = 0$. If $W(y) \in \{0, n-2\}$, then DJ$'(x) = 1$. The remaining question is exactly the Deutsch-Jozsa promise problem [17] and we can get the answer with 1 query as follows: we use the subalgorithm $\mathcal{B}$ to solve the remaining promise problem using $n-2$ quantum basis states $|1\rangle, \ldots, |n-2\rangle$ that will work as follows:
    (a) $\mathcal{B}$ begins in the state $|1\rangle$ and performs on it a unitary transformation U_3 such that

$$U_3|1\rangle = \sum_{k=1}^{n-2} \frac{1}{\sqrt{n-2}}|k\rangle. \tag{11}$$

    (b) $\mathcal{B}$ performs a query Q:

$$\sum_{k=1}^{n-2} \frac{1}{\sqrt{n-2}}|k\rangle \rightarrow \sum_{k=1}^{n-2} \frac{1}{\sqrt{n-2}}(-1)^{y_k}|k\rangle \tag{12}$$

(c) $\mathcal{B}$ performs a unitary transformation $U_4 = U_3^{-1}$ and

$$U_3^{-1} \sum_{k=1}^{n-2} \frac{1}{\sqrt{n-2}} (-1)^{y_k} |k\rangle = \frac{1}{n-2} \sum_{k=1}^{n-2} (-1)^{y_k} |1\rangle + \sum_{k=2}^{n-2} \beta_k |k\rangle, \quad (13)$$

where β_k are amplitudes that we do not need to be specified exactly.

(d) $\mathcal{B}$ measures the resulting state in the standard basis and outputs 1 if the measurement outcome is $|1\rangle$ and 0 otherwise.

According to [7], the unitary mapping U_2 exists. The rest of the proof is easy to verify. Obviously, the algorithm $\mathcal{A}$ uses 2 queries.

4   Communication Complexity of EQ$'(x, y)$

In this section, we will prove that $Q_E(\text{EQ}')$ is $\mathbf{O}(\log n)$ while $D(\text{EQ}')$ is $\mathbf{\Omega}(n)$.

Theorem 1. $Q_E(EQ') \in \mathbf{O}(\log n)$.

Proof. Assume that Alice is given an input $x = x_1, \cdots, x_n$ and Bob an input $y = y_1, \cdots, y_n$. The following quantum communication protocol $\mathcal{P}$ computes EQ$'$ using $\mathbf{O}(n^2)$ quantum basis states $|0, 0\rangle$, $|i, 0\rangle$, $|i, j\rangle$ and $|k\rangle$ with $0 \leq i < j \leq n$ and $1 \leq k \leq n - 2$ as follows:

1. Alice begins with the quantum state $|\psi_0\rangle = |0, 0\rangle$ and performs on it the unitary map U_1. The quantum state is changed to

$$|\psi_1\rangle = U_1 |0, 0\rangle = \frac{1}{\sqrt{n}} \sum_{i=1}^{n} |i, 0\rangle. \quad (14)$$

2. Alice applies the unitary map U_x to the current state such that $U_x |i, 0\rangle = (-1)^{x_i} |i, 0\rangle$ for $i > 0$ and the quantum state is changed to

$$|\psi_2\rangle = U_x |\psi_1\rangle = \frac{1}{\sqrt{n}} \sum_{i=1}^{n} (-1)^{x_i} |i, 0\rangle. \quad (15)$$

3. Alice then sends her current quantum state $|\psi_2\rangle$ to Bob.

4. Bob applies the unitary map U_y to the state that he has received such that $U_y |i, 0\rangle = (-1)^{y_i} |i, 0\rangle$ for $i > 0$ and the quantum state is changed to

$$|\psi_3\rangle = U_y |\psi_2\rangle U_x = \frac{1}{\sqrt{n}} \sum_{i=1}^{n} (-1)^{x_i + y_i} |i, 0\rangle. \quad (16)$$

5. Bob applies the unitary map U_2 to his quantum state and the quantum state is changed to

$$|\psi_4\rangle = U_2 |\psi_3\rangle = \frac{1}{n} \sum_{i=1}^{n} (-1)^{x_i + y_i} |0, 0\rangle + \frac{1}{n} \sum_{1 \leq i < j} ((-1)^{x_i + y_i} - (-1)^{x_j + y_j}) |i, j\rangle. \quad (17)$$

6. Bob measures the resulting state in the standard basis and outputs 1 if the measurement outcome is $|0,0\rangle$. Otherwise, suppose that the outcome is $|i,j\rangle$. Bob sends i and j to Alice using classical bits.

7. After Alice receives i and j, let $x' = x_1 \ldots x_{i-1}x_{i+1} \ldots x_{j-1}x_{j+1} \ldots x_n$. (In convenience, we write $x' = x'_1 \ldots x'_{n-2}$). Alice applies U_3 to the basis state $|1\rangle$ such that the quantum state is changed to

$$|\psi_5\rangle = U_3|1\rangle = \frac{1}{\sqrt{n-2}} \sum_{k=1}^{n-2} |k\rangle. \tag{18}$$

8. Alice then applies $U_{x'}$ to the current state such that $U_{x'}|k\rangle = (-1)^{x'_k}|k\rangle$ for $k > 0$ and the quantum state is changed to

$$|\psi_6\rangle = \frac{1}{\sqrt{n-2}} \sum_{k=1}^{n-2} (-1)^{x'_k}|k\rangle. \tag{19}$$

9. Alice sends her current quantum state $|\psi_6\rangle$ to Bob.

10. Bob applies the unitary map $U_{y'}$ to the state that he has received such that $U_{y'}|k\rangle = (-1)^{y'_k}|k\rangle$ for $k > 0$, where $y' = y_1 \ldots y_{i-1}y_{i+1} \ldots y_{j-1}y_{j+1} \ldots y_n$. (In convenience, we write $y' = y'_1 \ldots y'_{n-2}$). The quantum state is changed to

$$|\psi_7\rangle = \frac{1}{\sqrt{n-2}} \sum_{k=1}^{n-2} (-1)^{x'_k+y'_k}|k\rangle. \tag{20}$$

11. Bob performs a unitary transformation $U_4 = U_3^{-1}$ to the current state and the quantum state is changed to

$$|\psi_8\rangle = U_4|\psi_7\rangle = \frac{1}{n-2} \sum_{k=1}^{n-2} (-1)^{x'_k+y'_k}|1\rangle + \sum_{k=2}^{n-2} \beta_k|k\rangle, \tag{21}$$

where β_k are amplitudes that we do not need to be specified exactly.

12. Bob measures the resulting state in standard basis and outputs 1 if the measurement outcome is $|1\rangle$ and outputs 0 otherwise.

The unitary transformations U_1, U_2, U_3 and U_4 are the same ones as defined in Section 3.

If $H(x,y) \in \{0,n\}$, then the quantum state in Step 5 is

$$|\psi_4\rangle = \frac{1}{n} \sum_{i=1}^{n} (-1)^{x_i+y_i}|0,0\rangle = \pm|0,0\rangle. \tag{22}$$

Bob will get the quantum state $|0,0\rangle$ after the measurement in Step 6 and output 1 as the result of $EQ'(x,y)$.

If $H(x,y) \in \{1, n-1\}$, then there are two cases:

a) If the measurement outcome in Step 6 is $|0,0\rangle$ and Bob outputs 1 as the result of $EQ'(x,y)$.

b) If the measurement outcome in Step 6 is $|i, j\rangle$, then $H(x', y') \in \{0, n-2\}$ and the quantum state in Step 11 is

$$|\psi_8\rangle = \frac{1}{n-2} \sum_{k=1}^{n-2} (-1)^{x'_k + y'_k} |1\rangle = \pm |1\rangle \tag{23}$$

Bob will get the quantum state $|1\rangle$ after the measurement in Step 12 and output 1 as the result of $EQ'(x, y)$.

If $H(x, y) = \frac{n}{2}$, then Bob will output 0 as the result of $EQ'(x, y)$ in Step 12. In Step 3 Alice sends $\lceil \log(n^2) \rceil$ qubits, in Step 6 Bob sends $2\lceil \log(n) \rceil$ bits and in Step 9 Alice sends $\lceil \log(n-2) \rceil$ qubits. Since we can use qubits to send bits, it is clear that this protocol uses only $\mathbf{O}(\log n)$ qubits for communication.

The proof for deterministic communication lower bound is similar to the ones in [15,16]. In order to obtain an exponential quantum speed-up in [16], $\frac{n}{2}$ must be an even integer in the distributed Deutsch-Jozsa promise problem (see [23] for argument). However, $\frac{n}{2}$ can be arbitrary integer in the promise problem EQ' in this paper.

We use so called "rectangles" lower bound method [27] to prove the result.

A *rectangle* in $X \times Y$ is a subset $R \subseteq X \times Y$ such that $R = A \times B$ for some $A \subseteq X$ and $B \subseteq Y$. A rectangle $R = A \times B$ is called 1(0)-rectangle of a function $f : X \times Y \to \{0, 1\}$ if for every $x \in A$ and $y \in B$ the value of $f(x, y)$ is 1 (0). Moreover, $C^i(f)$ is defined as the minimum number of i-rectangles that partition the space of i-inputs (such inputs x and y that $f(x, y) = i$) of f.

Lemma 1. [27] $D(f) \geq \max\{\log C^1(f), \log C^0(f)\}$.

Remark 1. For a partial function $f : X \times Y \to \{0, 1\}$ with domain $\mathcal{D}$, a rectangle $R = A \times B$ is called 1(0)-rectangle if the value of $f(x, y)$ is 1(0) for every $(x, y) \in \mathcal{D} \cap (A \times B)$ – we do not care about values for $(x, y) \notin \mathcal{D}$. The above lemma still holds for promise problems (that is for partial functions). .

Theorem 2. $D(EQ') \in \mathbf{\Omega}(n)$.

Proof. Let $\mathcal{P}$ be a deterministic protocol for EQ'. There are two cases:

Case 1: $\frac{n}{2}$ is even. We consider the set $E = \{(x, x), (x, \overline{x}) \mid W(x) = \frac{n}{2}\}$. For every $(x, y) \in E$, we have $\mathcal{P}(x, y) = 1$. Suppose there is a 1-monochromatic rectangle $R = A \times B \subseteq \{0, 1\}^n \times \{0, 1\}^n$ such that $\mathcal{P}(x, y) = 1$ for every promise pair $(x, y) \in R$. Let $S = R \cap E$. For $x, y \in \{0, 1\}^n$, let us denote $|x \wedge y| = \sum_{i=1}^n x_i \wedge y_i$. We now prove that for any distinct $(x, x'), (y, y') \in S$, $|x \wedge y| \neq \frac{n}{4}$.

According to the assumption that $(y, y') \in S \subset E$, we have $y' = y$ or $y' = \overline{y}$. If $|x \wedge y| = \frac{n}{4}$, then $H(x, y) = 2(\frac{n}{2} - \frac{n}{4}) = \frac{n}{2} = H(x, \overline{y})$ and $\mathcal{P}(x, y') = 0$. Since $(x, x') \in R$ and $(y, y') \in R$, we have $(x, y') \in R$ and $\mathcal{P}(x, y') = 0$, which is a contradiction.

According to Corollary 1.2 from [18], we have $|S| \leq 1.99^n$. Therefore, the minimum number of 1-monochromatic rectangles that partition the space of inputs is

$$C^1(EQ') \geq \frac{|E|}{|S|} \geq \frac{2\binom{n}{n/2}}{(1.99)^n} > \frac{2^{n+1}/n}{(1.99)^n}. \tag{24}$$

The deterministic communication complexity is then

$$D(EQ') \geq \log C^1(EQ') > \log \frac{2^{n+1}/n}{(1.99)^n} > 0.0073n. \tag{25}$$

Case 2: $\frac{n}{2}$ is odd. We assume that $n = 4k + 2$. We consider the set $E = \{(x, x') \mid W(x) = \frac{n}{2}\}$, where $x'_n = x_n = 1$ and $x'_i = 1 - x_i$ for $i < n$. For every $(x, x') \in E$, we have $H(x, x') = n - 1$ and $\mathcal{P}(x, x') = 1$. Suppose there is a 1-monochromatic rectangle $R = A \times B \subseteq \{0, 1\}^n \times \{0, 1\}^n$ such that $\mathcal{P}(x, y) = 1$ for every promise pair $(x, y) \in R$. Let $S = R \cap E$. We now prove that for any distinct $(x, x'), (y, y') \in S$, $\sum_{i=1}^{n-1} |x_i \wedge y_i| \neq k$, that is $|x \wedge y| \neq k + 1$.

If $|x \wedge y| = k+1$, without a lost of generality, let $x = \overbrace{1\cdots1}^{k}\overbrace{1\cdots1}^{k}\overbrace{0\cdots0}^{k}\overbrace{0\cdots01}^{k+1}$,

and $y = \overbrace{1\cdots10}^{k}\overbrace{\cdots01}^{k}\overbrace{\cdots10}^{k}\overbrace{\cdots01}^{k+1}$. We have $H(x, y') = k + k + 1 = \frac{n}{2}$ and $\mathcal{P}(x, y') = 0$. Since $(x, x') \in R$ and $(y, y') \in R$, we have $(x, y') \in R$ and $\mathcal{P}(x, y') = 0$, which is a contradiction.

According to Corollary 1.2 from [18], we have $|S| \leq 1.99^n$. Therefore, the minimum number of 1-monochromatic rectangles that partition the space of inputs is

$$C^1(EQ') \geq \frac{|E|}{|S|} \geq \frac{\binom{n-1}{n/2-1}}{(1.99)^{n-1}} > \frac{2^{n-1}/(n-1)}{(1.99)^{n-1}}. \tag{26}$$

The deterministic communication complexity is then

$$D(EQ') \geq \log C^1(EQ') > \log \frac{2^{n-1}/(n-1)}{(1.99)^{n-1}} > 0.0073n. \tag{27}$$

Therefore the theorem has been proved.

5   State Succinctness Results

Now we are ready to derive the state succinctness result.

Theorem 3. *The promise problem $A(n)$ can be solved exactly by a 1QCFA $\mathcal{A}(n)$ with $\mathbf{O}(n^2)$ quantum basis states and $\mathbf{O}(n^3)$ classical states, whereas the sizes of the corresponding 1DFA are $2^{\Omega(n)}$.*

Proof. Let $x = x_1 \cdots x_n$ and $y = y_1 \cdots y_n$ be in $\{0, 1\}^n$. The input word on the tape will be $w = \mathrm{\mathcal{c}}x\#y\#\#x\#y\$$. Let us consider a 1QCFA $\mathcal{A}(n)$ with $\mathbf{O}(n^2)$ quantum basis states $\{|0, 0\rangle, |i, 0\rangle, |i, j\rangle, |k\rangle : 0 \leq i < j \leq n, 1 \leq k \leq n - 2\}$ and

$\mathbf{O}(n^3)$ classical states $\{S_{ijp} : 0 \le i, j, p \le n+1\}$ (some of the states may be not used in the automaton actions).

$\mathcal{A}(n)$ starts in the initial quantum state $|0, 0\rangle$ and the initial classical state S_{000}. We use classical states S_{ijp} $(1 \le p \le n+1)$ to point out the positions of the tape head that will provide some information for quantum transformations. If the classical state of $\mathcal{A}(n)$ will be S_{ijp} $(1 \le p \le n)$ that will mean that the next scanned symbol of the tape head is the p-th symbol of $x(y)$ and S_{ijn+1} means that the next scanned symbol of the tape head is #($\$$).

The behavior of $\mathcal{A}(n)$ is composed of two parts. The first part is the behavior of $\mathcal{A}(n)$ when reading the prefix of the input, namely ¢x#y#. In this part, $\mathcal{A}(n)$ uses quantum basis state $\{|0, 0\rangle, |i, 0\rangle, |i, j\rangle : 0 \le i < j \le n\}$ and classical states S_{00p} $(0 \le p \le n+1)$ to simulate Steps 1 to 6 in the proof of Theorem 1. After the measurement at the end of the first part, if the outcome is $|0, 0\rangle$, then the input is accepted. Otherwise, suppose that the outcome is $|i, j\rangle$, the classical state will be changed to S_{ij0} $(1 \le i < j \le n$, which means that $H(x_i x_j, y_i y_j) = 1$ and the input bits x_i, x_j, y_i, y_j will be skipped during the second part of the behavior of $\mathcal{A}(n)$. The second part is the behavior of the automation when reading the second part of the input #x#$y$$. In this part, $\mathcal{A}(n)$ uses quantum basis states $\{|k\rangle : 1 \le k \le n-2\}$ and classical states S_{ijp} $(0 \le p \le n+1)$ to simulate Steps 7 to 12 in the proof of Theorem 1. The automaton proceeds as follows:

1. $\mathcal{A}(n)$ reads the left end-marker ¢, performs U_1 on the initial quantum state $|0, 0\rangle$, changes its classical state to $\delta(S_{000},$ ¢$) = S_{001}$, and moves the tape head one cell to the right.
2. Until the currently scanned symbol σ is not #, $\mathcal{A}(n)$ does the following:
   (a) Applies $\Theta(S_{00p}, \sigma) = U_{p,\sigma}$ to the current quantum state.
   (b) Changes the classical state S_{00p} to S_{00p+1} and moves the tape head one cell to the right.
3. $\mathcal{A}(n)$ changes the classical state S_{00p+1} to S_{001} and moves the tape head one cell to the right.
4. Until the currently scanned symbol σ is not #, $\mathcal{A}(n)$ does the following:
   (a) Applies $\Theta(S_{00p}, \sigma) = U_{p,\sigma}$ to the current quantum state.
   (b) Changes the classical state S_{00p} to S_{00p+1} and moves the tape head one cell to the right.
5. When # is reached, $\mathcal{A}(n)$ performs U_2 on the current quantum state.
6. $\mathcal{A}(n)$ measures the current quantum state in the standard basis. If the outcome is $|0, 0\rangle$, $\mathcal{A}(n)$ accepts the input; otherwise, suppose that the outcome is $|i, j\rangle$, $\mathcal{A}(n)$ changes the classical state to S_{ij0}, moves the tape head one cell to the right.
7. $\mathcal{A}(n)$ reads #, applies $\Theta(S_{ij0}, \#) = U_3 U_{ij}$ to the current quantum state, changes its classical state to S_{ij1}, and moves the tape head one cell to the right.
8. Until the currently scanned symbol σ is not #, $\mathcal{A}(n)$ does the following:
   (a) Applies $\Theta(S_{ijp}, \sigma) = U_{ijp,\sigma}$ to the current quantum state.
   (b) Changes the classical state S_{ijp} to S_{ijp+1} and moves the tape head one cell to the right.

9. $A(n)$ changes the classical state S_{ijp+1} to S_{ij1} and moves the tape head one cell to the right.
10. While the currently scanned symbol σ is not the right end-marker \$, $A(n)$ does the following:
    (a) Applies $\Theta(S_{ijp}, \sigma) = U_{ijp,\sigma}$ to the current quantum state.
    (b) Changes the classical state S_{ijp} to S_{ijp+1} and moves the tape head one cell to the right.
11. When the right end-marker is reached, $A(n)$ performs U_4 on the current quantum state.
12. $A(n)$ measures the current quantum state in the standard basis. If the outcome is $|1\rangle$, $A(n)$ accepts the input; otherwise, rejects the input.

where unitary transformations U_1, U_2, U_3, U_4 are the ones defined in the proof of Theorem 1 and

$$U_{p,\sigma}|i,j\rangle = (-1)^\sigma |i,j\rangle \text{ if } i = p;$$
$$U_{p,\sigma}|i,j\rangle = |i,j\rangle \text{ if } i \neq p;$$
$$U_{ij}|i,j\rangle = |1\rangle;$$
$$U_{ijp,\sigma}|k\rangle = (-1)^\sigma |k\rangle \text{ if } p < i \text{ and } k = p;$$
$$U_{ijp,\sigma}|k\rangle = |k\rangle \text{ if } p < i \text{ and } k \neq p;$$
$$U_{ijp,\sigma}|k\rangle = |k\rangle \text{ if } p = i;$$
$$U_{ijp,\sigma}|k\rangle = (-1)^\sigma |k\rangle \text{ if } i < p < j \text{ and } k = p - 1;$$
$$U_{ijp,\sigma}|k\rangle = |k\rangle \text{ if } i < p < j \text{ and } k \neq p - 1;$$
$$U_{ijp,\sigma}|k\rangle = |k\rangle \text{ if } p = j;$$
$$U_{ijp,\sigma}|k\rangle = (-1)^\sigma |k\rangle \text{ if } p > j \text{ and } k = p - 2;$$
$$U_{ijp,\sigma}|k\rangle = |k\rangle \text{ if } p > j \text{ and } k \neq p - 2.$$

It is easy to verify that unitary transformation $U_{p,\sigma}$, U_{ij} and $U_{ijp,\sigma}$ exist. The rest of the proof is analogues to the proof in Theorem 1.

According to Theorem 2 , $D(EQ') \in \Omega(n)$. Therefore, it is easy to see that the sizes of the corresponding 1DFA for $A(n)$ are $2^{\Omega(n)}$ [27].

Acknowledgments. The first author would like to thank Jozef Gruska for having a most constructive influence on him, teaching him how to think and write in a clear way, and for continuous support during his postdoctoral research with him.

References

1. Ambainis, A., Watrous, J.: Two-way finite automata with quantum and classical states. Theoretical Computer Science **287**, 299–311 (2002)
2. Ambainis, A., Freivalds, R.: One-way quantum finite automata: strengths, weaknesses and generalizations. In: Proceedings of the 39th FOCS, pp. 332–341 (1998).
3. Ambainis, A., Nayak, A., Ta-Shma, A., Vazirani, U.: Dense quantum coding and quantum automata. Journal of the ACM **49**(4), 496–511 (2002)

4. Ambainis, A., Nahimovs, N.: Improved constructions of quantum automata. Theoretical Computer Science **410**, 1916–1922 (2009)
5. Ambainis, A., Yakaryilmaz, A.: Superiority of exact quantum automata for promise problems. Information Processing Letters **112**(7), 289–291 (2012)
6. Ambainis, A.: Superlinear advantage for exact quantum algorithms. In: Proceedings of 45th STOC, pp. 891–900 (2013).
7. Ambainis, A., Iraids, A., Smotrovs, J.: Exact quantum query complexity of EXACT and THRESHOLD. In: Proceedings of 8th TQC, pp. 263–269 (2013)
8. Ambainis, A., Gruska, J., Zheng, S.G.: Exact query complexity of some special classes of Boolean functions, arXiv:1404.1684 (2014)
9. Beals, R., Buhrman, H., Cleve, R., Mosca, M., de Wolf, R.: Quantum lower bounds by polynomials. Journal of the ACM **48**, 778–797 (2001)
10. Bertoni, A., Mereghetti, C., Palano, B.: Small size quantum automata recognizing. Theoretical Computer Science **340**, 394–407 (2005)
11. Bertoni, A., Mereghetti, C., Palano, B.: Some formal tools for analyzing quantum automata. Theoretical Computer Science **356**, 14–25 (2006)
12. Brassard, G., Høyer, P.: An exact quantum polynomial-time algorithm for Simon's problem. In: Proceedings of the Israeli Symposium on Theory of Computing and Systems, pp. 12–23 (1997).
13. Brodsky, A., Pippenger, N.: Characterizations of 1-way quantum finite automata. SIAM Journal on Computing **31**, 1456–1478 (2002)
14. Buhrman, H., Cleve, R., Wigderson, A.: Quantum vs. classical communication and computation. In: Proceedings of 30th STOC, pp. 63–68 (1998).
15. Buhrman, H., de Wolf, R.: Complexity measures and decision tree complexity: a survey. Theoretical Computer Science **288**, 21–43 (2002)
16. Buhrman, H., Cleve, R., Massar, S., de Wolf, R.: Nonlocality and Communication Complexity. Rev. Mod. Phys. **82**, 665–698 (2010)
17. Deutsch, D., Jozsa, R.: Rapid solution of problems by quantum computation. Proceedings of the Royal Society of London **A439**, 553–558 (1992)
18. Frankl, P., Rödl, V.: Forbidden intersections. Trans. Amer. Math. Soc. **300**(1), 259–286 (1987)
19. Freivalds, R., Ozols, M., Mancinska, L.: Improved constructions of mixed state quantum automata. Theoretical Computer Science **410**, 1923–1931 (2009)
20. Gruska, J.: Foundations of computing. Thomson International Computer Press (1997).
21. Gruska, J.: Quantum Computing. McGraw-Hill, London (1999)
22. Gruska, J.: Descriptional complexity issues in quantum computing. J. Automata, Languages Combin. 5(3), 191–218 (2000).
23. Gruska, J., Qiu, D.W., Zheng, S.G.: Generalizations of the distributed Deutsch-Jozsa promise problem, arXiv:1402.7254 (2014)
24. Gruska, J., Qiu, D.W., Zheng, S.G.: Potential of quantum finite automata with exact acceptance, arXiv:1404.1689 (2014)
25. Hromkovič, J., Schintger, G.: On the Power of Las Vegas for One-Way Communication Complexity. OBDDs, and Finite Automata, Information and Computation **169**, 284–296 (2001)
26. Klauck, H.: On quantum and probabilistic communication: Las Vegas and one-way protocols. In: Proceedings of the 32th STOC, pp. 644–651 (2000).
27. Kushilevitz, E.: Communication Complexity. Cambridge University Press (1997).
28. Kondacs, A., Watrous, J.: On the power of quantum finite state automata. In: Proceedings of the 38th FOCS, pp. 66–75 (1997).

29. Le Gall, F.: Exponential separation of quantum and classical online space complexity. In: Proceedings of SPAA 2006, pp. 67–73 (2006)

30. Mereghetti, C., Palano, B., Pighizzini, G.: Note on the Succinctness of Deterministic, Nondeterministic, Probabilistic and Quantum Finite Automata. RAIRO-Inf. Theor. Appl. **35**, 477–490 (2001)

31. Mereghetti, C., Palano, B.: On the size of one-way quantum finite automata with periodic behaviors. RAIRO-Inf. Theor. Appl. **36**, 277–291 (2002)

32. Montanaro, A., Jozsa, R., Mitchison, G.: On exact quantum query complexity. Algorithmica, 1–22 (2013) doi:10.1007/s00453-013-9826-8

33. Moore, C., Crutchfield, J.P.: Quantum automata and quantum grammars. Theoretical Computer Science **237**, 275–306 (2000)

34. Qiu, D.W., Li, L.Z., Zou, X.F., Mateus, P., Gruska, J.: Multi-letter quantum finite automata: decidability of the equivalence and minimization of states. Acta Inf. **48**, 271–290 (2011)

35. Qiu, D.W., Li, L.Z., Mateus, P., Gruska, J.: Quantum finite automata. In: Finite State Based Models and Applications, CRC Handbook, pp. 113–144. CRC Press (2012).

36. Yao, A.C.: Some Complexity Questions Related to Distributed Computing. In: Proceedings of 11th STOC, pp. 209–213 (1979)

37. Yu, S.: State Complexity: Recent Results and Open Problems. Fundamenta Informaticae **64**, 471–480 (2005)

38. Yakaryilmaz, A., Cem Say, A.C.: Unbounded-error quantum computation with small space bounds. Information and Computation **209**, 873–892 (2011)

39. Yakaryilmaz, A., Cem Say, A.C.: Succinctness of two-way probabilistic and quantum finite automata. Discrete Mathematics and Theoretical Computer Science **12**(4), 19–40 (2010)

40. Zheng, S.G., Qiu, D.W., Li, L.Z.: Some languages recognized by two-way finite automata with quantum and classical states. International Journal of Foundation of Computer Science **23**(5), 1117–1129 (2012)

41. Zheng, S.G., Qiu, D.W., Li, L.Z., Gruska, J.: One-Way Finite Automata with Quantum and Classical States. In: Bordihn, H., Kutrib, M., Truthe, B. (eds.) Languages Alive. LNCS, vol. 7300, pp. 273–290. Springer, Heidelberg (2012)

42. Zheng, S.G., Qiu, D.W., Gruska, J., Li, L.Z., Mateus, P.: State succinctness of two-way finite automata with quantum and classical states. Theoretical Computer Science **499**, 98–112 (2013)

43. Zheng, S.G., Gruska, J., Qiu, D.W.: On the state complexity of semi-quantum finite automata. In: Dediu, A.-H., Martín-Vide, C., Sierra-Rodríguez, J.-L., Truthe, B. (eds.) LATA 2014. LNCS, vol. 8370, pp. 601–612. Springer, Heidelberg (2014)

44. Zheng, S.G., Gruska, J., Qiu, D.W.: Power of the interactive proof systems with verifiers modeled by semi-quantum two-way finite automata, arXiv:1304.3876 (2013)

Computing with Controlled Resources

Small Universal Devices

Artiom Alhazov[1], Yurii Rogozhin[1], and Sergey Verlan[1,2](✉)

[1] Institute of Mathematics and Computer Science,
Academy of Sciences of Moldova Academiei 5, Chişinău MD-2028, Moldova
artiom@math.md
[2] LACL, Département Informatique, Université Paris Est,
61, av. Général de Gaulle, 94010 Créteil, France
verlan@u-pec.fr

Abstract. In this paper we overview several universal universality constructions for different type of devices based on (circular) string rewriting, multiset rewriting and splicing operations. We consider systems that have relatively small description and that are or can be effectively used for subsequent constructions of (small) universal devices.

1 Introduction

The concept of universality was first formulated by A. Turing in [45]. He constructed a universal (Turing) machine capable of simulating the computation of any other (Turing) machine. This universal machine takes as input a description of the machine to simulate, the contents of its input tape, and computes the result of its execution on the given input.

More generally, the universality problem for a class of computing devices (or functions) $\mathfrak{C}$ consists in finding a fixed element $\mathcal{M}$ of $\mathfrak{C}$ able to simulate the computation of any element $\mathcal{M}'$ of $\mathfrak{C}$ using an appropriate fixed encoding. More precisely, if $\mathcal{M}'$ computes y on an input x (we will write this as $\mathcal{M}'(x) = y$), then $\mathcal{M}'(x) = f(\mathcal{M}(g(\mathcal{M}'), h(x)))$, where h and f are the encoding and decoding functions, respectively, and g is the function retrieving the number of $\mathcal{M}'$ in some fixed enumeration of $\mathfrak{C}$. These functions should not be too complicated, otherwise the universal machine will be trivial, e.g. when f is partially recursive the machine can contain only one instruction – stop. It is commonly admitted that (general) recursive functions can be used for encoding and decoding. We remark that $\mathcal{M}$ can be also considered as a unary function by using an appropriate encoding of $\mathcal{M}'$ and x.

Let us stress here an important distinction between *computational completeness* and *universality*. Given a class $\mathfrak{C}$ of computability models, we say that $\mathfrak{C}$ is computationally complete if the devices in $\mathfrak{C}$ can characterize the power of Turing machines (or of any other type of equivalent devices). This means that given a Turing machine M one can find an element C in $\mathfrak{C}$ such that C is equivalent with M. Thus, completeness refers to the capacity of covering the level

The author acknowledges the project STCU 5384 awarded by the Scientific and Technology Center Ukraine.

C.S. Calude et al. (Eds.): Gruska Festschrift, LNCS 8808, pp. 249–263, 2014.
DOI: 10.1007/978-3-319-13350-8_19

of computability (in grammatical terms, this means to generate all recursively enumerable languages). Universality is an internal property of $\mathfrak{C}$ and it means the existence of a fixed element $\mathcal{M}$ of $\mathfrak{C}$ which is able to simulate any given element E (of $\mathfrak{C}$), providing that an appropriate encoding of E and of the input is given. If $\mathfrak{C}$ does not have a universal element, then there is a family $\mathfrak{C}' \supset \mathfrak{C}$ that contains an element $\mathcal{M}$ universal for $\mathfrak{C}$. We note that $\mathfrak{C}'$ is not necessarily universal for RE. We remark that these notions refer to the classical computing models. When additional features are present, like for example in quantum computing, the notions of the universality and completeness become completely different [17, 18].

In 1956 Shannon [44] considered the question of finding the smallest possible universal Turing machine where the size is calculated as the number of states and symbols. In the early sixties, Minsky and Watanabe had a running competition to see who could find the smallest universal Turing machine [30, 47]. Later, Rogozhin showed the construction of several small universal Turing machines [40]. An overview of recent results on this topic can be found in [33]. Other computational models were also considered, e.g. cellular automata [46] with a construction of universal cellular automata of rather small size; see [34, 48] for an overview.

Small universal devices have mostly theoretical importance as they demonstrate the minimal ingredients needed to achieve a complex (universal) computation. Their construction is a long-standing and fascinating challenge involving a lot of interconnections between different models, constructions, and encodings.

In this paper we adopt a unified view on computational devices and consider four classes of models based on different underlying operations: (1) string rewriting; (2) circular string rewriting; (3) multiset rewriting; and (4) splicing. Turing machines are well known examples of the models from the first class, Post systems are a representative of the second class. The third class contains such models as Petri nets and the fourth class contains for example time varying distributed H systems. We remark that models dealing with integer numbers directly can be interpreted in terms of multiset rewriting, which offers a representation of an arbitrary integer mapping. For each considered model we give a sketch of its definition and of the corresponding universality construction.

2   Models Based on String Rewriting

In this section we consider the operation of string rewriting $r : u \rightarrow v$, which is applicable to a string $w_1 u w_2$ yielding $w_1 v w_2$ (we denote this as $w_1 u w_2 \Rightarrow_r w_1 v w_2$). It can be seen that a Turing machine can be considered as instance of such an operation, especially if the string representation of the configuration is used. We also remark that considering a string rewriting operation on multiple strings in parallel yields multi-tape Turing machines and using a matrix or a graph controlled framework permits to represent multi-head machines.

2.1   Turing Machines

We will consider a standard definition of a Turing machine, e.g. from [16, 40]. We will use the notation $M = (Q, T, a_0, q_0, F, \delta)$, where Q is a finite set of states, T is the tape alphabet, $a_0 \in T$ is the blank symbol, $q_0 \in Q$ is the initial state, $F \subseteq Q$ is the set of final states and where δ is a transition function. A *configuration* of the Turing machine M is the following word $w_1 q_i a_k w_2$, where $w_1 a_k w_2$ is the part of the tape which is not empty, q_i is the state of the machine and a_k is the cell which is examined by the head of the machine.

It can be easily seen that the transition from configuration $w_1 q_i a_k w_2$ to $w_1 a_l q_j w_2$ corresponds to the application of rewriting rule $q_i a_k \rightarrow a_l q_j$. Similarly, a left move corresponds to a set of rewriting rules $a q_i a_k \rightarrow q_j a a_l$, for all $a \in T$ and a stationary move corresponds to the rewriting $q_i a_k \rightarrow q_j a_l$. For the result it is sufficient to consider rules that erase a final state $q_f \rightarrow \lambda$, $q_f \in F$.

The topic related to universal Turing machines is very well covered in the literature. We refer to some good overviews from this area [27, 33] for more discussion on the subject. We only give in Figure 1 the sizes of known constructions of universal Turing machines [33].

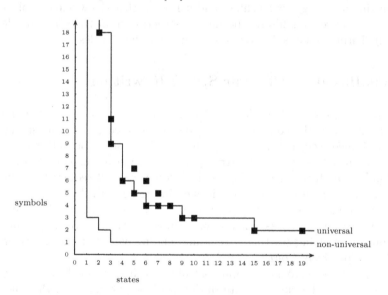

Fig. 1. State-symbol plot of known results on small universal Turing machines

We remark that when translating Turing machines to string rewriting, the number of left instructions and the number of symbols mostly counts for a universal construction. In this case, universal type-0 grammars with 68 rules can be constructed based on universal Turing machine with 18 states and 2 symbols.

2.2 Networks of Evolutionary Processors

In this subsection we would like to give another example of a universal construction based on a string rewriting. The model of a network of evolutionary processors is obtained as a restriction of the model of networks of language processors. The main idea is that the rewriting system is composed of several components (groups) arranged in a (communication) graph and containing simple rewriting rules (inserting or deleting or substituting one symbol in the string). Each component also have two regular input and output filters (languages). The computation is performed as a sequence of two subsequent steps. At the *computation* step, one of the applicable rewriting rules is performed. At the *communication* step the string being processed by component i can be further processed by a component j if it belongs to the regular language of the output filter of i and of the input filter of j (of cause we suppose that i and j are connected on the communication graph). This is quite powerful feature similar to regulated rewriting using target languages. The result consists of all strings that reach some final component. We refer to [8,10] for more details.

In the article [23] a universal construction using only 4 rules is given. This construction simulates register machines and it is clear that the whole complexity is hidden in the regular filter. Another construction from the same article simulates any Turing machine in polynomial time and has 7 rules.

3 Models Based on Circular String Rewriting

While the models considered in this section are based on the circular string rewriting, the result of the computation is often considered as a linear string. This can be obtained by considering that each string has a start (or end) marker, say, $\#$, that permits to linearize the string, this marker being usually omitted from the final result. In the remaining of this section we will require that the marker $\#$ shall be present once at both sides of any rewriting rule.

Consider a circular rewriting rule $x\#u \to v\#y$, where $u, x, y, v \in V^*$. Note that this rule may be viewed as synchronized (linear) string rewriting at both ends: it applies to a string starting with u and ending with x, replacing them with y and v, respectively ($uwx \Rightarrow ywv$).

Moreover, it is possible to use a graph-controlled mechanism for the rewriting. In this case we track the current state during the computation and the rules from each state indicate what is the next state. We will write such a rule as $(x\#u \to v\#y, p \to q)$, where p, q are states. This rule is applied to a string uwx in state p, resulting in string ywv in state q. Such a rule can be written in a very simple way, writing states p and q instead of $\#$ marker: $x\mathbf{p}u \to v\mathbf{q}y$.

The following are important special case of circular rewriting rules, where at least x and y are empty.

Post normal rewriting rule $P[u/v] \equiv \#u \to v\#$, $u, v \in V^*$, deletes u after the marker (i.e., at the left end of the string) and inserts v before the marker (i.e., at the right end of the string in the linear interpretation): $uw \Rightarrow wv$, $w \in V^*$.

Left deletion rule $D_L[u] \equiv P[u/\lambda] \equiv \#u \to \#$, where $u \in V^*$, deletes u after the marker: $uw \Rightarrow w$, $w \in V^*$.

Right insertion rule $I_R[v] \equiv P[\lambda/v] \equiv \# \to v\#$, where $v \in V^*$, inserts u before the marker: $I_R[v](u) = wv$, $w \in V^*$.

Normal Post systems consist of a set of Post normal rewriting rules. They compute by applying the rules iteratively over an initial string until no more application is possible. It is known that such systems are computationally complete and there are universal constructions having 194 rules [11].

3.1   Tag Systems

Tag systems [9,31,35] are special normal Post systems, obtained in the following way. Let $V = \{a_1, \cdots, a_{n+1}\}$ and consider words P_i, $1 \leq i \leq n$ and a number $m > 0$. Then, the rules of a tag system are exactly $\#a_i u \to P_i\#$, $1 \leq i \leq n$ for all $u \in V^{m-1}$. Words u are not reflected in the notation of tag system rules that are given directly as $a_i \to P_i$. The computation is performed on an input word and halts when either a special *halting* symbol is encountered or the length of the string is smaller than m.

Tag systems are an important tool for universality constructions as they exhibit an extremely simple behavior. Most small universality constructions are based on a tag systems simulation. It is worth to note that there are no known concrete constructions for universal tag systems. By taking the constructions from [32] it is possible to estimate the size of such a system to around 400 rules.

3.2   Tag Systems with States

It is possible to use the graph control for tag systems. We say that a tag system is *graph-controlled* (also called a tag system *with states*), if the rules of the tag systems are accompanied by the edges of the control graph, and the initial/final states are distinguished. A rule $(a_i \to P_i, p \to q)$ is applicable to a string if it is in state p and if rule $a_i \to P_i$ is applicable as defined above. The resulting string is as defined above, (the first symbol a_i is removed together with the next $m - 1$ symbols, and P_i is appended to the right end of the string), and the new state is q. The graph-controlled tag systems are computationally complete already with degree 1 [42], however no bound on the number of rules is given.

3.3   Bi-tag and Cyclic Tag Systems

Bi-tag systems are Post normal systems with rules $P[a/a]$, $P[ea/be']$ and $P[ea/bce']$, where $a, b, c \in A$, $e, e' \in E$ and $A \cap E = \emptyset$.

Cyclic tag systems are graph-controlled 1-tag systems, where there are given $n \in \mathbb{N}$ and P_i, $0 \leq i \leq n - 1$, and the rules are $(0 \to \lambda, i \to (i + 1) \mod n)$ and $(1 \to P_i, i \to (i + 1) \mod n)$, $0 \leq i \leq n - 1$.

The advantage of above models is that it is shown that they are polynomial-time simulators of Turing machines. Moreover, smallest known universal Turing machines from [32] are constructed using a simulation of bi-tag and cyclic tag systems.

3.4   Circular Post Machines

Circular Post machines (CPMs) may be viewed as a special case of circular string rewriting systems, or as a special case of graph-controlled Post normal systems. There are several variants of these machines and the Table 1 shows the type of circular rewriting rules used by each variant. We recall that bold symbols correspond to a state represented by a special marker.

Table 1. Variants of circular Post machines

CPM0	CPM1	CPM2	CPM3	CPM4	CPM5
$p x \to q$	$p x \to q$	$p x \to q$	$p x \to q$	$p x \to q$	$p x \to q$
$p x \to y q$	$p x \to y q$	$p x \to y q$	$p x \to y q$	$p x \to y q$	
$p 0 \to y q 0$	$p x \to x q 0$	$p x \to y q 0$	$p x \to y z q$	$p x \to y x q$	$p \to y q$

Universal circular Post machines were considered for CPM0 variant where following results are obtained [4] (state/symbol pairs are given): $UPM0(2, 46)$, $UPM0(3, 22)$, $UPM0(4, 11)$, $UPM0(5, 8)$, $UPM0(6, 6)$, $UPM0(8, 5)$, $UPM0(11, 4)$, $UPM0(16, 3)$, $UPM0(32, 2)$.

4   Models Based on Multiset Rewriting

In this section we group models using multiset rewriting and models using numbers directly. These two classes are extremely similar, because multiset rewriting permits to represent any numerical mapping. The difference between two representations mostly relies in the encoding and decoding concepts as well as in the descriptional complexity issues.

In what follows we will use the term and the definitions related to the multiset rewriting, but we would like to remark that there is one-to-one correspondence between many models based on this operation, e.g. vector addition systems, Petri nets, population protocols and P systems. So, the constructions presented below can be easily interpreted in terms of any of these models.

We will recall the terminology considered by Korec [25] and call a construction strongly universal if the encoding and decoding functions are identities, otherwise the corresponding construction will be called (weakly) universal. Some authors [25,26] implicitly consider only the strong notion of universality as the encoding and decoding functions can perform quite complicated transformations, which are not necessarily doable in the original devices [7,43]. We refer to [25] for a more detailed discussion of different variants of the universality and to [27] for a survey on this topic.

4.1   Multiset Rewriting with Inhibitors

A multiset is a mapping M from a finite alphabet O of symbols to the natural numbers $\mathbb{N}$, called the multiplicities of these symbols. It is common to denote multisets by strings, the multiplicity $M(a)$ of each symbol a being represented by the corresponding number of occurrences $|w|_a$ of the symbol in the string w. In the following, we write $x \subseteq y$ for strings $x, y \in O^*$ if $|x|_a \leq |y|_a$.

A multiset rewriting rule can thus be written as $u \to v$, where $u, v \in O^*$. A rule $r : u \to v$ can be applied to a configuration w producing w' ($w \Rightarrow_r w'$), if $u \subseteq w$ and $|w'|_a = |w|_a - |u_a| + |v_a|$ for each $a \in O$.

A multiset rewriting rule with inhibitors is written as $u \to v|_{\neg x_1, \cdots, \neg x_m}$, where $u, v \in O^*$ and $x_i \in O$. It is applicable to w if $u \subseteq w$ and $x_j \not\subseteq w$ for $1 \leq j \leq m$. In the case of applicability, the application of such a rule would yield the same result as the rule $u \to v$.

A multiset rewriting system applies iteratively the rules on a starting multiset and does a projection (over a terminal alphabet) to obtain the result. By definition multiset rewriting systems are not deterministic, which offers interesting ways for their minimization.

In [21] several universal multiset rewriting systems are constructed exhibiting trade-offs between the cardinality of the alphabet, the number of rules, the total number of used inhibitors and the maximal size of the rule. Deterministic strong and weak universal constructions with following parameters (in the above order) are presented: $(30, 34, 13, 3)$, $(14, 31, 51, 8)$, $(11, 31, 79, 11)$, $(21, 25, 13, 5)$, $(67, 64, 8, 3)$, $(58, 55, 8, 5)$. Recently in [22] the following parameters are obtained for the non-deterministic case: $(5, 877, 1022, 729)$, $(5, 1024, 1316, 379)$, $(4, 668, 778, 555)$, $(4, 780, 1002, 299)$.

4.2   Register Machines

Suppose that we distinguish a subset $Q \subseteq O$ of symbols, which we call state symbols, and we restrict the considered systems of multiset rewriting with inhibitors to those where the set of projections of reachable configurations on the state symbols is finite (i.e., the number of state symbols in reachable configurations is bounded), while simultaneously requiring left side of every rule to contain at least one state symbol. This model is called *finite-state* multiset rewriting with inhibitors, and the elements of $O \setminus Q$ are called registers.

A register machine can be viewed as a particular case of (finite-state) multiset rewriting with inhibitors, where (at most) one state symbol is present in reachable configurations, and the rules have the following forms: $p \to aq$, $pa \to q$ and $p \to q'|_{\neg a}$, where $p, q, q' \in Q$ and $a \in O \setminus Q$. These forms are called increment, decrement and zero-test of register a, respectively. The last two instructions represent contrary applicability conditions (assuming p is present), so they are often considered in pairs. Increment is commonly written as as $p : (A(a), q)$, while a pair of corresponding decrement and zero-test instruction is viewed as one conditional decrement instruction, written as $p : (S(a), q, q')$. It is assumed that the system has at least one instruction associated to every state (exactly one in the deterministic case).

Register machines with the smallest number of instructions are published by Korec [25], where he gives a construction for a strongly universal (for the class of unary functions) register machine having 22 instructions and using 8 registers and a weakly universal register machine having 20 instructions. Same paper considers other type of machine instructions and gives corresponding small universal constructions.

It is known that machines with two registers can be only weakly universal [7,43], while with 3 registers the strong universality can be achieved. The article [22] mentions such constructions having 278 instructions (112 decrement and 165 increment) for the case of the 2-register machine and 365 instructions (147 decrement and 217 increment) for the case of the 3-register machine.

A related model, *counter automata*, is a generalization of register machines, where multiple registers can be tested for zero, or even for non-zero, incremented or decremented in one step (the original inspiration coming from non-writing Turing machines with empty tapes with marked origin). This clearly can be captured in the finite-state multiset rewriting model.

One can even consider generalized counter automata to allow register decrements and increments of any register by more than one. This is a useful tool for obtaining some small universal systems. In the case of register machines such a generalization permits to have only 13 (decrement and add) instructions for the strong universality, while in the case of counter automata this permits to obtain a construction with 16 instructions and 4 states [12].

4.3   Maximally Parallel Multiset Rewriting

The application of rules in the case of the maximally parallel multiset rewriting follows the maximality principle – a set of rules is maximally parallel if the rules are all applicable in parallel and no other rule can be added to this set maintaining this property.

A register machine viewed as a finite-state multiset rewriting system behaves sequentially even under maximal parallelism, because (at most one) state symbol is present in any configuration, and any rule contains a state symbol in its left side. Hence, only zero-test has to be argumented. Using maximal parallelism, we can (deterministically) simulate instruction $p : (S(a), q, q')$ by rules $p \to p_1 t_a$, $p_1 \to p_2$, $t_a a \to d_a$, $p_2 d_a \to q$, $p_2 t_a \to q'$. Fewer rules may be used in small universal machines than by direct application of this simulation.

In [6] a maximally parallel multiset rewriting system with 23 rules is given. The construction is based on the simulation of the universal register machine U_{32} from [25] and takes profit of the parallelism to encode efficiently the representation of states.

By grouping rules in several disjoint groups and by allowing at each step at most one rule from each group to be applied, while still acting in a maximally parallel way it is possible to construct universal systems having 80 context-free rules arranged in 21 groups. If the application of rules from a group is performed in a graph-controlled manner, then 61 context-free rules arranged in 8 groups are sufficient for an universality construction [2].

5   Models Based on Splicing

In this section we consider models based on an operation conceptually different from (string) rewriting. The splicing operation was first considered by T.
Head [19,20] and its main difference with respect to the rewriting is being a
binary operation. Splicing considers some specified context in each of two strings
entering the operation and performs a crossover of the two strings at the context
location. Hence, the methods used for universality constructions are substantially different as a parallel evolution of a set of strings (instead of a single
string) should be considered.

We consider the Păun definition of splicing operation, which is widely used
in the area. For more details on the other definitions of splicing as well as for
the biological motivation we refer to [24,38,49].

A *splicing rule* (over an alphabet V) is a 4-tuple (u_1, u_2, u_3, u_4) where $u_1, u_2,$
$u_3, u_4 \in V^*$. It is frequently written as $u_1 \# u_2 \$ u_3 \# u_4$, $\{\$, \#\} \notin V$. Two strings
$x = x_1 u_1 u_2 x_2$ and $y = y_1 u_3 u_4 y_2$ can enter a rule $r = u_1 \# u_2 \$ u_3 \# u_4$ (we also say
that they can be spliced by r), yielding as a result two other strings $w = x_1 u_1 u_4 y_2$
and $z = y_1 u_3 u_2 x_2$. We write this as follows: $(x, y) \vdash_r (w, z)$.

The pair $\sigma = (V, R)$ where V is an alphabet and R is a finite set of splicing
rules is called a *splicing scheme* or an *H scheme*. For a splicing scheme $\sigma = (V, R)$
and for a language $L \subseteq V^*$ we define the operation $\sigma(L)$ as:

$\sigma(L) = \{w, z \in V^* \mid \exists x, y \in L, \exists r \in R : (x, y) \vdash_r (w, z)\}$.

The closure of a language under splicing with respect to σ is defined as:

$$\sigma^0(L) = L, \quad \sigma^{i+1}(L) = \sigma^i(L) \cup \sigma(\sigma^i(L)), \ i \geq 0, \quad \sigma^*(L) = \cup_{i \geq 0} \sigma^i(L).$$

We remark that in the above definition $\sigma^i(L)$ is not equivalent to the iteration
of the σ operator. In subsection 5.2 we consider the iterative variant of σ. It is
known that σ^* preserves the regularity of a language.

A *Head-splicing-system* [19,20], or *H system*, is a construct $\mathcal{H} = (\sigma, A)$, where
σ is a splicing scheme and A is a set of initial words, called *axioms*. The language
generated by an $\mathcal{H}$ is defined as $L(\mathcal{H}) = \sigma^*(A)$.

Since the language generated by any H system is regular, several models
based on splicing introducing additional control mechanisms were proposed. In
most of the cases this leads to the computational completeness.

Example. Consider the H system $H = (\sigma, A)$, where $\sigma = (\{a, b, c\}, \{r\})$ with
$r : c \# a \$ a \# b$ and $A = \{cab\}$. At the first step it is possible to apply cab to itself
using rule r: $(cab, cab) \vdash_r (cb, caab)$. So $\sigma^1(A) = A \cup \{cb, caab\} = \{cb, cab, caab\}$.
At the next step 4 splicings are possible (cab with itself, $caab$ with itself, cab
with $caab$ and $caab$ with cab) yielding $\sigma^2(A) = \{ca^i b \mid 0 \leq i \leq 4\}$. It is clear that
$L(H) = \{ca^i b \mid i \geq 0\}$. We remark that the iteration of σ on A in the classical
sense as defined in subsection 5.2 yields the language $\{cb\} \cup \{ca^{2^n} b \mid n \geq 0\}$.

Descriptional complexity measures. In the case of splicing based systems there
are several natural descriptional complexity measures that are considered: the
alphabet of the system, the number of splicing rules, the maximal diameter
(size) of splicing rules, the number of axioms and the number of distributed

components in the case of a distributed model of splicing. We would like to remark that the number of splicing rules and their size are the most interesting parameters that permit to estimate the complexity of a splicing system.

Input and output. The original definition of splicing systems considers them as language generating devices. So, in order to construct universal systems the notions of *input* and *output* should be introduced. It is natural to consider that the input(s) of a splicing-based model is encoded by a set of strings that are added to the set of axioms (initial strings) of the system (eventually in some concrete location in the case of distributed systems) before starting the computation. In order to define the output of the system we will require that on any input the system generates either a singleton or an empty language. A more relaxed definition is also possible by requiring that the image of the generated language with respect to some fixed recursive function is singleton or λ. In the first case the word from the singleton language will be considered as the output of the system, while in the second case we will consider that the corresponding function is not defined for the given input. We remark that in the case of computationally complete models it is not decidable if for a given input a splicing system will produce an empty language. We also note that the definition of the output allows non-deterministic computations to be considered, however we will restrict this notion to the deterministic case.

Universality constructions idea. The small universal constructions known in the area of splicing systems are based on the simulation of tag systems. There are several other constructions using different ideas [1,11,13,14], but their complexity parameters are several order larger. Basically, a unary coding of the current configuration of a tag system is considered, so a configuration w is represented as $L11c(w)1R$, where $c(a_i) = 0^i1$. The simulation of a production $a_i \rightarrow P_i$, $2 \leq i \leq n$ is performed using the rotate-and-simulate method used for many proofs in this area. This method works as follows. First, suffixes $c(P_j)\bar{c}(a_j)$, $2 \leq j \leq n$ are attached to the string producing several strings $L0^i1c(a_kw')c(P_j)10^jR$. After that the number of symbols 0 at both ends is decreased simultaneously. Hence, only the string for which $j = i$ will remain at the end (the other strings will be eliminated from further computation), producing $L1c(a_kw')1R$. After that the symbol a_k is removed (by removing corresponding 0's) and a new round begins. The simulation stops when the first symbol is a_1. Technically, this transformation is performed using following set of rules applied in correct sequences (which should be enforced by some additional mechanism).

$$1 : \varepsilon\#1R\$Z'\#\varepsilon \qquad 2 : \varepsilon\#0R\$Z\#R \qquad 3 : L10\#\varepsilon\$L1\#Z$$
$$4 : L0\#\varepsilon\$L\#Z \qquad 5 : L11\#00\$L\#Z$$

The attachment of suffixes $c(P_j)\bar{c}(a_j)$ is performed using rule 1. Rules 2 and 3 permit to perform the rotate-and-simulate method to check that correct suffix was attached. Rule 4 erases the code of the second letter from the string

and rule 5 cleans two consecutive 1's at the beginning of the string allowing
to start a simulation of a new step. The corresponding rules require strings
$\{L1Z,\ ZR,\ Z'R', LZ\}$ to be present in the axioms of the system.

The code of the tag system to simulate is given to the system as the set of
axioms $\{Z'c(P_i)\bar{c}(a_i)R \mid a_i \to P_i \in P\}$. The input word w is also added to the
axioms in an encoded way as $L11c(w)1R$. The output of the system is retrieved
using a simple decoding function. We refer to [5,41] for more technical details.

5.1 Double Splicing

The double splicing operation is in some sense a counterpart of matrix grammars
for splicing systems. However, instead of sequences of prescribed rules the double
splicing operation is composed of two splicings and requires that the result of
the first splicing to be the input of the second one. More precisely, we define

$$(x, y) \vdash_{r_1, r_2} (w, z) \text{ iff } (x, y) \vdash_{r_1} (u, v) \text{ and } (u, v) \vdash_{r_2} (w, z).$$

We remark that in most cases (and in particular for universality proofs) it is
possible to take a word y of special form that guarantees that r_1 and r_2 can be
used in this sequence only. A universal construction using only 5 splicing rules
is exhibited in [5].

5.2 (E)TVDH Systems

Below we consider the adaptation of the idea of time-varying grammars to the
area of splicing. We recall that time-varying grammars can be seen as graph-
controlled grammars where the corresponding control graph has the form of a
ring. In the splicing case the definition is slightly different as one allows using
words that are simultaneously obtained to perform a splicing at each step. More
precisely, for an H system $\mathcal{H} = (V, T, A, R)$ consider a partition of R in n (not
necessary disjoint) subsets: $R = R_1, \ldots, R_n$. We call each R_i a component of $\mathcal{H}$
and n its degree. The language generated by $\mathcal{H}$ is defined as follows:

$$L_0(\mathcal{H}) = A$$
$$L_{i+1}(\mathcal{H}) = \sigma_k(L_i(\mathcal{H})), \text{ where } \sigma_k = (V, R_k), \quad i = k \pmod{n}$$
$$L(\mathcal{H}) = \cup_{i \geq 0} L_i(\mathcal{H}) \cap T^*$$

In the literature there are also considered enhanced time-varying distributed
H (ETVDH) systems, which differ from TVDH by the fact that σ_k^* is used at
each iteration instead of σ_k.

In the case of TVDH systems of degree 1 the set of rules is applied to the
result of the previous application. This corresponds to the iteration of the splicing
operation:

$$\bar{\sigma}^*(L) = \cup_{i \geq 0} \bar{\sigma}^i(L), \text{ where } (\bar{\sigma}^i(L) = \underbrace{\sigma(\sigma(\ldots\sigma(L)\ldots))}_{i}).$$

We remark that the operation $\bar{\sigma}^*$ is different from σ^* as it keeps only the
resulting strings of each iteration available for the next iteration. This provides

a powerful feature that permits to eliminate all strings that are not produced by a splicing operation at the corresponding step. It is somehow surprising that this modification suffices by itself to achieve the computational completeness [28,29].

Article [3] presents constructions for universal TVDH systems of degree 1 and 2 and having 17 and 15 splicing rules, respectively. Both constructions follow the general idea presented above and the higher number of rules is due to the implementation of the algorithm.

5.3   Test Tube Systems

Previously we considered models of splicing systems based on H systems. One of the particularities of these models is that the system starts from a single initial set of axioms and at each step the current set of words is replaced by a new one, computed according to the control of the system. In this subsection we consider splicing systems based on a different idea. Namely, instead of evolving a single set of words, a fixed number of such sets (a vector) is evolved. This corresponds to a distributed system containing some units that we call *components*. The computation is then divided in two different steps: a *computation* step and a *communication* step. During the computation step splicing rules are applied in each component, independently from each other according to the underlying control. During the communication step the contents of components is redistributed in the system according to some algorithm.

The model considered in this subsection is the splicing counterpart of the parallel communicating grammar systems with communication by command and in the literature it is also known under the name of *splicing test tube* systems. The idea is to consider a group of H systems, called (splicing) tubes, as components, use σ^* operation for the computational step in each component and use input permitting filters for the communication according to a communication graph.

So during the computation step, each component acts like an H system. At the communication step the contents of each component is redistributed among other components according to the communication graph and the permitting regular filters. More precisely, if a string from component i belongs to F_j (the filter of component j) and there is an edge (i, j) in the communication graph, then at the next step this string will belong to component j. Strings that cannot pass any input filter of a connected node remain in the component of their origin. We remark a subtle point here: if a string can go to some other component(s) then each of them will receive a copy of that string and the initial component will not contain any copy of this string, except the case of a communication graph with a self-loop at the corresponding node and positive filter check.

In [5] a construction of a universal test tube system having 8 rules distributed in 3 components is given. Universal constructions with 2 tubes and different filter restrictions are given in [3], but in this case 10 splicing rules are necessary.

5.4   Splicing P Systems

In this subsection we consider a distributed system that applies the operation σ in each component during the computation step and redistributes the contents during the communication step based on the splicing rule that has been applied. In some sense this corresponds to considering splicing rules that have two target indicators – the numbers of components where the corresponding splicing results shall be moved. With some reserve (because splicing is a binary operation) the model can be considered as graph-controlled splicing. The language consists of words over terminal alphabet collected in some designated node. The obtained model, called splicing P systems, was introduced in [36] and more details can be found in [37,39].

As in previous models the input is provided by adding strings to the axioms of the system corresponding to the input and the encoding of the program, while the output should be the unique string from the generated language. It is worth to note that splicing P systems allow one of the smallest universal constructions for the splicing area as well as for string-based universal devices. The construction from [5] has 5 splicing rules, 6 axioms, 3 components, and alphabet of 7 symbols and the diameter (3,2,2,1). The construction uses the algorithm presented above to simulate tag systems and due to the nature of the control it is simple to ensure that the rules are applied in correct sequences.

6   Conclusions

In this paper we gave an overview of several small universal constructions. Our main goal was to present models that can serve as a basis for future universality constructions. We made a nontraditional classification of computational models in four groups and we believe that this point of view could be helpful as it highlights the key concepts of each model that can help to choose new targets for future work.

We remark that for each model we mostly discussed the number of rules, as in our opinion this is the main descriptional complexity parameter. However, there are other interesting parameters like the size of the alphabet, the number of states etc. We refer to [15] for a discussion on the descriptional complexity and the trade-offs between parameters. Many papers exhibit such trade-offs, but a systematical study with respect to several models is still missing.

References

1. Alford, G.: An explicit construction of a universal extended H system. Technical Report CDMTCS-043, University of Auckland (August 1997)
2. Alhazov, A., Freund, R.: On universal P systems with catalysts with/without states. Fundamenta Informaticae (to appear, 2014)
3. Alhazov, A., Kogler, M., Margenstern, M., Rogozhin, Y., Verlan, S.: Small universal TVDH and test tube systems. International Journal of Foundations of Computer Science **22**(1), 143–154 (2011)

4. Alhazov, A., Kudlek, M., Rogozhin, Y.: Nine universal circular post machines. Computer Science Journal of Moldova 10(3(30)) (2002)
5. Alhazov, A., Rogozhin, Y., Verlan, S.: On small universal splicing systems. International Journal of Foundations of Computer Science **23**(07), 1423–1438 (2012)
6. Alhazov, A., Verlan, S.: Minimization strategies for maximally parallel multiset rewriting systems. Theoretical Computer Science **412**(17), 1581–1591 (2011)
7. Barzdin, I.M.: Ob odnom klasse machin Turinga (machiny Minskogo), russian. Algebra i Logika **1**, 42–51 (1963)
8. Castellanos, J., Martín-Vide, C., Mitrana, V., Sempere, J.M.: Solving np-complete problems with networks of evolutionary processors. In: Mira, J., Prieto, A.G. (eds.) IWANN 2001. LNCS, vol. 2084, pp. 621–628. Springer, Heidelberg (2001)
9. Cocke, J., Minsky, M.: Universality of tag systems with P=2. Journal of the ACM **11**(1), 15–20 (1964)
10. Dassow, J., Truthe, B.: On the power of networks of evolutionary processors. In: Durand-Lose, J., Margenstern, M. (eds.) MCU 2007. LNCS, vol. 4664, pp. 158–169. Springer, Heidelberg (2007)
11. Ferretti, C., Mauri, G., Kobayashi, S., Yokomori, T.: On the universality of post and splicing systems. Theoretical Computer Science **231**(2), 157–170 (2000)
12. Freund, R., Oswald, M.: A small universal antiport P system with forbidden context. In: Leung, H., Pighizzini, G. (eds.) Proceedingsof the 8th International Workshop on Descriptional Complexity of Formal Systems, DCFS 2006, pp. 259–266. New Mexico State University, Las Cruces (2006)
13. Frisco, P.: Direct constructions of universal extended H systems. Theoretical Computer Science **296**(2), 269–293 (2003)
14. Frisco, P., Hoogeboom, H.J., Sant, P.: A direct construction of a universal P system. Fundamenta Informaticae **49**(1–3), 103–122 (2002)
15. Gruska, J.: Descriptional complexity (of languages) - a short survey. In: Mazurkiewicz, A. (ed.) Mathematical Foundations of Computer Science 1976. LNCS, vol. 45, pp. 65–80. Springer, Heidelberg (1976)
16. Gruska, J: Foundations of computing. Thomson Learning (1997)
17. Gruska, J.: Quantum challenges. In: Bartosek, M., Tel, G., Pavelka, J. (eds.) SOFSEM 1999. LNCS, vol. 1725, pp. 1–28. Springer, Heidelberg (1999)
18. Gruska, J.: Quantum Computing. Osborne/McGraw-Hill (1999)
19. Head, T.: Formal language theory and DNA: an analysis of the generative capacity of specific recombinant behaviors. Bull. Mathematical Biology **49**(6), 737–759 (1987)
20. Head, T.: Splicing languages generated with one sided context. In: Computing with Bio-Molecules. Theory and Experiments, pp. 158–181 (1998)
21. Ivanov, S., Pelz, E., Verlan, S.: Small universal Petri nets with inhibitor arcs. arXiv, CoRR, abs/1312.4414 (2013)
22. Ivanov, S., Pelz, E., Verlan, S.: Small universal non-deterministic petri nets with inhibitor arcs. In: Jürgensen, H., Karhumäki, J., Okhotin, A. (eds.) DCFS 2014. LNCS, vol. 8614, pp. 186–197. Springer, Heidelberg (2014)
23. Ivanov, S., Rogozhin, Y., Verlan, S.: Small universal networks of evolutionary processors. Fundamenta Informaticae (to appear, 2014)
24. Kari, L.: DNA computing: Arrival of biological mathematics. The Mathematical Intelligencer **19**(2), 9–22 (1997)
25. Korec, I.: Small universal register machines. Theoretical Computer Science **168**(2), 267–301 (1996)
26. Malcev, A.I.: Algorithms and Recursive Functions. Wolters-Noordhoff Pub. Co., Groningen (1970)

27. Margenstern, M.: Frontier between decidability and undecidability: a survey. Theoretical Computer Science **231**(2), 217–251 (2000)
28. Margenstern, M., Rogozhin, Y.: Time-varying distributed H systems of degree 1 generate all recursively enumerable languages. In: Ito, M., Păun, G., Yu, S., (eds.) Words, Semigroups, and Transductions, pp. 329–339. World Scientific (2001)
29. Margenstern, M., Rogozhin, Y., Verlan, S.: Time-varying distributed H systems with parallel computations: the problem is solved. In: Chen, J., Reif, J.H. (eds.) DNA 2003. LNCS, vol. 2943, pp. 48–53. Springer, Heidelberg (2004)
30. Minsky, M.: Size and structure of universal Turing machines using tag systems. In: Recursive Function Theory: Proceedings, Symposium in Pure Mathematics, Provelence, vol. 5, pp. 229–238 (1962)
31. Minsky, M.: Computations: Finite and Infinite Machines. Prentice Hall, Englewood Cliffts (1967)
32. Neary, T., Woods, D.: Four small universal turing machines. Fundam. Inform. **91**(1), 123–144 (2009)
33. Neary, T., Woods, D.: The Complexity of Small Universal Turing Machines: A Survey. In: Bieliková, M., Friedrich, G., Gottlob, G., Katzenbeisser, S., Turán, G. (eds.) SOFSEM 2012. LNCS, vol. 7147, pp. 385–405. Springer, Heidelberg (2012)
34. Ollinger, N.: The Quest for Small Universal Cellular Automata. In: Widmayer, P., Triguero, F., Morales, R., Hennessy, M., Eidenbenz, S., Conejo, R. (eds.) ICALP 2002. LNCS, vol. 2380, pp. 318–329. Springer, Heidelberg (2002)
35. Post, E.: Formal reductions of the general combinatorial decision problem. American Journal of Mathematics **65**(2), 197–215 (1943)
36. Păun, G.: Computing with membranes. Journal of Computer and System Sciences 1(61), 108–143 (2000) (Also TUCS. Report No. 208, 1998)
37. Păun, G.: Membrane Computing, An Introduction. Springer-Verlag (2002)
38. Păun, G., Rozenberg, G., Salomaa, A.: DNA Computing: New Computing Paradigms. Springer (1998)
39. Păun, G., Rozenberg, G., Salomaa, A.: The Oxford Handbook Of Membrane Computing. Oxford University Press (2009)
40. Rogozhin, Y.: Small universal Turing machines. Theoretical Computer Science **168**(2), 215–240 (1996)
41. Rogozhin, Y., Verlan, S.: On the rule complexity of universal tissue p systems. In: Freund, R., Păun, G., Rozenberg, G., Salomaa, A. (eds.) WMC 2005. LNCS, vol. 3850, pp. 356–362. Springer, Heidelberg (2006)
42. Rogozhin, Y., Verlan, S.: P systems based on tag operations. Computer Science Journal of Moldova **20**(3), 366–373 (2012)
43. Schroeppel, R.: A two counter machine cannot calculate 2N. In: AI Memos. MIT AI Lab (1972)
44. Shannon, C.E.: A universal Turing machine with two internal states. Automata Studies, Annals of Mathematics Studies **34**, 157–165 (1956)
45. Turing, A.M.: On computable numbers, with an application to the Entscheidungsproblem. Proc. of the London Mathematical Society **42**(2), 230–265 (1936)
46. von Neumann, J.: Theory of Self-Reproducing Automata. Univ. Illinois Press (1966)
47. Watanabe, S.: 5-symbol 8-state and 5-symbol 6-state universal Turing machines. Journal of the ACM **8**(4), 476–483 (1961)
48. Wolfram, S.: A New Kind of Science. Wolfram Media Inc., (2002)
49. Zizza, R.: Splicing systems. Scholarpedia **5**(7), 9397 (2010)

A Technique to Obtain Hardness Results for Randomized Online Algorithms – A Survey

Hans-Joachim Böckenhauer, Juraj Hromkovič[✉], and Dennis Komm

Department of Computer Science, ETH Zürich,
Universtitätsstrasse 6, 8092 Zürich, Switzerland
{hjb,juraj.hromkovic,dennis.komm}@inf.ethz.ch

Abstract. We survey how the advice complexity of online algorithms can be used to obtain lower bounds on the performance of randomized online algorithms. Online algorithms with advice may query an oracle that knows the whole input from the start to solve some instance of an online problem. This is done by reading a finite prefix of some infinite binary *advice tape*, which is created by the oracle before the first piece of input is processed. Similarly, a randomized online algorithm may use a binary tape where every bit is chosen uniformly at random.

In this survey, we review a technique, similar to Yao's principle, which allows statements on the advice complexity of some given online problem to translate to results on the power of randomization for this problem in terms of lower bounds. We give some examples where this technique works and how it is applied, and show its limitations and that it is tight in a very general sense.

1 Introduction

In online computation, an adversary produces some hard input of an optimization problem that is fed to an online algorithm, denoted by A, piece by piece over a number of discrete time steps. In every such time step, A needs to produce a corresponding piece of output which cannot be changed afterwards. In this paper, we focus on a class of problems where the objective is to minimize some cost function which is associated with the given online problem.

Many real-world problems such as the paging problem or many routing and scheduling problems are modeled this way; for instance, suppose you want to assign jobs to a fixed number of resources, e. g., processors. Such a service is offered to a large number of customers and processor time can be booked at any given point in time. But this means that assignments should be made long before all requests are known. Still, the objective is to minimize the waiting time for, say, the customer that waits the longest. Such a situation is a typical online scenario.

At first, we formally define the term *online minimization problem*, where the input consists of *requests* that arrive in consecutive time steps and the output is created piecewise as a sequence of *answers* to these requests.

© Springer International Publishing Switzerland 2014
C.S. Calude et al. (Eds.): Gruska Festschrift, LNCS 8808, pp. 264–276, 2014.
DOI: 10.1007/978-3-319-13350-8_20

Definition 1 (Online Minimization Problem). *An* online minimization problem *consists of a set $\mathcal{I}$ of inputs and a cost function. Every input $I \in \mathcal{I}$ is a sequence $I = (x_1, \ldots, x_n)$ of requests. Furthermore, a set of feasible outputs (or solutions) is associated with every I; every output is a sequence $O = (y_1, \ldots, y_n)$ of answers. The* cost function *assigns a positive real value $\mathrm{cost}(I, O)$ to every input I and any feasible output O. For every input I, we call any feasible output O for I that has smallest possible cost (i. e., that minimizes the cost function) an* optimal solution *for I.*

Classically, one searches for online algorithms that perform well in the sense that they produce output which has a cost that is as small as possible compared to the cost of an optimal solution. The study of such online algorithms is coined "competitive analysis" [11]. Note that the optimal solution can usually not be computed with full accuracy in an online manner. We therefore speak of an optimal "offline" solution. In a recent model considered in this paper one asks an advanced question that is beyond pure competitive analysis. In particular, we are interested in the (amount of) information that is both needed and sufficient to outperform purely deterministic or even randomized online algorithms. In a sense, we want to know which information about the yet unknown parts of the input is crucial to obtain a low competitive ratio or even an optimal solution. Let us first give a formal framework to study *online algorithms with advice*. To this end, we use the standard definition as first given in [9,26]. The intuitive idea is that, after the adversary created an input for a given online problem, an oracle inspects this input and writes binary information about it on a tape (the *advice tape*). Then, an online algorithm starts processing the input as usual, but it may, with every request, read some part of the tape (sequentially) to get additional information about the input. The minimum length of the prefix that the algorithm needs to read while guaranteeing some quality on every input, is then the advice complexity of this algorithm.

Definition 2 (Online Algorithm with Advice). *Consider an input I of an online minimization problem. An* online algorithm $\mathtt{A}$ with advice *computes the output sequence $\mathtt{A}^\phi(I) = (y_1, \ldots, y_n)$ such that y_i is computed from $\phi, x_1, \ldots, x_i$, where ϕ is the content of the advice tape, i. e., an infinite binary sequence. $\mathtt{A}$ is c-competitive with advice complexity $b(n)$ if there exists a non-negative constant α such that, for every n and for any input sequence I of length at most n, there exists some advice string ϕ such that*

$$\mathrm{cost}(\mathtt{A}^\phi(I)) \leq c \cdot \mathrm{cost}(\mathrm{OPT}(I)) + \alpha$$

and at most the first $b(n)$ bits of ϕ have been accessed during the computation of the solution $\mathtt{A}^\phi(I)$. If the above inequality holds with $\alpha = 0$, we call $\mathtt{A}$ strictly c-competitive with advice complexity $b(n)$. $\mathtt{A}$ is called optimal *if it is strictly 1-competitive.*

A first model of online computation with advice was introduced by Dobrev et al. [18]. As this model was not precise enough to measure the number of advice bits needed, Hromkovič et al. proposed the general model used here, and discussed its relation to the general notion of the *information content* of a problem [26]. The fruitfulness of this model was for the first time explored by Böckenhauer et al. [9], where it was applied to paging, disjoint path allocation, and job shop scheduling. At the same time, Emek et al. [20] proposed a similar model and studied the k-server problem and metrical task systems. Since then, new results on job shop scheduling [28], the k-server problem [8,23,32], and disjoint path allocation [2] were obtained. Additionally, many other online problems were studied including buffer management [14], online set cover [29], string guessing [7], graph exploration [17], online independent set [15], online knapsack [10], online makespan scheduling [19,33], online bin packing [12,33], online Steiner tree [1], list update [13] and online graph coloring [3,4,22,34]. Online algorithms using both advice and randomization were investigated by Böckenhauer et al. [6]. Further connections between computing online with advice and randomized online computation where, e. g., observed by Komm and Královič [28]. Our main observation on the topic of this paper was first made by Böckenhauer et al. [8], it establishes a non-trivial relationship between randomized online algorithms and online algorithms with advice for a given online minimization problem.

Note the resemblance between Definition 2 and the definition of the expected competitive ratio of a randomized online algorithm, which we give in what follows to fix our notation.

Definition 3. *Randomized Online Algorithm] Consider an input I of an online minimization problem. A* randomized online algorithm R *computes the output sequence* $R^\phi(I) = (y_1, \ldots, y_n)$ *such that y_i is computed from $\phi, x_1, \ldots, x_i$, where ϕ is the content of a* random tape, *i. e., an infinite binary sequence, where every bit is chosen uniformly at random and independently of all the others. By* $\mathrm{cost}(R^\phi(I))$, *we denote the random variable expressing the cost of the solution computed by R on I. R is c-competitive in expectation if there exists a non-negative constant α such that, for every I,*

$$\mathbb{E}\big[\mathrm{cost}(R^\phi(I))\big] \leq c \cdot \mathrm{cost}(\mathrm{OPT}(I)) + \alpha,$$

where, as above, OPT is an optimal offline algorithm for the problem.

Throughout this paper, since ϕ is always clear from context, we omit it and simply write, e. g., R instead of R^ϕ. We observe that the basic change is from speaking of "one best solution" (i. e., there always is one binary sequence ϕ that guarantees some success) to speaking of "all solutions *on average*" (i. e., in expectation, we can guarantee some success).

Let us take another point of view which will come in handy later. We consider a function $b \colon \mathbb{N} \to \mathbb{N}$ that measures the number of advice bits some randomized online algorithm uses on inputs of size n, for any $n \in \mathbb{N}$. For the ease of presentation, we will assume that R uses *exactly* $b(n)$ random bits on every input of size n. For any fixed bit string on R's random tape, the algorithm's decisions are fully determined by the input. As a result, we can think of R as a probability distribution over a set of $2^{b(n)}$ deterministic strategies. We denote this set by

$\text{Alg}(\text{R}) = \{\text{A}_1, \ldots, \text{A}_{2^{b(n)}}\}$. We further assume from now on that R picks a deterministic strategy uniformly at random from $\text{Alg}(\text{R})$. We are now ready to present the key theorem for proving lower bounds on the expected competitive ratio of randomized online algorithms.

2   The Main Theorem

As already mentioned, we want to focus on the relationship between advice and randomization. Before revisiting the main theorem [8], we make the following two observations, which are immediate.

1. If there is a randomized online algorithm R for some online problem Π such that R uses b random bits and achieves an expected competitive ratio of c, then there also is an online algorithm with advice for Π that is c-competitive and uses b advice bits.
2. Conversely, if there is provably no online algorithm with advice for Π that is c-competitive while using b advice bits, then there also is no randomized online algorithm using b random bits while being c-competitive in expectation.

If we follow our intuition, advice bits seem to be a lot more powerful than random bits. After all, we compare a situation where we always pick a best strategy for any instance, to a situation where we pick strategies with a fixed distribution; in essence, we compare the best to the average. We therefore ask whether there exists a scenario in which it is possible to save some bits if they are supplied by an oracle and not a random source. In what follows, we give a positive answer to this question. More specifically, we show that, if there is some randomized online algorithm R for some online minimization problem Π, then there also is some online algorithm with advice that is almost as good while using a number of advice bits (and that is the interesting part) which does not depend on the number of random bits R uses. However, the bound does depend on the number of possible instances of Π of given length. The proof uses some ideas that are similar to the proof of Yao's theorem [35].

Theorem 1 (Böckenhauer et al. [8]). *Let Π be an online minimization problem for which we have $m(n)$ different inputs of length n. Moreover, suppose there is a randomized online algorithm R for Π, which achieves an expected competitive ratio of c. Then there is an online algorithm A with advice for Π, which achieves a competitive ratio of $(1 + \varepsilon)c$, for any $\varepsilon > 0$, while using at most*

$$\lceil \log n \rceil + 2\lceil \log \lceil \log n \rceil \rceil + \log\left(\left\lfloor \frac{\log(m(n))}{\log(1 + \varepsilon)} \right\rfloor + 1\right)$$

advice bits.

$$\begin{array}{c|cccc} & A_1 & A_2 & A_3 & \cdots \\ \hline I_1 & c_{1,1} & c_{1,2} & c_{1,3} & \cdots \\ I_2 & c_{2,1} & c_{2,2} & c_{2,3} & \\ I_3 & c_{3,1} & c_{3,2} & c_{3,3} & \\ \vdots & \vdots & & & \ddots \end{array}$$

Fig. 1. An example matrix $\mathcal{M}$ as used in the proof

Proof. We suppose that, for any input length $n \in \mathbb{N}$, R uses $b(n)$ random bits. As observed above, this is equivalent to choosing uniformly at random a deterministic strategy from a set $\mathrm{Alg}(R) = \{A_1, \ldots, A_{2^{b(n)}}\}$. Since R is c-competitive in expectation, there is a constant α such that for every instance I, we have

$$\mathbb{E}[\mathrm{cost}(R(I))] \le c \cdot \mathrm{cost}(\mathrm{OPT}(I)) + \alpha$$

or, equivalently,

$$\frac{\mathbb{E}[\mathrm{cost}(R(I))] - \alpha}{\mathrm{cost}(\mathrm{OPT}(I))} \le c.$$

Now, for each deterministic strategy A_j and for each instance I_i of length n, $1 \le j \le 2^{b(n)}$ and $1 \le i \le m(n)$, we set

$$c_{i,j} := \max\left\{1, \frac{\mathrm{cost}(A_j(I_i)) - \alpha}{\mathrm{cost}(\mathrm{OPT}(I_i))}\right\},$$

and we call $c_{i,j}$ the *performance* of A_j on I_i. Next, we construct an $(m(n) \times 2^{b(n)})$-matrix $\mathcal{M}$ that we fill with these entries as shown in Fig. 1. As a result, the entry in the ith row and the jth column gives the performance of R on the input I_i if R chooses the deterministic strategy A_j. The central idea of the proof is to show that we are able to cleverly choose a small number of columns of $\mathcal{M}$ such that the performances of the corresponding deterministic strategies are small for many instances, and the sets of the chosen strategies together cover all input instances. We collect these algorithms in a set $\mathcal{S}$ and A gets as advice the index of the algorithm from $\mathcal{S}$ that should be used for the input at hand (and some additional information we describe later).

One row i of $\mathcal{M}$ corresponds to exactly one input I_i. Thus, by the definition of $c_{i,j}$ and the expected competitive ratio of R, for every i, $1 \le i \le m(n)$, we get

$$\frac{1}{2^{b(n)}} \sum_{j=1}^{2^{b(n)}} c_{i,j} = \frac{1}{2^{b(n)}} \sum_{j=1}^{2^{b(n)}} \frac{\mathrm{cost}(A_j(I_i)) - \alpha}{\mathrm{cost}(\mathrm{OPT}(I_i))}$$

$$= \frac{\frac{1}{2^{b(n)}} \sum_{j=1}^{2^{b(n)}} \mathrm{cost}(A_j(I_i)) - \alpha}{\mathrm{cost}(\mathrm{OPT}(I_i))}$$

$$= \frac{\mathbb{E}[\mathrm{cost}(R(I_i))] - \alpha}{\mathrm{cost}(\mathrm{OPT}(I_i))}$$

$$\le c$$

or, equivalently,

$$\sum_{j=1}^{2^{b(n)}} c_{i,j} \leq c \cdot 2^{b(n)},$$

and for the sum of all entries in all cells of $\mathcal{M}$, we get

$$\sum_{i=1}^{m(n)} \sum_{j=1}^{2^{b(n)}} c_{i,j} \leq \sum_{i=1}^{m(n)} c \cdot 2^{b(n)} \leq c \cdot 2^{b(n)} \cdot m(n).$$

Since there are $2^{b(n)}$ columns in $\mathcal{M}$, there is one column (deterministic strategy) j' such that

$$\sum_{i=1}^{m(n)} c_{i,j'} \leq c \cdot m(n).$$

The online algorithm $\mathsf{A}_{j'}$ is then included in $\mathcal{S}$ and it is used for every instance I_i, for which $c_{i,j'} \leq (1+\varepsilon)c$. Let s denote the number of these instances. In what follows, we want to estimate how large s is, i. e., for how many instances A can use $\mathsf{A}_{j'}$. Clearly, the performance of $\mathsf{A}_{j'}$ is larger than $(1+\varepsilon)c$ on $m(n) - s$ instances.

Summing up, this gives a total of $(m(n) - s)(1 + \varepsilon)c$ for the corresponding rows and we have

$$(m(n) - s)(1 + \varepsilon)c < \sum_{i=1}^{m(n)} c_{i,j'}.$$

From this, it follows that $(m(n) - s)(1 + \varepsilon)c < m(n) \cdot c$ and therefore $s > \varepsilon/(1 + \varepsilon) \cdot m(n)$, which means we can use the deterministic strategy $\mathsf{A}_{j'}$ for a fraction of $\varepsilon/(1 + \varepsilon)$ of the instances as we know that on these its performance is not larger than $(1 + \varepsilon)c$.

After $\mathsf{A}_{j'}$ is put into the set $\mathcal{S}$, we delete the column j' from $\mathcal{M}$ together with all rows that correspond to inputs on which $\mathsf{A}_{j'}$ achieves a sufficiently small performance. There remain

$$\left(1 - \frac{\varepsilon}{1+\varepsilon}\right) m(n) = \left(\frac{1}{1+\varepsilon}\right) m(n)$$

rows for which we need to find another algorithm from $\mathrm{Alg}(\mathsf{R})$. For every remaining row, the deleted entry in column j' was larger than c. It follows that, after removing this column, the average over all entries of remaining rows is still not larger than c. Therefore, we can repeat the aforementioned method with the remaining

$$\left(\frac{1}{1+\varepsilon}\right) m(n)$$

rows of $\mathcal{M}$. This way, we find another deterministic online algorithm $\mathsf{A}_{j''}$, which has a sufficiently small performance on a fraction of $\varepsilon/(1 + \varepsilon)$ of the remaining instances.

Now we compute how often we have to iterate this strategy at most until we have found an algorithm for every input. This means that we want to find a natural number r such that

$$\left(\frac{1}{1+\varepsilon}\right)^r m(n) < 1.$$

We get

$$\left(\frac{1}{1+\varepsilon}\right)^r < \frac{1}{m(n)} \iff (1+\varepsilon)^r > m(n) \iff r > \log_{1+\varepsilon}(m(n)),$$

which means that we have to make at most

$$\left\lfloor \frac{\log(m(n))}{\log(1+\varepsilon)} \right\rfloor + 1$$

iterations, i. e., we need that many deterministic algorithms from Alg(R). This immediately gives an upper bound on the size of $\mathcal{S}$.

Finally, we calculate the number of advice bits needed for this approach.

1. First, A needs to know the input length n, which can be encoded on the advice tape using $\log n$ bits. However, this must be done in a self-delimiting fashion, using, e. g., Elias encoding [21], summing up to a total of $2\lceil \log\lceil \log n\rceil\rceil + \lceil \log n\rceil$ advice bits at most.
2. Knowing n, A constructs $\mathcal{M}$ by simulating the randomized online algorithm R on any possible input. Then, A constructs $\mathcal{S}$ and enumerates all algorithms from $\mathcal{S}$ in, e. g., canonical order. After reading another

$$\log\left(\left\lfloor \frac{\log(m(n))}{\log(1+\varepsilon)} \right\rfloor + 1\right)$$

advice bits, A can pick one algorithm from $\mathcal{S}$, which is then simulated for the input at hand.

It follows that the competitive ratio of A on any instance is at most $(1+\varepsilon)c$ and A uses as much as advice as claimed by the theorem.   □

The contraposition of Theorem 1 is particularly interesting. Suppose we can show that any online algorithm with advice needs an amount of advice that is asymptotically larger than the value from the theorem statement to be c-competitive. The it follows that no randomized online algorithm can be c-competitive in expectation. We will apply this approach to $L(2, 1)$-coloring and to the k-server problem in Section 4.

3   Limits of this Approach

As we will see in the next section, the above mentioned technique is widely applicable. However, before giving examples, we want to point out some limitations and drawbacks.

First, note that the online algorithm A with advice does not run in polynomial time (even if R is efficient) if $m(n)$ is large with respect to the input length n, because A needs to construct the whole matrix $\mathcal{M}$. Clearly, $\mathcal{M}$ cannot be a part of A as it depends on n, which, of course, is not known by A, but is part of the advice.

Second, the online algorithm A is worse than the original randomized online algorithm R, even if the difference is very small. A natural question is whether it is possible to improve Theorem 1 such that A obtains the same competitive ratio as R. Intriguingly, this is not possible, so we really need this small gap. Consider the following online problem. The input $I = (x_1, \ldots, x_n)$ starts with a request $x_1 = 0$. All other requests are bits, i.e., $x_i \in \{0, 1\}$, for $2 \le i \le n$. Moreover, all answers must be bits, i.e., $y_i \in \{0, 1\}$, for $1 \le i \le n - 1$. If $y_i = x_{i+1}$, for all i, $1 \le i \le n - 1$, the total cost of the corresponding solution is 1, else it is 2. Thus, an optimal algorithm pays 1 and every other solution pays 2. Obviously, a best randomized online algorithm chooses every answer such that it is either 0 or 1 with a probability of $1/2$ each. This algorithm uses $n - 1$ random bits and its expected competitive ratio is not larger than

$$\frac{\frac{2^{n-1}-1}{2^{n-1}} \cdot 2 + \frac{1}{2^{n-1}} \cdot 1}{1} = 2 - \frac{1}{2^{n-1}}.$$

Conversely, every online algorithm with advice that uses less than $n - 1$ advice bits is at most 2-competitive. It follows that there are problems such that any online algorithm with advice needs as many advice bits as a randomized online algorithm needs random bits, or it is worse off.

Third, in this paper as well as in [8], we only considered online minimization problems. With a similar argument, however, it can be shown that an analogous statement for online maximization problems is possible [16].

4 Applications

In this section, we show how to apply Theorem 1 both directly and indirectly, thus creating both online algorithms with advice and lower bounds for randomized online algorithms for a selection of online problems.

4.1 Job Shop Scheduling

First, we study the online job shop scheduling problem with l machines and k jobs that consist of l unit length tasks each, denoted by (k, l)-JSS. More precisely, we are given k different jobs that need to use l different machines in some fixed order. A machine can only process one task at a time. Since every job asks for every machine exactly once, we can view a job as a permutation of the machine indices. Thus, an example input for $(4, 8)$-JSS is

$$\mathrm{Job}_1 = (1, 2, 3, 4, 5, 6, 7, 8), \quad \mathrm{Job}_2 = (3, 8, 4, 1, 2, 7, 6, 5),$$
$$\mathrm{Job}_3 = (7, 1, 5, 6, 8, 3, 4, 2), \quad \mathrm{Job}_4 = (8, 2, 4, 5, 3, 1, 6, 7),$$

which means that, e. g., the second job first needs the third machine, then the eighth, and so on. An algorithm for (k, l)-JSS must assign the machines to the jobs in the given order. In an online framework, these permutations arrive in consecutive time steps such that the $(i + 1)$th machine index of a job is revealed after the ith request is satisfied (i. e., assigned to a machine). In the example above, all four machines ask for four different machines in the first time step. Therefore, machine 1 can be assigned to Job_1, machine 3 is assigned to Job_2, and so on. In time step 2, however, two jobs, namely Job_1 and Job_4, ask for the same machine 2. In such a situation, an online algorithm needs to delay one of the two. Obviously, an optimal choice depends on future time steps.

The advice complexity of $(2, l)$-JSS was studied before by Böckenhauer et al. [9] and Komm and Královič [28]. Hromkovič et al. [27] constructed a randomized online algorithm which achieves a competitive ratio of $1 + 2k/\sqrt{l}$ in expectation. Now let us apply Theorem 1. There are $(l!)^k$ distinct instances of (k, l)-JSS of length $n = kl$, i. e., k-tuples of permutations of length l each. Using Stirling's approximation [24], we therefore get

$$m(n) = (l!)^k \leq \left(\left(1 + \frac{1}{11l} \right) \left(\frac{l}{e} \right)^l \sqrt{2l\pi} \right)^k$$

different inputs. Applying Theorem 1, it follows that, for any $\varepsilon > 0$, there is a $((1 + 2k/\sqrt{l}) \cdot (1 + \varepsilon))$-competitive online algorithm with advice that uses at most

$$\lceil \log n \rceil + 2\lceil \log \lceil \log n \rceil \rceil + \log \left(\left\lfloor \frac{\log(m(n))}{\log(1 + \varepsilon)} \right\rfloor + 1 \right)$$
$$\leq 2\lceil \log kl \rceil + \log \left(dk \log \left(\left(\frac{l}{e} \right)^l \sqrt{2l\pi} \right) \right)$$
$$\leq 2\lceil \log kl \rceil + \log(d'kl \log l)$$
$$\leq d'' \log(d'''kl)$$
$$\leq d'' \log(kl) + d'''$$

advice bits, for some constants d, d', d'', d'''. Thus, the advice complexity grows merely logarithmically in k and l. Note that, since the input length n is fully determined by these two parameters, the advice complexity can even be reduced further by a constant factor since we do not need a self-delimiting encoding of n.

Theorem 2. *There is a $(1 + 2k/\sqrt{l})$-competitive online algorithm A with advice for (k, l)-JSS which reads $\mathcal{O}(\log kl)$ advice bits.*

This is the first time, an upper bound of the general version of the problem (i. e., for k different jobs) was studied in terms of advice complexity. So far, the case for $k = 2$ was investigated by Böckenhauer et al. [9] and Komm and Královič [28].

4.2 $L(2, 1)$-Coloring

Another application of Theorem 1 is a version of graph coloring that arises in the context of assigning frequencies to transmitters in a multihop radio network. The difference between the frequencies that are used by the transmitters should be anti-proportional to their proximity to avoid interference. A simple graph-theoretic model of the frequency assignment problem has been introduced by Griggs and Yeh [25]. Here, the transmitters are the vertices of a graph and the frequencies are modeled by colors from a finite, ordered set, usually $\{0, 1, \ldots, \lambda\}$, for some natural number λ. In the easiest case, two levels of proximity are considered, neighboring vertices have to be assigned colors with a distance of at least 2 in the given order, and vertices at distance 2 in the graph still have to get different colors. The resulting problem of finding a coloring minimizing the color range λ is called $L(2, 1)$-coloring. The advice complexity of the online version of the $L(2, 1)$-coloring problem was studied by Bianchi et al. [4]. Here, a graph is given online, one vertex after another, and together with every vertex, exactly those edges are uncovered that are adjacent to vertices that are already known. If a vertex is revealed in some time step, an online algorithm must immediately assign it a color.

Among other results, Bianchi et al. [4] showed that every online algorithm with advice for $L(2, 1)$-coloring with a competitive ratio of 5/4 needs to read at least $3.9402 \cdot 10^{-10} n$ advice bits, even if the online graph has a maximum degree of 2, i.e., is a collection of paths and cycles. Although the constant factor in this linear lower bound is very small, the following lower bound on the expected competitive ratio of any randomized online algorithm was proven using Theorem 1.

Theorem 3 (Bianchi et al. [4]). *For arbitrarily small $\delta > 0$, every randomized algorithm for the online $L(2, 1)$-coloring problem on graphs with maximum degree 2 has a worst-case expected competitive ratio of at least $\frac{5}{4}(1 - \delta)$ on sufficiently large instances.*

Proof sketch. By an easy counting argument, there are $m(n) \leq 2^{\binom{n}{2}} n!$ online graphs on n vertices. It is easy to see that there exists a threshold n_0 on the input length such that the bound from Theorem 1 with this value of $m(n)$ plugged in exceeds $3.9402 \cdot 10^{-10} n$ for all $n \geq n_0$ (see the original paper [4] for the details of the calculation).

Since we already know that (even when restricting the considered online graphs to paths), with this number of advice bits, no online algorithm with advice can be better than 5/4, the result follows immediately by Theorem 1.   □

4.3   The k-Server Problem

The k-server problem is one of the most prominent online minimization problems. In this setup, we are given a metric space and k so-called servers that can be moved through this space. In every time step, a request is made that is given by some point. An answer is given by a server that is moved to this point, incurring a cost that is given by the distance between the original position of the server and the requested point.

Introduced in 1988 by Manasse et al. [31], the k-server problem is still not fully understood. There are, so far, two conjectures about the best possible deterministic and randomized online algorithms for the problem. Here, we want to focus on the *randomized k-server conjecture* which claims that there is a randomized online algorithm which is $\Theta(\log k)$-competitive in expectation. The following theorem shows how our technique could possibly be used to disprove the conjecture.

Theorem 4 (Böckenhauer et al. [8]). *If every online algorithm with advice for the k-server problem needs to use at least $\omega(\log n)$ advice bits to be $\mathcal{O}(\log k)$-competitive, the randomized k-server conjecture does not hold.*

Proof. Let us only consider inputs for k-server such that the size of the metric space is bounded from above by 2^n, where n is the input length. As above, let $m(n)$ denote the number of inputs of length n. In every time step, a point is requested, thus

$$m(n) = (2^n)^n.$$

Consider a randomized online algorithm R that is $\mathcal{O}(\log k)$-competitive in expectation on all of these instances. Then, there exists a constant $c > 0$ such that R is $(c \cdot \log k)$-competitive. Let $\varepsilon = 1$. Following Theorem 1, there also is a $(2 \cdot c \cdot \log k)$-competitive online algorithm with advice, which uses at most

$$\lceil \log n \rceil + 2\lceil \log \lceil \log n \rceil \rceil + \log(\lfloor \log ((2^n)^n) \rfloor + 1) \in \mathcal{O}(\log n)$$

advice bits.

If we could prove that any online algorithm with advice needs asymptotically more advice, this is a contradiction to the existence of R.   □

Note that, so far, the best known randomized online algorithm for k-server for arbitrary metric spaces is the $(2k - 1)$-competitive algorithm of Koutsoupias and Papadimitriou [30]. Considering the advice complexity, a lower bound is only known for optimality (approximately $n \log k$ advice bits are necessary [8]). Furthermore, Renault and Rosén [32] constructed a $\lceil \lceil \log k \rceil / (b - 2) \rceil$-competitive online algorithm with advice which reads b advice bits per request (this improves a previous result by Böckenhauer et al. [8] by a factor of 2). To be $\mathcal{O}(\log k)$-competitive, this algorithm thus needs a number of advice bits that is linear in n. As shown in the proof of Theorem 4, if the randomized k-server conjecture holds, there is an $\mathcal{O}(\log k)$-competitive online algorithm with advice that uses $\mathcal{O}(\log n)$ advice bits as long as the size of the metric space is at most 2^n. Thus, there remains an interesting exponential gap. A step towards proving the conjecture was made by Bansal et al. who constructed a randomized online algorithm with an expected competitive ratio of $\mathcal{O}((\log l)^3 (\log k)^2 \log \log n)$ in expectation [5], where l is the number of points of the underlying metric space. This algorithm improves over the one by Koutsoupias and Papadimitriou if $l \in o(2^{(2k)^{-(3+\varepsilon)}})$ and its competitive ratio is polylogarithmic in k if l is polynomial in k.

References

1. Barhum, K.: Tight Bounds for the Advice Complexity of the Online Minimum Steiner Tree Problem. In: Geffert, V., Preneel, B., Rovan, B., Štuller, J., Tjoa, A.M. (eds.) SOFSEM 2014. LNCS, vol. 8327, pp. 77–88. Springer, Heidelberg (2014)
2. Barhum, K., Böckenhauer, H.-J., Forišek, M., Gebauer, H., Hromkovič, J., Krug, S., Smula, J., Steffen, B.: On the Power of Advice and Randomization for the Disjoint Path Allocation Problem. In: Geffert, V., Preneel, B., Rovan, B., Štuller, J., Tjoa, A.M. (eds.) SOFSEM 2014. LNCS, vol. 8327, pp. 89–101. Springer, Heidelberg (2014)
3. Bianchi, M.P., Böckenhauer, H.-J., Hromkovič, J., Keller, L.: Online Coloring of Bipartite Graphs with and without Advice. In: Gudmundsson, J., Mestre, J., Viglas, T. (eds.) COCOON 2012. LNCS, vol. 7434, pp. 519–530. Springer, Heidelberg (2012)
4. Bianchi, M.P., Böckenhauer, H.-J., Hromkovič, J., Krug, S., Steffen, B.: On the Advice Complexity of the Online $L(2,1)$-Coloring Problem on Paths and Cycles. In: Du, D.-Z., Zhang, G. (eds.) COCOON 2013. LNCS, vol. 7936, pp. 53–64. Springer, Heidelberg (2013)
5. Bansal, N., Buchbinder, N., Madry, A., Naor, J.: A polylogarithmic-competitive algorithm for the k-server problem (extended abstract). In: Proc. of FOCS 2011, pp. 267–276 (2011)
6. Böckenhauer, H.-J., Hromkovič, J., Komm, D., Královič, R., Rossmanith, P.: On the Power of Randomness versus Advice in Online Computation. In: Bordihn, H., Kutrib, M., Truthe, B. (eds.) Languages Alive. LNCS, vol. 7300, pp. 30–43. Springer, Heidelberg (2012)
7. Böckenhauer, H.-J., Hromkovič, J., Komm, D., Krug, S., Smula, J., Sprock, A.: The String Guessing Problem as a Method to Prove Lower Bounds on the Advice Complexity. In: Du, D.-Z., Zhang, G. (eds.) COCOON 2013. LNCS, vol. 7936, pp. 493–505. Springer, Heidelberg (2013)
8. Böckenhauer, H.J., Komm, D., Královič, R., Královič, R.: On the advice complexity of the k-server problem. In: Aceto, L., Henzinger, M., Sgall, J. (eds.): ICALP 2011, Part I. LNCS, vol. 6755, pp. 207–218. Springer, Heidelberg (2011)
9. Böckenhauer, H.-J., Komm, D., Královič, R., Královič, R., Mömke, T.: On the Advice Complexity of Online Problems. In: Dong, Y., Du, D.-Z., Ibarra, O. (eds.) ISAAC 2009. LNCS, vol. 5878, pp. 331–340. Springer, Heidelberg (2009)
10. Böckenhauer, H.-J., Komm, D., Královič, R., Rossmanith, P.: On the Advice Complexity of the Knapsack Problem. In: Fernández-Baca, D. (ed.) LATIN 2012. LNCS, vol. 7256, pp. 61–72. Springer, Heidelberg (2012)
11. Borodin, A., El-Yaniv, R.: Online Computation and Competitive Analysis. Cambridge University Press (1998)
12. Boyar, J., Kamali, S., Larsen, K.S., López-Ortiz, A.: Online bin packing with advice. In: Proc. of STACS 2014. LIPIcs 25, pp. 174–186. Schloss Dagstuhl (2014)
13. Boyar, J., Kamali, S., Larsen, K.S., López-Ortiz, A.: On the List Update Problem with Advice. In: Dediu, A.-H., Martín-Vide, C., Sierra-Rodríguez, J.-L., Truthe, B. (eds.) LATA 2014. LNCS, vol. 8370, pp. 210–221. Springer, Heidelberg (2014)
14. Dorrigiv, R., He, M., Zeh, N.: On the Advice Complexity of Buffer Management. In: Chao, K.-M., Hsu, T., Lee, D.-T. (eds.) ISAAC 2012. LNCS, vol. 7676, pp. 136–145. Springer, Heidelberg (2012)
15. Dobrev, S., Královič, R., Královič, R.: Independent Set with Advice: The Impact of Graph Knowledge. In: Erlebach, T., Persiano, G. (eds.) WAOA 2012. LNCS, vol. 7846, pp. 2–15. Springer, Heidelberg (2013)

16. I. Seleceniova. Personal communication.
17. Dobrev, S., Královič, R., Markou, E.: Online Graph Exploration with Advice. In: Even, G., Halldórsson, M.M. (eds.) SIROCCO 2012. LNCS, vol. 7355, pp. 267–278. Springer, Heidelberg (2012)
18. Dobrev, S., Královič, R., Pardubská, D.: How Much Information about the Future Is Needed? In: Geffert, V., Karhumäki, J., Bertoni, A., Preneel, B., Návrat, P., Bieliková, M. (eds.) SOFSEM 2008. LNCS, vol. 4910, pp. 247–258. Springer, Heidelberg (2008)
19. Dohrau, J.: Online makespan scheduling with sublinear advice. Technical Report, ETH Zurich (2013)
20. Emek, Y., Fraigniaud, P., Korman, A., Rosén, A.: Online Computation with Advice. In: Albers, S., Marchetti-Spaccamela, A., Matias, Y., Nikoletseas, S., Thomas, W. (eds.) ICALP 2009, Part I. LNCS, vol. 5555, pp. 427–438. Springer, Heidelberg (2009)
21. Elias, P.: Universal codeword sets and representations of the integers. IEEE Transactions on Information Theory 21(2), 194–203 (1975)
22. Forišek, M., Keller, L., Steinová, M.: Advice Complexity of Online Coloring for Paths. In: Dediu, A.-H., Martín-Vide, C. (eds.) LATA 2012. LNCS, vol. 7183, pp. 228–239. Springer, Heidelberg (2012)
23. Gupta, S., Kamali, S., López-Ortiz, A.: On Advice Complexity of the k-server Problem under Sparse Metrics. In: Moscibroda, T., Rescigno, A.A. (eds.) SIROCCO 2013. LNCS, vol. 8179, pp. 55–67. Springer, Heidelberg (2013)
24. Graham, R.L., Knuth, D.E., Patashnik, O.: Concrete Mathematics, 2nd ed. Addison-Wesley (1994)
25. Griggs, J.R., Yeh, R.K.: Labelling graphs with a condition at distance 2. SIAM Journal on Discrete Mathemtics 5(4), 586–595 (1992)
26. Hromkovič, J., Královič, R., Královič, R.: Information Complexity of Online Problems. In: Hliněný, P., Kučera, A. (eds.) MFCS 2010. LNCS, vol. 6281, pp. 24–36. Springer, Heidelberg (2010)
27. Hromkovič, J., Mömke, T., Steinhöfel, K., Widmayer, P.: Job shop scheduling with unit length tasks: Bounds and algorithms. Algorithmic Operations Research 2(1), 1–14 (2007)
28. Komm, D., Královič, R.: Advice complexity and barely random algorithms. Theoretical Informatics and Applications (RAIRO) 45(2), 249–267 (2011)
29. Komm, D., Královič, R., Mömke, T.: On the Advice Complexity of the Set Cover Problem. In: Hirsch, E.A., Karhumäki, J., Lepistö, A., Prilutskii, M. (eds.) CSR 2012. LNCS, vol. 7353, pp. 241–252. Springer, Heidelberg (2012)
30. Koutsoupias, E., Papadimitriou, C.H.: On the k-server conjecture. Journal of the ACM 42(5), 971–983 (1995)
31. Manasse, M.S., McGeoch, L.A., Sleator, D.D.: Competitive algorithms for on-line problems. In: Proc. of STOC 1998, pp. 322–333 (1988)
32. Renault, M.P., Rosén, A.: On Online Algorithms with Advice for the k-Server Problem. In: Solis-Oba, R., Persiano, G. (eds.) WAOA 2011. LNCS, vol. 7164, pp. 198–210. Springer, Heidelberg (2012)
33. Renault, M.P., Rosén, A., van Stee, R.: Online algorithms with advice for bin packing and scheduling problems. CoRR abs/1311.7589 (2013)
34. Seibert, S., Sprock, A., Unger, W.: Advice Complexity of the Online Coloring Problem. In: Spirakis, P.G., Serna, M. (eds.) CIAC 2013. LNCS, vol. 7878, pp. 345–357. Springer, Heidelberg (2013)
35. Yao, A.C.-C.: Probabilistic computations: Toward a unified measure of complexity (extended abstract). In: Proc. of FOCS 1977, pp. 222–227. IEEE Computer Society (1977)

Integral Difference Ratio Functions on Integers

Patrick Cégielski[1], Serge Grigorieff[2], and Irène Guessarian[2(⊠)]

[1] LACL, EA 4219, Université Paris-Est Créteil,
IUT Fontainebleau-Sénart, Fontainebleau, France
[2] LIAFA, CNRS UMR 7089, Université Paris 7 Denis Diderot, Paris, France
ig@liafa.univ-paris-diderot.fr

To Jozef, on his 80th birthday, with our gratitude for sharing with us his prophetic vision of "Informatique"

Abstract. Various problems lead to the same class of functions from integers to integers: functions having integral difference ratio, i.e. verifying $f(a) - f(b) \equiv 0 \pmod{(a-b)}$ for all $a > b$. In this paper we characterize this class of functions from $\mathbb{Z}$ to $\mathbb{Z}$ via their *à la Newton* series expansions on a suitably chosen basis of polynomials (with rational coefficients). We also exhibit an example of such a function which is not polynomial but Bessel like.

Keywords: Number Theory · Theoretical Computer Science

1 Introduction

We deal with the following class of functions.

Definition 1. *Let $X \subseteq \mathbb{Z}$ (where $\mathbb{Z}$ denotes the set of integers). A map $f \colon X \to \mathbb{Z}$ has* integral difference ratio *if $\dfrac{f(i) - f(j)}{i - j} \in \mathbb{Z}$ for all distinct $i, j \in X$.*

Observe the following simple properties about these maps.

Proposition 1. *1. The set of maps $f \colon X \to \mathbb{Z}$ having integral difference ratio is closed under addition and multiplication. In particular, it contains all polynomials with integral coefficients.*
2. The set of maps $f \colon X \to \mathbb{Z}$ having integral difference ratio is closed under composition.

Which non-polynomial maps have integral difference ratio? This is the question we deal with. In our paper [2] we characterized the functions $f \colon \mathbb{N} \to \mathbb{Z}$ having integral difference ratio in terms of their Newton expansions over the "binomial polynomials". In §2 we give a similar characterization for functions $f \colon \mathbb{Z} \to \mathbb{Z}$ (Theorem 1). This is the main result of the paper, its proof runs through §3 to §5.

Partially supported by TARMAC ANR agreement 12 BS02 007 01.
Irène Guessarian: Emeritus at UPMC Université Paris 6.

C.S. Calude et al. (Eds.): Gruska Festschrift, LNCS 8808, pp. 277–291, 2014.
DOI: 10.1007/978-3-319-13350-8_21

2   Integral Difference Ratio and Newton Series

Definition 2. *The* $\mathbb{Z}$*-Newtonian polynomials are defined as follows:*

$$P_0(x) = 1 \ , \ P_{2k}(x) = \frac{1}{(2k)!} \prod_{i=-k+1}^{i=k} (x-i) \ , \ P_{2k+1}(x) = \frac{1}{(2k+1)!} \prod_{i=-k}^{i=k} (x-i)$$

Proposition 2. *The* $\mathbb{Z}$*-Newtonian polynomials define maps on* $\mathbb{Z}$ *which take values in* $\mathbb{Z}$ *and satisfy the following equations for* $k, n \in \mathbb{N}$,

$$P_{2k+1}(n) = \begin{cases} \binom{k+n}{2k+1} & \text{if } n > k \\ 0 \text{ if } 0 \leq n \leq k \end{cases} \qquad P_{2k}(n) = \begin{cases} \binom{k+n-1}{2k} & \text{if } n > k \\ 0 \text{ if } 0 \leq n \leq k \end{cases} \qquad (1)$$

$$P_{2k+1}(-n) = -P_{2k+1}(n) \qquad P_{2k}(-n) = \begin{cases} \binom{k+n}{2k} & \text{if } n \geq k \\ 0 \text{ if } 0 \leq n < k \end{cases} \qquad (2)$$

Definition 3. *A family* $(\varphi_n)_{n \in \mathbb{N}}$ *of functions* $\mathbb{Z} \to \mathbb{Z}$ *is a Newton basis for maps* $\mathbb{Z} \to \mathbb{Z}$ *if*

1. *For every* $x \in \mathbb{Z}$, *the set* $\{n \in \mathbb{N} \mid \varphi_n(x) \neq 0\}$ *is finite,*
2. *Every function* $f : \mathbb{Z} \to \mathbb{Z}$ *has a Newton expansion*

$$\forall x \in \mathbb{Z} \quad f(x) = \sum_{n \in \mathbb{N}} a_n \varphi_n(x) \qquad (3)$$

where $(a_n)_{n \in \mathbb{N}}$ *is a sequence in* $\mathbb{Z}^{\mathbb{N}}$.

Proposition 3. *The* $\mathbb{Z}$*-Newtonian polynomials are a Newton basis for maps* $\mathbb{Z} \to \mathbb{Z}$.

Proof. Conditions (1), (2) in Proposition 2 insure that equation (3) of Definition 3 reduces to

$$f(x) = \sum_{n \in \{0,\dots,2|x|+1\}} a_n P_n(x) \qquad (4)$$

which involves a finite sum.

To prove the converse, look at the instances of equation (4):

$$f(0) = a_0 \qquad f(1) = a_0 + a_1 \qquad f(2) = a_0 + 2a_1 + a_2 + a_3 \qquad \cdots$$
$$f(-1) = a_0 - a_1 + a_2 \qquad f(-2) = a_0 - 2a_1 + 3a_2 - a_3 + a_4 \ \cdots$$

In general, for $k \geq 1$, Proposition 2 yields

$$f(2k) = L_{2k}(a_0, \dots, a_{4k-2}) + a_{4k-1}$$
$$f(2k+1) = L_{2k+1}(a_0, \dots, a_{4k}) + a_{4k+1}$$
$$f(-2k) = L_{-2k}(a_0, \dots, a_{4k-1}) + a_{4k}$$
$$f(-2k-1) = L_{-2k-1}(a_0, \dots, a_{4k+1}) + a_{4k+2}$$

where $L_n(a_0, ..., a_{2n-2})$ and $L_{-n}(a_0, ..., a_{2n-1})$ are linear combinations of the a_i's with coefficients in $\mathbb{Z}$. This shows that, given any $f : \mathbb{Z} \rightarrow \mathbb{Z}$, there is a unique sequence of coefficients $(a_n)_{n\in\mathbb{N}}$ making equation (3) of Definition 3 true, and all these coefficients are in $\mathbb{Z}$. $\qquad\square$

Theorem 1. *Let $\sum_{k\in\mathbb{N}} a_k P_k(x)$ be the $\mathbb{Z}$-Newtonian expansion of a function $f : \mathbb{Z} \rightarrow \mathbb{Z}$. Then the following conditions are equivalent:*

1. *f has integral difference ratio,*
2. *$lcm(k)$ divides a_k for all k.*

3   Unary *lcm* and Binomial Coefficients

Definition 4. *For $k \in \mathbb{N}$, $k \geq 1$, $lcm(k)$ is the least common multiple of all positive integers less than or equal to k. By convention, $lcm(0) = 1$.*

The unary least common multiple function *lcm* (cf. Definition 4) has recently regained interest, cf. [3–5,8,10]. In this section, we prove three lemmas linking the *lcm* function and binomial coefficients.

Lemma 1. ([2]) *If $0 \leq n - k < p \leq n$ then p divides $lcm(k) \binom{n}{k}$.*

Lemma 2. *If $p \geq 0$ then $2(p+k)$ divides $lcm(2k) \binom{p + 2k - 1}{2k - 1}$.*

Proof. For $x \geq 1$, let $Val(x)$ denote the 2-valuation of x, i.e. the largest i such that 2^i divides x. The Lemma is proved through a series of claims. Throughout the proof, B will denote $\binom{p + 2k - 1}{2k - 1}$.

Claim 1. The number $p + k$ divides $B\, lcm(2k - 1)$.

Proof. Let $p' = p + k$, $n' = p + 2k - 1$ and $k' = 2k - 1$ and apply Lemma 1. $\qquad\square$

Claim 2. If k is a power of 2 then $2(p + k)$ divides $B\, lcm(2k)$.

Proof. Observe that $lcm(2k) = 2\, lcm(2k - 1)$ if k is a power of 2 and apply Claim 1. $\qquad\square$

Claim 3. The number $2^{Val(k)+1}$ divides $lcm(2k)$.

Proof. Since $2^{Val(k)}$ divides k it also divides $lcm(k)$. To conclude, observe that $Val(2k) = Val(k) + 1$. $\qquad\square$

Claim 4. The 2-valuation of B is the number of carries when adding $2k - 1$ and p in base 2.

Proof. This is an instance of Kummer's theorem (1852, cf. [6]) for base $s = 2$: if s is prime and $b \leq a$, the largest i such that s^i divides $\binom{a}{b}$ is the number of carries when adding b and $a - b$ in base s. $\qquad\square$

In the next claims we consider binary expansions with possibly non significant zeros ahead to get some prescribed large enough length.

Claim 5. Let $t \geq 1$ be the 2-valuation of $(2k' + 1) + (2p' + 1)$, i.e. $(2k' + 1) + (2p' + 1) = 2^t (2q + 1)$ for some q. For n large enough (e.g., $2^n \geq 2^t (2q + 1)$), let $k_n \ldots k_1 1$ and $p_n \ldots p_1 1$ be the length $n + 1$ binary expansions of $2k' + 1$ and $2p' + 1$. Then $k_i + p_i = 1$ for $1 \leq i \leq t - 1$ and $p_t = k_t$.

Proof. Let $q_n \ldots q_{t+1} 1 0 \ldots 0$ (with a tail of t zeros) be the length $n + 1$ binary expansion of $2^t (2q + 1)$. Consider the addition of $2k' + 1$ and $2p' + 1$ in base 2:

digit rank :	r	$\cdots$	$t+1$	t	$t-1$	$\cdots$	3	2	1	0
$(2k' + 1)$:	$\cdots$	$\cdots$	k_{t+1}	k_t	k_{t-1}	$\cdots$	k_3	k_2	k_1	1
$+ (2p' + 1)$:	$\cdots$	$\cdots$	p_{t+1}	p_t	p_{t-1}	$\cdots$	p_3	p_2	p_1	1
$= 2^t (2q + 1)$:	q_r	$\cdots$	q_{t+1}	1	0	$\cdots$	0	0	0	0

Observe that adding the digits $k_0 = 1$ and $p_0 = 1$ leads to $q_0 = 0$ and creates a carry. An easy induction on $i = 1, \ldots, t - 1$ shows that, in order to get the tail of t zeros in the sum, the incoming carry has to propagate from rank i to rank $i + 1$ and equality $k_i + p_i = 1$ holds. Finally, since $q_t = 1$ and there is an incoming carry at rank t, we have $p_t = k_t$.   □

Claim 6. Let p, k have the same 2-valuation ℓ, i.e. $p = 2^\ell (2p' + 1)$ and $k = 2^\ell (2k' + 1)$. Let t be the 2-valuation of $(2k' + 1) + (2p' + 1)$. For n large enough (say $2^n \geq p + 2k - 1$), let $p_n \cdots p_1 1$ be the length $n + 1$ binary expansion of $2p' + 1$. Let N be the number of 1's in $p_t \cdots p_1 1$. Then 2^N divides $B = \dbinom{p + 2k - 1}{2k - 1}$.

Proof. Let $k_n \cdots k_1 1$ be the length $n + 1$ binary expansion of $2k' + 1$. Applying Claim 5 to $2k' + 1$ and $2p' + 1$ we see that $k_i + p_i = 1$ for $1 \leq i \leq t - 1$ and $k_t = p_t$. By Claim 4, to show that 2^N divides B we reduce to prove that the number of carries when adding p and $2k - 1$ is at least N. The binary expansions of $k = 2^\ell (2k' + 1)$, $2k - 1$ and $p = 2^\ell (2p' + 1)$ are as follows:

rank: $\ldots$	$t+\ell+1$	$t+\ell$	$t+\ell-1$	$\ldots$	$\ell+2$	$\ell+1$	ℓ	$\ell-1$	$\ldots$	0
$k :$ $\ldots$	k_{t+1}	k_t	k_{t-1}	$\ldots$	k_2	k_1	1	0	$\ldots$	0
$2k-1 :$ $\ldots$	k_t	k_{t-1}	k_{t-2}	$\ldots$	k_1	0	1	1	$\ldots$	1
$p :$ $\ldots$	p_{t+1}	p_t	p_{t-1}	$\ldots$	p_2	p_1	1	0	$\ldots$	0

In the addition of $2k - 1$ and p the first carry occurs at rank ℓ. Hence, the number of carries in this addition is equal to the number of carries in the addition of the integers obtained by deleting the ℓ last digits, i.e. the numbers $\lambda = 2^{-\ell}((2k - 1) - (2^\ell - 1))$ and $2p' + 1$. We thus reduce to show that there are at least N carries in the addition of λ and $2p' + 1$. Their binary expansions are

rank:	$n+1$	n	$\ldots$	$t+2$	$t+1$	t	$t-1$	$\ldots$	3	2	1	0
$\lambda :$	k_n	k_{n-1}	$\ldots$	k_{t+1}	k_t	k_{t-1}	k_{t-2}	$\ldots$	k_2	k_1	0	1
$2p'+1 :$	$\ldots$	$\ldots$	$\ldots$	p_{t+2}	p_{t+1}	p_t	p_{t-1}	$\ldots$	p_3	p_2	p_1	1

with $k_i = 1 - p_i$ for $i = 1, \ldots, t - 1$ and $k_t = p_t$. We prove by induction on the rank $i = 0, \ldots, t$ that, in the addition of λ and $2p' + 1$, for all $0 \le i \le t$, if $p_i = 1$ then there is a carry at rank i.

Case $i = 0$. Since the added digits at rank 0 are both equal to 1, there is a carry.

Case $1 \le i \le t$ and $p_i = 0$. There is nothing to prove.

Case $i = 1$ and $p_1 = 1$. The added digits at rank 1 are 0 and 1 (since $p_1 = 1$). Since there is an incoming carry (that from rank 0) a carry is created at rank 1.

Case $1 \le i \le t$ and $p_i = 1$ and $p_{i-1} = 0$. Since $i - 1 < t$ we have $k_{i-1} + p_{i-1} = 1$ hence $k_{i-1} = 1$. Thus, the added digits at rank i (namely k_{i-1} and p_i) are both equal to 1 hence there is a carry.

Case $1 \le i \le t$ and $p_i = 1$ and $p_{i-1} = 1$. By the induction hypothesis, a carry occurs at rank $i - 1$. Thus, at rank i there is an incoming carry (the one from rank $i - 1$) and the digit p_i is 1, hence (whatever be the digit of λ at rank i) there is a carry at rank i.

Hence there are at least N carries in the addition of λ and $2p + 1$.   □

Claim 7. Let p, k, ℓ, t, N be as in Claim 6. Then $2^{\ell+t+1-N}$ divides $lcm(2k)$.

Proof. There are N ones in $p_t p_{t-1} \cdots p_1 1$, hence there are at most $N - 1$ ones and at least $t + 1 - N$ zeros in $p_{t-1} \cdots p_1$. By Claim 5, $k_{t-1} \cdots k_1$ contains at least $t + 1 - N$ ones. Thus, the number of significant digits of $k_{t-1} \cdots k_1 01$ is at least $t + 3 - N$. The binary expansion of $2k - 1$ is $k_n \cdots k_t k_{t-1} \cdots k_1 01$ followed by ℓ ones hence $2k - 1$ has at least $\ell + t + 3 - N$ significant digits. Consequently, $2k - 1 \ge 2^{\ell+t+2-N}$ and $2^{\ell+t+2-N}$ divides $lcm(2k-1)$ and, a fortiori, $lcm(2k)$.   □

Recall that integers a, b are coprime if 1 is their unique positive common divisor, i.e. $gcd(a, b) = 1$. The last claim is elementary number theory.

Claim 8. Let a, b, c be integers. If a, b are coprime and divide c, then ab also divides c.

We can now proceed with the proof of Lemma 2. We argue by cases.

- *Case $Val(p) \ne Val(k)$.*

  Let $m = \inf(Val(p), Val(k))$. Exactly one of the two integers $p \, 2^{-m}$ and $k \, 2^{-m}$ is odd so that $p + k = 2^m(2^{-m}p + 2^{-m}k) = 2^m(2q + 1)$ for some q. Now,

  - Since $m \le Val(k)$, Claim 3 insures that 2^{m+1} divides $lcm(2k)$.
  - Claim 1 insures that $p + k = 2^m(2q+1)$ divides $B \, lcm(2k-1)$. A fortiori $(2q+1)$ divides $B \, lcm(2k)$.

  As 2^{m+1} and $(2q+1)$ are coprime, Claim 8 implies that $2(p+k) = 2^{m+1}(2q+1)$ divides $B \, lcm(2k)$.

- *Case $Val(p) = Val(k) = \ell$.*

  Then $p + k = 2^\ell(2k' + 1) + 2^\ell(2p' + 1) = 2^{\ell+t}(2q + 1)$ with $t \ge 1$. There are three subcases.

  - *Subcase $k \ge 2^{\ell+t}$.* Then $2^{\ell+t+1} \le 2k$, hence $2^{\ell+t+1}$ divides $lcm(2k)$. Claim 1 insures that $p + k = 2^{\ell+t}(2q+1)$ divides $B \, lcm(2k-1)$, A fortiori $2q + 1$ divides $B \, lcm(2k)$. Finally, by Claim 8 we conclude that $2(p+k) = 2^{\ell+t+1}(2q+1)$ divides $B \, lcm(2k)$.

  - *Subcase k is a power of 2.* Apply Claim 2.

- *Subcase* $k = 2^\ell(2k'+1) < 2^{\ell+t}$ *for some* $k' \neq 0$. Claims 6 and 7 insure that 2^N divides B and $2^{\ell+t+1-N}$ divides $lcm(2k)$. Thus, $2^{\ell+t+1}$ divides $B\, lcm(2k)$. By Claim 1, $p + k = 2^{\ell+t}(2q+1)$ divides $B\, lcm(2k-1)$. A fortiori $(2q+1)$ divides $B\, lcm(2k)$. Finally by Claim 8, $2(p+k) = 2^{\ell+t+1}(2q+1)$ divides $B\, lcm(2k)$. □

Lemma 3. *If* $b \geq k$ *then* n *divides* $A_{k,b}^n = lcm(k)\left(\binom{b+n}{k} - \binom{b}{k}\right).$

Proof. We argue by double induction on k and b with the conditions

$$(\mathcal{P}_{k,b}) \quad \forall n \in \mathbb{N}, \ n \text{ divides } A_{k,b}^n \quad, \quad (\mathcal{P}_k) \quad \forall b \geq k, \ \forall n \in \mathbb{N}, \ n \text{ divides } A_{k,b}^n.$$

Conditions $(\mathcal{P}_0)$ and $(\mathcal{P}_1)$ are trivial since $A_{0,b}^n = 0$ and $A_{1,b}^n = n$.
Suppose $k \geq 1$ and $(\mathcal{P}_k)$ is true. To prove $(\mathcal{P}_{k+1})$, we prove by induction on $b \geq k+1$ that $(\mathcal{P}_{k+1,b})$ holds.

In the base case $b = k+1$, applying Pascal's rule, we have

$$
\begin{aligned}
A_{k+1,k+1}^n &= lcm(k+1)\left(\binom{k+1+n}{k+1} - \binom{k+1}{k+1}\right) \\
&= lcm(k+1)\left(\binom{k+n}{k} + \binom{k+n}{k+1} - 1\right) \\
&= lcm(k+1)\left(\binom{k+n}{k} - \binom{k}{k}\right) + lcm(k+1)\binom{k+n}{k+1} \\
&= \frac{lcm(k+1)}{lcm(k)}A_{k,k}^n + lcm(k+1)\binom{k+n}{k+1}
\end{aligned}
$$

Since $(\mathcal{P}_{k,k})$ holds (induction hypothesis on k), n divides $A_{k,k}^n$ hence n divides the first term. If $n \leq k+1$ then n divides $lcm(k+1)$ hence n also divides the second term. If $n > k+1$, applying Lemma 1 with $n' = k+n$, $p' = n$ and $k' = k+1$, we see that $n = p'$ divides the second term. Thus, in both cases n divides $A_{k+1,k+1}^n$ and $(\mathcal{P}_{k+1,k+1})$ holds.

Suppose now that $(\mathcal{P}_{k+1,c})$ holds for $k+1 \leq c \leq b$. We prove $(\mathcal{P}_{k+1,b+1})$. Using Pascal's rule, we get

$$
\begin{aligned}
A_{k+1,b+1}^n &= lcm(k+1)\left(\binom{b+1+n}{k+1} - \binom{b+1}{k+1}\right) \\
&= lcm(k+1)\left(\binom{b+n}{k} + \binom{b+n}{k+1} - \binom{b}{k} - \binom{b}{k+1}\right) \\
&= lcm(k+1)\left(\left(\binom{b+n}{k} - \binom{b}{k}\right) + \left(\binom{b+n}{k+1} - \binom{b}{k+1}\right)\right) \\
&= \left(\frac{lcm(k+1)}{lcm(k)}A_{k,b}^n\right) + A_{k+1,b}^n
\end{aligned}
$$

Since $(\mathcal{P}_{k,b})$ and $(\mathcal{P}_{k+1,b})$ hold, n divides both terms of the above sum, hence n divides $A_{k+1,b+1}^n$ and $(\mathcal{P}_{k+1,b+1})$ holds. □

Lemma 4. *Let*
$$
\begin{cases}
B(n,k,i) = \dbinom{n+k-1}{2k} - \dbinom{i+k}{2k} \\[2mm]
C(n,k,i) = \dbinom{n+k}{2k+1} + \dbinom{i+k}{2k+1}
\end{cases}.
$$

For all $n \geq 2$, and $1 \leq i \leq n-1$, the following hold

$$n+i \text{ divides} \quad lcm(2k)\, B(n,k,i) \quad \text{for } 1 \leq k \leq i \tag{5}$$

$$n+i \text{ divides} \quad lcm(2k+1)\, C(n,k,i) \quad \text{for } 0 \leq k \leq i \tag{6}$$

Proof. By induction on $n \geq 2$. Base case: $n = 2$ clear as $n-1 = 1 = i$. Induction: assuming that (5) and (6) hold for n, we first prove that (5) holds for $n+1$, and we then prove that (6) holds for $n+1$.

- Proof that (5) holds for $n+1$.

Let $1 \leq i \leq n$ and $1 \leq k \leq i$. Then, applying Pascal's rule,

$$
\begin{aligned}
B(n+1,k,i) &= \binom{n+k}{2k} - \binom{i+k}{2k} \\
&= \left[\binom{n+k-1}{2k} + \binom{n+k-1}{2k-1}\right] - \left[\binom{i+k+1}{2k} - \binom{i+k}{2k-1}\right] \\
&= \left[\binom{n+k-1}{2k} - \binom{i+1+k}{2k}\right] + \left[\binom{n+k-1}{2k-1} + \binom{(i+1)+(k-1)}{2k-1}\right] \\
B(n+1,k,i) &= B(n,k,i+1) + C(n,k-1,i+1)
\end{aligned}
\tag{7}
$$

By the induction hypothesis, applied for n and $i+1$, provided that $i+1 \leq n-1$, i.e. $i \leq n-2$:

- (5) holds for n hence $n+i+1$ divides $lcm(2k)\, B(n,k,i)$
- (6) holds for n hence $n+i+1$ divides $lcm(2k-1)\, C(n,k-1,i+1)$

Since $lcm(2k-1)$ divides $lcm(2k)$, we see that $n+i+1$ divides $lcm(2k)\, C(n,k-1,i+1)$ for $i \leq n-2$. Summing and using (7), we obtain that $n+i+1$ divides $lcm(2k)\, B(n+1,k,i)$ for $i \leq n-2$.

It remains to prove the same result for $i = n-1$ and $i = n$.

For $i = n$, it is clear since $B(n+1,k,n) = \binom{n+1+k-1}{2k} - \binom{i+k}{2k} = 0$.

For $i = n-1$, $B(n+1,k,n-1) = \binom{n+k}{2k} - \binom{n-1+k}{2k} = \binom{n-1+k}{2k-1}$ by Pascal's rule. As $k \leq n$, $n-k \geq 0$ and we can apply Lemma 2 with $p = n-k$, hence: $2n = 2(p+k)$ divides $lcm(2k)\binom{p+2k-1}{2k-1} = lcm(2k)\binom{n-1+k}{2k-1} = lcm(2k)\, B(n+1,k,n-1)$. To conclude, observe that $n+1+i = n+1+n-1 = 2n$.

- Proof that (6) holds for $n+1$.

Assume that (5) and (6) hold for n. Let $1 \leq i \leq n$, by Pascal's rule

$$C(n+1,k,i) = \binom{n+k+1}{2k+1} + \binom{i+k}{2k+1}$$

$$= \left[\binom{n+k}{2k+1} + \binom{n+k}{2k}\right] + \left[\binom{i+1+k}{2k+1} - \binom{i+k}{2k}\right]$$

$$= \left[\binom{n+k}{2k+1} + \binom{i+1+k}{2k+1}\right] + \left[\binom{n+k}{2k} - \binom{i+k}{2k}\right]$$

$$C(n+1,k,i) = C(n,k,i+1) + B(n+1,k,i) \tag{8}$$

We know that (5) holds for $n+1$. Thus, for $1 \le i \le n$ and $1 \le k \le i$, $n+1+i$ divides $lcm(2k)B(n+1,k,i)$ hence also $lcm(2k+1)B(n+1,k,i)$. This also trivially holds for $k=0$ as $B(n+1,0,i)=0$. By the induction hypothesis (6) holds for n. Thus, $n+(i+1)$ divides $lcm(2k+1)C(n,k,i+1)$ for $1 \le i+1 \le n-1$, i.e. $0 \le i \le n-2$, and $0 \le k \le i+1$. Summing and using (8), we obtain that $n+i+1$ divides $lcm(2k+1)C(n+1,k,i)$ for $1 \le i \le n-2$ and $0 \le k \le i$. It remains to prove the same result for $i=n-1$ and $i=n$.

For $i=n-1$, we have $n+1+i=2n$ and $C(n+1,k,n-1) = 2\binom{n+k}{2k+1}$. Lemma 1, applied with $p'=n$, $n'=n+k$ and $k'=2k+1$, shows that n divides $lcm(2k+1)\binom{n+k}{2k+1}$, hence $2n$ divides $lcm(2k+1)C(n+1,k,n-1)$.

For $i=n$ we have $n+1+i=2n+1$ and

$$C(n+1,k,n) = \binom{n+k+1}{2k+1} + \binom{n+k}{2k+1}$$

$$= \frac{(n+k+1)!}{(2k+1)!\,(n-k)!} + \frac{(n+k)!}{(2k+1)!\,(n-k-1)!}$$

$$= \frac{(n+k)!}{(2k+1)!\,(n-k-1)!}\left(\frac{n+k+1}{n-k}+1\right)$$

$$= \frac{(n+k)!}{(2k)!\,(n-k)!}\,\frac{2n+1}{2k+1}$$

$$lcm(2k+1)C(n+1,k,n) = \frac{lcm(2k+1)}{2k+1} \times \binom{n+k}{2k} \times (2n+1)$$

As the first two factors are integers $2n+1$ divides $lcm(2k+1)\,C(n+1,k,n)$. □

4   Proof of Implication (1) $\Rightarrow$ (2) in Theorem 1

In this subsection we assume that $f : \mathbb{Z} \to \mathbb{Z}$ has integral difference ratio and that $f(x) = \sum_{k \in \mathbb{N}} a_k P_k(x)$ is its $\mathbb{Z}$-Newtonian expansion. To prove that $lcm(n)$ divides a_n we have to prove that i divides a_n for all $i \le n$.

By induction on $n \ge 1$, we prove the property

$\mathcal{I}(n)$: $lcm(2n-1)$ *divides* a_{2n-1} *and* $lcm(2n)$ *divides* a_{2n}.

The cases $n=1,2$ have just been done. The inductive step is split in four cases corresponding to Lemmas 5 to 8. Assuming $\mathcal{I}(j)$ for all $j < n$, Lemmas 5, 6, 7 and 8 respectively deal with the four possible cases:

Middle number n	n divides a_{2n-1} and n divides a_{2n}
Below the middle	If $2 \leq i < n$ then i divides a_{2n-1} and a_{2n}.
Above the middle, case a_{2n-1}	If $1 \leq i \leq n-1$ then $n+i$ divides a_{2n-1}
Above the middle, case a_{2n}	If $1 \leq i \leq n$ then $n+i$ divides a_{2n}

The following equations follow from Proposition 2 (equation (1)) and will be used to prove the lemmas.

$$f(n) = \sum_{j=0}^{2n-1} a_j P_j(n) \quad \text{with}$$

$$P_j(n) = \left\{ \begin{array}{ll} P_{2k}(n) = \binom{k+n-1}{2k} & \text{for } j = 2k \\ P_{2k+1}(n) = \binom{k+n}{2k+1} & \text{for } j = 2k+1 \end{array} \right\} = \binom{n + \lfloor (j-1)/2 \rfloor}{j} \quad (9)$$

Lemma 5. *If condition $\mathcal{I}(s)$ holds for all $s < n$ then n divides a_{2n-1} and a_{2n}.*

Proof. 1. We first show that n divides $2n-1$. The case $n \leq 2$ has been done above. Suppose $n \geq 2$. By the integral difference ratio property, n divides $f(n) - f(0)$. As $P_j(0) = 0$ for all $j \geq 1$ we have $f(0) = a_0$. Also, $P_{2n-1}(n) = 1$. Thus, $f(n) - f(0) = \left(\sum_{j=1}^{2n-2} a_j P_j(n) \right) + a_{2n-1}$ where the $P_j(n)$ are given in Equation (9). As $0 \leq n + \lfloor (j-1)/2 \rfloor - j < n \leq n + \lfloor (j-1)/2 \rfloor$, Lemma 1 insures that n divides $lcm(j)P_j(n)$. Now, by the induction hypothesis $\mathcal{I}(s)$ holds for all $s < n$ and thus $lcm(j)$ divides a_j for $j = 1, \ldots, 2n-2$. Therefore n divides all the terms in the sum $\sum_{j=1}^{2n-2} a_j P_j(n)$. Hence n divides a_{2n-1}.

2. Similarly, using equation (2) in Proposition 2, we get $f(-n) = \sum_{j=0}^{2n} a_j P_j(-n)$. An analogous use of Lemma 1 and the fact that n divides $f(-n) - f(0)$ allows to conclude that n divides a_{2n}. $\square$

Lemma 6. *If condition $\mathcal{I}(s)$ holds for all $s < n$ then i divides a_{2n-1} and a_{2n} for all $2 \leq i < n$.*

Proof. 1. Fix i such that $2 \leq i < n$. We first prove that i divides a_{2n-1}. By the integral difference ratio property, i divides $f(n) - f(n-i)$. Equation (1) yields

$$f(n) - f(n-i) = \sum_{j=0}^{2n-1} a_j P_j(n) - \sum_{j=0}^{2n-2i-1} a_j P_j(n-i)$$

$$= \left(\sum_{j=1}^{2n-2i-1} a_j \big(P_j(n) - P_j(n-i)\big) \right)$$

$$+ \left(\sum_{j=2n-2i}^{i-1} a_j P_j(n) \right) + \left(\sum_{j=i}^{2n-2} a_j P_j(n) \right) + a_{2n-1} \quad (10)$$

- *Third sum.* The induction hypothesis $\mathcal{I}(s)$, for $s < n$, imply that $lcm(j)$ divides a_j $j \leq 2s \leq 2n - 2$: a fortiori, for $i \leq j \leq 2n - 2$, i divides a_j: hence, i divides $a_i, a_{i+1}, \ldots, a_{2n-2}$ and also all terms in the third sum.
- *Second sum.* Let $n' = n + \lfloor (j - 1)/2 \rfloor$, $k' = j$, and $p = i$. For $j \leq i - 1$ we have $0 \leq n' - k' < p \leq n'$ hence Lemma 1 applies and insures that i divides $lcm(k') \binom{n'}{k'} = lcm(j) \binom{n + \lfloor (j-1)/2 \rfloor}{j} = lcm(j) P_j(n)$ (by equation (9)). Again $\mathcal{I}(s)$, $s < n$, insure that $lcm(j)$ divides a_j for $j < 2n$, hence i a fortiori divides all the terms $a_j P_j(n)$ in the second sum.
- *First sum.* Its terms are of the form, for $k < n - i$,

$$a_{2k} \left[\binom{k+n-1}{2k} - \binom{k+n-i-1}{2k} \right] \text{ or } a_{2k+1} \left[\binom{k+n}{2k+1} - \binom{k+n-i}{2k+1} \right].$$

Thus the hypothesis of Lemma 3, namely $2k \leq k+n-i-1$ (resp. $2k+1 \leq k+n-i$) hold for each term $\left(P_j(n) - P_j(n - i) \right)$, $j < 2n - 2i$ of the first sum, implying that i divides each term $lcm(j) \left(P_j(n) - P_j(n - i) \right)$. Since conditions $\mathcal{I}(s)$, $s < n$, insure that $lcm(j)$ divides a_j for $j \leq 2s < 2n - 2$, we see that i divides all terms $a_j \left(P_j(n) - P_j(n - i) \right)$ in the first sum.

Since i divides the left member and all terms of the three sums in equation (10) it must divide a_{2n-1}.

2. The proof for a_{2n} is similar using $f(-n) - f(-n + i)$ and equation (2) of Proposition 2. $\qquad \square$

Lemma 7. *If condition $\mathcal{I}(s)$ holds for all $s < n$ then $n + i$ divides a_{2n-1} for all $1 \leq i \leq n - 1$.*

Proof. By the integral difference ratio property, $n+i$ divides $D = f(n) - f(-i) = \sum_{j=0}^{2n-1} a_j P_j(n) - \sum_{j=0}^{2i} a_j P_j(-i)$. D can be split into four sums

$$D = \left(\sum_{k=0}^{i-1} a_{2k+1} \left(P_{2k+1}(n) - P_{2k+1}(-i) \right) \right) + \left(\sum_{k=1}^{i} a_{2k} \left(P_{2k}(n) - P_{2k}(-i) \right) \right)$$

$$+ \left(\sum_{j=2i+1}^{2n-2} a_j P_j(n) \right) + a_{2n-1}$$

Using equations (1), (2) and (9), we rewrite D as

$$D = \sum_{k=0}^{i-1} a_{2k+1} \left(\binom{n+k}{2k+1} + \binom{i+k}{2k+1} \right) + \sum_{k=1}^{i} a_{2k} \left(\binom{n+k-1}{2k} - \binom{i+k}{2k} \right)$$

$$+ \left(\sum_{j=2i+1}^{2n-2} a_j \binom{n + \lfloor (j-1)/2 \rfloor}{j} \right) + a_{2n-1}$$

- *First/second sum.* Induction conditions $\mathcal{I}(s)$, for all $s < n$, insure that $lcm(2k)$ divides a_{2k} and $lcm(2k + 1)$ divides a_{2k+1} for $k \leq i < n$; Moreover, as $1 \leq i \leq$

$n-1$, Lemma 4 shows that $n+i$ divides $lcm(2k+1)\left(\binom{n+k}{2k+1}+\binom{i+k}{2k+1}\right)$ and $lcm(2k)\left(\binom{n+k-1}{2k}-\binom{i+k}{2k}\right)$. Hence, $n+i$ divides all terms in the first and the second sum.

- *Third sum.* Let $n'=n+\lfloor(j-1)/2\rfloor$, $k'=j$, and $p=n+i$. Since $i\leq n-1$, for $2i+1\geq j\leq 2n-2$ we have $0\leq n'-k'<p\leq n'$ hence we can apply Lemma 1 which insures that $n+i$ divides $lcm(j)\,P_j(n)$; moreover, the induction conditions $\mathcal{I}(j)$ hold for all $j<n$, hence $lcm(j)$ divides a_j for all $j\leq 2n-2$. Thus, $n+i$ divides all terms in the third sum.

Since it divides the left member and all terms in the above three sums, $n+i$ must divide a_{2n-1}. □

Lemma 8. *If condition $\mathcal{I}(s)$ holds for all $s<n$ then $n+i$ divides a_{2n} for all $1\leq i\leq n$.*

Proof. By the integral difference ratio property, $n+i$ divides $f(-n)-f(i)$. Equations (1) and (2) yield

$$f(-n)-f(i) = \sum_{j=0}^{2n} a_j P_j(-n) - \sum_{j=0}^{2i} a_j P_j(i)$$
$$= \left(\sum_{k=0}^{i-1} a_{2k+1}\left(P_{2k+1}(-n)-P_{2k+1}(i)\right)\right) + \left(\sum_{k=1}^{i} a_{2k}\left(P_{2k}(-n)-P_{2k}(i)\right)\right)$$
$$+ \left(\sum_{j=2i+1}^{2n-1} a_j P_j(-n)\right) + a_{2n}$$

- *First sum.* Since P_{2k+1} is odd, by equation (2) of Proposition 2 the first sum is the opposite of the first sum in the proof of Lemma 7, hence it is divided by $n+i$.
- *Second sum.* Equations (1), (2) insure that $P_{2k}(-n)-P_{2k}(i)=\binom{k+n}{2k}-\binom{k+i-1}{2k}$. In case $2\leq i\leq n$ we let $n'=n+1$ and $i'=i-1$. We have $1\leq i'\leq n'-1$, $P_{2k}(-n)-P_{2k}(i)=P_{2k}(n-1)-P_{2k}(i)=P_{2k}(n')-P_{2k}(i'+1)$ and we can apply Lemma 4. Exactly as in the proof of Lemma 7, we deduce that $n+i=n'+i'$ divides each term of the second sum.

Consider now the case $i=1$. The second sum reduces to one term:
$$a_2(P_2(-n)-P_2(1))=a_2 n(n+1)/2.$$
As 2 divides a_2, we see that $n+1$ divides this term.

- *Third sum.* Let $j=2k$ or $j=2k+1$, and $2i+1\leq j\leq 2n-1$, equation (2) shows that $P_{2k+1}(-n)=-\binom{k+n}{2k+1}$ and $P_{2k}(-n)=\binom{k+n}{2k}$. Let $n'=k+n$, $k'=2k$, and $p=n+i$, as $i\leq n$ and $2k\leq 2n-1$ we have $0\leq n'-k'<p\leq n'$, hence we can apply Lemma 1 which insures that $n+i$ divides $lcm(2k)\,P_{2k}(-n)$. Then, as $\mathcal{I}(j)$ hold for all $j<n$, $lcm(2k)$ divides a_{2k} for $2k<2n$ and $n+i$ divides $a_{2k}P_{2k}(-n)$. The case $k''=2k+1$ is similar. Thus, $n+i$ divides all terms in the third sum.

Since $n+i$ divides the left member and all terms in the above three sums, it must divide a_{2n}. □

Lemmas 5, 6, 7, 8 together with the base cases complete the proof of Theorem 1.

5   Proof of Implication (2) $\Rightarrow$ (1) in Theorem 1

We assume that the $\mathbb{Z}$-Newton expansion $\sum_{n\in\mathbb{N}} a_k\, P_k(x)$ of $f : \mathbb{Z} \to \mathbb{Z}$ is such that $lcm(n)$ divides a_n for all n. We want to prove that f has integral difference ratio. As for given $i, j \in \mathbb{Z}$, $f(i)-f(j)$ is a sum of finitely many $a_n P_n(i)-a_n P_n(j)$, it suffices to prove that each function $x \mapsto lcm(n)P_n(x)$ has integral difference ratio. Let $j < i$, $i, j \in \mathbb{Z}$. To prove that $i - j$ divides $lcm(n)(P_n(i) - P_n(j))$, we argue by disjunction of cases on the parity of n and the signs of i, j, i.e. relative to the positions of i, j with respect to the intervals $]-\infty, -k]$, $[-k, k]$, $[k, +\infty[$ for $k = \lfloor n/2 \rfloor$. We rely on conditions 1, 2 in Proposition 2.

1. *Case $n = 2k$ and $i, j \in] - \infty, -k]$.* Then $P_{2k}(i) - P_{2k}(j) = \begin{pmatrix} k + |i| \\ 2k \end{pmatrix} - \begin{pmatrix} k + |j| \\ 2k \end{pmatrix}$ and Lemma 3 applied with $b = k + |i| \geq 2k$, $n = |j| - |i|$ insures that $|j| - |i| = i - j$ divides $lcm(2k)(P_{2k}(j) - P_{2k}(i))$.

2. *Case $n = 2k$ and $j \in] - \infty, -k]$ and $i \in] - k, k]$.* Then $P_{2k}(i) - P_{2k}(j) = -\begin{pmatrix} k + |j| \\ 2k \end{pmatrix}$. Let $n' = k + |j|$, $k' = 2k$ and $p' = i - j = i + |j|$. Then $0 \leq n' - k' < p' \leq n'$, and Lemma 1 insures that $i - j$ divides $lcm(k')\binom{n'}{k'} = lcm(2k)(P_{2k}(j) - P_{2k}(i))$.

3. *Case $n = 2k$ and $j \in] - \infty, -k]$ and $i \in]k, +\infty[$.* Then $P_{2k}(i) - P_{2k}(j) = \begin{pmatrix} k + i - 1 \\ 2k \end{pmatrix} - \begin{pmatrix} k + |j| \\ 2k \end{pmatrix}$.
– *subcase $|j| \leq i - 1$* Let $n' = i$ and $i' = |j|$. As $i' \leq n' - 1$ Lemma 4 (5) applies and insures that $n' + i' = i + |j| = i - j$ divides $lcm(2k)B(n', k, i') = lcm(2k)(P_{2k}(i) - P_{2k}(j))$.
– *subcase $|j| \geq i$* Let $n' = |j| + 1$ and $i' = i - 1$. Again by Lemma 4 (5), $n' + i' = i + |j| = i - j$ divides $lcm(2k)B(n', k, i') = lcm(2k)(P_{2k}(j) - P_{2k}(i))$.

4. *Case $n = 2k$ and $i, j \in] - k, -k]$.* Clear as $P_{2k}(i) = P_{2k}(j) = 0$.

5. *Case $n = 2k$ and $j \in] - k, -k]$ and $i \in]k, +\infty[$.* Then $P_{2k}(i) - P_{2k}(j) = \begin{pmatrix} k + i \\ 2k \end{pmatrix}$. Let $n' = k + i$, $k' = 2k$ and $p' = i - j$. We have $0 \leq n' - k' < p' \leq n'$, hence by Lemma 1, $p' = i - j$ divides $lcm(2k)\binom{k+i}{2k}$.

6. *Case $n = 2k$ and $i, j \in]k, +\infty[$.* Then $P_{2k}(i) - P_{2k}(j) = \begin{pmatrix} k + i - 1 \\ 2k \end{pmatrix} - \begin{pmatrix} k + j - 1 \\ 2k \end{pmatrix}$ with $2k \leq k + j - 1$, we can thus conclude using Lemma 3.

7. *Case $n = 2k+1$ and $i, j \in] -\infty, -k[$.* Then $P_{2k+1}(i)-P_{2k+1}(j) = -\begin{pmatrix} k + |i| \\ 2k + 1 \end{pmatrix} + \begin{pmatrix} k + |j| \\ 2k + 1 \end{pmatrix}$: applying Lemma 3 with $b = |i|$, $n = |j|-|i|$ we conclude that $n = i-j$ divides $lcm(2k + 1)\big(P_{2k+1}(i) - P_{2k+1}(j)\big)$.

8. *Case $n = 2k+1$ and $j \in]-\infty, -k[$ and $i \in [-k, k]$.* Then $P_{2k+1}(i)-P_{2k+1}(j) = \begin{pmatrix} k + |j| \\ 2k + 1 \end{pmatrix}$. We conclude as in case 2. above, with Lemma 1.

9. *Case $n = 2k+1$ and $j \in]-\infty, -k[$ and $i \in]k, +\infty[$.* Then $P_{2k+1}(i) - P_{2k+1}(j) = \binom{k+i}{2k+1} + \binom{k+|j|}{2k+1}$. – *subcase $|j| \leq i - 1$* : let $n' = i$, $i' = |j|$ and apply Lemma 4 (6).

– *subcase $i \leq |j| - 1$* : let $n' = |j|$, $i' = i$ and apply Lemma 4 (6).

– *subcase $i = |j|$* : then $P_{2k+1}(i) - P_{2k+1}(j) = 2\binom{k+i}{2k+1}$; Lemma 1, applied with $n' = k+i$, $k' = 2k+1$ and $p' = i$ ($0 \leq n' - k' < p' \leq n'$ hold), implies that i divides $lcm(2k+1)\binom{k+i}{2k+1}$, hence $2i = i - |j|$ divides $lcm(2k+1)\big(P_{2k+1}(i) - P_{2k+1}(j)\big)$.

10. *Case $n = 2k+1$ and $i, j \in [-k, -k]$.* Trivial since then $P_{2k+1}(i) = P_{2k+1}(j) = 0$.

11. *Case $n = 2k+1$ and $j \in [-k, k]$ and $i \in]k, +\infty[$.* Then $P_{2k+1}(i) - P_{2k+1}(j) = \binom{k+i}{2k+1}$. Let $n' = k+i$, $k' = 2k+1$, and $p' = i - j$: as $0 \leq n' - k' = i - k - 1$, as $|j| \leq k$ and $i > k$, $i - k - 1 < p' = i - j \leq n'$, the hypothesis of Lemma 1 hold and Lemma 1 yields $i - j$ divides $lcm(2k+1)\big(P_{2k+1}(i) - P_{2k+1}(j)\big)$.

12. *Case $n = 2k+1$ and $i, j \in]k, +\infty[$.* Similar to Case 7: use Lemma 3 since then $P_{2k+1}(i) - P_{2k+1}(j) = \binom{k+i}{2k+1} - \binom{k+j}{2k+1}$. $\square$

6 Non Polynomial Functions Having Integral Difference Ratio

Let us mention a straightforward consequence of Theorem 1.

Corollary 1. *There are non polynomial functions $\mathbb{Z} \to \mathbb{Z}$ having integral difference ratio.*

Proof. In fact there are uncountably many such functions: let a_n be any non null element of $lcm(n)\mathbb{N}$. $\square$

We now explicit some non polynomial functions having integral difference ratio. We first briefly recall such examples $\mathbb{N} \to \mathbb{Z}$ obtained in [2] and then explicit functions $\mathbb{Z} \to \mathbb{Z}$ (Theorem 2).

Remark 1. Function $\lfloor e\, x! \rfloor$ does *not* have integral difference ratio (cf. [2]). The following functions $\mathbb{N} \to \mathbb{Z}$ have integral difference ratio (see [2]):

$$f : x \mapsto \begin{cases} 1 & \text{if } x = 0 \\ \lfloor e\, x! \rfloor & \text{if } x \in \mathbb{N} \setminus \{0\} \end{cases} \qquad f_h : x \mapsto \begin{cases} \lfloor \sinh(1)\, x! \rfloor & \text{if } x \text{ odd} \\ \lfloor \cosh(1)\, x! \rfloor & \text{if } x \text{ even} \end{cases}$$

It is easy to lift the integral difference ratio property from functions $\mathbb{N} \to \mathbb{Z}$ to functions $\mathbb{Z} \to \mathbb{Z}$.

Proposition 4. *Suppose $f : \mathbb{N} \to \mathbb{Z}$ has integral difference ratio and let $g : \mathbb{Z} \to \mathbb{Z}$ be such that $g(x) = f(x^2)$. Then g has integral difference ratio. In particular, there is a function $g : \mathbb{Z} \to \mathbb{Z}$ having integral difference ratio and such that $g(x) \in \{\lfloor e\,(x^2)! \rfloor, \lfloor e\,(x^2)! \rfloor - 1\}$.*

Proof. Since $a^2 - b^2 =$ divides $f(a^2) - f(b^2) = g(a) - g(b)$ so does $a - b$.   □

Here is an example of a non polynomial function $\mathbb{Z} \to \mathbb{Z}$ having integral difference ratio and which is not relevant to Proposition 4.

Lemma 9. *For all k, we have $lcm(k)$ divides $\dfrac{(2k)!}{k!}$.*

Proof. We have $lcm(2k) = \prod_{p \text{ prime}} p^{N(p)}$ with $N(p) = \sup\{i \mid p^i \leq 2k\}$. For p prime, let $M(p)$ be the largest integer divided by $p^{N(p)}$ and $\leq 2k$. Then $2M(p) > 2k$ hence $M(p) > k$. In particular, $M(p)$ hence $p^{N(p)}$ divides $(2k)!/k!$. As a product of pairwise coprime integers, $lcm(2k) = \prod_{p \text{ prime}} p^{N(p)}$ also divides $(2k)!/k!$.   □

Theorem 2. *The function defined on $\mathbb{Z}$ by*

$$f(n) = \begin{cases} \sqrt{\dfrac{e}{\pi}} \times \dfrac{\Gamma(1/2)}{2 \times 4^n \times n!} \int_1^\infty e^{-t/2}(t^2 - 1)^n dt & \text{for } n \geq 0 \\ -f(|n| - 1) & \text{for } n < 0 \end{cases}$$

maps $\mathbb{Z}$ into $\mathbb{Z}$ and has integral difference ratio.

Proof. Let $f : \mathbb{Z} \to \mathbb{Z}$ have $\mathbb{Z}$-Newton expansion $f(x) = \sum_{k \in \mathbb{N}} \dfrac{(2k)!}{k!} P_{2k}(x)$, i.e. $a_{2k} = (2k)!/k!$ and $a_{2k+1} = 0$. It is clearly nonpolynomial and, by Theorem 1, it has integral difference ratio.

Using Grashteyn & I. M. Ryzhik Tables [7], page 2, formula 0.126, and page 917 formulas 8.432 1 & 3, we see that, for $n \geq 0$ we have

$$f(n) = \sum_{k=0}^n \frac{2k!}{k!} \frac{(n+k)(n+k-1)\cdots(n-k+2)(n-k+1)}{(2k)!} = \sum_{k=0}^n \frac{(n+k)!}{k!\,(n-k)!}$$

$$= \sqrt{\frac{e}{\pi}} \times K_{n+\frac{1}{2}}\left(\frac{1}{2}\right) = \sqrt{\frac{e}{\pi}} \times \frac{\Gamma(\frac{1}{2})}{2 \times 4^n \times n!} \int_1^\infty e^{-\frac{t}{2}}(t^2 - 1)^n dt$$

$$f(-n) = \sum_{k=0}^n \frac{2k!}{k!} \frac{(-n+k)(-n+k-1)\cdots(-n-k+2)(-n-k+1)}{(2k)!}$$

$$= \sum_{k=0}^n (-1)^{2k} \frac{(n+k-1)\cdots(n-k)}{k!} = \sum_{k=0}^n \frac{(n+k-1)!}{k!\,(n-k-1)!} = f(n-1)$$

where $K_\nu(x) = \int_0^\infty e^{-x \cosh t} \cosh(\nu t) dt$ is associated with the Bessel function of the third kind.   □

7   Conclusion

We characterized the class of integral difference ratio functions from $\mathbb{Z}$ to $\mathbb{Z}$ via their Newton series expansions on a basis of polynomials with rational coefficients: the $\mathbb{Z}$-Newtonian polynomials. This enabled us to exhibit non polynomial such functions. Integral difference ratio functions can be seen as the solution for algebra $\mathbb{Z}$ of a general problem: which functions preserve a family of congruences on a given structure? Functions preserving all congruences on an algebra have been studied in universal algebra; it was known [9] that there exist such functions from $\mathbb{Z}$ to $\mathbb{Z}$ which are *polynomials with non-integer coefficients*. Our contribution to the study of congruence preserving functions on $\mathbb{Z}$ is (i) to *characterize the congruence preserving functions from $\mathbb{Z}$ to $\mathbb{Z}$* as the integral difference ratio functions and (ii) to give an example of a *non polynomial* Bessel like congruence preserving function.

References

1. Cégielski, P., Grigorieff, S., Guessarian, I.: On Lattices of Regular Sets of Natural Integers Closed under Decrementation. Information Processing Letters **114**(4), 197–202 (2014). Preliminary version on arXiv, 2013
2. Cegielski, P., Grigorieff, S., Guessarian, I.: Newton expansion of functions over natural integers having integral difference ratios. To be published in Int. J. Number Theory, Preliminary version on arXiv (2013)
3. Dusart, P.: Estimates of some functions over primes without Riemann hypothesis, unpublished. Preprint version on arXiv (2010)
4. Farhi, B.: Nontrivial lower bounds for the least common multiple of some finite sequences of integers. Journal of Number Theory **125**, 393–411 (2007)
5. Farhi, B., Kane, D.: New Results on the Least Common Multiple of Consecutive Integers. Proceedings of the AMS **137**(6), 1933–1939 (2009)
6. Granville, A.: Binomial coefficients modulo prime powers. Conference Proceedings of the Canadian Mathematical Society **20**, 253–275 (1997)
7. Grashteyn, I.S., Ryzhik, I.M.: Table of Integrals, Series, and Products, 7th edn. Academic Press (2007)
8. Hong, S., Qian, G., Tan, Q.: The least common multiple of a sequence of products of linear polynomials. Acta Mathematica Hungarica **135**(1–2), 160–167 (2011)
9. Pixley, A.F.: Functional and affine completeness and arithmetical varieties. In: Rosenberg, J., Sabidussi, G. (eds.) Algebras and Orders, pp. 317–357. Kluwer Acad. Pub. (1993)
10. Qian, G., Hong, S.: Asymptotic behavior of the least common multiple of consecutive arithmetic progression terms. Archiv der Mathematik **100**(4), 337–345 (2013)

Conditional Lindenmayer Systems
with Conditions Defined by Bounded Resources

Jürgen Dassow[(✉)]

Fakultät für Informatik, Otto-von-Guericke-Universität Magdeburg,
PSF 4120, D-39016 Magdeburg, Germany
`dassow@iws.cs.uni-magdeburg.de`

Abstract. An extended conditional tabled Lindenmayer systems is an
ET0L systems where each table is associated with a regular set, the
so-called condition. A table can only be applied to a sentential form if
the form belongs to its associated regular set. We study the power of
conditional ET0L systems if the conditions are given by regular languages with a limited state or nonterminal complexity. We show that
conditions obtained by regular grammars with two nonterminals and
finite automata with three states are sufficient to generate all recursively
enumerable languages. Similar results are given for the generation of all
context-sensitive languages. Moreover, in the non-extended case, one gets
infinite hierarchies for both complexity measures.

1 Introduction

In the theory of formal languages one imposes very often conditions to perform
a step in the generation of words. By practical reasons – but also by theoretical
considerations – it is very useful that one can check the condition by an efficient
procedure. Thus one relates the condition to regular languages, for which the
membership problem can be decided in linear time. We mention here as examples
regularly controlled context-free grammars, conditional context-free grammars,
tree controlled context-free grammars, and contextual grammars with selection
languages (for details see [6], [15], and [14]).

In these cases the process of checking the condition given by a regular language is now very simple and efficient, however, the increase of generative power
is considerable (for instance, for the first three devices, one has an increase from
context-free languages to recursively enumerable languages). Since on the one
hand practical requirements do not ask for arbitrary regular languages and on
the other hand theoretical studies – for instance proofs – show that only special
regular languages are used, it is very natural to study the devices with subregular
languages for the control. Investigations on the change of the generative power,
if subregular restrictions defined by combinatorial and algebraic properties are
done e. g. in [4] and [3] for conditional grammars, in [10] for tree controlled
grammars, and in [2], [5], and [13] for contextual grammars.

Furthermore, one can also restrict the regular languages by requiring that
they have bounded complexities. The most well-known complexity for regular

© Springer International Publishing Switzerland 2014
C.S. Calude et al. (Eds.): Gruska Festschrift, LNCS 8808, pp. 292–306, 2014.
DOI: 10.1007/978-3-319-13350-8_22

languages is the state complexity which is given as the number of states of a minimal deterministic automaton that accepts the given language. It is well-known that, for any natural number n, there is a regular language with state complexity n.

Other measures were defined for context-free languages but are also of interest for regular languages. Examples are the nonterminal and production complexity which were introduced by J. GRUSKA in [11] and [12]. Moreover, J. GRUSKA also proved that, for any natural number n, there is a regular language with nonterminal or production complexity n.

Therefore, the question arises which hierarchies are obtained if one restricts to regular languages with limited state, nonterminal, and production complexities. Results in this direction can be found in [1] for conditional grammars, in [9] for tree controlled grammars, and in [5], and [13] for contextual grammars.

The topic of this paper are conditional tabled Lindenmayer systems which were introduced in [16]. Here a table can only be applied to a sentential form if the form belongs to a regular set, which is associated with the table and is called its condition. In the extended case, such systems are very powerful; they can generate all recursively enumerable languages. If one restricts to special subregular families defined by combinatorial or algebraic properties, one gets almost the same hierachy as for the subregular families in the non-extended case, and e. g. further characterizations for the families of recursively enumerable languages, context-sensitive languages, matrix languages, and ET0L languages as shown in [7] and [8].

In this paper we study the power of conditional ET0L systems if the conditions are given by regular languages with a limited state or nonterminal complexity. We show that conditions obtained by regular grammars with two nonterminals and finite automata with three states are sufficient to generate all recursively enumerable languages. Similar results are given for the generation of all context-sensitive languages. Moreover, in the non-extended case, one gets infinite hierarchies for both complexity measures.

2 Preliminaries and Definitions

We assume that the reader is familiar with the basic concepts of the theory of formal languages and automata. In this section we only recall some notations and some definitions such that a reader can understand the results. We refer to [15] and [6].

For an alphabet V, i. e, V is a finite non-empty set, the sets of all words and of all non-empty words over V are denoted by V^* and V^+, respectively. The empty word is denoted by λ. For a word $w \in V^*$ and a letter $a \in V$, $|w|$ and $|w|_a$ denote the length of w and the number of occurrences of a in w, respectively.

By $\mathcal{L}(\text{CS})$ and $\mathcal{L}(\text{RE})$ we denote the families of all context-sensitive and recursively enumerable languages, respectively.

Let $\mathcal{A} = (X, Z, z_0, F, \delta)$ be a deterministic finite automaton (with the set X of input symbols, the set Z of states, the initial state z_0, the set F of accepting states, and the transition function δ). By $T(\mathcal{A})$ we denote the language accepted by $\mathcal{A}$. We define the state complexity $s(\mathcal{A})$ of $\mathcal{A}$ as the number of states of $\mathcal{A}$, i.e.,

$$s(\mathcal{A}) = \#(Z).$$

Let $G = (N, T, P, S)$ be a grammar (with the set N of nonterminals, the set T of terminals, the set P of rules or productions, and the start symbol S). We say that G is regular, if all rules of P have the form $A \to wB$ or $A \to w$ with $A, B \in N$ and $w \in T^*$.[1] The nonterminal complexity $n(G)$ of G is defined as the number of its nonterminals[2], i.e.,

$$v(G) = \#(N).$$

We recall the notion of a matrix grammar.

A *matrix grammar* is a quintuple $G = (N, T, M, S, Q)$ where
- N and T are disjunct alphabets of nonterminals and terminals,
- $M = \{m_1, m_2, \ldots, m_r\}$ is a finite set of finite sequences m_i of context-free rules, i.e.,

$$m_i = (A_{i,1} \to v_{i,1}, A_{i,2} \to v_{i,2}, \ldots A_{i,r_i} \to v_{i,r_i})$$

for $1 \le i \le r$ (the elements of M are called matrices),
- S is an element of N, and
- Q is a subset of the productions occurring in the matrices of M.

The application of a matrix m_i is defined as a sequential application of the rules of m_i in the given order where a rule of Q can be ignored if its left-hand side does not occur in the current sentential form, i.e., $x \Longrightarrow_{m_i} y$ holds iff there are words w_j, $1 \le j \le r_i + 1$ such that $x = w_1$, $y = w_{r_i+1}$ and, for $1 \le j \le r_i$,

$$w_j = x_j A_{i,j} y_j \text{ and } w_{j+1} = x_j v_{i,j} y_j \tag{1}$$

or

$$w_j = w_{j+1} \text{ and } A_{i,j} \text{ does not occur in } w_j \text{ and } A_{i,j} \to v_{i.j} \in Q. \tag{2}$$

The language $L(G)$ generated by G consists of all words $z \in T^+$ such that there is a derivation

$$S \Longrightarrow_{m_{i_1}} v_1 \Longrightarrow_{m_{i_2}} v_2 \Longrightarrow_{m_{i_3}} \cdots \Longrightarrow_{m_{i_t}} v_t = z$$

for some $t \ge 1$.

By $\mathcal{L}(\text{MAT})$ we denote the families of languages generated by matrix grammars. It is known that $\mathcal{L}(\text{MAT}) = \mathcal{L}(\text{RE})$.

We need the following normal form for matrix grammars.

---

[1] Sometimes such grammars are called right-linear, and then, for regularity, it is required that $w \in T \cup \{\lambda\}$.

[2] If regularity is defined by $w \in T \cup \{\lambda\}$, then state complexity and nonterminal complexity only differ by 1.

Lemma 1. *For any matrix grammar G, there is a matrix grammar $G' = (N \cup U \cup \{S\}, T, M, S, Q)$ such that all matrices of M have one of the following forms*

$$(S \to XA), \ (A \to w, \ X \to Y), \ (A \to w, \ X \to \lambda)$$

with $X, Y \in U$, $A \in N$, $w \in (N \cup T)^*$, the rules in Q are of the form $A \to w$ with $A \in N$ and $w \in (N \cup T)^*$, and $L(G') = L(G)$ holds.

Proof. We follow the proof of Lemma 1.2.3 in [6]. The only difference is that we start with rules $(S \to XA)$ instead of rules $(S \to AX)$.

Except the initial sentential form S and the finally generated terminal word, all intermediate sentential forms generated by a matrix G' of Lemma 1 start with a letter from U, and this letter is the only one from U in the word.

We now introduce central notion of this paper.

Definition 1. *An extended conditional tabled Lindenmayer system without interaction (ECT0L system, for short) is an $(n+3)$-tuple*

$$H = (V, T, \mathcal{P}, w),$$

where
- *V is an alphabet, T is a subset of V,*
- *$\mathcal{P}$ is a finite set of pairs (P, R), where*
    - *P is a finite set of rules $a \to v$ with $a \in V$ and $v \in V^*$ such that, for any $b \in V$, there is a word v_b with $b \to v_b \in P_i$, and*
    - *R is a regular language over V, and*
- *$w \in V^+$.*
  For $x \in V^+$ and $y \in V^*$, we say that x derives y in H, written as $x \Longrightarrow_H y$, if and only if there is a pair $(P, R) \in \mathcal{P}$ such that
- *$x = a_1 a_2 \ldots a_t$ with $a_i \in V$ for $1 \leq i \leq t$,*
- *$y = y_1 y_2 \ldots y_t$,*
- *$a_i \to y_i \in P$ for $1 \leq i \leq t$, and*
- *$x \in R$.*
  The language $L(H)$ generated by H is defined as

$$L(H) = \{z \mid z \in T^*, \ w \Longrightarrow_H^* z\}$$

where $\Longrightarrow_H^*$ is the reflexive and transitive closure of $\Longrightarrow_H$.

The sets P are called the tables of the system. By definition, in a ECT0L system, a regular set R is associated with any table P, and P is only applicable to a sentential form x, if x belongs to the associated language R. Therefore, R is called the condition of P.

It is required that, for any (P, R) and any $a \in V$, there is rule $a \to v_a$ in P. However, if we give an ECT0L system, we shall only mention the rules for letters a, for which a rule $a \to v_a$ with $v_a \neq a$ exists in P, i.e., if we mention no rule, then $a \to a$ is the only in P for a.

Let $H = (V, T, \{(P_1, R_1), (P_2, R_2), \ldots, (P_n, R_n)\}, w)$ be an ECT0L system. It is called a propagating (ECPT0L system, for short) if, for $1 \le i \le n$ and any $a \in V$, P_i does not contain the rule $a \to \lambda$. It is called a CT0L system if $V = T$. Furthermore, it is called an ET0L system if, for $1 \le i \le n$, $R_i = V^*$ (i. e., any table P_i can be apply at any moment). We can combine the restrictions; for instance, we can have propagating T0L system or (PT0L systems, for short).

Let

$$\mathcal{G} = \{ \text{ECT0L, ECPT0L, ET0L, EPT0L, CT0L, CPT0L, T0L, PT0L} \}.$$

For $X \in \mathcal{G}$, $\mathcal{L}(X)$ denotes the family of languages generated by X systems.

It is known that

$$\mathcal{L}(\text{EPT0L}) = \mathcal{L}(\text{ET0L}) \subset \mathcal{L}(\text{ECPT0L}) = \mathcal{L}(\text{CS})$$
$$\subset \mathcal{L}(\text{ECT0L}) = \mathcal{L}(\text{MAT}) = \mathcal{L}(\text{RE}). \qquad (3)$$

Example 1. We consider the ECT0L system

$$H = (V, \{a, b\}, \{(P_1, R_1), (P_2, R_2), (P_3, R_3), (P_4, R_4), (P_5, R_5)\}, SD)$$

with

$$V = \{S, A, B_1, B_2, C, D, a, b\},$$
$$(P_1, R_1) = (\{S \to ASC\}, V^*\{D\}),$$
$$(P_2, R_2) = (\{S \to AC, D \to \lambda\}, V^*\{D\}),$$
$$(P_3, R_3) = (\{A \to Ab, C \to B_1, C \to B_2\}, V^*\{C\}),$$
$$(P_4, R_4) = (\{B_1 \to \lambda, B_2 \to C\}, V^*\{B_1\}),$$
$$(P_3, R_3) = (\{A \to a\}, V^*\{b\}).$$

We start with SD, have to apply sometimes P_1 and then once P_2 (the only rules where the words in the associated language end with D). This yields $A^n C^m$. Now we have to apply P_3 and get $(Ab)^n z$ where z is a word of length n over $\{B_1, B_2\}$. If z ends with B_2, then the derivation cannot be continued. If B_1 is the last letter of z, we can only apply P_4 and obtain $(Ab)^n C^r$ with $r < n$ (since we cancel at least the last letter of z). This process can be iterated, in each step we add a letter b after each A, and cancel at least one C. Finally, we get $(Ab^m)^n$ with $m \ge n$ (m gives the number of iterations, for which $1 \le m \le n$ holds). Now, by the use of P_5 we get $(ab^m)^n$ with $n \ge 1$ and $1 \le m \le n$. Thus

$$L(H) = \{(ab^m)^n \mid 1 \le m \le n\}.$$

We note that it is well-known that $L(H)$ cannot be generated by an ET0L system.

For $X \in \mathcal{G}$, by $\mathcal{L}(X, s, n)$ we denote the family of all languages which can be generated by X systems $H = (V, T, \{(P_1, R_1), (P_2, R_2), \ldots, (P_n, R_n)\}, w)$, where

$R_i = T(\mathcal{A}_i)$ for some deterministic finite automaton $\mathcal{A}_i = (V, Z_i, z_{0i}, F_i, \delta_i)$ with $s(\mathcal{A}_i) \leq n$.

For $X \in \mathcal{G}$, by $\mathcal{L}(X, v, n)$ we denote the family of all languages which can be generated by X systems $H = (V, T, \{(P_1, R_1), (P_1, R_1), \ldots, (P_n, R_n)\}, w)$, where $R_i = L(G_i)$ for some regular grammar $G_i = (N_i, V, Q_i, S_i)$ with $v(G_i) \leq n$.

Because a set $V^*\{x\}$ with $x \in V$ can be accepted by the automaton

$$\mathcal{A} = (V, \{z_0, z_1\}, z_0, \{z_1\}, \delta)$$

with

$$\delta(z_0, x) = \delta(z_1, x) = z_1 \text{ and } \delta(z_0, a) = \delta(z_1, a) = z_0 \text{ for } a \in V \setminus \{x\}$$

and can be generated by the regular grammar

$$G = (\{S\}, V, \{S \to aS \mid a \in V\} \cup \{S \to x\}, S),$$

we see that the language of Example 1 is contained in $\mathcal{L}(\text{ECT0L}, s, 2)$ and in $\mathcal{L}(\text{ECT0L}, v, 1)$.

The following relations follow immediately from the definitions.

Lemma 2. *i) For all $X \in \{$ ECT0L, CT0L, ECPT0L, CPT0L $\}$, all $k \in \{s, v\}$, and all natural numbers $n \geq 1$,*

$$\mathcal{L}(X, k, n) \subseteq \mathcal{L}(X, k, n + 1).$$

The aim of this paper is a more detailed study of the hierarchies of Lemma 2.

3 Extended Conditional T0L Systems

We start with the investigation of ECT0L systems where the conditions are defined by a bounded number of nonterminals. First, we show that conditions which can be generated by regular grammars with two nonterminals are sufficient to generate all recursively enumerable languages.

Lemma 3. $\mathcal{L}(\text{RE}) = \mathcal{L}(\text{ECT0L}, v, 2)$.

Proof. By (3), it is sufficient to prove that any recursively enumerable language L can be generated by an ECT0L system with conditions which can be accepted by automata with at most two nonterminals.

Let $L \in \mathcal{L}(\text{RE})$. Then there is a grammar $G = (N, T, P, S)$ in Kuroda normal form generating L, i.e., any rule of P has one of the following forms: $A \to B$, $A \to BC$, $AB \to CD$, $A \to a$ or $A \to \lambda$ with $A, B, C, D \in N$ and $a \in T$.

Let $N' = \{A' \mid A \in N\} \cup \{A'' \mid A \in N\}$ such that $N' \cap (N \cup T) = \emptyset$ and $V = N \cup N' \cup T$. We now consider the ECT0L system $H = (N \cup N' \cup T, T, \mathcal{P}, S)$ where $\mathcal{P}$ consist of the pairs constructed as follows:

$$(P_1, R_1) = (\{A \to A \mid A \in N\} \cup \{A \to A' \mid A \in N\} \cup \{A \to A'' \mid A \in N\}, V^*)$$

(some symbols of N are replaced by a primed version),

$$(P_{A\to w}, R_{A\to w}) = (\{A' \to w\}, (N \cup T)^*\{A'\}(N \cup T)^*) \text{ for } A \to w \in P$$

(the only existing primed letter in the word is replaced by w, all other letters are not changed)

$$(P_{AB\to CD}, R_{AB\to CD}) = (\{A' \to C, B'' \to D\}, (N \cup T)^*\{A'B''\}(N \cup T)^*)$$
$$\text{for } AB \to CD \in P$$

(if the word contains the subword $A'B''$ and all its other letters belong to N or T, then $A'B''$ is replaced by CD).

If a sentential form contains at least two occurrences of letters of N' which do not form a subword $A'B''$, then we are not able to decrease the number of occurrences of letters of N' (but we can increase it by using (P_1, R_1)), i.e., we cannot terminate the derivation. Thus to a word in $(N \cup T)^*$ we can only apply (P_1, R_1) producing exactly one primed letter A' or exactly two primed letters which form a subword $A'B''$ (otherwise we cannot terminate) and then we apply some $(P_{A\to w}, R_{A\to w})$ or $(P_{AB\to CD}, R_{AB\to CD})$, respectively. We obtain a word over $(N \cup T)^*$, again. It is easy to see that this simulates an application of $A \to w$ or $AB \to CD$ in G. Obviously, any application of a rule in G can be simulated. Therefore, $L(H) = L(G)$.

Since R_1, $R_{A\to w}$, and $R_{AB\to CD}$ can be generated by regular grammars with the production sets $\{S_1 \to aS_1 \mid a \in V\} \cup \{S_1 \to \lambda\}$,
$\{S_1 \to aS_1 \mid a \in N \cup T\} \cup \{S_1 \to A'S_2\} \cup \{S_2 \to aS_2 \mid a \in N \cup T\} \cup \{S_2 \to \lambda\}$,
$\{S_1 \to aS_1 \mid a \in N \cup T\} \cup \{S_1 \to A'B''S_2\} \cup \{S_2 \to aS_2 \mid a \in N \cup T\} \cup \{S_2 \to \lambda\}$,
respectively, where S_1 and S_2 are the nonterminals. Therefore, two nonterminals are sufficient.   □

Since the Kuroda normal form for context-sensitive grammars differs from that for general phrase structure grammars only by omitting $A \to \lambda$, we obtain the following statement by repeating the proof.

Lemma 4. $\mathcal{L}(\text{CS}) = \mathcal{L}(\text{ECPT0L}, v, 2)$.   □

We now turn to ECT0L systems where the conditions are defined by a bounded number of states.

We start with a simple lemma showing that conditional systems with conditions which can be accepted by automata with only one state generate only ET0L languages.

Lemma 5. $\mathcal{L}(\text{ECT0L}, s, 1) = \mathcal{L}(\text{ECPT0L}, s, 1) = \mathcal{L}(\text{ET0L})$.

Proof. Let $L \in \mathcal{L}(\text{ECT0L}, s, 1)$. Then L is generated by a ECT0L system H where all conditions can be accepted by automata with one state. Obviously, if an automaton $\mathcal{A}$ has only one state, then $T(\mathcal{A}) = V^*$ or $T(\mathcal{A}) = \emptyset$. Therefore, $H = (V, T, \{(P_1, V^*), (P_2, V^*), \ldots, (P_n, V^*)\}, w)$. Thus H is an ET0L system and $\mathcal{L}(\text{ECT0L}, s, 1) \subseteq \mathcal{L}(\text{ET0L})$ follows.

The converse inclusion follows by analogous arguments.

Moreover, we can repeat the proof to obtain $\mathcal{L}(\text{ECPT0L}, s, 1) = \mathcal{L}(\text{EPT0L})$. Now the statement follows by $\mathcal{L}(\text{ET0L}) = \mathcal{L}(\text{EPT0L})$. □

We mention that such a statement does not hold for nonterminal complexity. By the same arguments, we have $\mathcal{L}(\text{ET0L}) \subseteq \mathcal{L}(\text{ECT0L}, v, 1)$ and $\mathcal{L}(\text{EPT0L}) \subseteq \mathcal{L}(\text{ECPT0L}, v, 1)$, but the first inclusion is proper by Example 1.

We now show that conditions acceptable with four states are sufficient to generate all context-sensitive languages in the propagating case.

Lemma 6. $\mathcal{L}(\text{CS}) = \mathcal{L}(\text{ECPT0L}, s, 4)$.

Proof. We repeat again the proof of Lemma 3 (without rules $A \to \lambda$). However, for $R_{AB \to CD}$, we need an automaton with four states. More precisely, $R_{AB \to CD}$ is accepted by the finite automaton $\mathcal{A} = (V, \{z_0, z_1, z_2, z_3\}, z_0, \{z_2\}, \delta)$ with

$$\delta(z_0, A') = z_1, \ \delta(z_0, x) = z_0 \text{ for } x \in N \cup T, \ \delta(z_0, y) = z_3 \text{ for } y \in N' \setminus \{A'\},$$
$$\delta(z_1, B'') = z_2, \ \delta(z_1, x) = z_3 \text{ for } x \in V \setminus \{B''\},$$
$$\delta(z_2, x) = z_2 \text{ for } x \in N \cup T, \ \delta(z_2, y) = z_3 \text{ for } y \in N',$$
$$\delta(z_3, x) = z_3 \text{ for } x \in V.$$

By an analogous automaton one can show that $R_{A \to w}$ can be accepted by an automaton with three states, and obviously R_1 can be accepted by an automaton with one state. □

If erasing rules $A \to \lambda$ are allowed we can improve the result.

Lemma 7. $\mathcal{L}(\text{RE}) = \mathcal{L}(\text{ECT0L}, s, 3)$.

Proof. By (3), it is sufficient to prove that any recursively enumerable language L can be generated by an ECT0L system with conditions which can be accepted by automata with at most three states.

Let L be a recursively enumerable language. By (3), there is a matrix grammar $G = (N \cup U \cup \{S, F\}, T, M, S, Q)$ in the normal form of Lemma 1 such that $L(G) = L$.

Let $N' = \{A' \mid A \in N\}$ and $V = N \cup N' \cup U \cup \{S\}$. We now construct the ECT0L system $H = (V, T, \mathcal{P}, S)$ where the pairs of $\mathcal{P}$ are determined as follows:

$$(\{S \to XA\}, V^*) \text{ for } (S \to XA) \in M$$

(in the first derivation step we do the same replacement as in G),

$$(\{A \to A \mid A \in N\} \cup \{A \to A' \mid A \in N\}, V^*),$$
$$(\{A' \to w, X \to Y\}, \{X\}(N \cup T)^*\{A'\}(N \cup T)^*) \text{ for } (A \to w, X \to Y) \in M$$

(first we replace some symbols of N by its primed version; we cannot decrease the number of occurrences of letters of N' and thus not terminate, if at least two symbols of N' are generated; if only one A' occurs, we can replace it by w and the only letter of X of U is replaced by Y, i.e., an application of $(A \to w, X \to Y)$ is simulated, where both rules are applied according (1)),

$(\{A \to F, X \to Y\}, (N \cup U \cup T)^*)$ for $(A \to w, X \to Y) \in M$, $A \to w \in Q$

(we only change a letter of U, if A is not present in the word, which is a simulation of an application of $(A \to w, X \to Y)$ where the first rule is used according to (2) and the second rule according to (1); and we introduce F, if A is present, and then we cannot replace F, i.e., we cannot terminate). By the explanations given in brackets, it is clear that we simulate exactly the matrix applications in G. Thus $L(H) = L(G) = L$ follow.

Again, V^* can be accepted by an automaton with one state. The condition $(N \cup U \cup T)^*$ is accepted by $\mathcal{A} = (V, \{z_0, z_1\}, z_0, \{z_0\}, \delta)$ with

$$\delta(z_0, x) = z_0 \text{ for } x \in N \cup U \cup T, \quad \delta(z_0, y) = z_1 \text{ for } y \in N', \quad \delta(z_1, v) = z_1 \text{ for } v \in V.$$

To handle $(\{A' \to w, X \to Y\}, \{X\}(N \cup T)^*\{A'\}(N \cup T)^*)$ we consider the automaton

$$\mathcal{A}' = (V, \{q_0, q_1, q_2\}, q_0, \{q_2\}, \delta')$$

with

$$\delta(z_0, B) = z_1, \quad \delta(z_0, x) = z_0 \text{ for } x \in V \setminus \{B\},$$
$$\delta(z_1, A') = z_2, \quad \delta(z_1, x) = z_1 \text{ for } x \in N \cup T, \quad \delta(z_1, y) = z_0 \text{ for } y \in B \cup N',$$
$$\delta(z_2, x) = z_2 \text{ for } x \in N \cup T, \quad \delta(z_2, y) = z_0 \text{ for } y \in B \cup N'.$$

Since any sentential form of G contains only one letter of U, this letter is its first letter, and any sentential form of H only differs from those of G by priming some letters, a sentential form of H is accepted by $\mathcal{A}'$ if and only if it has the form $X w_1 A' w_2$ with $X \in U$, $w_1, w_2 \in (N \cup T)^*$, and $A' \in N'$. (We note that $\mathcal{A}'$ accepts words which cannot occur as sentential forms and, thus, are not of interest.) Because the conditions have to hold only for sentential forms, we can use the pair $(\{A' \to w, X \to Y\}, T(\mathcal{A}'))$ instead of $(\{A' \to w, X \to Y\}, \{X\}(N \cup T)^*\{A'\}(N \cup T)^*)$ without changing the set of words generated by H.

Therefore three states are sufficient.   □

We now summarize our result in the following statement.

Theorem 1. *For any $n \geq 2$, $m \geq 3$ and $k \geq 4$,*

$$\mathcal{L}(\mathrm{ET0L}) \subset \mathcal{L}(\mathrm{ECT0L}, v, 1) \subseteq \mathcal{L}(\mathrm{ECT0L}, v, n) = \mathcal{L}(\mathrm{RE}),$$
$$\mathcal{L}(\mathrm{ET0L}) \subseteq \mathcal{L}(\mathrm{ECPT0L}, v, 1) \subseteq \mathcal{L}(\mathrm{ECT0L}, v, 2) = \mathcal{L}(\mathrm{CS}),$$
$$\mathcal{L}(\mathrm{ET0L}) = \mathcal{L}(\mathrm{ECT0L}, s, 1) \subseteq \mathcal{L}(\mathrm{ECT0L}, s, 2) \subseteq \mathcal{L}(\mathrm{ECT0L}, s, m) = \mathcal{L}(\mathrm{RE}),$$
$$\mathcal{L}(\mathrm{ET0L}) = \mathcal{L}(\mathrm{ECPT0L}, s, 1) \subseteq \mathcal{L}(\mathrm{ECT0L}, s, 2) \subseteq \mathcal{L}(\mathrm{ECT0L}, s, 3)$$
$$\subseteq \mathcal{L}(\mathrm{ECT0L}, s, k) = \mathcal{L}(\mathrm{CS}).$$

It is open whether our bounds are optimal, i.e., we do not know whether some of the inclusion given in Theorem 1 are strict.

4   Non-Extended Conditional T0L Systems

We start with the estimation of number of states necessary for a special language.

Lemma 8. *For $n \geq 4$, let*

$$L_n = \{a^3ccb^3, d^nccb^n\} \cup \{a^mxb^m \mid m \geq 3, x \in \{acac, accb, cbac, cbcb\}\}.$$

i) *For $n \geq 4$, $L_n \in \mathcal{L}(\text{CPT0L}, s, n+4)$.*
ii) *For any prime number $p \geq 5$, $L_p \notin \mathcal{L}(\text{CT0L}, s, p)$*

Proof. i) The language L_n is generated by the CPT0L system

$$H_n = (\{a, b, c, d\}, \ \{a, b, c, d\}, \ \mathcal{P}_n, \ a^3ccb^3)$$

with

$$\mathcal{P}_n = \{((\{c \to ac, c \to cb\}, \{a\}^*\{cc\}\{b\}^*), (\{a \to d\}, \{a^ncc\}\{b\}^*).$$

Since $\{a\}^*\{cc\}\{b\}^*$ and $\{a^ncc\}\{b\}^*$ are accepted by the automata

$$\mathcal{A}_1 = (\{a, b, c, d\}, \{z_0, z_1, z_2, z_3\}, z_0, \{z_2\}, \delta_1)$$

with

$$\delta_1(z_0, a) = z_0, \ \delta_1(z_0, c) = z_1, \ \delta_1(z_0, b) = \delta_1(z_0, d) = z_3,$$
$$\delta_1(z_1, c) = z_2, \ \delta_1(z_1, a) = \delta_1(z_1, b) = \delta_1(z_1, d) = z_3,$$
$$\delta_1(z_2, b) = z_2, \ \delta_1(z_2, a) = \delta_1(z_2, c) = \delta_1(z_2, d) = z_3,$$
$$\delta_1(z_3, x) = z_3 \text{ for } x \in \{a, b, c, d\}$$

and

$$\mathcal{A}_2 = (\{a, b, c, d\}, \{z_0, z_1, \ldots, z_{n+3}\}, z_0, \{z_{n+2}\}, \delta_2)$$

with

$$\delta_2(z_i, a) = z_{i+1}, \ \delta_2(z_i, b) = \delta_2(z_i, c) = \delta_2(z_i, d) = z_{n+3} \text{ for } 0 \leq i \leq n-1,$$
$$\delta_2(z_j, c) = z_{j+1}, \ \delta_2(z_j, a) = \delta_2(z_j, b) = \delta_2(z_j, d) = z_{n+3} \text{ for } n \leq j \leq n+1,$$
$$\delta_2(z_{n+2}, b) = z_{n+2}, \ \delta_2(z_{n+2}, a) = \delta_2(z_{n+2}, c) = \delta_2(z_{n+2}, d) = z_{n+3},$$
$$\delta_2(z_{n+3}, x) = z_{n+3} \text{ for } x \in \{a, b, c, d\},$$

respectively, $n + 4$ states are sufficient, which proves $L_n \in \mathcal{L}(\text{CPT0L}, s, n+4)$.

ii) We assume that there is a CT0L system $H = (\{a, b, c, d\}, \{a, b, c, d\}, \mathcal{P}, w)$ where, for all (P, R) in $\mathcal{P}$, R is accepted by a finite automaton with at most p states, which generates L_p. We first discuss possible derivations in H. Assume that there is a derivation $a^mxb^m \Longrightarrow a^nyb^n$ for some $m \geq 3$, $n \geq 3$, and $x, y \in \{acac, accb, cbac, cbcb\}$ by the application of some table P with the associated condition R (this means $(P, R) \in \mathcal{P}$). Let $a \to v_a$ be a rule in P. Then v_a cannot contain c. Otherwise, we can produce a word z with at least three occurrences of c (because $m \geq 3$). Then $z \in L(H) = L_p$, but $z \notin L_p$ by the definition of L_p, which is a contradiction. If v_a starts with b, we can derive a word in $L(H)$ which starts with b, which is impossible. If v_a contains a b and starts with a, then we can generate in H a word with three occurrences of the subword ab which is impossible, too. Hence we have $v_a \in \{a\}^*$. Analogously, we can prove that $v_b \in \{b\}^*$ for $b \to v_b \in P$. Thus the two occurrences of c in $a^n y b^n$ are derived from the two occurrences of c in $a^m x b^m$. Hence $c \to v_c \in P$ implies $|v_c|_c = 1$ (if $|v_c|_c = 0$ or $|v_c|_c \geq 2$, we can derive a word in $L(H)$ which contains no c or at least four cs which is impossible by $L(H) = L_p$). If $v_a = \lambda$, then the first c in $a^m x b^m$ has to produce at least three occurrences of a. Applying this rule to both occurrences of c we get a word with three occurrences of a between the two cs which is impossible again. This gives $v_a \in \{a\}^+$, and analogously, we also get $v_b \in \{b\}^+$. Hence P is propagating.

Similarly, we can prove that a pair (P, R) which allows a derivation $d^p ccb^p \Longrightarrow a^m y b^m$ has a propagating table P.

Thus $w = a^3 ccb^3$ since it is the shortest word in L_p.

Hence $d^p ccb^p$ has to be generated from some word $a^m x b^m$ using some pair (P, R). As above we get $u_a \in \{d\}^+$, $u_b \in \{b\}^+$, and $|u_c|_c = 1$ for any $a \to u_a$, $b \to u_b$, $c \to u_c \in P$. If $x \in \{acac, cbac, cbcb\}$ or v_c contains a letter d and/or a letter b, then we can derive a word with an occurrence of d or b between the two occurrences of c and at least one occurrence of d (coming from an a), which is impossible. Thus we get $v_c = c$ and $x = cc$. Now assume P contains two rules $a \to d^r$ and $a \to d^s$ for a. Then $r, s \geq 1$ by our above considerations. Let us assume that $a^m ccb^m \Longrightarrow d^p ccb^p$ is obtained by replacing the first a by d^r, i.e., $d^p ccb^p = d^r d^{p-r} ccb^p$. We now use $a \to d^s$ for the first a and do not change the applied rule for all other letters. Then we get $d^s d^{p-r} ccb^p$ which is not in L_p since $p + s - r \neq p$. This shows that there is only one rule for a and, similarly to prove, there is only one rule for b. Let $a \to d^r$ and $b \to b^s$ be these two rules. Then $a^m ccb^m \Longrightarrow (d^r)^m cc(b^s)^m$. Because $d^p ccb^p$ is the only word in L_p containing d, we get $mr = ms = p$. Because $m \geq 3$ and p is a prime number, $m = p$ and $r = s = 1$. Therefore we get $a^p ccb^p \in R$.

Let $\mathcal{A} = (\{a, b, c, d\}, Z, z_0, F, \delta)$ be an automaton accepting R with at most p states. Let

$$z_i = \delta(z_0, a^i) \text{ for } 1 \leq i \leq p \text{ and } q_i = \delta(z_0, a^p ccb^i) \text{ for } 0 \leq i \leq p.$$

Then there are indexes $e, f, g, h \in \{0, 1, 2, \ldots, p\}$ such that $e < f$, $z_e = z_f$ and $g < h$, $q_g = q_h$. Therefore $\delta(z_e, a^{f-e}) = z_f = z_e$ and $\delta(z_g, b^{h-g}) = z_h = z_g$. Now it follows that

$$\delta(z_0, a^p ccb^p) = \delta(z_0, a^e a^{f-e} a^{p-f} ccb^g b^{h-g} b^{p-h})$$
$$= \delta(z_0, a^e (a^{f-e})^{h-g+1} a^{p-f} ccb^g (b^{h-g})^{f-e+1} b^{p-h})$$
$$= \delta(z_0, a^{p+(f-e)(h-g)} ccb^{p+(f-e)(h-g)}).$$

Hence $a^{p+(f-e)(h-g)} ccb^{p+(f-e)(h-g)}$ is in R as well as in L_p. Thus we can apply P to $a^{p+(f-e)(h-g)} ccb^{p+(f-e)(h-g)}$ which results in $d^{p+(f-e)(h-g)} ccb^{p+(f-e)(h-g)}$, which is not in L_p.

This contradiction shows that our assumption is false and $L_p \notin \mathcal{L}(\text{CT0L}, s, p)$ holds. $\qquad\qquad\qquad\qquad\qquad\qquad\qquad\qquad\qquad\qquad\qquad\qquad\qquad\qquad\qquad\square$

From this lemma we get immediately the following statement.

Theorem 2. *Let $p_1, p_2, \ldots, p_n, \ldots$ be an infinite sequence of prime numbers such that $p_{i+1} - p_i \geq 4$ for $i \geq 1$. Then*

$$\mathcal{L}(\text{CT0L}), s, p_i + 4 \subset \mathcal{L}(\text{CT0L}), s, p_{i+1} + 4$$

and

$$\mathcal{L}(\text{CPT0L}), s, p_i + 4 \subset \mathcal{L}(\text{CPT0L}), s, p_{i+1} + 4.$$

By Theorem 2 we obtain an infinite hierarchy with respect to the state complexity, but it remains open whether $\mathcal{L}(\text{CPT0L}), s, n \subset \mathcal{L}(\text{CPT0L}), s, n + 1$ for $n \geq 1$.

We now prove an analogous result for the nonterminal complexity.

Lemma 9. *For $n \geq 2$ and a letters $x_1, x_2, \ldots, x_n, x_1' x_2', \ldots, x_n', c$, let*

$$L_n' = \{x_1^3 x_2^3 \ldots x_n^3 ccb^3\} \cup \{x_1^3 x_2^3 \ldots x_n^3 x_{i_1} x_{i_2} \ldots x_{i_k} xb^{k+3} \mid$$
$$k \geq 0, x \in \{cbcb\} \cup \bigcup_{1 \leq i \leq n} \{x_i cx_i c, x_i ccb, cbx_i c\}\}$$
$$\cup \{\{(x_1')^3 (x_2')^3 \ldots (x_n')^3 (x_1')^{k_1} (x_2')^{k_2} \ldots (x_n')^{k_n} ccb^{3+k_1+k_2+\cdots+k_n} \mid$$
$$k_i \geq 3 \text{ for } 1 \leq i \leq n\}.$$

Then

i) $L_n' \in \mathcal{L}(\text{CPT0L}, v, n + 2)$.
ii) $L_n' \notin \mathcal{L}(\text{CT0L}, v, n - 1)$

Proof. i) Let $V = \{x_1, x_2, \ldots, x_n, x_1' x_2', \ldots, x_n', c, b\}$. The CPT0L system

$$H_n' = (V, V, \mathcal{P}_n', x_1^3 x_2^3 \ldots x_n^3 ccb^3)$$

with

$$\mathcal{P}_n' = \{(\{c \to x_i c, c \to cb\}, \{x_1, x_2, \ldots, x_n\}^* \{cc\} \{b\}^*) \mid 1 \leq i \leq n\}),$$
$$(\{x_i \to x_i' \mid 1 \leq i \leq n\},$$
$$\{x_1^3 x_2^3 \ldots x_n^3 x_1^{k_1} x_2^{k_2} \ldots x_n^{k_n} cc \mid k_i \geq 3 \text{ for } 1 \leq i \leq n\} \{b^3\} \{b\}^*)$$

generates L_n'.

Since the two conditions can be generated by the regular grammars

$$G_1 = (\{S, B\}, V, \{S \to x_i S \mid 1 \leq i \leq n\} \cup \{S \to ccB, B \to bB, B \to \lambda\}, S)$$

and

$$G_2 = (\{S, A_1, A_2, \ldots A_n, B\}, V, P, S))$$

with

$$P = \{S \to x_1^3 x_2^3 \ldots x_n^3 A_1\} \cup \{A_i \to x_i A_i, A_i \to x_i^3 A_{i+1} \mid 1 \leq i \leq n-1\}$$
$$\cup \{A_n \to x_n A_n, A_n \to x_n^3 ccB, B \to bB, B \to b^3\}.$$

Thus $n+2$ nonterminals are sufficient, which proves $L_n' \in \mathcal{L}(\text{CPT0L}, v, n+2)$.

ii) Let us assume that $H = (V, V, \mathcal{P}, w)$ is a CT0L system which generates L_n' and all its conditions can be generated by regular grammars with at most $n-1$ nonterminals.

By similar arguments as used in the proof of Lemma 8 we can show that any table which can be used is propagating. Thus $w = x_1^3 x_2^3 \ldots x_n^3 ccb^3$. Therefore, any word $z = (x_1')^3 (x_2')^3 \ldots (x_n')^3 (x_1')^{k_1} (x_2')^{k_2} \ldots (x_n')^{k_n} ccb^{3+k_1+k_2+\cdots+k_n}$ has to be derived from some word z' in L_n' which differs from z. Let us assume that

$$z' = (x_1')^3 (x_2')^3 \ldots (x_n')^3 (x_1')^{t_1} (x_2')^{t_2} \ldots (x_n')^{t_n} ccb^{3+t_1+t_2+\cdots+t_n} \Longrightarrow z$$

holds by some pair (P, R). Again, similar to the proof of Lemma 8, we can show that

$$P = \{c \to c, b \to b\} \cup \{x_i' \to x_i' \mid 1 \leq i \leq n\}.$$

This contradicts $z' \neq z$. Therefore

$$z' = x_1^3 x_2^3 \ldots x_n^3 x_1^{t_1} x_2^{t_2} \ldots x_n^{t_n} xb^{3+t_1+t_2+\cdots+t_n}$$

with $x = cc$ or $x = c_i x c_i x$ or $x = x_i ccb$ or $x = cb x_i c$ for some i, $1 \leq i \leq n$. In the three latter cases, we can prove that $x_i \to x_i' \in P$ for $1 \leq i \leq n$ and $b \to b \in P$, and we can produce a word q containing some primed letter and a letter between the occurrences of c, which is not in $L_n' = L(H)$. Therefore the former case holds for z' and we can show that

$$P = \{c \to c, b \to b\} \cup \{x_i \to x_i' \mid 1 \leq i \leq n\}.$$

Now it follows that $t_i = k_i$ for $1 \leq i \leq n$.

Let $R_1, R_2, \ldots, R_n$ be the regular sets such that $(P, R_i) \in \mathcal{P}$. Moreover, for $1 \leq i \leq n$, let $G_i = (V_i, V, P_i, S_i)$ be a regular grammar which generates R_i with at most $n-1$ nonterminals. Let

$$r = \max\{|v| \mid A \to v \in P_i, 1 \leq i \leq n\}$$

and $s \geq 2r$.

We consider the word $u' = (x_1')^3 (x_2')^3 \ldots (x_n')^3 (x_1')^s (x_2')^s \ldots (x_n')^s ccb^{3+ns}$ which is generated from $u = x_1^3 x_2^3 \ldots x_n^3 x_1^s x_2^s \ldots x_n^s ccb^{3+ns}$ by some (P, R_i). Then $u \in R$ and it has a derivation

$$S \Longrightarrow^* x_1^3 x_2^3 \ldots x_n^3 x_1^{s_1} A_1$$
$$\Longrightarrow^* x_1^3 x_2^3 \ldots x_n^3 x_1^s x_2^{s_2} A_2$$
$$\Longrightarrow^* x_1^3 x_2^3 \ldots x_n^3 x_1^s x_2^s x_3^{s_3} A_3$$

$$\Longrightarrow^* \dots$$
$$\Longrightarrow^* x_1^3 x_2^3 \dots x_n^3 x_1^s x_2^s \dots x_{n-1}^s x_n^{s_n} A_n$$
$$\Longrightarrow^* x_1^3 x_2^3 \dots x_n^3 x_1^s x_2^s \dots x_{n-1}^s x_n^s ccb^{r_1} B_1$$
$$\Longrightarrow^* x_1^3 x_2^3 \dots x_n^3 x_1^s x_2^s \dots x_{n-1}^s x_n^s ccb^{r_2} B_2$$
$$\Longrightarrow^* \dots$$
$$\Longrightarrow^* x_1^3 x_2^3 \dots x_n^3 x_1^s x_2^s \dots x_{n-1}^s x_n^s ccb^{r_n} B_n$$
$$\Longrightarrow^* x_1^3 x_2^3 \dots x_n^3 x_1^s x_2^s \dots x_{n-1}^s x_n^s ccb^{3+sn}$$

with $1 \leq s_i \leq r$ for $1 \leq i \leq n$ and $r_{j+1} - r_j > r$ for $1 \leq j \leq n-1$. Since the R_i has at most $n-1$ nonterminals, we get that there are indices $e, f, g, h \in \{1, 2, \dots, n\}$ such that $e < f$ and $A_e = A_f$ and $g < h$ and $B_g = B_h$. Thus there are derivations

$$A_e \Longrightarrow^* x_e^t x_{e+1}^s \dots x_{f-1}^s x_f^{s_f} A_f = x_e^t x_{e+1}^s \dots x_{f-1}^s x_f^{s_f} A_e, \quad B_g \Longrightarrow^* b^{t'} B_h = b^{t'} B_g \tag{4}$$

with $t, t' \geq 1$. Let $t'' = t + s(f - e - 1) + s_f$. If we now perform the two derivations (4) $t' + 1$ and $t'' + 1$ times, respectively, we obtain

$$x_1^3 x_2^3 \dots x_n^3 x_1^s x_2^s \dots x_e^{s_e} (x_e^t x_{e+1}^s \dots x_{f-1}^s x_f^{s_f})^{t'} x_f^{s-s_f} x_{f+1}^s \dots x_{n-1}^s x_n^s ccb^{3+sn+t't''},$$

which is R_i as well as in L_n'. Thus we can apply R and get a word not in L_n'. This contradiction shows that $n-1$ nonterminals are not sufficient.

Theorem 3. *Let $n_1, n_2, \dots, n_m, \dots$ be an infinite sequence of numbers such that $n_{i+1} - n_i \geq 3$ for $i \geq 1$. Then*

$$\mathcal{L}(\mathrm{CT0L}), v, n_i \subset \mathcal{L}(\mathrm{CT0L}), v, n_{i+1}$$

and

$$\mathcal{L}(\mathrm{CPT0L}), v, n_i \subset \mathcal{L}(\mathrm{CPT0L}), v, n_{i+1}.$$

We mention that it is open whether $\mathcal{L}(\mathrm{CPT0L}), v, n \subset \mathcal{L}(\mathrm{CPT0L}), v, n + 1$ holds for $n \geq 1$.

For nonterminal complexity, we get a strict increase of the power if we increase the complexity by 3. In contrast, for state complexity, sometimes, an increase by a large number is necessary to get a strict increase of the power. Moreover, in the case of nonterminal complexity, we use alphabets with unlimited number of letters, whereas for state complexity four letters were sufficient.

References

1. Dassow, J.: Conditional grammars with restrictions by syntactic parameters. In: Ito, M., Păun, Gh, Yu, Sh (eds.) Words, Semigroups, Transductions, pp. 59–68. World Scientific, Singapore (2001)
2. Dassow, J.: Contextual grammars with subregular choice. Fundamenta Informaticae **64**, 109–118 (2005)

3. Dassow, J.: Grammars with commutative, circular, and locally testable conditions. In: Automata, Formal Languages, and Related Topics - Dedicated to Ferenc Gécseg on the occasion of his 70th birthday, University of Szeged, 27–37 (2009)

4. Dassow, J., Hornig, H.: Conditional grammars with subregular conditions. In: Proc. Internat. Conf. Words, Languages and Combinatorics II, World Scientific Singapore, 71–86 (1994)

5. Dassow, J., Manea, F., Truthe, B.: On external contextual grammars with subregular selection languages. Theoretical Computer Science **449**, 64–73 (2012)

6. Dassow, J., Păun, G.: Regulated Rrewriting in Formal Language Theory. Springer-Verlag, Berlin (1989)

7. Dassow, J.: Rudolf, St.: Conditional Lindenmayer systems with subregular conditions: the non-extended case. RAIRO -. Theor. Inf. Appl. **48**, 127–147 (2014)

8. Dassow, J., Rudolf, St.: Conditional Lindenmayer systems with subregular conditions: the extended case. Submitted

9. Dassow, J., Stiebe, R., Truthe, B.: Two collapsing hierarchies of subregularly tree controlled languages. Theoretical Computer Science **410**, 3261–3271 (2009)

10. Dassow, J., Stiebe, R., Truthe, B.: Generative capacity of subregularly tree controlled grammars. International Journal of Foundations of Computer Science **21**, 723–740 (2010)

11. Gruska, J.: On a classification of context-free languages. Kybernetika **1**, 22–29 (1967)

12. Gruska, J.: Some classifications of context-free languages. Information and Control **14**, 152–179 (1969)

13. Manea, F., Truthe, B.: On internal contextual grammars with subregular selection languages. In: Kutrib, M., Moreira, N., Reis, R. (eds.) DCFS 2012. LNCS, vol. 7386, pp. 222–235. Springer, Heidelberg (2012)

14. Păun, G.: Marcus Contextual Grammars. Kluwer Publ. House, Doordrecht (1998)

15. Rozenberg, G., Salomaa, A.: Handbook of Formal Languages. Springer-Verlag, Berlin (1997)

16. Rozenberg, G., von Solms, S.H.: Priorities on context conditions in rewriting systems. Inform. Sci. **14**, 15–51 (1978)

Symmetries and Dualities in Name-Passing Process Calculi

Daniel Hirschkoff[1]([✉]), Jean-Marie Madiot[1], and Davide Sangiorgi[2]

[1] ENS Lyon, Université de Lyon CNRS, INRIA, Lyon, France
Daniel.Hirschkoff@ens-lyon.fr
[2] INRIA/Università di Bologna, Bologna, Italy

Abstract. We study symmetries and duality between input and output in the π-calculus. We show that in dualisable versions of π, including π and fusions, duality breaks with the addition of ordinary input/output types. We illustrate two proposals of calculi that overcome these problems. One approach is based on a modification of fusion calculi in which the name equivalences produced by fusions are replaced by name preorders, and with a distinction between positive and negative occurrences of names. The resulting calculus allows us to import subtype systems, and related results, from the pi-calculus. The second approach consists in taking the minimal symmetrical conservative extension of π with input/output types.

1 Introduction

Process calculi are algebraic models employed for understanding systems of processes: linguistic constructs for concurrency, as well as techniques for reasoning about the behaviour of processes. The π-calculus [15] (sometimes simply called π below) is one of the most studied process calculi. In particular, it is the paradigmatical *name-passing* calculus, that is, a calculus where names (a synonymous for "channels") may be passed around. Key aspects for the success of the π-calculus are the minimality of its syntax — its grammar is made of a handful of operators — and its expressiveness — it can model a variety of entities, such as protocols for distributed systems, functions, objects, and so on.

It is common in mathematics to look for symmetries and dualities; dualities may reveal underlying structure and lead to simpler theories. In turn, dualities can be used to relate different mathematical entities. This paper is a summary of work on the π-calculus aimed at studying symmetries and dualities in the π-calculus, particularly those arising in connection with type systems.

In the π-calculus, computation, or reduction, is interaction. This is achieved when an input and an output on the same name meet. If the name is a, then the output, $\bar{a}c.P$, emits a name c along a; in the matching input $a(x).Q$, name x is bound: it is a placeholder for the object c that is received. The input prefix both sequentialises a behaviour *and* binds a name. Correspondingly, in an interaction two processes are synchronised and, simultaneously, a substitution is performed. The π-calculus features another binder, the restriction operator. These operators, together with parallel composition, are the main operators of the calculus.

© Springer International Publishing Switzerland 2014
C.S. Calude et al. (Eds.): Gruska Festschrift, LNCS 8808, pp. 307–322, 2014.
DOI: 10.1007/978-3-319-13350-8_23

Reasoning about processes usually involves proving behavioural equivalences. In the case of the π-calculus, there is a well-established theory of equivalences and proof techniques. In some cases, it is necessary to work in a *typed* setting. Types allow one to express constraints about the observations available to the context when comparing two processes. Indeed, in practice the π-calculus is hardly ever used untyped: a π programmer has always an intended discipline for the use of names in mind; making such discipline explicit by means of types may allow one to validate important behavioural properties which would otherwise fail.

For a simple example, consider a process P that implements two services, for computing the factorial and the exponentiation (n^n) of an integer. The two services are accessible using channels a and b, that must be communicated to clients of the services. We assume here only two clients, that receive the channels via a_1 and a_2:

$$P \stackrel{\text{def}}{=} (\boldsymbol{\nu}a, b)\, (\overline{a_1}\langle a, b\rangle.\, \overline{a_2}\langle a, b\rangle.\, (\mathsf{A} \mid \mathsf{B})) \tag{1}$$

We expect that outputs at a or b from the clients are eventually received and processed by the appropriate service. But this is not necessarily the case: a malign client can disrupt the expected protocol by simply offering an input at a or b and then throwing away the values received, or forwarding the values to the wrong service. These misbehaviours are ruled out by a capability type system imposing that the clients only obtain the output capability on the names a and b when receiving them from a_1 and a_2. The typing rules are straightforward, and mimick those for the typing of references in imperative languages with subtyping. These types, called *capability types*, or i/o-types, are one of the simplest and widely used type disciplines in π.

In the π-calculus, the natural form of duality comes from the symmetry between input and output. There are several variants of π where processes can be 'symmetrised' by replacing inputs with outputs and vice versa. The π-calculus with internal mobility, πI [13], is a subcalculus of π where only bound outputs are allowed (a bound output, that we shall note $\overline{a}(x).\,P$, is the emission of a private name x on some channel a). In πI, duality can be expressed at an operational level, by exchanging (bound) inputs and bound outputs: the dual of $a(x).\,\overline{x}(y).\,0$ is $\overline{a}(x).\,x(y).\,0$.

Other well-known variants of π with dualities are the calculi in the fusion family [2,3,10]. In fusions, a construct for *free input* acts as the dual of the free output construct of π, and the calculus has only one binder, restriction. Interaction on a given channel has the effect of *fusing* (that is, identifying) names.

As for the π-calculus, however, the amazing expressiveness of the fusion calculi makes desirable behavioural properties fail. The examples we introduced for the π-calculus can be used. For instance, the problems of misbehaving clients of the services (1) remain. Actually, in fusion calculi additional problems arise; for example a client receiving the two channels a and b could fuse them. Now a and b are indistinguishable, and an emission on one of them can reach any of the two services (moreover, if a definition of a service is recursive, a recursive call could be redirected towards the other service).

The i/o-types, while being important for reasoning, bring in some inherent asymmetry. Let us give some intuitions about why it is so. In i/o-types, types are assigned to channels and express *capabilities*: a name of type oT can be used only to emit values of type T, and similarly for the input capability (iT). This is expressed by the following typing rules for i/o-types in π:

$$\frac{\Gamma \vdash a : iT \quad \Gamma, x : T \vdash P}{\Gamma \vdash a(x).P} \qquad \frac{\Gamma \vdash a : oT \quad \Gamma \vdash b : T \quad \Gamma \vdash P}{\Gamma \vdash \overline{a}b.P}$$

The rule for input can be read as follows: process $a(x).P$ is well-typed provided (i) the typing environment, Γ, ensures that the input capability on a can be derived, and (ii) the continuation of the input can be typed in an environment where x is used according to T. The typing rule for output checks that (i) the output capability on a is derivable, (ii) the emitted value, b, has the right type, and (iii) the continuation P can be typed. As an example, $a : i(iT) \vdash a(x).\overline{x}t.0$ cannot be derived, because only the input capability is received on a, which prevents $\overline{x}t.0$ from being typable.

I/o-types come with a notion of subtyping, that makes it possible to relate type $\sharp T$ (which stands for both input and output capabilities) with input and output capabilities (in particular, we have $\sharp T \leq iT$ and $\sharp T \leq oT$). We stress an asymmetry between the constraints attached to the transmitted name in the two rules above. Indeed, while in a reception we somehow enforce a "contract" on the usage of the received name, in the rule for output this is not the case: we can use subtyping in order to derive type, say, iU for b when typechecking the output, while b's type can be $\sharp U$ when typechecking the continuation P.

The main technical point that is discussed in this work is the conflict between the asymmetry inherent to i/o-types and the symmetries we want to obtain via duality. For example i/o-types can be adapted to πI, but duality cannot be applied to the resulting typings. In fusion calculi, the conflict with the asymmetry of i/o-types is even more dramatic. Indeed, subtyping in i/o-types is closely related to substitution, since replacing a name with another makes sense only if the latter has a more general type. Fusions are intuitively substitutions operating in both directions, which leaves no room for subtyping. We explain in Section 3 the problems with symmetries, and why i/o-types cannot be extended easily to fusions.

We discuss two ways to conciliate symmetries and types. The first approach is based on a refinement of fusion calculi. Intuitively, the problems of fusion calculi with types arise because at the heart of the operational semantics for fusion calculi is an equivalence relation on names, generated through name fusions. In contrast, subtyping and capability systems are based on a preorder relation (subtyping, set inclusion among subsets of capabilities). The equivalence on names forces one to have an equivalence also on types, instead of a preorder.

The crux of the solution we propose is the replacement of the equivalence on names by a preorder, and a distinction on occurrences of names, between 'positive' and 'negative'. In the resulting single-binder calculus, πP ('π with Preorder'), reductions generate a preorder. The basic reduction rule is

$$\bar{c}a.\, P \mid cb.\, Q \longrightarrow P \mid Q \mid a/b \ .$$

The particle a/b, called an *arc*, sets a to be above b in the name preorder. Such a process may redirect a prefix at b (which represents a 'positive' occurrence of b) to become a prefix at a. In the processes written above, all visible occurrences of a and c (resp. b) are positive (resp. negative). We show that the i/o (input/output) capability systems of the π-calculus can be reused in πP, following a generalisation of the typing rules of the π-calculus that takes into account the negative and positive occurrences of names. A better understanding of type systems with subtyping in name-passing calculi is a by-product of this study. For instance, the study suggests that it is essential for subtyping that substitutions produced by communications (in πP, the substitutions pro-duced by arcs) only affect the positive occurrences of names.

A property of certain fusion calculi (Fusion, Explicit Fusion) is a semantic duality induced by the symmetry between input and output prefixes. In πP, the syntax still allows us to swap inputs and outputs, but in general the original and final processes have incomparable behaviours.

The second approach to conciliating dualities and types possibility is illustrated by formalising a calculus named $\overline{\pi}$. This is an extension of π with constructs for free input and bound output (note that bound output is not seen as a derived construct in $\overline{\pi}$). In $\overline{\pi}$, we rely on substitutions as the main mechanism at work along interactions. To achieve this, we forbid interactions involving a free input and a free output: the type system rules out processes that use both kinds of prefixes on the same channel.

Calculus $\overline{\pi}$ contains π, and any π process that can be typed using i/o-types can be typed in exactly the same way in $\overline{\pi}$. Moreover, $\overline{\pi}$ contains a 'dualised' version of π: one can choose to use some channels in free input and bound output. For such channels, the typing rules intuitively enforce a 'contract' on the usage of the transmitted name *on the side of the emitter* (dually to the typing rules presented above).

Further Related Work. Central to πP is the preorder on names, that breaks the symmetry of name equivalence in fusion-like calculi. Another important ingredient for the theory of πP is the distinction between negative and positive occurrences of a name. In Update [11] and (asymmetric versions of) Chi [2], reductions produce ordinary substitutions on names. In practice, however, substitutions are not much different from fusions: a substitution $\{a/b\}$ fuses a with b *and* makes a the representative of the equivalence class. Still, substitutions are directed, and in this sense Update and Chi look closer to πP than the other fusion calculi. For instance Update and Chi, like πP, lack the duality property on computations. Update was refined to the Fusion calculus [10] because of difficulties in the extension with polyadicity. Another major difference for Update and Chi with respect to πP is that in the former calculi substitutions replace all occurrences of names, whereas πP takes into account the distinction between positive and negative occurrences.

The question of controlling the fusion of private names has been addressed in [1], in the U-calculus. This calculus makes no distinction between input and output, and relies on two forms of binding to achieve a better control of scope extrusion, thus leading to a sensible behavioural theory that encompasses fusions and π. It is unclear how capability types could be defined in this calculs, as it does not have primitive constructs for input and output.

Structure of the Paper. Section 2 gives some background on calculi for mobile processes. Section 3 shows that, in typed languages with fusions, it is impossible to have a non-trivial subtyping, assuming a few simple and standard typing properties of name-passing calculi. Section 4 refines the fusion calculi by replacing the equivalence relation on names generated through communication by a preorder, yielding the calculus πP. Finally, Section 5 presents $\overline{\pi}$, the extension of the π-calculus with capability types that enjoys duality properties.

2   Background on Name-Passing Calculi

In this section we group terminology and notation that are common to all the calculi discussed in the paper. For simplicity of presentation, all calculi in the paper are finite. The addition of operators like replication for writing infinite behaviours goes as expected. The results in the paper would not be affected.

We informally call *name-passing* the calculi in the π-calculus tradition, which have the usual constructs of parallel composition and restriction, and in which computation is interaction between input and output constructs. *Names* identify the pairs of matching inputs/outputs, and the values transmitted may themselves be names. Restriction is a binder for the names; in some cases the input may be a binder too. Examples of these calculi are the π-calculus, the asynchronous π-calculus, the Join calculus, the Distributed π-calculus, the Fusion calculus, and so on. Binders support the usual alpha-conversion mechanism, and give rise to the usual definitions of free and bound names.

To simplify the presentation, throughout the paper, in all statements (including rules), we assume that the bound names of the entities in the statements are different from each other and different from the free names *(Barendregt convention on names). Similarly, we say that a name is* fresh *or* fresh for a process, *if the name does not appear in the entities of the statements or in the process.*

We use $a, b, \ldots$ to range over names. In a free input $ab.\,P$, bound input $a(b).\,P$, free output $\overline{a}b.\,P$, and bout output $\overline{a}(b)$, we call a the *subject* of the prefix, and b the *object*. We sometimes abbreviate prefixes as $a.\,P$ and $\overline{a}.\,P$ when the object carried is not important. We omit trailing $\mathbf{0}$, for instance writing $\overline{a}b$ in place of $\overline{a}b.\,\mathbf{0}$. We write $P\{a/b\}$ for the result of applying the substitution of b with a in P.

The semantics of the calculi studied in the paper are given in the reduction style, by defining structural congruence and reduction relations. Structural congruence, $\equiv$, is defined as the usual congruence produced by the monoidal rules for parallel composition and the rules for commuting and extruding restriction

3   Typing and Subtyping with Fusions

Calculi Having Fusions. When restriction is the only binder (hence the prefixes are not binding), we say that the calculus *has a single binder*. If in addition interaction involves fusion between names, so that we have ($\Longrightarrow$ stands for an arbitrary number of reduction steps, and in the right-hand side P, Q can be omitted if they are $\mathbf{0}$)

$$(\boldsymbol{\nu} c)\,(\overline{a}b.\,P \mid ac.\,Q \mid R) \Longrightarrow (P \mid Q \mid R)\{b/c\}\ , \tag{2}$$

we say that the calculus *has name-fusions*, or, more briefly, has *fusions*. (We are not requiring that (2) is among the rules of the operational semantics of the calculus, just that (2) holds. The shape of (2) has been chosen so to capture the existing calculi; the presence of R allows us to capture also the Solos calculus.) All single-binder calculi in the literature (Update [11], Chi [2], Fusion [10], Explicit Fusion calculus [3], Solos [8]) have fusions. In Section 4 we will introduce a single-binder calculus without fusions.

In all calculi in the paper, (reduction-closed) barbed congruence will be our reference behavioural equivalence. Its definition only requires a reduction relation, $\longrightarrow$, and a notion of barb on names, $\downarrow_a$. Intuitively, a barb at a holds for a process if that process can accept an offer of interaction at a from its environment. We write $\simeq_{\mathcal{L}}$ for (strong) reduction-closed barbed congruence in a calculus $\mathcal{L}$. Informally, $\simeq_{\mathcal{L}}$ is the largest relation that is context-closed, barb-preserving, and reduction-closed. Its weak version, written $\approx_{\mathcal{L}}$, replaces the relation $\longrightarrow_{\mathcal{L}}$ with its reflexive and transitive closure $\Longrightarrow_{\mathcal{L}}$, and the barbs $\downarrow_a^{\mathcal{L}}$ with the weak barbs $\Downarrow_a^{\mathcal{L}}$, where $\Downarrow_a^{\mathcal{L}}$ is the composition of the relations $\Longrightarrow_{\mathcal{L}}$ and $\downarrow_a^{\mathcal{L}}$ (i.e., the barb is visible after some internal actions).

We consider typed versions of languages with fusions. We show that in such languages it is impossible to have a non-trivial subtyping, assuming a few simple and standard typing properties of name-passing calculi.

We use T, U to range over types, and Γ to range over type environments, i.e., partial functions from names to types. We write $\mathrm{dom}(\Gamma)$ for the set of names on which Γ is defined. In name-passing calculi, a type system assigns a type to each name. Typing judgements are of the form $\Gamma \vdash P$ (process P respects the type assignments in Γ), and $\Gamma \vdash a : T$ (name a can be assigned type T in Γ).[1] The following are the standard typing rules for parallel composition and restriction:

$$\frac{\Gamma \vdash P_1 \qquad \Gamma \vdash P_2}{\Gamma \vdash P_1 \mid P_2} \qquad \frac{\Gamma, x : T \vdash P}{\Gamma \vdash (\boldsymbol{\nu} x : T)\,P} \tag{3}$$

The first rule says that any two processes typed in the same type environment can be composed in parallel. The second rule handles name restriction.

---

[1] We consider in this paper basic type systems and basic properties for them; more sophisticated type systems exist where processes have a type too, e.g., behavioural type systems.

In name-passing calculi, the basic type construct is the channel (or connection) type $\sharp T$. This is the type of a name that may carry, in an input or an output, values of type T. Consequently, we also assume that the following rule for prefixes $ab.\,P$ and $\bar{a}b.\,P$ is admissible.

$$\frac{\Gamma(a) = \sharp T \qquad \Gamma(b) = T \qquad \Gamma \vdash P}{\Gamma \vdash \alpha.\,P} \quad \alpha \in \{ab, \bar{a}b\} \tag{4}$$

(Prefixes may not have a continuation, in which case P would be missing from the rule.) In the rule, the type of the subject and of the object of the prefix are compatible. Again, these need not be the typing rules for prefixes; we are just assuming that the rules are valid in the type system. The standard rule for prefix would have, as hypotheses, $\Gamma \vdash a : \sharp T$ and $\Gamma \vdash b : T$. These imply, but are not equivalent to, the hypotheses in (4), for instance in presence of subtyping.

Fundamental properties of type systems are:

- Subject Reduction (or Type Soundness): if $\Gamma \vdash P$ and $P \to P'$, then $\Gamma \vdash P'$;
- Weakening: if $\Gamma \vdash P$ and a is fresh, then $\Gamma, a : T \vdash P$;
- Strengthening: whenever $\Gamma, a : T \vdash P$ and a is fresh for P, then $\Gamma \vdash P$;
- Closure under injective substitutions: if $\Gamma, a : T \vdash P$ and b is fresh, then $\Gamma, b : T \vdash P\{b/a\}$.

Definition 1. *A typed calculus with single binder is* plain *if it satisfies Subject Reduction, Weakening, Strengthening, Closure under injective substitutions, and the typing rules (3) and (4) are admissible.*

If the type system admits subtyping, then another fundamental property is narrowing, which authorises, in a typing environment, the specialisation of types:

- (Narrowing): if $\Gamma, a : T \vdash P$ and $U \leq T$ then also $\Gamma, a : U \vdash P$.

When narrowing holds, we say that the calculus *supports narrowing*.

A typed calculus *has trivial subtyping* if, whenever $T \leq U$, we have $\Gamma, a : T \vdash P$ iff $\Gamma, a : U \vdash P$. When this is not the case (i.e., there are T, U with $T \leq U$, and T, U are not interchangeable in all typing judgements) we say that the calculus has *meaningful* subtyping.

Under the assumptions of Definition 1, a calculus with fusions may only have trivial subtyping.

Theorem 1. *A typed calculus with fusions that is plain and supports narrowing has trivial subtyping.*

In the proof, given in [5], we assume a meaningful subtyping and use it to derive a contradiction from type soundness and the other hypotheses. An additional theorem is presented in [5], showing that any form of narrowing, on one prefix object, would force subtyping to be trivial.

4   A Calculus with Name Preorders

4.1   Preorders, Positive and Negative Occurrences

We now refine the fusion calculi by replacing the equivalence relation on names generated through communication by a preorder, yielding πP. As the preorder on types given by subtyping allows promotions between related types, so the preorder on names of πP allows promotions between related names. Precisely, if a is below a name b in the preorder, then a prefix at a may be promoted to a prefix at b and then interact with another prefix at b. Thus an input $av.\,P$ may interact with an output $\bar{b}w.\,Q$; and, if also c is below b, then $av.\,P$ may as well interact with an output $\bar{c}z.\,R$.

The ordering on names is introduced by means of the *arc* construct, a/b, that declares the *source* b to be below the *target* a. The remaining operators are as for fusion calculi.

$$P ::= \mathbf{0} \;\Big|\; P \mid P \;\Big|\; \bar{a}b.\,P \;\Big|\; ab.\,P \;\Big|\; \nu a P \;\Big|\; a/b \;.$$

We explain the effect of reduction by means of contexts, rather than separate rules for each operator. Contexts yield a more succinct presentation. An *active context* is one in which the hole may reduce. Thus the only difference with respect to ordinary contexts is that the hole may not occur underneath a prefix. We use C to range over (ordinary) contexts, and E for active contexts.

The rules for reduction are as follows:

$$\text{R-SCon}: \quad \frac{P \equiv E[Q] \qquad Q \longrightarrow Q' \qquad E[Q'] \equiv P'}{P \longrightarrow P'}$$

$$\text{R-Inter}: \quad \bar{a}b.\,P \mid ac.\,Q \longrightarrow P \mid Q \mid b/c$$

$$\text{R-SubOut}: \quad a/b \mid \bar{b}c.\,Q \longrightarrow a/b \mid \bar{a}c.\,Q$$

$$\text{R-SubInp}: \quad a/b \mid bc.\,Q \longrightarrow a/b \mid ac.\,Q$$

Rule R-Inter shows that communication generates an arc. Rules R-SubOut and R-SubInp show that arcs only act on the subject of prefixes; moreover, they only act on *unguarded* prefixes (i.e., prefixes that are not underneath another prefix). The rules also show that arcs are persistent processes. Acting only on prefix subjects, arcs can be thought of as particles that "redirect prefixes": an arc a/b redirects a prefix at b towards a higher name a. (Arcs remind us of special π-calculus processes, called forwarders or wires [7], which under certain hypotheses allow one to model substitutions; as for arcs, so the effect of forwarders is to replace the subject of prefixes.)

We write $\Longrightarrow$ for the reflexive and transitive closure of $\longrightarrow$. Here are some examples of reduction.

$$\bar{a}c.\bar{c}a.e.P \mid ad.de.\bar{a}.Q$$

R-INTER $\longrightarrow$	$\bar{c}a.e.P \mid$	$de.\bar{a}.Q \mid c/d$
R-SUBINP $\longrightarrow$	$\bar{c}a.e.P \mid$	$ce.\bar{a}.Q \mid c/d$
R-INTER $\longrightarrow$	$e.P \mid$	$\bar{a}.Q \mid c/d \mid a/e$
R-SUBINP $\longrightarrow$	$a.P \mid$	$\bar{a}.Q \mid c/d \mid a/e$
R-INTER $\longrightarrow$	$P \mid$	$Q \mid c/d \mid a/e$

Reductions can produce multiple arcs that act on the same name. This may be used to represent certain forms of choice, as in the following processes:

$$(\nu h, k)\, (bu.\, cu.\bar{u} \mid \bar{b}h.\, h.\, P \mid \bar{c}k.\, k.\, Q)$$
$$\Longrightarrow (\nu h, k)\, (\bar{u} \mid h/u \mid k/u \mid h.\, P \mid k.\, Q)\ .$$

Both arcs may act on $\bar{u}$, and are therefore in competition with each other. The outcome of the competition determines which process between P and Q is activated. For instance, reduction may continue as follows:

$$\text{R-SUBOUT} \longrightarrow (\nu h, k)\, (\bar{k} \mid h/u \mid k/u \mid h.\, P \mid k.\, Q)$$
$$\text{R-INTER} \longrightarrow (\nu h, k)\, (h/u \mid k/u \mid h.\, P \mid Q)\ .$$

Definition 2 (Positive and negative occurrences). *In an input $ab.\, P$ and an arc a/b, the name b has a* negative *occurrence. All other occurrences of names in input, output and arcs are* positive *occurrences.*

An occurrence in a restriction (νa) is neither negative nor positive, intuitively because restriction acts only as a binder, and does not stand for an usage of the name (in particular, it does not take part in a substitution).

Negative occurrences are particularly important, as by properly tuning them, different usages of names may be obtained. For instance, a name with zero negative occurrence is a constant (i.e., it is a channel, and may not be substituted); and a name that has a single negative occurrence is like a π-calculus name bound by an input (see [5]).

4.2 Types

We now show that the i/o capability type system and its subtyping can be transplanted from π to πP.

In the typing rules for i/o-types in the (monadic) π-calculus [12], two additional types are introduced: $o\,T$, the type of a name that can be used only in output and that carries values of type T; and $i\,T$, the type of a name that can be used only in input and that carries values of type T. The subtyping rules stipulate that i is covariant, o is contravariant, and $\sharp$ is invariant. The subsumption rule injects subtyping in the typing rules. The most important typing rules are those for input and output prefixes; for input we have:

$$\text{T-INPBOUND}: \quad \frac{\Gamma \vdash a : i\,T \qquad \Gamma, b : T \vdash P}{\Gamma \vdash a(b).\, P}$$

Table 1. The type system of πP

Types (**1** is the unit type): $\qquad\qquad T ::= \mathtt{i}\,T \mid \mathtt{o}\,T \mid \sharp\,T \mid \mathbf{1}$

Subtyping rules:

$$\frac{}{\sharp T \leq \mathtt{i}\,T} \qquad \frac{}{\sharp T \leq \mathtt{o}\,T} \qquad \frac{S \leq T}{\mathtt{i}\,S \leq \mathtt{i}\,T} \qquad \frac{S \leq T}{\mathtt{o}\,T \leq \mathtt{o}\,S} \qquad \frac{}{T \leq T}$$

$$\frac{S \leq T \qquad T \leq U}{S \leq U}$$

Typing rules:

$$\text{Tv-Name}\ \frac{}{\Gamma, a : T \vdash a : T} \qquad \text{Subsumption}\ \frac{\Gamma \vdash a : S \qquad S \leq T}{\Gamma \vdash a : T} \qquad \text{T-Res}\ \frac{\Gamma, a : T \vdash P}{\Gamma \vdash \nu a P} \qquad \text{T-Par}\ \frac{\Gamma \vdash P \qquad \Gamma \vdash Q}{\Gamma \vdash P \mid Q}$$

$$\text{T-Nil}\ \frac{}{\Gamma \vdash \mathbf{0}} \qquad \text{T-Out}\ \frac{\Gamma \vdash a : \mathtt{o}\,T \qquad \Gamma \vdash b : T \qquad \Gamma \vdash P}{\Gamma \vdash \overline{a}b.\,P} \qquad \text{T-InpFree}\ \frac{\Gamma \vdash a : \mathtt{i}\,\Gamma(b) \qquad \Gamma \vdash P}{\Gamma \vdash ab.\,P}$$

$$\text{T-Arc}\ \frac{\Gamma \vdash a : \Gamma(b)}{\Gamma \vdash a/b}$$

The type system for πP is presented in Table 1. With respect to the π-calculus, only the rule for input needs an adjustment, as πP uses free, rather than bound, input. The idea in rule T-InpFree of πP is however the same as in rule T-InpBound of π: we look up the type of the object of the prefix, say T, and we require $\mathtt{i}\,T$ as the type for the subject of the prefix. To understand the typing of an arc a/b, recall that such an arc allows one to replace b with a. Rule T-Arc essentially checks that a has at least as many capabilities as b, in line with the intuition for subtyping in capability type systems.

Common to the premises of T-InpFree and T-Arc is the look-up of the type of names that occur negatively (the source of an arc and the object of an input prefix): the type that appears for b in the hypothesis is precisely the type found in the conclusion (within the process or in Γ). In contrast, the types for positive occurrences may be different (e.g., because of subsumption $\Gamma \vdash a : \mathtt{i}\,T$ may hold even if $\Gamma(a) \neq \mathtt{i}\,T$).

We cannot type inputs like outputs: consider

$$\text{T-InpFree2-Wrong} : \qquad \frac{\Gamma \vdash a : \mathtt{i}\,T \qquad \Gamma \vdash b : T}{\Gamma \vdash ab}$$

Rule T-InpFree2-Wrong would accept, for instance, an input ab in an environment Γ where $a : \mathtt{i}\,\mathtt{i}\,\mathbf{1}$ and $b : \sharp\mathbf{1}$. By subtyping and subsumption, we could then derive $\Gamma \vdash b : \mathtt{i}\,\mathbf{1}$. In contrast, rule T-INPFREE, following the input rule of the π-calculus, makes sure that the object of the input does not have too many capabilities with respect to what is expected in the type of the subject of the input. This constraint is necessary for subject reduction. As a counterexample, assuming rule T-INPFREE2-WRONG, we would have $a : \sharp\,\mathtt{i}\,\mathbf{1}, b : \sharp\,\mathbf{1}, c : \mathtt{i}\,\mathbf{1} \vdash P$, for $P \stackrel{\text{def}}{=} ab \mid \bar{a}c \mid \bar{b}$. However, $P \longrightarrow c/b \mid \bar{b} \longrightarrow c/b \mid \bar{c}$, and the final derivative is not typable under Γ (as Γ only authorises inputs at c).

In πP, the direction of the narrowing is determined by the negative or positive occurrences of a name.

Theorem 2 (Polarised narrowing). *Let T_1, T_2 be types such that $T_1 \leq T_2$.*

1. *If a occurs only positively in P, then $\Gamma, a : T_2 \vdash P$ implies $\Gamma, a : T_1 \vdash P$.*
2. *If a occurs only negatively in P, then $\Gamma, a : T_1 \vdash P$ implies $\Gamma, a : T_2 \vdash P$.*
3. *If a occurs both positively and negatively in P, then it is in general unsound to replace, in a typing $\Gamma \vdash P$, the type of a in Γ with a subtype or supertype.*

Theorem 2 (specialised to prefixes) does not contradict Theorem 1, because in πP, reduction does not satisfy (2) (from Section 2). We have subject reduction:

Theorem 3. *If $\Gamma \vdash P$ and $P \longrightarrow P'$ then also $\Gamma \vdash P'$.*

4.3   Other Results

Behavioural equivalences for πP and the fusion calculi, in the form of barbed congruence, are considered in [5]. It is shown that the modification from fusion calculi to πP also brings in behavioural differences. For instance, both in the π-calculus and in πP, a process that creates a new name a has the guarantee that a will remain different from all other known names, even if a is communicated to other processes (only the creator of a can break this, by using a in negative position). This is not true in fusion calculi, where the emission of a may produce fusions between a and other names. To demonstrate the proximity with the π-calculus we show that the embedding of the asynchronous π-calculus into πP is fully abstract (full abstraction of the encoding of the π-calculus into fusion calculi fails). We also exhibit an encoding of Explicit Fusions into πP, where fusions become bi-directional arcs. Indeed πP is closer to the π-calculus than to fusion calculi, not only in typing, but also behaviourally.

The reduction semantics for πP that we have presented ma considered *eager*, in that arcs may freely act on prefixes. An alternative, *by-need*, semantics, is possible, where arcs act on prefixes only when interactions occur. See [5] for a comparison between the two semantics, as well as for further comparison with semantics based on name fusion. The behavioural theory of πP, under by-need semantics, is further studied in [6]. Two characterisations of barbed congruence, using a labelled transition system and using equations, are presented. Also, see [5] for examples concerning behavioural laws and expressiveness results for πP.

5 $\overline{\pi}$, a Symmetric π-Calculus

In this section, we present $\overline{\pi}$, a π-calculus with i/o-types that enjoys duality properties. We define the syntax and operational semantics for $\overline{\pi}$ processes in Section 5.1, introduce types and barbed congruence in Section 5.2, establish duality in Section 5.3. We finally discuss other results, and an application to the encoding of functions, in Section 5.4.

5.1 Syntax and Operational Semantics

The syntax of $\overline{\pi}$ is as follows:

$$P ::= 0 \;\Big|\; P \mid P \;\Big|\; \alpha.\,P \;\Big|\; (\nu a)P \qquad\qquad \alpha ::= \rho b \mid \rho(x) \qquad\qquad a ::= a \mid \overline{a}$$

$\overline{\pi}$ differs from the usual π-calculus by the presence of the free input ab and bound output $\overline{a}(x)$ prefixes. Note that in $\overline{\pi}$, the latter is *not* a notation for $(\nu x)\overline{a}x.\,P$, but a primitive construct. These prefixes are the symmetric counterpart of $\overline{a}b$ and $a(x)$ respectively. Given ρ of the form a or $\overline{a}$, $\mathrm{n}(\rho)$ is defined by

Reduction is defined by law R-SCON from Section 4.1, as well as the following axioms, to allow communication involving two prefixes *only if at least one of them is bound*:

$$\overline{a}b.\,P \mid a(x).\,Q \;\to\; P \mid Q[b/x] \qquad\qquad ab.\,P \mid \overline{a}(x).\,Q \;\to\; P \mid Q[b/x]$$

$$\overline{a}(x).\,P \mid a(x).\,Q \;\to\; (\nu x)(P \mid Q)$$

$\Rightarrow$ denotes the reflexive transitive closure of $\to$. Note that the $\overline{\pi}$ process $\overline{a}b \mid ab$ has no reduction; this process is ruled out by the type system presented below.

5.2 Types and Behavioural Equivalence

Types in $\overline{\pi}$ are a refinement of standard i/o-types: in addition to capabilities (ranged over using c), we annotate types with *sorts* (s), that specify whether a name can be used in free input (sort $\mathbf{e}$) or in free output ($\mathbf{r}$) — note that a name cannot be used to build both kinds of free prefixes.

$$T ::= c^s T \mid 1 \qquad\qquad c ::= i \mid o \mid \sharp \qquad\qquad s ::= \mathbf{e} \mid \mathbf{r}$$

If name a has type $c^{\mathbf{r}}T$, we shall refer to a as a $\mathbf{r}$-*name*, and similarly for $\mathbf{e}$.

The subtyping relation is the smallest reflexive and transitive relation $\leq$ satisfying the rules of Figure 1. As in the π-calculus $i^{\mathbf{r}}$ is covariant and $o^{\mathbf{r}}$ is contravariant. Dually, $i^{\mathbf{e}}$ is contravariant and $o^{\mathbf{e}}$ is covariant. Note that sorts ($\mathbf{e}$, $\mathbf{r}$) are not affected by subtyping.

The type system is given by the rules of Figure 2. We write $\Gamma(a)$ for the type associated to a in Γ. There is a dedicated typing rule for every kind of prefix (free, ρb, or bound, $\rho(x)$), according to the sort of the involved name. $T^{\leftrightarrow}$ stands for T where we switch the toplevel capability: $(c^s T)^{\leftrightarrow} = \overline{c}^s T$ where

$$\overline{\sharp^s T \leq i^s T} \qquad\qquad \overline{\sharp^s T \leq o^s T}$$

$$\frac{T_1 \leq T_2}{i^r T_1 \leq i^r T_2} \qquad \frac{T_1 \leq T_2}{o^r T_2 \leq o^r T_1} \qquad \frac{T_1 \leq T_2}{i^e T_2 \leq i^e T_1} \qquad \frac{T_1 \leq T_2}{o^e T_1 \leq o^e T_2}$$

Fig. 1. Subtyping in $\overline{\pi}$

$$\frac{\Gamma \vdash a : i^r T \quad \Gamma, x : T \vdash P}{\Gamma \vdash a(x).P} \qquad\qquad \frac{\Gamma \vdash a : i^e T \quad \Gamma, x : T^{\leftrightarrow} \vdash P}{\Gamma \vdash a(x).P}$$

$$\frac{\Gamma \vdash a : o^e T \quad \Gamma, x : T \vdash P}{\Gamma \vdash \overline{a}(x).P} \qquad\qquad \frac{\Gamma \vdash a : o^r T \quad \Gamma, x : T^{\leftrightarrow} \vdash P}{\Gamma \vdash \overline{a}(x).P}$$

$$\frac{\Gamma \vdash a : i^e T \quad \Gamma \vdash b : T \quad \Gamma \vdash P}{\Gamma \vdash ab.P} \qquad\qquad \frac{\Gamma \vdash a : o^r T \quad \Gamma \vdash b : T \quad \Gamma \vdash P}{\Gamma \vdash \overline{a}b.P}$$

$$\frac{\Gamma, a : T \vdash P}{\Gamma \vdash (\nu a)P} \qquad \frac{\Gamma \vdash P \quad \Gamma \vdash Q}{\Gamma \vdash P \mid Q} \qquad \overline{\Gamma \vdash 0} \qquad \frac{\Gamma(a) \leq T}{\Gamma \vdash a : T}$$

Fig. 2. $\overline{\pi}$: Typing rules

$\overline{o} = i, \overline{i} = o, \overline{\sharp} = \sharp$. The typing rules for **r**-names impose a constraint on the receiving side: all inputs on a **r**-channel should be bound. Note that $\overline{a}(x).P$ and $(\nu x)\overline{a}x.P$ are *not* equivalent from the point of view of typing: typing a bound output on a **r**-channel (a) imposes that the transmitted name (x) is used according to the "dual constraint" w.r.t. what a's type specifies: this is enforced using $T^{\leftrightarrow}$ (while names received on a are used according to T). Symmetrical considerations hold for **e**-names, that impose constraints on the emitting side.

Remark 1 ("Double contract"). We could adopt a more liberal typing for bound outputs on **r** names, and use the rule

$$\frac{\Gamma \vdash a : o^r T \quad \Gamma, x : T' \vdash P \quad T' \leq T}{\Gamma \vdash \overline{a}(x).P}$$

(and its counterpart for inputs on **e**-names). This would have the effect of typing $\overline{a}(x).P$ like $(\nu x)\overline{a}x.P$. We instead chose to enforce what we call a *"double contract"*: the same way a receiving process uses the bound name according to the type specified in the channel that is used for reception, the continuation of a bound output uses the emitted name according to $T^{\leftrightarrow}$, the *symmetrised version* of T. This corresponds to a useful programming idiom in π, where it is common to create a name, transmit one capability on this name and use locally the other, dual capability. This choice moreover simplifies reasoning about $\overline{\pi}$.

Observe that when a typable process reduces according to

$$\overline{a}(x).\,P \mid a(x).\,Q \rightarrow (\nu x)(P \mid Q) \ ,$$

if a has type, say, $\sharp^{\mathbf{r}}(o^s T)$, then in the right hand side process, name x is given type $\sharp^s T$, and the $\sharp$ capability is "split" into $i^s T$ (used by P) and $o^s T$ (used by Q). It would be the other way around if a's sort were $\mathbf{e}$.

Proposition 1 (Subject reduction). *If $\Gamma \vdash P$ and $P \rightarrow Q$ then $\Gamma \vdash Q$.*

We now move to the definition of behavioural equivalence.

Definition 3 (Contexts). *Contexts are processes with one occurrence of the hole, written $[-]$. They are defined by the following grammar:*

$$C ::= [-] \mid C \mid P \mid C \mid P \mid \alpha.\,C \mid (\nu a)C \ .$$

Definition 4. *Let Γ, Δ be typing environments. We say that Γ extends Δ if the support of Δ is included in the support of Γ, and if $\Delta \vdash x : T$ entails $\Gamma \vdash x : T$ for all x. A context C is a (Γ/Δ)-context, written $\Gamma/\Delta \vdash C$, if C can be typed in the environment Γ, the hole being well-typed in any context that extends Δ.*

Definition 5 (Barbs). *Given $\rho \in \{a, \overline{a}\}$, where a is a name, we say that P exhibits barb ρ, written P_ρ, if $P(\nu c_1 \ldots c_n)(\alpha.\,Q \mid R)$ where $\alpha \in \{\rho(x), \rho b\}$ with $a \notin \{c_1, \ldots, c_n\}$. We extend the definition to weak barbs: $P \Downarrow_\rho$ stands for $P \Rightarrow \rho$.*

Definition 6 (Typed barbed congruence). *Barbed bisimilarity is the largest symmetric relation $\dot{\approx}$ such that whenever $P \dot{\approx} Q$,*

1. *if P_ρ then $Q \Downarrow_\rho$, and*
2. *if $P \rightarrow P'$ then $Q \Rightarrow \dot{\approx} P'$.*

When $\Delta \vdash P$ and $\Delta \vdash Q$, we say that P and Q are barbed congruent at Δ, written $\Delta \triangleright P \cong^c Q$, if for all (Γ/Δ)-context C, $C[P] \dot{\approx} C[Q]$.

5.3   Duality

Definition 7 (Dual of a process). *The dual of a process P, written $\overline{P}$, is the process obtained by transforming prefixes as follows: $\overline{\overline{a}b} = ab$, $\overline{ab} = \overline{a}b$, $\overline{\overline{a}(x)} = a(x)$, $\overline{a(x)} = \overline{a}(x)$, and applying dualisation homeomorphically to the other constructs.*

Lemma 1 (Duality for reduction). *If $P \rightarrow Q$ then $\overline{P} \rightarrow \overline{Q}$.*

Dualising a type means swapping i/o capabilities and $\mathbf{e}/\mathbf{r}$ sorts.

Definition 8 (Dual of a type). *The dual of T, written $\overline{T}$, is defined as follows:*

$$\overline{c^s T} = \overline{c}^{\,\overline{s}}\, \overline{T} \qquad \text{with} \qquad \overline{\mathbf{r}} = \mathbf{e}, \quad \overline{\mathbf{e}} = \mathbf{r}, \quad \overline{i} = o, \quad \overline{o} = i \ .$$

We extend the definition to typing environments, and write $\overline{\Gamma}$ for the dual of Γ.

Lemma 2 (Duality for typing). *The type system enjoys the following duality properties: If $T_1 \leq T_2$ then $\overline{T_1} \leq \overline{T_2}$. Moreover, if $\Gamma \vdash P$ then $\overline{\Gamma} \vdash \overline{P}$. Finally, if $\Gamma/\Delta \vdash C$ then $\overline{\Gamma}/\overline{\Delta} \vdash \overline{C}$.*

Most importantly, duality holds for typed barbed congruence. The result is easy in the untyped case, since duality preserves reduction and dualises barbs. On the other hand, we are not aware of the existence of another system having this property in presence of i/o-types.

Theorem 4 (Duality for $\cong^c$). *If $\Delta \triangleright P \cong^c Q$ then $\overline{\Delta} \triangleright \overline{P} \cong^c \overline{Q}$.*

5.4 Further Results and Applications

It is shown in [4] that $\overline{\pi}$ can be related to π, by translating $\overline{\pi}$ into a variant of the π-calculus with i/o-types in a a fully abstract way. This result shows that π and $\overline{\pi}$ are rather close in terms of expressiveness.

As an application of $\overline{\pi}$, its dualities, and its behavioural theory, the calculus is used in [4] to relate two encodings of call-by-name λ-calculus. The first one is the ordinary encoding by Milner [9], the second one, more recent, is by van Bakel and Vigliotti [16]. The two encodings are syntactically quite different. Milner's is *input-based*, in that an abstraction interacts with its environment via an input. In contrast, van Bakel and Vigliotti's is *output-based*.

We exploit $\overline{\pi}$ (in fact the extension of $\overline{\pi}$ with delayed input) to prove that the two encodings are the dual of one another. This is achieved by first embedding the π-terms of the λ-encodings into $\overline{\pi}$, and then applying behavioural laws of $\overline{\pi}$. The correctness of these transformations is justified using i/o-types (essentially to express the conditions under which a link can be erased in favour of a substitution). As a consequence, correctness results for one encoding can be transferred onto the other one. For instance, we derive that the equivalence induced on λ-terms by Milner's encoding (whereby two λ-terms are equal if their π-calculus images are behaviourally equivalent) is the same as that induced by van Bakel and Vigliotti's encoding. And since for Milner's encoding this equivalence coincides with the Levy-Longo tree equality [14], the same holds for van Bakel and Vigliotti's encoding, a question that is not addressed in [16].

Acknowledgments. The authors acknowledge support from the ANR projects 2010-BLAN-0305 PiCoq and 12IS02001 PACE.

The third author, Davide Sangiorgi, would like to add special thanks to Jozef Gruska: my current research is quite remote from the systolic automata and systems on which I collaborated with Jozef when I was a student; I have learned a lot from Jozef's papers and from our collaboration, and it is a pleasure to contribute a paper in this volume.

References

1. Boreale, M., Buscemi, M.G., Montanari, U.: A General Name Binding Mechanism. In: De Nicola, R., Sangiorgi, D. (eds.) TGC 2005. LNCS, vol. 3705, pp. 61–74. Springer, Heidelberg (2005)

2. Fu, Y.: The χ-calculus. In: Proc. APDC, pp. 74–81. IEEE Computer Society Press (1997)
3. Gardner, P., Wischik, L.: Explicit fusions. In: Nielsen, M., Rovan, B. (eds.) MFCS 2000. LNCS, vol. 1893, p. 373. Springer, Heidelberg (2000)
4. Hirschkoff, D., Madiot, J.-M., Sangiorgi, D.: Duality and i/o-types in the π-calculus. In: Koutny, M., Ulidowski, I. (eds.) CONCUR 2012. LNCS, vol. 7454, pp. 302–316. Springer, Heidelberg (2012)
5. Hirschkoff, D., Madiot, J.M., Sangiorgi, D.: Name-Passing Calculi: From Fusions to Preorders and Types. long version of the paper presented at LICS'13, in preparation (2014)
6. Hirschkoff, D., Madiot, J.M., Xu, X.: A behavioural theory for a π-calculus with preorders. submitted (2014)
7. Honda, K., Yoshida, N.: On reduction-based process semantics. Theor. Comp. Sci. 152(2), 437–486 (1995)
8. Laneve, C., Victor, B.: Solos in Concert. Mathematical Structures in Computer Science 13(5), 657–683 (2003)
9. Milner, R.: Functions as processes. Mathematical Structures in Computer Science 2(2), 119–141 (1992)
10. Parrow, J., Victor, B.: The fusion calculus: expressiveness and symmetry in mobile processes. In: Proc. of LICS, pp. 176–185. IEEE (1998)
11. Parrow, J., Victor, B.: The update calculus (extended abstract). In: Johnson, M. (ed.) AMAST 1997. LNCS, vol. 1349, pp. 409–423. Springer, Heidelberg (1997)
12. Pierce, B.C., Sangiorgi, D.: Typing and subtyping for mobile processes. Mathematical Structures in Computer Science 6(5), 409–453 (1996)
13. Sangiorgi, D.: π-calculus, internal mobility, and agent-passing calculi. In: Selected papers from TAPSOFT '95, pp. 235–274. Elsevier (1996)
14. Sangiorgi, D.: Lazy functions and mobile processes. In: Proof, Language, and Interaction, pp. 691–720. The MIT Press (2000)
15. Sangiorgi, D., Walker, D.: The Pi-Calculus: a theory of mobile processes. Cambridge University Press (2001)
16. van Bakel, S., Vigliotti, M.G.: An Implicative Logic based encoding of the λ-calculus into the π-calculus (2014). http://www.doc.ic.ac.uk/~svb/

Learning from Positive Data and Negative Counterexamples: A Survey

Sanjay Jain[1] and Efim Kinber[2(✉)]

[1] School of Computing, National University of Singapore,
Singapore 117417, Singapore
sanjay@comp.nus.edu.sg
[2] Department of Computer Science, Sacred Heart University,
Fairfield, CT 06432-1000, USA
kinbere@sacredheart.edu

Abstract. The article presents state of the art on learning languages in the limit from full positive data and negative counterexamples to overextending conjectures. In the main model, the learner can store in its long-term memory all data seen so far. Variants of this model are considered where the learner always gets least counterexamples, or counterexamples bounded by the maximal size of positive data seen. All these variants are also considered for the model, where the learner does not have long-term memory, but can use the last conjecture. Capabilities, properties, and relationships between these models (and some other variations) are surveyed. Also, a variant of the main model restricted to learning classes definable by finite automata by learners definable by finite automata is considered.

1 Introduction

The paper surveys recent results on algorithmic learning languages from all correct words of the language (full positive data) and a finite number of negative counterexamples. A popular formal model for study of learning languages from full positive data was introduced by M. Gold in his seminal paper [Gol67]. In this model, motivated largely by theories of language acquisition by children, a learner gets access to growing segments of the target language (where words appear in no particular order and can be repeated) and outputs a (potentially infinite) sequence of grammars, settling eventually on a grammar correctly representing the target language. In the sequel, we refer to this model as **TxtEx**, where **Txt** stands for "text", which is a complete positive data presentation, and "**Ex**" stands for "explanatory learning". The impact of this model on understanding of human language acquisition has been discussed in [Pin79], [WC80], and [OSW86], among others. Another popular variant of this model, **TxtBc**, where a learner eventually outputs only correct grammars of the target language, but not necessarily the same grammar, was introduced by J. Barzdin [Bār74] and J. Case and C. Smith [CS83] ("**Bc**" here stands for "behaviourally correct").

Sanjay Jain—Supported in part by NUS grant number C-252-000-087-001.

On the other hand, some studies point out that children, when learning languages, do use some, limited, negative information (incorrect words/sentences) about the target language ([DPS86], [BH70], [HPTS84]). The major question is how access to some limited negative data can be formalized within the framework of learning languages from primarily positive, potentially full, data. In [Shi86], [BCJ95] and some other works, the authors considered a situation when a learner, in addition to full positive data, has immediate access to a finite number of selected negative examples. This approach, while being interesting from theoretical standpoint — as it gives opportunity to explore the impact of finite negative data on the limits of learnability — does not really model a real process of learning a language, whereby a learner receives negative data from time to time, when the learning process progresses. In such a process, a learner would typically receive negative datum in form of a "counterexample" to incorrectly conjectured grammar/description of the target language (note that such incorrect conjecture, in some sense, "overextends" — hypothesizes something that not only was not in the positive data seen so far, but is not in the target language at all). Thus the learning process is an interaction between a learner and a "teacher": the learner offers its next conjecture, and the teacher returns a counterexample if the conjecture overextends. Learning paradigm of this sort was formalized by D. Angluin in her seminal paper [Ang88]. Specifically, D. Angluin suggested to consider learning processes based on *queries* to a "teacher" (formally, an oracle) of different kinds. In one type of queries, *subset queries*, a learner can ask if a language M is a subset of a target language L, and if the answer is negative, the oracle returns a counterexample that is in M, but not in L. In an important variant of such queries, the learner asks if a current conjecture H is a subset of L, thus addressing the aforementioned problem of "overextension". In [JK08] the authors combined this variant of Angluin's learning via subset queries and **TxtEx** into the model **NCEx** — the main model being reviewed in this paper — whereby the learner receives full positive data and counterexamples to each conjecture that is not a subset of the target language (note that if a learner is successful, the number of negative counterexamples is finite). In the same paper [JK08], the authors introduced a variant of this model, **NCBc**, combining the Angluin' subset queries model and **TxtBc**.

Later, the authors suggested and studied few more variants of this model:

— in [JK07a] the learner is *iterative* [Wie76] (see also [LZ96]) — unlike general **NCEx**-type learners, which, at any moment, have access to all the data seen so far, an iterative learner, in order to produce a new conjecture, can only use the current conjecture and next positive and negative (if any) data items; this model, while strongly limiting long-term memory of a learner, still preserves incremental character of learning in the limit; certain variants of iterative learning proved to be quite useful in the context of applied machine learning (for example, [LZ06] use the idea of iterative learning in the context of training Support Vector Machines).

— in [JK12, JKS14] classes of languages to be learnt are *automatic* — that is, each class is defined by a finite automaton — and the learners, while using access to full positive data and negative counterexamples to conjectures, are also automatic.

In the basic **NCEx** model, it is assumed that the learner is provided arbitrary counterexamples. In addition to this model, [JK08], introduces two more variants: in one of them, **LNCEx**, the learner always gets *the least counterexamples*; in another one, **BNCEx**, the learner always gets the counterexamples (if any) which is bounded by the largest positive datum seen so far (the latter condition is influenced by possible complexity constraints of the "teacher"). In the sequel, we will refer to the counterexamples of the latter type as *bounded*.

The paper is a survey of theoretical studies of the model **NCEx** and its aforementioned variants. We hope that this survey, presenting most salient results in this field, will give robust advice to researches working in more practical areas of algorithmic and machine learning, as well as to cognitive scientists.

2   Notation and Preliminaries

The set of natural numbers $\{0, 1, 2, \ldots\}$ is denoted by N. We let $\emptyset$, $\subseteq$, $\supseteq$, $\subset$ and $\supset$ denote emptyset, subset, superset, proper subset and proper superset respectively. χ_A denotes the characteristic function of A, that is $\chi_A(x) = 1$, if $x \in A$ and $\chi_A(x) = 0$, if $x \notin A$. For two sets A and B, $A =^n B$ means, $(A - B) \cup (B - A)$ has at most n elements; $A =^* B$ means that $(A - B) \cup (B - A)$ has at most finitely many elements. Maximum and minimum of a set S is denoted by $\max(S)$ and $\min(S)$ respectively, where $\min(\emptyset) = \infty$ and $\max(\emptyset) = 0$.

We let $\mathcal{E}$ denote the class of all recursively enumerable (r.e.) sets. We let L, with or without decorations, range over $\mathcal{E}$ and $\mathcal{L}$, with or without decorations, range over subsets of $\mathcal{E}$.

$\mathcal{L} = \{L_0, L_1, \ldots\}$ is said to be an *indexed family* of languages (with the corresponding indexing $L_0, L_1, \ldots$) if the question $x \in L_i$ is uniformly decidable (i.e., there exists a recursive function f such that $f(i, x) = \chi_{L_i}(x)$).

2.1   Concepts from Language Learning Theory

In the introduction we considered models of learning from texts (positive data only). In the sequel, we will also consider learning from informants (both full positive and full negative data, see [Gol67]).

A *text* T is a mapping from N to $N \cup \{\#\}$ (see [Gol67]). Intuitively, a text is an infinite sequence of elements from N, with $\#$'s denoting pauses in the presentation of data. For a text T, $T(i)$ thus denotes the $(i + 1)$-th element of the sequence. We let T, with or without decorations, range over texts. For a text T, we let $T[n]$ denote the initial finite portion $T(0)T(1) \ldots T(n - 1)$ of the text T. Let content$(T) = $ range$(T) - \{\#\}$. A text T is for a language L iff content$(T) = L$.

An *informant* I is a mapping from N to $(N \times \{0, 1\}) \cup \{\#\}$ such that for no x both $(x, 0)$ and $(x, 1)$ are in the range of I (see [Gol67]). Let content$(I) = $ range$(I) - \{\#\}$. I is an informant for L iff content$(I) = \{(x, \chi_L(x)) : x \in N\}$.

Intuitively, informants give both all positive and all negative data for the language being learned. For an informant I, we let $I[n]$ denote the initial finite portion $I(0)I(1)\ldots I(n-1)$ of the text I. We let σ and τ range over initial finite sequences of texts and informants. We define content(σ) analogously. Λ denotes the empty finite sequence. SEQ (respectively, SEG) denotes the set of all finite initial sequences of texts (respectively, informants). The *length* of a finite sequence σ is denoted by $|\sigma|$. $\sigma\diamond\tau$ denotes the concatenation of sequences σ and τ. For ease of notation, we denote the concatenation of sequence σ with a sequence containing just one element x by $\sigma\diamond x$. If it is clear from context, then we often denote $\sigma\diamond\tau$ by just $\sigma\tau$.

Intuitively, a learner receives as input a text (informant) for a language, one element of the text at a time. As it receives more and more data, it updates its memory and conjecture about what the input language might be. Thus, the learner can be considered as an algorithmic mapping from previous memory and current datum to a new memory and a hypothesis. This hypothesis of the learner is interpreted in some hypothesis space $(H_i)_{i\in J}$. We will always assume (without explicitly stating it) that the hypothesis space is recursively enumerable, that is, $\{(i,x) : x \in H_i\}$ is recursively enumerable. In some cases hypothesis spaces are more restricted. At any moment, the (finite) content of the (long-term) memory of the learner is from some set Δ. More formally a learner is defined as follows.

Definition 1. (Based on [Gol67]) Suppose $(H_i)_{i\in J}$ is a hypothesis space, and Δ is a set of possible memory contents (or simply memories).

(a) A *learning machine or learner from texts* is an algorithmic mapping from $\Delta \times (N \cup \{\#\})$ to $\Delta \times (J \cup \{?\})$.
A learner has an initial memory $mem_0 \in \Delta$ and initial hypothesis $hyp_0 \in J \cup \{?\}$.

(b) Suppose a learner $\mathbf{M}$ with initial memory mem_0 and initial hypothesis hyp_0 is given. Below, $\sigma \in SEQ$ and $x \in N \cup \{\#\}$. Extend the definition of $\mathbf{M}$ to finite sequences by inductively defining
$\mathbf{M}(\Lambda) = (mem_0, hyp_0)$;
$\mathbf{M}(\sigma\diamond x) = \mathbf{M}(mem, x)$, where $\mathbf{M}(\sigma) = (mem, hyp)$, for some $hyp \in J \cup \{?\}$.

(c) $\mathbf{M}$ converges on a text T to a hypothesis β (written: $\mathbf{M}(T){\downarrow}_{hyp} = \beta$) iff there exists a t such that,
(i) $\mathbf{M}(T[t]) \in (N \cup \{?\}) \times \{\beta\}$, and
(ii) for all $t' \geq t$, $\mathbf{M}(T[t]) \in (N \cup \{?\}) \times \{\beta, ?\}$.

One can similarly define learning machines (learners) from informants. We let $\mathbf{M}$, with or without decorations, range over learning machines.

$\mathbf{M}(\sigma) = (mem, hyp)$ in the definition above indicates that, after having seen the input σ, the memory and hypothesis of the learner $\mathbf{M}$ are mem and hyp respectively. The convergence of a learner on a text T to a hypothesis is thus its final conjecture (if any) on the input text T. If this conjecture is for the input language $L = $ content(T), then one can consider the learner to have learnt the language (from the text T). This is basically the notion of **TxtEx** learning first considered by Gold [Gol67] (see Definition 2. below). There have been several variations of this model considered in the literature, and we define some of them in the definitions below.

Definition 2. (Based on [Gol67, CL82]) Suppose $\mathcal{H} = (H_i)_{i \in N}$ is a hypothesis space. Suppose $a \in N \cup \{*\}$.

(a) We say that **M TxtEx^a**-learns the language L (using hypothesis space $\mathcal{H}$) from a text T iff $\mathbf{M}(T){\downarrow}_{hyp} = \beta$ such that $H_\beta =^a L$.
(b) We say that **M TxtEx^a**-learns a language L (using hypothesis space $\mathcal{H}$) iff **M TxtEx^a**-learns L from all texts for the language L (using hypothesis space $\mathcal{H}$).
(c) We say that **M TxtEx^a**-learns $\mathcal{L}$ (using hypothesis space $\mathcal{H}$) iff **M TxtEx^a**-learns all languages in $\mathcal{L}$ (using hypothesis space $\mathcal{H}$).
(d) **TxtEx^a** $= \{\mathcal{L} : (\exists \mathbf{M})[\mathbf{M} \ \mathbf{TxtEx}^a$-learns $\mathcal{L}$ using some hypothesis space$]\}$.

Definition 3. (Based on [CL82]) Suppose $\mathcal{H} = (H_i)_{i \in N}$ is a hypothesis space. Suppose $a \in N \cup \{*\}$.

(a) We say that **M TxtBc^a**-learns the language L (using hypothesis space $\mathcal{H}$) from a text T iff for some n, (i) $\mathbf{M}(T[n]) = (mem, \beta)$ such that $H_\beta =^a L$ and (ii) for all $m \geq n$, if $\mathbf{M}(T[m]) = (mem, \beta)$, where $\beta \neq ?$, then $H_\beta =^a L$.
(b) We say that **M TxtBc^a**-learns a language L (using hypothesis space $\mathcal{H}$) iff **M TxtBc^a**-learns L from all texts for the language L (using hypothesis space $\mathcal{H}$).
(c) We say that **M TxtBc^a**-learns $\mathcal{L}$ (using hypothesis space $\mathcal{H}$) iff **M TxtBc^a**-learns all languages in $\mathcal{L}$ (using hypothesis space $\mathcal{H}$).
(d) **TxtBc^a** $= \{\mathcal{L} : (\exists \mathbf{M})[\mathbf{M} \ \mathbf{TxtBc}^a$-learns $\mathcal{L}$ using some hypothesis space$]\}$.

One can similarly define **InfEx^a** and **InfBc^a**, where instead of text T as input one considers informant I as input to the learner. Note that for both the above criterion of learning, the learner needs to be defined on all initial segments of the text to be able to learn it.

Definition 4. [Wie76, LZ96] A learner **M** is said to be an *iterative learner* if its hypothesis depends only on its last conjecture and current input. That is, (i) if its initial memory mem_0 and hypothesis hyp_0 are same, and (ii) for all σ, if $\mathbf{M}(\sigma) = (mem, hyp)$, then $mem = hyp$.

TxtIt^a and **InfIt^a**-criterion are **TxtEx^a** and **InfEx^a**-criteria where the learners are restricted to be iterative.

Note that, although it is not stated explicitly, an **It**-type learner might store some input data in its conjecture (thus serving as a limited long-term memory). However, the amount of stored data cannot grow indefinitely, as the learner must stabilize to one (right) conjecture.

When the error allowed, a is 0, then we often drop it from the superscript of the learning criterion, that is, for example, we write **TxtEx** instead of **TxtEx^0**.

3   Learning with Negative Counterexamples

We now consider learning using negative counterexamples. In this model, the learner in addition to getting a text for the target language L, also gets negative counterexamples (if any) to its conjectures. That is, if the previous hypothesis of the learner is hyp, then in addition to getting a datum x, the learner also gets a datum y, where $y = \#$, if $H_{hyp} \subseteq L$, and $y \in L - H_{hyp}$, otherwise. By constraining the kind of counterexample given, different variations of the model were considered by [JK04],[JK08].

Definition 5. (Based on [JK08]) Suppose Δ is the set of allowed memories, and $(H_i)_{i \in J}$ is a hypothesis space.

(a) A *learner* learning using negative counterexamples examples is a mapping from $\Delta \times (N \cup \{\#\}) \times (N \cup \{\#\})$ to $\Delta \times (J \cup \{?\})$.
   A learner has an initial memory $mem_0 \in \Delta$, and initial hypothesis $hyp_0 \in J \cup \{?\}$.
(b) Suppose a learner $\mathbf{M}$ with initial memory mem_0 and initial hypothesis hyp_0 is given. Below, σ, τ are sequences over $N \cup \{\#\}$ with $|\sigma| = |\tau|$, and $x, y \in N \cup \{\#\}$. Extend the definition of $\mathbf{M}$ to sequences as follows.
   $\mathbf{M}(\Lambda, \Lambda) = (mem_0, hyp_0)$;
   $\mathbf{M}(\sigma \diamond x, \tau \diamond y) = \mathbf{M}(mem, x, y)$, where $\mathbf{M}(\sigma, \tau) = (mem, hyp)$, for some $hyp \in J \cup \{?\}$.
(c) $\mathbf{M}$ converges on text T with negative counterexample text T' to a hypothesis β (written: $\mathbf{M}(T, T')\!\downarrow_{hyp} = \beta$) iff there exists a t such that
   (i) $\mathbf{M}(T[t], T'[t]) \in \Delta \times \{\beta\}$, and
   (ii) for all $t' \geq t$, $\mathbf{M}(T[t], T'[t]) \in \Delta \times \{\beta, ?\}$.

$\mathbf{M}(\sigma, \tau) = (mem, hyp)$ in the definition above means that the memory and the hypothesis of the learner $\mathbf{M}$, after having seen the sequence σ and the corresponding negative counterexample sequence τ, is mem and hyp, respectively.

$\mathbf{NC}$ in the name of the criteria defined below means "from negative counterexample". $\mathbf{BNC}$ denotes "bounded negative counterexample" and $\mathbf{LNC}$ denotes "least negative counterexample."

Definition 6. (Based on [JK08]) Suppose $\mathcal{H} = (H_i)_{i \in J}$ is a hypothesis space, and Δ is the set of allowed memory.
   For ease of notation in the text below, let $H_? = \emptyset$.

(a) (i) T' is called a *counterexample text* for a learner $\mathbf{M}$ (with initial memory and hypothesis being mem_0 and hyp_0 respectively) on an input text T for a language L iff for all n, where $\mathbf{M}(T[n], T'[n]) = (mem, hyp)$,
      if $H_{hyp} \subseteq L$, then $T'(n) = \#$, and
      if $H_{hyp} \not\subseteq L$, then $T'(n) \in H_{hyp} - L$.
   (ii) T' is a *least-counterexample text* for $\mathbf{M}$ on an input text T for a language L iff for all n, where $\mathbf{M}(T[n], T'[n]) = (mem, hyp)$,
      if $H_{hyp} \subseteq L$, then $T'(n) = \#$, and
      if $H_{hyp} \not\subseteq L$, then $T'(n) = \min(H_{hyp} - L)$.

(iii) T' is a *bounded counterexample text* for **M** on an input text T for a language L iff for all n, where $\mathbf{M}(T[n], T'[n]) = (mem, hyp)$, if $H_{hyp} \cap \{x \in \Sigma^* : x \leq \max(\text{content}(T[n]))\} \subseteq L$, then $T'(n) = \#$, and if $H_{hyp} \cap \{x \in \Sigma^* : x \leq \max(\text{content}(T[n]))\} \not\subseteq L$, then $T'(n) \in H_{hyp} \cap \{x \in \Sigma^* : x \leq \max(\text{content}(T[n]))\} - L$.

(Intuitively, in bounded counterexample text, we bound the counterexample given by the largest positive datum seen so far. Thus, if the least counterexample exceeds this bound, then no counterexample is given — that is the corresponding value given in the counterexample text is $\#$.)

(b) **M NCEx**-*learns* a language L (using hypothesis space $\mathcal{H}$) iff for all texts T for L, for all counterexample texts T' for **M** on input text T, $\mathbf{M}(T, T')\!\downarrow_{hyp} = \beta$ such that $H_\beta = L$.

(c) We say that **M NCEx**-learns $\mathcal{L}$ (using a hypothesis space $\mathcal{H}$) if it **NCEx**-learns all languages in $\mathcal{L}$ (using the hypothesis space $\mathcal{H}$).

(d) **NCEx** $= \{\mathcal{L} : (\exists \mathbf{M})[\mathbf{M}\ \mathbf{NCEx}$-learns $\mathcal{L}$ using some hypothesis space $]\}$.

Learning criteria **LNCEx** and **BNCEx** for learning from least counterexamples or bounded counterexamples can be defined similarly.

4   NCEx and NCBc Models

The results in this section are from [JK08].

It is well known (a folklore, see [LZ94]) that all indexed classes can be learned from full positive and negative data (informants). As it turns out, in fact, just a finite number of negative counterexamples is necessary if full positive data is available.

Theorem 7. *Suppose $\mathcal{L}$ is an indexed family. Then $\mathcal{L} \in$ **NCEx**.*

It is also well known that some indexed classes are not **TxtEx**-learnable (see [Gol67]), thus, to learn any indexed class, a finite amount of negative data is necessary.

Still, **NCEx**-learners (and even **NCBc**-learners) are not as powerful as learners from informants (despite the fact that any **NCEx**-learner can test membership problem for any element w — making $\{w\}$ its conjecture and querying the oracle).

Theorem 8. *(a)* **NCEx** $\subseteq$ **InfEx***;*
(b) **InfEx** $-$ **NCEx**$^* \neq \emptyset$ *and* **InfEx** $-$ **NCBc** $\neq \emptyset$.

Moreover, some **Bc**-style learnable classes (without negative data) cannot be **NCEx**-learned.

Theorem 9. **TxtBc** $-$ **NCEx**$^* \neq \emptyset$.

Yet, while being more powerful than **NCEx**-learners, **NCBc**-style learners (without errors in the almost all correct conjectures) are not as powerful as the learners having access to full positive and full negative data.

Theorem 10.   *(a)* $\mathbf{NCBc} \subseteq \mathbf{InfBc}$;
(b) $\mathbf{InfEx} - \mathbf{NCBc} \neq \emptyset$.

Note that, as it follows from Theorem 9., $\mathbf{NCEx}^*$-learners, even making an arbitrary finite number of errors in the final correct conjecture, cannot learn some classes of recursively enumerable languages. On the other hand, it turns out that $\mathbf{NCBc}^1$-learners, making just one error in almost all conjectures, reach the ultimate learning power — such a learner can learn every class of recursively enumerable languages!

Theorem 11. $\mathcal{E} \in \mathbf{NCBc}^1$.

The proof of the above theorem is very interesting. A $\mathbf{NCBc}^1$-learner is, naturally, allowed to ask a subset query $W \subseteq L$, where W is any recursively enumerable language and L is the target language. However, the learner suggested in the proof needs answers to completely different type of subset queries: for any arbitrary initial segment of the input $T[n]$ and some r.e. set $W \subseteq L$, whether $\mathrm{content}(T[n]) \not\subseteq W$. As W might not be the target language, the learner cannot expect the oracle to answer such queries directly. However, the learner finds a way to encode this problem into a current conjecture and then query if the current conjecture is a subset of the target language. In order to do this, the learner (potentially) makes one deliberate error in its conjecture!

Now $\mathbf{NCEx}$ is compared with $\mathbf{LNCEx}$ and $\mathbf{BNCEx}$. Similarly, $\mathbf{NCBc}$ is compared with $\mathbf{LNCBc}$ and $\mathbf{BNCBc}$. $\mathbf{LNCEx}$-learners using least negative counterexamples are shown to have no advantage over $\mathbf{NCEx}$-learners. Same is true for the $\mathbf{Bc}$-style learning. Note here that for $\mathbf{LNCBc}^a$, with $a \geq 1$, $\mathbf{LNCBc}^a = \mathbf{NCBc}^a$ follows from $\mathcal{E} \in \mathbf{NCBc}^a$.

Theorem 12.   *Suppose* $a \in N \cup \{*\}$. *Then,* $\mathbf{NCEx}^a = \mathbf{LNCEx}^a$ *and* $\mathbf{NCBc} = \mathbf{LNCBc}$.

Yet $\mathbf{BNCEx}$-learners using counterexamples of bounded size turn out to be weaker than $\mathbf{NCEx}$-learners.

Theorem 13.   *(a) For any* $a \in N \cup \{*\}$, $\mathbf{BNCEx}^a \subset \mathbf{NCEx}^a$;
(b) $\mathbf{NCEx} - \mathbf{BNCBc}^* \neq \emptyset$.

Yet when learning just infinite classes of languages is considered, $\mathbf{BNCEx}$ model turns out to be as powerful as $\mathbf{NCEx}$. The same is true for $\mathbf{BNCBc}$ and $\mathbf{NCBc}$-learners (when no errors in almost all conjectures are allowed).

Theorem 14.   *Suppose* $\mathcal{L}$ *consists of only infinite languages. Then*
(a) $\mathcal{L} \in \mathbf{NCEx}^a$ *iff* $\mathcal{L} \in \mathbf{BNCEx}^a$;
(b) $\mathcal{L} \in \mathbf{NCBc}$ *iff* $\mathcal{L} \in \mathbf{BNCBc}$.

As a corollary to Theorem 13., we can conclude that $\mathbf{BNCBc}$-learners are weaker than $\mathbf{NCBc}$-learners and, though $\mathbf{NCBc}^1$-learners can learn any class of r.e. languages, $\mathbf{BNCBc}$-style learners cannot do this, even if an arbitrary finite number of errors is allowed in almost all conjectures (moreover, such learners are shown to be unable to learn even all indexed classes of languages). Yet, based on the ideas similar to the ones in the proof of Theorem 11., it has been shown that there is a **BNCBc**^{1}-learner that can learn all infinite r.e. languages.

According to Theorem 8., **NCEx** are weaker than learners from full positive and full negative data in terms of what classes they can learn. However, interestingly, for some **NCEx**-learnable classes, **NCEx**-learners can provide huge complexity advantage over the learners using full positive and full negative data. This advantage can be achieved when the number of mind changes is used as the complexity measure. It can be shown that, in some cases, one can learn a class in **NCEx** model using only n mind changes, whereas learning with informants requires exponentially many mind changes. In a variation of the **NCEx** model, where least negative counterexamples are given, one can even show that there are classes which are learnable using just 1 mind change, whereas learning with informants requires unbounded number of mind changes! In general, whereas several variations of negative counterexample types do not change learning power of the **NCEx** model, there is often complexity (mind change) advantage which may result from a particular variation.

5   Learning with a Limited Number of Bounded Counterexamples

In [JK07b], several variants of **BNCEx** model are explored that allow only uniformly bounded number of bounded negative counterexamples. Specifically,

— in the model **BNC^{n}Ex**, a learner makes a subset query for every new conjecture until n negative counterexamples have been received (still the learner can change its mind if new positive data have been received)

— in the model **BGNC^{n}Ex**, a learner is allowed to make subset queries (not necessarily for every conjecture) until n counterexamples have been received.

For both above variants of **BNCEx**, the versions where an oracle returns the least counterexamples have also been considered. Notation for each of these model is obtained by adding the prefix **L** — for example, **LBNC^{n}Ex**. Also, for all these models, restrictive variants, where a learner does not get a counterexample — just the answer "no" if the tested conjecture is incorrect and a bounded counterexample exists — have been considered; such models are denoted by adding **Res** as the prefix for the names of all three models in question. All these concepts are also considered for the **Bc**-style of learning.

The paper [JK07b] is devoted to a study of relationships between all these models and how they are related to the similar models when counterexamples are of arbitrary size (specifically, the variants **NC^{n}Ex** and **GNC^{n}Ex** corresponding to the above **BNC^{n}Ex** and **BGNC^{n}Ex** are considered). Some related results are also proved in [JK06] and some proofs in [JK07b] are based on the proofs in [JK06]. The results of this section are from the above papers.

The first problem studied in [JK07b] is the following: under which circumstances, more limited learners of the above types can simulate more capable learners. The major result is that **BNCEx**-type and **BNCBc**-type learners getting up to n least bounded counterexamples can be simulated by the learners of the same type and getting up to $2n - 1$ just answers "yes" if a bounded counterexample exists and "no", otherwise.

For $a \in N \cup \{*\}$, let $\mathbf{I} \in \{\mathbf{Ex}^a, \mathbf{Bc}^a\}$.

Theorem 15. *For all* $n \in N, n \geq 1$,
 (a) $\mathbf{LBNC}^n\mathbf{I} \subseteq \mathbf{ResBNC}^{2n-1}\mathbf{I}$.
 (b) $\mathbf{LBGNC}^n\mathbf{I} \subseteq \mathbf{ResBGNC}^{2n-1}\mathbf{I}$.

The bound $2n - 1$ turns out to be tight for the $\mathbf{Ex}^*$ and $\mathbf{Bc}^m$ types of learnability in the strongest possible way: it is shown that **BNC**-learners using n least short counterexamples cannot be simulated by **BGNC**-learners using $2n - 2$ (arbitrary short) counterexamples.

Theorem 16. *Suppose* $n \in N$ *and* $n \geq 1$.
 (a) $\mathbf{LBNC}^n\mathbf{Ex} - \mathbf{BGNC}^{2n-2}\mathbf{Bc}^m \neq \emptyset$.
 (b) $\mathbf{LBNC}^n\mathbf{Ex} - \mathbf{BGNC}^{2n-2}\mathbf{Ex}^* \neq \emptyset$.

The bound $2n-1$ on the number of negative answers turns out to be tight also for $\mathbf{Bc}$ and $\mathbf{Ex}^*$ types of learnability when **ResBNC**-learners try to simulate $\mathbf{BNC}^n$-learners. It is shown in the strongest possible way: there are $\mathbf{BNC}^n\mathbf{Ex}$-learners that cannot be simulated by $\mathbf{ResBNC}^{2n-2}\mathbf{Bc}^m$ or $\mathbf{ResBNC}^{2n-2}\mathbf{Ex}^*$-learners.

Theorem 17. *Suppose* $n \in N$ *and* $n \geq 1$.
 $\mathbf{BNC}^n\mathbf{Ex} - (\mathbf{ResBNC}^{2n-2}\mathbf{Bc}^m \cup \mathbf{ResBNC}^{2n-2}\mathbf{Ex}^*) \neq \emptyset$.

Interestingly, if one considers behaviorally correct learners that are allowed to make any finite number of errors in almost all correct conjectures, then n short (even least) counterexamples can be always substituted by just n 'no' answers. (For the general model **NC**, the lower bound $2n - 1$ for the simulation by **Res**-type learners still holds even for $\mathbf{Bc}^*$-learnability, as shown in [JK06]).

Theorem 18. *For all* $n \in N$, $\mathbf{LBGNC}^n\mathbf{Bc}^* \subseteq \mathbf{ResBNC}^n\mathbf{Bc}^*$.

Another issue addressed in [JK07b] is how short counterexamples fair against arbitrary or least counterexamples (this includes also the cases when just answers 'no' are returned instead of counterexamples). As it was established in [JK06], one answer 'no' used by an **NCEx**-learner can sometimes do more than unbounded number of least (short) counterexamples used by $\mathbf{Bc}^*$-learners.

Theorem 19. *[JK06]* $\mathbf{ResNC}^1\mathbf{Ex} - \mathbf{LBGNCBc}^* \neq \emptyset$.

Whereas, it would, perhaps, be natural to expect the above result, the next result, showing that one short counterexample can sometimes give a learner more than any bounded number of least counterexamples, may be perceived as surprising. However, note that a **LNC**-learner does *always* get least counterexamples if the conjecture overextends, and a **BNC** learner gets just a counterexample if *there exists one* below the maximal positive datum seen so far. On the surface, a **BNC**-learner seems to be at disadvantage, as it is likely to get less (negative) data. In fact, this disadvantage is salient if the number of allowed negative counterexamples is not limited: it is shown in [JK06] that, for $a \in N \cup \{*\}$, for $\mathbf{I} \in \{\mathbf{Ex}^a, \mathbf{Bc}^a\}$, **LBNCI** $\subset$ **ResNCI**. However, when the number of allowed counterexamples is uniformly bounded, there is a *charge* for every counterexample used. Consequently, a **BNC**-learner is not being charged for (unnecessary) negative data, if it does not receive it! As a result, the possibility of getting negative data which are $\leq$ largest positive datum seen in the input so far can be turned to an advantage — in terms of cost of learning, which is exploited in the proof the following result.

Theorem 20. *For all $n \in N$,* $\mathbf{ResBNC}^1\mathbf{Ex} - \mathbf{LGNC}^n\mathbf{Bc}^* \neq \emptyset$.

Some results in [JK07b] compare learnability from full positive data and a limited number of bounded counterexamples with learnability from full positive data and a limited number of other types of queries (as defined in [Ang88]).

6   Iterative Learning Using Negative Counterexamples

The paper [JK07a] introduces an *iterative* variant of learning from full positive data and negative counterexamples discussed above — the **NCIt**-model. The results of this section are mainly from the above paper. As for the general **NCEx** and **NCBc** models, the variants **LNCIt** and **BNCIt** are defined to denote learning using least counterexamples and, respectively, the bounded ones. As in the case of **NCEx**, least counterexamples are shown to have no advantage over the arbitrary ones.

Theorem 21. *For all $a \in N \cup \{*\}$,* $\mathbf{LNCIt}^a = \mathbf{NCIt}^a$.

On the other hand, contrary to the immediate intuition, "short" counterexamples sometimes can provide advantage over the arbitrary ones! The proof of the following result exploits the fact that sometimes actually *absence* of bounded counterexamples can help in a situation when arbitrary counterexamples are useless! Note that if a bounded counterexample is available to a learner, then an arbitrary counterexample is trivially available, and **NCEx**-learners can easily utilize this circumstance to simulate any **BNCEx**-learner — however, this is not the case with **NCIt**-learners: the fact that **NCIt**-learners are not able to memorize all data seen so far becomes of crucial importance.

Theorem 22. $\mathbf{BNCIt} - \mathbf{NCIt}^* \neq \emptyset$.

General capabilities of **NCIt** and **BNCIt** are compared with capabilities of some other popular learning models. First, it is shown that the **Ex**-style learners, being capable of storing in their memory all positive data seen so far, can sometimes learn more than any **NCIt** or **BNCIt**-learner.

Theorem 23. *(a)* $\mathbf{TxtEx} - \mathbf{NCIt}^* \neq \emptyset$;
(b) $\mathbf{TxtEx} - \mathbf{BNCIt}^* \neq \emptyset$.

Still, perhaps, also not surprisingly, some classes of languages in **NCIt** (even in **BNCIt**) cannot be learned from full positive data without negative counterexamples to conjectures, even if a learner always has access to full positive data seen so far (**Ex** or **Bc**-style). However, **NCIt** and **BNCIt**-learners can sometimes learn classes that are not learnable iteratively even from full positive and *full negative* data! — negative counterexamples, obtained when necessary to the learner, may provide more learning power than full negative data, appearing on the input when it might not be of use for the learner.

Theorem 24. $(\mathbf{BNCIt} \cap \mathbf{NCIt}) - \mathbf{InfIt}^* \neq \emptyset$.

In fact, **NCIt** is a proper superset of **InfIt**.

Theorem 25. $\mathbf{InfIt} \subset \mathbf{NCIt}$.

Another important result is that all indexed classes are **NCIt**-learnable. This result contrasts the well-known fact (established yet by Gold in [Gol67]) that not all indexed classes are in **TxtEx** — that is, when all positive data are stored in the memory, but no negative data is available.

Theorem 26. *Every indexed class of languages is in* **NCIt**.

Interestingly, whereas all indexed classes are **NCIt**-learnable, not every indexed class is **NCIt**-learnable *class-preservingly* ([ZL95]) — that is, when conjectures can be only from the numbering defining the target class. As it is shown in [JK11] all indexed classes are **NCIt**-learnable class-preservingly if a learner has access to additional information of certain types.

In [JK11], the extensions of **NCIt** model — using additional information of the following four different types — have been introduced and studied:

(a) when memorizing up to n input data seen so far is allowed;

(b) when up to n *feedback* membership queries (testing if an item belongs to the input seen so far) are allowed;

(c) when the number of the elements seen so far is memorized by the learner;

(d) when the maximum element seen so far is memorized by the learner.

(In the context of learning languages just from full positive data, the first two types of additional information for iterative learners were introduced and studied in [LZ96], and then reformulated and thoroughly studied and discussed in [CJLZ99]). It turned out that if the additional information of the types (c) or (d) is available to a **NCIt**-learner, then every indexed class can be learned class-preservingly. It has been also established how these four types of additional information influence capabilities of **NCIt**-learners, how they fair against each other, and how memorizing $n+1$ input data items and $n+1$ feedback membership queries fair over memorizing n input data items and n feedback membership queries, respectively.

7   Automatic NCEx-Learning

The automatic learnability model for learning from full positive data was introduced, motivated, and explored in [JLS10, JLS12]. For automatic learnability, one requires the input/output behaviour of the learner to be recognizable by a finite automata. Thus, the languages are considered to be sets of strings over some alphabet, and the memory and conjectures are also strings over some alphabet. By input/output behaviour to be recognizable by finite automata we mean that if the input and output of the learner is given in parallel (one character at a time, with the characters # used to pad the shorter input/output if any), then the automaton accepts it iff the learner on the input produces the corresponding output. (Due to space limitations, we present this model rather informally; the formal details can be found in [JLS12] and also in [JKS14]). The classes of languages learnable by automatic learners are *automatic* themselves: specifically, a family of target languages is defined by a regular index set, and the membership problem in these languages is regular in the sense that one finite automaton recognizes a combination (so-called "convolution") of an index and a word if and only if the word is in the language defined by the index.

The automatic analogue of **NCEx** has been introduced and studied first in [JK12]. We refer to this model as **AutoNCEx**. Similarly, we will refer to the automatic analogue of **NCIt**-model as **AutoNCIt**. The results of this section are from the full version of the above mentioned paper [JKS14].

The paper [JLS12] exhibits some examples of automatic classes of languages learnable from full positive data, however, as it has been established in [JLS12], not every automatic class is learnable from full positive data. A natural question is what additional information is needed to learn every automatic class. The following result gives the answer: a finite number of counterexamples to overextending conjectures. Moreover, the learner may be iterative.

Theorem 27. *Every automatic class is in* **AutoNCIt**.

On the other hand, interestingly, conjectures of the learners exhibited in the proof of the above theorem might not always be consistent with the input seen so far, and it is an open question if such consistency may be achieved. Yet, it has been shown that such consistency can be achieved if **AutoNCIt**-learners always receive the least negative counterexamples. On the other hand, as it follows from a result in [JK08], there are automatic classes that cannot be learned even by non-automatic **BNCEx**-learners. Still, with this bound on the size of counterexamples, **AutoNCEx**-learners with memory limited by the size of the longest positive input datum seen so far can learn automatic classes consisting only of infinite languages. Similar result holds for **AutoNCIt**-learners.

It is also shown that some automatic classes cannot be **AutoNCEx**-learned using bounded negative counterexamples with memory limited by the size of the current hypothesis (and, thus, when only the last hypothesis can be stored in the memory), but can be automatically learned with memory limited by the size of the longest positive datum seen so far even without negative counterexamples.

References

[Ang88] Angluin, D.: Queries and concept learning. Machine Learning **2**(4), 319–342 (1988)

[Bār74] Bārzdiņš, J.: Two theorems on the limiting synthesis of functions. In: Theory of Algorithms and Programs, vol. 1, pp. 82–88. Latvian State University (1974). In Russian

[BCJ95] Baliga, G., Case, J., Jain, S.: Language learning with some negative information. Journal of Computer and System Sciences **51**(5), 273–285 (1995)

[BH70] Brown, R., Hanlon, C.: Derivational complexity and the order of acquisition in child speech. In: Hayes, J.R. (ed.) Cognition and the Development of Language, Wiley (1970)

[Blu67] Blum, M.: A machine-independent theory of the complexity of recursive functions. Journal of the ACM **14**(2), 322–336 (1967)

[CJLZ99] Case, J., Jain, S., Lange, S., Zeugmann, T.: Incremental concept learning for bounded data mining. Information and Computation **152**(1), 74–110 (1999)

[CL82] Case, J., Lynes, C.: Machine inductive inference and language identification. In: Nielsen, M., Schmidt, E.M. (eds.) Automata, Languages and Programming. LNCS, vol. 140, pp. 107–115. Springer, Heidelberg (1982)

[CS83] Case, J., Smith, C.: Comparison of identification criteria for machine inductive inference. Theoretical Computer Science **25**, 193–220 (1983)

[DPS86] Demetras, M., Post, K., Snow, C.: Feedback to first language learners: The role of repetitions and clarification questions. Journal of Child Language **13**, 275–292 (1986)

[Gol67] Gold, E.M.: Language identification in the limit. Information and Control **10**(5), 447–474 (1967)

[HPTS84] Hirsh-Pasek, K., Treiman, R., Schneiderman, M.: Brown and Hanlon revisited: Mothers' sensitivity to ungrammatical forms. Journal of Child Language **11**, 81–88 (1984)

[JK04] Jain, S., Kinber, E.: Learning Languages from Positive Data and Negative Counterexamples. In: Ben-David, S., Case, J., Maruoka, A. (eds.) ALT 2004. LNCS (LNAI), vol. 3244, pp. 54–68. Springer, Heidelberg (2004)

[JK06] Jain, S., Kinber, E.: Learning languages from positive data and a finite number of queries. Information and Computation **204**(1), 123–175 (2006)

[JK07a] Jain, S., Kinber, E.: Iterative learning from positive data and negative counterexamples. Information and Computation **205**(12), 1777–1805 (2007)

[JK07b] Jain, S., Kinber, E.: Learning languages from positive data and a limited number of short counterexamples. Theoretical Computer Science **389**(1–2), 190–218 (2007)

[JK08] Jain, S., Kinber, E.: Learning languages from positive data and negative counterexamples. Journal of Computer and System Sciences **74**(4), 431–456 (2008). Special Issue: Carl Smith memorial issue

[JK11] Jain, S., Kinber, E.: Iterative learning from texts and counterexamples using additional information. Machine Learning **84**, 291–333 (2011)

[JK12] Jain, S., Kinber, E.: Automatic Learning from Positive Data and Negative Counterexamples. In: Bshouty, N.H., Stoltz, G., Vayatis, N., Zeugmann, T. (eds.) ALT 2012. LNCS (LNAI), vol. 7568, pp. 66–80. Springer, Heidelberg (2012)

[JKS14] Jain, S., Kinber, E., Stephan, F.: Automatic learning from positive data and negative counterexamples (2014). Manuscript

[JLS10] Jain, S., Luo, Q., Stephan, F.: Learnability of Automatic Classes. In: Dediu, A.-H., Fernau, H., Martín-Vide, C. (eds.) LATA 2010. LNCS, vol. 6031, pp. 321–332. Springer, Heidelberg (2010)

[JLS12] Jain, S., Luo, Q., Stephan, F.: Learnability of automatic classes. Journal of Computer and System Sciences **78**(6), 1910–1927 (2012)

[LZ94] Lange, S., Zeugmann, T.: Characterization of language learning from informant under various monotonicity constraints. Journal of Experimental and Theoretical Artificial Intelligence **6**, 73–94 (1994)

[LZ96] Lange, S., Zeugmann, T.: Incremental learning from positive data. Journal of Computer and System Sciences **53**(1), 88–103 (1996)

[LZ06] Li, Y., Zhang, W.: Simplify support vector machines by iterative learning. Neural Processsing Information - Letters and Reviews **10**(1), 11–17 (2006)

[OSW86] Osherson, D., Stob, M., Weinstein, S.: Systems that Learn: An Introduction to Learning Theory for Cognitive and Computer Scientists. MIT Press (1986)

[Pin79] Pinker, S.: Formal models of language learning. Cognition **7**, 217–283 (1979)

[Rog67] Rogers, H.: Theory of Recursive Functions and Effective Computability. McGraw-Hill (1967). Reprinted by MIT Press in 1987

[Shi86] Shinohara, T.: Studies on Inductive Inference from Positive Data. PhD thesis, Kyushu University, Kyushu, Japan (1986)

[WC80] Wexler, K., Culicover, P.: Formal Principles of Language Acquisition. MIT Press (1980)

[Wie76] Wiehagen, R.: Limes-Erkennung rekursiver Funktionen durch spezielle Strategien. Journal of Information Processing and Cybernetics (EIK) **12**(1–2), 93–99 (1976)

[ZL95] Zeugmann, T., Lange, S.: A guided tour across the boundaries of learning recursive languages. In: Lange, S., Jantke, K.P. (eds.) GOSLER 1994. LNCS, vol. 961, pp. 190–258. Springer, Heidelberg (1995)

One-Sided Random Context Grammars: A Survey

Alexander Meduna and Petr Zemek[✉]

Faculty of Information Technology, IT4Innovations Centre of Excellence,
Brno University of Technology, Božetěchova 2, 612 66 Brno, Czech Republic
{meduna,izemek}@fit.vutbr.cz

Abstract. Recall that the notion of a *one-sided random context grammar* is based upon a finite set of context-free rules, each of which may be extended by finitely many *permitting* and *forbidding nonterminal symbols*. The set of all these rules is divided into two sets—the set of *left random context rules* and the set of *right random context rules*. When applying a left random context rule, the grammar checks the existence and absence of its permitting and forbidding symbols, respectively, in the prefix to the left of the rewritten nonterminal. Analogically, when applying a right random context rule, it checks the existence and absence of its permitting and forbidding symbols, respectively, only in the suffix to the right of the rewritten nonterminal.

This paper gives a survey of the established results concerning one-sided random context grammars. These results concern their generative power, normal forms, size reduction, and conceptual modifications, which represent both restricted and generalized versions of their standard concepts. Perhaps most importantly and surprisingly, the paper points out that propagating versions of one-sided random context grammars characterize the family of context-sensitive languages, and with erasing rules, they characterize the family of recursively enumerable languages; as a result, they are stronger than ordinary random context grammars. Many open problem areas are suggested.

Keywords: Formal language theory · Regulated rewriting · Random context grammars · One-sided random context grammars · Generative power · Normal forms · Reduction · Leftmost derivations · Generalized versions · Survey

1 Introduction

The present paper deals with regulated grammars referred to as *random context grammars* (see Section 1.1 in [2]). In essence, these grammars regulate the language generation process so they require the presence of some prescribed symbols and, simultaneously, the absence of some others in the rewritten sentential forms. More precisely, random context grammars are based upon context-free rules, each of which may be extended by finitely many *permitting* and *forbidding*

© Springer International Publishing Switzerland 2014
C.S. Calude et al. (Eds.): Gruska Festschrift, LNCS 8808, pp. 338–351, 2014.
DOI: 10.1007/978-3-319-13350-8_25

nonterminal symbols. A rule like this can rewrite the current sentential form provided that all its permitting symbols occur in the sentential form while all its forbidding symbols do not.

As a matter of fact, this paper concerns *one-sided random context grammars* (see [7]) as slightly modified versions of ordinary random context grammars. That is, while random context grammars verify the presence and absence of symbols in sentential forms in their entirety, one-sided random context grammars perform this verification only in their prefixes or suffixes. More precisely, in every one-sided random context grammar, the set of rules is divided into the set of *left random context rules* and the set of *right random context rules*. When applying a left random context rule, the grammar checks the existence and absence of its permitting and forbidding symbols, respectively, only in the prefix to the left of the rewritten nonterminal. Similarly, when applying a right random context rule, it checks the existence and absence of its permitting and forbidding symbols, respectively, only in the suffix to the right of the rewritten nonterminal. Otherwise, it works just like any random context grammar.

The present paper gives a survey of the crucially important results concerning one-sided random context grammars. It points out that propagating versions of one-sided random context grammars characterize the family of context-sensitive languages, and with erasing rules, they characterize the family of recursively enumerable languages. Therefore, they are stronger than random context grammars, and this result comes as a surprise because one-sided random context grammars actually verify the presence and absence of symbols only in parts of sentential forms, not in their entirety. The paper also gives an overview concerning normal forms and reduction of these grammars.

In addition, the paper considers several restricted versions of these grammars. Specifically, it shows that *one-sided permitting grammars*, which have only permitting rules, are more powerful than context-free grammars; on the other hand, they are no more powerful than propagating scattered context grammars (see [4]). *One-sided forbidding grammars*, which have only forbidding rules, are equivalent to selective substitution grammars (see [5,15]), and *left forbidding grammars*, which have only left forbidding rules, are only as powerful as context-free grammars.

Apart from restricted versions of one-sided random context grammars, the paper also makes remarks on their generalized versions. In fact, the paper even suggests introducing one-sided versions of completely different formal models than random context grammars. Finally, it formulates many open problem areas related to one-sided random context grammars.

This paper is organized as follows. Section 2 gives all the necessary notation and terminology to follow the rest of the paper. Then, Section 3 defines one-sided random context grammars and their variants, and illustrates these definitions by examples. After that, Section 4 gives an overview of the established results concerning these grammars, including many references. Section 5 closes the paper by mentioning several open problems.

2   Preliminaries

In this paper, we assume that the reader is familiar with formal language theory (see [17]). For a set Q, card(Q) denotes the cardinality of Q, and 2^Q denotes the power set of Q. For an alphabet (finite nonempty set) V, V^* represents the free monoid generated by V under the operation of concatenation. The unit of V^* is denoted by ε. For $x \in V^*$, $|x|$ denotes the length of x and alph(x) denotes the set of symbols occurring in x.

A *random context grammar* (see Section 1.1 in [2]) is a quadruple, $G = (N, T, P, S)$, where N and T are two disjoint alphabets of *nonterminals* and *terminals*, respectively, $S \in N$ is the *start symbol*, and $P \subseteq N \times (N \cup T)^* \times 2^N \times 2^N$ is a finite relation, called the set of *rules*. Set $V = N \cup T$. Each rule $(A, x, U, W) \in P$ is written as $(A \to x, U, W)$ throughout this paper. The *direct derivation relation* over V^*, symbolically denoted by $\Rightarrow_G$, is defined as follows: if $u, v \in V^*$, $(A \to x, U, W) \in P$, $U \subseteq$ alph(uAv), and $W \cap$ alph(uAv) $= \emptyset$, then $uAv \Rightarrow_G uxv$. U is called the *permitting context* and W is called the *forbidding context*. Let $\Rightarrow_G^*$ denote the reflexive-transitive closure of $\Rightarrow_G$. The *language of G* is denoted by $L(G)$ and defined as $L(G) = \{w \in T^* \mid S \Rightarrow_G^* w\}$.

Let $G = (N, T, P, S)$ be a random context grammar. Rules of the form $(A \to \varepsilon, U, W)$ are called *erasing rules*. If $(A \to x, U, W) \in P$ implies that $|x| \geq 1$, then G is a *propagating random context grammar*. If $(A \to x, U, W) \in P$ implies that $W = \emptyset$, then G is a *permitting grammar*. If $(A \to x, U, W) \in P$ implies that $U = \emptyset$, then G is a *forbidding grammar*. By analogy with propagating random context grammars, we define a *propagating permitting grammar* and a *propagating forbidding grammar*, respectively.

Denotation of Language Families

Throughout the rest of this paper, the language families under discussion are denoted in the following way. **RC**, **P**, and **F** denote the language families generated by random context grammars, permitting grammars, and forbidding grammars, respectively. The notation with the upper index $-\varepsilon$ stands for the corresponding propagating family. For example, **RC**$^{-\varepsilon}$ denotes the family of languages generated by propagating random context grammars. **CF**, **CS**, and **RE** denote the families of context-free languages, context-sensitive languages, and recursively enumerable languages, respectively. **SC**$^{-\varepsilon}$, **S**, and **S**$^{-\varepsilon}$ denote the language families generated by propagating scattered context languages (see [4]), selective substitution grammars (see [5,15]), and propagating selective substitution grammars—that is, selective substitution grammars without erasing rules—, respectively.

3   Definitions and Examples

Next, we formally define one-sided random context grammars and their variants. In addition, we illustrate them by examples.

Definition 1. A *one-sided random context grammar* is a quintuple

$$G = (N, T, P_L, P_R, S)$$

where N and T are two disjoint alphabets, $S \in N$, and

$$P_L, P_R \subseteq N \times (N \cup T)^* \times 2^N \times 2^N$$

are two finite relations. Set $V = N \cup T$. The components V, N, T, P_L, P_R, and S are called the *total alphabet*, the alphabet of *nonterminals*, the alphabet of *terminals*, the set of *left random context rules*, the set of *right random context rules*, and the *start symbol*, respectively. Each $(A, x, U, W) \in P_L \cup P_R$ is written as

$$(A \to x, U, W)$$

throughout this paper. For $(A \to x, U, W) \in P_L$, U and W are called the *left permitting context* and the *left forbidding context*, respectively. For $(A \to x, U, W) \in P_R$, U and W are called the *right permitting context* and the *right forbidding context*, respectively.   □

   When applying a left random context rule, the grammar checks the existence and absence of its permitting and forbidding symbols, respectively, only in the prefix to the left of the rewritten nonterminal in the current sentential form. Analogously, when applying a right random context rule, it checks the existence and absence of its permitting and forbidding symbols, respectively, only in the suffix to the right of the rewritten nonterminal. The following definition states this formally.

Definition 2. Let $G = (N, T, P_L, P_R, S)$ be a one-sided random context grammar. The *direct derivation relation* over V^* is denoted by $\Rightarrow_G$ and defined as follows. Let $u, v \in V^*$ and $(A \to x, U, W) \in P_L \cup P_R$. Then,

$$uAv \Rightarrow_G uxv$$

if and only if

$$(A \to x, U, W) \in P_L, U \subseteq \mathrm{alph}(u), \text{ and } W \cap \mathrm{alph}(u) = \emptyset$$

or

$$(A \to x, U, W) \in P_R, U \subseteq \mathrm{alph}(v), \text{ and } W \cap \mathrm{alph}(v) = \emptyset$$

Let $\Rightarrow_G^*$ denote the reflexive-transitive closure of $\Rightarrow_G$.   □

   The language generated by a one-sided random context grammar is defined as usual—that is, it consists of strings over the terminal alphabet that can be generated from the start symbol.

Definition 3. Let $G = (N, T, P_L, P_R, S)$ be a one-sided random context grammar. The *language of G* is denoted by $L(G)$ and defined as

$$L(G) = \{w \in T^* \mid S \Rightarrow_G^* w\}$$ □

Next, we define several special variants of one-sided random context grammars.

Definition 4. Let $G = (N, T, P_L, P_R, S)$ be a one-sided random context grammar. Rules of the form $(A \to \varepsilon, U, W)$ are called *erasing rules*. If $(A \to x, U, W) \in P_L \cup P_R$ implies that $|x| \geq 1$, then G is a *propagating one-sided random context grammar*. If $(A \to x, U, W) \in P_L \cup P_R$ implies that $W = \emptyset$, then G is a *one-sided permitting grammar*. If $(A \to x, U, W) \in P_L \cup P_R$ implies that $U = \emptyset$, then G is a *one-sided forbidding grammar*. By analogy with propagating one-sided random context grammars, we define a *propagating one-sided permitting grammar* and a *propagating one-sided forbidding grammar*, respectively.   □

Definition 5. Let $G = (N, T, P_L, P_R, S)$ be a one-sided random context grammar. If $P_R = \emptyset$, then G is a *left random context grammar*. By analogy with one-sided permitting and forbidding grammars, we define a *left permitting grammar* (see [1]) and a *left forbidding grammar* (see [3]), respectively. Their propagating versions are defined analogously as well.   □

Next, we illustrate the above definitions by three examples.

Example 1. Consider the one-sided random context grammar

$$G = (\{S, A, B, \bar{A}, \bar{B}\}, \{a, b, c\}, P_L, P_R, S)$$

where P_L contains the following four rules

$$(S \to AB, \emptyset, \emptyset) \qquad (\bar{B} \to B, \{A\}, \emptyset)$$
$$(B \to b\bar{B}c, \{\bar{A}\}, \emptyset) \qquad (B \to \varepsilon, \emptyset, \{A, \bar{A}\})$$

and P_R contains the following three rules

$$(A \to a\bar{A}, \{B\}, \emptyset) \qquad (\bar{A} \to A, \{\bar{B}\}, \emptyset) \qquad (A \to \varepsilon, \{B\}, \emptyset)$$

It is rather easy to see that every derivation that generates a nonempty string of $L(G)$ is of the form

$$
\begin{aligned}
S &\Rightarrow_G AB \\
&\Rightarrow_G a\bar{A}B \\
&\Rightarrow_G a\bar{A}b\bar{B}c \\
&\Rightarrow_G aAb\bar{B}c \\
&\Rightarrow_G aAbBc \\
&\Rightarrow_G^* a^n Ab^n Bc^n \\
&\Rightarrow_G a^n b^n Bc^n \\
&\Rightarrow_G a^n b^n c^n
\end{aligned}
$$

where $n \geq 1$. The empty string is generated by

$$S \Rightarrow_G AB \Rightarrow_G B \Rightarrow_G \varepsilon$$

Based on the previous observations, we see that G generates the non-context-free language $\{a^n b^n c^n \mid n \geq 0\}$.   □

Example 2. Consider $K = \{a^n b^m c^m \mid 1 \leq m \leq n\}$. This non-context-free language is generated by the one-sided permitting grammar

$$G = (\{S, A, B, X, Y\}, \{a, b, c\}, P_L, \emptyset, S)$$

with P_L containing the following seven rules

$(S \rightarrow AX, \emptyset, \emptyset)$	$(A \rightarrow a, \emptyset, \emptyset)$	$(X \rightarrow bc, \emptyset, \emptyset)$
	$(A \rightarrow aB, \emptyset, \emptyset)$	$(X \rightarrow bYc, \{B\}, \emptyset)$
	$(B \rightarrow A, \emptyset, \emptyset)$	$(Y \rightarrow X, \{A\}, \emptyset)$

Notice that G is, in fact, a propagating left permitting grammar. Observe that $(X \rightarrow bYc, \{B\}, \emptyset)$ is applicable if B, produced by $(A \rightarrow aB, \emptyset, \emptyset)$, occurs to the left of X in the current sentential form. Similarly, $(Y \rightarrow X, \{A\}, \emptyset)$ is applicable if A, produced by $(B \rightarrow A, \emptyset, \emptyset)$, occurs to the left of Y in the current sentential form. Consequently, we see that every derivation that generates $w \in L(G)$ is of the form[1]

$$\begin{aligned}
S &\Rightarrow_G AX \\
&\Rightarrow_G^* a^u AX \\
&\Rightarrow_G a^{u+1} BX \\
&\Rightarrow_G a^{u+1} BbYc \\
&\Rightarrow_G a^{u+1} AbYc \\
&\Rightarrow_G^* a^{u+1+v} AbYc \\
&\Rightarrow_G a^{u+1+v} AbXc \\
&\quad\vdots \\
&\Rightarrow_G^* a^{n-1} Ab^{m-1} Xc^{m-1} \\
&\Rightarrow_G ab^{m-1} Xc^{m-1} \\
&\Rightarrow_G a^n b^m c^m = w
\end{aligned}$$

where $u, v \geq 0$, $1 \leq m \leq n$. Hence, $L(G) = K$. $\qquad\square$

Example 3. Consider the one-sided forbidding grammar

$$G = (\{S, A, B, A', B', \bar{A}, \bar{B}\}, \{a, b, c\}, P_L, P_R, S)$$

where P_L contains the following five rules

$(S \rightarrow AB, \emptyset, \emptyset)$	$(B \rightarrow bB'c, \emptyset, \{A, \bar{A}\})$	$(B' \rightarrow B, \emptyset, \{A'\})$
	$(B \rightarrow \bar{B}, \emptyset, \{A, A'\})$	$(\bar{B} \rightarrow \varepsilon, \emptyset, \{\bar{A}\})$

and P_R contains the following four rules

---

[1] Notice that after X is rewritten to bc by $(X \rightarrow bc, \emptyset, \emptyset)$, more *as* can be generated by $(A \rightarrow aB, \emptyset, \emptyset)$. However, observe that this does not affect the generated language.

$$(A \to aA', \emptyset, \{B'\}) \qquad (A' \to A, \emptyset, \{B\})$$
$$(A \to \bar{A}, \emptyset, \{B'\}) \qquad (\bar{A} \to \varepsilon, \emptyset, \{B\})$$

Notice that G is, in fact, a one-sided forbidding grammar, and that every derivation that generates a nonempty string of $L(G)$ is of the form

$$
\begin{aligned}
S &\Rightarrow_G AB \\
&\Rightarrow_G aA'B \\
&\Rightarrow_G aA'bB'c \\
&\Rightarrow_G aAbB'c \\
&\Rightarrow_G aAbBc \\
&\Rightarrow_G^* a^n Ab^n Bc^n \\
&\Rightarrow_G a^n \bar{A}b^n Bc^n \\
&\Rightarrow_G a^n \bar{A}b^n \bar{B}c^n \\
&\Rightarrow_G a^n b^n \bar{B}c^n \\
&\Rightarrow_G a^n b^n c^n
\end{aligned}
$$

where $n \geq 1$. The empty string is generated by

$$S \Rightarrow_G AB \Rightarrow_G \bar{A}B \Rightarrow_G \bar{A}\bar{B} \Rightarrow_G \bar{B} \Rightarrow_G \varepsilon$$

Based on the previous observations, we see that G generates the non-context-free language $\{a^n b^n c^n \mid n \geq 0\}$. $\qquad\square$

Denotation of Language Families

Throughout the rest of this paper, the language families under discussion are denoted in the following way. **ORC**, **OP**, and **OF** denote the language families generated by one-sided random context grammars, one-sided permitting grammars, and one-sided forbidding grammars, respectively. **LRC**, **LP**, and **LF** denote the language families generated by left random context grammars, left permitting grammars, and left forbidding grammars, respectively.

The notation with the upper index $-\varepsilon$ stands for the corresponding propagating family. For example, **ORC**$^{-\varepsilon}$ denotes the family of languages generated by propagating one-sided random context grammars.

4   Results

In this section, we give an overview of the established results concerning one-sided random context grammars. More details can be found in the cited papers and in Chapter 6 of [14].

Generative Power

First, we investigate the generative power of one-sided random context grammars. In [7], it is proved that one-sided random context grammars characterize the family of recursively enumerable languages, and that their propagating versions characterize the family of context-sensitive languages.

Theorem 1 (see Theorem 2 in [7]). $\mathbf{ORC} = \mathbf{RE}$ □

Theorem 2 (see Theorem 1 in [7]). $\mathbf{ORC}^{-\varepsilon} = \mathbf{CS}$ □

Since $\mathbf{RC}^{-\varepsilon} \subset \mathbf{CS}$ and $\mathbf{RC} = \mathbf{RE}$ (see [2]), we have that one-sided random context grammars are equally powerful as random context grammars, while propagating one-sided random context grammars are more powerful than propagating random context grammars.

Theorem 3 (see Corollary 3 in [7]). $\mathbf{RC}^{-\varepsilon} \subset \mathbf{ORC}^{-\varepsilon} \subset \mathbf{RC} = \mathbf{ORC}$ □

The power of one-sided forbidding grammars is investigated in [9]. In there, it is proved that they have the same power as selective substitution grammars (see [5,15]).

Theorem 4 (see Theorem 3.7 in [9]). $\mathbf{OF} = \mathbf{S}$ □

Theorem 5 (see Theorem 3.8 in [9]). $\mathbf{OF}^{-\varepsilon} = \mathbf{S}^{-\varepsilon}$ □

It is not known whether one-sided forbidding grammars or selective substitution grammars characterize the family of recursively enumerable languages. Also, it is not known whether these grammars without erasing rules characterize the family of context-sensitive languages.

Moreover, [9] proves the following two results concerning the generative power of one-sided forbidding grammars, where the set of left random context rules coincides with the set of right random context rules.

Theorem 6 (see Theorem 3.11 in [9]). *A language K is context-free if and only if there is a one-sided forbidding grammar, $G = (N, T, P_L, P_R, S)$, satisfying $K = L(G)$ and $P_L = P_R$.* □

Theorem 7 (see Corollary 3.12 in [9]). *Let $G = (N, T, P_L, P_R, S)$ be a one-sided forbidding grammar satisfying $P_L = P_R$. Then, there is a propagating one-sided forbidding grammar H such that $L(H) = L(G) - \{\varepsilon\}$.* □

One-sided forbidding grammars are at least as powerful as forbidding grammars. This is stated in the next two theorems.

Theorem 8 (see Theorem 5 in [7]). $\mathbf{F} \subseteq \mathbf{OF}$ □

Theorem 9 (see Corollary 1 in [7]). $\mathbf{F}^{-\varepsilon} \subseteq \mathbf{OF}^{-\varepsilon}$ □

In terms of left forbidding grammars and their power, [3] proves that they are no more powerful than context-free grammars.

Theorem 10 (see Theorem 1 in [3]). $\mathbf{LF}^{-\varepsilon} = \mathbf{LF} = \mathbf{CF}$ □

From Theorems 9 and 10 above and from the fact that $\mathbf{CF} \subset \mathbf{F}^{-\varepsilon}$ (see [2]), we obtain the following corollary, which relates the language families generated by left forbidding grammars, one-sided forbidding grammars, and forbidding grammars.

Corollary 1. $\mathbf{LF^{-\varepsilon}} = \mathbf{LF} \subset \mathbf{F^{-\varepsilon}} \subseteq \mathbf{OF^{-\varepsilon}} \subseteq \mathbf{OF}$ □

Finally, the following two theorems relate the language families generated by propagating one-sided permitting grammars and propagating left permitting grammars to other families of languages.

Theorem 11 (see Theorem 7 in [7]). $\mathbf{CF} \subset \mathbf{OP^{-\varepsilon}} \subseteq \mathbf{SC^{-\varepsilon}} \subseteq \mathbf{CS} = \mathbf{ORC^{-\varepsilon}}$ □

Theorem 12 (see Corollary 2 in [7]). $\mathbf{CF} \subset \mathbf{LP^{-\varepsilon}} \subseteq \mathbf{SC^{-\varepsilon}} \subseteq \mathbf{CS} = \mathbf{ORC^{-\varepsilon}}$ □

Recall that it is not known whether propagating scattered context grammars characterize the family of context-sensitive languages—that is, whether the inclusion $\mathbf{SC^{-\varepsilon}} \subseteq \mathbf{CS}$ above is, in fact, an identity (see [6]).

Normal Forms

Formal language theory has always struggled to turn grammars into *normal forms*, in which grammatical rules satisfy some prescribed properties or format because they are easier to handle from a theoretical as well as practical standpoint. Concerning context-free grammars, there exist two famous normal forms—the Chomsky and Greibach normal forms. In the former, every grammatical rule has on its right-hand side either a terminal or two nonterminals. In the latter, every grammatical rule has on its right-hand side a terminal followed by zero or more nonterminals. Similarly, there exist normal forms for general grammars, such as the Kuroda, Penttonen, and Geffert normal forms. In this section, we present four normal forms for one-sided random context grammars.

In the first normal form, the set of left random context rules coincides with the set of right random context rules.

Theorem 13 (see Theorems 3 and 4 in [7]). *Let $G = (N, T, P_L, P_R, S)$ be a one-sided random context grammar. Then, there is a one-sided random context grammar, $H = (N', T, P'_L, P'_R, S)$, such that $L(H) = L(G)$ and $P'_L = P'_R$. Furthermore, if G is propagating, so is H.* □

The second normal form represents a dual normal form to that in Theorem 13. Indeed, every one-sided random context grammar can be turned into an equivalent one-sided random context grammar with the sets of left and right random context rules being disjoint.

Theorem 14 (see Theorem 4 in [18]). *Let $G = (N, T, P_L, P_R, S)$ be a one-sided random context grammar. Then, there is a one-sided random context grammar, $H = (N', T, P'_L, P'_R, S)$, such that $L(H) = L(G)$ and $P'_L \cap P'_R = \emptyset$. Furthermore, if G is propagating, so is H.* □

The third normal form represents an analogy of the well-known Chomsky normal form for context-free grammars. However, since one-sided random context grammars with erasing rules are more powerful than their propagating versions, we allow the presence of erasing rules in the transformed grammar.

Theorem 15 (see Theorem 2 in [18]). *Let* $G = (N, T, P_L, P_R, S)$ *be a one-sided random context grammar. Then, there is a one-sided random context grammar,* $H = (N', T, P_L', P_R', S)$, *such that* $L(H) = L(G)$ *and* $(A \rightarrow x, U, W) \in P_L' \cup P_R'$ *implies that* $x \in N'N' \cup T \cup \{\varepsilon\}$. *Furthermore, if* G *is propagating, so is* H. □

In the fourth normal form, every rule has its permitting or forbidding context empty.

Theorem 16 (see Theorem 3 in [18]). *Let* $G = (N, T, P_L, P_R, S)$ *be a one-sided random context grammar. Then, there is a one-sided random context grammar,* $H = (N', T, P_L', P_R', S)$, *such that* $L(H) = L(G)$ *and* $(A \rightarrow x, U, W) \in P_L' \cup P_R'$ *implies that* $U = \emptyset$ *or* $W = \emptyset$. *Furthermore, if* G *is propagating, so is* H. □

Reduction

Recall that one-sided random context grammars characterize the family of recursively enumerable languages (see Theorem 1). Of course, it is more than natural to ask whether the family of recursively enumerable languages is characterized by one-sided random context grammars with a limited number of nonterminals or rules. The present section gives an affirmative answer to this question.

The next theorem states that ten nonterminals suffice to generate any recursively enumerable language by a one-sided random context grammar.

Theorem 17 (see Theorem 1 in [8]). *For every recursively enumerable language* K, *there exists a one-sided random context grammar,* $H = (N, T, P_L, P_R, S)$, *such that* $L(H) = K$ *and* $\mathrm{card}(N) = 10$. □

The number of nonterminals can be also limited in terms of one-sided random context grammars satisfying the normal form from Theorem 13.

Theorem 18 (see Corollary 1 in [8]). *For every recursively enumerable language* K, *there exists a one-sided random context grammar,* $H = (N, T, P_L, P_R, S)$, *such that* $L(H) = K$, $P_L = P_R$, *and* $\mathrm{card}(N) = 13$. □

To approach the reduction of the number of nonterminals in a finer way, in [8], the notion of a *right random context nonterminal* is introduced. It is defined as a nonterminal that appears on the left-hand side of a right random context rule. That paper has demonstrated how to convert any one-sided random context grammar to an equivalent one-sided random context grammar with two right random context nonterminals. This result has been proved also for propagating one-sided random context grammars.

Let us first define the above-mentioned measure formally.

Definition 6. Let $G = (N, T, P_L, P_R, S)$ be a one-sided random context grammar. If $(A \rightarrow x, U, W) \in P_R$, then A is a *right random context nonterminal*.

The *number of right random context nonterminals* of G is denoted by $\mathrm{nrrcn}(G)$ and defined as

$$\mathrm{nrrcn}(G) = \mathrm{card}\big(\{A \mid (A \to x, U, W) \in P_R\}\big) \qquad \square$$

The next two theorems state that two right random context nonterminals suffice to keep the power of one-sided random context grammars unchanged.

Theorem 19 (see Theorem 2 in [8]). *For every recursively enumerable language K, there is a one-sided random context grammar H such that $L(H) = K$ and $\mathrm{nrrcn}(H) = 2$.* $\qquad \square$

Theorem 20 (see Theorem 4 in [8]). *For every context-sensitive language J, there is a propagating one-sided random context grammar H such that $L(H) = J$ and $\mathrm{nrrcn}(H) = 2$.* $\qquad \square$

By analogy with Definition 6, we may define a *left random context nonterminal* and their number in one-sided random context grammars. Then, in [8], it is shown that Theorems 19 and 20 can be reformulated in terms of left random context nonterminals and their number. That paper also proves that we may limit both the total number of right and left random context nonterminals at the same time.

Finally, apart from reducing the overall number of nonterminals and right random context nonterminals, a reduction of the number of right random context rules has been investigated in [13]. Recall that a right random context rule is a rule that checks the presence and absence of symbols to the right of the rewritten nonterminal (see Definition 1).

Theorem 21 (see Theorem 1 in [13]). *For every recursively enumerable language K, there exists a one-sided random context grammar, $H = (N, T, P_L, P_R, S)$, such that $L(H) = K$ and $\mathrm{card}(P_R) = 2$.* $\qquad \square$

That is, we know that two right random context rules suffice to keep the generative power of one-sided random context grammars unchanged.

The next theorem says that it is possible to simultaneously reduce both the number of nonterminals and the number of right random context rules.

Theorem 22 (see Corollary 1 in [13]). *For every recursively enumerable language K, there exists a one-sided random context grammar, $H = (N, T, P_L, P_R, S)$, such that $L(H) = K$, $\mathrm{card}(N) = 13$, $\mathrm{nrrcn}(H) = 2$, and $\mathrm{card}(P_R) = 2$.* $\qquad \square$

Other Topics of Investigation

We conclude this section by briefly mentioning other topics related to one-sided random context grammars that have been investigated.

Leftmost Derivations. By analogy with the three well-known types of leftmost derivations in regulated grammars (see [2]), three types of leftmost derivation restrictions placed upon one-sided random context grammars have been defined and studied in [10]. In the *type-1 derivation restriction*, during every derivation step, the leftmost occurrence of a nonterminal has to be rewritten. In the *type-2 derivation restriction*, during every derivation step, the leftmost occurrence of a nonterminal which can be rewritten has to be rewritten. In the *type-3 derivation restriction*, during every derivation step, a rule is chosen, and the leftmost occurrence of its left-hand side is rewritten. In [10], the following three results are demonstrated.

(I) One-sided random context grammars with type-1 leftmost derivations characterize the family of context-free languages.

(II) One-sided random context grammars with type-2 and type-3 leftmost derivations characterize the family of recursively enumerable languages.

(III) Propagating one-sided random context grammars with type-2 and type-3 leftmost derivations characterize the family of context-sensitive languages.

Generalized One-Sided Random Context Grammars. We may generalize the concept of one-sided context from symbols to strings. Obviously, as one-sided random context grammars already characterize the family of recursively languages, such a generalization cannot increase their strength. However, a generalization likes this makes sense in terms of variants of one-sided random context grammars. In [11], one-sided forbidding grammars that can forbid strings instead of single symbols are studied, and it has been proved that they are computationally complete, even if all strings are formed by at most two symbols.

One-Sided Versions of Other Formal Models. One-sided random context grammars are based upon context-free grammars. It is only natural to consider other types of grammars and equip them with one-sided random context. Some preliminary results in this direction have been achieved in [12], where ET0L grammars (see [16]) and their variants enhanced with left random context are studied.

5   Open Problems

In this concluding section, we mention several open problems concerning one-sided random context grammars and their variants. Some of them are mentioned in [19].

(I) What is the generative power of left random context grammars? What is the role of erasing rules in this left variant? That is, are left random context grammars more powerful than propagating left random context grammars?

(II) What is the generative power of one-sided forbidding grammars? We only know that they are equally powerful as selective substitution grammars (see Theorems 4 and 5). Thus, by establishing the generative power of one-sided forbidding grammars, we would establish the power of selective substitution grammars, too.

(III) By Theorem 17, ten nonterminals suffice to generate any recursively enumerable language by a one-sided random context grammar. Is this limit optimal? In other words, can Theorem 17 be improved?

(IV) Recall that propagating one-sided random context grammars characterize the family of context-sensitive languages (see Theorem 2). Can we also limit the overall number of nonterminals in terms of this propagating version like in Theorem 17?

(V) What is the generative power of one-sided forbidding grammars and one-sided permitting grammars? Moreover, what is the power of left permitting grammars? Recall that every propagating scattered context grammar can be turned to an equivalent context-sensitive grammar (see Theorem 3.21 in [6]), but it is a longstanding open problem whether these two kinds of grammars are actually equivalent—the *PSC = CS problem*. If in the future one proves that propagating one-sided permitting grammars and propagating one-sided random context grammars are equivalent, then so are propagating scattered context grammars and context-sensitive grammars (see Theorem 11), so the PSC = CS problem would be solved.

(VI) By Theorem 19, any recursively enumerable language is generated by a one-sided random context grammar having no more than two right random context nonterminals. Does this result hold with one or even zero right random context nonterminals? Notice that by proving that no right random context nonterminals are needed, we would establish the generative power of left random context grammars.

(VII) By Theorem 21, any recursively enumerable language is generated by a one-sided random context grammar having no more than two right random context rules. Does this result hold with one or even zero right random context rules? Again, notice that by proving that no right random context rules are needed, we would establish the generative power of left random context grammars.

Acknowledgments. This work was supported by the following grants: MŠMT CZ1.1.00/02.0070, BUT FIT-S-11-2, and TAČR TE01020415.

References

1. Csuhaj-Varjú, E., Masopust, T., Vaszil, G.: Cooperating distributed grammar systems with permitting grammars as components. Romanian Journal of Information Science and Technology **12**(2), 175–189 (2009)

2. Dassow, J., Păun, G.: Regulated Rewriting in Formal Language Theory. Springer (1989)

3. Goldefus, F., Masopust, T., Meduna, Λ.: Left-forbidding cooperating distributed grammar systems. Theoretical Computer Science **20**(3), 1–11 (2010)
4. Greibach, S.A., Hopcroft, J.E.: Scattered context grammars. Journal of Computer and System Sciences **3**(3), 233–247 (1969)
5. Kleijn, H.C.M.: Basic ideas of selective substitution grammars. In: Kelemenová, A., Kelemen, J. (eds.) Trends, Techniques, and Problems in Theoretical Computer Science. LNCS, vol. 281, pp. 75–95. Springer, Heidelberg (1987)
6. Meduna, A., Techet, J.: Scattered Context Grammars and Their Applications. WIT Press, Southampton (2010)
7. Meduna, A., Zemek, P.: One-sided random context grammars. Acta Informatica **48**(3), 149–163 (2011)
8. Meduna, A., Zemek, P.: Nonterminal complexity of one-sided random context grammars. Acta Informatica **49**(2), 55–68 (2012)
9. Meduna, A., Zemek, P.: One-sided forbidding grammars and selective substitution grammars. International Journal of Computer Mathematics **89**(5), 586–596 (2012)
10. Meduna, A., Zemek, P.: One-Sided Random Context Grammars with Leftmost Derivations. In: Bordihn, H., Kutrib, M., Truthe, B. (eds.) Languages Alive. LNCS, vol. 7300, pp. 160–173. Springer, Heidelberg (2012)
11. Meduna, A., Zemek, P.: Generalized one-sided forbidding grammars. International Journal of Computer Mathematics **90**(2), 127–182 (2013)
12. Meduna, A., Zemek, P.: Left random context ET0L grammars. Fundamenta Informaticae **123**(3), 289–304 (2013)
13. Meduna, A., Zemek, P.: One-sided random context grammars with a limited number of right random context rules. Theoretical Computer Science **516**(1), 127–132 (2014)
14. Meduna, A., Zemek, P.: Regulated Grammars and Automata. Springer, New York (2014)
15. Rozenberg, G.: Selective substitution grammars (towards a framework for rewriting systems). Part 1: Definitions and examples. Elektronische Informationsverarbeitung und Kybernetik **13**(9), 455–463 (1977)
16. Rozenberg, G., Salomaa, A.: Mathematical Theory of L Systems. Academic Press, Orlando (1980)
17. Rozenberg, G., Salomaa, A. (eds.) Handbook of Formal Languages, vol. 1 through 3. Springer (1997)
18. Zemek, P.: Normal forms of one-sided random context grammars. In: Proceedings of the 18th Conference STUDENT EEICT 2012, vol. 3, pp. 430–434. Brno University of Technology, Brno, CZ (2012)
19. Zemek, P.: One-sided random context grammars: Established results and open problems. In: Proceedings of the 19th Conference STUDENT EEICT 2013, vol. 3, pp. 222–226. Brno University of Technology, Brno, CZ (2013)

How Can We Construct Reversible Machines Out of Reversible Logic Element with Memory?

Kenichi Morita[✉] and Tsuyoshi Ogiro

Hiroshima University, Higashi-Hiroshima 739-8527, Japan
km@hiroshima-u.ac.jp

Abstract. Reversible computing is a paradigm of computation closely related to physical reversibility. In this survey/tutorial paper, we discuss topics on reversible logic elements with memory (RLEM), which are used to build reversible computing machines. It is known that any reversible sequential machine (RSM) can be constructed systematically and simply from a rotary element (RE), a typical 2-state RLEM. It is also known that "all" non-degenerate 2-state RLEMs except only four are universal. Thus, RSMs can be built by any one of universal RLEMs. However, so far, no concise construction method has been given except the method of using RE. Here, we show a new simple method of composing RSMs from 2-state RLEMs of ID numbers 4-31 and 3-7.

1 Introduction

A reversible computing system is a one such that every computational configuration has at most one predecessor, and thus its evolution is described by a one-to-one mapping. Though its definition is rather simple, it has a close relation to physical reversibility. It is also noted that reversible computing can be regarded as a special subcase of quantum computing, since evolution of a quantum system is expressed by a unitary operator (the reference [4] by Gruska is a good introductory book on quantum computing).

So far, various kinds of reversible computing models have been proposed and investigated. There are several levels of models ranging from a microscopic one to a macroscopic one. In the bottom level, i.e., in the most microscopic level, there is a physically reversible model like the billiard ball model (BBM) of computing [3]. In the next level, there exist reversible logic elements, from which reversible logic circuits are built, such as Fredkin gate [3], Toffoli gate [18,19], and reversible logic elements with memory [7]. In the still higher level, there are reversible logic circuits that can be used as building modules for reversible computers. In the top level, there are models of reversible computers such as reversible Turing machines [1], reversible cellular automata [17], and others.

Although reversible computing systems have only classical states rather than quantum states, they still have several interesting features. First, in spite of the

---

This work was supported by JSPS KAKENHI Grant Number 24500017.

© Springer International Publishing Switzerland 2014
C.S. Calude et al. (Eds.): Gruska Festschrift, LNCS 8808, pp. 352–366, 2014.
DOI: 10.1007/978-3-319-13350-8_26

strong constraint of reversibility, even very simple reversible systems have computational universality (see e.g. [9] for the survey). Second, reversible computing systems can be often constructed in a method that is very different from the ones found in the traditional design techniques of computing systems. Thus, they will give new insights and ideas for future computing.

In this survey/tutorial paper, we focus on the topics of reversible logic elements with memory (RLEM) and circuits composed of them. In the conventional design theory of logic circuits, logic gates (i.e., elements without memory) are used as primitives for composing logic circuits (but in the study of asynchronous circuits, logic elements with memory are sometimes used [2,5]). On the other hand, in the case of reversible computing, RLEMs are also known to be useful. The main reason is that if we use an appropriate RLEM, we can construct various kinds of reversible computing models, e.g., reversible Turing machines and reversible sequential machines, very simply [7,8,10].

Here, we investigate 2-state RLEMs, i.e., RLEMs with 1-bit memory. In Section 2, we give definitions and classifications of 2-state RLEMs. In Section 3, we explain how reversible sequential machines (RSMs) can be constructed systematically from a rotary element (RE), a typical 2-state RLEM [8]. In Section 4, we show the result that "all" non-degenerate 2-state RLEMs except only four are universal [16]. Thus, RSMs can be built by any one of universal RLEMs. However, so far, no concise construction method has been given except the method of using RE. In Section 5, we give a new simple method of composing RSMs from 2-state RLEMs of ID numbers 4-31 and 3-7.

2   Reversible Logic Element with Memory (RLEM)

A sequential machine (SM) of Mealy type is a finite automaton with an output as well as an input. A reversible logic element with memory (RLEM) is nothing but a reversible sequential machine.

Definition 1. *A sequential machine (SM) is defined by $M = (Q, \Sigma, \Gamma, \delta)$, where Q is a finite set of internal states, Σ and Γ are finite sets of input and output symbols, and $\delta : Q \times \Sigma \rightarrow Q \times \Gamma$ is a move function. If δ is injective, M is called a* reversible sequential machine *(RSM). More specifically, M is called a $|Q|$-state $|\Gamma|$-symbol RSM, for convenience. Note that $|\Sigma| \leq |\Gamma|$ must hold, if M is reversible. A reversible logic element with memory (RLEM) is an RSM such that $|\Sigma| = |\Gamma|$, and it is also called a $|Q|$-state $|\Gamma|$-symbol RLEM.*

The move function δ of an SM M determines the next state of M and the output symbol from the present state and the input symbol. Hence, if the present state is p, the input symbol is a_i, and $\delta(p, a_i) = (q, s_j)$, then the next state is q and the output is s_j as shown in Fig. 1 (a). To use an SM as a logic element for composing a logic circuit, we interpret the SM as a machine having "decoded" input and output ports as in Fig. 1 (b). Namely, for each input symbol, there is a unique input port, to which a signal (or particle) can be given. Likewise, for each output symbol, there is a unique output port, from which a signal can

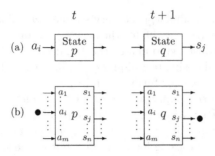

Fig. 1. (a) A sequential machine $M = (Q, \{a_1, \ldots, a_m\}, \{s_1, \ldots, s_n\}, \delta)$ such that $\delta(p, a_i) = (q, s_j)$, and (b) an interpretation of a sequential machine as a system having decoded input ports and output ports

appear. When making a logic circuit using such SMs, we assume the following: each output port of an SM can be connected to only one input port of another (maybe the same) SM. Thus, fan-out of an output is not allowed.

Hereafter, we investigate only 2-state RLEMs. We first give two examples of 2-state 4-symbol RLEMs with ID numbers 4-31 and 4-289 (the numbering method will be explained later). They are $M_{4\text{-}31} = (\{0, 1\}, \{a, b, c, d\}, \{s, t, u, v\}, \delta_{4\text{-}31})$ and $M_{4\text{-}289} = (\{0, 1\}, \{a, b, c, d\}, \{s, t, u, v\}, \delta_{4\text{-}289})$. The move functions $\delta_{4\text{-}31}$ and $\delta_{4\text{-}289}$ are given in Table 1. For example, $\delta_{4\text{-}31}(0, d) = (1, s)$. It is easy to verify that $\delta_{4\text{-}31}$ and $\delta_{4\text{-}289}$ are injective. In the following, we denote the move functions of 2-state RLEMs by a pictorial notation as shown in Fig. 2 instead of tables as in Table 1. Each of two states is represented by a rectangle having input ports and output ports. The relation between input and output is indicated by solid and dotted lines. We assume a signal is given to at most one input port at a time. If a signal is given to some input port, it travels along the line connected to the port. In the case that a signal goes through a dotted line, the state does not change (Fig. 3 (a)). On the other hand, if it goes through a solid line, the state changes to the other (Fig. 3 (b)).

Table 1. The move functions $\delta_{4\text{-}31}$ and $\delta_{4\text{-}289}$ of the 2-state RLEMs 4-31 and 4-289

Present state	Input				Present state	Input			
	a	b	c	d		a	b	c	d
State 0	0 s	0 t	0 u	1 s	State 0	0 s	0 t	1 s	1 t
State 1	1 t	0 v	1 v	1 u	State 1	0 u	0 v	1 v	1 u
$\delta_{4\text{-}31}$ of RLEM 4-31					$\delta_{4\text{-}289}$ of RLEM 4-289				

2-state RLEMs are classified as follows. Since the move function δ of a 2-state k-symbol RLEM $M = (\{0, 1\}, \Sigma, \Gamma, \delta)$ is identified by a permutation of $\{0, 1\} \times \Gamma$, the total number of 2-state k-symbol RLEMs is $(2k)!$. They are numbered from 0 to $(2k)! - 1$ in the lexicographic order of permutations [13]. To indicate it is

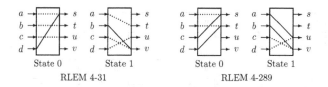

Fig. 2. A pictorial representation of the 2-state RLEMs 4-31 and 4-289

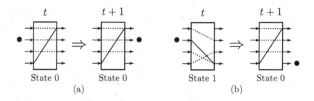

Fig. 3. Examples of operations of the 2-state RLEM 4-31. (a) If a particle passes a dotted line, then the state remains to be the same. (b) If a particle passes a solid line, then the state changes to the other.

a k-symbol RLEM, the prefix "k-" is attached to its serial number like RLEM 4-31. Two RLEMs are said to be *equivalent* if one can be obtained by renaming the states and/or the input/output symbols of the other. It has been shown that the numbers of equivalence classes of 2-state 2-, 3-, and 4-symbol RLEMs are 8, 24, and 82, respectively [13]. Fig. 4 shows all representative RLEMs in the equivalence classes of 2- and 3-symbol RLEMs. The representatives are chosen so that it has the smallest number in the class.

Among RLEMs, there are *degenerate* ones, each of which is either equivalent to simple connecting wires (e.g., RLEM 3-3), or equivalent to an RLEM with fewer symbols (e.g., RLEM 3-6). Its precise definition is in [12]. In Fig. 4, they are indicated by "eq. to wires" or "eq. to 2-n". Thus, *non-degenerate k-symbol* RLEMs are the main concern of the study. It is known that the numbers of non-degenerate 2- 3- and 4-symbol RLEMs are 4, 14, and 55, respectively.

A *rotary element* (RE) [7] is a 2-state 4-symbol RLEM defined by $M_{RE} = (\{H, V\}, \{n, e, s, w\}, \{n', e', s', w'\}, \delta_{RE})$, where δ_{RE} is given in Table 2. RE is equivalent to RLEM 4-289, since the latter is obtained by the following renaming of states and input/output symbols: $H \mapsto 0, V \mapsto 1, n \mapsto c, s \mapsto d, e \mapsto a, w \mapsto b, n' \mapsto u, s' \mapsto v, e' \mapsto t, w' \mapsto s$. Its behavior can be very easily understood,

Table 2. The move function δ_{RE} of rotary element (RE)

Present state	Input			
	n	e	s	w
H	$V\,w'$	$H\,w'$	$V\,e'$	$H\,e'$
V	$V\,s'$	$H\,n'$	$V\,n'$	$H\,s'$

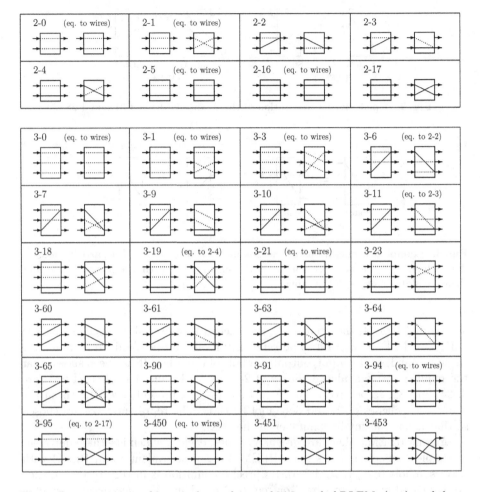

Fig. 4. Representatives of 8 equivalence classes of 24 2-symbol RLEMs (top), and those of 24 equivalence classes of 720 3-symbol RLEMs (bottom). The indications "eq. to wires" and "eq. to 2-n" mean it is equivalent to connecting wires, and it is equivalent to RLEM 2-n, respectively. Thus they are degenerate ones.

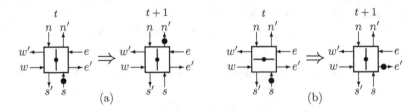

Fig. 5. Operations of rotary element (RE): (a) the parallel case, and (b) the orthogonal case

since it has the following interpretation on its operation. RE is depicted by a box that contains a rotatable bar inside (Fig. 5). Two states of an RE are distinguished by the direction of the bar corresponding to states H and V. There are four input lines and four output lines corresponding to the sets of input symbols $\{n, e, s, w\}$ and output symbols $\{n', e', s', w'\}$. The rotatable bar is used to control the move direction of an input signal (or particle). When no particle exists, nothing happens on the RE. If a particle comes from the direction parallel to the rotatable bar, then it goes out from the output line of the opposite side without affecting the direction of the bar (Fig. 5 (a)). If a particle comes from the direction orthogonal to the bar, then it makes a right turn, and rotates the bar by 90 degrees (Fig. 5 (b)). In the next section we use RE for composing circuits that simulate RSMs.

We now give a short remark how RLEMs are related to reversible physical systems. The billiard ball model (BBM) proposed by Fredkin and Toffoli [3] is an idealized model of Newtonian mechanics in which reversible logic gates can be embedded. In [9,11], it is shown that RE can be directly and simply simulated in BBM without using reversible logic gates. It is also proved that any m-state k-symbol RLEM can be realized in BBM in a systematic way if $k \leq 4$ [15].

3 Constructing Reversible Machines by RE

In [8] it is shown that there is a systematic method of composing an RE circuit that simulates a given RSM. Here, we explain it by an example. Assume an RSM $M_0 = (\{q_1, q_2, q_3\}, \{a_1, a_2, a_3\}, \{s_1, s_2, s_3\}, \delta_0)$ is given, where δ_0 is described in Table 3. Then, we first prepare three columns of REs each of which consists of four REs, and connect them as shown in Fig. 6 (a). This is a "framework circuit" that can be used for any 3-state 3-symbol RSM. More generally, for an m-state n-symbol RSM, we prepare m columns of REs each of which consists of $n + 1$ REs. Here, the j-th column corresponds to the state q_j of M_0 ($j \in \{1, 2, 3\}$). If M_0's state is q_j, then the bottom RE of the j-th column is set to state H. All other REs are set to V. In Fig. 6, it is in the state q_2. The REs of the i-th row corresponds to the input symbol a_i as well as the output symbol s_i ($i \in \{1, 2, 3\}$). If a particle is given to an input port e.g. a_1 of Fig. 6 (a), then after setting the bottom RE of the second column to state V, the particle finally comes out from the port "$q_2 a_1$". Namely, the crossing point of the second column and the first row is found. Then, since $\delta_0(q_2, a_1) = (q_3, s_2)$, the bottom RE of the third column

Table 3. The move function δ_0 of an example of an RSM M_0

Present state	Input		
	a_1	a_2	a_3
q_1	$q_2 s_2$	$q_3 s_1$	$q_1 s_2$
q_2	$q_3 s_2$	$q_2 s_1$	$q_1 s_3$
q_3	$q_3 s_3$	$q_2 s_3$	$q_1 s_1$

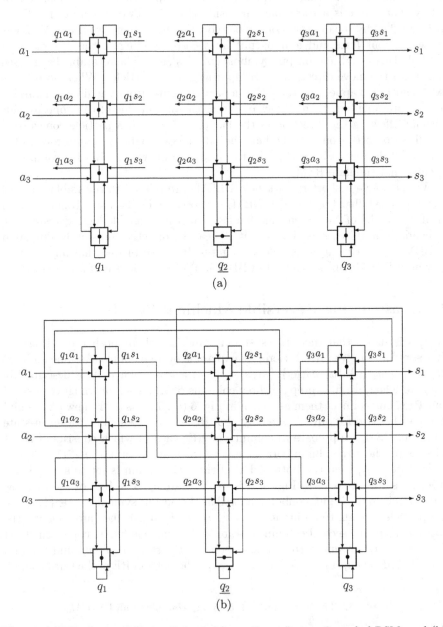

Fig. 6. (a) The framework circuit for implementing a 3-state 3-symbol RSM, and (b) the RSM M_0 realized by RE. Here, M_0 is in the state q_2 since the bottom RE of the second column is in state H.

should be set to state H, and the particle must go out from the output port s_2. This can be done by giving a particle to the line "q_3s_2". Hence, each line "q_ja_i" in Fig. 6 (a) is connected to the line "$q_{j'}s_{i'}$", if $\delta_0(q_j, a_i) = (q_{j'}s_{i'})$. Connecting all such lines appropriately according to δ_0 in Table 3, we finally obtain the circuit in Fig. 6 (b) that simulates M_0.

We can also see that any *reversible Turing machine* (RTM) is constructed only of REs. An RTM is a machine having backward deterministic property (see [1,9] for its definition), and it is known that for any irreversible TM, there is an RTM that simulates the former and leaves no garbage information when it halts [1]. In [7,10], a design method of a finite state control and a memory cell of an RTM is given. Fig. 7 is a circuit that simulates an example of an RTM T_{parity} that accepts the language $\{1^{2n} | n = 0, 1, \ldots\}$ [10]. The move function of T_{parity} is specified by the following set of quintuples: $\{[q_0, 0, 1, R, q_1], [q_1, 0, 1, L, q_{\text{acc}}], [q_1, 1, 0, R, q_2], [q_2, 0, 1, L, q_{\text{rej}}], [q_2, 1, 0, R, q_1]\}$. If we give a particle to the input port "Begin," then it starts to compute. Finally, the particle comes out from the output port "Accept" or "Reject" depending on the input. Detailed descriptions of this circuit is given in [10,11].

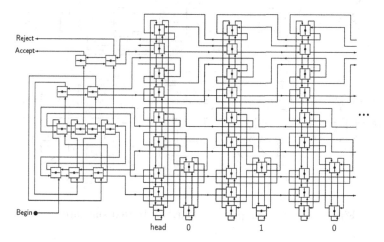

Fig. 7. A circuit made of RE that simulates an RTM T_{parity} that accepts $\{1^{2n} | n = 0, 1, \ldots\}$. An example of its whole computing process is shown in 4406 figures in [10].

4   Universality of 2-State RLEMs

As we have seen in Section 3, RE is "universal" in the sense that any RSM can be simulated by a circuit made only of REs. Since there are infinitely many kinds of RLEMs, it is important to know which 2-state RLEMs are universal, and which are not. Surprisingly, every non-degenerate 2-state RLEMs except only four are universal [12]. In the following, we explain its outline.

Definition 2. *An RLEM is called* universal *if any RSM is realized by a circuit composed only of copies of the RLEM.*

Theorem 1. [8] *RE (or equivalently RLEM 4-289) is universal.*

The following lemmas are on universality of RLEMs other than RE.

Lemma 1. [6,12] *RE can be simulated by a circuit composed of RLEM 3-10.*

Lemma 2. [6] *RLEM 3-10 can be simulated by a circuit composed of RLEMs 2-3 and 2-4.*

Lemma 3. [12] *RLEMs 2-3 and 2-4 can be simulated by any one of 14 non-degenerate 3-symbol RLEMs.*

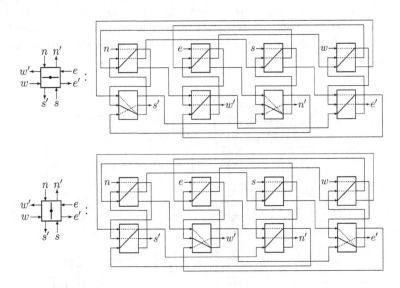

Fig. 8. A circuit composed of RLEM 3-10 that simulates RE

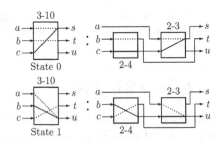

Fig. 9. A circuit composed of RLEMs 2-3 and 2-4 that simulates RLEM 3-10

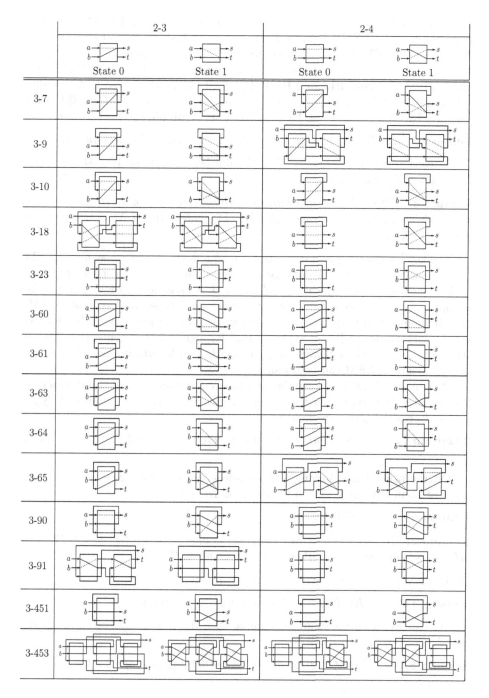

Fig. 10. Circuits composed of each of 14 non-degenerate 3-symbol RLEMs that simulate RLEMs 2-3 and 2-4

Lemmas 1–3 are proved by giving circuits composed of given RLEMs that simulate the target RLEMs. Lemma 1 was first proved in [6] by a circuit made of 20 copies of RLEM 3-10 that simulates RE. Later, a simpler circuit in Fig. 8 was given in [12]. Lemma 2 is proved by a circuit in Fig. 9 made of RLEMs 2-3 and 2-4 that simulates RLEM 3-10 [6]. Finally, Lemma 3 is proved by 28 circuits shown in Fig. 10 composed of each of 14 non-degenerate 3-symbol RLEMS that simulate RLEMs 2-3 and 2-4. By Lemmas 1–3, we obtain the next lemma.

Lemma 4. [12] *Every non-degenerate 2-state 3-symbol RLEM is universal.*

A relation between k-symbol RLEMs and $(k-1)$-symbol RLEMs is shown in the following lemma.

Lemma 5. [12] *Let M_k be an arbitrary non-degenerate k-symbol RLEM ($k > 2$). Then, there exists a non-degenerate $(k-1)$-symbol RLEM M_{k-1} that can be simulated by M_k.*

The key idea of the proof of Lemma 5 is as follows. When a k-symbol RLEM is given, we choose one output line and one input line, and connect them to make a feedback loop. By this, we obtain a $(k-1)$-symbol RLEM. If we make an appropriate feedback loop, we can get a non-degenerate 3-symbol RLEM. But, if we make an inappropriate feedback, then the resulting 3-symbol RLEM is a degenerate one. In [12], it is proved that for a given non-degenerate k-symbol RLEM ($k > 2$), we can always find a feedback loop by which a non-degenerate $(k-1)$-symbol RLEM can be obtained.

By Lemmas 4 and 5 we have the next theorem stating that all non-degenerate 2-state RLEMs except only four 2-state 2-symbol RLEMs are universal. Note that universal RLEMs can simulate each other.

Theorem 2. [12] *Every non-degenerate 2-state k-symbol RLEM is universal if $k > 2$.*

On the other hand, among four non-degenerate 2-state 2-symbol RLEMs, three of them have been shown to be non-universal.

Lemma 6. [16] *RLEM 2-2 can simulate neither RLEM 2-3, 2-4, nor 2-17.*

Lemma 7. [16] *RLEM 2-3 can simulate neither RLEM 2-4, nor 2-17, and RLEM 2-4 can simulate neither RLEM 2-3, nor 2-17.*

By Lemmas 6 and 7, we have the following theorem.

Theorem 3. [16] *RLEMs 2-2, 2-3, and 2-4 are non-universal.*

We can see, from the following lemma, RLEM 2-2 is the weakest one among non-degenerate 2-state RLEMs.

Lemma 8. [16] *RLEM 2-2 can be simulated by any one of RLEMs 2-3, 2-4, and 2-17.*

Fig. 11 summarizes the above results. It is an open problem whether RLEM 2-17 is universal or not. On the other hand, it is shown that any combination of two among RLEMs 2-3, 2-4, and 2-17 is universal [6,16].

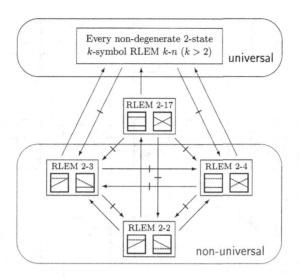

Fig. 11. A hierarchy among non-degenerate 2-state RLEMs. Here, $A \rightarrow B$ ($A \nrightarrow B$, respectively) indicates that A can (cannot) be simulated by B.

5   Constructing RSMs by RLEMs 4-31 and 3-7

By Lemmas 1–3 and 5, we can construct RSMs by any universal RLEM in a systematic way. For example, if we want to construct an RSM M_0 in Section 3 by RLEM 3-7, it can be done as follows. First, make RLEMs 2-3 and 2-4 as the circuit of RLEM 3-7 shown in the first row of Fig. 10. Next, make RLEM 3-10 as in Fig. 9. Then, compose a circuit out of RLEM 3-7 that simulates RE according to Fig. 8. This circuit consists of 16 copies of RLEM 3-7. Finally, replace each RE in Fig. 6 (b) by this circuit. We thus obtain a circuit composed of RLEM 3-7 that simulates the RSM M_0. However, the above method is not good with respect to the number of RLEMs, since there is a simpler circuit consisting only four (instead of 16) copies of RLEM 3-7 that simulates RE (Fig. 12).

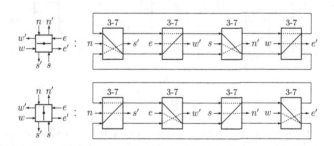

Fig. 12. A circuit composed of four copies of RLEM 3-7 that simulates RE

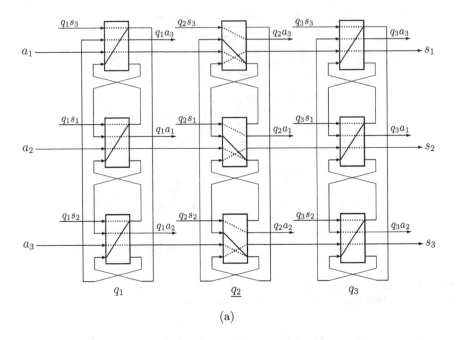

(a)

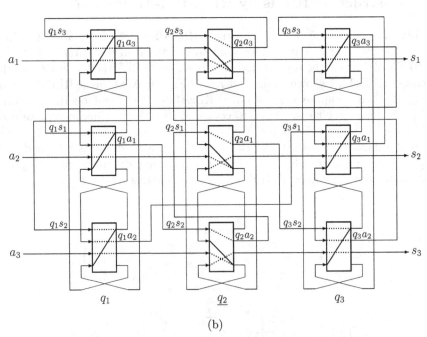

(b)

Fig. 13. (a) A framework circuit for implementing a 3-state 3-symbol RSM, and (b) the RSM M_0 realized by RLEM 4-31. Here, M_0 is in the state q_2 since all the RLEMs in the second column are in state 1.

Here, we give a new method of constructing RSMs concisely by RLEM 4-31, and then by RLEM 3-7. We take again the example of the RSM M_0 whose move function δ_0 is given in Table 3. As in Section 3, we first prepare a "framework circuit" consisting of three rows and three columns of RLEM 4-31 as shown in Fig. 13 (a). Generally, for an m-state n-symbol RSM, we prepare an $n \times m$ array of RLEM 4-31. As in the case of Fig. 6 (a), the j-th column corresponds to the state q_j of M_0 ($j \in \{1, 2, 3\}$). If M_0's state is q_j, then all the RLEMs of the j-th column is set to state 1. All other RLEMs are set to state 0. In Fig. 13, it is in the state q_2. The RLEMs of the i-th row corresponds to the input symbol a_i as well as the output symbol s_i ($i \in \{1, 2, 3\}$). If a particle is given to an input port e.g. a_1 of Fig. 13 (a), then after setting the all RLEMs of the second column to state 0, the particle finally comes out from the port "q_2a_1". Hence, the crossing point of the second column and the first row is found, though the port "q_2a_1" is shifted downward by one row cyclically. Since $\delta_0(q_2, a_1) = (q_3, s_2)$, the RLEMs of the third column should be set to state 1, and the particle must go out from the output port s_2. This can be performed by giving a particle to the line "q_3s_2". Again, the port "q_3s_2" is shifted downward by one row. Connecting all such lines appropriately according to δ_0 in Table 3, we finally obtain the circuit composed of RLEM 4-31 shown in Fig. 13 (b) that simulates M_0.

Next, we consider a problem of constructing RSMs by RLEM 3-7. It is easily done, since RLEM 4-31 is implemented by a circuit consisting only two copies of RLEM 3-7 as shown in Fig. 14. By this method, an m-state n-symbol RSM can be constructed using $2mn$ copies of RLEM 3-7.

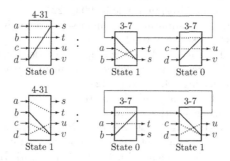

Fig. 14. A circuit composed of two copies of RLEM 3-7 that simulates RLEM 4-31

6   Concluding Remarks

In this paper, we discussed universality of RLEMs, in particular, how RSMs are implemented by circuits made of universal RLEMs. We proposed a new method of realizing RSMs concisely by RLEMs 4-31 and 3-7. If we use RLEM 4-31 (or 3-7, respectively), an m-state n-symbol RSM can be realized by a circuit consisting of mn (or $2mn$) copies of it. As for reversible Turing machines, a compact realization method by RLEM 4-31 is given in [14]. Finding other construction methods by simpler (i.e., 3- or 2-symbol) RLEMs is left for the future study.

References

1. Bennett, C.H.: Logical reversibility of computation. IBM J. Res. Dev. **17**, 525–532 (1973)
2. Büning, H., Priese, L.: Universal asynchronous iterative arrays of Mealy automata. Acta Informatica **13**, 269–285 (1980)
3. Fredkin, E., Toffoli, T.: Conservative logic. Int. J. Theoret. Phys. **21**, 219–253 (1982)
4. Gruska, J.: Quantum Computing. McGraw-Hill, London (1999); Japanese translation: Morikita Publishing Co., Ltd, Tokyo (2003)
5. Keller, R.: Towards a theory of universal speed-independent modules. IEEE Trans. Computers **C–23**, 21–33 (1974)
6. Lee, J., Peper, F., Adachi, S., Morita, K.: An Asynchronous Cellular Automaton Implementing 2-State 2-Input 2-Output Reversed-Twin Reversible Elements. In: Umeo, H., Morishita, S., Nishinari, K., Komatsuzaki, T., Bandini, S. (eds.) ACRI 2008. LNCS, vol. 5191, pp. 67–76. Springer, Heidelberg (2008)
7. Morita, K.: A Simple Universal Logic Element and Cellular Automata for Reversible Computing. In: Margenstern, M., Rogozhin, Y. (eds.) MCU 2001. LNCS, vol. 2055, pp. 102–113. Springer, Heidelberg (2001)
8. Morita, K.: A new universal logic element for reversible computing. In: Martin-Vide, C., Mitrana, V. (eds.) Grammars and Automata for String Processing, pp. 285–294. Taylor and Francis, London (2003)
9. Morita, K.: Reversible computing and cellular automata – A survey. Theoret. Comput. Sci. **395**, 101–131 (2008)
10. Morita, K.: Constructing a reversible Turing machine by a rotary element, a reversible logic element with memory. Hiroshima University Institutional Repository (2010). http://ir.lib.hiroshima-u.ac.jp/00029224
11. Morita, K.: Reversible Computing (in Japanese). Kindai Kagaku-sha Co., Ltd, Tokyo (2012). ISBN: 978-4-7649-0422-4
12. Morita, K., Ogiro, T., Alhazov, A., Tanizawa, T.: Non-degenerate 2-state reversible logic elements with three or more symbols are all universal. J. Multiple-Valued Logic and Soft Computing **18**, 37–54 (2012)
13. Morita, K., Ogiro, T., Tanaka, K., Kato, H.: Classification and Universality of Reversible Logic Elements with One-Bit Memory. In: Margenstern, M. (ed.) MCU 2004. LNCS, vol. 3354, pp. 245–256. Springer, Heidelberg (2005)
14. Morita, K., Suyama, R.: Compact Realization of Reversible Turing Machines by 2-State Reversible Logic Elements. In: Ibarra, O.H., Kari, L., Kopecki, S. (eds.) UCNC 2014. LNCS, vol. 8553, pp. 280–292. Springer, Heidelberg (2014)
15. Mukai, Y., Morita, K.: Realizing reversible logic elements with memory in the billiard ball model. Int. J. of Unconventional Computing **8**(1), 47–59 (2012)
16. Mukai, Y., Ogiro, T., Morita, K.: Universality problems on reversible logic elements with 1-bit memory. Int. J. Unconventional Computing (to appear)
17. Toffoli, T.: Computation and construction universality of reversible cellular automata. J. Comput. Syst. Sci. **15**, 213–231 (1977)
18. Toffoli, T.: Reversible computing. Automata, Languages and Programming. LNCS, vol. 85, pp. 632–644. Springer, Heidelberg (1980)
19. Toffoli, T.: Bicontinuous extensions of invertible combinatorial functions. Math. Syst. Theory **14**, 12–23 (1981)

On Evolutionary Approximation of Logic Circuits

Lukas Sekanina[✉] and Zdenek Vasicek

IT4Innovations Centre of Excellence, Faculty of Information Technology,
Brno University of Technology, Bozetechova 2, 61266 Brno, Czech Republic
{sekanina,vasicek}@fit.vutbr.cz

Abstract. The concept of approximation has intensively been studied, developed and applied not only in computer science, but also in mathematics and engineering disciplines. The never ending requirement for low power consumption led to making approximate circuits and computer systems even in the areas in which only accurately working solutions have traditionally been accepted. Approximate circuits are the circuits relaxing the requirement on the functional equivalence between the specification and implementation in order to reduce the area on a chip, delay or energy consumption. Approximate computing machines further exploit and apply this idea at all system levels. This paper introduces the field of approximate computing and shows how evolutionary design methods can automate the design process of approximate computing systems, in particular, approximate logic circuits.

1 Introduction

The notion of *approximation* is well established in computer science, mathematics and engineering [1]. However, the reasons for approximations can be different.

In computer science, *approximation algorithms* are algorithms used to find approximate solutions to NP-hard optimization problems. As it is intractable to find an optimal solution, the goal is to find polynomial-time exact algorithms and guarantee provable solution quality in provable run-time bounds. An interesting discovery is that, in spite of the isomorphism between NP-complete problems, good approximation algorithms can be surprisingly different for particular problem classes. A detailed overview of the theory of approximation algorithms can be found in [2].

One of the classic utilizations of the concept of approximation is approximate string matching. Finding strings that match a pattern approximately rather than exactly is crucial for spell checking, bioinformatics, spam filtering and other applications.

In bio-inspired artificial intelligence, models of computation, such as artificial neural networks, have been developed which inherently exploit the concept of approximation. For example, a feed-forward network with a single hidden layer containing a finite number of neurons can approximate continuous functions [3].

In mathematics, it is investigated how certain (usually complex) functions can be approximated by means of basic functions that are inexpensive or suitable

© Springer International Publishing Switzerland 2014
C.S. Calude et al. (Eds.): Gruska Festschrift, LNCS 8808, pp. 367–378, 2014.
DOI: 10.1007/978-3-319-13350-8_27

according to a given purpose. In order to do so, traditional approaches (such as Taylor series or Newton's method) utilize only elementary operations: addition, subtraction and multiplication. But multiplication can still be very expensive. As a hardware multiplier is a relatively complex and slow component, multiplierless methods have been discovered in computer engineering to inexpensively and quickly approximate mathematical functions. The most prominent example is the CORDIC algorithm (COordinate Rotation DIgital Computer), developed by Jack E. Volder, which is capable of calculating hyperbolic and trigonometric functions using addition, subtraction, bit shift and table lookup [4]. We will see later that even the adders are approximated in modern computing devices.

All approaches to approximations suppose that an *error measure* is defined in order to quantify how far a given approximation is from an optimal (or known) solution. The aforementioned example dealing with hardware resources shows that the error measure is not the only measure in engineering applications. For example, speed of processing and area on a chip are fundamental measures used for hardware components. Moreover, if a sequence of successive approximations can be constructed, the rate of convergence and stability are other important measures of the approximation method.

It can be seen that the concept of approximation is thus relevant for both algorithms as well as solutions produced by algorithms. One has to carefully distinguish *algorithms* (i.e. problem solving mechanisms, such as the quicksort) from *solutions* to particular problems (e.g. a sorted sequence of integers), because an algorithm can often be a solution produced by another algorithm (e.g. in genetic programming).

In the recent five years, we could observe a lot of work around approximations in a different context, mainly in a connection with *energy consumption*. A new research direction – *approximate computing* – has been established to investigate how computer systems can be made better – more energy efficient, faster, and less complex – by relaxing the requirement that they are exactly correct. Approximate computing exploits the fact that the requirement of perfect functional behavior (i.e. accuracy) can be relaxed because some applications are inherently *error resilient* [5]. The errors are not recognizable because human perception capabilities are limited (e.g. in multimedia applications), no golden solution is available for validation of results (e.g. in data mining applications), or users are willing to accept some inaccuracies (e.g. when battery of a mobile phone is almost depleted, but at least a basic functionality is still requested). Therefore, the accuracy can be used as a design metric, traded for area on a chip, delay, throughput, or power consumption.

In approximate computing systems, approximations can be introduced at all design levels, starting from the circuit via the architecture and operating system to programming language. Taking approximate computing closer to mainstream adoption requires a deeper understanding of inherent application resilience across a broader range of applications, which has partially been investigated, e.g. in [6]. As a manual re-design of fully functional (exact) systems is not an efficient design method, several *automated approaches* have been proposed to particular problem classes.

The goal of this paper is to introduce the nascent field of approximate computing and show how *evolutionary design* methods can automate the design process of approximate computing systems, in particular, approximate digital circuits. Note that no support for the design of approximate circuits is available in common circuit design and optimization tools [7,8]. Because of the nature of approximate circuits (in fact, partially working circuits are sought) and principles of evolutionary circuit design (evolutionary-based improving of partially working circuits), evolutionary computing seems to be a promising design method.

The rest of the paper is organized as follows. Section 2 briefly surveys the field of approximate computing and approximate circuit design. In Section 3, evolutionary computing is introduced as a method for approximate circuit design. Section 4 specifically deals with a multi-objective approach to approximate circuit design. Concluding remarks are given in Section 5.

2   Approximate Computing

In the introduction, we have shown that approximate computing is a much wider concept than approximation algorithms and numerical approximation. It deals with new approaches to circuits, components, microarchitectures, operating systems, programming languages, compilers and their interactions.

Approximate computing should not also be confused with stochastic computing and probabilistic computing [5,9]. In stochastic computing, values are represented by streams of random bits. On the other hand, probabilistic computing utilizes random behavior of circuit elements under presence of thermal noise.

The number of papers dealing with approximate computing is rapidly increasing and the field is now very active. Approximate solutions have been applied at various levels of computer systems, including:

- elementary circuits (e.g. adders [10], multipliers [11]);
- high-level processing blocks (e.g. image compression [11], discrete cosine transform, finite and infinite impulse response filters [12]);
- computer architecture (approximate pipelines in microprocessors [13]);
- general purpose approximate computing machines [14];
- programming languages [15].

Considering the energy efficiency as the main driving factor for introducing inaccurate solutions, approximate computing is thus primarily relevant to physical design of circuits and development of software. In the case of software, a key challenge is how to isolate parts of the program that must be precise from those that can be approximated so that a program execution is correct even if quality of the output degrades [15].

Approximate computing is definitely a promising way in computer engineering as small imperfections in functionality can be tolerated in many domains and obtained benefits (especially in terms of power consumption) are impressive. At the same time, future fabrication technologies operating with atomic-scale elements will inherently lead to imperfectly working circuits and thus majority of circuits will have to be considered as approximate circuits. However, there is not still a well-established methodology for automated construction of approximate systems and circuits which could provide a good trade-off among key parameters. A recent comprehensive survey [16] clearly states in its "Implications for Circuits and Architectures" section that

> Much research needs to be done to functionally or parametrically underdesign large general class of circuits automatically. Mechanisms to pass application intent to physical implementation flow (especially to logic synthesis in case of functional underdesign) need to be developed.

2.1   Approximate Circuits

Before a *digital circuit* is implemented using gates and transistors, it is initially represented at the logic level. There is a huge number of possibilities to map the logic behavior onto available gates. In past decades, various optimization techniques were proposed to find the most suitable mapping according to a preselected *metric*, typically reflecting the area on a chip, power consumption and delay [7,8]. The circuits which are intentionally designed in such a way that the specification is not met in terms of functionality and some savings are expected in terms of energy, performance or area are called *approximate circuits*.

Power consumption reduction methods have been developed for decades [17]. However, new technology-level optimizations such as downsizing of gates (i.e. creating smaller than normally sized gates to reduce power consumption, in exchange for increased delay) on critical paths and voltage over-scaling (i.e. using deliberately lower power supply voltage for which the circuit is known to occasionally produce erroneous outputs) enabled additional power savings.

Another technique which is, to some extent, technology-independent is *functional approximation*. An accurate computing circuit is modified so that it does not fully implement the logic behavior given by the specification. A natural way is eliminating the least significant bits in the case of arithmetic circuits. However, this technique leads to insignificant area (and so power consumption) savings for some key circuits such as multipliers. Hence more drastic changes have to be introduced into the circuit structure.

The problem of *circuit approximation* can be formulated as a multiobjective optimization problem: Let C be a combinational circuit (a feed-forward network composed of elementary logic gates) implementing a multiple-output logic function $\{0, 1\}^m \rightarrow \{0, 1\}^n$ which satisfies the specification S (given by, e.g., truth table, algebraic expressions, netlist etc.), where m and n is the number of inputs and outputs. The goal is to generate a circuit C', implementing S with errors never exceeding predefined threshold error values ϵ_i according to a set of chosen error (constraint) functions E_i and minimizing a set of objective functions F_j.

The role of fabrication technology has to be emphasized in this task. The relation between the area and power consumption can be highly non-linear. A simple assumption that a small circuit will have low power consumption does not always apply. As circuit power consumption in static and dynamic mode depends on a particular technology, detailed simulations of power consumption have to always be performed for the chosen technology in order to get trustworthy results from the circuit approximation process.

2.2 Systematic Design Methods

The design of approximate circuits is typically based on manual modifications of fully functional circuits [11]. Only a few research groups have worked on an automated approach for approximate circuit synthesis.

The Systematic methodology for Automatic Logic Synthesis of Approximate circuits (SALSA) starts with a description of the exact version of the circuit and an error constraint that specifies the type and amount of error that the implementation can exhibit [12]. The methodology introduces the so-called Q-function which takes the outputs from both the original circuit and approximate circuit and decides if the quality constraints are satisfied. The Q-function outputs a single Boolean value. The SALSA algorithm attempts to modify the approximate circuit with the goal of keeping the output of the Q-function unchanged. The execution times of SALSA (on a server with an AMD Opteron 6176, 2.29 GHz processor) ranged from 4 minutes to 2.5 hours for circuits such as multipliers, filters and discrete cosine transform blocks [12].

Another systematic approach, Substitute-And-SIMplIfy (SASIMI), tries to identify signal pairs in the circuit that exhibit the same value with a high probability, and substitutes one for the other [18]. These substitutions introduce functional approximations. Unused logic can be eliminated from the circuit which results in area and power savings.

In both cases, the design process is controlled by a predefined acceptable error, and hence we call the approaches *error-oriented*.

3 Evolutionary Approach to Approximate Circuits

The *evolutionary circuit design*, which has been developed in the framework of modern bio-inspired artificial intelligence, is the use of bio-inspired search algorithms for automated synthesis and optimization of circuit designs. The method has been utilized for digital as well as analogue circuits [19].

3.1 Evolutionary Circuit Design

Electronic circuits encoded as strings of symbols are constructed and optimized by the *evolutionary algorithm* (EA) in order to obtain a circuit implementation satisfying the specification. In order to evaluate a candidate circuit, a reconfigurable circuit (or its simulator if evolution is performed using a circuit simulator) is reconfigured using a new configuration created on the basis of the chromosome content. The configured device is then evaluated and its behavior is compared with the desired behavior. The fitness score is calculated which reflects to what extent the candidate circuit satisfies the specification.

Among various branches of EAs, *multiobjective* EAs (MOEA) have been recognized as a very valuable method in systems design as they naturally provide a set of candidate solutions showing various trade-offs among conflicting design objectives. The circuit design problem is thus transformed into the search problem.

The main reason why evolutionary circuit design has been studied and developed is its ability to (i) provide novel designs hardly reachable by means of conventional methods; (ii) deliver good solutions for problems where the specification is inherently incomplete and any golden solution does not exist; and (iii) achieve adaptation/fault tolerance directly at the hardware level. John Koza, the influential proponent of genetic programming, surveyed dozens of human-competitive designs produced by EA [20].

The main challenge is to overcome the *scalability issues* emerging in real-world applications of evolutionary circuit design, which primarily means developing EA-based methods capable of evolving complex circuits. Another disadvantage is that EA-based methods do not guarantee obtaining a solution with a predefined quality.

3.2   Cartesian Genetic Programming

Cartesian genetic programming (CGP) is one of the most suitable and popular methods for evolutionary circuit design [21].

A candidate circuit is modeled by means of a directed acyclic graph whose nodes (gates) are organized in c columns and r rows. The circuit utilizes m primary inputs and n primary outputs. Primary inputs and processing node outputs are labeled $0, 1, \ldots, m - 1$ and $m, m + 1, \ldots, m + c \cdot r - 1$, respectively. Each node input can be connected either to the output of a node placed in previous l columns or to one of the primary circuit inputs, where l is one of CGP parameters. Figure 1 shows the CGP grid of nodes.

A candidate solution consisting of two-input nodes is represented in the chromosome by $r \cdot c$ triplets (x_1, x_2, ψ) determining for each processing node its function ψ ($\psi \in \Gamma$), and addresses of nodes x_1 and x_2 which its inputs are connected to. The last part of the chromosome contains n integers specifying either the nodes where the primary outputs are connected to or logic constants ('0' and '1') which can directly be connected to the primary output. While the chromosome size is constant for a given product $r \cdot c$, the phenotype size is variable and measured as the number of used nodes (gates).

The initial population of CGP is created either randomly or by means of existing circuits. Calculating the fitness value is a two-phase process. Firstly, the circuit functionality is determined, e.g. by computing responses for all possible assignments to the inputs. After reaching a satisfactory accuracy in the course of evolution or when CGP is seeded by fully functional designs, the second phase is initiated in which the circuit size (or other objectives) can be optimized. CGP employs a $(1 + \lambda)$ evolution strategy whose pseudo-code is given in Algorithm 1. This search method is based on a point mutation operator which modifies h randomly selected genes (integers) of the parent circuit. The role of mutation is

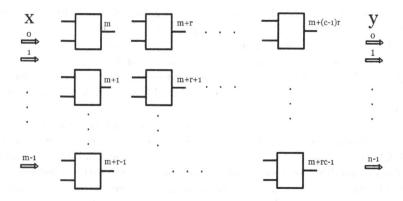

Fig. 1. An array of $r \cdot c$ 2-input nodes used in CGP. The number of inputs and outputs is m and n.

Algorithm 1. CGP

    Input: CGP parameters, fitness function
    Output: The highest scored individual p and its fitness

1 $P \leftarrow$ randomly generate parent p and its λ offspring;
2 EvaluatePopulation(P);
3 **while** ⟨*terminating condition not satisfied*⟩ **do**
4      $\alpha \leftarrow$ highest-scored-individual(P);
5   **if** *fitness(α)* $\geq$ *fitness(p)* **then**
6         $p \leftarrow \alpha$;
7      $P \leftarrow$ create λ offspring of p using mutation;
8   EvaluatePopulation(P);
9 **return** p, fitness(p);

---

substantial because even a single modified gene (integer) can significantly change the phenotype.

3.3   Evolution of Approximate Circuits

The CGP-based design methods were introduced for the design of approximate circuits because it was expected that they can provide much better solutions (i.e. approximate circuits) for a larger class of circuits and multiple conflicting objectives than existing design methods. We will briefly introduce our previous work, in which we proposed two approaches to the evolutionary design of approximate circuits by means of CGP.

In paper [22], we exploited the facts that power consumption is often highly correlated with occupied resources and the evolutionary design is capable of constructing partially working solutions even if sufficient resources (required for finding a fully functional solution) are not available. Let z be the (minimum) number of gates required for obtaining an accurate function. CGP is employed to minimize the error providing that only $z - 1$ gates are available. The process can be repeated for $z - 2$, $z - 3$ etc. gates. The user thus obtains a set of approximate combinational circuits, each of which typically exhibits different trade-off between the functionality and the number of gates. This approach can be considered as an *area-oriented* method because the user can control the used area (and so power consumption) more comfortably than by means of the error-oriented methods.

In paper [23], we proposed a complementary design approach. The user is supposed to define a required error level e_{max} (e.g. the average error magnitude). CGP, which is seeded by a conventional fully functional implementation, is utilized to modify the seed in order to obtain a circuit with predefined e_{max}. After obtaining that circuit, CGP can minimize the mean error, the number of gates or other criteria providing that e_{max} is left unchanged.

Because the utilized power estimation algorithm is very time consuming, it has not been included into the fitness function directly. Power consumption was calculated at the end of evolution for the best evolved approximate circuits. In both cases we demonstrated that for the cost of runtime the proposed methods provide better trade-offs for elementary arithmetic circuits (such as adders and multipliers) than conventional methods. The error-oriented approach tends to be less computationally demanding.

4 Multiobjective Approximate Circuit Evolution

Both aforementioned approaches are the single-objective optimization methods. In this section, we will demonstrate how truly multiobjective evolutionary optimization algorithms can be employed to approximate circuits design.

4.1 Multiobjective Optimization

Multiobjective evolutionary algorithms are utilized if multiple conflicting objective functions are formulated. Contrasted to the single-objective EAs, they internally sort individuals according to the dominance relation, build archives of so-called non-dominating solutions, and ensure population diversity to avoid converging to a single solution. In order to compare two solutions, the *dominance relation* is defined as follows: Solution x dominates another solution y if two conditions are satisfied:

1. The solution x is no worse than y in all objectives.
2. The solution x is strictly better than y in at least one objective.

In the set of solutions P, the non-dominated subset of solutions P' contains those solutions that are not dominated by any member of P. The non-dominated subset of all possible solutions is called the Pareto-optimal set. The ultimate goal of a multiobjective optimization is to find all Pareto-optimal solutions in a single run of MOEA.

Instead of evolving for every possible number of gates or error (as we have seen in Section 3.3), various trade-offs can be obtained in a single run of a suitable MOEA. Hence we combined CGP encoding with a typical multiobjective evolutionary algorithm NSGA-II [24]. The proposed MOEA will be seeded by a fully functional circuit. The goal is to simultaneously minimize the error and the number of gates, providing that solutions showing the error higher than E_{max} are infeasible.

4.2   Case Study

The proposed MOEA is evaluated in the task of a 4-bit multiplier approximation. The conventional 4-bit multiplier considered in this study consists of 59 gates and calculates an 8-bit product from two unsigned 4-bit operands. The error criterion is a mean absolute error between the produced outputs and correct outputs for all possible assignments to the inputs (2^8 vectors). The CGP parameters are initialized as follows: $r = 1$, $c = 59$, $l = c$, $\lambda = 4$, $h = 5\%$, $E_{max} = 5000$. The set of available gates is $\Gamma = \{$NOT, AND, OR, XOR, NAND, NOR, XNOR$\}$. The evolutionary algorithm operates with a 50 member population and stops when $g_{max} = 32 \cdot 10^6$ generations are spent. This corresponds with a four hour run on an Intel Xeon processor running at 3 GHz. The setting of these values is based on our previous experiments.

Fig. 2 shows all the trade-offs obtained from 100 independent runs of the proposed MOEA. It can be seen that several solutions have been discovered for

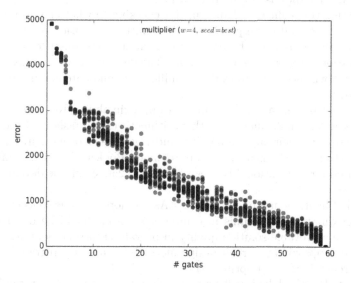

Fig. 2. Trade-offs between the number of gates and error for the 4-bit approximate multiplier (59 gates corresponds to the perfect functionality).

every possible number of gates. A single run led to 16.97 different solutions on average. A detailed analysis of the best evolved approximate circuits revealed that a circuit containing k gates can exhibit a higher error than a circuit containing $k-1$ gates (see, e.g., the error for 24 and 25 gates). It is, however, assumed that a smaller error is obtained if more gates are allowed in the circuit. Hence the current version and setting of the method seems to be inefficient. On the other hand, the method is capable of producing many useful trade-offs much faster than multiple runs of single-objective EAs from [22, 23].

5   Conclusions

The field of approximate computing in general and approximate circuits in particular is in an early stage of development. Only a few systematic design methodologies have been proposed for the approximate circuit design so far. Despite the interesting preliminary results obtained by EAs, it is a well-known problem that EAs utilize very time consuming algorithms, the scalability of resulting solutions is limited and the whole process is too non-deterministic for the community of "conventional" designers. On the other hand, even conventional approaches have to employ heuristics and time-consuming procedures in order to approximate circuit designs.

In the context of approximate circuit design methodologies, the future research should mainly deal with the following issues:

- More efficient and accurate multiobjective EAs, employing more scalable circuit representations and efficient genetic operators should be introduced specifically for the task of approximation.
- Discovering time-efficient algorithms for checking to what extent a complex approximate circuit corresponds with the exact specification is a challenging task. Current approaches based on testing circuit's responses for all possible combinations of inputs are not scalable. The desired algorithm must be fast, because it will be called to evaluate millions of candidate circuits produced by MOEA.
- NP-hard problems vary greatly in their approximability. Key circuit classes (such as adders, multipliers and other arithmetic circuits) should be analyzed with respect to their approximability under various error measures and constraints. Complexity measures of approximate Boolean functions, similar to those used for conventional Boolean functions [25], should be developed and exploited.
- Instead of heuristic methods (such as EAs), a more rigorous concept, similar to approximation algorithms in computer science, should be developed to guarantee a provable solution quality in provable run-time bounds.
- Resulting approximate circuit design methods should be integrated to standard circuit design and optimization tools.
- Automated methodologies allowing designers to identify those system's components that can be replaced by their approximate counterparts should be developed.

All these issues have to be seen in the context of hardware, because very good circuit approximations obtained for a given fabrication technology can become useless when another fabrication technology is considered.

Approximate computing is a promising emerging paradigm which is quite important for future low power and resources-efficient computers. However, a lot of work has to be done in order to be widely accepted.

Acknowledgments. This work was supported by the Czech science foundation project 14-04197S.

References

1. Gruska, J.: Foundations of Computing. Int. Thomson Publishing Computer Press (1997)
2. Vazirani, V.V.: Approximation Algorithms. Springer Verlag (2001)
3. Cybenko, G.: Approximation by superpositions of a sigmoidal function. Mathematics of Control, Signals and Systems **2**(4), 303–314 (1989)
4. Volder, J.E.: The birth of cordic. Journal of VLSI Signal Processing Systems for Signal, Image and Video Technology **25**(2), 101–105 (2000)
5. Han, J., Orshansky, M.: Approximate computing: An emerging paradigm for energy-efficient design. In: Proc. of the 18th IEEE European Test Symposium, pp. 1–6. IEEE (2013)
6. Chippa, V.K., Chakradhar, S.T., Roy, K., Raghunathan, A.: Analysis and characterization of inherent application resilience for approximate computing. In: The 50th Annual Design Automation Conference, DAC 2013, pp. 1–9. ACM (2013)
7. Mishchenko, A.: ABC: A system for sequential synthesis and verification, Berkley logic synthesis and verification group (2012)
8. Kahng, A.B., Lienig, J., Markov, I.L., Hu, J.: VLSI Physical Design: From Graph Partitioning to Timing Closure. Springer-Verlag (2011)
9. Shanbhag, N.R., Abdallah, R.A., Kumar, R., Jones, D.L.: Stochastic computation. In: The 47th Annual Design Automation Conference, DAC 2010, pp. 859–867. ACM (2010)
10. Gupta, V., Mohapatra, D., Raghunathan, A., Roy, K.: Low-power digital signal processing using approximate adders. IEEE Trans. on CAD of Integrated Circuits and Systems **32**(1), 124–137 (2013)
11. Kulkarni, P., Gupta, P., Ercegovac, M.D.: Trading accuracy for power in a multiplier architecture. J. Low Power Electronics **7**(4), 490–501 (2011)
12. Venkataramani, S., Sabne, A., Kozhikkottu, V.J., Roy, K., Raghunathan, A.: Salsa: systematic logic synthesis of approximate circuits. In: The 49th Annual Design Automation Conference, DAC 2012, pp. 796–801. ACM (2012)
13. Lu, S.L.: Speeding up processing with approximation circuits. IEEE Computer **37**(3), 67–73 (2004)
14. Esmaeilzadeh, H., Sampson, A., Ceze, L., Burger, D.: Neural acceleration for general-purpose approximate programs. In: Proc. of the 2012 45th Annual IEEE/ACM International Symposium on Microarchitecture, pp. 449–460. IEEE Computer Society (2012)
15. Sampson, A., Dietl, W., Fortuna, E., Gnanapragasam, D., Ceze, L., Grossman, D.: Enerj: Approximate data types for safe and general low-power computation. In: Proc. of the 32nd ACM SIGPLAN Conference on Programming Language Design and Implementation, pp. 164–174. ACM (2011)

16. Gupta, P., Agarwal, Y., Dolecek, L., Dutt, N., Gupta, R.K., Kumar, R., Mitra, S., Nicolau, A., Rosing, T.S., Srivastava, M.B., Swanson, S., Sylvester, D.: Under-designed and opportunistic computing in presence of hardware variability. IEEE Trans. on CAD of Integrated Circuits and Systems **32**(1), 8–23 (2013)
17. Venkatachalam, V., Franz, M.: Power reduction techniques for microprocessor systems. ACM Computing Surveys **37**(3), 195–237 (2005)
18. Venkataramani, S., Roy, K., Raghunathan, A.: Substitute-and-simplify: A unified design paradigm for approximate and quality configurable circuits. In: Design, Automation and Test in Europe, DATE 2013, EDA Consortium San Jose, CA, USA, pp. 1–6 (2013)
19. Lohn, J.D., Hornby, G.S.: Evolvable hardware: Using evolutionary computation to design and optimize hardware systems. IEEE Computational Intelligence Magazine **1**(1), 19–27 (2006)
20. Koza, J.R.: Human-competitive results produced by genetic programming. Genetic Programming and Evolvable Machines **11**(3–4), 251–284 (2010)
21. Miller, J.F.: Cartesian Genetic Programming. Springer-Verlag (2011)
22. Sekanina, L., Vasicek, Z.: Approximate circuits by means of evolvable hardware. In: 2013 IEEE International Conference on Evolvable Systems, Proceedings of the 2013 IEEE Symposium Series on Computational Intelligence (SSCI), pp. 21–28. IEEE CIS (2013)
23. Vasicek, Z., Sekanina, L.: Evolutionary design of approximate multipliers under different error metrics. In: IEEE International Symposium on Design and Diagnostics of Electronic Circuits and Systems 2013, pp. 135–140. IEEE (2014)
24. Deb, K., Pratap, A., Agarwal, S., Meyarivan, T.: A fast and elitist multiobjective genetic algorithm: Nsga-II. IEEE Transactions on Evolutionary Computation **6**(2), 182–197 (2002)
25. Buhrman, H., de Wolf, R.: Complexity measures and decision tree complexity: A survey. Theoretical Computer Science **288**(1), 21–43 (2002)

A Distributed Computing Model for Dataflow, Controlflow, and Workflow in Fractionated Cyber-Physical Systems

Mark-Oliver Stehr$^{(\boxtimes)}$, Minyoung Kim, and Tim McCarthy

SRI International, Menlo Park, California, USA
{mark-oliver.stehr,minyoung.kim,tim.mcCarthy}@sri.com

Abstract. With the ongoing trend to parallelize computations for scalability, better performance, and reliability, distributed dataflow models are attracting interest at all design levels, ranging from processor architectures to local- and wide-area computing clusters in the cloud. Data-driven computation has also been an important paradigm in sensor networks and embedded systems, which have evolved into a larger research effort on networked cyber-physical systems (NCPS), that can sense and affect their environment. Fractionated cyber-physical systems (FCPS) are an interesting subclass of NCPS where the redundancy and diversity of many unreliable and potentially heterogeneous networked components is exploited to improve scalability, reliability, and verifiability of the overall system. In this paper we present the theory of a new distributed computing model for such systems as a first step toward a model-based design methodology for FCPS. To uniformly capture dataflow, controlflow, and workflow, we use a subclass of Petri nets as an intuitive high-level model, which is translated into a weaker model — namely, a new variant of Petri nets that does not make any atomicity assumptions but instead uses a partial order to ensure eventual consistency. In the full version of this paper, we briefly discuss an application to unmanned aerial vehicle (UAV) swarms, which has been implemented on top of a prototype of our theory for both simulation models and real world deployments.

Dedication

The first author is dedicating this paper to Jozef Gruska, who in his role as visiting professor was his early advisor during his studies at the University of Hamburg. One topic was Carl Adam Petri's theory of concurrency, which has influenced this paper to a great degree, although in an unexpected direction. This paper explores a world in which atomic non-deterministic choices do not exist or are too expensive to implement with high reliability. The motivating application domain are loosely coupled distributed systems, such as wireless networks of mobile cyber-physical devices, which can be regarded as the new computing resources of our time. Interestingly, observable non-determinism is also a challenge in quantum computing, a potential computing resource of the

© Springer International Publishing Switzerland 2014
C.S. Calude et al. (Eds.): Gruska Festschrift, LNCS 8808, pp. 379–393, 2014.
DOI: 10.1007/978-3-319-13350-8_28

future, due to the associated and often undesirable collapse of the quantum state. Hence, potential applications of our model in this domain would be worthwhile to explore, but they are beyond the scope of this paper.

1   Introduction

Dataflow models have a long history in computer science as witnessed by the large body of literature on dataflow graphs, Kahn networks, stream processing languages, and Petri nets. Dataflow models come in many flavors. Some use graphical representations, while others are presented as formal systems, such as linear logic [14] or rewriting logic [25]. Such models have been used not only to describe software and hardware designs but also workflow in various domains from manufacturing to government, where the individual tasks of a workflow are not computational but may entail interaction with the physical world or the social/organizational context. Dataflow models make explicit the information flow and hence the causal structure of computations, which is only implicitly represented in traditional algorithms. Explicitly representing the structure of a distributed computation is a form of partial reflection that enables the runtime system to make better decisions on how to map computation to the available resources. Another attractive feature of dataflow/workflow models is that they are declarative, in the sense that data objects, functions, and causal dependencies can be specified, e.g., in the form of a Petri net, and at the same time they can be operational, i.e., executable.

Distributed dataflow approaches are gaining popularity, most recently because of their potential to exploit the parallelism offered by modern many-core architectures (stream processing) and cloud computing. Google's MapReduce framework [7] can be seen as an execution engine for distributed dataflow graphs of a certain two-level shape. Programming languages for the distributed execution of larger classes of dataflow graphs are being developed, as for instance CIEL [28]. Stream processing frameworks such as OpenCL [1] can express data-parallel programs in terms of kernel functions that can be efficiently mapped to many-core architectures such as modern graphical processing units (GPUs). Thanks to their capability to separate timing and functionality, dataflow models enable scalability and are also becoming increasingly popular in hardware design as witnessed by approaches such as BlueSpec [2], which is influenced by Petri nets and rewriting-based approaches, and is becoming a real competitor for VHSIC hardware description language (VHDL) and Verilog. Data-oriented approaches have also traditionally been used in sensor networks with in-network processing (mostly asynchronous) and model-based design of embedded systems (mostly synchronous), which have become part of a larger research effort on sensor/actor networks [10] or networked cyber-physical systems (NCPS). There is also a parallel trend to make general-purpose networking architectures more data oriented and aware of the semantics of the data, as witnessed by recent efforts such as disruption-tolerant networking [11], declarative networking [24], and content-based networking [16,21].

The real potential of distributed dataflow models for programming or model-based design has not been reached yet, because existing dataflow engines are implemented as classical distributed algorithms that can operate successfully only in very constrained and cooperative environments. Although some traditional fault tolerance can be offered by dataflow engines, operating under high failure rates, with highly unreliable connectivity, or even in the context of node mobility is still a major challenge arising in many real-world large-scale distributed systems or systems operating in hostile/uncontrollable environments. The objective of this paper is to develop a dataflow model for fractionated software and hardware systems. Such systems are motivated by the strong trend toward a truly distributed world in which potentially unreliable and resource-constrained devices and powerful computing resources coexist without assuming continuous network connectivity, and where a large number of such components need to be operating as an ensemble to produce sufficient performance and reliability.

Background

1.1 Fractionated Cyber-Physical Systems

NCPS are distributed systems consisting of heterogeneous software and hardware components that can sense and affect the environment. Typically, the environment plays an important role and can have many dimensions. For instance, manufacturing systems, process control systems, automobiles, aircraft, satellites, and robots are classical examples of NCPS, but also systems that support social interaction or collaborative activities with humans in the loop. The notion of fractionated software is inspired by hardware fractionation in DARPA's F6 space program [5] and has been proposed in [37] as a new basis to improve reliability and verifiability of systems and for future systems built on fundamentally unreliable components. Fractionated cyber-physical systems (FCPS) can be seen as a class of NCPS in which the operation of the system is fully distributed without tying a function to a particular piece of hardware, which can also be regarded as an extreme form of virtualization. Hardware is highly redundant so that functions can be performed even in the presence of continuous failures without the need for global coordination. FCPS should operate in a meaningful way even if network communication is extremely unreliable and network partitioning may occur. FCPS also need to provide scalability in the sense that the amount of hardware/software elements (so-called fracments) can be adjusted, without requiring changes in the application. Many classical distributed algorithms that may be sufficient for NCPS are not suitable for FCPS, because they make strong assumptions about the network — e.g., have bounded delays, use nonscalable primitives such as transactions, or introduce temporary bottlenecks, e.g., synchronization or leader election phases. Aspects of FCPS can be found in sensor networks, ensembles or swarms of vehicles, or biological systems, more generally systems of a large number of unreliable components that are beyond the reach of classical distributed algorithms.

1.2   Partially Ordered Knowledge Sharing

The partially ordered knowledge sharing model for loosely coupled distributed computing was introduced in [18], which presents a prototypical implementation of what we call the *cyber-application framework*, a software framework for NCPS. A logical version of this model was studied in [19,34] and a particular instance was used for disruption-tolerant networking [36].

In a nutshell, this model postulates an NCPS with a finite set of so-called *cyber-nodes* that provide *computing* resources, can have volatile and/or persistent *storage*, and are all equipped with *networking* capabilities. Cyber-nodes can have additional devices such as *sensors* and *actuators*, through which they can observe and control their environment, but only to a limited degree (including possibly their own physical state, e.g., their orientation/position). Cyber-nodes can be fixed or mobile, and for the general model no assumption is made about the computing or storage resources or about the network and the communication capabilities or opportunities that it provides. Hence, this model covers a broad range of *heterogeneous* technologies (e.g., wireless/wired, unicast/broadcast) and potentially challenging environment conditions, where networking characteristics can range from high-quality persistent connectivity to intermittent/episodic connectivity. The cyber-physical system is *open* in the sense that new nodes can join and leave the network at any time. Permanent or temporary communication or node *failures* are admitted by this model.

As a step toward semantic networking [29], partially ordered knowledge sharing allows the network to be aware of the application semantics (in this paper, the semantics of our workflow model), and hence a real-world distributed implementation of our model has a well-defined behavior under network partitioning and network merging, and can tolerate unbounded network delays and node mobility. Due to the transactionless nature of our model, disconnections do not have to be announced or predicted as in distributed tuple space models such as [27]. Thanks to in-network caching, delay- and disruption-tolerant communication scenarios — e.g., highly unreliable wireless networks, short windows of opportunity, and message ferrying — can be supported. There is no need for continuous clock synchronization, as long as logical time [23] is respected.

Applications are event-driven; that is, they can post and respond to local events. For coordination, knowledge can be posted into the network by a *semantic broadcast* that can be implemented by many different protocols, ranging from physical broadcast to gossip-style protocols. Knowledge can also be cached in the network by intermediate nodes and at the endpoints. To partially capture the semantics of knowledge for the purpose of distributed knowledge sharing, we assume an application-specific strict partial order $\prec$ on units of knowledge that we refer to as *replacement order*, with the intuition that $k \prec k'$ means that k' replaces/overwrites k, and hence if k has not been delivered yet to the application, the knowledge-sharing model may discard it without delivering it, if k' has already been received.

1.3   Petri Nets

Petri nets are the prototypical model for dataflow that has inspired many other formalisms. Here, we use nets with individual tokens, specifically colored nets, as a common specification of dataflow, controlflow, and workflow. We begin with some basic notation and Petri net terminology.

A *finite multiset* over a set S is a function m from S to $\mathbb{N}$ such that its support $\mathcal{S}(m) = \{s \in S \mid m(s) > 0\}$ is finite. We denote by $\mathcal{MS}(S)$ the set of finite multisets over S. We write $\emptyset_S$ for the empty multiset over S and $\langle e_1, \dots, e_n \rangle_S$ for the multiset containing the listed elements (we usually omit S if it is clear from the context), and, overloading some set operators, we use the standard definitions of multiset membership $\in$, inclusion $\subseteq$, union $+$, and difference $-$.

A *net* $\mathcal{N}$ consists of a finite set of *places* $P_\mathcal{N}$, a finite set of *transitions* $T_\mathcal{N}$ disjoint from $P_\mathcal{N}$, and a *flow relation* $F_\mathcal{N} \subseteq (P_\mathcal{N} \times T_\mathcal{N}) \cup (T_\mathcal{N} \times P_\mathcal{N})$ such that the *preset* ${}^\bullet t$ and the *postset* $t^\bullet$ are nonempty for each $t \in T_\mathcal{N}$, where the *preset* ${}^\bullet x$ and *postset* $x^\bullet$ of $x \in P \cup T$ are defined as $\{y \mid y\ F_\mathcal{N}\ x\}$ and $\{y \mid x\ F_\mathcal{N}\ y\}$, respectively. A net is *pure* iff $x^\bullet \cap {}^\bullet x = \emptyset$ for all $x \in P \cup T$.

Whenever we use nonpure nets, we interpret symmetric pairs of the flow relation to represent what is usually called test or read arcs, rather then self-loops, which have a different concurrency and refinement semantics.

Let $\mathcal{N}$ be a net. A *(black) token* is simply defined by a place $p \in P_\mathcal{N}$. A *marking* is a multiset of tokens. An *occurrence* is defined by a transition $t \in T_\mathcal{N}$. The sets of *tokens*, *markings*, and *occurrences* of $\mathcal{N}$ are denoted by $\mathcal{K}_\mathcal{N}$, $\mathcal{M}_\mathcal{N}$ and $\mathcal{O}_\mathcal{N}$, respectively. The *semantics* of a net $\mathcal{N}$ is given by the labeled transition system that has $\mathcal{M}_\mathcal{N}$ as its set of states, $\mathcal{O}_\mathcal{N}$ as its set of labels, and a transition relation $\longrightarrow$ given by the *occurrence transition relation* $\longrightarrow_o \subseteq \mathcal{M}_\mathcal{N} \times \mathcal{O}_\mathcal{N} \times \mathcal{M}_\mathcal{N}$ defined by $m_1 \xrightarrow{t}_o m_2$ iff there is a marking m such that $m_1 = m + {}^\bullet t$ and $m_2 = m + t^\bullet$. Writing the occurrence rule in the way given above makes it evident that the occurrence of a transition t replaces its preset by its postset, whereas the remainder of the marking, here denoted by m, is not involved in this process. We say that a transition t is *enabled* at a marking m iff $m \xrightarrow{t}_o m'$ for some marking m'. We also define a *binary transition relation* $\longrightarrow \subseteq \mathcal{M}_\mathcal{N} \times \mathcal{M}_\mathcal{N}$ by $m_1 \longrightarrow m_2$ iff $m_1 \xrightarrow{l}_o m_2$ for some label l, its transitive closure $\xrightarrow{+}$, and its reflexive and transitive closure $\xrightarrow{*}$. We say that m_2 is *reachable from* m_1 iff $m_1 \xrightarrow{*} m_2$. We write $\mathcal{R}(\mathcal{N}, m)$ to denote the set of markings reachable from m.

An *execution* of a net $\mathcal{N}$ is a finite sequence $\pi = m_0, l_0, m_1, l_1, \dots, l_n, m_{n+1}$, or an infinite sequence $\pi = m_0, l_0, m_1, l_1, \dots$ of markings m_i and labels l_i such that $m_i \xrightarrow{l_i}_o m_{i+1}$ for all indices $i, i+1$ of π. Typically, a net $\mathcal{N}$ is specified together with an initial marking m_0, giving rise to a *net system* $(\mathcal{N}, m_0)$, in which case executions of $(\mathcal{N}, m_0)$ are the subset of executions of $\mathcal{N}$ starting with m_0.

Let $(\mathcal{N}, m_0)$ be a net system. We say that $(\mathcal{N}, m_0)$ is *safe* iff for each marking $m \in \mathcal{R}(\mathcal{N}, m_0)$ we have $m(p) \leq 1$ for all $p \in P_\mathcal{N}$. Furthermore, $(\mathcal{N}, m_0)$ is *live* iff for each marking $m \in \mathcal{R}(\mathcal{N}, m_0)$ and each transition $t' \in T_\mathcal{N}$ there exists m' with $m \xrightarrow{*}_o m'$ such that t' is enabled at m'. Safety and liveness imply boundedness and deadlock freedom, respectively [9].

Abstract workflows of many different kinds [32,39] are often modeled using free-choice nets [4,9], which exhibit the property that conflicts are localized and structurally defined. A *free-choice (FC) net* $\mathcal{N}$ is a net[1] such that for all transitions $t, t' \in T_\mathcal{N}$ with ${}^\bullet t \cap {}^\bullet t' \neq \emptyset$, we have ${}^\bullet t = {}^\bullet t' = \{p\}$ for some $p \in P_\mathcal{N}$.

Motivated by our application, we will only consider safe and live free-choice (SLFC) net systems (i.e. nets sytems with an underlying FC net) in this paper. In our proofs, we frequently exploit their well-understood structural properties that can be most intuitively captured by reduction or synthesis rules [9].

Colored nets [17] are nets with places, transitions, and arcs inscribed with additional information given by functions C and W. The color set $C(p)$ of a place p is the set of possible objects p can carry. The color set $C(t)$ of a transition t can be seen as a set of bindings (also called modes) under which t may occur. We use a specialization of colored nets, where the arc inscription W defines individual objects ("colored" tokens) that are transported by an arc when the associated transition occurs. In fact, this object may depend on the binding under which the transition occurs, which is why $W(p, t)$ and $W(t, p)$ take the form of functions in the definition below. In a graphical representation, W is represented by variables or terms on the arcs, and the color set of a transition is implicitly defined by all the possible bindings of all its local variables, which can be restricted by an optional condition.

A *colored net* N consists of (1) a net $N_\mathcal{N}$; (2) a set of *color sets* $CS_\mathcal{N}$; (3) a *color function* $C_\mathcal{N} : P_\mathcal{N} \cup T_\mathcal{N} \to CS_\mathcal{N}$; and (4) an *arc inscription* $W_\mathcal{N}$ on $F_\mathcal{N}$ such that $W_\mathcal{N}(p, t) : C_\mathcal{N}(t) \to C_\mathcal{N}(p)$ and $W_\mathcal{N}(t, p) : C_\mathcal{N}(t) \to C_\mathcal{N}(p)$. $W_\mathcal{N}$ is extended to a function on $(P_\mathcal{N} \times T_\mathcal{N}) \cup (T_\mathcal{N} \times P_\mathcal{N})$ in such a way that $(p, t) \notin F_\mathcal{N}$ implies $W_\mathcal{N}(p, t)(b) = \emptyset$, and $(t, p) \notin F_\mathcal{N}$ implies $W_\mathcal{N}(t, p)(b) = \emptyset$ for each $b \in C_\mathcal{N}(t)$. A colored net N is *pure* iff the underlying net $N_\mathcal{N}$ is pure.

The semantics of colored nets can be reduced to that of ordinary nets by a flattening operation [35], but we give a direct definition for the purpose of this paper. Let $\mathcal{N}$ be a colored net. A *token* is of the form (p, d) where $p \in P_\mathcal{N}$ and $d \in C(p)$, also called a *data object* for p. A *marking* is a multiset of tokens. An *occurrence* is of the form (t, b) where $t \in T_\mathcal{N}$ and $b \in C(t)$, also called a *binding* for t. The sets of *tokens*, *markings*, and *occurrences* of $\mathcal{N}$ are denoted by $\mathcal{K}_\mathcal{N}$, $\mathcal{M}_\mathcal{N}$, and $\mathcal{O}_\mathcal{N}$, respectively. Given a marking m we define the projection on $p \in P_\mathcal{N}$, written $p(m)$, by $p(m)(p, d) = m(p, d)$ and $p(m)(p', d') = 0$ if $p' \neq p$. Given an occurrence (t, b) we define the multisets ${}^\bullet(t, b)$ and $(t, b)^\bullet$ by ${}^\bullet(t, b)(p, d) = W(p, t)(b)(d)$ and $(t, b)^\bullet(p, d) = W(t, p)(b)(d)$. The *semantics* of a colored net $\mathcal{N}$ is given by the labeled transition system that has $\mathcal{M}_\mathcal{N}$ as its set of states, $\mathcal{O}_\mathcal{N}$ as its set of labels and a transition relation $\longrightarrow$ given by the *occurrence transition relation* $\longrightarrow_o \subseteq \mathcal{M}_\mathcal{N} \times \mathcal{O}_\mathcal{N} \times \mathcal{M}_\mathcal{N}$ defined by $m_1 \xrightarrow{(t,b)}_o m_2$ iff there is a marking m such that $m_1 = m + {}^\bullet(t, b)$ and $m_2 = m + (t, b)^\bullet$. We say that a transition t is *enabled* under a binding b or equivalently that the occurrence (t, b) is *enabled* at a marking m iff $m \xrightarrow{(t,b)}_o m'$ for some marking m'. Typically, a colored net $\mathcal{N}$ is specified together with an initial marking m_0, giving

---

[1] To simplify the treatment we do not consider the slightly more general class of extended free-choice nets in this paper.

rise to a *colored net system* $(\mathcal{N}, m_0)$. The *binary transition relation, reachable markings*, and *executions* are defined as for nets and net systems, respectively.

Given a colored net system $(\mathcal{N}, m_0)$, we define the *flow abstraction* $(\hat{\mathcal{N}}, \hat{m}_0)$ as the net system consisting of the underlying net $\hat{\mathcal{N}}$ of $(\mathcal{N}, m_0)$ and a marking $\hat{m}_0$ of $\hat{\mathcal{N}}$ that is defined as $\eta(m_0)$ where $\eta : \mathcal{M}_{\mathcal{N}} \to \mathcal{M}_{\hat{\mathcal{N}}}$ lifts $\eta : \mathcal{K}_{\mathcal{N}} \to \mathcal{K}_{\hat{\mathcal{N}}}$ to multisets, which maps each token (p, d) in $\mathcal{N}$ to a (black) token p in $\hat{\mathcal{N}}$, abstracting from the data. A corresponding function $\eta : \mathcal{O}_{\mathcal{N}} \to \mathcal{O}_{\hat{\mathcal{N}}}$ maps each occurrence (t, b) in $\mathcal{N}$ to an occurrence t in $\hat{\mathcal{N}}$, abstracting from the binding. From our definitions, it is obvious that η preserves the semantics — i.e., every $m \xrightarrow{o}_o m'$ implies $\eta(m) \xrightarrow{\eta(o)}_o \eta(m')$, but the converse does not typically hold.

2 Toward a Truly Distributed Workflow Model for Fractionated Systems

We introduce two Petri-net-based models, a high-level workflow model, and an implementation-level model, and establish a formal correspondence. We begin with the latter, but we first enrich colored nets with a notion of timestamps that will enable the mapping between these models.

A colored net system $(\mathcal{N}, m_0)$ *maintains timestamps* iff there is a function $ts : \mathcal{K} \cup \mathcal{O} \to \mathbb{R}$ such that the following timestamp conditions hold: (1) $ts(p, d) = 0$ for all $(p, d) \in m_0$ and (2) for each occurrence $(t, b) \in \mathcal{O}$ we have $ts(p', d') = ts(t, b) > ts(p, d)$ for each $(p, d) \in {}^\bullet(t, b)$ and $(p', d') \in (t, b)^\bullet$. Since we are interested in fully distributed executions of nets, we cannot assume the existence of a global clock. Instead, we are using the weaker logical time [23].

For colored nets that maintain timestamps we canonically restrict the sets of *tokens* $\mathcal{K}_{\mathcal{N}}$ so that $ts(k) = ts(k')$ implies $k = k'$ for all $k, k' \in \mathcal{K}_{\mathcal{N}}$, and similarly we restrict the set of *occurrences* $\mathcal{O}_{\mathcal{N}}$ so that $ts(o) = ts(o')$ implies $o = o'$ for all $o, o' \in \mathcal{O}_{\mathcal{N}}$. Furthermore, we canonically restrict the *occurrence transition relation* $\longrightarrow_o \subseteq \mathcal{M}_{\mathcal{N}} \times \mathcal{O}_{\mathcal{N}} \times \mathcal{M}_{\mathcal{N}}$ so that $m \xrightarrow{o}_o m' \xrightarrow{*}_o m''$ and $ts(o) = ts(o')$ implies that o' is not enabled at m'', which in particular entails that the timestamps of occurrences on each execution are distinct. Such requirements of distinct timestamps are satisfied in practice with arbitrary high probability if the timestamp precision is sufficiently high.

Lemma 1. *Given a colored net system $(\mathcal{N}, m_0)$ there is an equivalent colored net system $(\bar{\mathcal{N}}, \bar{m}_0)$ that maintains timestamps in the sense that there are functions $\phi : \mathcal{M}_{\bar{\mathcal{N}}} \to \mathcal{M}_{\mathcal{N}}$ and $\phi : \mathcal{O}_{\bar{\mathcal{N}}} \to \mathcal{O}_{\mathcal{N}}$ such that for all $\bar{m} \in \mathcal{R}(\bar{\mathcal{N}}, \bar{m}_0)$ we have (1) $\bar{m} \xrightarrow{\bar{o}}_o \bar{m}'$ implies $\phi(\bar{m}) \xrightarrow{\phi(\bar{o})}_o \phi(\bar{m}')$, and (2) $\phi(\bar{m}) = m$ and $m \xrightarrow{o}_o m'$ implies $\bar{m} \xrightarrow{\bar{o}}_o \bar{m}'$ for some $\bar{o}$ and $\bar{m}'$ with $\phi(\bar{o}) = o$ and $\phi(\bar{m}') = m'$.*

A colored net $\mathcal{N}$ is *monotonic* iff $(p, t) \in F_{\mathcal{N}}$ implies $(t, p) \in F_{\mathcal{N}}$ for all $p \in P_{\mathcal{N}}$ and $t \in T_{\mathcal{N}}$ and $W(p, t) = W(t, p)$ for all $(p, t) \in F_{\mathcal{N}}$. Given a pure colored net $\mathcal{N}$ we define the *monotonic closure* $\bar{\mathcal{N}}$ as the colored net that is identical to $\mathcal{N}$ except that $F_{\bar{\mathcal{N}}} = F_{\mathcal{N}} \cup \{(t, p) \mid (p, t) \in F_{\mathcal{N}}\}$, $W_{\bar{\mathcal{N}}}$ is identical to $W_{\mathcal{N}}$ on $F_{\mathcal{N}}$, and $W_{\bar{\mathcal{N}}}(t, p)(b) = W_{\mathcal{N}}(p, t)(b)$ for all $(p, t) \in F_{\mathcal{N}}$.

Clearly, monotonic nets have monotonic executions where the markings can only grow, because tokens cannot be removed by transition occurrences. Different from Petri nets with test or read arcs, monotonic nets require that the preset of a transition is exclusively accessed through read arcs. The only way to eliminate tokens is by means of an ordering, which leads to the next definition.

A *partially ordered net* $(\mathcal{N}, \prec_{\mathcal{N}})$ consists of a colored net $N_{\mathcal{N}}$ and a strict partial order $\prec_{\mathcal{N}} \subseteq \mathcal{K}_{\mathcal{N}} \times \mathcal{K}_{\mathcal{N}}$ called the *replacement order*. The *occurrence semantics* of $(\mathcal{N}, \prec_{\mathcal{N}})$ extends the occurrence semantics of $\mathcal{N}$ by an additional *replacement transition relation* $\longrightarrow_r \subseteq \mathcal{M}_{\mathcal{N}} \times \mathcal{K}_{\mathcal{N}} \times \mathcal{M}_{\mathcal{N}}$ defined by $m_1 \xrightarrow{(p,d)}_r m_2$ iff $(p, d) \in m_1$, $(p', d') \in m_1$, $(p, d) \prec (p', d')$, and $m_2 = m_1 - \langle (p, d) \rangle$. In this case, we also write $m_1 \longrightarrow_r m_2$. A *partially ordered net system* $(\mathcal{N}, \prec_{\mathcal{N}}, m_0)$ is a partially ordered net $(\mathcal{N}, \prec_{\mathcal{N}})$ with an initial marking $m_0 \in \mathcal{M}_{\mathcal{N}}$. The *semantics* of a partially ordered net $(\mathcal{N}, \prec_{\mathcal{N}})$ and a partially ordered net system $(\mathcal{N}, \prec_{\mathcal{N}}, m_0)$ is defined as for colored nets or net systems but using an extended transition relation $\longrightarrow$, which is the union of the occurrence transition relation $\longrightarrow_o$ and the replacement transition relation $\longrightarrow_r$.

Partially ordered net systems with an underlying monotonic net will serve as our implementation-level model, which allows inconsistencies to enable efficient distributed execution as long as they can be resolved when needed. Hence, our approach can be best characterized as optimistic, in contrast to a pessimistic approach, which would block progress to make sure that inconsistencies can never arise. Our high-level workflow model is introduced next.

A *multiround workflow system* $(\mathcal{N}, m_0)$ is a colored net system with an initial place p_0 and an initial data object $d_0 \in C(p_0)$, giving rise to an initial marking $m_0 = \langle (p_0, d_0) \rangle$, such that the following conditions are satisfied. (1) The flow abstraction of $(\mathcal{N}, m_0)$ is a pure SLFC net system. (2) For each marking $m \in \mathcal{R}(\mathcal{N}, m_0)$ we have $|m| = 1$ whenever $m(p_0) \neq \emptyset$. (3) There exists a function $r : \mathcal{K} \to \mathbb{N}$ such that $r(p_0, d_0) = 0$ and (3a) for each occurrence $(t, b) \in \mathcal{O}$ and for all $(p, d), (p', d') \in {}^\bullet(t, b)$ we have $r(p', d') = r(p, d)$ and (3b) for all $(p, d) \in {}^\bullet(t, b)$, $(p', d') \in (t, b)^\bullet$ we have $r(p', d') = r(p, d) + 1$ if $p' = p_0$ and $r(p', d') = r(p, d)$ otherwise.

From this definition it follows that $\langle p_0 \rangle$ is a home marking in the flow abstraction, meaning that it is reachable from any reachable marking [9]. If should be noted that although the flow abstraction is live, it is only an overapproximation of the behavior of $(\mathcal{N}, m_0)$, which due to conditional transitions (as expressed by valid bindings) may terminate (possibly after a number of rounds).

To explicitly track causality and define an appropriate replacement ordering, we enrich each token in our workflow system with some local provenance information.

A multiround workflow system $(\mathcal{N}, m_0)$ *maintains provenance* iff it maintains timestamps and there is a function $h : \mathcal{K} \to 2^{\mathcal{K} \cup \mathcal{O}}$ such that the following provenance conditions hold: (1) $h(p_0, d) = \emptyset$ for $d \in C(p_0)$ and (2) for each occurrence $(t, b) \in \mathcal{O}$ and $(p', d') \in (t, b)^\bullet$ with $p' \neq p_0$ we have $h(p', d') = \bigcup \{ h(p, d) \mid (p, d) \in {}^\bullet(t, b) \} \cup \{ (t, b) \} \cup \{ (p', d') \}$.

We note that provenance is represented by the past causality cone within each round and gives rise to a causal order on tokens defined by set-theoretic inclusion. Our multiround scheme together with Condition (1) ensures that the accumulated provenance information remains bounded, which is essential for any implementation.

Lemma 2. *Given a multiround workflow system $(\mathcal{N}, m_0)$ there is an equivalent colored net system $(\bar{\mathcal{N}}, \bar{m}_0)$ that maintains provenance in the sense that there are functions $\phi : \mathcal{M}_{\bar{\mathcal{N}}} \to \mathcal{M}_{\mathcal{N}}$ and $\phi : \mathcal{O}_{\bar{\mathcal{N}}} \to \mathcal{O}_{\mathcal{N}}$ such that for all $\bar{m} \in \mathcal{R}(\bar{\mathcal{N}}, \bar{m}_0)$ we have (1) $\bar{m} \xrightarrow{\bar{o}}_o \bar{m}'$ implies $\phi(\bar{m}) \xrightarrow{\phi(\bar{o})}_o \phi(\bar{m}')$, and (2) $\phi(\bar{m}) = m$ and $m \xrightarrow{o}_o m'$ implies $\bar{m} \xrightarrow{\bar{o}}_o \bar{m}'$ for some $\bar{o}$ and $\bar{m}'$ with $\phi(\bar{o}) = o$ and $\phi(\bar{m}') = m'$.*

Utilizing the embedded provenance information we can define a replacement ordering that has two purposes and hence two components. First, the system should move forward in time by making sure that more recent tokens replace obsolete tokens (causal replacement). Second, inconsistencies — e.g., violations of mutual exclusion — must be eventually resolved (conflict replacement).

Given a multiround workflow system $(\mathcal{N}, m_0)$ that maintains provenance we define a *causal replacement relation* $\prec_{li} \subseteq \mathcal{K} \times \mathcal{K}$, where $\mathcal{K} = \mathcal{K}(\mathcal{N}, m_0)$ is defined as the union of the support of all reachable markings $\mathcal{R}(\mathcal{N}, m_0)$, as follows: $k \prec_{li} k'$ iff $r(k) < r(k')$, or $k \in h(k')$ and $r(k) = r(k')$. We also define a *conflict replacement relation* $\prec_{al} \subseteq \mathcal{K} \times \mathcal{K}$ as follows: $k \prec_{al} k'$ iff $r(k) = r(k')$ and (1) $p(k) = p(k') = p_0$ and $ts(k) > ts(k')$ or (2) there exists a timestamp-minimal pair (o, o') of occurrences $o \in h(k)$ and $o' \in h(k')$ such that ${}^\bullet o \cap {}^\bullet o' \neq \emptyset$ and $ts(o) > ts(o')$. Here, a pair of occurrences is *timestamp-minimal* in a set of pairs if $ts(o, o')$ is minimal, where the *timestamp* $ts(o, o')$ of a pair (o, o') is defined as $\min(ts(o), ts(o'))$. The *full replacement relation* $\prec_{\mathcal{N}}$ is defined as $\prec_{li} \cup \prec_{al}$.

The overall coherence of our previous definitions — namely, that $\prec$ results in a strict partial order — is essential and hence established in the subsequent theorem.

Theorem 1 (Well-Formedness). *A monotonic multi-round workflow system $(\mathcal{N}, m_0)$ that maintains provenance together with $\prec_{\mathcal{N}}$ forms a partially ordered net system $(\mathcal{N}, \prec_{\mathcal{N}}, m_0)$.*

For the reminder of this section, we assume a multiround workflow system $(\mathcal{N}, m_0)$ that maintains provenance and the partially ordered net system $(\bar{\mathcal{N}}, \prec_{\bar{\mathcal{N}}}, m_0)$ where $\bar{\mathcal{N}}$ is the monotonic closure of $\mathcal{N}$. Note that $\mathcal{M}_{\bar{\mathcal{N}}} = \mathcal{M}_{\mathcal{N}}$ and $\mathcal{O}_{\bar{\mathcal{N}}} = \mathcal{O}_{\mathcal{N}}$. For better readability, we use a few conventions. The notation ${}^\bullet x$ and $x^\bullet$ will always refer to $\mathcal{N}$. If not otherwise noted, transition relations will refer to $\mathcal{N}$, except in the case where they are used with variables like $\bar{m}$ and $\bar{m}'$, in which case they refer to $\bar{\mathcal{N}}$.

As a first observation stated in the following theorem, a causality cone does not contain inconsistencies, and hence conflicts are never visible in provenance of individual tokens (and hence this set is preserved).

Theorem 2. $\mathcal{K}(\mathcal{N}, m_0) = \mathcal{K}(\bar{\mathcal{N}}, m_0)$.

In the following, we use $\psi(m)$ to denote the submarking given by the maximal elements of m w.r.t. $\prec$. This gives rise to an induced equivalence relation $\equiv$ defined by $m \equiv m'$ iff $\psi(m) = \psi(m')$. The following theorems use ψ to state equivalence modulo replacement between our high-level model, the multiround workflow system, and the implementation-level model, given by a monotonic partially ordered net system. By using the function ψ we can state eventual consistency results for the global state, in the sense that when all knowledge would be accumulated by some observer, the replacement ordering will ensure consistency of the observation. Of course, the goal of using this ordering at runtime is to ensure local consistency after each step while the system is running, so that inconsistencies are unlikely to propagate and computational and networking resources are not wasted.

Completeness as formulated in the following theorem means that our implementation-level model can capture each step of our workflow.

Theorem 3 (Completeness). *Let $\bar{m} \in \mathcal{R}(\bar{\mathcal{N}}, \prec_{\bar{\mathcal{N}}}, m_0)$. Then $\psi(\bar{m}) = m$ and $m \xrightarrow{o}_o m'$ (in $\mathcal{N}$) implies $\bar{m} \xrightarrow{o}_o \bar{m}'$ (in $\bar{\mathcal{N}}$) for some $\bar{m}'$ with $\psi(\bar{m}') = m'$.*

The following result shows that the implementation-level model is sound. Each of its steps corresponds to a step in the workflow, possibly after rolling back (i.e., eliminating) some redundant occurrences.

Theorem 4 (Soundness). *Let $\bar{m} \in \mathcal{R}(\bar{\mathcal{N}}, \prec_{\bar{\mathcal{N}}}, m_0)$. Then we have (1) $\bar{m} \xrightarrow{o}_o \bar{m}'$ (in $\bar{\mathcal{N}}$) implies $\psi(\bar{m}) \xleftarrow{*}_o \circ \xrightarrow{o}_o \psi(\bar{m}')$ (in $\mathcal{N}$) or $\psi(\bar{m}) = \psi(\bar{m}')$, and (2) $\bar{m} \longrightarrow_r \bar{m}'$ (in $\bar{\mathcal{N}}$) implies $\psi(\bar{m}) = \psi(\bar{m}')$.*

Theorems 4 and 3 can be composed with Lemma 2 to see that every multiround workflow system can be equipped with provenance information and by taking the monotonic closure executed in a distributed fashion while preserving the behavior of the original workflow specification. Usually, the workflow specification already uses a notion of time, but by an additional composition with Lemma 1 it is also possible to first add timestamps if the original workflow specification is untimed.

The following theorem is a concise summary of our results in terms of reachable markings:

Theorem 5. $\psi(\mathcal{R}(\bar{\mathcal{N}}, \prec_{\bar{\mathcal{N}}}, m_0)) = \mathcal{R}(\mathcal{N}, m_0)$.

We have implemented a distributed execution engine on top of our NCPS framework [18] that allows the user to specify the multiround workflow system and synthesizes a partially ordered net system under the hood. It also allows the specification of the timing distributions of transitions to allow for randomized delays that reduce the likelihood of conflicts (in fact, it is traded against speed).

Redundancy and diversity as they occur in biological systems are key features of fractionated systems. For example, randomized scheduling of transition occurrences allows us to reduce the likelihood of inconsistencies without coordination overhead by exploiting relative timing. Hence, asynchronous distributed operation, which is often considered as a challenge, is turned into an advantage. FCPS can be designed with a suitable degree of redundancy, but we cannot generally assume that each logical function can be executed by any hardware/device, at any node/location, or by any agent/person. Hence, some transitions may have additional constraints that could be captured as part of their conditions.

Given that a higher-level model is automatically mapped into a lower-level model that can be directly implemented, our approach is a first step toward model-based design for fractionated systems. The high-level workflow model has a well-defined semantics and can be analyzed or verified using many existing Petri net tools or through a mapping into other formalisms such as rewriting logic [35], which is implemented in the Maude system. In this way, it is possible to perform structural analysis, reachability and deadlock analysis, and more generally model checking of temporal logic properties at a high level of abstraction.

3 Related Work

The adequate modeling of distributed systems, ranging from information processing systems to workflow in organizations and most notably physical processes, has always been a primary concern for C. A. Petri. One thread of his research was to axiomatize certain classes of Petri nets [30] and to study their causal structure [22], because not all instances correspond to physical phenomena or adequate models of reality, or might simply not be implementable. To lift the level of abstraction, various kinds of high-level nets have been proposed, including colored nets [17] and algebraic nets [31], which can be seen as compact notations for classical Petri nets. Because of their expressiveness, the proper use of Petri nets for the modeling of distributed algorithms remains an important concern; see, e.g., [31]. In addition, various extensions have been studied, which cannot be directly reduced to the classical Petri net model by means of homomorphisms. For instance, the need to model shared resources and nondestructive access — e.g., for applications in delay-tolerant designs (e.g., asynchronous circuits) — has led to the study of Petri nets with test/read arcs (e.g., [40]), which have also been studied under the name contextual nets in [26]. Petri nets and such extensions are also closely related to linear logic and rewriting logic (e.g., [15,35]). Not surprisingly, Petri nets with read arcs have been found to be important in the modeling of biological systems [38], which are real-world examples of highly distributed and fractionated systems. Monotonic and partially ordered net systems, as introduced in this paper, can be seen as a very fundamental attempt to tame the expressiveness of Petri nets. They can only use read arcs to access tokens and allow tokens to be replaced by means of a partial order. The key idea is to give up the concept of a resource as an atomic object with the rationale that a fully distributed (in fact, fractionated) implementation must always be possible for a large well-defined class of models.

Petri nets have been used to support the model-based design of embedded software (see, e.g., [32] for an approach utilizing free-choice nets to model dataflow). Furthermore, various approaches to the distributed execution of Petri nets have been developed including [3,6,12,20] but all of them use a more or less fine-grained partitioning of the net, in contrast to our fractionated approach that relies on an inherently distributed model that does not require any partitioning. In FCPS, each computing resource can (in the absence of other constraints) execute any transition in an opportunistic and optimistic fashion.

Undirected causality, concurrency, and conflict relations were studied by C.A. Petri in various unpublished lectures as symmetric relational structures (X, li, co, al), and the consistent orientation of causality was investigated in [22]. The conflict relation has also been studied in the context of event structures [41], which are partial orders equipped with a symmetric conflict relation. In this paper, we combine causality and conflict relations into a single consistent ordering by embedding provenance information (also referred to as lineage) in each token to capture its causality cone. Enriching systems with provenance can be seen as a form of distributed reflection, because it allows runtime awareness about the computational process, which in our case is exploited to resolve inconsistencies in a fractionated implementation. Systems for maintaining distributed provenance for other purposes are emerging [8], and the early work [13] uses a bounded tree structure as a representation, similar to our causality cones.

4   Conclusion and Future Work

The trend toward model-based design has been a primary driver for executable models, but most work is currently concerned with synchronous systems or systems that can be viewed as such by means of a suitable transformation. This paper investigates the other end of the spectrum — namely, loosely coupled asynchronous systems, and a possible direction for model-based design of fractionated software and more generally FCPS. The idea is that the correct and timely functioning of the system becomes a statistical property if sufficiently many networked resources are available to overcome failures and other deficiencies in the environment.

We introduced a subclass of nets that can be executed in a fully fractionated fashion by means of a partially ordered net model that, unlike traditional models, does not rely on the atomicity of tokens and a corresponding transactional semantics. All proofs, some additional results, and our application to the distributed control of UAV swarms can be found in the full version of this paper [33]. The most interesting research question is how far can this class be generalized while maintaining these key results. We conjecture that the multiround structure and the free-choice assumptions can be relaxed. It might be possible to cover an even-larger class by relaxing the key theorems. It is also clear that only a subclass of fractionated systems based on the partially ordered knowledge-sharing model can be captured in a Petri net style model, which makes the generalization of our ideas to other well-known formalisms, such as classical logics, linear logic, term rewriting, or process algebra, a natural long-term goal. A purely logical approach to distributed control for a different class of NCPS in [19,34] can be an alternative. Studying the precise relationship and possible integration of these approaches would be another interesting direction.

Our framework already supports different forms of probabilistic analysis, which can be applied to fractionated systems before system deployment. To improve verifiability of systems, more work is needed on the theoretical side to develop new runtime verification methods such as those proposed in [37], because fractionated systems are typically incrementally deployed, are highly reconfigurable, and operate in a broad range of different environments.

On the practical side, a more efficient implementation and a quantitative evaluation of performance are important next steps. To test our theory in an experimental real-world deployment with distributed-control applications such as those described in the appendix, we are currently building an NCPS testbed consisting of micro-UAVs. Specifically, we are extending inexpensive quadricopters (Parrot AR.Drones) running an on-board Linux system (running low-level flight control software) with additional hardware and sensing capabilities, such as an additional on-board computer (Gumstix), a WiFi module, a digital compass, and a GPS module. The additional on-board computer will enable us to run high-level flight control software and the cyber-application framework with networking and workflow execution capabilities.

Already there are many other applications that could benefit from fractionated software, fractionated hardware, or more generally FCPS at a coarse-grained level. Two particular areas of interest are robotic teams that operate in microfactories and scientific satellite missions involving a large number of inexpensive pico-satellites (e.g., CubeSats), which can act as distributed sensors in space. In the longer-term future, there might be potential to apply these ideas at a more fine-grained level. Since today's hardware designs are essentially networks of subsystems (e.g., many-core architectures), it would be natural to ask if by utilizing sufficient redundancy and diversity, a form of fractionated software can perform useful computations on high-density chips that contain so many highly unreliable components that failure becomes a normal part of every computation. In this case, we would like to have a clear high-level specification of the computation (e.g., a workflow describing a multistage processing pipeline with many branches), but the mapping and binding to the actual hardware must happen at runtime without the need for explicit global coordination.

An open source prototype is available as part of our multi-platform cyber-application framework at http://ncps.csl.sri.com.

Acknowledgments. Support from National Science Foundation Grant 0932397 (A Logical Framework for Self-Optimizing Networked Cyber-Physical Systems) and Office of Naval Research Grant N00014-10-1-0365 (Principles and Foundations for Fractionated Networked Cyber-Physical Systems) is gratefully acknowledged. Any opinions, findings, and conclusions or recommendations expressed in this material are those of the author(s) and do not necessarily reflect the views of NSF or ONR.

References

1. OpenCL 1.1 Specification (September 2010)
2. Arvind, B.: A language for hardware design, simulation, synthesis and verification. In: Proc. First ACM/IEEE Int. Conf. Formal Methods and Models for Co-Design, MEMOCODE 2003, pp. 249 (2003)

3. Baccelli, F., Furmento, N., Gaujal, B.: Parallel and distributed simulation of free choice Petri nets. SIGSIM Simul. Dig. **25**, 3–10 (1995)
4. Best, E.: Structure theory of Petri nets: The free choice hiatus. In: Advances in Petri Nets 1986, Part I on Petri Nets: Central Models and Their Properties, pp. 168–205. Springer-Verlag (1987)
5. Brown, O., Eremenko, P.: Fractionated space architectures: A vision for responsive space. In: 4th Responsive Space Conf. (2006)
6. Chiola, G., Ferscha, A.: Distributed simulation of timed Petri nets: Exploiting the net structure to obtain efficiency. In: 14th Int. Conf. Application and Theory of Petri Nets, pp. 14–6 (1993)
7. Dean, J., Ghemawat, S.: MapReduce: Simplified data processing on large clusters. Commun. ACM **51**, 107–113 (2008)
8. Deelman, E., Singh, G., Su, M.-H., Blythe, J., Gil, Y., Kesselman, C., Mehta, G., Vahi, K., Berriman, G.B., Good, J., Laity, A., Jacob, J.C., Katz, D.S.: Pegasus: A framework for mapping complex scientific workflows onto distributed systems. Sci. Program. **13**, 219–237 (2005)
9. Desel, J., Esparza, J.: Free Choice Petri Nets. CUP (1995)
10. Dressler. F.: Self-Organization in Sensor and Actor Networks. Wiley (2008)
11. Farrell, S., Cahill, V.: Delay- and Disruption-Tolerant Networking. Artech House Inc, Norwood, MA, USA (2006)
12. Ferscha, A.: Optimistic distributed execution of business process models. In: Proc. 31st Annual Hawaii Int. Conf. System Sciences-Volume 7, HICSS (1998)
13. Gehani, A., Lindqvist, U.: Bonsai: Balanced lineage authentication. In: IEEE Annual Computer Security Applications Conf. (ACSAC) (2007)
14. Girard, J.-Y.: Linear logic. Theor. Comput. Sci. **50**, 1–102 (1987)
15. Girault, C., Valk, R.: Petri Nets for System Engineering: A Guide to Modeling, Verification, and Applications. Springer-Verlag (2001)
16. Jacobson, V., Smetters, D.K., Thornton, J.D., Plass, M.F., Briggs, N.H., Braynard, R.L.: Networking named content. In: Proc. 5th Int. Conf. Emerging Networking Experiments and Technologies, CoNEXT 2009, pp. 1–12 (2009)
17. Jensen, K.: Coloured Petri Nets: Basic Concepts, Analysis Methods and Practical Use, Vol. 1. Springer-Verlag (1995)
18. Kim, M., Stehr, M.O., Kim, J., Ha, S.: An application framework for loosely coupled networked cyber-physical systems. In: IEEE/IFIP Int. Conf. Embedded and Ubiquitous Computing, EUC 2010, pp. 144–153 (2010)
19. Kim, M., Stehr, M.-O., Talcott, C.: A distributed logic for networked cyber-physical systems. In: Arbab, F., Sirjani, M. (eds.) FSEN 2011. LNCS, vol. 7141, pp. 190–205. Springer, Heidelberg (2012)
20. Knoke, M., Zimmermann, A.: Distributed simulation of colored stochastic Petri nets with timenet 4.0. In: Proc. 3rd Int. Conf. Quantitative Evaluation of Systems, pp. 117–118 (2006)
21. Koponen, T., Chawla, M., Chun, B.-G., Ermolinskiy, A., Kim, K.H., Shenker, S., Stoica, I.: A data-oriented (and beyond) network architecture. SIGCOMM Comput. Commun. Rev. **37**, 181–192 (2007)
22. Kummer, O., Stehr, M.O.: Petri's axioms of concurrency- a selection of recent results. In: Proc. 18th Int. Conf. Application and Theory of Petri Nets, pp. 195–214. Springer-Verlag (1997)
23. Lamport, L.: Time, clocks, and the ordering of events in a distributed system. Commun, ACM **21**, 558–565 (1978)

24. Loo, B.T., Condie, T., Garofalakis, M., Gay, D.E., Hellerstein, J.M., Maniatis, P., Ramakrishnan, R., Roscoe, T., Stoica, I.: Declarative networking: Language, execution and optimization. In: Proc. 2006 ACM SIGMOD Int. Conf. Management of Data, pp. 97–108 (2006)

25. Meseguer, J.: Conditional rewriting logic as a unified model of concurrency. Theo. Comput. Sci. **96**, 73–155 (1992)

26. Montanari, U., Rossi, F.: Contextual nets. Acta Informatica, 32(6) (1995)

27. Murphy, A.L., Picco, G.P., Roman, G.-C.: Lime: A coordination model and middleware supporting mobility of hosts and agents. ACM Trans. Softw. Eng. Methodol. **15**(3), 279–328 (2006)

28. Murray, D.G., Schwarzkopf, M., Smowton, C., Smith, S., Madhavapeddy, A., Hand, S.: CIEL: A universal execution engine for distributed data-flow computing. In: Proc. 8th USENIX Conf. Networked Systems Design and Implementation, NSDI 2011 (2011)

29. Pereira, J., Rodrigues, L., Oliveira, R.: Semantically reliable multicast: Definition, implementation, and performance evaluation. IEEE Trans. Comput. **52**(2), 150–165 (2003)

30. Petri, C.A.: Nets, time and space. Theor. Comput. Sci. **153**, 3–48 (1996)

31. Reisig, W.: Elements of Distributed Algorithms: Modeling and Analysis with Petri Nets. Springer-Verlag (1998)

32. Sgroi, M., Lavagno, L., Watanabe, Y., Sangiovanni-Vincentelli, A.: Synthesis of embedded software using free-choice Petri nets. In: Proc. ACM/IEEE Design Automation Conf., DAC 1999, pp. 805–810 (1999)

33. Stehr, M.O., Kim, M., McCarthy, T.: A distributed computing model for dataflow, controlflow, and workflow in fractionated cyber-physical systems (full version) (2014). http://ncps.csl.sri.com/papers/cpsflows.pdf

34. Stehr, M.-O., Kim, M., Talcott, C.: Toward distributed declarative control of networked cyber-physical systems. In: Yu, Z., Liscano, R., Chen, G., Zhang, D., Zhou, X. (eds.) UIC 2010. LNCS, vol. 6406, pp. 397–413. Springer, Heidelberg (2010)

35. Stehr, M.-O., Meseguer, J., Ölveczky, P.C.: Rewriting Logic as a Unifying Framework for Petri Nets. In: Ehrig, H., Juhás, G., Padberg, J., Rozenberg, G. (eds.) APN 2001. LNCS, vol. 2128, pp. 250–303. Springer, Heidelberg (2001)

36. Stehr, M.O., Talcott, C.: Planning and learning algorithms for routing in disruption-tolerant networks. In: IEEE Military Communications Conf. (2008)

37. Stehr, M.-O., Talcott, C., Rushby, J., Lincoln, P., Kim, M., Cheung, S., Poggio, A.: Fractionated software for networked cyber-physical systems: research directions and long-term vision. In: Agha, G., Danvy, O., Meseguer, J. (eds.) Formal Modeling: Actors, Open Systems, Biological Systems. LNCS, vol. 7000, pp. 110–143. Springer, Heidelberg (2011)

38. Talcott, C., Dill, D.L.: Multiple representations of biological processes. Trans. Computational Systems Biology (2006)

39. van der Aalst, W.M.P.: The application of Petri nets to workflow management. J. of Circuits, Systems, and Computers 8(1), 21–66 (1998)

40. Vogler, W., Semenov, A., Yakovlev, A.: Unfolding and finite prefix for nets with read arcs. In: Sangiorgi, D., de Simone, R. (eds.) CONCUR 1998. LNCS, vol. 1466, pp. 501–516. Springer, Heidelberg (1998)

41. Winskel, G.: Event structures. In: Advances in Petri Nets 1986, Part II on Petri nets: Applications and Relationships to Other Models of Concurrency, pp. 325–392. Springer (1987)

On the Limit of Some Algorithmic Approach
to Circuit Lower Bounds

Osamu Watanabe[✉]

Department of Mathematical and Computing Sciences,
Tokyo Institute of Technology, Tokyo 152-8552, Japan
watanabe@is.titech.ac.jp

Abstract. We propose a framework — generic algorithm framework —
for studying the limit of a certain algorithmic approach for showing circuit lower bounds. We show some illustrative examples for explaining the
motivation/justification of our framework while leaving one key technical and very challenging problem open. We hope that this framework
is useful for investigating the limit of algorithmic approaches to define
computationally hard problems.

1 Introduction

This is a paper on some question that I have been considering from time to
time since I published a paper [KW98]. It is about some important topic in
computational complexity theory, which is also important in general, I believe,
to understand the nature of computation. Unfortunately, though, the question
is not in the area of quantum computing nor parallel/distributed computing.
Furthermore, as we will see, I realized that solving this question leads to the resolution of the P $\neq$ NP conjecture! But we may consider this as some new insight
for the P $\neq$ NP conjecture, and a person like Prof. Gruska with challenging mind
would appreciate such very challenging open questions. I hope that this paper
is yet suitable for this celebrated book.

Now let me start the introduction *as if* I had solved the question ;-)

✳ ✳ ✳ ✳ ✳ ✳ ✳ ✳ ✳

Showing a nonlinear circuit lower bound is one of the fundamental tasks in computational complexity theory; it is also important in general for understanding
the nature of computation. Clearly, one can define a problem that is not solved
by, say, square-size circuit (or more precisely, by a family of n^2-size circuits). An
important task is to show such a problem from those that we would like to solve.
For example, we want to know whether the 3SAT problem, one of the standard
NP-complete problems, has no square-size circuit, or more generally, we ask
whether there exists *any* NP problem with no square-size circuit. One possible
approach for showing such an NP problem is to design some NP-algorithm that
defines a problem that is "hard" and that has no square-size circuit. Here we
discuss the limit of some type of algorithmic approach.

Based on the idea of Shannon, one can show the existence of hard problem
that has no square-size circuits. This is a proof of the existence of hard problem.

© Springer International Publishing Switzerland 2014
C.S. Calude et al. (Eds.): Gruska Festschrift, LNCS 8808, pp. 394–405, 2014.
DOI: 10.1007/978-3-319-13350-8_29

By "algorithmic approach" we mean here a way to define such a hard problem by giving some algorithm specifying it. Since Shannon's argument is not specific to the model of computation, we intuitively assume that such an algorithm does not need to use any property that is specific to the standard computation model. For example, consider the standard circuit model where we are allowed to use only $\wedge$- $\vee$-, and $\neg$-gates. Then we cannot compute $x \oplus y$ by using less than three $\wedge$- or $\vee$-gates. We would not need to use properties of this type for implementing Shannon's argument algorithmically (if it is indeed possible). Here we introduce the notion of "generic algorithm" in order to discuss this intuition formally, and show the limit of an algorithmic approach of this type by showing the impossibility of designing a generic, say, NP-algorithm to define a problem with no square-size circuit.

Relativization [Betal75] is a framework for discussing whether a proof for showing some property of computation uses properties of computation that are not so specific to our usual/standard model of computation. Our generic algorithm is regarded as one type of relativized computation model. In fact, it is easy to show that any proof showing a circuit lower bound by giving a generic algorithm is relativizable. But its converse is not true. That is, there may be some relativizable proof for a circuit lower bound that does not seem to be achieved by any generic algorithm. Here we claim that Kannan's famous proof for a non-fixed-poly-size circuit lower bound is one of its typical examples.

In his seminal paper [Kan82] Ravi Kannan proved[1] the existence of a problem in $\Sigma_2^p \cap \Pi_2^p$ that does not have n^2-size circuits. Some years later, Köbler-Watanabe pointed out [KW98] that the learning technique of Bshouty et al. [Betal96] can be used to improve the Kannan's result, showing such a hard problem in ZPP^{NP}, which has been improved further to S_2 by [Cai01]. These techniques are relativizable[2]. But we show that it is in a sense stronger than the algorithmic approach by proving (*well, not yet proved though*) that it is impossible to define any generic algorithm that gives the same result. We hope that this reveals the importance of the argument of Kannan, which may be useful for proving some other lower bounds.

Preliminaries

We use standard notions and notation in the computational complexity theory except for using somewhat simpler notions for circuit complexity explained below. By a "problem" we mean a *recognition problem* of a given set $L \subseteq \{0,1\}^*$; that is, the task for a given input $x \in \{0,1\}^*$ is to determine whether it belongs to L or not. Throughout this paper we assume that a circuit is a device computing one bit output when some bit data is given to each of its input gates. As

---

[1] In fact, his argument shows that, for any $d > 0$, there exists a problem in $\Sigma_2^p \cap \Pi_2^p$ that has no family of n^d-size circuits. But here for the simplicity, we use n^2 as our target circuit size lower bound.

[2] And it has been shown, unfortunately, that one cannot improve this upper bound to, e.g., P^{NP} by any relativizable proof technique; see, e.g., an excellent extended survey of Arronson [Aar06] for this and related results.

usual, we consider this computation as a function mapping a binary string of $\{0,1\}^n$ to $\{0,1\}$, where n is the number of input gates of the circuit. A circuit family $C = \{c_n\}_{n \geq 1}$ is regarded as a computation device recognizing some set L of strings if for each $n \geq 1$, and for any $x \in \{0,1\}^n$, $c_n(x) = 1$ if and only if $x \in L$. We fix some standard way to encode circuits as binary strings of $\{0,1\}^*$, and we identify a circuit and its encoding, which is usually denoted by using symbol c. By the size of a circuit c (denoted as $|c|$) we simply mean the length of this binary string encoding c. The standard circuit size that is measured by the number of gates would be smaller than our circuit size; but since the difference is within some fixed polynomial, we will ignore this difference for the sake of simplicity. We may assume that $|c|$ is larger than the number n of c's input gates. For any complexity bound $s(n)$, we say that a set L *has $s(n)$-size circuits* if it is recognized by a family $C = \{c_n\}_{n \geq 1}$ such that $|c_n| = s(n)$ holds for all sufficiently large[3] n. Now w.r.t. this complexity measure, we define complexity class SIZE$[s(n)]$ by

$$\text{SIZE}[s(n)] = \{ L \mid L \text{ has } s(n)\text{-size circuits} \}.$$

We use PSIZE to denote $\cup_{d>0}\text{SIZE}[n^d]$, a class of problems with polynomial-size circuits.

We assume some circuit evaluator/interpreter $\text{Int}_{m,n}$, an algorithm that takes a circuit c (encoded in $\{0,1\}^m$) and an input x (in $\{0,1\}^n$) and outputs $c(x)$, the output value of c on x. We may assume that $\text{Int}_{m,n}$ runs in $O(m)$ steps. For simplicity, we assume that $\text{Int}_{m,n}(c,x)$ is defined for all $c \in \{0,1\}^m$ and $x \in \{0,1\}^n$; that is, every string in $\{0,1\}^m$ is regarded as a code of some circuit for $\{0,1\}^n$.

We use the standard (length-wise) lexicographic order on $\{0,1\}^*$, which will be denoted by $\leq_{\text{lex}}$. For our discussion, we sometimes express a set of strings as a *characteristic sequence*. For any $L \subseteq \{0,1\}^*$, let χ_L denote its characteristic sequence, that is, an infinite $0,1$-sequence whose each ith bit indicates the membership of lexicographically the ith string of $\{0,1\}^*$ in L. For each string $x \in \{0,1\}^*$, the ith bit of χ_L corresponding to x will be sometimes called *the xth bit of χ_L*. By $\chi_L[x]$ (and respectively, by $\chi_L[x:y]$) we denote the xth bit of χ_L (resp., the subsequence of χ_L from its xth to yth bits). For example, by $\chi_L[0^n : 1^n]$, we mean the subsequence of χ_L corresponding to $L^{=n}$ ($\overset{\text{def}}{=} L \cap \{0,1\}^n$).

In our discussion we will often consider, e.g., a Σ_2^p-algorithm, a Δ_3^p-algorithm, etc. These are defined in terms of a polynomial-time deterministic/nondeterministic Turing machine using some lower-level algorithm as a subroutine. For example, a Δ_3^p-algorithm is a polynomial-time deterministic Turing machine that uses some Σ_2^p-algorithm as a subroutine, where this Σ_2^p-algorithm is a polynomial-time nondeterministic Turing machine using some polynomial-time nondeterministic Turing machine as a subroutine. We will use a symbol D to

---

[3] For simplifying our discussion, we measure the size of circuit exactly. On the other hand, we allow to have some exceptions for small n.

denote algorithms for decision problems, and for such an algorithm D, we denote by $L(D)$ the set of strings accepted by D.

2   A Typical Example

In [Kan82] Kannan proved the existence of a problem L in $\Sigma_2^p \cap \Pi_2^p$ that does not have n^d-size circuits for any given constant $d > 0$. This is a typical example for our discussion.

Theorem 1. *(Kannan [Kan82]) For any constant $d > 0$, there exists a set in $\Sigma_2^p \cap \Pi_2^p$ that does not have n^d-size circuits; that is, we have $\Sigma_2^p \cap \Pi_2^p \not\subseteq \mathrm{SIZE}[n^d]$.*

For our later explanation we give a proof outline of this theorem. Here, and in the following discussion, just for simplicity, we will fix our target hardness to n^2- circuit-size; that is, our goal is to show a set (in a target complexity class) that does not have a family of n^2-size circuits. Hence, for the theorem, we show the relation $\Sigma_2^p \cap \Pi_2^p \not\subseteq \mathrm{SIZE}[n^2]$.

Proof. First we point out that one can construct a set L_0 in Σ_4^p (in fact, in Δ_3^p) that is not in $\mathrm{SIZE}[n^2]$ as stated in Lemma 1 below. Then for any standard NP-complete set, say, SAT, consider two cases depending on the circuit complexity of SAT. First consider the case where SAT has no polynomial-size circuits, that is, SAT $\notin$ PSIZE. In this case, SAT itself is the desired set satisfying the theorem.

Next consider the case where SAT has some polynomial-size circuits. In this case we can use the famous theorem of Karp and Lipton [KL82] proving that the polynomial-time hierarchy PH $\stackrel{\text{def}}{=} \cup_{k \geq 1} \Sigma_k^p$ collapses to $\Sigma_2^p \cap \Pi_2^p$ from the assumption that SAT $\in$ PSIZE. Then clearly the above constructed set L_0 is in $\Sigma_2^p \cap \Pi_2^p$; hence, L_0 is our desired set.   □

This proof has an interesting structure. It considers two cases depending on the circuit complexity of SAT, and two different sets are used for each case as a witness for $\Sigma_2^p \cap \Pi_2^p \not\subseteq \mathrm{SIZE}[n^2]$. That is, we used some additional knowledge (namely, the circuit complexity of SAT) in order to give an algorithm specifying a computationally hard problem such as L_0. Is such an additional knowledge necessary? Can we give an algorithmic way to define a hard problem in $\Sigma_2^p \cap \Pi_2^p$? Here is the current upper bound where some algorithmic way is possible. (Though this theorem and its proof have been known as a folklore, we state it here for the sake of completeness and for our later explanation.)

Theorem 2. *For any constant $d > 0$, we have some Σ_2^p-algorithm D_d such that $L(D_d) \notin \mathrm{SIZE}[n^d]$.*

The statement itself is immediate from Theorem 1 because the class Σ_2^p has a complete set and $\Sigma_2^p \cap \Pi_2^p \subseteq \Sigma_2^p$; hence, from Theorem 1, we have, e.g., $\Sigma_2^p \not\subseteq \mathrm{SIZE}[n^2]$, and then any Σ_2^p-algorithm recognizing any complete set in Σ_2^p satisfies the theorem. But here we give a direct way to design a Σ_2^p-algorithm recognizing a hard set not in $\mathrm{SIZE}[n^2]$. We begin with the construction of L_0 used in the previous proof; see, e.g., [CW04] for this construction.

Lemma 1. *There is a Δ_3^p-algorithm recognizing $L_0 \notin \mathrm{SIZE}[n^2]$.*

Proof. Consider any $n \geq 1$ and define $L_0^{=n}$. We define it in terms of its characteristic subsequence $\chi_{L_0}[0^n : 1^n] \in \{0,1\}^{2^n}$.

Let $m = n^2$. Recall that each circuit with n input gates of size m is encoded by a binary string of length m (exactly). Hence, there are at most 2^m circuits of this type. Thus, there must be some sequence in $\{0,1\}^{m+1}0^{2^n-(m+1)}$ that is not consistent with any circuit of size $\leq m$ as a characteristic subsequence for the domain $\{0,1\}^n$. We define $\chi_{L_0}[0^n : 1^n]$ by the lexicographically the smallest one among all such sequences. In order to identify it computationally, we introduce some tools. First we define a predicate that checks whether a given circuit c (encoded in $\{0,1\}^{\leq m}$) is consistent with a given $\omega \in \{0,1\}^{m+1}$, a "nontrivial prefix" of sequences in $\{0,1\}^{m+1}0^{2^n-(m+1)}$.

$$\mathrm{cons}_{m,n}(c,\omega) \;\Leftrightarrow\; [\,\forall i, 1 \leq i \leq m+1\,[\,\mathrm{Int}(c, z_i) = \omega[i]\,]\,],$$

where z_i is the ith string in $\{0,1\}^n$ by the lexicographic order. Note that the predicate is $O(m^2)$-time computable, which is polynomial-time in n. We then define H_n and PreH_n by

$$\mathrm{H}_n \;=\; \{\,\omega \in \{0,1\}^{m+1} \,|\, \forall c : |c| = m\,[\,\neg\mathrm{cons}_{n,m}(c,\omega)\,]\,\},$$
$$\mathrm{PreH}_n \;=\; \{\,\alpha \in \{0,1\}^* \,|\, \alpha \text{ is a prefix of some } \omega \in \mathrm{H}_n\,\}.$$

Then it is easy to see that $\cup_{n \geq 1}\mathrm{H}_n$ is in coNP and that $\cup_{n \geq 1}\mathrm{PreH}_n$ is in Σ_2^p. Furthermore, the lexicographically the smallest one in H_n, that is, the nontrivial prefix of $\chi_{L_0}[0^n : 1^n]$, is computable in polynomial-time by using PreH_n as an oracle. Therefore, we have some Δ_3^p-algorithm that for a given $x \in \{0,1\}^*$ (where we may assume that x is one of the first $m+1$ strings of $\{0,1\}^n$ for some $n \geq 1$), first computes the nontrivial prefix of $\chi_{L_0}[0^n : 1^n]$, and then determines whether $x \in L_0$ by using this prefix. $\qquad\square$

By using the predicate cons defined above, we introduce a predicate preC and an algorithm A_C that will be used in the following discussion. Let n be any input length, and here again we use $m = n^2$ for our target circuit size bound. For any sequence $\omega \in \{0,1\}^{m+1}$ and any c', $|c'| \leq m$, define preC_n by

$$\mathrm{preC}_n((\omega, c')) \;\Longleftrightarrow\; \exists c : |c| = m\,[\,\mathrm{cons}_{n,m}(c,\omega) \wedge c' \text{ is a prefix of } c\,].$$

Here we assume some appropriate encoding for (ω, c') in $\{0,1\}^*$ so that $|(\omega, c')| = 2m - 1$ holds for all $\omega \in \{0,1\}^{m+1}$ and $c' \in \{0,1\}^{\leq m}$. Precisely speaking, preC_n takes such encoding of (ω, c') as an input. Note that ω has no n^2-size circuit (i.e., $\omega \in \mathrm{H}_n$) if and only if $\neg\mathrm{preC}_n((\omega, \lambda))$ holds for the empty string λ. It is also easy to show a polynomial-time algorithm that computes some n^2-size circuit c (if it exists) for a given ω by using preC_n as a subroutine. We denote it as A_C. More specifically, by $A_C^{\mathrm{preC}_n}(\omega)$ we mean the output of the algorithm computed on ω by using preC_n as a subroutine; that is, $A_C^{\mathrm{preC}_n}(\omega)$ is some n^2-size circuit c of ω (if it exists). We assume that $A_C^{\mathrm{preC}_n}(\omega) = \lambda$ if ω has no n^2-size circuit. We may generalize this notation to write, e.g., $A_C^f(\omega)$ for denoting the output of the algorithm by using a function f on $\{0,1\}^{2m-1}$ as a subroutine. We also introduce a set PreC corresponding to preC. For any n, define PreC_n $= \{(\omega, c')|\text{preC}((\omega, c'))\}$. Let $\text{PreC} = \cup_{n \geq 1}\text{PreC}_n$. Clearly $\text{PreC} \in \text{NP}$.

Proof of Theorem 2. We first give a rough structure of our desired hard set $L_1 \notin \text{SIZE}[n^2]$. For each $n \geq 1$ such $n = 2(n')^2$ for some n', $L_1^{=n}$ is defined by

$$L_1^{=n} = 1\text{PreC}_{n'} \cup (L_0')^{=n},$$

where $(L_0')^{=n}$ is either the empty set or $L_0^{=n}$, depending the hardness of PreC_n. Note that we may assume that $(L_0')^{=n} \subseteq 0\{0,1\}^{n-1}$ because $L_0^{=n}$ is defined by only lexicographically the first $m + 1$ strings of $\{0,1\}^n$.

We give a Σ_2^P-algorithm D_1 for L_1 with which the L_0' part is defined precisely. Consider and fix any n such that $n = 2(n')^2$ holds for some n', and we explain the execution of D_1 on inputs of length n. Let $m = n^2$. First for any input $x = 1x'$ for some $x' \in \{0,1\}^{n-1}$, D_1 accepts x iff $x' \in \text{PreC}_{n'}$; clearly, this computation is implemented as some Σ_2^P-algorithm.

Next consider any $x \in 0\{0,1\}^{n-1}$; in particular, we assume that x is one of lexicographically the first $m + 1$ strings of $\{0,1\}^n$. We would like to accept x iff $x \in L_0^{=n}$. On the other hand, we only know that $L_0 \in \Delta_3^P$. Here we (tentatively) assume that 1PreC_n has a square-size circuit c_* (and we can somehow obtain this circuit); that is, we have some circuit that computes the predicate preC_n. Recall that the input string length of 1PreC_n is $2m$; hence, "square-size" means $(2m)^2$-size. With such a circuit we can recognize H_n in polynomial-time since $\omega \in H_n$ iff $\neg\text{preC}_n((\omega, \lambda))$. Thus, by using this circuit, we can define a Δ_2^P-algorithm for $L_0^{=n}$. We implement this idea as a two level quantified formula.

For a given circuit c for $\{0,1\}^n$, let $f_{\text{omg}}(c)$ denote $c(z_1)c(z_2)\cdots c(z_{m+1})$, where $z_1,\ldots,z_{m+1}$ are lexicographically the first $m + 1$ strings of $\{0,1\}^n$. Now consider the following formula.

$$\exists c_* : |c_*| = (2m)^2, \exists \omega_* : |\omega_*| = m + 1$$
$$\forall c : |c| = n^2, \forall \omega : |\omega| = m + 1 \land \omega < \omega_*$$
$$(1)\ \text{cons}_{m,n}(A_C^{c_*'}(f_{\text{omg}}(c)), f_{\text{omg}}(c)),$$
$$(2)\ \neg c_*(1(\omega_*, \lambda)),$$
$$(3)\ c_*(1(\omega, \lambda)),\ \text{and}$$
$$(4)\ \omega_*[x] = 1\ (\text{i.e., the } x\text{th bit of } \omega_* \text{ is } 1).$$

We guess a circuit c_* for 1PreC_n of size $(2m)^2$; since it is for deciding $1(\omega, c') \in 1\text{PreC}_n$, we define a subroutine c_*' computing preC_n by using c_*. The correctness of c_* is checked by (1); that is, c_* is regarded correct if c_*' can be used as a subroutine of A_C to produce some n^2-size circuit for any set that is indeed defined by some n^2-size circuit c. Assuming that c_* passes the check (1) w.r.t. all c, we determine the smallest partial characteristic sequence ω_* of length $m+1$ defining a set $\subseteq \{0,1\}^n$ with no n^2-size circuit. First by (2), we check whether the set defined by ω_* has no n^2-size circuit. Then by (3), we confirm that all smaller partial characteristic sequence ω has n^2-sice circuits. Then finally we determine whether a given input x should be accepted or not by using the xth bit of the obtained partial characteristic sequence w_*. Our algorithm D_1 test whether $x \in L_1$ following this formula; it is easy to see that this execution can be implemented as a Σ_2^p-algorithm.

We show that $L_1 = L(M)$ indeed is not in $\mathrm{SIZE}[n^2]$. This clearly holds if $\mathrm{PreC} \notin \mathrm{SIZE}[n^2]$. Suppose then $\mathrm{PreC} \in \mathrm{SIZE}[n^2]$; that is, preC_n has $(2m-1)^2$-size circuit for all sufficiently large n. Then for sufficiently large n such that $n = 2(n')^2$ for some n', D on input $x \in 0\{0,1\}^{n-1}$ nondeterministically finds such a circuit c_* for $1\mathrm{PreC}_n$ to accepts x if and only if $x \in L_0$. Therefore, we have $L(D_1) \notin \mathrm{SIZE}[n^2]$. $\qquad\square$

3   Our Framework

We introduce a framework for investigating a certain algorithmic approach for defining computationally hard problems. Here we explain the framework focusing on our target task, i.e., to define a hard problem that cannot be solved by square-size circuits.

Our framework is natural; we abstract "circuit interpreter" and use it as a "black box." A (generalized) *circuit interpreter* is nothing but a family of *total* functions $\{I_{m,n}\}_{m,n \geq 1}$, where each $I_{m,n}$ is a mapping from $\{0,1\}^m \times \{0,1\}^n$ to $\{0,1\}$ and its value $I_{m,n}(c,x)$ is regarded as the output of circuit c (with n input gates) encoded in $\{0,1\}^m$ on input $x \in \{0,1\}^n$. Again we consider only $\{I_{n^2,n}\}_{n \geq 1}$ for the case $m = n^2$; since $I_{n^2,n}$ is total, any $c \in \{0,1\}^{n^2}$ can be regarded as a circuit for $\{0,1\}^n$. We say that a set L has a *(family of)* n^2-size *circuits w.r.t.* I if there exists $\{c_n\}_{n \geq 1}$ such that for almost all $n \geq 1$, we have (i) $|c_n| = n^2$, and (ii) $\forall x \in \{0,1\}^n$ [$x \in L \Leftrightarrow c_n(x) = 1$ (i.e., $I_{n^2,n}(c_n,x) = 1$)]. Then we define $\mathrm{SIZE}^{(I)}[n^2]$ by a family of sets with n^2-size circuits w.r.t. I.

Now we define the notion of "generic algorithm" for defining hard problems with no square-size circuit. For any complexity class $\mathcal{C}$, consider $\mathcal{C}$-algorithms, algorithms corresponding to the class $\mathcal{C}$; for example, Σ_2^p-algorithms for the class Σ_2^p. We extend such algorithms by allowing them to use a given circuit interpreter $\{I_{n^2,n}\}_{n \geq 1}$ as a black box; that is, algorithms can use interpreter functions as subroutines and they can get the value of $I_{(n')^2,n'}(c',x')$ for any n', $c' \in \{0,1\}^{(n')^2}$, and $x' \in \{0,1\}^{n'}$ during their computation by calling $I_{(n')^2,n'}$ on (c',x'). In this paper we assume[4] that the cost of one call of $I_{(n')^2,n'}$ is n'. Intuitively, we require that the algorithm achieves some task and/or satisfies some property w.r.t. any interpreter I. We call such an algorithm a *generic algorithm* in this paper. A generic algorithm of type $\mathcal{C}$ is called a $\mathcal{C}^{(\cdot)}$-*algorithm*.

---

[4] Precisely speaking, we would have to assume that the cost is $c_0(n')^2$ for some constant c_0, which corresponds to the standard circuit interpreter. But since we are discussing within the polynomial-time range, this difference does not seem so critical.

For any generic algorithm A and for any circuit interpreter I we use $A^{(I)}$ to denote the instantiated algorithm A that uses I as a circuit interpreter. For example, for a given circuit interpreter I_*, by $A^{(I_*)}(x)$ we mean the execution of A on input x using I_*. Also for any generic algorithm D for a decision problem, by $L(D^{(I_*)})$ we mean the set of strings accepted by the computation of D using the interpreter I_*.

As a corollary to the proof of Lemma 1, we can show the following generic algorithm.

Theorem 3. *(Corollary to the proof of Lemma 1)   There is a generic $\Delta_3^{p,(\cdot)}$-algorithm D satisfying*

$$\forall^\infty n \ \left[L(D^{(I)})^{=n} \text{ has no } n^2\text{-size circuit} \right] \tag{1}$$

for any circuit interpreter I. (Here by "$\forall^\infty n$", we mean "all sufficiently large n.")

On the other hand, we conjecture that this type of hardness cannot be shown by any generic $\Sigma_2^{p,(\cdot)}$-algorithm.

Conjecture 1. *There is no generic $\Sigma_2^{p,(\cdot)}$-algorithm D that satisfies (1) for any circuit interpreter I.*

We have not had a proof for this conjecture yet. Nevertheless, we explain some possible proof outline so that we can see what is the technical key for completing this proof outline.

Consider any generic $\Sigma_2^{p,(\cdot)}$-algorithm D for a decision problem. Fix any sufficiently large n, and let $\ell = n^d$ be a polynomial time bound for D, and let $m = n^2$. Let $L = 2^{(m+1)\ell}$, $M = 2^{m+n}$, and $N = 2^n$. Our task is to define $I = \{I_{(n')^2,n'}\}_{n' \geq 1}$ appropriately so that $L(D^{(I)})^{=n}$ has some m-size circuit. That is, we have some $c_0 \in \{0,1\}^m$ such that

$$\forall x \in \{0,1\}^n \ \left[x \in L(D^{(I)})^{=n} \ \Leftrightarrow \ I(c_0, x) = 1 \right] \tag{2}$$

holds. In other words, we need to define the values $I_{(n')^2,n'}(c',x')$ appropriately to guarantee the existence of such c_0. Without losing generality, we may fix $I_{(n')^2,n'}(c',x') = 0$ for all $n' \neq n$ and focus on the values of $I_{m,n}(c,x)$ for all $c \in \{0,1\}^m$ and $x \in \{0,1\}^n$.

Consider any $x \in \{0,1\}^n$ and the execution of $D^{(I)}$ on x. Since D is a $\Sigma_2^{p,(\cdot)}$-algorithm that halts in ℓ steps on x, we can express its computation by

$$D^{(I)} \text{ accepts } x \Leftrightarrow \exists u : |u| = \ell, \ \forall v : |v| = \ell \ \left[A^{(I)}(x,u,v) = 1 \right]$$
$$\Leftrightarrow \exists u : |u| = \ell, \ \forall v : |v| = \ell, \ \forall w = ((c_1,x_1,b_1),\dots,(c_\ell,x_\ell,b_\ell))$$
$$\neg \left[A'(x,u,v,w) = 0 \ \wedge \ \bigwedge_{1 \leq i \leq \ell} I_{m,n}(c_i,x_i) = b_i \right].$$

Here A is some polynomial-time deterministic generic algorithm; we may assume that $A(x, u, v)$ calls $I_{m,n}$ exactly ℓ times. For any $w = ((c_1, x_1, b_1), \ldots, (c_\ell, x_\ell, b_\ell))$, $A'(x, u, v, w)$ simulates A by assuming that the first call of $I_{m,n}$ in the execution of $A(x, u, v)$ is (c_1, x_1) by which A gets b_1 as an answer from $I_{m,n}$, and so on for all $(c_2, x_2, b_2), \ldots, (c_\ell, x_\ell, b_\ell)$. Here we explain the case when A' yields 0 (i.e., reject). A' first confirms w is correct in the sense that A in fact calls $I_{m,n}$ with $(c_1, x_1), \ldots, (c_\ell, x_\ell)$ assuming that $b_1, \ldots, b_\ell$ are the answers from $I_{m,n}$. Then it yields output 0 if and only if this correctness of w is confirmed *and* A yields 0 by this simulation. It is clear that the computation of $x \in L(D^{(I)})$ is characterized in this way. We note here that the number of nondet. branches corresponding to "$\exists u$" and "$\forall v, \forall w$" is respectively 2^ℓ and $2^{\ell + m\ell} = 2^{(m+1)\ell}$; we will simply use $L = 2^{(m+1)\ell}$ to bound both numbers.

Note that this last expression can be regarded as a depth three Boolean formula F_x over $M = 2^{m+n}$ Boolean variables $X_{c', x'}$, for $c' \in \{0, 1\}^m$ and $x' \in \{0, 1\}^n$, where each $X_{c', x'}$ corresponds to the value of $I_{m,n}(c', x')$. That is, for any assignment $\mathbf{a} \in \{0, 1\}^M$, we have $F_x(\mathbf{a}) = 1$ if and only if the above expression holds by using the interpreter $I_{m,n}$ such that $I_{m,n}(c', x') = \mathbf{a}_{c', x'}$, i.e., the value of $\mathbf{a}$ on the corresponding Boolean variable $X_{c', x'}$ for each c' and x'. Furthermore, F_x has the following structure: it has one $\vee$-gate with $\leq L$ fan-in as a top gate, at most L $\wedge$-gates with $\leq L$ fan-in as the 2nd level gates, and at most L^2 $\vee$-gates with $\leq \ell$ fan-in as the 3rd level (bottom) gates. We have such a Boolean formula F_x for each $x \in \{0, 1\}^n$.

Now as our working hypothesis, suppose that we can fix all the values of such Boolean formulas by some partial assignment that fixes the values of only limited number of Boolean variables. More precisely, we consider the following assumption.

Working Assumption. *For a given size parameter n, let $\ell = n^d$ for some constant $d > 0$ and let $m = n^2$. Let $L = 2^{(m+1)\ell}$, $M = 2^{m+n}$, and $N = 2^n$. Consider any set of N depth three formulas $\{F_1, \ldots, F_N\}$ over a set of M Boolean variables such that each F_i consists of an $\vee$-gate with $\leq L$ fan-in as a top gate, at most L $\wedge$-gates with $\leq L$ fan-in as the 2nd level gates, and at most L^2 $\vee$-gates with $\leq \ell$ fan-in as the 3rd level (bottom) gates. Then there exists a partial assignment α to Boolean variables that determines the value of all F_i's by fixing the values of less than 2^m variables.*

For defined N formulas $\{F_x\}_{x \in \{0,1\}^n}$, let us assume that there exists some partial assignment α by assigning less than 2^m variables. Fix values $I_{m,n}(c', x')$ according to α for pairs of (c', x') corresponding to the variables that are assigned values by α. Then there should be some $c_0 \in \{0, 1\}^m$ for which the value of $I_{m,n}(c_0, x')$ is not fixed for all $x' \in \{0, 1\}^n$ by α. Because otherwise (that is, if for any c', the value of $I_{m,n}(c', x')$ is fixed at some x'), α fixes at least 2^m values, contradicting the condition of α. We then simply define the values of $I_{m,n}(c_0, x)$ so that $I_{m,n}(c_0, x) = F_x(\alpha)$ holds, which means that c_0 can be used as a circuit recognizing $L(D^{(I)})^{=n}$. That is, we have some I such that $L(D^{(I)})^{=n}$ has a n^2-size circuit. This is the proof outline that we propose for Conjecture 1.

Unfortunately, we have not yet obtained the proof for the Working Assumption; in fact, it may be the case that this does not hold (see also the discussion of Concluding Remarks). On the other hand, for formulas with a slightly simpler structure, we can show the existence of "short" partial assignment. For example, the following proposition shows the existence of such a "short" partial assignment if the bottom fan-in is restricted to 1. That is, when $F_1, \ldots, F_N$ are depth two formulas.

Proposition 1. *For a given size parameter n, let $\ell = n^d$ for some constant $d > 0$ and let $m = n^2$. Let $L = 2^{(m+1)\ell}$, $M = 2^{m+n}$, and $N = 2^n$. Consider any set of N depth two formulas $\{F_1, \ldots, F_N\}$ over a set of M Boolean variables such that each F_i consists of an $\vee$-gate with $\leq L$ fan-in as a top gate, and at most L $\wedge$-gates with $\leq L$ fan-in as the 2nd level gates. Then there exists a partial assignment α to Boolean variables that determines the value of all F_i's by fixing the values of less than $2^m/N$ variables.*

Proof. Consider (initially) a set S of $\wedge$-gates at the 2nd level of $F_1, \ldots, F_N$, and let N_S denote the number of elements of S. Note that $N_S \leq N_0 \stackrel{\text{def}}{=} NL = 2^{n+(m+1)\ell}$. We say a gate in S is *fat* if it consists of more than $M2^{-3n-1}$ literals. Consider here a process of assigning a value to a variable (at each step) to falsify (and hence remove from S) such fat gates until no fat gate exists or the value of all F_i's are fixed. During the process, if some formula F_i has a non-fat $\wedge$-gate, then we fix assignment to all its literals so that the gate is evaluated true, which determines $F_i = 1$ (and allows us to remove all its $\wedge$-gates from S). Note that the total number of variables that are assigned a value in this way is at most $N \cdot M2^{-3n-1} = 2^{m+n}2^{-2n-1} \ (= 2^m/2N)$.

Consider the situation that all $\wedge$-gates in S are fat. Then there must be some literal that appears more than $N_S \cdot 2^{-3n-1}$ times. Thus, by fixing the value of such a literal as 0 we can falsify at least $(1 - 2^{-3n-1})N_S$ gates of S. Thus, assignments of this type are made at most $2^{3n+1} \log_e N_0 \leq 2^{3n+1}(n + (m+1)\ell) \log_2 e$ times, which is much less than $2^m/2N$. Therefore, altogether the process stops fixing all values of $F_1, \ldots, F_N$ by assigning at most $2^m/N$ variables. $\square$

Note that the proof of Theorem 2 should work for our generic algorithm framework. That is, the Σ_2^p-algorithm D_1 can be modified to $D_1^{(\cdot)}$ that runs with a given circuit interpreter I to define a hard set w.r.t. I. Does it contradict to the above proof outline for Conjecture 1? In the above proof outline, we tried to define $I_{m,n}$ so that $L(D^{(I)})^{=n}$ indeed has a n^2-size circuit for any $\Sigma_2^{p,(\cdot)}$-algorithm D. This *does not* contradict to the algorithm D_1. In fact, since any $L(D^{(I)})^{=n}$ has a n^2-size circuit, $1\mathrm{PreC}_{n'} \ (\subseteq \{0,1\}^n)$ has a n^2-size circuit for n' such that $n = 2(n')^2$; hence, $D_1^{(I)}$ should define $L(D_1^{(I)})^{=n'}$ that has no $(n')^2$-size circuit. That is, our choice of $I_{m,n}$ indeed leads to the existence of a hard set at length n'. If we wanted to guarantee that any D including D_1 defines a set with (n')-size circuit on $\{0,1\}^{n'}$, we should have to define $I_{m,n} \ (= I_{2(n')^2,2(n')^2})$ appropriately so that $1\mathrm{PreC}_{n'}$ does not have a $(2(n')^2)^2$-size circuit w.r.t. $I_{m,n}$. In summary, while we conjecture that the a.e.-hardness cannot be achieve by any

$\Sigma_2^{\mathrm{p},(\cdot)}$-algorithm, the i.e.-hardness is in fact shown as a corollary to the proof of Theorem 2.

Theorem 4. *(Corollary to the proof of Theorem 2)   There is a generic $\Sigma_2^{\mathrm{p},(\cdot)}$-algorithm D_1 such that $L(D_1^{(I)}) \notin \mathrm{SIZE}^{(I)}[n^2]$ for any circuit interpreter $I = \{I_{n^2,n}\}_{n \geq 1}$.*

Aaronson [Aar06] introduced a notion of "black box" learning algorithm, an algorithm that finds a relatively small circuit (for a target function f) by asking queries on the values of f. We can use this algorithm for our generic algorithm. Then from the following result, we can see that it is extremely difficult to resolve Conjecture 1 because it implies P $\neq$ NP!

Theorem 5. *(Theorem 11 of [Aar06])*
If P $=$ NP, then there exists a black box Δ_2^{p}-algorithm (more precisely, $\mathrm{P}_{||}^{\mathrm{NP}}$-algorithm) solving the black box learning problem, which implies that there is a $\Delta_2^{\mathrm{p},(\cdot)}$-algorithm achieving (1) for any circuit interpreter I.

Now we look back the proof of Kannan. The key point for obtaining a hard problem in $\Sigma_2^{\mathrm{p}} \cap \Pi_2^{\mathrm{p}}$ is to consider two cases depending on the condition whether SAT has polynomial-size circuits or not. In our argument above, the set PreC has the same role as SAT. In this case, we consider more specifically whether PreC is in $\mathrm{SIZE}^{(I)}$ or not. If not, we can simply use PreC, that is, an $\mathrm{NP}^{(I)}$-algorithm recognizing PreC w.r.t. I. On the other hand, if PreC has some square-size circuits, then we use the $\Sigma_2^{\mathrm{p},(I)}$-algorithm that we designed for recognizing L_0'. Since we assume that PreC has square-size circuits, L_0' is indeed L_0 and this algorithm is also used to rejecting a string not in L_0. That is, this is a $\Sigma_2^{\mathrm{p},(I)} \cap \Pi_2^{\mathrm{p},(I)}$-algorithm for L_0. It seems that using two different algorithms is essential unless we have some algorithmic way to distinguish two cases. This leads us to the following conjecture.

Conjecture 2. *There is no generic $\Sigma_2^{\mathrm{p},(\cdot)} \cap \Pi_2^{\mathrm{p},(\cdot)}$-algorithm D such that $L(D^{(I)}) \notin \mathrm{SIZE}^{(I)}[n^2]$ holds for any circuit interpreter $I = \{I_{n^2,n}\}_{n \geq 1}$. (Cf. There is a relativizable proof showing that $\mathrm{SIZE}^{(I)}[n^2] \not\subset \Sigma_2^{\mathrm{p},(I)} \cap \Pi_2^{\mathrm{p},(I)}$ for any circuit interpreter $I = \{I_{n^2,n}\}_{n \geq 1}$.)*

Here again we can show that the same relation to the P $\neq$ NP conjecture; solving this conjecture implies P $\neq$ NP.

4   Concluding Remarks

We propose some framework for discussing the limit of a certain algorithmic approach to prove a nonlinear circuit size lower bound for classes below Σ_2^{p}. We explain a way to show some limit by using some working assumption. On the other hand, it is shown that the solution of the conjecture implies P $\neq$ NP.

Then one would feel fishy about the working assumption proposed above. It may be possible this working assumption could be too strong to hold. But it should be noted here that this assumption is for deriving one of the simplest way to encode $\Sigma_2^{\mathrm{p},(\cdot)}$-computations on $\{0,1\}^n$ so that they are decodable by some n^2-size circuit. Certainly there are many other ways to achieve this; see, e.g., the one used in [CW04]. And I believe that one can think of some very sophisticated coding in future, solving the P $\neq$ NP conjecture at the same time! Note that designing such a coding method leads to the fundamental lower bound result. This may be an interesting view point.

References

[Aar06] Aaronson, S.: Oracles are subtle but not malicious. In: Proc. IEEE Conference on Computational Complexity (CCC 2006), pp. 340–354. IEEE (2006)

[Betal75] Baker, T., Gill, J., Solovay, R.: Relativizations of the P=?NP question. SIAM J. Comput. **4**, 431–442 (1975)

[Betal96] Bshouty, N.H., Cleve, R., Gavaldà, R., Kannan, S.: Oracles and queries that are sufficient for exact learning. J. Comput. Sys. Sci. **52**(3), 421–433 (1996)

[Cai01] Cai, J.Y.: $S_2^p \subseteq \mathrm{ZPP^{NP}}$. In: Proc. of the 42nd Annual Sympos. on Foundations of Comp. Sci. pp. 620–629. IEEE (2001)

[CW04] Cai, J., Watanabe, O.: On proving circuit lower bounds against the polynomial-time hierarchy. SIAM Journal on Computing **33**(4), 984–1009 (2004)

[Kan82] Kannan, R.: Circuit-size lower bounds and non-reducibility to sparse sets. Information and Control **55**(1), 40–56 (1982)

[KL82] Karp, R.M., Lipton, R.J.: Turing machines that take advice. Enseign. Math. **28**, 191–201 (1982)

[KW98] Köbler, J., Watanabe, O.: New collapse consequences of np having small circuits. SIAM Journal on Computing **28**(1), 311–324 (1998)

Computing with Unconventional Resources

P Systems with Anti-Matter

Rudolf Freund[1] and Gheorghe Păun[2]([✉])

[1] Faculty of Informatics, Vienna University of Technology,
Favoritenstr. 9, 1040 Vienna, Austria
rudi@emcc.at
[2] Institute of Mathematics of the Romanian Academy,
PO Box 1-764, 014700 Bucharest, Romania
curteadelaarges@gmail.com

Abstract. After a quick introduction to the area of membrane computing (a branch of natural computing), recalling the basic notions of cell-like and spiking neural P systems, we introduce the concept of anti-matter in membrane computing. First we consider spiking neural P systems with anti-spikes, and then we show the power of anti-matter in cell-like P systems. As expected, the use of anti-matter objects and especially of matter/anti-matter annihilation rules, turns out to be rather powerful: computational completeness of P systems with anti-matter is obtained immediately, even without using catalysts. Finally, some open problems are formulated, too.

1 Introduction

First we give a brief introduction to membrane computing, a branch of natural computing having widely developed during the more than fifteen years since its initiation, see [19]. In some details we present a specific class of membrane systems (usually called *P systems*) with motivation coming from the way neurons interact, the spiking neural (in short, SN) P systems. In particular, we discuss SN P systems with *anti-spikes*, and then we generalize this idea, considering P systems of any type with *anti-objects*: for an object a, we say that $\bar{a}$ is an anti-object if an *annihilation rule* $a\bar{a} \rightarrow \lambda$ is assumed to exist in all membranes, which may either be an explicit rule or else act in an implicit way by removing a pair $a, \bar{a}$ in zero time. These annihilation rules turn out to be rather powerful, as somehow expected if, for example, we look at the λ-rules as the only non-context-free rules in the Geffert normal forms, e.g., see [22].

2 Elements of Membrane Computing

Membrane computing is a branch of natural computing, aiming to abstract computing models from the structure and the functioning of living cells. The models obtained in that way are called *P systems*. Single cells (leading to *cell-like P systems*) as well as communities of cells, like tissues or organs (leading to *tissue-like P systems*), or neural cells (the associated models are called *spiking neural P*

© Springer International Publishing Switzerland 2014
C.S. Calude et al. (Eds.): Gruska Festschrift, LNCS 8808, pp. 409–420, 2014.
DOI: 10.1007/978-3-319-13350-8_30

systems; these are one of the main topics in the present survey paper) have been considered in the literature. Basically, a P system consists of an arrangement of *membranes* (arranged in a hierarchical manner in the cell-like case and placed in the nodes of an arbitrary graph in the tissue-like case), which determine *compartments* where *multisets of objects* are placed, together with *evolution rules* inspired from biochemistry. Using these rules, the objects evolve, and these evolutions of objects are considered as *computations*. A result is associated with certain computations, hence, a computing device is obtained (working in the generative, the accepting, or the computing mode).

This very general framework lead to a large number of specific classes of P systems. Details can be found, for example, in [20] and [21]; recent information is available at the membrane computing website [27].

As objects in a P system we may use multisets of symbols from a given (finite) alphabet, strings, or more complex structures, such as graphs or *d*-dimensional arrays. In the case of spiking neural P systems, only multisets over a single object – the *spike*, an electrical impulse used by neurons to communicate with each other – are used. The rules used in a P system are of various types: multiset rewriting rules (similar to chemical reactions), string processing rules, specific rules for handling spikes, or rules directly inspired from biology, such as symport/antiport rules (for moving coupled symbol objects through membranes, corresponding to the functioning of selective protein channels in biology), or rules for handling membranes (dividing or creating membranes, exocytosis, endocytosis, etc.). The rules can be used sequentially or in parallel; the basic strategy in membrane computing is to use the rules in the maximally parallel way (in each step, a maximal multiset of rules is used in each compartment, in the multiset inclusion sense: no rule can be added to a chosen multiset of rules such that the resulting multiset of rules would still be applicable). Most of the investigations carried out in the literature concern synchronized P systems, but also non-synchronized systems were considered. In what concerns the ways to associate a result to a computation, there also are several possibilities: usually, only halting computations are considered to be successful (those computations which reach a configuration of the system where no rule can be applied any more). When dealing with multisets (which is also the case when dealing with SN P systems), the natural result of a computation is a number, but also strings can be associated in various ways.

The computing power of these devices is rather large: Turing computability can be obtained by many classes of P systems. In the cases when an exponential working space can be created during the computation in polynomial time, then, by a time-space trade-off, polynomial, often even linear, solutions to computationally hard problems (typically, **NP**-complete problems, but sometimes even **PSPACE**-problems) can be obtained.

Power and efficiency are computer science issues. Membrane computing proved to be rather attractive as a modeling framework, too. The reader can consult [3] and [4] in this respect. The most numerous and advanced applications are those in biology and biomedicine, but there are also well-investigated applications in approximate optimization, computer graphics, robot control, etc.

In this paper, we formally introduce only the basic model of membrane computing, the cell-like P systems with symbol objects (which will also be considered in Section 5 below). Hierarchical membrane structures (which can be described by a tree) are represented by strings of labeled matching parentheses, and the multisets over an alphabet V are represented by strings over V; a string and all its permutations represent the same multiset. For an alphabet V, by V^* we denote the set of all strings over V, including the empty string. The length of $x \in V^*$ is denoted by $|x|$; the empty string, of length zero, is denoted by λ. Basic knowledge in formal language theory as well as some familiarity with basic elements of membrane computing is assumed in what follows.

A *cell-like P system*, of degree m, with catalysts, is a construct

$$\Pi = (O, C, \mu, w_1, \ldots, w_m, R_1, \ldots, R_m, i_{in}, i_{out})$$

where O is the alphabet of objects, $C \subset O$ is the set of catalysts, μ is the *membrane structure* (with m membranes), $w_1, \ldots, w_m$ are strings over O representing multisets of objects present in the m regions of μ at the beginning of a computation, $R_1, \ldots, R_m$ are finite sets of evolution rules associated with the regions of μ, and i_{in} and i_{out} are the labels of the input and output regions, respectively; if the input or output is taken from the environment, this is indicated by taking the label 0 for i_{in} or i_{out}, respectively.

The *evolution rules* are multiset rewriting rules of the form $u \to v$, where u is a non-empty multiset over O and $v = (b_1, tar_1) \ldots (b_k, tar_k)$ with $b_i \in O$ and $tar_i \in \{here, out, in\}$, i.e., the objects b_i in v have associated a *target indication* tar_i. Using such a rule means "consuming" the objects of u and "producing" the objects from $b_1, \ldots, b_k$ of v, where the target indication *here* means that the objects remain in the same region where the rule is applied, *out* means that they are sent out of the respective membrane (in this way, objects can also be sent to the environment, when the rule is applied in the skin region), and *in* means that they are sent to one of the immediately inner membranes, chosen in a non-deterministic way; in general, the target indication *here* is omitted.

A rule $u \to v$ with $|u| = 1$ is said to be *non-cooperative*. A rule of the form $ca \to cv$, where $c \in C$, $a \in O \setminus C$, and the objects in v are from $O \setminus C$, too, is called *catalytic*; C is the set of catalysts, objects which are not changed by evolution rules. Arbitrary rules are called *cooperative*.

If the system is used in the generative mode, then i_{in} is omitted, and if the system is used in the accepting mode, then i_{out} is omitted. The number m of membranes in μ is called the *degree* of Π.

In the generative case, the set of numbers computed by Π (in the maximally parallel non-deterministic mode) is denoted by $N(\Pi)$. The family of all sets $N(\Pi)$ computed by systems Π of degree at most $m \geq 1$ and using rules of form α is denoted by $NOP_m(\alpha)$; if there is no bound on the degree of the systems, then the subscript m is replaced by $*$. According to the previous classification, $\alpha \in \{ncoo, cat, coo\}$, with the obvious meaning.

It is known that $NOP_1(coo) = NOP_1(cat_2) = NRE$, where cat_2 indicates the fact that only two catalysts are used with catalytic rules together with non-cooperative rules, and NRE is the family of recursively enumerable (Turing computable) sets of natural numbers. In turn, $NOP_*(ncoo) = NREG$, where $NREG$ is the family of length sets of regular languages (i.e., the family of semi-linear sets of natural numbers).

3   Spiking Neural P Systems

Spiking neural P systems, see [8], have a completely different architecture and functioning, as they are not based on the standard eukaryotic cell, but on brain biology. Here we only consider the neurons cooperating by means of spikes, electrical impulses of identical forms, moving along axons. Spiking neurons are also investigated in the current neural computing area (e.g., see [11]). We do not define SN P systems in a formal way, instead we only describe such a system and then also introduce anti-spikes, and we will give a simple example.

In short, an SN P system consists of a set of *neurons* (represented by membranes) placed in the nodes of a directed graph (the arcs are called *synapses*) and containing *spikes*, denoted by copies of the symbol a. Thus, the architecture is that of a tissue-like P system, with only one kind of objects present in the cells. The objects evolve by means of *spiking rules*, which are of the form $(E/a^c \rightarrow a; d)$, where E is a regular expression over a and c, d are natural numbers, $c \geq 1$, $d \geq 0$. The meaning is that a neuron containing k spikes such that $a^k \in L(E)$, $k \geq c$, can consume c spikes and produce one spike, after a delay of d steps. This spike is sent to all neurons to which a synapse exists outgoing from the neuron where the rule was applied. There also are *forgetting rules*, of the form $a^s \rightarrow \lambda$, with the meaning that $s \geq 1$ spikes are removed, provided that the neuron contains exactly s spikes. The system works in a synchronized manner, i.e., in each time unit, every neuron which can use a rule should do that, but the work of the system is sequential in each neuron: only (at most) one rule is used in each neuron. One of the neurons is considered to be the *output* one, and its spikes are also sent to the environment. The moments of time when a spike is emitted by the output neuron are marked with 1, the other moments are marked with 0. This binary sequence is called the *spike train* of the system; it might be infinite if the computation does not stop.

The result of a computation is encoded in the distance between the first two spikes sent to the environment by the (output neuron of the) system. Other ways to associate a result with a computation were considered, for instance, the total number of spikes emitted by the output neuron during a halting computation, or else the number of spikes contained in the output neuron at the end of a halting computation; the spike train itself can be taken as the result of the computation, and in this way the system generates a binary sequence (a finite string, if the computation halts).

There are several classes of SN P systems, using various combinations of ingredients – rules of restricted forms, for example, without a delay (i.e., with all rules $E/a^c \rightarrow a; d$ having $d = 0$, a case when the rules are written in the simplified form $E/a^c \rightarrow a$), without forgetting rules, or extended rules, e.g., producing more than one spike, as well as asynchronous SN P systems (no clock is considered, any neuron may use a rule or not), with exhaustive use of rules (when enabled, a rule is used as many times as made possible by the spikes present in a neuron), with certain further conditions imposed on the halting configuration, with the same sets of rules in each neuron (the system then is called *homogeneous*), containing further biological ingredients, such as *astrocytes*, with inhibitory synapses, etc. For most SN P systems with unbounded neurons (arbitrarily many spikes can be found in each of them), characterizations of Turing computable sets of natural numbers are obtained. When the neurons are bounded, usually characterizations of the family $NREG$ are obtained. SN P systems can also be used in the accepting and in the computing modes.

4   SN P Systems with Anti-Spikes

A natural feature added to an SN P system is that of *anti-spikes*, proposed in [17] and then investigated in a series of papers. For the reader's convenience, the bibliography below contains many titles of papers dealing with this subject, yet not all of them are explicitly referred to in the present suvey paper.

The main point of the new notion is to interpret the "anti-spikes" as "anti-matter", hence to assume that when a piece of matter meets the corresponding piece of anti-matter, they will annihilate each other. This corresponds to the existence of rules of the form $a\bar{a} \to \lambda$, which are used immediately when a and $\bar{a}$ are present in the same neuron.

Thus, in an SN P system with anti-spikes, the spiking rules and the forgetting rules are of the forms $E/b^c \to b'^c$ and $b^c \to \lambda$ where E is a regular expression over a or over $\bar{a}$, while $b, b' \in \{a, \bar{a}\}$ and $c \geq 1$. If $L(E) = b^c$, then we write the first rule as $b^c \to b'$. As usual, a delay can be added to the spiking rules, too.

Note that we have four categories of rules, identified by $(b, b') \in \{(a, a), (a, \bar{a}), (\bar{a}, a), (\bar{a}, \bar{a})\}$. Of course, it is of interest to restrict the type of rules, and this is the case in most papers found in the literature.

The rules are used as usual in SN P systems, with the additional fact that a and $\bar{a}$ "cannot stay together", they instantaneously annihilate each other: if in a neuron there are either objects a or objects $\bar{a}$, and further objects of either type (maybe both) arrive from other neurons, such that we end with a^r and $\bar{a}^s$ inside, then immediately the rule of the form $a\bar{a} \to \lambda$ is applied in the maximal manner, so that either the multiset of spikes a^{r-s} – if $r \geq s$ – or of anti-spikes $\bar{a}^{s-r}$ – if $s \geq r$ – remains.

In the definition from [17], the mutual annihilation of spikes and anti-spikes takes no time, so that the neurons always contain either only spikes or only anti-spikes. That is why, for instance, the regular expressions of the spiking rules are defined either over a or over $\bar{a}$, but not over both symbols. Moreover, annihilation has priority over spiking and forgetting rules. Later, also the case when the annihilation takes one time unit was considered, with explicitly using the rule $a\bar{a} \to \lambda$, eventually even without priority over other rules.

The computations and the results of computations are defined in the same way as for usual SN P systems. In most investigations, the restriction was considered that the output neuron produces only spikes, not also anti-spikes. The anti-spikes are sometimes used to encode, in a natural way, negative numbers.

By $N_2(\Pi)$ we denote the set of numbers generated by an SN P system (with anti-spikes) as the distance between the first two spikes sent to the environment by the output neuron, and by $N_2 S_a N P_m$ the families of all sets $N_2(\Pi)$, computed by SN P systems with anti-spikes and at most $m \geq 1$ neurons. When the number of neurons is not bounded, we replace the subscript m by $*$.

We illustrate the previous definition by an example recalled from [17]; it is, in fact, part of the proof showing computational completeness of SN P systems with anti-spikes (i.e., $N_2 S_a N P_* = NRE$), namely, the module which simulates a SUB-instruction of a register machine. We present the module in the graphical form, a usual way of presentation in membrane computing: neurons are given as ovals containing spiking and forgetting rules, and in addition indicating the initial spikes and anti-spikes; the synapses are represented by arrows linking the neurons.

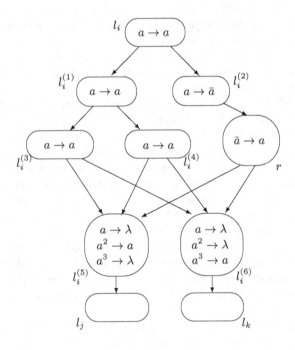

Fig. 1. Module SUB, simulating $l_i : (\text{SUB}(r), l_j, l_k)$.

Figure 1 shows the module associated with an instruction $l_i : (\text{SUB}(r), l_j, l_k)$. The module is activated when neuron σ_{l_i} receives a spike. Initially, no neuron contains any spike, except for the neuron σ_{l_0} associated with l_0, the initial label of the register machine; each label has such an associated neuron, and also each register r has associated a neuron σ_r. Neuron σ_{l_i} sends a spike to neurons $\sigma_{l_i^{(1)}}$ and $\sigma_{l_i^{(2)}}$. In the next step, neuron $\sigma_{l_i^{(2)}}$ sends an anti-spike to neuron σ_r, which corresponds to register r; at the same time, $\sigma_{l_i^{(1)}}$ sends a spike to the neurons $\sigma_{l_i^{(3)}}$ and $\sigma_{l_i^{(4)}}$. If register r is non-empty, that is, neuron σ_r contains at least one a, then $\bar{a}$ removes one occurrence of a, which corresponds to subtracting one from register r, and no rule is applied in σ_r. This means that $\sigma_{l_i^{(5)}}$ and $\sigma_{l_i^{(6)}}$ receive only two spikes, from $\sigma_{l_i^{(3)}}$ and $\sigma_{l_i^{(4)}}$, hence, σ_{l_j} is activated, whereas σ_{l_k} is not activated. If register r is empty, then the rule $\bar{a} \to a$ is used in σ_r, hence, $\sigma_{l_i^{(5)}}$ and $\sigma_{l_i^{(6)}}$ receive three spikes, and this leads to the activation of σ_{l_k}, which is the correct continuation in this case.

The reader is referred to [17] for further details concerning the functioning of this module, and in general, for the proof of the universality of SN P systems with anti-spikes.

We cannot present all the developments concerning SN P systems with anti-spikes; most of the titles of the related articles listed at the end of the paper are self-explanatory. We only mention an important research direction in membrane computing in general and in the SN P systems area in particular, reminding the "old times" of investigations in formal language theory (see a survey in [7]) concerning the *descriptional complexity* of grammars and languages: considering size parameters for P systems. Because most of the classes of P systems are universal, for those classes the basic question is to find the smallest number of membranes in order to get the equivalence with Turing machines. For subuniversal classes, an important question of interest is whether or not the number of membranes induces an infinite hierarchy.

These questions are of interest for SN P systems, too, with or without anti-spikes. Further questions appear, resembling those mentioned in [7]: How many rules per neuron are needed? How many different types of neurons are needed? Can rules of a specific type be avoided?

Another question of interest is to find universal systems for a given class of devices with a small descriptional complexity; like in the case of universal Turing machines, we search for fixed P systems which can simulate any P system from a given class, as soon as the code of a particular system is introduced as an input to the universal one. For SN P systems, the "race" was started in [18], with several subsequent papers succeeding to decrease the complexity of the universal systems constructed there.

According to our knowledge, for SN P systems with anti-spikes the best results currently available are those from [24]: a universal system is constructed, for the case of computing functions, having 75 neurons and 125 rules, with 6 types of neurons and 8 types of rules. A related result is reported in [12], where a similar system is described, containing 91 neurons, each of them containing only one rule, of one of the simple forms $a \to a$ and $a \to \bar{a}$. This once again proves the power of annihilation rules.

5 P Systems with Anti-Matter

The idea of considering "anti-matter" objects and their corresponding matter/anti-matter annihilation rules can be extended to all types of P systems. We briefly discuss it here for cell-like P systems.

Formally, a cell-like P system (of degree m, with catalysts) with anti-matter is a construct

$$\Pi = (O, A_O, C, \mu, w_1, \ldots, w_m, R_1, \ldots, R_m, i_{in}, i_{out})$$

where all the components are as in a usual P system and A_O is a set of symbols $\bar{a}$, for $a \in O \setminus C$ (obviously, we do not allow the catalysts to have anti-objects). In each compartment of μ we assume the matter/anti-matter annihilation rules $a\bar{a} \to \lambda$ to be present, for all $\bar{a} \in A_O$. As in SN P systems we might assume that these rules are used "automatically", in zero time, as soon as they can be applied. Yet in the following we assume the annihilation rules to be used as other rules, yet eventually with *weak priority* (e.g., see [2]) over all other rules, i.e., other rules then also may be applied if objects cannot be bound by some annihilation rule any more. In both cases, the rules in the sets R_i, $1 \leq i \leq m$, of the form $u \to v$ have to obey to the condition that neither u nor v may contain both the symbol a and its anti-matter object $\bar{a}$ for any $\bar{a} \in A_O$.

The functioning of such a system is as usual in membrane computing, keeping in mind that the annihilation rules have to be added to all sets of rules R_i, $1 \leq i \leq m$. By $NO_a P_m(ncoo, pri)$ we denote the family of sets of numbers generated by P systems with at most m membranes, using anti-objects, with non-cooperative rules. The parameter pri indicates the use of annihilation rules with priority over the other rules; it is omitted if we do not use this implicit priority. If in addition to non-cooperative rules we also allow catalytic rules and at most k catalysts, $ncoo$ is replaced by cat_k in these notations.

Although the annihilation rules are expected to add a lot of computational power, it is still surprising that together with giving the annihilation rules priority over all other rules, non-cooperative rules are already sufficient to obtain computational completeness, whereas without this priority condition, in addition we need catalytic rules with one catalyst; in both cases rather simple proofs can be obtained, whereas without these matter/anti-matter annihilation rules, non-cooperative rules together with catalytic rules with two catalysts are needed, see the rather complex proof given in [5].

Theorem 1. $NO_a P_1(ncoo, pri) = NRE$.

Proof. Let $M = (3, H, l_0, l_h, I)$ (number of registers, labels of instructions, initial label, halt label, set if instructions) be a register machine with three registers; register 1 is the output register containing the result at the end of a successful computation, it is never decremented; registers 2 and 3 are empty at the begin and at the end of a successful computation. We now construct the (generating, hence, we omit i_{in}) P system with anti-matter

$$\Pi = (O, A_O, [\ ]_1, l_0, R_1, 1)$$

with only one membrane and the following components:

$$O = \{l, l' \mid l \in H\} \cup \{a_r \mid r \in \{1, 2, 3\}\} \cup \{\#\},$$
$$A_O = \{\bar{a}_2, \bar{a}_3, \bar{\#}\};$$

the non-cooperative rules in R_1 are described below.

The contents of register r is represented by the number of copies of the object a_r, $r \in \{1, 2, 3\}$, in the system. The P system starts with the object l_0 representing the initial label of M.

For each instruction $l_i : (\text{ADD}(r), l_j, l_k)$ in I, $r \in \{1, 2, 3\}$, we take the rules

$$l_i \to l_j a_r \text{ and}$$
$$l_i \to l_k a_r,$$

which obviously simulate the given ADD-instruction.

For each instruction $l_i : (\text{SUB}(r), l_j, l_k)$ in I, $r \in \{2, 3\}$, we consider the three rules

$$l_i \to l_j \bar{a}_r,$$
$$l_i \to l_i' \bar{a}_r,$$
$$l_i' \to \# l_k.$$

We also add the rules $\bar{a}_r \to \bar{\#}$, $r \in \{2, 3\}$, the annihilation rules $a_r \bar{a}_r \to \lambda$ and $\# \bar{\#} \to \lambda$, as well as the trap rules $\# \to \# \#$ and $\bar{\#} \to \# \#$.

When simulating a SUB-instruction $l_i : (\text{SUB}(r), l_j, l_k)$, we have to make a non-deterministic choice between the decrement case and the zero-test. The decrement case of the SUB-instruction $l_i : (\text{SUB}(r), l_j, l_k)$ is simulated by the rule $l_i \to l_j \bar{a}_r$ and the subsequent application of the annihilation rule $a_r \bar{a}_r \to \lambda$. If this rule is not applicable, i.e., if register r is empty, the rule $\bar{a}_r \to \bar{\#}$ will be applied instead, which in absence of its counterpart $\#$ immediately evolves to $\# \#$ and thus leads to an infinite computation.

The zero-test is initiated with the rule $l_i \to l_i' \bar{a}_r$. If register r is empty, then $\bar{a}_r$ cannot be annihilated and therefore evolves to $\bar{\#}$, which then annihilates the symbol $\#$ generated by the rule $l_i' \to \# l_k$; if register r is not empty, $\bar{a}_r$ is annihilated by some copy of a_r, hence, the trap symbol $\#$ generated by the rule $l_i' \to \# l_k$ does not find its anti-matter $\bar{\#}$ and therefore evolves to $\# \#$, thus leading to an infinite computation. Here we find the crucial situation where we need the constraint that annihilation rules have priority over all other rules, i.e., $\bar{a}_r \to \bar{\#}$ cannot be applied if the annihilation rule $a_r \bar{a}_r \to \lambda$ can be applied.

The rule $l_h \to \lambda$ is applied at the end of a successful simulation of the instructions of the register machine M, and the computation halts if no trap symbol $\#$ is present; the number of symbols a_1 in the skin membrane then represents the result of this halting computation. In conclusion, we obtain $N(M) = N(\Pi)$. $\square$

Returning to descriptional complexity issues, it is worth noting that the P system constructed in the preceding proof has only one membrane and only three matter/anti-matter annihilation rules.

If we look for small universal systems, we may start with the universal register machine U_{32} from [9], with 8 registers which are decremented during the computations, and apply the construction given in the preceding proof, thus needing $8 + 1$ matter/anti-matter annihilation rules. An optimized P system with matter/anti-matter annihilation rules having priority over all other rules can be found in [1].

Without this priority of the annihilation rules, the construction is not working, hence, a characterization of the class $NO_aP_1(ncoo)$ remains as an open problem. Yet in addition using catalytic rules with one catalyst again allows us to obtain computational completeness:

Theorem 2. $NO_aP_1(cat_1) = NRE.$

Proof. We again consider a register machine $M = (3, H, l_0, l_h, I)$ as in the previous proof, and construct the (generating) catalytic P system

$$\Pi = (O, A_O, [\ ]_1, \{c\}, cl_0, R_1, 0)$$

with only one membrane (containing the single catalyst c) and the following components:

$$O = \{l, l', l'' \mid l \in H\} \cup \{a_r \mid r \in \{1, 2, 3\}\} \cup \{\#, d\},$$
$$A_O = \{\bar{a}_2, \bar{a}_3, \bar{\#}\};$$

the non-cooperative rules in R_1 are described below. The output symbols a_1 now are sent to the environment, in order not to have to count the catalyst in the skin membrane; for that purpose, we simply use the rule $a_1 \to (a_1, out)$.

For each instruction $l_i : (\text{ADD}(r), l_j, l_k)$ in I, $r \in \{1, 2, 3\}$, we again take the rules

$$l_i \to l_j a_r \text{ and}$$
$$l_i \to l_k a_r.$$

For each instruction $l_i : (\text{SUB}(r), l_j, l_k)$ in I, $r \in \{2, 3\}$, we now consider the following four rules:

$$l_i \to l_j \bar{a}_r,$$
$$l_i \to l_i'' d\bar{a}_r,$$
$$l_i'' \to l_i',$$
$$l_i' \to \# l_k.$$

We also add the annihilation rules $a_r \bar{a}_r \to \lambda$ and $\#\bar{\#} \to \lambda$, the trap rules $\# \to \#\#$ and $\bar{\#} \to \#\#$, $d \to \#\#$, as well as the catalytic rules $cd \to c$ and $c\bar{a}_r \to c\bar{\#}$, $r \in \{2, 3\}$.

The decrement case of the SUB-instruction $l_i : (\text{SUB}(r), l_j, l_k)$ is simulated as in the previous proof, by using the rule $l_i \to l_j \bar{a}_r$ and then applying the annihilation rule $a_r \bar{a}_r \to \lambda$. If this rule is not applicable, i.e., if register r is empty, the rule $\bar{a}_r \to \bar{\#}$ will be applied instead, which in absence of its counterpart $\#$ immediately evolves to $\#\#$ and thus leads to an infinite computation.

The zero-test now is initiated with the rule $l_i \to l_i'' d\bar{a}_r$ thus introducing the (dummy) symbol d which keeps the catalyst busy for one step, where the catalytic rule $cd \to c$ has to be applied in order to avoid the application of the trap rule

$d \rightarrow \#\#$. If register r is empty, then $\bar{a}_r$ cannot be annihilated and therefore evolves to $\bar{\#}$ in the third step by the application of the catalytic rule $c\bar{a}_r \rightarrow c\bar{\#}$, which symbol $\bar{\#}$ then annihilates the symbol $\#$ generated by the rule $l'_i \rightarrow \#l_k$ in the same step; if register r is not empty, $\bar{a}_r$ is annihilated by some copy of a_r already in the first step, hence, the trap symbol $\#$ generated by the rule $l'_i \rightarrow \#l_k$ does not find its anti-matter $\bar{\#}$ and therefore evolves to $\#\#$, thus leading to an infinite computation. Altough the annihilation rule $a_r\bar{a}_r \rightarrow \lambda$ now does not have priority over the catalytic rule $c\bar{a}_r \rightarrow c\bar{\#}$, maximal parallelism enforces $a_r\bar{a}_r \rightarrow \lambda$ to be applied, if possible, already in the first step instead of $c\bar{a}_r \rightarrow c\bar{\#}$, as in a successful derivation the catalyst c first has to eliminate the dummy symbol d.

The rule $l_h \rightarrow \lambda$ is applied at the end of a successful simulation of the instructions of the register machine M, and the computation halts if no trap symbol $\#$ is present; the number of symbols a_1 sent out to the environment during the computation represents the result of this halting computation. In sum, we obtain $N(M) = N(\Pi)$. □

6   Concluding Remarks

In this paper we have briefly recalled some basic ideas of membrane computing, and especially have given some information about spiking neural P systems, including spiking neural P systems with anti-spikes. We have also extended this idea of anti-objects ("anti-matter") to cell-like P systems with symbol objects, which can be proved to be computationally complete when the annihilation rules are applied with having priority over the remaining non-cooperative rules; without this priority, in addition catalytic rules with a single catalyst are needed to obtain computational completeness.

Several problems are still open in this area of P systems with anti-matter. Some of them have been formulated in this paper; the interested reader can find many more in the literature, for instance, in [6].

Acknowledgments. Thanks are due to an anonymous referee for a careful reading of the paper.

References

1. Alhazov, A., Aman, B., Freund, R., Păun, G.: Matter and anti-matter in membrane systems. Brainstorming Week in Membrane Computing, Sevilla, pp. 1–26 (2014)
2. Alhazov, A., Sburlan, D.: Static Sorting P Systems. In: Ciobanu, G., Păun, G., Pérez-Jiménez, M.J. (eds.) Applications of Membrane Computing, pp. 215–252. Springer, Natural Computing Series (2006)
3. Ciobanu, G., Păun, G., Pérez-Jiménez, M.J. (eds.): Applications of Membrane Computing. Springer, Berlin (2006)
4. Frisco, P., Gheorghe, M., Pérez-Jiménez, M.J., (eds.): Applications of Membrane Computing in Systems and Synthetic Biology. Springer, Berlin (2014)
5. Freund, R., Kari, L., Oswald, M., Sosík, P.: Computationally universal P systems without priorities: two catalysts are sufficient. Theoretical Computer Science **330**, 251–266 (2005)

6. Gheorghe, M., Păun, G., Pérez-Jiménez, M.J., Rozenberg, G.: Frontiers of membrane computing: Open problems and research topics. Intern. J. Found. Computer Sci. **24**(5), 547–623 (2013)
7. Gruska, J.: Descriptional complexity of context-free languages, pp. 71–83. High Tatras, Proc. Symp. Math. Found. Computer Sci. (1973)
8. Ionescu, M., Păun, G., Yokomori, T.: Spiking neural P systems. Fundamenta Informaticae **71**(2–3), 279–308 (2006)
9. Korec, I.: Small universal Turing machines. Theoretical Comp. Sci. **168**, 267–301 (1996)
10. Krithivasan, K., Metta, V.P., Garg, D.: On string languages generated by spiking neural P systems with anti-spikes. Intern. J. Found. Computer Sci. **22**, 1 (2011)
11. Maass, W., Bishop, C. (eds.): Pulsed Neural Networks. MIT Press, Cambridge (1999)
12. Metta, V.P., Kelemenova, A.: More on universality of spiking neural P systems with anti-spikes. Manuscript (2013)
13. Metta, V.P., Krithivasan, K., Garg, D.: Some characteristics of spiking neural P systems with anti-spikes. In: Proc. 11th Intern. Conf. on Membrane Computing, Jena, Germany, 291–303 (August 2010)
14. Metta, V.P., Krithivasan, K., Garg, D.: Modelling and analysis of spiking neural P systems with anti-spikes using Pnet lab. Nano Comm. Networks **1**(2), 141–149 (2011)
15. Metta, V.P., Krithivasan, K., Garg, D.: Computability of spiking neural P systems with anti-spikes. New Math. and Natural Comput. **8**(3), 283–295 (2012)
16. Metta, V.P., Krithivasan, K., Garg, D.: Spiking neural P systems with anti-spikes as transducers. Romanian J. Info. Sci. and Tehnology **14**(1), 20–30 (2011)
17. Pan, L., Păun, Gh: Spiking neural P systems with anti-spikes. Int. J. Comoputers, Comm. and Control **4**(3), 273–282 (2009)
18. Păun, A., Păun, G.: Small universal spiking neural P systems. BioSystems **90**, 48–60 (2007)
19. Păun, Gh: Computing with membranes. Journal of Computer and System Sciences **61**(1), 108–143 (2000). (and Turku Center for Computer Science-TUCS Report 208, November 1998, www.tucs.fi).
20. Păun, G.: Membrane Computing. An Introduction. Springer, Berlin (2002)
21. Păun, Gh., Rozenberg, G., Salomaa, A. (eds.): The Oxford Handbook of Membrane Computing. Oxford. Univ. Press (2010)
22. Rozenberg, G., Salomaa, A. (eds.): Handbook of Formal Languages, 3 vols. Springer, Berlin (1997)
23. Song, T., Pan, L., Wang, J., Venkat, I., Subramanian, K.G., Abdullah, R.: Normal forms for spiking neural P systems with anti-spikes. IEEE Trans. Nanobioscience **22**(4), 352–359 (2012)
24. Song, T., Jiang, Y., Shi, X., Zeng, X.: Small universal spiking neural P systems with anti-spikes. J. Comput. and Th. Nanoscience **10**(4), 999–1006 (2013)
25. Song, T., Wang, X., Zhang, Z., Chen, Z.: Homogeneous spiking neural P systems with anti-spikes. Neural Comput. and Applic. (June 2013). doi:10.1007/s00521-0123-1397-8
26. Tan, G., Song, T., Chen, Z., Zeng, X.: Spiking neural P systems with anti-spikes and without annihilating priority working in a "flip-flop" way. Intern. J. Computing Sci. and Math **4**(2), 152–162 (2013)
27. The P Systems Website: www.ppage.psystems.eu

A Robust Universal Flying Amorphous Computer

Lukáš Petrů and Jiří Wiedermann[✉]

Institute of Computer Science, Academy of Sciences of the Czech Republic,
Pod Vodárenskou věží 2, 182 07 Prague 8, Czech Republic
Lukas.Petru@seznam.cz, jiri.wiedermann@cs.cas.cz

Abstract. Amorphous computers are systems that derive their computational capability from the operation of vast numbers of simple, identical, randomly distributed and locally communicating units. The wireless communication ability and the memory capacity of the computational units is severely restricted due to their minimal size. Moreover, the units originally have no identifiers and can only use simple asynchronous communication protocols that cannot guarantee a reliable message delivery. In this work we concentrate on a so-called robust flying amorphous computer whose units are in a constant motion. The units are modelled by miniature RAMs communicating via radio. For this model we design a distributed probabilistic communication protocol and an algorithm enabling a simulation of a RAM in finite time. Our model is robust in the sense that if one or several computational units fail the computer will autonomously restart and reconfigure itself in order to initiate the computation anew. The underlying algorithms make use of a number of original ideas having no counterpart in the classical theory of distributed computing.

1 Introduction

Amorphous computing systems are a relatively recent phenomenon. Apart from the sci-fi literature where various forms of such systems have been envisaged in diverse futuristic scenarios (cf. an interstellar intelligent mobile cloud in [2], or a mentally controlled flying dust serving as an extension of human senses and as an interface to a very distant offspring of today's Internet in [8]), amorphous computing systems as a subject of scientific research emerged by the end of the 1990s. For an overview of the respective developments, cf. [13], [15].

The common issue in all visions and research projects was the fact that all of them considered a vast amount of very simple autonomous devices. These devices were randomly placed in a target area — there was no regular topology assumed as, e.g., in the case of cellular automata. Another joint idea was that, using local communication, the respective devices should self–organize in order to perform a coordinated action none of the elements alone was able to realize.

This research was partially supported by RVO:67985807 and the GA ČR grant No. P202/10/1333.

C.S. Calude et al. (Eds.): Gruska Festschrift, LNCS 8808, pp. 421–435, 2014.
DOI: 10.1007/978-3-319-13350-8_31

The prevailing focus of research mentioned above was on engineering or technological aspects of amorphous computing systems, almost completely ignoring theoretical questions related to computational power and efficiency of such systems. Obviously, without knowing their theoretical limits, one cannot have a complete picture of the potential abilities and limitations of such systems. This was the starting point of the project of the present authors devoted to studies of theoretical issues in amorphous computing initiated in 2004. Since that time various models of amorphous systems have been investigated, roughly in the order of their increased generality (cf. [9], [10], [11], [12], [13], [14], [15]). In all cases computational universality of the underlying systems has been proved. This points to the versatility of such systems in various computational or robotic applications.

The present paper makes a further step towards more general and computationally more efficient amorphous systems: we will consider amorphous systems with randomly moving mobile processors communicating via a radio. The processors take a form of miniature finite-memory RAMs. The transition from systems with a static communication pattern to systems with an unpredictably changing communication pattern brings a number of new problems that have been encountered formerly neither in the classical theory of distributed systems nor in the previous models of amorphous systems. Namely, the situation is further complicated by a continuously changing communication topology in which new communication paths keep emerging while the old ones keep vanishing unpredictably. Moreover, some processors may become temporarily unaccessible. This may lead to problems with data consistency maintenance over the entire system at times when the nodes become again accessible. These changes call for novel approaches in the design of communicating protocol resulting in unusual time complexity estimation of the simulation algorithm: without additional assumptions on the nature of processor movements one cannot come with a better than a finite upper bound on the time complexity of this algorithm.

In its class of minimalist amorphous systems communicating over radio, our model of a flying amorphous computer presents the first model for which the computational universality in the efficient sense has been proven.

In our previous papers we have always assumed ideal conditions when all nodes are always available and faultless during a computation, in this paper we will specifically focus on the question how can an amorphous computer be made more robust, resilient to the events that can cause loss or damage of some of its nodes.

The structure of the paper is as follows. In Section 2 the definition of the flying amorphous computer is given along with the scenario of its use. In Section 3 we sketch the main ideas of simulation of a RAM computer under simplifying assumptions that will enable a clear exposition of the main design ideas. In Section 4 we give the details of a so-called setup phase in which the amorphous computer is preprocessed in order to be able to perform a simulation. In Section 5 the communication protocol is described enabling a probabilistic communication among the nearest processors. The additional features necessary for obtaining required robustness are described in Section 6. Finally, conclusions are in Section 7.

A preliminary short version of this paper dealing only with the case of faultless processors appeared in [6]. A full, extended version of this paper has appeared as a technical report in [7].

2 Flying Amorphous Computer

Definition 1. *A flying amorphous computer is a septuple* $C = [N, A, P, r, s, T, v]$. *The model has the following properties:*

General properties:

(i) The computer consists of N nodes (or processors); there is one distinguished node called the base node.

(ii) Each node is modelled as a point in a square target area A. *The initial positions of nodes in A are determined by a process P assigning a random initial position independently to each node.*

Node properties:

(iii) Each node is a RAM with a fixed number of memory registers *of size s bits; initially, all registers contain zeros. There is a predefined subset of so-called* input and output registers *used in message transmission among a node's neighbors. There also is a single register providing an s-bit* random number *between 0 and 1 upon request.*

(iv) In each node there is a control unit *operating over all registers. The control unit operates according to a fixed program.*

(v) The nodes are not synchronized but they operate at nearly the same clock rate. An operation taking time t on the fastest node takes at most $(1 + \varepsilon_t)t$ on the slowest node, for a fixed $\varepsilon_t > 0$.

Movement:

(vi) Initially, a non-zero random direction vector u *is assigned to each node. Thereafter, each node moves with a constant speed v in the direction of its vector u. A node does not know and cannot influence its direction vector.*

(vii) If a node is about to leave the target area A, then on the boundary of A its direction vector is mirrored as a billiard ball bounced off a wall.

Communication properties:

(viii) Each node is equipped with a radio transceiver *by which it communicates with other nodes via a shared channel up to the distance r (called* communication radius*); all nodes at distance r are called the* neighbors *of the node at hand.*

(ix) Transmission of each message takes time T.

(x) A node receives message m if and only if exactly one of its neighbors sends m during transmission time T. While sending, a node cannot receive a message. If two or more neighbors of a node are simultaneously sending a message, a collision *occurs and the node receives no message.*

(xi) A node cannot detect a collision, the radio receiver cannot distinguish the case when multiple neighbors send messages from the case when no neighbor sends a message.

The target area of a squared shape has been chosen for simplicity of the definition and of simulations.

The communication properties of a node are among the weakest possible and are enforced by requirements of the maximal technological simplicity of the underlying receiver.

3   Simulation

In order to solve a computational task a flying amorphous computer operates according to the following scenario in which we assume the existence of an external operator. The scenario consists of three subsequent phases.

First, the operator deploys the nodes in the target area and powers on the computer so that the nodes start moving and operating.

In the second phase, the operator performs a setup of the computer. During the setup addresses are assigned to all nodes that are unique with high probability and the input data of the computational task are loaded into the computer.

In the final phase, after the setup is finished, the computer's own computation can start. At that time, the operator may disconnect from the computer and the computer carries out the computation autonomously. From time to time, the operator may reconnect to check the outcome of the computation.

The universality of our model will be proved by showing that it can simulate any computation of a bounded RAM machine. We will be using the standard model of a unit cost RAM, cf. [1] with registers of roughly the same size s as the registers of our flying computer (cf. Theorem 1). The program, the input and the output data are also stored in these registers.

For the sake of clarity of our exposition, we first sketch the main steps of the simulation algorithm postponing the details how the previous two phases of the computational scenario are implemented. The simplifying assumptions are: first, we will suppose that uniques addresses have been assigned to all nodes in the setup phase and second, there is a broadcast algorithm guaranteeing a message delivery between two concrete nodes in a finite time.

In order to start a simulation of a RAM with M registers we will require that the simulating flying amorphous computer also has at least M registers loaded with the same initial data as the RAM. This will happen in the setup phase to be described in Section 4.

Definition 2. *We say that a flying amorphous computer A is* set up *with respect to a RAM R with initial data $i_1, i_2, \ldots, i_M$ in its registers if A contains at least M nodes with unique addresses in the range 1 to M and if the j-th node of A contains the same data i_j as the register j in R does, for $j = 1, 2, \ldots, M$.*

The nodes of a flying amorphous computer communicate using broadcast from one node to its neighbors within their communication radius thus forming a multi-hop communication network. A broadcast operation is started at one node and delivers the message, possibly using many hops, to all nodes in a connected communication component. However, as the nodes are moving, not all nodes may be reachable (not even through several intermediary nodes due to the fact that they moved away too far) from the originating node at times when needed. In order to exclude such an improbable situation we will assume that this situation can never occur for an infinitely long time, that is, the nodes are moving in such a way that it will never happen that two nodes remain forever in different connected components of the underlying communication graph.

Definition 3. *Let A be a flying amorphous computer, B a broadcasting protocol, and n_1, n_2 two nodes of A. Assume that in A message m is being repeatedly broadcast from node n_1. We say that flying amorphous computer A with protocol B is* lively flying *if after a finite amount of broadcast attempts message m is eventually delivered to n_2.*

Note that in a lively flying computer the similar process of message delivery from n_1 to n_2 works also in the reverse direction, from n_2 to n_1. This can be used for a message delivery acknowledging.

We are ready to show how the simulation proceeds.

Theorem 1. *Let R be a RAM with M registers of size b, $M + 1 \leq N$. Let $I = i_1, i_2, \ldots i_M$ be the input data in R's registers. Let C be a computation on R taking time T_1 on input data I. Let A be a lively flying amorphous computer with broadcasting protocol B and register size $s = O(\log_2 M + \log_2 N + b)$ bits. Let the nodes of A except of the base node have memory capacity of at least $O(\log_2 M + \log_2 N + b)$ bits. Let A be set up with initial configuration I. Then A can simulate computation C in a finite time.*

Proof sketch: The amorphous computer will simulate the computation of R by simulating the individual instructions one after the other. During the simulation, the base node controls the computation and plays the role of the control unit of R. The values of registers of R are stored in other nodes of A : the j-th register is stored in the j-th node of A.

For simulating an instruction the base node must be able to perform two kinds of operations. First, it must be able to simulate reading from and writing to memory registers what it does by communicating with the other nodes using broadcasts. Second, it has to simulate arithmetic operations, branching, and choosing of the next instruction to be processed. These operations are encoded in the internal fixed program of the base node. Each register to which a new value is written must send an *acknowledgment* to the base node.

Obviously, a broadcast to some node may fail due to a temporary inaccessibility of that node. If, within a certain a priori given time interval, the base node does not receive an acknowledgement from the target node, the broadcast is repeated until an acknowledgement is received. Thanks to the amorphous computer being lively flying, at most a finite number of retries is required. It follows that one instruction can be simulated in finite time and, therefore, any finite computation can be simulated in finite time, too.

Further details of the simulation process and its complexity analysis are described in the extended version of this paper in [7]. □

4   Setup

Now we describe how the amorphous computer should be formed initially in order to be able to perform a simulation described in the previous section.

The setup has two phases: address assignment and input data loading.

Address assignment. The purpose of the address assignment process is to allocate unique addresses to the nodes of amorphous computer which are initially indistinguishable, all having zeroed memory. This process is controlled by the base node using the following program (on the left side):

```
for a = 1 to M             |      procedure PickSingleNode()
    PickSingleNode()       |          broadcast(Initialize, 0)
    AssignAddress(a, h)    |          for i = 1 to h
                           |              broadcast(RandomGroup, i)
                           |              broadcast(WhichGroup?)
                           |              g = receive()
                           I              broadcast(Choose, g)
```

To pick a single node, the base node makes use of the algorithm on the right side of the previous picture. In this algorithm, procedure `broadcast()` represents a call of the broadcast protocol of the flying amorphous computer, which is described in the next section. In general, a broadcast can fail, but for the moment let us assume that the broadcast messages are always successfully delivered to all nodes. Namely, under this assumption it is easier to describe procedure `PickSingleNode` which makes use of the well-known method of probabilistic halving the set of candidates until a single one remains. The general case counting on the possibility of broadcast procedure failure is substantially more complicated since it must also handle the cases of temporary inaccessibility of some nodes and the problems of data consistency maintenance after the return of such nodes. This more involved case will be described later.

Procedure `PickSingleNode` initializes the nodes via the `Initialize` message. After receiving this message, all nodes not yet having an allocated address participate in the node selection procedure. In this procedure, the base node performs h of so-called splitting rounds. During each round, all nodes receiving `RandomGroup` message (for the time being, forget about the second parameter which starts to be important in the case of failed broadcasts to be described later) randomly choose number 0 or 1 assigning themselves in this way to either of the two groups, 0 or 1. Then, all such nodes broadcast the number g of the group they selected. From the received answers the base node randomly picks one group number and reports it back to all nodes. In the forthcoming round participate only nodes that are in the selected group. It is expected that by each such split the number of candidate nodes is roughly halved. If value of h is sufficiently high this algorithm selects exactly one node with high probability. The procedure `AssignAddress(a, h)` then assigns address a to a node that went through all of h rounds.

Theorem 2. *Let there be N nodes participating in the* `PickSingleNode()` *algorithm. The probability of selecting more than one node after h splitting rounds is at most $N/2^h$.*

Proof. Consider the cardinality of the set of nodes after the last splitting round. After each round for each node the probability that another node remained in the same group is $1/2$. The probability that after h rounds a node still participates in the algorithm is $1/2^h$; therefore for all N nodes the probability that the cardinality of the remaining set is greater than 1 is at most $N/2^h$.   □

Now we return to a rather peculiar general case in which broadcasts in the address assignment phase can fail.

Recall that our goal—selection of exactly one node with high probability—is now complicated by the fact that there is no guarantee that a message sent to a certain subset of nodes will always reach all its members. However, for the correctness of the `PickSingleNode` algorithm it has been necessary that a single node is picked from among the nodes that have passed all splitting rounds.

For instance, if a node participating in a splitting round would not receive the `RandomGroup` message, then answering the subsequent `WhichGroup?` message that the node might later obtain would spoil the correctness of the entire algorithm. Namely, such a node could only provide an old value of g, not the current one. Thus, should a node miss a message, which is important for the correctness of selection process and which is addressed also to that node, the node must no longer participate in the algorithm.

In order to enable for a node to detect whether it has missed some round we make use of parameter i in `RandomGroup` message that was not important in the previous faultless communication case. This parameter stores the number of the current splitting round. A node is allowed to participate in round $i + 1$ if and only if the node has already passed successfully round i, i.e., if and only if it had first received message (`RandomGroup`,i) followed by (`Choose`,g), with g being the same as was the number of the node's chosen splitting group. In order to implement this idea it is enough for each node to remember the number of the last round in which it has participated. Then, upon receiving a (`RandomGroup`,i) message a node can discover whether it has missed the previous message (i.e., the previous round) or not.

Upon detecting a missed message, the node at hand acts as if it was in the group that was not chosen, i.e., it stops participating in the next rounds of the splitting algorithm. This puts us on the safe side as far as the probability of selecting more than one node is concerned.

However, a premature termination of a node's further participation in the selection process could in an extreme case lead to a situation when all nodes stop participating eventually. In such a case we end up with an empty set from which no node can be selected. In order to recognize this situation we introduce a mechanism of message acknowledgements. After performing a step in a computation, a node expected to perform such a step sends an acknowledging `OK` message back to the base node. The base node proceeds to the next step if and only if it hears at least one acknowledgement. Otherwise it repeats the current step. Technically, instead of performing, for example, a simple broadcast(RandomGroup,i), the base node makes use of the following code (on the left side):

```
repeat                          |      repeat
  broadcast(RandomGroup,i)      |        broadcast(Write, a, x)
  m = receive()                 |        m = receive()
until m not empty               |      until m not empty
```

With these changes, the probability of selecting exactly one node holds as in Theorem 2.

Input data loading. After the addresses were assigned to nodes but before starting the RAM simulation the input data must be stored into the respective nodes. The base node stores data x to a node with address a using the algorithm from the right side of the previous picture. Upon receiving the respective message, a node with address a stores x in its memory and responds with the OK message.

5 Communication

As mentioned in Section 2, from technological reasons the communication capabilities of the individual nodes are as simple as possible. This, however, complicates the communication issues. For instance, when a node transmits a message, it cannot determine if there are none, one, or several other nodes around which might hear its message. Neither can a node determine if the sent message was successfully received by an other node. In order to transmit a message from one node to other nodes with high probability even under these restrictive conditions the nodes must obey a communication protocol that coordinates the actions of the nodes.

The nodes communicate using broadcasting and each message reaches all other nodes using a so-called *flooding* which works as follows. A message originates in one node and is subsequently transmitted to (potentially) all other nodes of the computer. The algorithm is relatively simple. The first node sends a message which is received by the node's immediate neighbors. These neighbors again send the message so that their neighbors receive it, etc. Note that whenever several nodes share a common neighbor, they should not send the message simultaneously since in such a case the message could not be delivered due to the collisions (cf. item x and xi in Definition 1). In order to minimize the probability of collisions each node sends its message randomly with a fixed probability p and repeatedly during a certain time slot.

The key idea here is that the processors should broadcast a message sporadically in order to prevent message delivery (i.e., broadcast) conflicts, and repeatedly in order to maximize the likelihood of a successful delivery. The analysis of such a protocol reveals that the above mentioned probability p of sending should depend inversely on the expected number of a node's neighbors at that time and should be repeated more times in order to handle the case of more processors in a node's neighborhood (cf. [11]).

The resulting protocol used by the nodes (the base node included) is described by the following code.

```
procedure broadcast(m,k)
  while k <= B
    if random() < p then
        send(m,k+1)
        wait(2T)
    k := k+2
```

In the above procedure, calling `send(m,k+1)` causes one-shot sending of both message m and parameter $k+1$ from the node at hand. Parameter k of `broadcast` procedure keeps track of how many time slots have elapsed, in multiples of T, until the current moment. For the node where the message originates the starting value of k is 0. For other nodes, the current value of k is derived from the corresponding value in the lastly received message. The value of k is incremented by 2 on each time slot. Hencefore, all nodes stop broadcasting when k reaches the value of B which is a global constant known in advance to all nodes of the whole flying amorphous computer. Termination of broadcasting will happen at about the same time; small variations due to different clock speeds are possible.

In fact, the value of B influences how far from the originating node the message will spread. With too small a value, the message will not reach the nodes that are far away from the originating node; with too large a value, the excessive message sending after all nodes have already received the message just wastes time and energy.

We assume that the external operator is able to choose a reasonable value of constant B. This value should take into account the number of nodes and their density in the target area. Asymptotically, the value rises as $O(\sqrt{N})$. In other words, it rises as the distance between the opposite corners of the target area if measured in units of r (the communication radius). The operator can find a reasonable value either by using a computer simulation of the system or by trying out several values on the actual flying amorphous computer.

Theorem 3. *Let all nodes of an amorphous computer be in a quiet state (i.e. not sending anything). Let X be a node that starts broadcasting a message using procedure* `broadcast` *at time t. Then, at time $t+BT(1+\varepsilon_T)$ all nodes are again in a quiet state.*

Proof. The first node runs procedure `broadcast` with parameter k initially equal to 0. Each time through the loop the node waits for time $2T$ and the value of k is increased by 2. So, at most after time $BT(1 + \varepsilon_T)$ the node stops re-sending the message at hand. Transmitting a message takes time T. Therefore, whenever a neighbor node receives a message, value $k+1$ corresponds to the running time of the procedure up to now, and hence also this node ends transmitting after at most $(B - k - 1)(1 + \varepsilon_T)$ time steps. By induction, all nodes terminate their sending activities in time $BT(1 + \varepsilon_T)$.   □

Note that in order to start a new broadcast it is necessary for all nodes to wait until the current broadcast ends. Namely, should a broadcast of two different messages have started simultaneously, then we cannot be sure which of the two messages would be delivered first. Therefore, the end of a current call to broadcast must be known to all nodes.

In order to guarantee the condition of non-concurrent broadcasts after the base node has started broadcasting a message, all other nodes must wait for time $B\varepsilon_T$ to be sure that in total time $B(1 + \varepsilon_T)$ has passed. Only thereafter a node can broadcast another message.

6   Making the Simulation Robust

In practice we can expect that amorphous computers will be deployed outdoors under unfriendly conditions. Clearly, under such a circumstance some nodes of the computer could be destroyed or moved out of reach of other nodes. In such a situation the model just described would not work correctly Therefore we will introduce an improved model which is more robust to accidental damage or removal of nodes.

We will consider two types of damages that can happen. The first type occurs when a node is destroyed or moved away from other nodes and stays forever inaccessible. The second type happens when a node is away for a long time but eventually returns back to the vicinity of other nodes. We would like our model to work under both types of errors.

We expect that during a computation accidental damages only occur with vanishing probability. Nevertheless, if a limited scope damage occurs affecting but a few nodes the robust computer must be able to restart and finish its computation, albeit with some time overhead.

In order to make our amorphous computer robust we must store additional data in its nodes and modify its communication protocol accordingly. Moreover, for restarting the computer a new protocol will be used.

The previous model of amorphous computer made use of such a number of nodes that was sufficient for accommodating the contents of all RAM registers. In order for a robust computer to cope with the fact that some of its nodes could be damaged we will need extra nodes. These spare nodes will be ready to replace the previously damaged nodes. We will also have to back-up the initial data (in another nodes) so that a computation can be restarted even in the case when the original input data are lost.

To that end we will make use of four types of nodes. Bellow we list for each type the data contained in a node of that type:

Memory nodes: they keep the data during a computation. They contain the address of the respective RAM register, data stored in the RAM register, version number and leader version number (the latter two parameters will be described in the sequel).

Base node: this is a single node that controls the computation. It contains a pointer to the address of the current instruction, an accumulator, version number and a leader version number.

Spare nodes which can substitute any damaged node. They contain merely a leader version number plus empty space needed for storing information in the nodes to be replaced.

Backup nodes keeping copies of the RAM registers containing the initial data.

The first three types of nodes containing the leader version numbers are called *potential leaders*. The leader version numbers are unique and in the initialization phase are assigned once for all times to all nodes except of backup nodes. Each of these nodes may become the base node in case when a computation is restarted (see the subsequent explanation). The version number is the leader version number of the current base node.

Each backup node will keep its function permanently for the whole existence of the amorphous computer. Other nodes can switch their type during the lifetime of the amorphous computer.

The overall structure of the operation of a robust amorphous computer will be the same as in the previous non-robust model. First, we perform the initialization step, then the computation, and finally we obtain the result and halt. That is in the case when no error occurs. On the other hand, if there was an error, the computation is stopped, the computer is reorganized and the computation is restarted from its very beginning, this time hopefully running till the very end.

Initialization

At the beginning, all nodes start as spare nodes with their memory zeroed.

Then an external operator connects to the computer. First, the operator starts preparing the data redundancy. Backup nodes are allocated exploiting the address assignment protocol. This protocol assigns addresses 1 to M to M different spare nodes that will then become backup nodes. The input data are stored into these nodes. Then the operator again assigns addresses 1 to M and sets another set of M nodes. This is repeated so that finally there are u different nodes for each address mirroring the same data. The purpose of this is to store the input data in several copies so that the input data can be retrieved even if some of the respective nodes get damaged during a computation.

Next, using the address assignment protocol, the operator assigns to each of the remaining spare nodes a different leader version number (starting from 1). Finally, the operator sends a message to a node with leader version number 1 instructing it to start the computation. This node becomes the current base node.

Computation

Generally, the computation runs in a similar way as in the previous non-robust model, with a few exceptions. We describe the differences in a communication protocol and the new protocols for starting and restarting a computation.

Adjustments to the communication protocol

When the base node tries to read data from some memory node and the reading fails several times (i.e., no acknowledgments are received) it may mean that the target node is damaged or inaccessible. Therefore, a limit on the number of reading attempts to a node must be set (and similarly for writing attempts). This limit should not be too small, because sometimes the communication with a node may fail due to random network conditions. Such conditions can only be temporary, possibly improving in a short time. A good strategy is to set this limit to a much larger value than is the average time of a temporary communication network disconnection. Such a value will depend on various properties of the amorphous computer (like number of nodes, average number of neighbors, movement speed) and can be determined in a simulation of the underlying model under corresponding conditions.

Let's assume we have chosen this limit to be ℓ. When the base node has made ℓ unsuccessful attempts to read data from a node, it will stop operation of all available nodes. This is because nothing else can be done since the computer does not have all the necessary data to complete the current computation. Similarly, if it is the base node that is damaged or removed, the computation will have also to be terminated since without the base node no other node can start any communication by itself. The necessity of restarting a computation is detected by the following mechanism.

All potential leaders monitor each sending activity in the amorphous computer. If time of length $2\ell BT$ (corresponding to ℓ broadcasts) has elapsed since a node lastly had heard any message or a message from the base node, , this particular node deduces that the amorphous computer cannot continue in its current setting any longer and needs to be restarted. To that end the node starts sending message (leader v), where v is the node's leader version number. The semantics of this message is *"the computation lead by the current base node has possibly failed and I am proposing myself to become a new base node with version number v"*. By this, the new leader selection process starts.

Leader election

It is necessary that exactly one leader (acting as the base node in the near future) is selected (with high probability). For this a simple protocol is used whose idea is to choose from among all potential leaders the one with the lowest version number. Such a unique leader always exists thanks to the fact that all of them possess different version numbers.

Therefore, while sending (leader v) message all potential leaders also listen messages sent by other potential leaders. If a potential leader receives a message from another leader with a lower leader version number, this leader stops proposing itself as a leader and stops sending its message while a node with the lower number keeps on sending its message. All other nodes that are not potential leaders forward the message as in normal broadcasting procedure and also these nodes stop sending the old message when they receive a message with a lower leader version number.

This leader announcing process proceeds for time $2\ell BT$. After that time there is a very small probability that more than one node assumes its being a leader. Thus, after time $2\ell BT$ the last remaining active potential leader node makes itself the new leader and starts working according to the steps described below. Note that with a high probability this is a node with the lowest version number from among all "living" nodes. This node will also set internal flag in its memory recording that it is not a potential leader for any later leader selection. This is because a node can become a leader only once since otherwise, when a leader with a lower version number would be selected in some future restart, "forgotten" nodes with the same version number might participate again in the current computation and lead it astray.

Computation start/restart

The leader first discards all the memory nodes remaining from a previous computation. It does so by broadcasting a message (discard) to all nodes. Note that it is not guaranteed that all memory nodes will receive this message, but at least a large part of them will. The memory nodes that receive the discard message change their type to spare node.

Then, the leader has to select new nodes that will act as memory nodes for the new computation. The leader uses the address assignment algorithm, assigning addresses 1 to N to N different spare nodes. Each spare node after receiving an address changes its type to memory node. The address has two components—a version number and an actual address. The version number is the unique leader version number and the leader will broadcast it as a part of all its messages.

Next, the leader copies initial data to the first M memory nodes from the backup nodes (we assume $M \leq N$). It does it by first sending (read,backup:a) message to read contents of memory with address a from a backup node. If at least one backup node for that address is available, the read will be successfull. The leader than sends (write,v:a,x) message (where v is the version number component of the address) to assign the value x to memory node with address a.

Finally, the leader becomes the base node. The new base node runs the computation in a standard way. If no error occurs the computation finishes by executing the *HALT* instruction.

Note that it is necessary to send in each message the version number because it is possible that some memory node from some past computation has not received the inactivating message. Such a node must not participate in a later computation. This is achieved thanks to the fact that nodes only respond to messages having the same version as the node's own address.

Theorem 4. *If there are enough backup nodes to recover the initial configuration and there are enough spare nodes for running the computation and from this time on no node is damaged then the computer eventually finishes its computation successfully.*

Robustness Analysis

The computation of the amorphous computer is influenced by randomly occuring damaging events. As a result the number of restarts that happen during the computation is a random variable. A computation can either finish successfully with some probability or fail. This leads to a geometric distribution for the number of restarts.

Theorem 5. *Let T_1 be the average time needed by the amorphous computer to finish a computation in case that no damaging event occurs. Let p_e be the probability that a damaging event occurs within time T_1. Assume the damaging events are independent. The expected number of restarts of the amorphous computer is $1/(1 - p_e) - 1$.*

Proof sketch: The number of restarts follows a geometric distribution (number of unsuccessful trials before the first success) with success rate $1 - p_e$. $\quad\square$

This shows that the amorphous computer can finish only if the probability of failures is low, which is exactly the case in which we wanted the computer to work. Obviously, in case of permanently occurring damages this model of amorphous computer would never finish its computation.

Now let's look at how well the backup nodes can survive the damaging events.

Theorem 6. *Let the backup nodes of an amorphous computer contain M addresses, each in u copies. Let each node be damaged during time T_1 with probability p_d. The probability that for address a after time hT_1 the input data cannot be recovered is $p_1 = (1 - (1 - p_d)^h)^u$. The probability that data from some address cannot be recovered is $1 - (1 - p_1)^M$.*

Proof sketch: After time hT_1 the probability that a node is not damaged is $p_{node} = (1 - p_d)^h$. The probability that a complete set of u nodes is damaged is $p_1 = (1 - p_{node})^u$. Of the M sets the probability that none of them is completely damaged is $(1 - p_1)^M$. The complement, i.e. the probability that at least one set is completely damaged, is $1 - (1 - p_1)^M$. $\quad\square$

7   Conclusion

A unique property of every amorphous computer is that its nodes are all structurally identical. Therefore, in case when some nodes are damaged or become inaccessible other nodes can take over the function of the damaged ones. This enables the whole computer to carry out a computation robustly in a possibly harsh working environment. We have shown how to implement these features — mainly how to store data redundantly in the backup nodes and how to perform a reset of the computer after a vital node was damaged. As a result, we have shown a computational universality and robustness of our model of flying amorphous computer.

An unusual feature of our simulation algorithm is its time complexity estimation in terms of finite time. This is due to the unpredictability of the communication paths formation. Interestingly, real computer simulations have revealed that within a flying amorphous computer a message is delivered to all nodes quite efficiently, in a wide range of velocities of node movements and parameters of the broadcast algorithm [4]. The simulations have also confirmed intuition that there is a tradeoff between the amount of nodes' mixing in a flying amorphous computer and the frequency of message repetition sendings in the broadcast protocol.

More research is needed in order to better understand and exploit the respective phenomena. In particular, a more efficient algorithm for recovering from a failed computation might exist. Our results present but the first steps in this direction.

References

1. Aho, A.V., Hopcroft, J.E., Ullman, J.D.: The Design and Analysis of Computer Algorithms, Reading. Addison-Wesley, MA (1974)
2. Hoyle, F.: The Black Cloud. Penguin Books, 219 p. (1957)
3. Kurzweil R.: The Singularity is Near. Viking Books, 652 pages (2005)
4. Petrů, L.: Universality in Amorphous Computing. PhD Dissertation Thesis, Dept. of Math. and Physics, Charles University, Prague (2009)
5. Petrů, L., Wiedermann, J.: A Model of an Amorphous Computer and Its Communication Protocol. In: van Leeuwen, J., Italiano, G.F., van der Hoek, W., Meinel, C., Sack, H., Plášil, F. (eds.) SOFSEM 2007. LNCS, vol. 4362, pp. 446–455. Springer, Heidelberg (2007)
6. Petrū, L., Wiedermann, J.: A Universal Flying Amorphous Computer. In: Calude, C.S., Kari, J., Petre, I., Rozenberg, G. (eds.) UC 2011. LNCS, vol. 6714, pp. 189–200. Springer, Heidelberg (2011)
7. Petů, L., Wiedermann, J..: Flying Amorphous Computer: A Robust Model. Technical report No. 1173, Institute of Computer Science, Academy of Sciences of the Czech Republic (December 2012)
8. Vinge, V.: A Deepness in the Sky. Tor Books, 800 p. (January 2000)
9. Wiedermann, J., Petru, L.: Computability in Amorphous Structures. In: Cooper, S.B., Löwe, B., Sorbi, A. (eds.) CiE 2007. LNCS, vol. 4497, pp. 781–790. Springer, Heidelberg (2007)
10. Wiedermann, J., Petrů, L.: Communicating Mobile Nano-Machines and Their Computational Power. In: Cheng, M. (ed.) NanoNet 2008. LNICST, vol. 3, pp. 123–130. Springer, Heidelberg (2009)
11. Wiedermann, J., Petrů, L.: On the Universal Computing Power of Amorphous Computing Systems. Theory of Computing Systems 46(4), 995–1010 (2009)
12. Wiedermann, J.: Nanomachine Computing by Quorum Sensing. In: Kelemen, J., Kelemenová, A. (eds.) Computation, Cooperation, and Life. LNCS, vol. 6610, pp. 203–215. Springer, Heidelberg (2011)
13. Wiedermann, J.: Amorphous Computing: A Research Agenda for the Near Future. Natural Computing 11(1), 59–63 (2012)
14. Wiedermann, J.: Computability and Non-computability Issues in Amorphous Computing. In: Baeten, J.C.M., Ball, T., de Boer, F.S. (eds.) TCS 2012. LNCS, vol. 7604, pp. 1–9. Springer, Heidelberg (2012)
15. Wiedermann, J.: The many forms of amorphous computational systems. In: H. Zenil (Ed.): A Computable Universe. Understanding Computation and Exploring Nature As Computation, p. 243–256. World Scientific, Singapore (2013)

Minimal Reaction Systems Defining Subset Functions

Arto Salomaa[⊠]

Turku Centre for Computer Science,
Joukahaisenkatu 3–5 B, 20520 Turku, Finland
asalomaa@utu.fi

Abstract. In *reaction systems* introduced by Ehrenfeucht and Rozenberg the number of resources is essential when various questions concerning generative capacity are investigated. While almost all functions from the set of subsets of a finite set S into itself can be defined by unrestricted reaction systems, only a specific subclass of such functions is defined by minimal reaction systems. In this paper we show that also minimal reaction systems suffice for defining all such functions, provided repetitive use is allowed. Specifically, everything generated by an arbitrary reaction system is generated by a minimal one in three steps. In this way also some functions not at all definable by reaction systems can be generated by minimal reaction systems. All subsets of S, in any prechosen order, appear in the sequence of a minimal reaction system.

Keywords: Reaction system · Reactant · Inhibitor · Universality of minimal resources · Subset function · Sequence

1 Introduction

Reaction systems introduced by Ehrenfeucht and Rozenberg, [4], constitute an interesting new model of computation. While originally motivated by applications to certain biochemical reactions, reaction systems have turned out to be suitable in many other, very diverse, setups. The reference [1] gives some idea of the various possibilities. However, the very active research in this area opens frequently new vistas. We refer to [5] for quite new developments.

Apart from various applications, reaction systems as such have been objected to many theoretical studies, [2,3,6,10–14]. The arising problems are mathematically very interesting, since the model is simple and clean. Additional interest is provided by the fact that reaction systems constitute a tool for investigating *subset functions*, that is, functions mapping the set 2^S of subsets of a finite set S into 2^S. Composition theory of subset functions is not understood in the same sense as that of functions from S to S, see for instance [8,9].

A reaction system consists of a finite number of *reactions*. Each reaction is characterized by its set of *reactants*, each of which has to be present for the reaction to take place, by its set of *inhibitors*, none of which is allowed to be

© Springer International Publishing Switzerland 2014
C.S. Calude et al. (Eds.): Gruska Festschrift, LNCS 8808, pp. 436–446, 2014.
DOI: 10.1007/978-3-319-13350-8_32

present, and by its set of *products*, each of which will be present after a successful reaction. Thus, a single reaction is based on facilitation and inhibition.

Everything happens within a fixed finite *background set* S. The sets of reactants, inhibitors and products, R, I and P, are nonempty subsets of S, the sets R and I being disjoint. A *reaction system* $\mathcal{A}$ consists of finitely many such triples (R, I, P), called *reactions*. The application of $\mathcal{A}$ to a subset T of S (to be explained in detail below) produces another subset T' of S and, thus, we have a *subset function*, that is, a function from subsets of S to subsets of S. Iterating the function we get a *sequence* of subsets of S. As a result, we have a new kind of mechanism for generating functions and sequences over a finite set.

We already emphasized that the model of reaction systems is suitable in a large variety of different setups, and the possibilities are by far not exhausted. Since this paper deals exclusively with the mathematical properties of the basic model, we do not go further into this more general aspect of reaction systems.

A brief outline of the contents of the paper follows. The paper is largely self-contained. The next two sections provide the necessary background by giving the formal definitions of the notions needed, as well as reviewing some earlier work, in particular work concerning the limitations of *minimal* reaction systems. Section 4 presents a method of enhancing minimal reaction systems beyond these limitations. Using this method, any subset function definable by any reaction system can be defined by a minimal one. In Section 5 the results are extended further to concern all subset functions, also ones not at all definable by reaction systems. A case study is also presented. Applications to sequences and cycles are discussed in Section 6. The final section presents a summary and possible research topics.

2   Reaction Systems and Functions Defined

We will now give the formal definitions of the basic notions. We begin with the central notion of a reaction system, as well as related operational notions.

Definition 1. *A reaction over the finite background set S is a triple*

$$\rho = (R, I, P),$$

where R, I and P are nonempty subsets of S such that R and I do not intersect. The three sets are referred as reactants, inhibitors *and* products, *respectively. A reaction system $\mathcal{A}_S$ over the base set S is a finite nonempty set*

$$\mathcal{A}_S = \{\rho_i \mid 1 \leq i \leq k\},$$

of reactions over S.

No specific assumptions are made about the set P. In particular, it may or may not contain elements of $R \cup I$. In this paper S will always denote the background set. We usually denote its elements by natural numbers or small letters from the beginning of the English alphabet. The *cardinality* of a finite set X is denoted by $\sharp X$. The *empty set* is denoted by $\emptyset$.

We will omit the index S from $\mathcal{A}_S$ whenever S is understood. We now come to the central definitions dealing with *functions* defined by reaction systems.

Definition 2. *Consider a reaction $\rho = (R, I, P)$ over S and a subset T of S. The set T is* enabled *(with respect to ρ), in symbols $en_\rho(T)$, if $R \subseteq T$ and $I \cap T = \emptyset$. If T is (resp. is not) enabled, then we define the* result *by*

$$res_\rho(T) = P \text{ (resp. } = \emptyset).$$

For a reaction system $\mathcal{A} = \{\rho_j \mid 1 \le j \le k\}$, we define the result by

$$res_{\mathcal{A}}(T) = \bigcup_{j=1}^{k} res_{\rho_j}(T).$$

The result is also called the function defined by the reaction system *and denoted $F_{\mathcal{A}}$.*

Thus, the range and domain of the function $F_{\mathcal{A}}$ are subsets of 2^S. Informally, the term "subset function" is used for such functions.

There are some minor terminological differences in the literature. Rather than subset functions, the reference [3] considers functions from S into S. Special attention to the function value $\emptyset$ is paid in the reference [11].

As an example, let $\mathcal{A}$ be a reaction system over the background set $\{1, 2, 3\}$, consisting of the three reactions

$$\rho_1 = (\{1, 2\}, \{3\}, \{1, 3\}), \quad \rho_2 = (\{2\}, \{3\}, \{2\}), \quad \rho_3 = (\{1\}, \{2\}, \{1, 3\}).$$

Consider $T = \{1, 2\}$. Then $en_{\rho_1}(T)$ and $en_{\rho_2}(T)$, whereas $en_{\rho_3}(T)$ does not hold. Consequently,

$$res_{\rho_3}(T) = \emptyset, \quad res_{\rho_1}(T) = \{1, 3\}, \quad res_{\rho_2}(T) = \{2\}, \quad res_{\mathcal{A}}(T) = \{1, 2, 3\}.$$

Definition 2 exhibits an important feature of reaction systems. Whenever an element is in a set, it is considered to be there always when needed. Thus, the element 2 of T is not "consumed" in the application of the reaction ρ_1 but is also available for ρ_2 when $res_{\mathcal{A}}(T)$ is computed. In this sense there is no "conflict" between ρ_1 and ρ_2. This feature makes reaction systems different from many other models of computation.

The function $F_{\mathcal{A}}$ defined by the reaction system $\mathcal{A}$ satisfies

$$F_{\mathcal{A}}\{1\} = \{1, 3\}, \quad F_{\mathcal{A}}\{2\} = \{2\}, \quad F_{\mathcal{A}}\{1, 2\} = \{1, 2, 3\},$$
$$F_{\mathcal{A}}\{1, 3\} = \{1, 3\}, \quad F_{\mathcal{A}}\{3\} = F_{\mathcal{A}}\{2, 3\} = \emptyset.$$

3   Resources in Reaction Systems. Sequences

Elements in the set $R \cup I$ are referred to as *resources*. Reaction systems are classified according to the maximal cardinalities of the sets of reactants and inhibitors, and also according to the cardinality of the set of resources.

Definition 3. *A reaction system $\mathcal{A}$ is a (k, l) system if the conditions $\sharp(R) \leq k$ and $\sharp(I) \leq l$ are satisfied for every reaction (R, I, P) in $\mathcal{A}$. A reaction system is minimal (resp. almost minimal if in every reaction the cardinality of the set of resources equals 2 (resp. is at most 3).*

Thus, minimal reaction systems are always $(1, 1)$ systems, whereas almost minimal reaction systems can be either $(2, 1)$ or $(1, 2)$ systems. Almost minimal reaction systems will not be considered in this paper.

For any $\mathcal{A}$ and T, the result $res_\mathcal{A}(T)$ is always a unique subset T' of S. If $res_\mathcal{A}(T) = T'$, we use the notation

$$T \Rightarrow_\mathcal{A} T',$$

or simply $T \Rightarrow T'$ if $\mathcal{A}$ is understood. If

$$res_\mathcal{A}(T_i) = T_{i+1}, \ 0 \leq i \leq m - 1,$$

we write

$$T_0 \Rightarrow T_1 \Rightarrow \ldots \Rightarrow T_m$$

and call $T_0, T_1, \ldots, T_m$ the *sequence* of *length* m generated (or defined) by the reaction system $\mathcal{A}$. Sometimes the sets T_i are referred to as *states* and the sequence itself as a *state sequence*.

Since $res_\mathcal{A}(T)$ is uniquely determined by T, and since there are only $2^{\sharp S}$ subsets of S, one of the following two alternatives always occurs, for large enough m, for sequences

$$T_0 \Rightarrow T_1 \Rightarrow \ldots \Rightarrow T_m.$$

1. $T_m = \emptyset$. Then we say that the sequence is a *terminating sequence* of length m. In this case $en_\rho(T_{m-1})$ holds for no reaction ρ in $\mathcal{A}$.
2. $T_m = T_{m_1}$, for some $m_1 < m$. In this case we say that the sequence has (or ends with) a *cycle* of length $m - m_1$.

While sequences of arbitrary length can be generated by unrestricted reaction systems, there are several results concerning long sequences and cycles generated by minimal reaction systems, [3, 11–13]. For instance, consider the minimal reaction system with the background set $S = \{1, 2, 3\}$ and reactions

$$(\{1\}, \{2\}, \{3\}), \ (\{1\}, \{3\}, \{1\}), \ (\{2\}, \{3\}, \{1\}),$$
$$(\{2\}, \{1\}, \{2\}), \ (\{3\}, \{1\}, \{2\}), \ (\{3\}, \{2\}, \{3\}).$$

We obtain the cycle

$$\{1\} \Rightarrow \{1, 3\} \Rightarrow \{3\} \Rightarrow \{2, 3\} \Rightarrow \{2\} \Rightarrow \{1, 2\} \Rightarrow \{1\}$$

of maximal length $2^{\#S} - 2$.

We conclude this section with a characterization due to [2] of functions definable by minimal reaction systems. The characterization is based on the following definition.

Definition 4. *A function f is*

- *union-subadditive if $f(X \cup Y) \subseteq f(X) \cup f(Y)$,*
- *intersection-subadditive if $f(X \cap Y) \subseteq f(X) \cup f(Y)$,*
- *for all subsets X and Y of S.*

We are now ready to state the characterization result given in [2].

Theorem 1. *A function F_A defined by a reaction system A is definable by a $(1,1)$ reaction system if and only if F_A is both union-subadditive and intersection-subadditive.*

The characterization given in Theorem 1 is exhaustive. However, since the two conditions needed seem rather hard to test computationally, it is not clear whether Theorem 1 simplifies the problem of deciding whether or not a given reaction system is equivalent to a minimal one. (Two reaction systems are termed *equivalent* if they define the same function.) The equivalence problem is clearly decidable but no simple algorithm for it is known.

4   Universality of Minimal Reaction Systems

We will now prove that, in spite of the restrictions due to Theorem 1, the value of the function defined by an arbitrary reaction system can be obtained as the third step in the sequence of a minimal reaction system. This shows that minimal reaction systems are, in fact, very powerful.

We want to connect this study with the study of subset functions. Thus, we consider subsets of a given background set S. Various cases arise, depending on whether all subsets, all nonempty subsets, or all proper nonempty subsets are taken into account. We will use the notations.

$$Z = 2^S, \ Z_1 = 2^S - \{\emptyset\}, \ Z_2 = 2^S - \{S, \emptyset\}.$$

(Since we are dealing with a fixed background set S, we use the simple notation Z rather than $Z(S)$.) The cardinalities of the three sets Z, Z_1, Z_2 are $2^{\#(S)}, 2^{\#(S)} - 1, 2^{\#(S)} - 2$, respectively.

Observe that the domain of the function defined by a reaction system can never include S or $\emptyset$. Otherwise, everything can be obtained. The following theorem is a reformulation of a result in [10].

Theorem 2. *Let G be a mapping of Z_2 into Z. Then there is a reaction system A_G such that, for all $x \in Z_2$,*

$$F_{A_G}(x) = G(x).$$

Proof. The reactions in the reaction system $\mathcal{A}_G$ (with the background set S) are:

$$(x, S - x, G(x)), \ x \in Z_2,$$

where $x \in Z_2$ is arbitrary satisfying the condition $G(x) \neq \emptyset$. (If $G(x) = \emptyset$, we cannot include the corresponding reaction since, by definition, the product set in a reaction is always nonempty.) Each reaction is enabled only for x, so the theorem follows. The conclusion holds also if $G(x) = \emptyset$, since in this case no reaction is enabled for x. $\square$

We are now ready to establish the main result. The idea is to extend the background set and define the reactions in such a way that every third state in the generated sequence, starting with a subset of the original background set S, contains only elements of S, whereas the other states contain no elements of S. The idea of using the *names of the reactions* as elements of the extended background set is due to [6]. Another nice idea is to use the names of the subsets of S, [7].

Theorem 3. *For any reaction system $\mathcal{A}$ (over the background set S), there is a minimal reaction system $\mathcal{A}_M$ (with a background set containing S) such that, for all $x \in Z_2$*

$$F_{\mathcal{A}}(x) = F^3_{\mathcal{A}_M}(x).$$

Thus, the function value $F_{\mathcal{A}}(x)$ appears as the third step in the sequence of $\mathcal{A}_M$ starting with x.

Proof. Assume that the reactions in the given reaction system $\mathcal{A}$ are

$$\rho_i = (R_i, I_i, P_i), \ 1 \leq i \leq k.$$

Define $\overline{S} = \{\overline{a} | a \in S\}$. (Thus, we consider "barred versions" of the elements in S.) The background set of $\mathcal{A}_M$ is defined to be

$$S \cup \overline{S} \cup \{\rho_1, \ldots, \rho_k\} \cup \{B, \$, E\}.$$

Consider now an arbitrary $a \in S$. Then all of the following are reactions in $\mathcal{A}_M$.

1. $(\{a\}, \{\$\}, \{\overline{a}, B\})$.
2. Let $\rho^a_{i_1}, \ldots, \rho^a_{i_{m(a)}}$ be all the reactions in $\mathcal{A}$ such that $a \in R_{i_t}$, for every t, $1 \leq t \leq m(a)$. If $m(a) \geq 1$, we include in $\mathcal{A}_M$ the reaction

$$(\{B\}, \{\overline{a}\}, \{\rho^a_{i_1}, \ldots, \rho^a_{i_{m(a)}}\}).$$

(If $m(a) = 0$, no reaction results from this point.)
3. Let $\rho^a_{j_1}, \ldots, \rho^a_{j_{n(a)}}$ be all the reactions in $\mathcal{A}$ such that $a \in I_{j_t}$, for every t, $1 \leq t \leq n(a)$. If $n(a) \geq 1$, we include in $\mathcal{A}_M$ the reaction

$$(\{\overline{a}\}, \{\$\}, \{\rho^a_{j_1}, \ldots, \rho^a_{j_{n(a)}}\}).$$

(If $n(a) = 0$, no reaction results from this point.)

4. $(\{B\}, \{\$\}, \{E\})$.
5. $(\{E\}, \{\rho_i\}, \{P_i\})$, $1 \leq i \leq k$.

Clearly, $\mathcal{A}_M$ is a minimal reaction system. Consider a sequence of $\mathcal{A}_M$ beginning with $x \in Z_2$. Only the reactions in point 1 are enabled. Consequently, the barred versions of the elements in x, as well as the element B constitute the first step in the sequence. Then reactions in points 2 and 3 produce the (names of the) reactions that are *not* enabled for x in $\mathcal{A}$. Besides, the element E is always produced by the reaction in point 4. Thus, the second step of the sequence consists of E and the names of the reactions *not* enabled for x in $\mathcal{A}$. This means that exactly the names of the reactions enabled in $\mathcal{A}$ for x miss the second step and, consequently, the reactions in point 5 produce the result $F_{\mathcal{A}}(x)$ to the third step. This holds true also in case $F_{\mathcal{A}}(x) = \emptyset$. □

Theorems 2 and 3 yield immediately the following result.

Corollary 1. *Let G be a mapping of Z_2 into Z. There is a minimal reaction system $\mathcal{A}_G$ such that, for all $x \in Z_2$*

$$G(x) = F^3_{\mathcal{A}_G}(x).$$

Thus, the function value $G(x)$ appears as the third step in the sequence of $\mathcal{A}_G$, starting with x.

The proof of Theorem 3 shows that the background set and the set of reactions grow only linearly in the transition from $\mathcal{A}$ to $\mathcal{A}_M$.

Corollary 2. *Let $\mathcal{A}$ and $\mathcal{A}_M$ be as in Theorem 3, and let $\mathcal{A}$ consist of $k \geq 1$ reactions. Then the cardinality of the background set (resp. the set of reactions) of $\mathcal{A}_M$ is at most $2 \cdot (\sharp(S)) + k + 3$ (resp. $3 \cdot (\sharp(S)) + k + 1$).*

5   Generalizations to Subset Functions

We now consider arbitrary subset functions, that is, arbitrary mappings 0f Z into Z. (As before, the background set S defining Z is given.) In particular, we study possible generalizations of Corollary 1. Clearly, if we work with reaction systems, then the argument value $\emptyset$ always maps to $\emptyset$. Consequently, Corollary 1 can be extended only to concern mappings of Z_1 into Z. This will be accomplished in the following theorem, formulated in analogy of Corollary 1.

Theorem 4. *Let G be a mapping of Z_1 into Z. There is a minimal reaction system $\mathcal{A}_G$ such that, for all $x \in Z_1$*

$$G(x) = F^3_{\mathcal{A}_G}(x).$$

Thus, the function value $G(x)$ appears as the third step in the sequence of $\mathcal{A}_G$, starting with x.

Proof. We follow the proof of Theorem 3. We have to take care of the case, where the whole background set S appears as an argument of the function G. Assume first that $G(S) = \emptyset$. Then the proof of Theorem 3 works without any changes. The second state of the sequence of $\mathcal{A}_M$, starting with S, is $\{E, \rho_1, \ldots, \rho_k\}$. Thus, none of the reactions in point 5 is enabled. This yields the third state $\emptyset$.

Assume, secondly, that $G(S) = x \neq \emptyset$. In this case we make the following additions to the reaction system $\mathcal{A}_M$. The element ρ_S is added to the background set of $\mathcal{A}_M$. For every element $a \in S$, the element ρ_S is added to the product set of each reaction in point 2. (The reactions in point 3 are left unchanged.) Finally, the reaction $(\{E\}, \{\rho_S\}, x)$ is added to the reactions in $\mathcal{A}_M$. Denote by $\mathcal{A}_G$. the minimal reaction system thus obtained.

It is now easy to verify that

$$G(S) = F^3_{\mathcal{A}_G}(S) = x,$$

whereas

$$F^3_{\mathcal{A}_G}(y) = F^3_{\mathcal{A}_M}(y),$$

for all proper subsets y of S. Indeed, the second state of the sequence of $\mathcal{A}_G$ does not contain the element ρ_S exactly in case the initial state equals S. Consequently, only in this case the reaction $(\{E\}, \{\rho_S\}, x)$ is enabled. $\square$

As a case study implementing the techniques we now consider the background set $S = \{a, b, c\}$ and the mapping G of Z_1 into Z, defined by

x	$\{a\}$	$\{b\}$	$\{c\}$	$\{a,b\}$	$\{a,c\}$	$\{b,c\}$	$\{a,b,c\}$
$G(x)$	$\emptyset$	$\{a,b,c\}$	$\{a,c\}$	$\emptyset$	$\{b\}$	$\{a,b\}$	$\{a,b\}$

We now define the minimal reaction system $\mathcal{A}_G$ as in Theorem 4. The reactions resulting from Theorem 2 are in this case

$$\rho_1 = (\{a,c\}, \{b\}, \{b\}), \quad \rho_2 = (\{b,c\}, \{a\}, \{a,b\}),$$
$$\rho_3 = (\{b\}, \{a,c\}, \{a,b,c\}), \quad \rho_4 = (\{c\}, \{a,b\}, \{a,c\}).$$

They are mentioned here to ease understanding; only their names ρ_j, $1 \leq j \leq 4$, are used in the sequel.

The minimal reaction system $\mathcal{A}_G$ has the background set

$$\{a, b, c, \bar{a}, \bar{b}, \bar{c}, \rho_1, \rho_2, \rho_3, \rho_4, \rho_S, B, \$, E\}$$

and reactions

$$(\{a\}, \{B\}, \{\bar{a}, B\}), \ (\{b\}, \{B\}, \{\bar{b}, B\}), \ (\{c\}, \{B\}, \{\bar{c}, B\}),$$
$$(\{\bar{a}\}, \{\$\}, \{\rho_2, \rho_3, \rho_4\}), \ (\{\bar{b}\}, \{\$\}, \{\rho_1, \rho_4\}), \ (\{\bar{c}\}, \{\$\}, \{\rho_3\}),$$
$$(\{B\}, \{\bar{a}\}, \{\rho_1, \rho_S\}), \ (\{B\}, \{\bar{b}\}, \{\rho_2, \rho_3, \rho_S\}), \ (\{B\}, \{\bar{c}\}, \{\rho_1, \rho_2, \rho_4, \rho_S\}),$$
$$(\{E\}, \{\rho_1\}, \{b\}), \ (\{E\}, \{\rho_2\}, \{a,b\}), \ (\{E\}, \{\rho_3\}, \{a,b,c\}),$$
$$(\{E\}, \{\rho_4\}, \{a,c\}), \ (\{E\}, \{\rho_S\}, \{a,b\}), \ (\{B\}, \{\$\}, \{E\}).$$

The first three steps in the sequence of $\mathcal{A}_G$ are listed below, for the 7 possible initial states.

$$\{a,b,c\} \Rightarrow \{\bar{a},\bar{b},\bar{c},B\} \Rightarrow \{\rho_1,\rho_2,\rho_3,\rho_4,E\} \Rightarrow \{a,b\}$$
$$\{a,b\} \Rightarrow \{\bar{a},\bar{b},B\} \Rightarrow \{\rho_1,\rho_2,\rho_3,\rho_4,\rho_S,E\} \Rightarrow \emptyset$$
$$\{a,c\} \Rightarrow \{\bar{a},\bar{c},B\} \Rightarrow \{\rho_2,\rho_3,\rho_4,\rho_S,E\} \Rightarrow \{b\}$$
$$\{b,c\} \Rightarrow \{\bar{b},\bar{c},B\} \Rightarrow \{\rho_1,\rho_2,\rho_4,\rho_S,E\} \Rightarrow \{a,b\}$$
$$\{a\} \Rightarrow \{\bar{a},B\} \Rightarrow \{\rho_1,\rho_2,\rho_3,\rho_4,\rho_S,E\} \Rightarrow \emptyset$$
$$\{b\} \Rightarrow \{\bar{b},B\} \Rightarrow \{\rho_1,\rho_2,\rho_4,\rho_S,E\} \Rightarrow \{a,b,c\}$$
$$\{c\} \Rightarrow \{\bar{c},B\} \Rightarrow \{\rho_1,\rho_2,\rho_3,\rho_S,E\} \Rightarrow \{a,c\}$$

In each case the function value $G(x)$ appears as the third state.

6   Minimal Reaction Systems Generating Long Sequences and Cycles

The construction discussed above can be applied repetitively. Consider an arbitrary listing of all subsets of S, ending with the empty set:

$$x_1, x_2, \ldots, x_{2^{\#S}} = \emptyset.$$

Using our earlier notation, the listing defines a mapping G of Z_1 onto Z:

$$G(x_j) = x_{j+1}, \ 1 \leq j \leq 2^{\#S} - 1, \ G(\emptyset) = \emptyset.$$

Consider now the *sequence* of the minimal reaction system $\mathcal{A}_G$ defined in Theorem 4, starting with x_1. The third state in the sequence is x_2, the sixth state x_3, and so forth. Altogether we obtain a terminating sequence of length $3 \cdot 2^{\#S}$, where all nonempty subsets of S appear in an arbitrary pre-chosen order at every third step of the sequence. The other steps contain no elements of S.

Consider next an arbitrary listing $y_1, \ldots, y_{2^{\#S}-1}$ of all nonempty subsets of S. We obtain now a mapping G of Z_1 onto Z_1 by

$$G(y_j) = y_{j+1}, \ 1 \leq j \leq 2^{\#S} - 2, \ G(y_{2^{\#S}-1}) = y_1.$$

Consider again the reaction system $\mathcal{A}_G$. Its sequence is a *cycle* of length $3 \cdot (2^{\#S-1})$. Again, all nonempty subsets of S appear at every third step in the cycle, in the arbitrary pre-chosen order, whereas the other steps contain no elements of S.

Altogether we have established the following theorem

Theorem 5. *Consider any ordering of all the $2^{\#S} - 1$ nonempty subsets of the background set S. Then there is a minimal reaction system (whose background set contains S) such that its sequence is a cycle of length $3 \cdot (2^{\#S} - 1)$, where every third state consists of the nonempty subsets of S in the chosen order, and the other states do not contain any elements of S. Add next $\emptyset$ to the end of* *the chosen ordering of nonempty subsets of S. Then there is a minimal reaction system with a terminating sequence of length $2^{\sharp S}$, where where every third state consists of the nonempty subsets of S in the chosen order, and the other states do not contain any elements of S.*

Theorem 5 improves the known results concerning long sequences and cycles of minimal reaction systems only in some special cases. This is due to the fact the background sets of the reaction systems $\mathcal{A}_M$ and $\mathcal{A}_G$ depend on the number k of reactions in the basic reaction system $\mathcal{A}$. Indeed, the cardinality of the background set of the reaction system $\mathcal{A}_G$ in Theorem 4 is at most $2 \cdot (\sharp S) + k + 4$, and $\mathcal{A}_G$ consists of at most $3 \cdot (\sharp S) + k + 2$ reactions. In the case study at the end of the preceding section we have $\sharp S = 3$ and $k = 4$, giving 14 background elements and 15 reactions.

7   Conclusion

Minimal reaction systems constitute mathematically a very natural object. However, their capabilities are limited in comparison with arbitrary reaction systems. The capabilities can be enhanced using an arbitrary sequence of inputs from the "environment", [4,10]. We have shown in this paper that minimal reaction systems can be enhanced to cover the capabilities of arbitrary reaction systems, and even more generally arbitrary subset functions, without any additional inputs by considering every third step in the state sequence. Because of Corollary 2, the approach is pleasing from the point of view of complexity.

An interesting problem area consists in trying to modify this method, or perhaps in finding other ways of enhancement. The problems are linked with characterizations of almost minimal reaction systems, and comparisons between minimal, almost minimal, and arbitrary reaction systems.

References

1. Brijder, R., Ehrenfeucht, A., Main, M., Rozenberg, G.: A tour of reaction systems. International Journal of Foundations of Computer Science **22**, 1499–1517 (2011)
2. Ehrenfeucht, A., Kleijn, J., Koutny, M., Rozenberg, G.: Minimal reaction systems. In: Priami, C., Petre, I., de Vink, E. (eds.) Transactions on Computational Systems Biology XIV. LNCS, vol. 7625, pp. 102–122. Springer, Heidelberg (2012)
3. Ehrenfeucht, A., Main, M., Rozenberg, G.: Functions defined by reaction systems. International Journal of Foundations of Computer Science **22**, 167–178 (2011)
4. Ehrenfeucht, A., Rozenberg, G.: Reaction systems. Fundamenta Informaticae **7**, 263–280 (2007)
5. Ehrenfeucht, A., Rozenberg, G.: Zoom structures and reaction systems yield exploration systems. International Journal of Foundations of Computer Science (to appear, 2014)
6. Formenti, E., Manzoni, L., Porreca, A.E.: On the complexity of occurrence and convergence problems for reaction systems. Natural Computing (to appear, 2014)
7. Montagna, F., Rozenberg, G.: On minimal reaction systems, forthcoming. (G. Rozenberg, personal communication.)

8. Piccard, S.: Sur les bases du groupe symétrique et les couples de substitutions qui engendrent un goupe régulier. Librairie Vuibert, Paris (1946)
9. Salomaa, A.: Composition sequences for functions over a finite domain. Theoretical Computer Science **292**, 263–281 (2003)
10. Salomaa, A.: On state sequences defined by reaction systems. In: Constable, R.L., Silva, A. (eds.) Logic and Program Semantics, Kozen Festschrift. LNCS, vol. 7230, pp. 271–282. Springer, Heidelberg (2012)
11. Salomaa, A.: Functions and sequences generated by reaction systems. Theoretical Computer Science **466**, 87–96 (2012)
12. Salomaa, A.: Functional constructions between reaction systems and propositional logic. International Journal of Foundations of Computer Science **24**, 147–159 (2013)
13. Salomaa, A.: Minimal and almost minimal reaction systems. Natural Computing **12**, 369–376 (2013)
14. Salomaa, A.: Compositions of reaction systems. Submitted for publication (2013)

History and Philosophy of Computing

Grand Challenges of Informatics

Jozef Gruska$^{(\boxtimes)}$

Faculty of Informatics, Masaryk University, Brno, Czech Republic
gruska@fi.muni.cz

Abstract. A view on grand challenges of broadly understood Informatics is presented and its importance for two mega-challenges of the science and technology is discussed.

1 Prologue

One way to get a good, motivating and inspiring understanding of the current state and potential of the science and technology in general, or of a their specific area in particular, is to try to determine their (current) grand challenges.[1]

This is important for several reasons. First of all, a good vision of grand challenges allows to specify short and long term research goals. Grand challenges make the research community worldwide to work together to meet them, and in this way accelerate the overall scientific and technological progress. In addition, grand challenges guide not only researchers, but also the science and technology supporting agencies.[2] Grand challenges are important also for education.

Intensively cooperating research initiatives create the potential for attacking successfully very broadly and ambitiously formulated challenges that are outside of the potential of individuals and also of the small-scale or even national research efforts. This starts to be well understood, in spite of the validity of the observation, captured well by the so called *black swan principle*, that a big portion of the progress in general and in science and technology in particular, is due to the impacts of highly improbable and unpredictable discoveries or events.

In order to meet the above goals and to identify important and reachable grand challenges, an area of science or technology needs to be perceived sufficiently deeply and broadly.

We present a *new* perception of Informatics, derived from the overall developments in sciences and technologies and in (especially nature-driven) information

---

[1] Historically, grand challenges used to be seen those problems that had resisted for long time to concentrated attempts to solve them and, in addition, they were expected to have, once solved, far-reaching consequences. However, due to the more and more important role science and technology play in the society, it is desirable to see grand challenges in much broader and more forward oriented ways and to consider challenges which can have not only scientific or technological, but actually very large societal (and sometimes especially economical) impacts.

[2] For any area of research a vision that a period of diminishing returns is coming is a nightmare.

© Springer International Publishing Switzerland 2014
C.S. Calude et al. (Eds.): Gruska Festschrift, LNCS 8808, pp. 449–461, 2014.
DOI: 10.1007/978-3-319-13350-8_33

processing. As a consequence, Informatics is seen not only as an area of science and technology that influences (currently) society in general, science and technology, as well as medicine, but also (to say it in a bit dramatic way), as a new powerful, wise, but nice, queen at the same time. Informatics is an incredibly useful, intelligent, powerful and diligent servant of all sciences and technologies (and most, if not all, of other major areas of society). In a more modest way *Informatics could and should be the area of science and technology transforming science, technology, medicine and society in a way hardly imaginable not long time ago.*

2   A Glance into the History of Grand Challenges

For centuries, unsolved mysteries, gaps in scientific knowledge provided researchers with motivations, directions and challenges. (A more modern way of saying that is: *The most important product of knowledge is ignorance* (David Gross (2005).)

In the past, when progress in science and technology used to be done mainly by individuals, or small groups, mainly driven by curiosity, challenges concentrated on problems believed to be solvable by individuals. Discovery, especially after the great success of science and technology in the Second World War, was captured well in Vannevar Bush report "Science - The Endless Frontiers" from 1945. An understanding has slowly emerged that it can be possible, and actually very profitable, both for society and the research community, to put before the research community huge challenges of immense importance for society, especially its economy.

The huge progress in the science and technology during the last 100, or even 50, years has increased the number of (very) interesting and important open problems and challenges – the more we know, the more we need to know. That naturally led to the concentration of the research funding to mainly on a few specific areas where returns could be seen as the largest.

Formulation of grand challenges for any area of science and technology is always subjective to a large degree, no matter whether done by individuals or small groups of knowledgeable experts. Behind this is, on one side, the well known fact that to ask good questions is very, very hard. On the other side, the problem is that for most of researchers it is in principle not easy to see beyond their research expertise, paradigms and scopes and so a revolution in the research goals is usually fully done and accepted by the majority only after a generation "dies out".

As an interesting example of an "old type" of the very influential grand challenges are Hilbert's 10 problems formulated at the Mathematical Congress in 1900 (out of his gathering of 23 problems). At that time Hilbert was considered as the last universal mathematician with a very broad knowledge of Mathematics and as the one having an idea how to put all Mathematics on a firm basis - after a turmoil in mathematics caused by the discovery of mathematical paradoxes and by the existence of many counter-intuitive phenomena in Mathematics. A recent example are "Millennium problems" (7 of them) in Mathematics formulated by a group of mathematicians at the Clay Mathematical Institute - as the final outcome of the original intention to publish, for a "Millennium book", 50 important and challenging mathematical problems, see [7]. The formulation of this new set of mathematical problems followed Hilbert's view of mathematical challenges. Grand challenges in Physics, as seen in [3,9,10], are already much more along these lines.

An excellent example of a successful attempt of a societal leader to formulate a great mega-challenge was Kennedy: *Let us put a man on the moon within this decade.* This shocked not only the whole society, but also the scientific and technological communities, and was perceived by some as science-fiction. The fact that this mega-challenge was achieved can now be seen as a shocking example of what can be done with a coordinated effort of scientists and engineers and a huge societal support.

3   Main Mega-challenges of Current Science and Technology

The first mega-challenge of modern science was actually to demonstrate geniality of God and to discover his laws for the objects and phenomena of the physical world. Namely, to show that the apparently mysterious and enormously complicated physical world, especially our celestial system, follows actually simple mathematical rules. At that time the main task of science and technology was more to support the religious view of the world and life before and after the death, than to make a contribution to the well being of society.

Mega-challenges of another level emerged after a big progress in natural sciences and the development of reductionist philosophy of (natural) sciences. That resulted in the view that Physics is the most fundamental natural science, Chemistry is an applied Physics and Biology can be seen as applied Chemistry. hence, it was natural to put as a new mega-challenge: get deep understanding of the space-time as well as of its structure and of the developments of universe. The mega-challenge therefore was to develop a theory of everything, integrating our understanding of the micro and macro levels of nature, its elements and forces, from which all understanding of nature could be derived, step by step.

Recent progress and the expected developments in the science and technology have allowed, and actually forced society, science and technology, to make another significant step in the direction of putting before the science and technology really huge mega-challenges. On one side, these mega-challenges could be seen as being feasible in the near future, and, on the other side, they could be expected to have enormous impacts on practically all areas of society - even if they would be reached only partially.[3] These new mega-challenges can be stated especially due to the enormous progress in the information processing, networking, Informatics (in general and in the Artificial Intelligence and Robotics in

---

[3] The following quote of Leo Burnett seems to capture well the value of such mega-challenges: *If you try to reach for the stars you may not always get one, but you won't come up with a handful of mud either.*

particular), Neuroscience, Biology, medicine, nanotechnology, and so on. The two new mega-challenges are:

– *To beat human intelligence.*[4]
– *To beat natural death.*[5]

In more details, the goal is: (1) to get deep insights into human intelligence, into what it means to be human, think intelligently and be creative; (2) to design systems/robots that could overcome human biological intelligence in an increasingly larger variety of tasks crucial for mankind; (3) to achieve a merge of the biological and non-biological intelligence in increasingly larger and more and more important degrees.

There are good reasons for such mega-challenges. One of them is the recent and foreseeable progress in Artificial Intelligence and Robotics and also in the understanding of human brains. Another one is in the progresses in the GNR-revolution, what stands for Genetics, Nanotechnology and Robotics, and in its expected developments. The main one is the exponential progress in the power, energy consummation and miniaturisation of the information processing tools that is expected, for good reasons, to be going on still for long (enough).

The recent launching of several big projects in the brain and genome research, such as *Human Brain Project*[6], initiated by EU in 2013 has very ambitious goals: to functionally simulate human brain, to apply that to the development of new information processing paradigms and technologies.

Another key reason why these mega-challenges seem to be feasible is the enormous increase, for huge masses of bright people worldwide, of access to all scientific, technological and medicine knowledge. That is already happening due to increasingly ubiquitous and powerful internet, web services and mobiles and rapidly growing potential for communication, computation and knowledge distribution and discovery. All that is expected to increase the pool of very bright people capable to produce innovations on one side, their connectivity and potential for collaboration on the other side.

The second mega-challenge has the goal to keep significantly increasing longevity and to achieve that in such a way that people's productive and enjoyable life is more and more prolonged. Progress in Genetics, Nanotechnology, Robotics, Medical diagnosis through (wearable/embedded) devices, implants, treatments, regenerative medicine and in creating models of human organs and

---

[4] Some food for thought: *It seems probable that once the machine thinking method had started, it will not take long to outstrip our feeble power. They would be able to converse with each other to sharpen their wits. At some stage therefore, we should have to expect machine to take control* (Alan M. Turing). *Since there is a real danger that computers will develop intelligence and take over, we urgently need to develop their direct connections to our brains so that computers can add to human intelligence rather than be in opposition* (Stephen Hawking).

[5] Another food for thought: *But there is nothing in Biology yet found that indicates the inevitability of death.* (Richard Feynman).

[6] It is almost 1.2 billion EUR project with 135 partners from 26 countries.

in producing them, suggests that longevity could be seen as an achievable. Quite surprisingly, longevity starts to be seen also as a desirable goal that could contribute significantly to the overall prosperity of mankind.

Of course, dealing with these mega-challenges requires work across traditional research disciplines boundaries at which Informatics, once properly, broadly and deeply understood and developed, could play a very significant role.

There are, of course, other interesting challenges for science and technology. For example: (1) To find out whether there are other civilisations in universe; (2) To make sun energy to replace all nonrenewable sources of energy and to create an *energy internet* making the use of all renewable sources of energy; (3) To find out whether our universe is a part of a "multiverse"; (4) To find initial conditions for Big Bang; (5) To find out whether time was also before Big Bang; (6) To determine the nature of black holes, dark matter and dark energy; (7) To find out what are the smallest building blocks of matter; (7) To find out whether we can and how animate extinct living beings; (8) To design live beings from lifeless matter; (9) To find out why we dream; (10) To find out .... Other interesting open problems/challenges has been recently compiled in the *Science* journal, see [8]. However, their overall impacts can hardly be seen as comparable to the potential impacts of the two mega-challenges discussed above. In addition, they can be seen as more easily and faster achievable once a significant progress on the way to deal with the two mega-challenges presented above is reached.

Society has two other mega-challenges that are, however of different nature: (1) To beat human wars as the ways to solve conflicts and pursue ambitions and to establish total and lasting peace; (2) To beat conflicts between demands of society and needs of nature.

4   Grand Challenges in Physics, Mathematics and Chemistry

Physics has made enormous progress in the last century (actually in the last 40 years), as the product of both curiosity and wars-driven research, by relatively small groups of researchers at the beginning. The outcomes have increased enormously our understanding of the evolution of the universe since its Big Bang, 13.798 ± 0.037 billions years ago, and also understanding of the elementary structures of matter, atoms and particles, powers and energy. Its current main grand challenges could be, for example, stated as follows:

- *The problem of the origin of universe.* Can we find out the initial conditions for Big Bang? A model for the very origin of universe? ...
- *The problem of very basic elements of universe.* What is universe made of? What is the nature of dark matter, dark energy, black holes, ... ? Can we create them experimentally? How can dark matter interact with "ordinary" matter? How do elements of universe - stars, planets,... - form?
- *The problem of the true nature of space-time?* What is their origin and structure? How many dimension has space? Is time an emerging concept? Are time

and space an illusion (N. Seiberg)? Are they doomed (E. Witten)? Was time before Big Bang? ...

- *The problem of the theory of everything.* To develop a theory that would unify all interactions (in particular, also the general relativity theory and quantum mechanics, as well as all particles and forces) into a single theory (that could be then seen as a complete theory of nature) – if such a theory can exist at all.

All these grand challenges are really fundamental and their significance can be seen easily also for laymen.

Observe that also Physics is starting to broaden its scope and grand challenges, in order to keep it in the frontiers of science. For example, in the recent list of the grand challenges of Physics, as stated by Nobel price (2004) winner David Gross in his CERN talk in 2005, see [3], the following grand questions are included: *(1) Complexity – behaviour of complex systems and emergence of various phenomena in their processes; (2) Biology – to help to build theoretical Biology, if this can be done; (3) Genomics – to find out whether theory of evolution can be quantitative and predictive; (4) Consciousness – to find out principles that underline the self-organisation responsible for memory an consciousness.*

Other grand challenges for the 21st century Physics have been formulated by Patel [9], the former president of the American Physical Society: *(1) Development of quantum and nano sciences and technologies; (2) To apply Physics to Biology and medicine; (3) To develop Physics in support of national security.*

In UK, Physics Grand Challenges Advisory Board suggested the following four grand challenges for Physics in UK in 2006 [10]: *(1) Emergence and Physics far from equilibrium; (2) Quantum Physics for new quantum technologies; (3) Nanoscale design of functional material and (4) Understanding of the Physics of life.* This list indicates a shift from those with quite short time impacts to areas where cooperation with other science and technology fields are needed and future impact on society and economy could be very important.

Concerning Mathematics, the situation is on one side different and on the other side quite similar. As the grand challenges one could try to see already mentioned the "Millennium problems", formulated at the end of the last century as the problems for the next century. Namely, the following problems, see [7]: *(1) P = NP problem.*[7] *(2) The Poincaré conjecture*[8] *(Solved in 2003, by Perelman.) (3) The Hodge conjecture*[9] *(4) The Riemann conjecture*[10] *(5) Soundness of quantum*

---

[7] Is it more difficult to prove theorems than to check their proofs?

[8] In topology, a sphere with a two-dimensional surface is characterised by the fact that it is compact and simply connected. The Poincare conjecture was that this is also true in higher dimensions.

[9] For projective algebraic varieties, Hodge cycles are rational linear combinations of algebraic cycles.

[10] To show that all nontrivial zeros of the analytical continuation of the Riemann zeta function have a real part of $1/2$.

Yang-Mills theory[11] *(6) Analysis of Navier-Stokes equation*[12] *(7) The Birch and Swinnerton-Dyer conjecture*[13]

All these problems have been open for a very long time. However, a layman cannot see their large importance and even most mathematicians can hardly see how these problems can have really a great impact on Mathematics, not to speak on society as the whole.

It seems that Mathematics has a problem to formulate such grand challenges. Can one see the formulation of such grand challenges in Mathematics as a grand challenge by itself?

Following [2], the Chemistry grand challenges are: *(1) To discover the chemical origin of life (to find out which substrates can provide life. Under which circumstances and how matter can come alive and, eventually, can know itself and how to bridge the gap from inanimate matter to self-replicating and self). (2) To understand chemical basis of memory and thoughts. (3) To develop chemical information technology - to see chemical world as consisting of chemical elements connected by chemical reactions and on this bases to develop chemical sensing, diagnosing, monitoring, signalling as well as information exchange between molecules and atoms and to integrate chemical phenomena and processes with the electronic ones, especially circuitry, to be used especially in biomedicine and in enhancing humans by implants and so on. (4) To develop the science and engineering of designing new molecules - in particular to develop good dynamic model of molecules. (5) To develop computational Chemistry capable to model efficiently behaviour of complex molecules, vast biomolecular systems, complex chemical processes and behaviours - to help to understand cells environments (where many molecules, large and small, interact, aggregate and react,...). (6) To develop artificial photosynthesis (to convert efficiently solar energy to chemical energy/fuel). (7) To develop efficiently biofuels. (8) To overcome limits of periodic table - to design new forms of matter. (9) To find the potential of graphene and carbon nanotechnology. (10) To understand the chemical basis of epigenetic.*

All of them can be easily seen as really fundamental and important ones.

5   A New Perception of Informatics

The first very influential perception of the science related to computers and information processing, written excellently by A. Newel, H. Simon and A. Perlis, was presented in 1967 in the *Science* journal and its basic idea reads as follows: *Whenever there are phenomena there can be a science dealing with these phenomena. Phenomena breed sciences. Since there are computers, there is computer science. The phenomena surrounding computers are varied, complex and rich.*

---

[11] For almost 50 years the standard model of particle Physics rested on quantum Yang-Mills theory, which links the behaviour of particles to structures found in geometry. Though theory is elegant and simple, no one so far has proved it is sound.

[12] To determine whether the equation has smooth solutions.

[13] This conjecture says how to determine the number of solutions have elliptic curves in the realm of rational numbers.

Such a perception corresponded well to the developments and understanding of the field in their time, but should be seen as not broad and deep enough nowadays. The first observation of narrowness of such a perception of the field was perhaps due to Dijkstra, who noted that *Computing science is no more about computers than astronomy is about telescopes*. The developments in the field at Dijkstra's time were enough for seeing what the underlying science and technology is not, but not yet how it should be perceived in its full depth and broadness, as discussed in the next.

The perception presented in the following has its roots in the recent developments in the understanding of the crucial role information processing has played in the evolution of universe and life, see [1], for example, and in getting deeper insights into the fundamental physical, chemical and biological as well as social phenomena.[14] The basic position presented in the following is also based on standpoints that *the main scientific goal of Physics is to study concepts, processes, laws and limitations of the physical worlds* and that *the main scientific goal of Informatics is to study concepts, processes, laws and limitations of the information precessing worlds*. As a consequence, Physics and Informatics could (and should) be seen as representing two windows through which we try to perceive, understand and develop our world.

5.1   A Perception of Scientific Informatics

As a scientific discipline of a very broad scope and deep nature, Informatics has many goals. Its main task is to discover, explore and exploit in depth, the laws, limitations, paradigms, concepts, models, theories, phenomena, structures and processes of natural and virtual information processing worlds.

To achieve its tasks, the scientific Informatics concentrates on the development of the information processing based understanding of the universe, evolution, nature, lives (natural and artificial), brain and mind processes, intelligence, creativity, information storing, processing and transmission systems and tools, complexity, security, and other basic phenomena of the information processing worlds.

In order to meet its goals, the scientific Informatics has developed close relations with other sciences and technology fields - currently especially with Physics, Biology and Chemistry, on one hand, and with electronics, optics, nano- and biotechnologies on the other hand.

The basis of the relationship between Informatics and natural sciences rests first of all on the fact that *information carriers are always elements of the physical, biological or chemical worlds*, and, consequently, information processing is governed and constrained by their laws and limitations. Of the importance is also that information processes are inherent parts of the basic processes of nature and life.

---

[14] For more on the analyses of the obsolete perceptions of computer science see [4] and [5].

Informatics as a science includes also numerous theories and subareas much needed for its development to depth and in broadness. Some of them are very abstract, others quite specific, and some are oriented on making better use of the outcomes of the scientific Informatics to create a scientific basis of the technological Informatics and Informatics-driven methodology.

Informatics is, without doubts, currently the leading science and technology discipline with enormous impacts on all other sciences, technologies, industry, economics, health and environment care, liberal art and so on - guiding them and serving them in their reasoning and doing.[15]

5.2 Grand Challenges of Scientific Informatics

Grand challenges of the scientific Informatics can be seen briefly as follows;

- To explore the ensemble of all potential information processing worlds and our real information processing worlds as points in such an ensemble.
- To explore basic laws and limitations of the information processing that govern universe, evolution, nature, life and society.
- To understand and model human brain, mind, consciousness, intelligence, creativity, reasoning, learning, body and their processes from the information processing and functional point of views.
- To study complexity - complex processes, their outcomes and emergent phenomena.
- To understand and manage all fundamental aspects of computations, communications, interactions and their complexities and feasibilities as well as the design and analysis of algorithms.
- To develop theoretical foundations for specification, design, analysis, verification, security, simulation, modelling and visualisation of huge information processing systems.
- To develop foundations for huge data sets and streams driven scientific approaches as well as for harvesting from incomplete and imprecise information.
- To help other sciences in their merge with Informatics and to help them to develop new information processing paradigms.
- To develop sound approaches to forecasting and understanding of the fast changing future.

5.3 Grand Challenges of Technological Informatics

An increasingly important feature of the current development of sciences and technologies in general is their convergence to the scientific and technological

---

[15] Science used to have (always?) a Queen. It used to be Theology in the middle age, Philology in the Renaissance, Mathematics in the Galileo's time and also Physics (at least for natural sciences) in modern time. This has been, in a condense way, well captured by remark of Ernest Rutherford (1912): *All science is either Physics or stamp collecting.*

Informatics, and also their merges. As the consequence, the current science can be seen as being, to a large extent, technology-driven and current technology as science-driven. This is also reflected in the following view of main grand challenges of the technological Informatics.

(1) To achieve sufficient security, privacy and reliability of and in huge information processing systems and networks; (2) To develop methods for specification, design, correctness proving, efficiency analysis, updating, maintenance and understanding of huge, distributed, parallel and reliable information processing and communication systems and networks; (3) To achieve steady miniaturisation of the size and energy consumption, as well as maximisation of performances, of the information processing systems - to give still quite long life to the Moore law; (4) To keep designing more and more perfect global computation and communication environment connecting all computation and communication systems with a new quality internet (of people, things and energy resources) and new quality webs; (5) To keep designing artificial intelligence systems (robots) beating (much) human intelligence and actions capabilities in important aspects; (6) To develop micro- and nano-scale robots and ways of their controlled self-assembly; (7) To develop bio- , brain- , cell- , molecule- and DNA-driven computers and computing and the merge of bio- and non-bio-computing technologies. (8) To develop fully and make full use of the GNR-revolution (G-genetics, N-nano-technology and R-robotic/AI); (9) To design and explore the virtual reality worlds and systems; (10) To develop global warning systems against natural disasters and terrorist attacks; (11) To keep developing more and more sophisticated information gathering, processing and sharing systems to make medicine knowledge global and models, as well as treatments, personalised; (12) To design advanced, especially mind controlled, human-computer interfaces; (13) To develop insights, methods and tools for management, analysis, processing and visualisation of huge (up to petabytes and exabytes) data sets and streams; (14) To achieve permanent and open access to the rapidly growing worldwide information and knowledge bases.

5.4   Informatics-Driven Methodology

Modern science and its two main methodologies, observations/experiments and theory/deduction, or induction and deduction, are usually seen as having its modern and fully worked out origin in the 16-17th century in the critical rationalism of René Descartes and in practical empiricism of Francis Bacon and Galileo - as well as in breathtaking contributions of Isac Newton. Galileo's philosophy was a concentration on measuring things quantitatively, thinking mathematically and submitting theoretical outcomes/hypothesis to repeatable verification/experiments by nature.[16] All that represented a big change in the science methodology.

---

[16] Well known is Galileo's dictum: *Measure what is measurable, and make measurable what is not.*

Indeed, before and in the golden era of Greek Mathematics/science, concentration was on *searches for causes of phenomena* and on the understanding *why things happen*. F. Bacon's, Descartes' and Galileo's points of view was that it is sufficient, in many cases, to concentrate on an understanding *how things happen* and in order to do that to find key and simple relations (expressed mathematically and fully understandable by men) between the key and simple quantitative characteristics of the underlying phenomena and processes (and by that to glorify God). That was also seen as sufficient for making useful and important predictions concerning the behaviour of the basic phenomena of physical nature and to understand quite enough *how things happen*.[17]

Developments in Informatics, as in a science and technology discipline, started to create another, fundamentally new, methodology. The starting and main assumption is that we often need to know neither causes of phenomena nor explicitly and fully relations between their important quantitative characteristics. In many important and also complex cases it is sufficient, to a large degree, to design an (evolving - capable to learn and improve) oraculum, *an information processing model of phenomena/processes*, that can be used to answer, through simulations, or even visually demonstrate, sufficiently well, answers to important questions about the phenomena and help to develop also their deeper understanding. That would also allow to pursue much a new, holistic, approach to science.

The main features of Informatics-driven methodology are:

- Modelling – Design of the information processing models of nature-made, men-made, and also virtual complex phenomena and processes.
- Simulation – Utilisation of the information processing models to study phenomena of nature-made, men-made and virtual objects and processes.
- Visualisation – Visual presentation of complex data, objects and processes in order to make them (better) understandable by humans.
- Virtualization – Design of virtual systems and processes including designs of virtual reality systems and worlds.
- Formalisation of reasoning – Design of formal systems for learning and for mechanised problem solving, reasoning and proofs making as well as for proof checking and creative actions.
- Searching – Design of special searching techniques (to use a sophisticated searching in data sets and structures as an alternative to sophisticated knowledge based reasoning).
- Methods for design and analysis of artificial systems, especially artificial intelligence and life systems, also as a way to understand and explore systems made by nature.

---

[17] Observe that, on a more philosophical level, scientists of those times were not yet completely able to ignore the role of God, not even Galileo. Their dominating view was that the all-powerful God-creator has designed the world (nature) describable in the mathematical language and let the nature run according to simple mathematical laws. The role of the science and scientists was to discover such laws and by that to demonstrate ingenuity and rationality of God.

- Development of (formal) methods to specify, design, analyse, verify, update and maintain complex (information processing) systems.
- Design of algorithms, study of their performances and inherent complexities of computational, communication and description problems and systems, as a way to get a deeper understanding of phenomena and their interrelations.
- Development of huge-data-driven approaches to problem solving.

The power of the new methodology could be summarised as follows: (1) It brings new dimensions to both old methodologies; (2) It brings into new heights an enormous power of modelling and simulations; (3) It utilises an enormous power of visualisation; (4) It utilises an enormous potential that the study of artificial and virtual worlds brings for an understanding of the real world; (5) It utilises an enormous power of (sophisticated) search techniques. (6) It allows to change the old vision of science - namely, that science is to achieve its goals mainly by discovering, isolating and studying the primitive phenomena and processes - and provides intellectual frameworks and tools to investigate also very complex and large systems, in their full complexity.

Informatics-driven methodology subsumes and extends the role Mathematics used to play in advising, guiding and serving other scientific and technology disciplines and society in general.

Another main challenges of Informatics-driven methodology is to develop "Informatics thinking" as an underlying basis of all education.

6   Relations Between Grand Challenges of Informatics and two Mega-Challenges

The grand challenges of Informatics discussed above are also to the large extent related to the two mega-challenges. Let us discuss this briefly.

On a meta level, three grand challenges of Informatics, which can significantly contribute to both mega-challenges are: (1) Developments of (especially communication) resources and tools that would allow most of the society members (also from the underdeveloped parts of the world) to get an easy access to the world open pool of knowledge and this way to speed up much frequency of innovations, and also the overall progress in science and technology. (2) Developments of the ways and tools for knowledge presentation as well as for distributed cooperation in the production of knowledge and tools that would allow much more effective use of all knowledge produced worldwide. (3) To increase quality of Informatics-driven thinking of the whole society, especially of the research and development communities.

The first five grand challenges of the scientific Informatics are closely related, on various levels of abstraction, to the two mega-challenges. The information processing exploration of life, brain, mind, intelligence, creativity, deduction and artificial intelligence as well as of the ways to speed up information processing and communications are directly relevant. Progress in the understanding of complex systems and emergent phenomena is also of the large importance.

In addition, most of grand challenges of technological Informatics are closely related to the two mega-challenges. Of special importance are challenges to increase much performance of information obtaining and processing tools, to decrease much size of very powerful information processing and communication tools as well as to decrease much their energy consumption. This is also related to the challenge to develop an information processing technology inspired by those used in nature especially in living beings. Grand challenges in artificial intelligent systems in general and in (nano)robotics in particular are of special importance, but so are many others. For example, so are tools needed to specify, design, verify and manage huge software systems.

Informatics-driven methodology paradigms and tools are of special importance to the development of knowledge and tools concerning the design and use of huge (especially discrete) models and their simulations as well as visualisations of their outcomes.

Less explicitly, but actually also deeply important for the two mega-challenges, are such grand challenges on "big-data science and technology", a well as the development of the science and technology of the science and technology development.

References

1. Avery, J.: Information Theory and Evolution. World Scientific (2003)
2. Ball, P.: 10 unsolved mysteries in chemistry. Scientific American **305**(I4), 48–53 (2011)
3. Gross, D.: 25 grand challenges of Physics, talk on a seminar in CERN on 26.01.2005, see cds.cern.ch/record/975368 (2005)
4. Gruska, J.: A new perception of Informatics, Academia Europaea 49 p. (2010). http://www.AE.Info.org/ae/User/Gruska.Jozef
5. Gruska J.: Impulses and roads to a new perception of Informatics, in Rainbow of Computer Science, edited by C. Calude, A. Salomaa and G. Rozenberg. Springer Verlag (2011)
6. Gruska, J., Calude, C.S.: Quantum Informatics and its relation to Informatics, Physics and Mathematics (A dialog between C. Calude and J. Gruska), Bulletin of EATCS, N92, 20–30, N93, 33–49 (2007)
7. Jaffe, A.M.: The millennium grand challenges in Mathematics. Notices of the AMS **53**(6), 652–660 (2006)
8. Kennedy, D., Norman, C.: What don't we know, special issue of Science, 75 (July 1, 2005)
9. Kumar, C., Patel, N., Jaudi, I.: 21st Century Physics: Grand challenges. The Journal of the Federation of American Scientists 56(2), 1, 9–12 (2003)
10. Physics Grand Challenges of UK Engineering and Physical Sciences Research Council. www.eprc.ac.uk/research/ourportfolio/themes/physicalsciences/introduction/Pages/grandcl

Konrad Zuse's Relationship to Informatics

Roland Vollmar[(⊠)]

Karlsruhe Institute of Technology, Institute of Theoretical
Informatics, D-76131 Karlsruhe, Germany
vollmar@ira.uka.de

Abstract. Konrad Zuse's self–identity was that of an engineer, as a
person who creates "means to purposes" [1]. In its German beginnings,
Informatics focused on theoretical aspects. In my opinion this goes a
long way to explaining Zuse's hesitant acceptance of this emergent discipline. Later, the solving of practical problems came to the fore. This
may explain his delayed affinity for this academic discipline.

1 Konrad Zuse (1910–1995)

In 1941 Konrad Zuse (1910–1995) completed the "first fully automatic program
controlled and freely programmable in a binary floating point working computing
device" (F.L. Bauer, in [20][1]). He went on to build one of the first process control devices, proposed a parallel computer, designed the first high level computer
language ("Plankalkül"), published considerations of the universe as a cellular
automaton ("Rechnender Raum"), founded the first computer factory in con-
tinental Europe, to mention only his major achievements. In my opinion this
justifies characterizing him as a visionary. His inventions were fundamental for
the birth of Informatics, the discipline founded in the 1960s. Although he never
held a full academic position – with the exception of an honorary professorship
at the University of Göttingen – he was in contact with Informatics scientists
and practitioners, and he observed the genesis of the corresponding studies with
critical attention. In this article I will try to refer to his (changing) positions on
the basis of his published comments. This (clearly incomplete) report also gives
some clues as to the different directions in which Informatics in Germany could
have developed.

2 The Beginning of Informatics in the Federal Republic of Germany

It should be remembered that "Informatics" was only "defined" at the universities of the Federal Republic of Germany (FRG) during the last third of Konrad
Zuse's life, and this establishment did not happen immediately or at the same
pace. Therefore it is worth describing this process, if only very briefly. Vollmar

---

[1] Translated by the author.

© Springer International Publishing Switzerland 2014
C.S. Calude et al. (Eds.): Gruska Festschrift, LNCS 8808, pp. 462–471, 2014.
DOI: 10.1007/978-3-319-13350-8_34

[15] gives a short survey of the genesis of the discipline in the FRG. Coy [5] gives more details from a critical point of view. Reuse [11] describes the political and financial decisions which led to the establishment of the field at universities and colleges of higher education.

Even in the late fifties and sixties computers were widespread in the sciences, industry and throughout the economy. Nevertheless, it was widely accepted that Informatics would be sufficiently represented as a minor field of study for mathematicians, physicists and electrical engineers. In 1969 the "responsible" federal ministry (Bundesministerium für Bildung und Wissenschaft) [2] initiated the development of Informatics in academia in the FRG under the title "Überregionales Forschungsprogramm Informatik" (supraregional Informatics research program) [11]. 13 topics were marked: automata theory and formal languages; programming and dialogue languages and their translators; computer organization and sequential circuits; operating systems; information processing systems; computer technology; digital processing of continuous signals and six application–oriented areas. At a first glance this list is quite impressive, but the listed fields were much narrower than they are today. The number of methods and results was quite small compared with the present situation.

In 1969 a so–called GAMM–NTG committee proposed framework examination regulations for the study of Informatics at universities. This committee was composed of leading German Informatics researchers, mainly mathematicians and electrical engineers. Due to the (numerical) predominance of mathematicians the introductory study period was dominated by mathematical courses. But the quite marginal provision of genuine Informatics courses at this time was realistic and pragmatic, because there were very few teachers available and the number of results was small. The prescribed mathematics courses were generally identical to those proposed for students of Mathematics. I believe two reasons were instrumental in making this choice: the limited capacity of the mathematics departments and differing opinions about the "right Mathematics", even among the Informatics professors. By the end of the seventies a (numerical) balance between courses in Mathematics and Informatics had already been attained at many universities. This adjustment is one example of the early changes to Informatics (or more precisely its instantiation at German universities). At a first glance the consequences of deciding in favour for a more mathematical orientation for the new discipline are far–reaching. But in the long run they may be negligible. The development of Computer Science in the USA dominated the discipline, at least in the Western World, and meant eventually Informatics would have the actual shape. I dare say it would have appealed more to Konrad Zuse if its aim had been the "mechanical engineering" of computers.

---

[2] It should be mentioned that the situation was complicate: In effect the federal government was not allowed to interfere educational topics, this was in the competence of the states (so–called "Kulturhoheit der Länder"). Therefore the given finances were declared as a support for research.

3   Domains of Informatics in Germany

It is obvious that an emerging branch of science needs some time to create its identity, cutting the cord from the areas it arose from and separating from neighbouring disciplines. "The new domain starts to forget its parentage and strike out on its own, and a consciousness emerges that a new field is starting to exist in its own right." [1] The dispute about the "right" Informatics was not limited to teaching concepts or to the importance of Mathematics; the impacts of the different areas were also discussed. Such conflicts arise for different reasons. Conceptions of a discipline may be strongly influenced by its application areas, and within these areas by divergent ideas about future development. But personal predilections tempered by education and experience also play a role. This situation is not restricted to new disciplines (even in such long standing departments such as Mathematics, discussions about the "rank" of the topics still take place), but in expanding disciplines with people with completely different backgrounds and histories such contentions are more virulent. The resulting essential changes to the discipline have often been emphasized, e.g. in [9]: "[...] since the beginning of the institutionalization of Computer Science since 1959/60 in the USA and since 1964/65 in Europe the debate about the focus, the basic theory and the paradigms of the science has not ended." From the beginning the word "Informatics" has been used in Germany.

The preface of the first edition (1970) of a standard course book [3] states: "Informatics is the German term for 'Computer Science', an area which has been developed during the sixties esp. in USA, but also in Great Britain, to become its own scientific discipline."[3]

To get a better understanding of Konrad Zuse's attitude to the discipline, a rough description of the content will be helpful [6]: "The major subdisciplines of computer science have traditionally been (1) architecture (including all levels of hardware design, as well as the integration of hardware and software components to form computer systems), (2) software (the programs [...]), here subdivided into software engineering, programming languages, operating systems, information systems and databases, artificial intelligence, and computer graphics, and (3) theory, which includes computational methods and numerical analysis on the one hand and data structures and algorithms on the other."

Although in my opinion some areas are missing, e.g. the social implications of computer applications, this "definition" was widely accepted from the mid-sixties until the nineties. There were also a lot of other influential proposals, e.g. the ACM recommendations of 1968 or the GAMM–NTG recommendations of 1969, but at least in the German academia they were controversially discussed (cf. e.g. [9]). When introducing this artificial word "Informatics" (analogous to the French term "informatique"), the restriction to computers (such as "Computer Science" or "Computing Science" may suggest) should be avoided.

Considering Zuse's attitude to Informatics this may provide one of many explanations for his different statements about the discipline. Although he was

---

[3] Translated by the author.

not strongly integrated within academia, Konrad Zuse pursued the development of the discipline, as the notes quoted below will prove.

4   Konrad Zuse's Situation at the End of the Sixties

Before discussing Konrad Zuse's relationship to Informatics, I will briefly consider his situation at the end of the sixties. Zuse's most important achievements by this time include (keywords only):

- Design and construction of computing devices, esp. Z1, Z2, Z3[4], Z4
- Conditional combinatorics (~ propositional logic)
- Design of a coding device
- Associative memory
- Process computer
- Concept for a higher programming language ("Plankalkül")
- Pipeline principle
- Plotter ("Graphomat")
- Self-reproducing systems
- Design of a parallel computer ("Feldrechner")
- "Computing universe" ("Rechnender Raum")

Details may be found in his autobiography [20] (English translation [21]), specifically in the original articles. Although he had published a remarkable number of papers about different topics, he was mainly acknowledged as the German computer pioneer. Even in 1984 he states: "My present-day standing is essentially predicated on the ten to twenty years of my pioneering work since 1934."[5][20] His economic situation was determined by his retirement from ZUSE KG, a company founded by him, which was taken over by BBC Mannheim in 1964. An unfortunate event in his life was the definite rejection of a very long pending application for a patent for "computers" by the Federal Patent Court in 1967.

5   Some Statements by Konrad Zuse Concerning Informatics

Konrad Zuse's main interests comprised the development of the computer technology and his "Plankalkül". On the basis of statements made by Zuse in various lectures and articles in the relevant period (the sixties and the first half of the seventies) I will discuss his opinions in two separate parts.

Most of Konrad Zuse's lectures were devoted to the development of computers. The talks had similar compositions, but were updated in each case. As an example I will outline the content of a lecture at the Technion (Haifa) in 1960:

---

[4] It may be remarkable that the Z3 was *in principle* a universal computer as Rojas [13] has shown by a sophisticated programming construction.

[5] Translated by the author.

Zuse started with mechanical computing devices, then he outlined program-controlled ones, starting with Babbage's Analytical Engine. Thereafter he outlined his most important ideas for computing devices since the mid-thirties and their realizations as Z1, Z2 and Z3. He emphasized the appropriateness of the logical design of the switching mechanisms for a mechanical realization as well as for relay and tube technologies. He states that he was convinced even in the early forties that the progress of program-controlled computing would eventually lead to an "artificial brain" and that for this purpose conditional instructions would become necessary, a feature he did not build into his first devices. [22] In an article [23] Zuse underlined the significance of program storage and control. A lecture in 1961 [32] follows the same line, but his main point is the demand on an academic direction of computer design and technology. I am unable to assess his opinion about Computer Science, which was under development in the USA at the time (cf. e.g. [9]). It is interesting that this talk was given at the Braunschweig Technical University, where at this time the establishment of a chair for data processing devices in the EE faculty had been discussed and were successfully completed in 1962. Konrad Zuse was later invited to accept the chair, but he "waved it aside" [14]. This is in line with a remark of his eldest son, Horst who states that his father never strived for a university position, instead pursuing his vision to build and sell computers. [16] Therefore it will not be surprising that most of his lectures were devoted to the development of computers – sometimes with elements of advertisement for his company, ZUSE KG – rather than programmatic aspects of the burgeoning field of Informatics. Yet there were exceptions: In an article from 1965 [24] he ascribes computers as "working material of the intelligence" ("Arbeitsmittel der Intelligenz"). Figure 1 is an illustration of his perception of the possible embodiment of a new discipline. His categorizations of "Formelsprachen (Plankalkül)"[6] as "Theory" and of "Programm-Sprachen (Algol, Fortran)" as "skill" points to his assessment of the second–rank value of the theoretical results of the formal languages for the systematics and analysis of programming languages. It is surprising that he renounces an explicit reference to operating systems and information systems – unless he tacitly subsumes them as "Systeme" in the "Technik" section. In his listing of theoretical topics, "Kybernetik" is listed as the last point. Nevertheless he had a special affinity to it. In another article titled "Thoughts about an institute for automation"[7] [28] he underlines the function of cybernetics: "Automation has a similar central place in industry and economy as cybernetics in science."[8] But there he considered it not as a self-contained domain but as a bridge between the sciences.

In other lectures (e.g. [26], [27]), Zuse laments the gap between theory and praxis in the computer development, but without an explicit elucidation of this

---

[6] To conserve the authenticity I don't try to translate the German notions, but due to their affinity to the English words they should be understandable.

[7] Translated by the author.

[8] Translated by the author.

Arbeitsmittel der Intelligenz

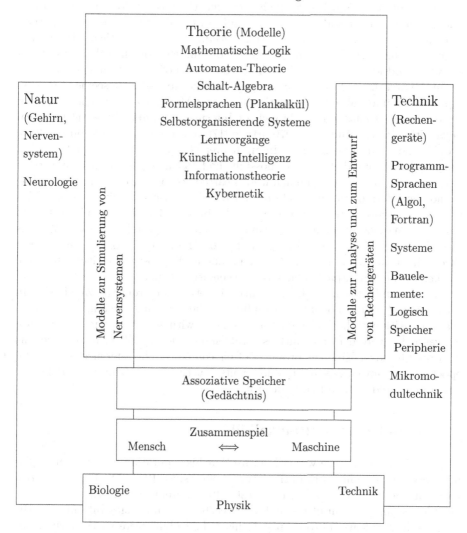

Fig. 1. Working material of the intelligence; after[24]

deficit. To clarify his attitude, the following citation may help [30]:[9] "In Informatics and the science of the computers, we have several directions and some are very practically oriented: there are the constructors, the designers of the computers, the pr[o]grammers and so on, and on the other side we have some very theoretically oriented disciplines, the informatic[s], the discipline of algor[i]thmic

---

[9] Unfortunately it is not dated (and not well edited), but it seems this lecture was given in 1973.

languages based on automata theory, and so on. Turing machines are very mathematically oriented and I have the feeling that these two fields, very practically
oriented informatics and very theoretically oriented, cannot be put together.
They are two worlds [...]. And I have the feeling that the practical informatic[s]
engineer cannot use these mathematical tools and that on the other hand there
are very good ideas in the field of the theoreticians of the automata theory."

In the first draft of his autobiography in 1968, Konrad Zuse seems to express
a positive opinion about Informatics studies: "After long discussions the plan
is now to eventually start a branch of Informatics studies at some technical
universities."[10] [25] But in a 1970 article [17], addressed to a wide public, Zuse
avoided the term "Informatics". In an answer [29] to a critical letter from F.L.
Bauer [2], he conceded that he possibly had taken a partial look at certain
developments, but in my opinion a wholehearted acceptance of the new discipline
cannot be inferred. In an article from 1972 [27], Zuse extensively reduced his
criticism: "Unfortunately however it can also be seen that theory and practice do
not cooperate closely enough and sometimes develop apart."[11] These quotations
should not be misinterpreted as contempt on the part of Konrad Zuse to the
theory in its entirety. E.g. he had a pronouncedly positive attitude to some
mathematical topics, particularly to mathematical logic.

At least until the mid–60s, i.e. until his retirement from the ZUSE KG, in
my opinion Zuse did not intend to influence the emerging discipline or even to
shape it. Although he had numerous contacts with scientists and universities,
he was not involved in committees establishing science policy; instead he was
dedicated to advertising the products of his company. The references to his own
epoch-making inventions and developments – at this time not universally known
and appreciated – should add authority.

6   Konrad Zuse's "Plankalkül"

Yet in 1984 Konrad Zuse was still aware that his reputation as a computer pioneer was reliant on his work in the 20 or so years since 1934 [20]. This was partly
based on the fact that his main interests after retirement from ZUSE KG were
outside the mainstream of research and teaching of university Informatics. His
longstanding endeavours to propagate his "Plankalkül" were particularly coun-
terproductive: "Efforts to the practical introduction of the 'Plankalkül' [...] did
not gain enough recognition; partly one can even speak from a closed defensive
front both from the industry and from the research."[12] [20] Since the scarce
uptake of the "Plankalkül" was a longstanding nuisance for Zuse – and possibly
provides an (emotional) reason for his hesitating attitude against Informatics –
I will discuss this work in greater detail. Konrad Zuse was aware early on that
his computers were not restricted to solving arithmetical tasks. In his proposal

---

[10] Translated by the author.
[11] Translated by the author.
[12] Translated by the author.

of a programming language, called "Plankalkül" (PK)[13], he demonstrated this via examples of sorting algorithms, graph algorithms and chess problem algorithms. The history of PK was strange: The manuscript was completed in 1945, but there was no publication of the full text before 1972 [18]. In the meantime two short papers appeared and he spoke about it in some lectures; however, he attracted almost no interest. Disregarding PK's meagre propagation, it also has some inherent difficulties. "[...] at first glance the programs of the PK are strange for us. The notation looks a bit two-dimensional [...]. Adapting this notation for the teletype writer, which was used in the early days to input the programs, appears rather difficult. [...] In addition to the notation of programs, the lack of 'goto', 'if then, else' and recursive procedures (usual in machine programming) discredited the PK with the few people that had known it. Another cause is deeper. PK's very rich data structures, which makes it so interesting now, make a technical realisation of this language seem unpromising."[14][10]

"John Backus comments on the Plankalkül: "Like most of the world (except perhaps Heinz Rutishauser and Corrado Böhm [...]), we were entirely unaware of the work of Konrad Zuse. Zuse's 'Plankalkül', which he completed in 1945, was, in some ways, a more elegant and advanced programming language than those that appeared 10 and 15 years later. (IEEE Annals of the History of Computing, Band 20, 1998, Heft 4, Seite 69 [...])" [4]

On various occasions Konrad Zuse recommended the use of PK. With the emergent multiple-access systems, he saw a chance for the PK [26]. Due to its universality he proposed PK as ideally suited to serving as a reference language between different systems and he considered it an adequate language for man-machine communication. Zuse also recommended PK to overcome the "software crisis", because it is designed to support structured programming [19].

Other concepts and proposals by Konrad Zuse, e.g. for an associative memory, an array computer or the "Computing Universe", also only garnered low attention. But this did not influence him as strongly as the disrespect for his PK.

7   Konrad Zuse, Viewed from Outside

We could see that Konrad Zuse doubted in his self–evaluation that he should be considered as an informatician, at least in the sense of the established discipline. This contrasts with the assessment of senior scientists. By 1969, when the aforementioned GAMM-NTG recommendations were formulated, Konrad Zuse was not only a computer pioneer; he had so many scientific results that he could have a competent voice in at least five of the areas of the corresponding report. This had been widely acknowledged – at least in Germany. E.g. F.L. Bauer [2]

---

[13] I could not find a clue about the naming; possibly it should be reminiscent to "Plansprache" which, according to Blanke, is an artificial language to facilitate the international communication.

[14] Translated by the author.

emphasizes that Zuse could be considered as the senior of Informatics. A statement by Giloi [7] conveys a similar appraisal: "Konrad Zuse, developing his "Plankalkül" in 1945, already had a clear conception of an abstract programming model with abstract data types and operations and of data representation suitable for numerical and non-numerical applications. Such concepts were only introduced into Informatics in the seventies. This gives him the rank of the first informatician."[15] In 1971 K. Steinbuch offered Zuse the chance to give a statement about Informatics (in a TV series entitled "Man, technology, future"). [31].

During his life Konrad Zuse received a lot of tributes and awards, including some honorary doctorates from Informatics faculties and the first honorary membership of the German Society for Informatics (GI). One award in particular should be mentioned: In 1965 he received together with George Stibitz the Harry H. Goode Memorial Award from the American Federation of Information Processing Societies (AFIPS), only a year after Howard H. Aiken has been distinguished with it. This also shows that his eminent role in the development of computers has also been acknowledged in the USA.

8   Conclusion

I have tried to show that Konrad Zuse was convinced that an "Informatics" discipline should also be established in Germany. He never fully agreed with its embodiment in the academic environment. He would have preferred a more engineering-based approach instead of a theory-oriented development. He also had emotional reservations concerning the discipline due to the extensive disregard for his "Plankalkül".

References

1. Arthur, W.B.: The Nature of Technology Penguin Books Ltd., London (2009)
2. Letter from F.L. Bauer to Konrad Zuse dated 11.5.1970 Literary remains "Konrad Zuse" in the archive of Deutsches Museum München, provisional no. 110/1
3. Bauer, F.L., Goos, G.: Informatik, 2nd edn. Springer, Heidelberg (1973)
4. Bruderer, H.: Konrad Zuse und die Schweiz Oldenbourg, München (2012)
5. Coy, W.: Was ist Informatik? Zur Entstehung des Faches an den deutschen Universitäten. In: [9], 473–498
6. The New Encyclopaedia Britannica Chicago, 15th ed., vol. 16, Macropaedia, 629 (2005)
7. Giloi, W.K.: Die Ungnade der frühen Geburt Konrad-Zuse-Zentrum für Informationstechnik Berlin Preprint SC 97–09, 15 pp. (Juni 1997)
8. Händler, W. (ed.): Computer Architecture. Springer, Heidelberg (1976); 1–8
9. Hellige, H.D. (ed.): Geschichten der Informatik. Springer, Heidelberg (2004)
10. Hotz Konrad Zuse, G.: Forschung und Entwicklung Informatik-Spektrum 3, 41–47 (1980), (slightly modified version of a lecture from 29.8.1979 in der GMD, Schloß Birlinghoven) Gesellschaft für Mathematik und Datenverarbeitung mbH (GMD) (Hrsg.): Der GMD-Spiegel 3/79, 22–39.

---

[15] Slightly modified translation by the author.

11. B. Reuse Schwerpunkte der Informatikforschung in Deutschlands in den 70er Jahren. In:[12], 3–26

12. Reuse, B., Vollmar, R. (eds.): Informatikforschung in Deutschland. Springer, Heidelberg (2008)

13. Rojas, R.: How to make Zuse's Z3 a universal computer. IEEE Annals of the History of Computing **20**(3), 51–54 (1998)

14. H.-G. Unger Personal communication

15. Vollmar, R.: Seit wann gibt es Informatik? Jahrbuch 2002 der Braunschweigischen Wissenschaftlichen Gesellschaft Cramer,. Braunschweig, 65–75 (2001)

16. Zuse, H.: Konrad Zuse Biographie: In (March 6, 2012). www.horst-zuse.homepage. t-online.de/kz-bio.html

17. Zuse, K.: Wissenschaft und Rechenmaschine. Bild der Wissenschaft **7**(3), 232–241 (1970)

18. Zuse, K.: Der Plankalkül Gesellschaft für Mathematik und Datenverarbeitung, Bonn (1972)

19. Zuse, K.: Rediscovery of buried ideas from the pioneer age of computers. In: [8], 1–8

20. Zuse, K.: Der Computer - Mein Lebenswerk. Springer, Heidelberg (1984)

21. Zuse, K.: The Computer - My Life. Springer, Heidelberg (1993)

22. Zuse, K.: Problems in the Computer Fields. Entwicklungslinien der Rechengeräteentwicklung. Lecture at the Technion Haifa, (Juni 2, 1960). http://www.zib.de/zuse[1] ZIANr 0630 ZuP 035/004 1960 (cf. [32])

23. Zuse, K.: Entwicklungslinien einer Rechengeräte- Entwicklung von der Mechanik zur Elektronik. http://www.zib.de/zuse[2] ZIANr 0086 ZuP 040/006 1960 (?)

24. Zuse, K.: Grundsätzliche Gedanken für die Entwicklung leistungsfähiger programm-gesteuerter Rechengeräte auf weite Sicht. http://www.zib.de/zuse[3] ZIANr 0304 ZuP 039/003 1965

25. Zuse, K.: Rechnender Raum (1967). http://www.de/zuse/[4]336-344 076 (038/015)

26. Zuse, K.: Wesen und Bedeutung der Elektronik in Gegenwart und Zukunft (1968). http://www.zib.de/zuse/[5] ZIANr 0632 ZuP 035/014

27. Zuse, K.: Erkennbare Entwicklungen der EDV-Systeme 1972. http://www.zib.de/zuse/[6] ZIANr 0096 ZuP 043/010

28. Literary remains "Konrad Zuse" in the archive of Deutsches Museum München, provisional no. 379/96 (May 12, 1965)

29. Literary remains "Konrad Zuse" in the archive of Deutsches Museum München, provisional no. 101/1/02, 15

30. Literary remains "Konrad Zuse" in the archive of Deutsches Museum München, provisional no. 080/23 o.D. Typescript lecture; Debate Paper Zuse Contains: Textualization of a debate to a lecture of Zuse; 23 pp. hektogr.;fre; eng

31. Literary remains "Konrad Zuse" in the archive of Deutsches Museum München, provisional no. 160/1

32. Literary remains "Konrad Zuse" in the archive of Deutsches Museum München, provisional no. 178/1a.

Author Index

Printed in the United States
By Bookmasters